Published for
OXFORD INTERNATIONAL AQA EXAMINATIONS

International GCSE
GEOGRAPHY

Simon Ross
Stephen Durman
Nicholas Rowles
David Holmes
Bob Digby

Great Clarendon Street, Oxford, OX2 6DP, United Kingdom

Oxford University Press is a department of the University of Oxford. It furthers the University's objective of excellence in research, scholarship, and education by publishing worldwide. Oxford is a registered trade mark of Oxford University Press in the UK and in certain other countries

© Oxford University Press 2018

First published in 2018

All rights reserved. No part of this publication may be reproduced, stored in a retrieval system, or transmitted, in any form or by any means, without the prior permission in writing of Oxford University Press, or as expressly permitted by law, by licence or under terms agreed with the appropriate reprographics rights organization. Enquiries concerning reproduction outside the scope of the above should be sent to the Rights Department, Oxford University Press, at the address above.

You must not circulate this work in any other form and you must impose this same condition on any acquirer

British Library Cataloguing in Publication Data
Data available

ISBN 978-0-19-841718-7

10 9 8 7 6 5 4 3 2 1

Paper used in the production of this book is a natural, recyclable product made from wood grown in sustainable forests. The manufacturing process conforms to the environmental regulations of the country of origin.

Printed in Great Britain by Ashford Colour Press Ltd.

Acknowledgements

The publisher and authors would like to thank the following for permission to use photographs and other copyright material:

Cover: Danita Delimont/Getty Images. All photos © Shutterstock, except: **p4:** ESDRAS NDIKUMANA/Getty Images; **p12(t):** MARTIN BERNETTI/Getty Images; **p13(t):** Manish Swarup/REX/Shutterstock; **p13(b):** ZUMA/REX/Shutterstock; **p25(b):** © Shelterbox 2017; **p26:** Neil Cooper/Alamy Stock Photo; **p27(t):** National Hurricane Center/National Oceanic and Atmospheric Administration; **p27(b):** Hayley Sharp; **p29(t):** Accent Alaska.com/Alamy Stock Photo; **p29(b), 30:** NASA; **p31(t):** FineArt/Alamy Stock Photo; **p31(b):** Contemporary illustration of the eruption of Tambora volcano in the Moluccas islands, 1815 (engraving), German School, (19th century)/© SZ Photo/Bridgeman Images; **p34:** EDF Energy; **p36(t):** 123RF; **p37(t):** Emma Stoner/Alamy Stock Photo; **p37(b):** ifish/iStockphoto; **p42:** martin meehan/Alamy Stock Photo; **p43:** Land and Water Services; **p46:** Universal Images Group North America LLC/Alamy Stock Photo; **p49(t):** 123RF; **p49(m):** Bazuki Muhammad/Reuters; **p50(t):** Ahmad Yahaya/EyeEm/Getty Images; **p53(b):** Francois ANCELLET/Getty Images; **p55(b):** Alex Hipkiss/RSPB; **p56:** Simon Ross; **p58:** PhotoAlto sas/Alamy Stock Photo; **p60(l):** Simon Ross; **p61(b):** Eye Ubiquitous/REX/Shutterstock; **p66(b):** Reuters/Mainichi Shimbun; **p68(t):** Rob Wilkinson/Alamy Stock Photo; **p70:** RooM the Agency/Alamy Stock Photo; **p72:** Simon Ross; **p73:** Schmerbeck/Alamy Stock Photo; **p74(t):** 123RF; **p76:** New Mindflow/Alamy Stock Photo; **p77:** Maroš Markovic/Alamy Stock Photo; **p78:** southeast asia/Alamy Stock Photo; **p79(t):** Minden Pictures/Alamy Stock Photo; **p79(b):** irwan Setiawan/Alamy Stock Photo; **p81(b):** David Sewell/Alamy Stock Photo; **p84(b):** Simon Ross; **p86:** imageBROKER/Alamy Stock Photo; **p88(b):** Mike P Shepherd/Alamy Stock Photo; **p89:** Michele Burgess/Alamy Stock Photo; **p90:** Frans Lemmens/Getty Images; **p92(t):** Tony Waltham Geophotos; **p93:** 123RF; **p95(b):** Franck METOIS/Alamy Stock Photo; **p97(t):** Frédéric Soltan/Getty Images; **p99:** Travel India/Alamy Stock Photo; **p100:** Raintree Photo/Alamy Stock Photo; **p102:** Travelmania/Alamy Stock Photo; **p104:** Victor Paul Borg/Alamy Stock Photo; **p106:** Global Warming Images/Alamy Stock Photo; **p108:** David Angel/Alamy Stock Photo; **p110(t):** Nick Hanna/Alamy Stock Photo; **p110(b):** Wild Trout Trust; **p111:** Jeff Morgan 01/Alamy Stock Photo; **p112:** Xinhua/Alamy Stock Photo; **p113:** Vmenkov/Wikimedia Commons/CC BY-SA 3.0; **p118(t):** Fredrik Renander/Alamy Stock Photo; **p121:** Dinodia Photo/Gettuy Images; **p124(t):** Realy Easy Star/Tullio Valente/Alamy Stock Photo; **p129:** JeffG/Alamy Stock Photo; **p130(tl):** ZUMA Press, Inc./Alamy Stock Photo; **p130(tm):** paul prescott/Alamy Stock Photo; **p130(tr):** ZUMA Press, Inc./Alamy Stock Photo; **p130(bl):** roger parkes/Alamy Stock Photo; **p130(bm):** ZUMA Press, Inc./Alamy Stock Photo; **p130(mr):** Keith J Smith./Alamy Stock Photo; **p131(t):** Dinodia Photos/Alamy Stock Photo; **p132(b):** ZUMA Press, Inc./Alamy Stock Photo; **p135:** Frank Bienewald/Alamy Stock Photo; **p136(b):** Maciej Dakowicz/Alamy Stock Photo; **p152(b):** Marcin Rogozinski/Alamy Stock Photo; **p156(t):** robertharding/Alamy Stock Photo; **p156(b):** David Ramkalawon/Alamy Stock Photo; **p158:** Avalon/Construction Photography/Alamy Stock Photo; **p159:** Commission Air/Alamy Stock Photo; **p161:** Mesmoland/Wikimedia Commons/CC BY 2.0; **p170:** Kingsnyc/Wikimedia Commons/Public Domain; **p176:** Xinhua/Alamy Stock Photo; **p186(t):** Mike Goldwater/Alamy Stock Photo; **p190:** Michael Honegger/Alamy Stock Photo; **p191(t):** ZSOLT SZIGETVARY/EPA/REX/Shutterstock; **p191(b):** Tim Scrivener/Alamy Stock Photo; **p193(t):** Asia Images Group Pte Ltd/Alamy Stock Photo; **p194:** Richard Hanson/TEARFUND; **p195(t):** Design Pics Inc/REX/Shutterstock; **p195(b):** Sean Sprague; **p196:** Robertharding/Alamy Stock Photo; **p197(t):** Fairtrade Foundation; **p197(b):** Simon Rawles; **p199:** Majority World/REX/Shutterstock; **p200:** Jon Arnold Images Ltd/Alamy Stock Photo; **p202(l):** Chris Hondros/Getty Images; **p204:** Jiang Xintong/Xinhua/Alamy Live News; **p205:** Tom Gilks/Alamy Stock Photo; **p206:** Jeremy sutton-hibbert/Alamy Stock Photo; **p207:** Str/EPA/REX/Shutterstock; **p208:** powderkeg stock/Alamy Stock Photo; **p209:** John Cole/Alamy Stock Photo; **p210(t):** Khalil Senosi/AP/REX/Shutterstock; **p210(b):** Adekunle Ajayi/Nur/Getty Images; **p211:** Eye Ubiquitous/Alamy Stock Photo; **p213:** ZUMA Press, Inc./Alamy Stock Photo; **p214(t):** Sipa Press/REX/Shutterstock; **p214(b):** Peeter Viisimaa/Getty Images; **p215(t):** powderkeg stock/Alamy Stock Photo; **p215(b):** Amnesty International; **p216:** jordi clave garsot/Alamy Stock Photo; **p217:** Stephen Chung/Alamy Stock Photo; **p224:** 123RF; **p228:** Image courtesy of TheWaterProject.org; **p229:** Cuhlik/Public Domain/Wikimedia Commons; **p230:** Dieter Telemans/Panos; **p231:** PACIFIC PRESS/Alamy Stock Photo; **p235:** ActionAid; **p240:** Highshot/Malmöstad; **p241(t):** Archimage/Alamy Stock Photo; **p242:** Tiago Fernandez/Alamy Stock Photo; **p243:** Practical Action/Peru; **p251:** Agencja Fotograficzna Caro/Alamy Stock Photo; **p273:** David R. Frazier Photolibrary, Inc./Alamy Stock Photo; **p275:** blickwinkel/Alamy Stock Photo; **p285(b):** Olli Geibel/Alamy Stock Photo; **p288:** Jpatokal/Wikimedia Commons/CC BY-SA 3.0; **p290:** Joerg Boethling/Alamy Stock Photo; **p311:** Olivier Asselin/Alamy Stock Photo; **p314(t):** Sooksan Kasiansin/Alamy Stock Photo; **p314(b):** Rick Piper/Alamy Stock Photo; **p316(t, b), 317, 321, 323:** David Holmes; **p324(t):** Kumar Sriskandan/Alamy Stock Photo; **p324(b):** Andi Kusuma Wahyudi/Alamy Stock Photo; **p333:** Peter Treanor/Alamy Stock Photo; **p341:** © Crown Copyright and database right 2018; **p342(t):** robertharding/Alamy Stock Photo; **p342(mt):** Xinhua/Alamy Stock Photo; **p342(mb):** View Stock/Getty Images; **p342(b):** NASA; **p343:** OUP; **p360:** © Crown Copyright and database right 2018.

Artwork by Kamae Design, Q2A Media Services Inc., Lovell Johns (p65), Barking Dog Art, and Giorgio Bacchin (p41, p42).

Every effort has been made to contact copyright holders of material reproduced in this book. Any omissions will be rectified in subsequent printings if notice is given to the publisher.

Contents

Unit 1 – Living with the physical environment

Section A – The challenge of natural hazards 2

1	**Natural hazards**	4
1.1	What are natural hazards?	4
2	**Tectonic hazards**	**6**
2.1	Distribution of earthquakes and volcanoes	6
2.2	Physical processes at plate margins	8
2.3	The effects of earthquakes	10
2.4	Responses to earthquakes	12
2.5	Living with the risk from tectonic hazards	14
2.6	Reducing the risk from tectonic hazards	16
3	**Weather hazards**	**18**
3.1	Global atmospheric circulation	18
3.2	Where and how are tropical storms formed?	20
3.3	The structure and features of tropical storms	22
3.4	Typhoon Haiyan – a tropical storm	24
3.5	Reducing the effects of tropical storms	26
4	**Climate change**	**28**
4.1	What is the evidence for climate change?	28
4.2	What are the natural causes of climate change?	30
4.3	What are the human causes of climate change?	32
4.4	Managing the impacts of climate change (1)	34
4.5	Managing the impacts of climate change (2)	36

Section B – The living world 38

5	**Ecosystems**	**40**
5.1	Introducing a small-scale ecosystem	40
5.2	How does change affect ecosystems?	42
5.3	Introducing global ecosystems	44
6	**Tropical rainforests**	**46**
6.1	Environmental characteristics of rainforests	46
6.2	Causes of deforestation in Malaysia	48
6.3	Impacts of deforestation in Malaysia	50
6.4	Managing tropical rainforests	52
6.5	Sustainable management of tropical rainforests	54

7	**Hot deserts**	**56**
7.1	Environmental characteristics of hot deserts	56
7.2	Causes of desertification in hot deserts	58
7.3	Reducing desertification in hot deserts	60

Section C – Physical landscapes 62

8	**Physical landscapes in the Middle and Far East**	**64**
8.1	The Middle and Far East	64
9	**Coastal landscapes**	**66**
9.1	Wave types and their characteristics	66
9.2	Weathering and mass movement	68
9.3	Coastal erosion processes	70
9.4	Coastal erosion landforms	72
9.5	Coastal deposition landforms	74
9.6	Coastal landforms in Indonesia (1)	76
9.7	Coastal landforms in Indonesia (2)	78
9.8	Coastal management strategies	80
9.9	Coastal management at Mactan Island	82
10	**Hot desert landscapes**	**84**
10.1	Aeolian (wind) processes	84
10.2	Water processes	86
10.3	Wind landforms	88
10.4	Water landforms	92
10.5	Opportunities for development in hot deserts	94
10.6	Challenges of development in hot deserts	96
11	**River landscapes**	**98**
11.1	Changes in rivers and their valleys	98
11.2	Fluvial (river) processes	100
11.3	River erosion landforms	102
11.4	River erosion and deposition landforms	104
11.5	Factors increasing flood risk	106
11.6	Managing floods – hard engineering	108
11.7	Managing floods – soft engineering	110
11.8	Managing floods in the Huai River Basin, China	112

iii

Contents

Unit 2 – Challenges in the human environment

Section A – Urban issues and challenges 114

12	**The urban world**	**116**
12.1	An increasingly urban world	116
12.2	The emergence of megacities	118
13	**Urban growth**	**120**
13.1	Exploring Mumbai	120
13.2	Mumbai: a growing city	122
13.3	Social opportunities	124
13.4	Economic opportunities	126
13.5	Managing urban growth	128
13.6	Providing basic resources and services	130
13.7	Managing waste, recycling and pollution	134
13.8	Managing traffic congestion	136
13.9	Improving the quality of life for the urban poor	138
14	**World cities**	**140**
14.1	What is a world city?	140
14.2	London: a world city	142
14.3	The importance of London as a world city	146
14.4	London's economic, social and environmental opportunities	148
14.5	London's economic and social challenges	150
14.6	London's environmental challenges	152
14.7	Managing London's resources	154
14.8	London Olympic Park: an urban regeneration project	158
14.9	New York: a world city	162
14.10	The importance of New York as a world city	166
14.11	New York's economic, social and environmental opportunities	168
14.12	New York's economic and social challenges	170
14.13	New York's environmental challenges	172

Section B – The changing economic world 176

15	**The development gap**	**178**
15.1	Our unequal world	178
15.2	Measuring development	180
15.3	The demographic transition model	182
15.4	Changing population structures	184
15.5	Causes of uneven development	186
15.6	Uneven development – wealth and health	188
15.7	Uneven development – migration	190
15.8	Reducing the gap	192
15.9	Reducing the gap – aid and intermediate technology	194
15.10	Reducing the gap – fair trade	196
15.11	Reducing the gap – debt relief	198
15.12	Reducing the gap – tourism	200
16	**Nigeria: newly emerging economy**	**202**
16.1	Exploring Nigeria (1)	202
16.2	Exploring Nigeria (2)	204
16.3	Nigeria in the wider world	206
16.4	Balancing a changing industrial structure	208
16.5	The impacts of transnational corporations	210
16.6	The impacts of international aid	212
16.7	Managing environmental issues	214
16.8	Quality of life in Nigeria	216

Section C – Global issues 218

17	**Water**	**220**
17.1	Global water supply	220
17.2	The impact of water insecurity	222
17.3	How can water supply be increased?	224
17.4	The Lesotho Highland Water Project	226
17.5	Sustainable water supplies	228
17.6	The Wakel River Basin project	230

18	**Energy**	**232**
18.1	Global energy supply and demand	232
18.2	Impacts of energy insecurity	234
18.3	Strategies to increase energy supply	236
18.4	Gas – a non-renewable resource	238
18.5	Sustainable energy use	240
18.6	The Chambamontera micro-hydro scheme	242

19	**Population**	**244**
19.1	The change in world population over time	244
19.2	Causes of global increase in population	248
19.3	Environmental and economic impacts of population change	254
19.4	Strategies to manage population growth	258
19.5	International migration	264
19.6	Causes and impacts of forced migration	268
19.7	Causes and impacts of voluntary migration	272

20	**Communication**	**276**
20.1	Development of ocean shipping and ports	276
20.2	Global patterns of movement by sea	280
20.3	The world's leading ports	282
20.4	Comparing ocean transport with air transport	284
20.5	Development of airports and global patterns	286
20.6	Advantages of international links for manufacturing, trade and tourism	290
20.7	Challenges of increasing airport development	292
20.8	Developments in ICT	296
20.9	Development of International phone links	300
20.10	ICT and economic growth in NEEs: call centres	302
20.11	ICT and economic growth in NEEs: TNC investment	306
20.12	ICT and economic growth in NEEs: trade and tourism	310

Unit 3 – Geographical applications and skills 314

21	**Fieldwork**	**314**
21.1	Investigating river processes and management	314
21.2	Primary data collection in river fieldwork	316
21.3	Processing and presenting river fieldwork	318
21.4	Analysis and conclusions – river enquiry	320
21.5	Evaluating your river enquiry	322
21.6	Investigating variations in urban quality of life	324
21.7	Primary data collection for urban fieldwork	326
21.8	Processing and presenting urban fieldwork	328
21.9	Analysis and conclusions – urban enquiry	330
21.10	Evaluating your urban enquiry	332

22	**Geographical skills**	**334**
22.1	Cartographic skills	334
22.2	Graphical skills	344
22.3	Statistical skills	350

Glossary	**354**
OS map symbols key	**360**
Index	**361**

Unit 1 Living with the physical environment

Section A The challenge of natural hazards

Collapsed buildings in Bhaktapur, Nepal, following the 2015 earthquake

Unit 1 Living with the physical environment is about physical processes and systems, how they change, and how people interact with them at a range of scales and in a range of places. It is split into three sections.

Section A The challenge of natural hazards includes:

- an introduction to natural hazards
- tectonic hazards
- weather hazards
- climate change.

You need to study all the topics in Section A – in your final exam you will have to answer questions on all of them.

What if...

1. you were caught up in a volcanic eruption?
2. your home was flattened in an earthquake?
3. you lived in the path of a tropical storm?
4. your region was hit by a tsunami?
5. the world ran out of fossil fuels?

Unit 1 Section A

Specification key ideas	Pages in this book
1 Natural hazards	**4–5**
• Natural hazards pose major risks to people and property.	4–5
2 Tectonic hazards	**6–17**
• Earthquakes and volcanic eruptions are the result of physical processes.	6–9
• The effects of, and responses to, earthquakes and volcanoes vary between areas of contrasting levels of wealth.	10–13
• Management can reduce the effects of a tectonic hazard.	14–17
3 Weather hazards	**18–27**
• Global atmospheric circulation helps to determine patterns of weather and climate.	18–19
• Tropical storms (hurricanes, cyclones, typhoons) develop as a result of particular physical conditions.	20–3
• Tropical storms have significant effects on people and the environment.	24–7
4 Climate change	**28–37**
• Climate change is the result of natural and human factors, and has a range of effects.	28–33
• Managing climate change involves both mitigation (reducing causes) and adaptation (responding to change).	34–7

Your key skills

To be a good geographer, you need to develop important geographical skills – in this section you will learn the following skills:

- Using different graphical techniques to present information.
- Carrying out personal research.
- Drawing and annotating diagrams and sketches.
- Describing and interpreting information from maps and graphs.
- Finding evidence from photographs.

Your key words

As you go through the chapters in this section, make sure you know and understand the key words shown in bold. Definitions are provided in the Glossary on page 354. To be a good geographer, you need to use good subject terminology.

Your exam

Section A makes up part of Paper 1 – a one and a half hour written exam worth 34 per cent of your GCSE.

1 Natural hazards

1.1 What are natural hazards?

On this spread you will find out about the risks from natural hazards

What is a natural hazard?

In March 2015 landslides struck Bujumbura in western Burundi, central Africa, killing several people and leaving thousands homeless. Following a period of heavy rain, mud and rocks plunged down hillsides destroying houses and damaging roads (photo **A**).

This event is an example of a natural hazard. It is a natural event that has had a huge **social impact**. If the landslide had occurred in a remote area where it did not pose any threat to people it would not be considered a hazard.

Landslides are not major killers. The most deadly natural hazards are floods, storms, earthquakes and droughts. Between 2002 and 2012, an average of 100 000 people worldwide were killed each year by natural hazards. In most years, flooding caused the greatest number of deaths.

Diagram **B** is called a Venn diagram. Notice that a natural hazard occurs when a natural event overlaps with human activities.

What are the different types of natural hazard?

There is a huge range of natural hazards. These include:

- volcanic eruptions
- earthquakes
- storms
- tsunami (huge waves caused by earthquakes)
- landslides
- floods.

Diagram **C** shows how natural hazards can be sorted into three main groups.

A Landslides affecting Bujumbura, Burundi, 2015

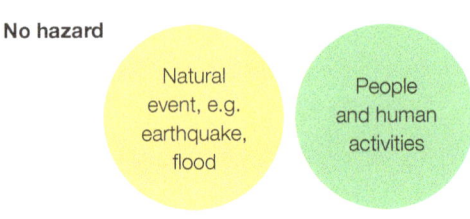

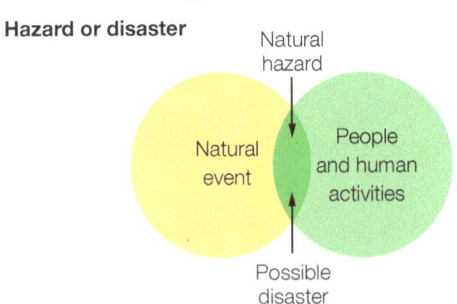

B When is a natural event a hazard?

C Different types of natural hazard

Did you know?
Hurricane Patricia (2015) was the most powerful tropical storm ever recorded, with winds reaching 320 km/h (200 mph).

Natural hazards

What is 'hazard risk'?

Hazard risk is the chance or probability of being affected by a natural event. People who choose to live close to a river may be at risk from flooding. Those who live close to the sea may be at risk from tropical cyclones or tsunami.

So why do people put themselves at risk by living in such places? They weigh up the advantages and disadvantages and, because such events don't happen very often, they may decide to accept the risk. Some people may have little choice of where to live or knowledge that where they are living is dangerous.

Think about it
*Are natural hazards occurring more frequently today than 100 years ago? Use diagram **B** to help you.*

What factors affect risk?

There are several factors that have led to an increase in the number of people at risk from natural events.

Urbanisation
Over 50 per cent of the world's population now live in cities. Some of the world's largest cities (e.g. Tokyo, Istanbul and Los Angeles) are at risk from earthquakes.
Densely populated urban areas are at great risk from natural events such as earthquakes and tropical cyclones. The 2010 Haiti earthquake destroyed much of the capital Port-au-Prince killing some 230 000 people.

Poverty
In poorer parts of the world poverty may force people to live in areas at risk. This is especially true in cities such as Lima in Peru or Caracas in Venezuela. Here, a shortage of housing has led to people building on unstable slopes prone to floods and landslides.

Factors increasing the risk from natural hazards

Farming
When a river floods it deposits fertile silt on its floodplain, which is excellent for farming. But when people choose to live there they are putting themselves at risk. In low-lying countries many people may live on floodplains, such as those of the River Ganges in Bangladesh.

Climate change
In a warmer world the atmosphere will have more energy leading to more intense storms and hurricanes. **Climate change** may cause some parts of the world to become wetter with an increased risk of flooding. Other areas may become drier and prone to droughts and famines.

ACTIVITIES

1. Describe what has happened in photo **A**.
2. a Make a copy of diagram **B**.
   b Explain in your own words how a 'natural event' becomes a 'natural hazard'.
3. a What are the three main groups of hazard shown in diagram **C**?
   b Why do you think more people are likely to be affected by river flooding than by landslides and mudflows?
4. In the future, why is it likely that increasing numbers of people will be at risk from natural hazards?

Stretch yourself

Find out about natural hazards in Bangladesh. What are the natural events that threaten the country? Why are so many people at risk from these events?

Maths skills

Use a divided bar chart or a pie chart to present the following information.

Percentage of fatalities (2014)
Hydrological events (e.g. floods)   66%
Meteorological events (e.g. storms)   17%
Geophysical events (e.g. earthquakes)   11%
Climatological events (e.g. drought)   6%

Practice question

Explain two human developments that would increase the risk of people being affected by natural hazards. *(4 marks)*

5

2 Tectonic hazards

2.1 Distribution of earthquakes and volcanoes

On this spread you will find out where earthquakes and volcanoes happen and link their location to plate tectonics

Why is there a pattern of earthquakes?

An **earthquake** is a sudden and violent period of ground shaking. It is most commonly caused by a sudden movement of rocks within the Earth's crust. This occurs mainly at the margins of *tectonic plates* (map **B**) where plates are moving and enormous pressures build up and are released.

Compare map **B** to map **A**. Notice the pattern of earthquakes along **plate margins**, for example along the western coast of North and South America. The occurrence of earthquakes around the edge of the Pacific Ocean follows the plate margins.

Some earthquakes do not occur at plate margins. These may be caused by human activity such as underground mining or oil extraction.

A *Earthquakes recorded during March 2015*

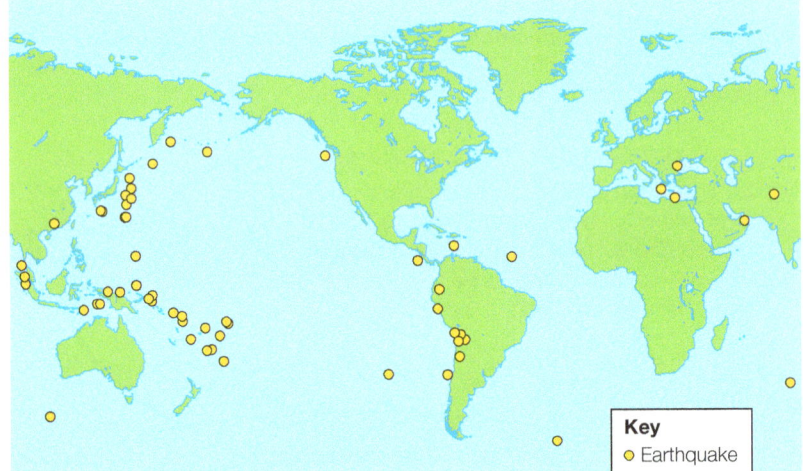

Tectonic plates

- The Earth's crust is split into a number of plates about 100 km thick.
- There are two types of crust – dense, thin oceanic crust and less dense, thick continental crust.
- Plates move in relation to each other due to convection (heat) currents from deep within the Earth. Gravitational pull may play a part.
- At a *constructive* plate margin plates move apart. New crust is formed as magma rises towards the surface. At a *destructive* margin, where plates are moving towards each other, the denser oceanic plate may sink (subduct) beneath a less dense continental plate. Gravity pulls the oceanic plate into the mantle, dragging the plate away from the constructive margin.
- Tectonic activity at plate margins causes earthquakes and volcanoes.

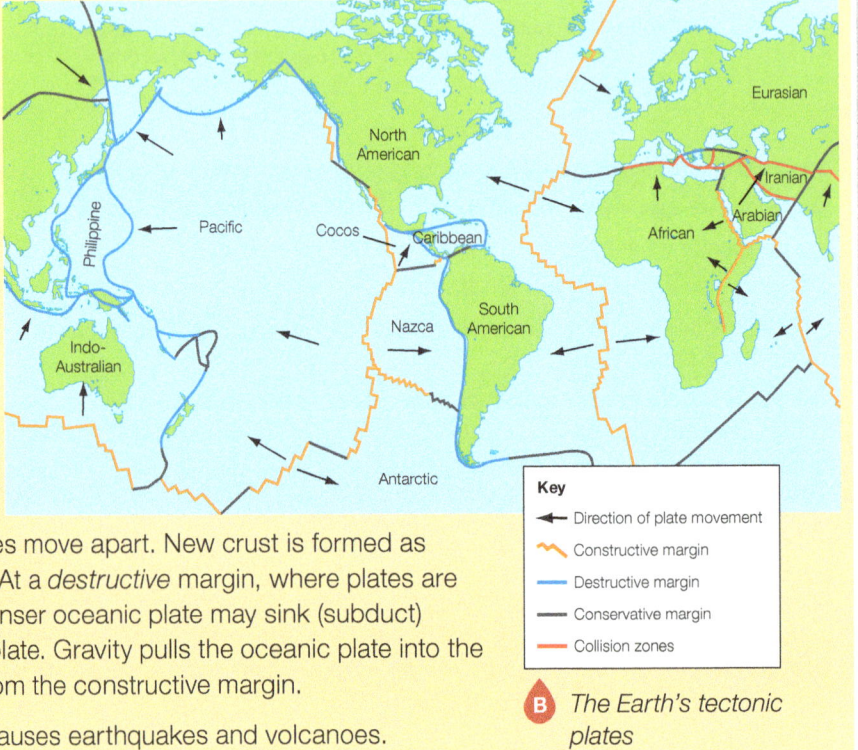

B *The Earth's tectonic plates*

Tectonic hazards

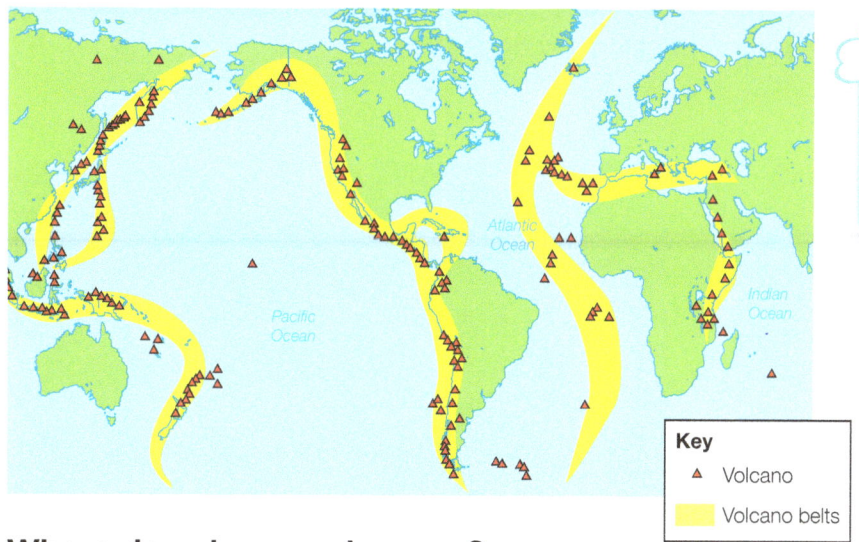

Think about it

Think about any major earthquakes or volcanoes that have been in the news recently. How does their location link to plate tectonics?

C The distribution of volcanoes

Where do volcanoes happen?

Look at map **C**, which shows the distribution of volcanoes. A **volcano** is a large and often conical-shaped landform usually formed over a long period of time by a series of eruptions. Like earthquakes, the majority of volcanoes occur in long belts that follow the plate margins, for example around the edge of the Pacific Ocean. This is known as the 'Pacific Ring of Fire'. There is also a belt of volcanoes through the middle of the Atlantic Ocean. This is the Mid-Atlantic Ridge which includes the Azores and Iceland, which are volcanic islands.

Why is there a pattern of volcanoes?

Volcanoes are fed by hot molten rock (magma) from deep within the Earth. This rises to the surface at *constructive* and *destructive* plate margins. Volcanoes also form at hot spots, where the crust is thin and magma is able to break through to the surface. The Hawaiian Islands in the Pacific Ocean are a good example of a hot spot.

Did you know?
The biggest volcanic eruption ever recorded was Mount Tambora, in Indonesia, in 1815. Volcanic ash from the eruption blocked the sun!

ACTIVITIES

1. Use map **A** to describe the pattern of earthquakes.
2. Use map **B** to answer the following questions.
   a. Which plate is the UK on?
   b. Name a country which is being split by two plates.
   c. Describe the movement of the plates at the margin of the Nazca and South American plates.
3. Describe the pattern of volcanoes (map **C**). Refer to names of oceans, continents and countries in your answer.
4. Why do the majority of earthquakes and volcanoes occur at plate margins?

Maths skills

A total of 1482 earthquakes occurred in a seven-day period at the end of April 2016. Work out the average number of earthquakes per day and per hour. Can you calculate the frequency of the earthquakes?

Practice question

Explain why the majority of earthquakes and volcanoes occur at plate margins. *(4 marks)*

Stretch yourself

Use the United States Geological Survey (USGS) website to find a map of recent earthquakes. You could look at a single day or a whole week. Copy and paste the map and write a few sentences (or use text boxes) to describe the pattern of earthquakes. Use map **B** to relate this to named plate margins.

2.2 Physical processes at plate margins

On this spread you will find out about the physical processes at plate margins

What happens at plate margins?

Iceland is a country in the North Atlantic Ocean. It is situated on the Mid-Atlantic Ridge, a plate margin where two plates are moving away from each other. There are several active volcanoes in Iceland including Eyjafjallajökull, which erupted in 2010 (photo **A**). It is possible to identify three main types of plate margin:

- **Constructive** – where two plates are moving apart.
- **Destructive** – where two plates are moving towards one another.
- **Conservative (transform)** – where two plates are sliding alongside each other.

A Eruption of Eyjafjallajökull, 2010

Maths skills

At a constructive plate margin, each plate moves at an average of 2 cm a year. Calculate the increase in the width of Iceland over a period of 1 million years.

Did you know?
Volcanic eruptions over millions of years mean that Iceland is growing outwards from the middle!

Constructive margin

At a constructive margin two plates are moving apart. Diagram **B** shows what is happening at the constructive margin in the mid-Atlantic. Magma is forcing its way to the surface along the Mid-Atlantic Ridge. As it breaks through the overlying crust it causes earthquakes. On reaching the surface it forms volcanoes such as Eyjafjallajökull in Iceland.

The magma at constructive margins is very hot and fluid. Lava erupting from a volcano will flow a long way before cooling. This results in typically broad and flat *shield volcanoes*.

B Constructive plate margin

Tectonic hazards

Destructive margin

At a destructive plate margin two plates are moving towards one another. Diagram **C** shows what is happening on the west coast of South America.

Where the two plates meet a deep ocean trench has formed. The oceanic Nazca Plate, which is relatively dense, is *subducted* beneath the less dense South American Plate. Friction between the two plates causes strong earthquakes. As the oceanic plate moves downwards it melts. This creates magma which is less fluid than at a constructive margin. It breaks through to the surface to form steep-sided *composite volcanoes*. Eruptions are often very violent and explosive.

Where two continental plates meet, there is no subduction. Instead, the two plates collide and the crust becomes crumpled and uplifted. This collision forms fold mountains such as the Himalayas. These mountain-building processes cause earthquakes. There are no volcanoes at these *collision* margins because there is no magma.

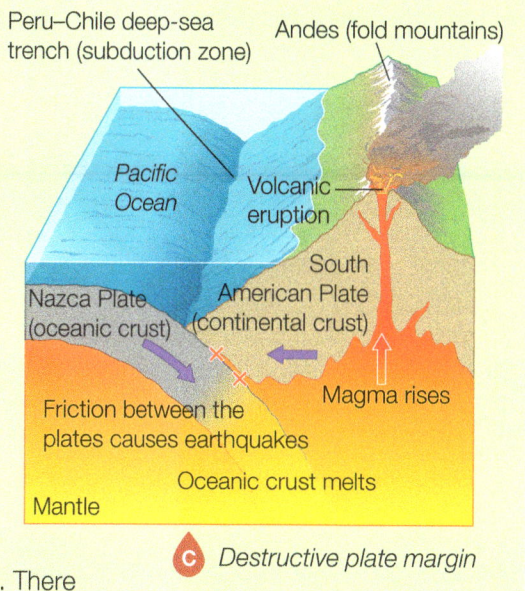

C Destructive plate margin

Conservative margin

At conservative plate margins, two plates are moving past each other. Friction between the plates then causes earthquakes. Map **D** shows the San Andreas Fault in California, a well-known example of a conservative margin. The faster-moving Pacific Plate is sliding in the same direction next to the slower-moving North American Plate.

Earthquakes happen along conservative margins as stresses gradually build up over many years. They can be destructive as they are close to the Earth's surface. These are released suddenly when the plates slip and shift.

There are no volcanoes because there is no magma.

D Conservative plate margin

ACTIVITIES

1. **a** What type of plate margin runs through the middle of Iceland?
   b Why do earthquakes occur in Iceland?
   c Explain why there are volcanoes like Eyjafjallajökull in Iceland.
2. Explain the formation of earthquakes and volcanoes at a destructive margin (diagram **C**).
3. Make a copy of map **D**.
   a Use crosses to show where you would expect earthquakes to happen.
   b Why are there no volcanoes at a conservative plate margin?

Stretch yourself

Find out about the North Anatolian Fault, one of the world's most active plate margins.
- Where is it?
- What type of plate margin is it?
- What are the hazards associated with the North Anatolian Fault?
- Which major city near this fault is at greatest risk from a natural disaster?

Practice question

Explain the physical processes that happen at constructive plate margins. *(4 marks)*

9

2.3 The effects of earthquakes

On this spread you will find out about the effects of two earthquakes in contrasting countries – Chile and Nepal

The earthquakes in Chile and Nepal

Earthquakes can have devastating effects on peoples' lives and activities. **Primary effects** are caused by ground shaking and can include deaths and injuries, and damage to roads and buildings. **Secondary effects** are the result of primary effects (ground shaking) and include tsunami, fires and landslides. Responses to earthquakes include emergency care and support, and help with longer-term reconstruction.

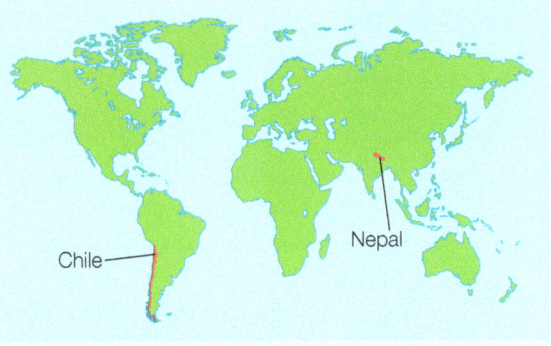

Indicator	Chile	Nepal	UK
Gross domestic product (GDP) – a measure of wealth	38th out of 193 countries	109th out of 193 countries	6th out of 193 countries
Human development index (HDI) – a measure of the level of development	41st out of 187 countries	145th out of 187 countries	14th out of 187 countries

A Contrasting Chile and Nepal

Chile

Imagine what it would be like if the ground shook underneath you for three minutes! This is what happened on 27 February 2010 when a very powerful earthquake measuring 8.8 on the Richter scale struck just off the coast of central Chile (map **B**). The earthquake occurred at a destructive plate margin where the Nazca Plate is moving beneath the South American Plate.

It was followed by a series of smaller aftershocks.

Because the earthquake occurred out to sea, tsunami warnings were issued as waves raced across the Pacific Ocean at speeds of up to 800 km per hour.

Nepal

On 25 April 2015 Nepal was struck by an earthquake measuring 7.9 on the Richter scale. The epicentre was about 80 km (50 miles) to the north-west of Nepal's capital Kathmandu in the foothills of the Himalayas (map **C**). This is a destructive plate margin where the Indo-Australian Plate is colliding with the Eurasian Plate at a rate of 45 mm per year. The collision and pressure at this margin are responsible for the formation of the Himalayas.

The earthquake was very shallow, just 15 km below the surface. This resulted in very severe ground shaking and widespread landslides and avalanches. The earthquake caused damage hundreds of kilometres away in India, Tibet and Pakistan.

B The Chile earthquake

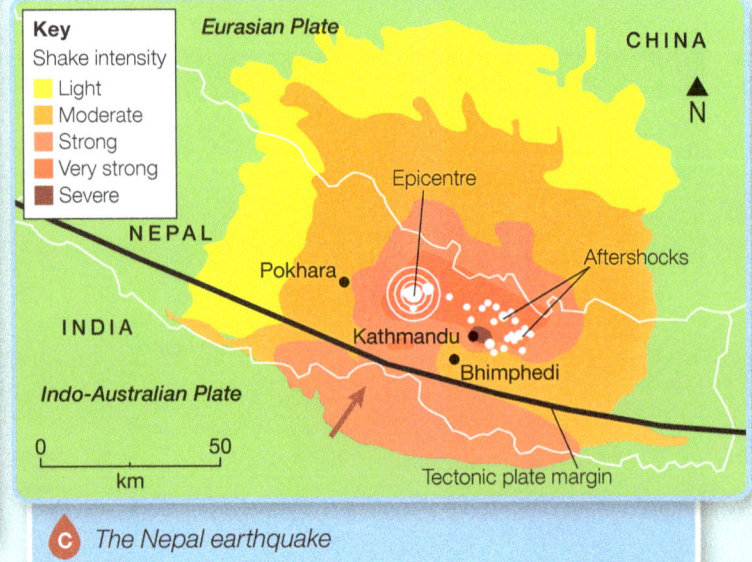

C The Nepal earthquake

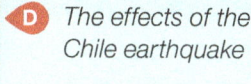
Tectonic hazards

Chile

Primary effects (caused by ground shaking)
- Around 500 people killed and 12 000 injured – 800 000 people affected.
- 220 000 homes, 4500 schools, 53 ports, 56 hospitals and other public buildings destroyed.
- Port of Talcahuanao and Santiago airport badly damaged.
- Much of Chile lost power, water supplies and communications.
- Cost of the earthquake estimated at US$30 billion.

D The effects of the Chile earthquake

Secondary effects (tsunamis, fires and landslides)
- 1500 km of roads damaged, mainly by landslides – remote communities cut off for many days.
- Several coastal towns devastated by tsunami waves.
- Several Pacific countries struck by tsunami – warnings prevented loss of life.
- A fire at a chemical plant near Santiago – the area had to be evacuated.

Nepal

Primary effects
- 9000 people died and 20 000 injured – over 8 million people (a third of Nepal's population) affected.
- 3 million people left homeless when homes were destroyed.
- Electricity and water supplies, sanitation and communications affected.
- 1.4 million people needed food, water and shelter in the days and weeks after the earthquake.
- 7000 schools destroyed and hospitals overwhelmed.
- International airport became congested as aid arrived.
- 50 per cent of shops destroyed, affecting food supplies and people's livelihoods.
- Cost of damage estimated at over US$5 billion.

Secondary effects
- Ground shaking triggered landslides and avalanches, blocking roads and hampering relief efforts.
- Avalanches on Mount Everest killed at least 19 people – the greatest loss of life on the mountain in a single incident.
- An avalanche in the Langtang region left 250 people missing.
- A landslide blocked the Kali Gandaki River, 140 km (90 miles) north-west of the capital, Kathmandu – many people evacuated in case of flooding.
- The earthquake occurred on land so did not cause a tsunami.

E The effects of the Nepal earthquake

ACTIVITIES

1. a What is the evidence that Nepal is poorer and less developed than Chile?
   b Why did the Nepal earthquake affect such a vast area?
   c Why did the Chile earthquake trigger a tsunami?
2. Describe the primary effects of the Nepal earthquake shown in figure **E**.
3. To what extent did the levels of wealth and development of the two countries affect the impacts of the earthquakes?
4. What were the effects of the tsunami waves caused by the Chilean earthquake?

Stretch yourself

A second powerful earthquake struck Nepal on 12 May 2015. How might this have affected the country's recovery?

Practice question

Explain how different levels of wealth and development affected the impact of the earthquakes in Chile and Nepal. *(6 marks)*

11

2.4 Responses to earthquakes

Example

On this spread you will find out about responses to earthquakes in Chile and Nepal

Responding to earthquakes

There are two different types of response to natural disasters such as earthquakes:

- **Immediate responses** – search and rescue and keeping survivors alive by providing medical care, food, water and shelter.
- **Long-term responses** – rebuilding and reconstruction, with the aim of returning people's lives back to normal and reducing future risk.

Did you know?
The last earthquake to hit Kathmandu was in 1934 when over 10 000 people were killed.

Comparing responses in Chile and Nepal

Earthquakes in Chile are quite common. Local communities and the government were prepared and knew how to respond quickly and effectively to the earthquake. Chile had the money to support people and to rebuild.

Earthquakes in Nepal are also common. Scientists have identified a pattern of large earthquakes in this region every 80 years or so. Despite these warnings and new building regulations, little had been done to prepare the city and its people for when the earthquake struck.

Chile: immediate responses

- Emergency services acted swiftly. International help needed to supply field hospitals, satellite phones and floating bridges.
- Temporary repairs made to the important Route 5 north–south highway within 24 hours, enabling aid to be transported from Santiago to affected areas.
- Power and water restored to 90 per cent of homes within 10 days.
- A national appeal raised US$60 million – enough to build 30 000 small emergency shelters (photo **A**).

A *Temporary wooden shelters for those made homeless by the earthquake*

Chile: long-term responses

- A month after the earthquake Chile's government launched a housing reconstruction plan to help nearly 200 000 households affected by the earthquake.
- Chile's strong economy, based on copper exports, could be rebuilt without the need for much foreign aid.
- The president announced it could take four years for Chile to recover fully from the damage to buildings and ports (photo **B**).

B *Buildings destroyed by the Chile earthquake*

Tectonic hazards

Nepal: immediate responses

- Search and rescue teams (photo **C**), water and medical support arrived quickly from countries such as UK, India and China.
- Helicopters rescued many people caught in avalanches on Mount Everest and delivered supplies to villages cut off by landslides.
- Half a million tents needed to provide shelter for the homeless.
- Financial aid pledged from many countries.
- Field hospitals set up to support overcrowded main hospitals.
- 300 000 people migrated from Kathmandu to seek shelter and support with family and friends.
- Social media widely used in search and rescue operations and satellites mapped damaged areas.

Rubble to be shifted · Rescue dogs · Listening for survivors · Local knowledge · Lifting equipment · Weak buildings – danger of collapse · Video cameras to see inside collapsed buildings

C *Searching a building for survivors in Kathmandu*

Nepal: long-term responses

- Roads repaired and landslides cleared. Lakes, formed by landslides damming river valleys, to be emptied to avoid flooding.
- Thousands of homeless people to be rehoused, and damaged homes repaired. Over 7000 schools to be rebuilt or repaired.
- Stricter controls on building codes.
- In June 2015 Nepal hosted an international conference to discuss reconstruction and seek technical and financial support from other countries.
- Tourism, a major source of income, to be boosted. By July 2015 some heritage sites reopened and tourists were starting to return.
- Repairs to Everest base camp (photo **D**) and trekking routes. By August 2015 new routes had been established and the mountain reopened for climbers.
- In late 2015 a blockade at the Indian border badly affected supplies of fuels, medicines and construction materials.

D *Everest base camp*

ACTIVITIES

1. **a** Why did the Chilean government focus on repairing the main north–south highway?
   b Why was the Chilean government able to respond quickly and effectively to the earthquake?
2. Describe how search and rescue teams locate and rescue people from collapsed buildings (photo **C**).
3. What were the immediate needs of the survivors of the Nepal earthquake?
4. What needs to be done to support Nepal's recovery following the earthquake?

Stretch yourself

Investigate the latest information about recovery in Chile and Nepal.

What has been done to reduce the impacts of future earthquakes in the two countries?

Practice question

Choose either the earthquake in Chile or Nepal. Describe the immediate and long-term responses to the disaster. *(6 marks)*

2.5 Living with the risk from tectonic hazards

On this spread you will find out why people continue to live in areas at risk from earthquakes and volcanoes

Living in the shadow of a volcano

In AD79 Mount Vesuvius in southern Italy erupted, burying the nearby cities of Pompeii and Herculaneum in volcanic ash and killing thousands of people. Today over 1 million people live in the shadow of the volcano, most of them in the city of Naples (photo **A**). Vesuvius last erupted in 1944. In the 300 years before then it erupted nearly every 20 years. Many people think that the next eruption is long overdue!

Living at risk from tectonic hazards

You have seen from the examples of Chile and Nepal how destructive earthquakes can be. So why do people choose to live in such dangerous places?

The majority of tectonic hazards occur at plate margins which criss-cross the Earth's surface. Some margins run through densely populated regions such as Japan, parts of China, and southern Europe (map **C**).

There are several reasons why people live in areas at risk from tectonic hazards, as shown below.

A *Naples in the shadow of Mount Vesuvius*

B *Fertile farmland on the slopes of Mount Merapi, Indonesia*

- Earthquakes and volcanic eruptions don't happen very often. They are not seen as a great threat in most people's lives.
- People living in poverty have other things to think about on a daily basis – money, food, security and family.
- Plate margins often coincide with very favourable areas for settlement, such as coastal areas where ports have developed.
- Better building design can withstand earthquakes so people feel less at risk.
- Why choose to live in hazardous areas?
- Some people may not be aware of the risks of living close to a plate margin.
- More effective monitoring of volcanoes and tsunami waves enable people to receive warnings and evacuate before events happen.
- Fault lines associated with earthquakes can allow water supplies to reach the surface. This is particularly important in dry desert regions.
- Volcanoes can bring benefits such as fertile soils, rocks for building, rich mineral deposits and hot water (photo **B**).

Tectonic hazards

Life on a plate margin in Iceland

Iceland lies on the Mid-Atlantic Ridge, a constructive plate margin that stretches through the middle of the Atlantic Ocean. There are several active volcanoes – an eruption occurs on average every five years. Earthquakes are common. Over 320 000 people live in Iceland and close to 1 million people visit the country each year.

While the tectonic activity does pose a threat, the people in Iceland consider it to be a low risk. This is mainly due to effective scientific monitoring and awareness of the potential dangers. In fact, tectonic activity brings huge benefits to the country (figure **D**).

C Tectonic plates and population density

Key
- Densely populated
- Moderately populated
- Sparsely populated
- Plate margins

D Geothermal power plant near Krafla volcano, Iceland

Hot water from within the Earth's crust provides heat and hot water for nearly 90 per cent of all buildings in Iceland.

Volcanic rocks are used in construction for roads and buildings.

Iceland's dramatic landscape with waterfalls, volcanoes and mountain glaciers has become a huge draw for tourists. Tourism provides jobs for many people.

The naturally occurring hot water – some of which reaches the surface through cracks created by earthquakes – is used to heat greenhouses and swimming pools.

Geothermal energy is used to generate 25 per cent of the country's electricity (most of the rest is generated by hydroelectric power).

Thousands of tourists visited Iceland after the recent eruption of Eyjafjallajökull in 2010.

ACTIVITIES

1. Why do you think 1 million people choose to live so close to one of Europe's most dangerous volcanoes (photo **A**)?
2. a Which areas of the world are most densely populated (map **C**)?
   b Which of these areas lie on active plate margins? Name some of these margins.
   c Why do you think so many people live in areas at risk from earthquakes and volcanic eruptions?
3. What evidence is there in photo **B** that people are making use of the land close to Mount Merapi?
4. How do the people of Iceland benefit from living on a plate margin (figure **D**)?

Stretch yourself

Carry out some research to find out how people in Iceland benefit from living in an area at risk from tectonic activity.
- What is geothermal energy and how is it used to generate electricity?
- How is Iceland's naturally occurring hot water used for heating?
- How has tectonic activity created attractions for tourists?

Practice question

Use figure **D** to evaluate the benefits of Iceland's location on a plate margin. *(6 marks)*

2.6 Reducing the risk from tectonic hazards

On this spread you will find out how the risks from tectonic hazards can be reduced

How can the risks from tectonic hazards be reduced?

There are four main **management strategies** for reducing the risk from tectonic hazards:

- **Monitoring** – using scientific equipment to detect warning signs of events such as a volcanic eruption.
- **Prediction** – using historical evidence and monitoring, scientists can make predictions about when and where a tectonic hazard may happen.
- **Protection** – designing buildings that will withstand tectonic hazards.
- **Planning** – identifying and avoiding places most at risk.

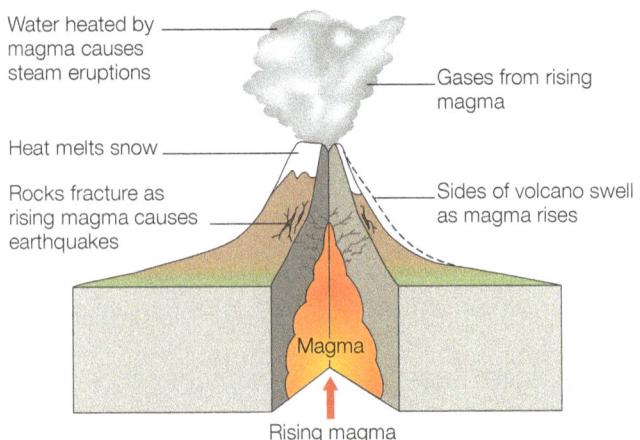

A Warning signs of a volcanic eruption

Monitoring

Volcanoes

As magma rises through a volcano it gives a number of warning signs that an eruption is likely to occur (diagram **A**).

All of the world's active volcanoes are closely monitored by scientists. If an eruption seems likely, warnings can be issued and action taken to evacuate surrounding areas. Modern hi-tech equipment is used, some of which is located on the volcano itself. Scientists monitor volcanoes in the following ways:

- *Remote sensing* – satellites detect heat and changes to the volcano's shape.
- *Seismicity* – seismographs record earthquakes.
- *Ground deformation* – changes to the shape of the volcano are measured using laser beams.
- *Geophysical measurements* – detect changes in gravity as magma rises to the surface.
- *Gas* – instruments detect gases released as magma rises.
- *Hydrology* – measurements of gases dissolved in water.

Earthquakes

Earthquakes generally occur without warning. While there is some evidence of changes in water pressure, ground deformation and minor tremors prior to an earthquake, scientists have yet to discover reliable ways to monitor and predict earthquakes.

Prediction

Volcanoes

The prediction of a volcanic eruption is based on scientific monitoring. In 2010 an increase in earthquake activity beneath the Eyjafjallajökull ice cap in Iceland enabled scientists to make an accurate prediction about the eruptions that took place in March and April that year.

Earthquakes

It is impossible to make accurate predictions about earthquakes due to the lack of clear warning signs. However, scientists studying historical records of earthquakes at plate margins have identified locations that they believe are at greatest risk. Map **B** shows why scientists believe the city of Istanbul in Turkey is at risk from an earthquake…soon!

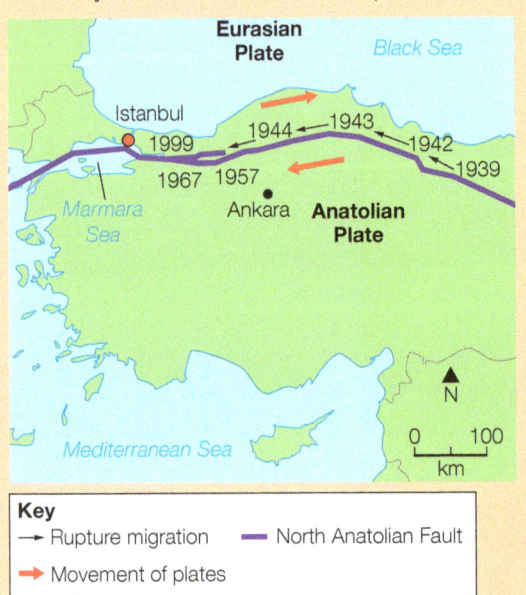

B Migration of earthquakes along the North Anatolian Fault, Turkey

Protection

Volcanoes

The sheer power of a volcanic eruption means that there is often little that can be done to protect people and property. However, it is possible to use earth embankments or explosives to divert lava flows away from property. This has been done on the slopes of Mount Etna in Italy.

Earthquakes

Earthquake protection is the main way to reduce risk. It is possible to construct buildings and bridges to resist the ground shaking associated with an earthquake (diagram **C**). In Chile, new buildings have reinforced concrete columns strengthened by a steel frame. Regular earthquake drills help people keep alert and be prepared.

It is possible to construct tsunami walls at the coast to protect people and important buildings such as nuclear power stations.

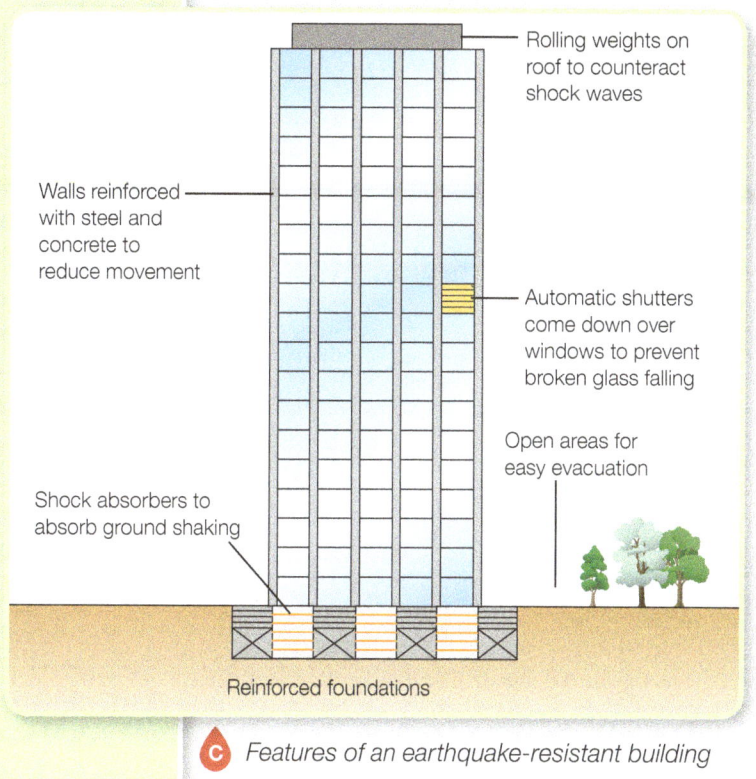

C Features of an earthquake-resistant building

Planning

Volcanoes

Hazard maps have been produced for many of the world's most dangerous volcanoes, showing the likely areas to be affected. They can be used in planning to restrict certain land uses or to identify which areas need to be evacuated when an eruption is about to happen.

Earthquakes

Maps can be produced to show the effects of an earthquake or identify those areas most at risk from damage. High-value land uses such as hospitals, reservoirs and office blocks can then be protected in these vulnerable areas.

ACTIVITIES

1. Why does rising magma cause earthquakes to occur?
2. a How can scientists monitor the changing shape of a volcano?
   b What are the other warning signs of an eruption?
3. Use map **B** to explain why Istanbul is at risk from a future earthquake.
4. How can buildings be made safer to withstand earthquakes (diagram **C**)?

Stretch yourself

What methods are used to monitor *either* Mount Vesuvius or Mount Etna?

Practice question

'Earthquakes don't kill people, buildings do.'
Use evidence to support this statement. *(4 marks)*

3 Weather hazards

3.1 Global atmospheric circulation

On this spread you will find out how global atmospheric circulation affects global weather and climate

What is global atmospheric circulation?

The cruising altitude (height) of an aeroplane is about 10 km above the ground surface. At this altitude the vast majority of the atmosphere's mass is below you (diagram **A**). The atmosphere – the air above our heads – is a highly complex swirling mass of gases, liquids and solids. These include water droplets, water vapour, ash, carbon dioxide and oxygen – just to mention a few!

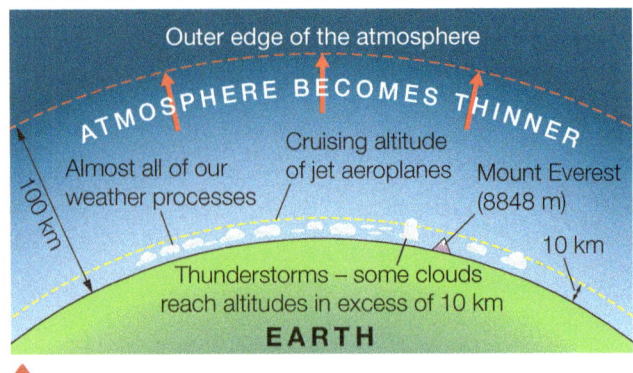

A The atmosphere

How does global atmospheric circulation work?

Diagram **B** shows global atmospheric circulation. This involves a number of circular air movements called cells. These cells all join together to form the overall circulation of the Earth's atmosphere.

- Air that is *sinking* towards the ground surface forms areas of *high pressure* (for example, at the North Pole). Winds on the ground move outwards from these areas.

- Air that is *rising* from the ground surface forms areas of *low pressure* on the ground, for example at the Equator. Winds on the ground move towards these areas of low pressure.

- Winds on the ground are distorted by the Earth's rotation. They curve as they move from areas of high pressure to areas of low pressure.

- Surface winds are very important in transferring heat and moisture from one place to another.

- The patterns of pressure belts and winds are affected by seasonal changes. The tilt and rotation of the Earth causes relative changes in the position of the overhead Sun. These seasonal changes cause pressure belts and winds to move north during our summer and then south during our winter.

B Global atmospheric circulation

Did you know?
The term 'trade winds' comes from the fourteenth century word 'trade' meaning path or track. It was centuries later that the winds became important for the spread of trade across the world.

How does global circulation affect the world's weather?

Global atmospheric circulation is what drives the world's weather. The circulation cells, pressure belts and surface winds (diagram **B**) affect the weather around the world. For example, the trade winds in the tropics are responsible for driving tropical storms (hurricanes) across these regions bringing chaos and destruction to coastal regions in their path.

Weather hazards

Cloudy and wet in the UK

The UK is located at about 55° north just below the 60° N line of latitude. This puts the UK close to the boundary of cold polar air moving down from the north and warm sub-tropical air moving up from the south.

The boundary between these two air masses is unstable. Here there is rising air and low-pressure belts (the *sub-polar low*) on the ground. Rising air cools, condenses and forms cloud and rain. This is why it is often cloudy and wet in the UK.

Surface winds in these mid-latitudes come from the south-west. These winds bring warm and wet conditions to the UK. But sometimes the cold polar air from the north moves down over the UK bringing snow and very cold winter weather.

C Wet weather in the UK

Hot and dry in the desert

Most of the world's hot deserts are found at about 30° north and south of the Equator. Here the air is sinking (diagram **B**), making a belt of high pressure (the sub-tropical high). Air isn't rising here, so there are few clouds forming and little rainfall. The lack of cloud makes it very hot during the day and very cold at night, as heat is quickly lost from the ground.

D Hot, dry weather in the desert

Hot and sweaty at the Equator

At the Equator the air is rising (diagram **B**) and there is another low-pressure belt (the *equatorial low*). This part of the world is very much hotter than the UK, with the sun directly overhead. Equatorial regions, such as central Africa and south-east Asia, experience hot, humid conditions. It is often cloudy with high rainfall. This is the region where tropical rainforests are found.

E Hot, humid weather at the Equator

ACTIVITIES

1. Copy diagram **B**. Draw the lines of latitude and label the Equator. Add the winds and circulation cells to your diagram. Use different colours to show the high- and low-pressure belts.
2. What do you notice about patterns of surface winds in relation to high- and low-pressure belts?
3. Explain why the patterns of pressure belts and surface winds move north and south during the year.
4. How does the atmospheric circulation system explain the UK's mild, cloudy and wet weather?
5. Draw a sketch to show how atmospheric circulation accounts for the high rainfall at the Equator.

Stretch yourself

Find a map to show the tracks followed by tropical storms. Use diagram **B** to add the Equator and the tropics. Draw on the trade winds to show how they are responsible for the east–west movement of the storms.

Practice question

Explain how the global atmospheric system affects the weather and climate of the tropics. *(6 marks)*

19

3.2 Where and how are tropical storms formed?

On this spread you will find out about the distribution and formation of tropical storms

What is a tropical storm?

A **tropical storm** is a huge storm that develops in the tropics (image **A**). In the USA and the Caribbean these are called hurricanes. In south-east Asia and Australia they are called cyclones, but in Japan and the Philippines they are called typhoons.

Tropical storms are incredibly powerful and can cause devastation to small islands and coastal regions. Photo **B** shows some of the damage caused by Hurricane Sandy on the east coast of the USA in 2012. It was the costliest and most deadly Atlantic storm of the year, killing 285 people.

A *Satellite image of Hurricane Sandy off the coast of Florida, USA, 2012*

Where do tropical storms form?

Map **C** shows the distribution of tropical storms. It also provides some useful clues about the formation of tropical storms.

- Tropical storms form over warm oceans (above 27 °C), which explains why they are found in the tropics.
- They form in the summer and autumn when sea temperatures are at their highest.
- Most tropical storms form 5–15° north and south of the Equator. This is because at the Equator there is not enough 'spin' from the rotation of the Earth. The effect of the Earth's rotation is called the *Coriolis effect*. A tropical storm is a spinning mass of clouds (photo **A**).
- In tropical regions the intense heat makes the air unstable causing it to rise rapidly. These unstable conditions are important in the formation of hurricanes.

B *The impact of Hurricane Sandy in Queens, New York*

C *The distribution of tropical storms*

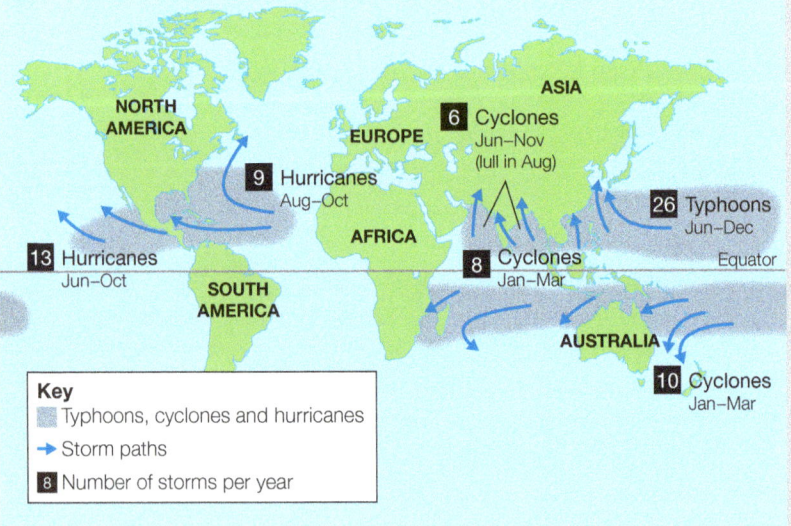

20

How do tropical storms form?

Scientists are not certain what causes the formation of a hurricane, but it involves the sequence of events shown below.

On reaching land the storm's energy supply (evaporated water) is cut off. Friction with the land slows it down and it begins to weaken. If the storm reaches warm seas after crossing the land, it may pick up strength again.

As the storm is carried across the ocean by the prevailing winds, it continues to gather strength.

The storm now develops an eye at its centre where air descends rapidly. The outer edge of the eye is the eye wall where the most intense weather conditions (strong winds and heavy rain) are felt.

Several smaller thunderstorms join together to form a giant spinning storm. When surface winds reach an average of 120 km per hour (75 miles per hour) the storm officially becomes a tropical storm.

As the air condenses it releases heat, which powers the storm and draws up more and more water from the ocean.

This evaporated air cools as it rises and condenses to form towering thunderstorm clouds.

A strong upward movement of air draws water vapour up from the warm ocean surface.

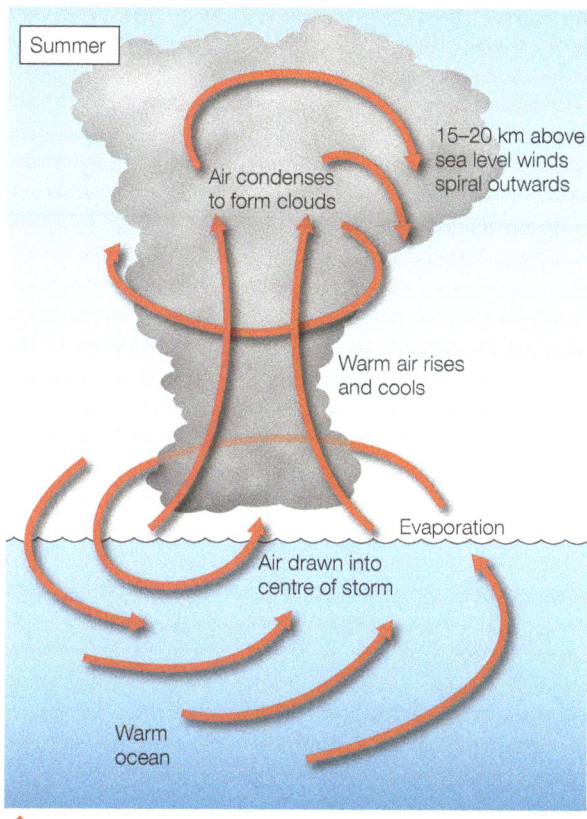

D Formation of a tropical storm

ACTIVITIES

1 a In which part of the world are tropical storms called cyclones?
   b During which months are hurricanes most likely to affect the east coast of the USA?
   c On average how many cyclones affect Australia each year?
   d Which countries are most likely to experience tropical storms during the year?
2 Why do tropical storms not form at the Equator?

Stretch yourself

Make a copy of diagram **D** showing how a tropical storm forms. Add detailed labels in the form of a sequence (1, 2, 3, etc.). Describe the formation of a tropical storm.

Practice question

Using map **C** and your own knowledge, describe the global distribution of tropical storms. *(4 marks)*

3.3 The structure and features of tropical storms

On this spread you will find out about the structure and features of tropical storms, and how climate change might affect tropical storms in the future.

What is the structure of a tropical storm?

Tropical storms can be huge, up to 480 km (300 miles) across. A tropical storm has a roughly symmetrical shape. Diagram **A** shows an imaginary cross-section (X–Y) through a tropical cyclone.

Did you know? A tropical storm can release the energy of 10 atom bombs every second!

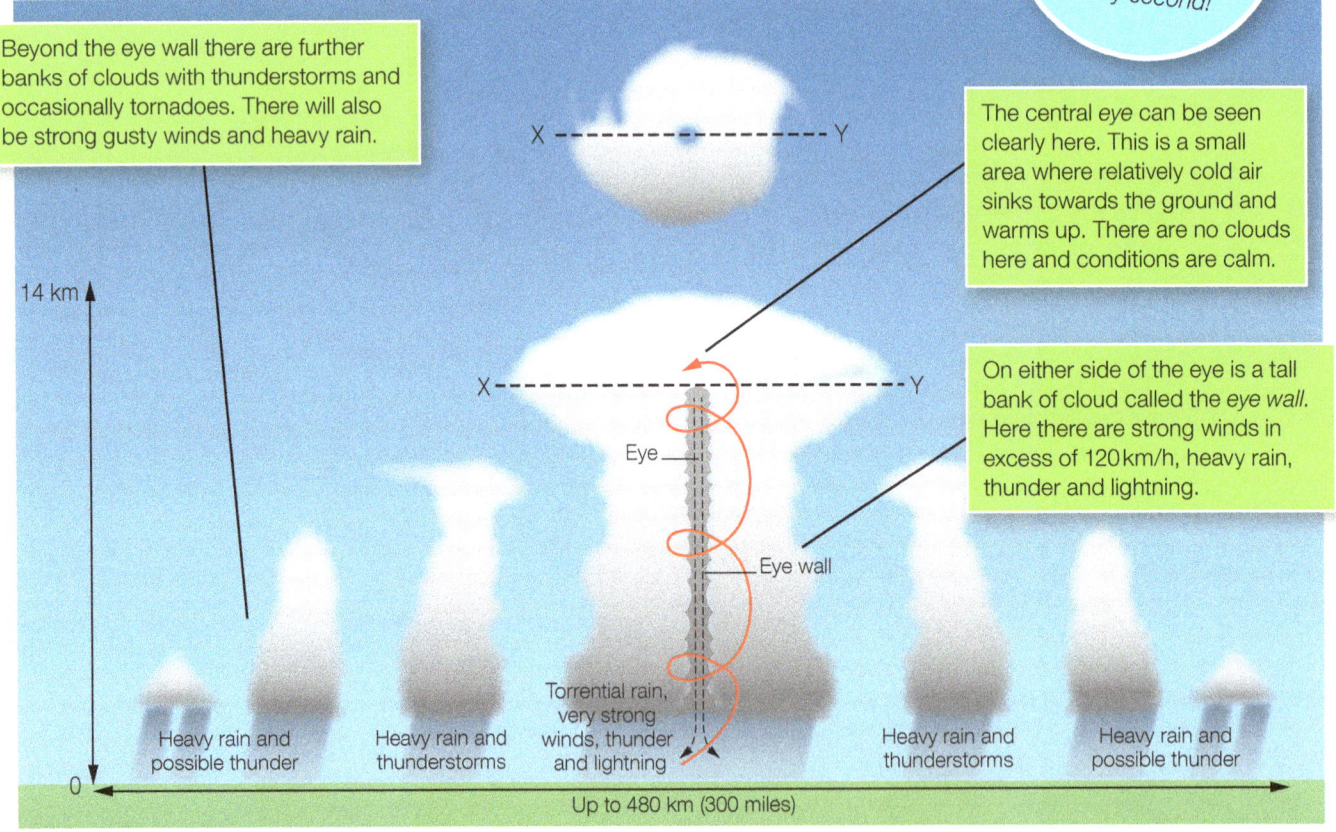

Beyond the eye wall there are further banks of clouds with thunderstorms and occasionally tornadoes. There will also be strong gusty winds and heavy rain.

The central *eye* can be seen clearly here. This is a small area where relatively cold air sinks towards the ground and warms up. There are no clouds here and conditions are calm.

On either side of the eye is a tall bank of cloud called the *eye wall*. Here there are strong winds in excess of 120 km/h, heavy rain, thunder and lightning.

A Structure of a tropical storm

Will climate change affect tropical storms?

There is strong scientific evidence that global temperatures have risen over the last few decades. These rises may be impacting on the world's natural systems. But what impact will they have on tropical storms?

Tropical storm facts

- Tropical storms are the most destructive storms on Earth.
- They are given names for identification. Hurricanes, for example, are given alternating male and female names each 'season'. The first hurricane starts with 'A', the second 'B', and so on. In 2020, Bertha will be the first named Atlantic hurricane, followed by Cristobal, Dolly and Edouard.
- Hurricane Camille in 1969 had the highest recorded wind speed, estimated at 304 km/h (190 mph).

How strong is a hurricane?

Hurricanes are measured using the Saffir–Simpson scale.

Category	Wind speeds
5	> 252 km/h
4	209–251 km/h
3	178–208 km/h
2	154–177 km/h
1	119–153 km/h

Weather hazards

Distribution

Over the last few decades sea surface temperatures in the tropics have increased by 0.25–0.5°C. As patterns of sea surface temperatures change, they may affect the distribution of tropical storms.

In the future, tropical storms may affect areas outside the current hazard zone, such as the South Atlantic and parts of the sub-tropics. Hurricanes may also become more powerful.

Hurricane Catarina (2004)

In March 2004, the south-east coast of Brazil was struck by a Category 2 hurricane, the first ever recorded there. Coastal communities were taken by surprise and extensive damage was done. Between three and 11 people died, 40 000 homes were damaged and 85 per cent of the region's banana plants were destroyed.

Hurricanes do not usually form in the South Atlantic (see map **C** on page 20). Cold ocean currents keep waters below the minimum temperature required for hurricane formation. Strong winds 'shear' rising air preventing storms from forming.

In March 2004, sea surface temperatures were unusually high. Conditions were right for a hurricane to form. Such events might become more common as sea surface temperatures change.

Frequency

Graph **B** shows the number of hurricanes recorded in the North Atlantic since 1878. Six of the 10 most active years since 1950 have happened since the mid-1990s. Some computer models indicate that the frequency of tropical storms may decrease in the future – but, their *intensity* might increase.

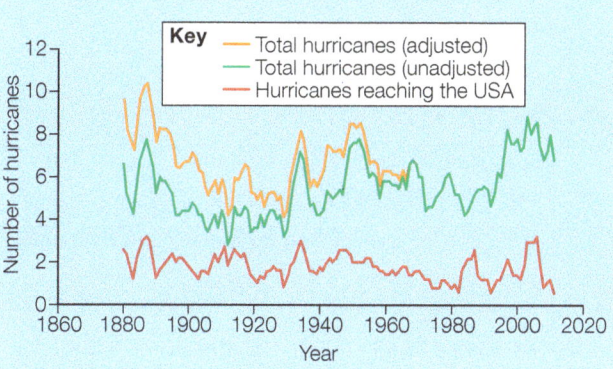

B Hurricanes in the North Atlantic, 1878–2013

Intensity

Graph **C** shows hurricane intensity in the North Atlantic has risen in the last 20 years. This appears to be linked to increases in sea surface temperatures. But comparisons with the past may not be completely reliable. More data will be needed over a longer period of time.

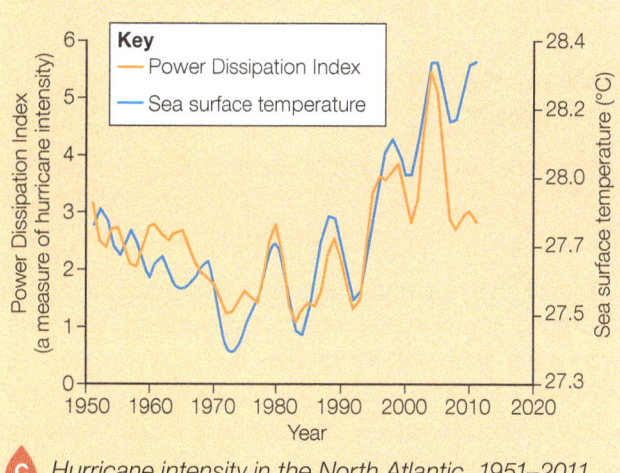

C Hurricane intensity in the North Atlantic, 1951–2011

ACTIVITIES

1. Make a copy of diagram **A**. Add labels to describe the main features of a tropical storm.
2. **a** What is the orange line on graph **B** and why is it important?
   b Describe the pattern of hurricanes reaching the USA since 1980.
   c Is there evidence of an overall trend since 1878?
3. Describe and explain the pattern of the Power Dissipation Index between 1950 and 2011 (graph **C**).

Stretch yourself

Carry out some research on Hurricane Catarina. Why did the formation of the storm make it so unusual?

Practice question

Study graph **C**. Has there been an increase in hurricane intensity in recent decades? Support your answer with evidence. *(4 marks)*

3.4 Typhoon Haiyan – a tropical storm

On this spread you will find out about the effects of and responses to Typhoon Haiyan

Example

Tropical storms can have devastating effects on people and property. The strong winds can tear off roofs, overturn cars and make large objects fly. Torrential rain can lead to flooding. Strong winds and low atmospheric pressure may cause the sea level to rise by several metres to form a destructive storm surge. These storm surges cause the most loss of life.

Tropical storms can be tracked and warnings given for people to evacuate coastal areas. In the aftermath, people need emergency support. Reconstruction may take many months.

A *The track of Typhoon Haiyan*

What happened?

In November 2013 'Super' Typhoon Haiyan – a Category 5 storm on the Saffir–Simpson scale – hit the Philippines (map **A**). Huge areas of coastline and several towns were devastated by winds of up to 275 km/h (170 mph) and waves as high as 15 m (45 ft). It was one of the strongest storms ever recorded.

What were the effects of Typhoon Haiyan?

The province of Leyte took the full force of the storm. The city of Tacloban was one of the worst affected places, with most of the 220 000 inhabitants left homeless.

Most of the destruction in Tacloban was caused by a 5 m high *storm surge*. This is a wall of water similar to a tsunami. The very low atmospheric pressure associated with the typhoon caused the level of the sea to rise. As the strong winds swept this water onshore, it formed a wall of water several metres high.

B *The destruction at Tacloban*

Primary effects (impacts of strong winds, heavy rain and storm surge)

- About 6300 people killed – most drowned by the storm surge.
- Over 600 000 people displaced and 40 000 homes damaged or flattened – 90 per cent of Tacloban city destroyed.
- Tacloban airport terminal badly damaged.
- The typhoon destroyed 30 000 fishing boats.
- Strong winds damaged buildings and power lines and destroyed crops.
- Over 400 mm of rain caused widespread **flooding**.

Secondary effects (longer-term impacts resulting from primary effects)

- 14 million people affected, many left homeless and 6 million people lost their source of income.
- Flooding caused landslides and blocked roads, cutting off aid to remote communities.
- Power supplies in some areas cut off for a month.
- Ferry services and airline flights disrupted for weeks, slowing down aid efforts.
- Shortages of water, food and shelter affected many people, leading to outbreaks of disease.
- Many jobs lost, hospitals were damaged, shops and schools were destroyed, affecting people's livelihoods and education.
- Looting and violence broke out in Tacloban.

What were the responses to Typhoon Haiyan?

Immediate responses

- International government and aid agencies responded quickly with food aid, water and temporary shelters.
- US aircraft carrier *George Washington* and helicopters assisted with search and rescue and delivery of aid.
- Over 1200 evacuation centres were set up to help the homeless.
- UK government sent shelter kits (photo **D**), each one able to provide emergency shelter for a family.
- French, Belgian and Israeli field hospitals set up to help the injured.
- The Philippines Red Cross delivered basic food aid, which included rice, canned food, sugar, salt and cooking oil.

C *A survivor in Tacloban*

Long-term responses

- The UN and countries including the UK, Australia, Japan and the US donated financial aid, supplies and medical support.
- Rebuilding of roads, bridges and airport facilities.
- 'Cash for work' programmes – people paid to help clear debris and rebuild the city.
- Foreign donors, including the US, Australia and the EU, supported new livelihood opportunities.
- Rice farming and fishing quickly re-established. Coconut production – where trees may take five years to bear fruit – will take longer.
- Aid agencies such as Oxfam supported the replacement of fishing boats – a vital source of income.
- Thousands of homes have been built away from areas at risk from flooding.
- More cyclone shelters built to accommodate people evacuated from coastal areas.

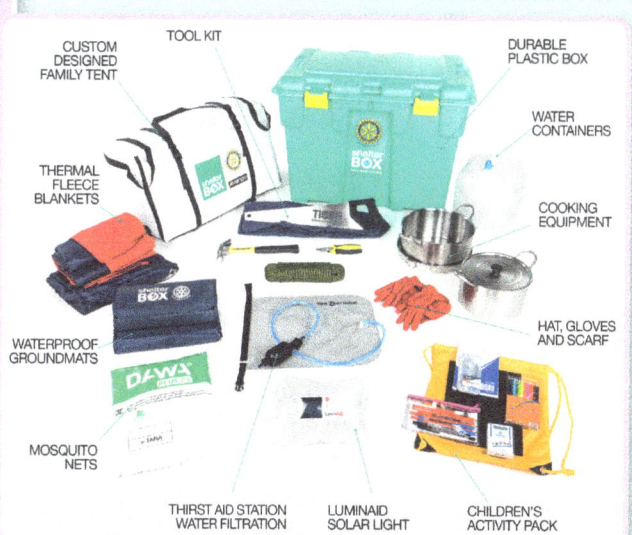

D *The contents of a Shelter Box*

ACTIVITIES

1. Describe the track of the typhoon (map **A**).
2. **a** Why do you think so many buildings were destroyed (photo **B**)?
   b What are the challenges facing the authorities in rebuilding this area?
3. **a** Describe the destruction caused by the tsunami.
   b What are his immediate needs and what are the challenges facing him in the future?
4. Describe the purpose of each of the items in the Shelter Box (photo **D**).

Stretch yourself

How has the city of Tacloban been rebuilt since the disaster struck? What is the situation like now? Is the city in a better position to cope with a future typhoon?

Practice question

Describe the primary and secondary effects of a tropical storm. Use a named example and your own knowledge.
(9 marks)

25

3.5 Reducing the effects of tropical storms

On this spread you will find out how the effects of tropical storms can be reduced

Monitoring and prediction

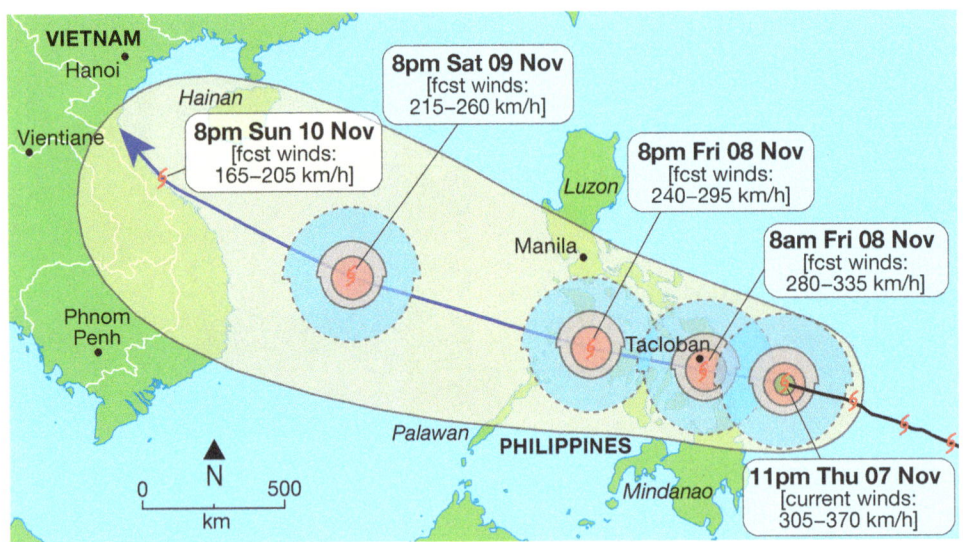

A The predicted track of Typhoon Haiyan

Map **A** shows the location of Typhoon Haiyan at 11 pm local time on Thursday 7 November 2013. This was just 9 hours before it struck Leyte and flattened most of the city of Tacloban. The map shows the predicted course (track) of the tropical storm across the Philippines. Notice that the area showing the predicted track becomes wider with time. This is because the future track of the tropical storm is uncertain.

Developments in technology have made it possible to predict and monitor tropical storms more accurately and effectively.

In the North Atlantic, there are two levels of warning issued by the National Hurricane Center in Miami:

- Hurricane Watch – advises that hurricane conditions are possible.
- Hurricane Warning – advises that hurricane conditions are expected and that people should take immediate action (e.g. evacuate to high ground or take shelter).

Think about it
Storm surges are often the greatest threat to life and property from a tropical storm. Why do you think this is?

Protection

There are a number of options available to protect people from the hazards associated with tropical storms.

- Windows, doors and roofs reinforced to strengthen buildings to withstand strong winds.
- Storm drains constructed in urban areas to take away excessive amounts of rainfall and prevent flooding.
- Sea walls built to protect key properties from storm surges.
- Houses close to the coast constructed on stilts so that a storm surge will pass beneath.
- In Bangladesh nearly 2000 cyclone shelters have been built (photo **B**).

B Cyclone shelter in Bangladesh

Weather hazards

Planning

It is unrealistic to stop the tens of millions of people living and working in coastal areas that are at risk from tropical storms. Many people rely upon fishing or tourism to make a living. Even in rich countries like the USA, vast urban developments have been allowed to take place on vulnerable barrier islands off the coast of Florida, for example Miami Beach. South Miami was hit by a powerful hurricane in 1992. However, building developments have still taken place on land at risk from flooding. It's only a matter of time before Miami is hit again.

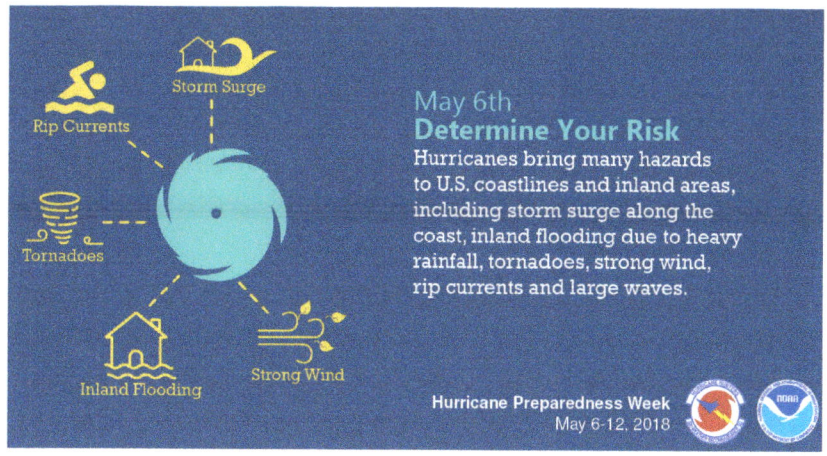

C *National Hurricane Preparedness Week (USA)*

Planning to reduce the tropical storm hazard is mostly about raising individual and community awareness. People need to understand the potential dangers and be able to respond. In the USA there is a National Hurricane Preparedness Week (image **C**), which focuses on educating people about potential dangers ahead of the next hurricane season. Families are encouraged to devise their own plan of action should a warning be issued.

D *Bikes carry cyclone warnings to rural communities in Bangladesh*

Bangladesh – a success story

Early warning systems, cyclone shelters (photo **B**) and greater awareness have helped reduce the death toll from tropical cyclones in Bangladesh. The number of deaths has decreased 100-fold over the past 40 years from 500 000 deaths in 1970 to 4234 in 2007.

Tropical cyclones are tracked by the Bangladesh Meteorological Department. Warnings are issued in several languages by radio, television and via social media. In rural areas, even the most remote communities are reached – sometimes by bike (photo **D**)!

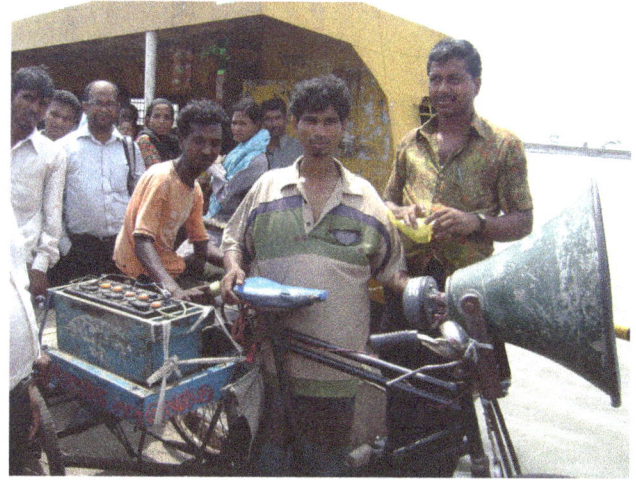

ACTIVITIES

1. **a** Use map **A** to describe the characteristics of Typhoon Haiyan at 11 pm on Thursday 7 November.
   b Describe the direction of the predicted track of the typhoon.
   c How many hours was the typhoon expected to take to cross the Philippines?
   d Where was the typhoon expected to make landfall after the Philippines?
2. In photo **B** what are the special features of the cyclone shelter designed to reduce the impacts of a storm surge?

Stretch yourself

Do some further research about the work of the National Hurricane Center in Miami.
- How are hurricanes forecast and predictions made?
- What advice is given to people who live in vulnerable areas to help them prepare?

Practice question

Explain why planning and being prepared is the best option for reducing the effects of tropical storms. *(4 marks)*

27

4 Climate change

4.1 What is the evidence for climate change?

On this spread you will consider the evidence for climate change from the beginning of the Quaternary period to the present day

It's not as cold as it used to be!

Graph **A** shows the pattern of global temperatures for the last 5.5 million years. This may sound like a long time but remember that the Earth was formed 4600 million years ago!

The graph shows how temperature has changed over time (purple line) compared to today's average temperature (shown by the dashed line at 0). The last 2.6 million years is called the *Quaternary period*. During this geological period temperatures have fluctuated a great deal. Despite these fluctuations the graph shows there has been a gradual cooling during this period.

In graph **B** the downward cold 'spikes' are *glacial periods* when ice covered parts of Europe and North America. The warmer periods in between are called *interglacial periods*. Notice that today's average temperature is higher than during almost all of the last 400 000 years.

Graph **C** shows that in the last few decades the average global temperature has increased relative to the 1901–2000 average. This has become known as 'global warming', the most recent indication of climate change.

Since 1880 the average global temperature has risen by 0.85 °C. Most of this increase has occurred since the mid-1970s.

Global effects of climate change

Climate change has already had significant effects on global ecosystems and on people's lives.

- Many of the world's glaciers and ice caps are shrinking.
- Arctic sea ice is less extensive than in the past, affecting wildlife such as polar bears. However, this may provide opportunities for ships to use the North-West Passage in the future.
- Low-lying Islands such as the Maldives and Tuvalu are under threat from sea-level rise.
- Sea levels may rise by 1 m by 2100, flooding agricultural land in Bangladesh, Vietnam, India and China.

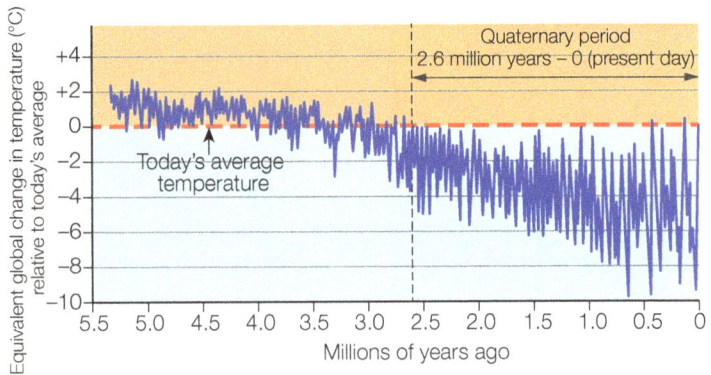

A Average global temperatures for the last 5.5 million years using information from sediment cores

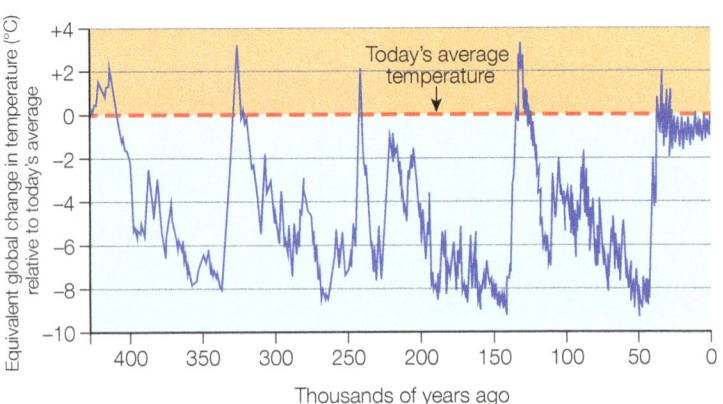

B Alternating cold (glacial) and warm (interglacial) periods experienced over the last 400 000 years

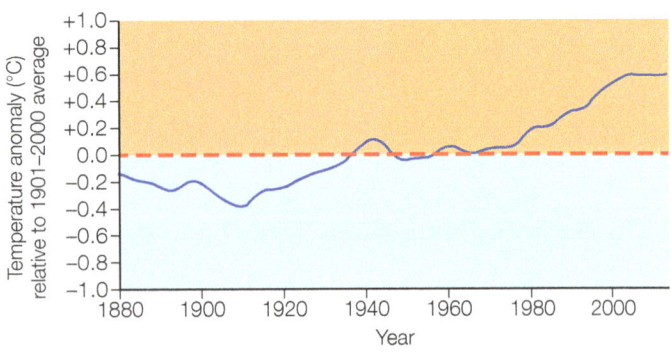

Key

☐ Warmer than today   ☐ Cooler than today

C Average global temperature (1880–2013) based on recorded temperature records

28

Climate change

What is the evidence for climate change?

Temperature is measured directly using an instrument called a thermometer. Reliable measurements using thermometers go back only about a hundred years. In the UK, for example, reliable weather records began in 1910. So, how do we know what temperatures were in the distant past?

Without the use of thermometers, scientists use indirect data stored as a fossil record. These are found in deep ocean sediments and frozen ice cores.

When layers of sediment or fresh falls of snow become buried they trap and preserve evidence of the global temperature at that time. Scientists can study the oxygen in ocean sediments or water molecules in ice to calculate temperature. They can be accurately dated and this information used to plot graphs, such as graphs **A** and **B**. Ice cores have been used to reconstruct temperature patterns from as long as 400 000 years ago (photo **D**).

D Extracting ice cores in Alaska

Things are heating up!

Direct measurements of temperature using thermometers have indicated a clear warming trend (graph **C**). There is other evidence that climate change is taking place.

Shrinking glaciers and melting ice
Glaciers throughout the world are shrinking and retreating. It is estimated that some may disappear completely by 2035. Arctic sea ice has thinned by 65 per cent since 1975 and in 2014 its extent was at an all-time low (photo **E**).

Rising sea level
According to the Intergovernmental Panel on Climate Change (IPCC), the average global sea level has risen between 10 and 20 cm in the past 100 years. There are two reasons why sea levels have risen:
- When temperatures rise and freshwater ice melts, more water flows to the seas from glaciers and ice caps.
- When ocean water warms it expands in volume – this is called thermal expansion.

What is the recent evidence for climate change?

Seasonal changes
Studies have suggested that the timing of natural seasonal activities such as tree flowering and bird migration is advancing. A study of bird nesting in the mid-1990s discovered that 65 species nested an average of 9 days earlier than in the 1970s. Could this be evidence of a warming world?

 Shrinkage of Arctic sea ice, 1979–2012 (yellow line indicates extent in 1979)

ACTIVITIES

1. Describe the pattern of temperatures during the Quaternary period (graphs **A** and **B**).
2. **a** Describe the trend of the average temperature between 1880 and 1940 (graph **C**).
   b Describe the trend in average temperature since 2000.
   c Do you think this graph provides strong evidence for global warming?
3. Briefly describe how ice cores provide scientists with data about past temperatures.

Stretch yourself

Research the shrinking of the world's glaciers and how this is providing evidence of climate change. Find images to show the changes that have taken place in the last few decades. What impact might the melting of glaciers have on people's lives?

Practice question

Study photo **E**. Explain how the shrinkage of Arctic sea ice could be evidence of climate change. *(4 marks)*

29

4.2 What are the natural causes of climate change?

On this spread you will find out about the natural causes of climate change

Natural causes of climate change

Scientists believe that there are several natural causes for climate change. These include:

- changes in the Earth's orbit
- variations in heat output from the Sun
- volcanic activity.

Orbital changes

Milutin Milankovitch was a Serbian geophysicist and astronomer. While he was imprisoned during the First World War (1914–18) he studied the Earth's orbit and identified three distinct *cycles* that he believed affected the world's climate. These are known as *Milankovitch cycles* (diagram **A**).

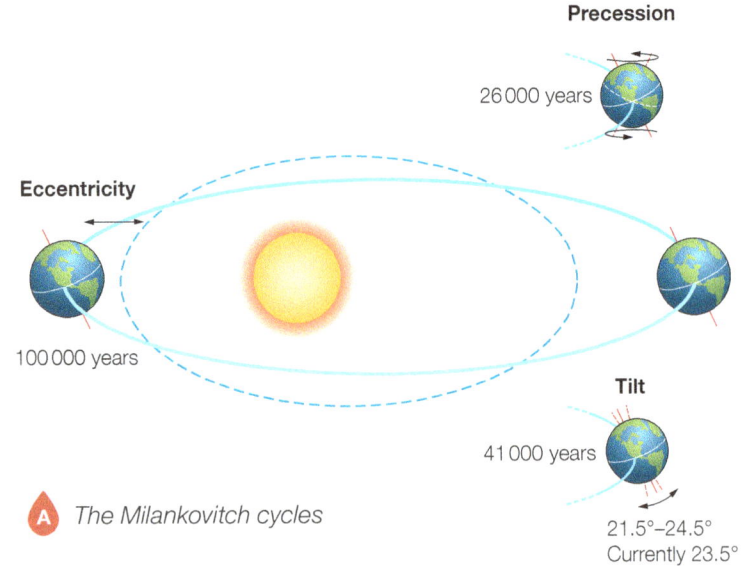

A The Milankovitch cycles

Scientists believe that these cycles affect the timings and seasons of the Earth's climate. In particular, the 100 000-year eccentricity cycle coincides closely with the alternating cold (glacial) and warm (interglacial) periods in the Quaternary period.

Eccentricity
This describes the path of the Earth as it orbits the Sun. The Earth's orbit is not fixed – it changes from being almost circular to being mildly elliptical. A complete cycle – from circular to elliptical and back to circular again – occurs about every 100 000 years.

Axial tilt
The Earth spins on its axis, causing night and day. The Earth's axis is currently tilted at an angle of 23.5°. However, over a period of about 41 000 years, the tilt of the Earth's axis moves back and forth between two extremes – 21.5° and 24.5°. You can see this on diagram **A**.

The Milankovitch cycles

Precession
This describes a natural 'wobble' rather like a spinning top. A complete wobble cycle takes about 26 000 years. The Earth's wobble accounts for certain regions of the world – such as northern Norway – experiencing very long days and very long nights at certain times of the year.

Solar activity

Scientists have identified cyclical changes in solar energy output linked to the presence of *sunspots*. A sunspot is a dark patch that appears from time to time on the surface of the Sun (photo **B**). The number of sunspots increases from a minimum to a maximum and then back to a minimum over a period of about 11 years. This 11-year period is called the *sunspot cycle*.

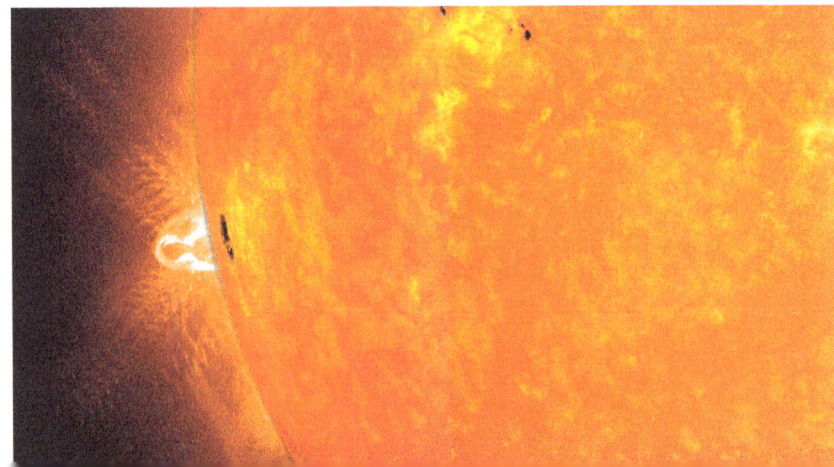

B Sunspot and solar flare on the surface of the Sun, 2014

30

Climate change

- When sunspot activity is at a *maximum*, the Sun gives off more heat.
  Large explosions occur on the surface of the Sun resulting in solar flares.
- When sunspot activity is at a *minimum* the solar output is reduced.
  This can lead to lower temperatures on Earth.

For example, very few sunspots were observed between the years 1645 and 1715. This coincided with the coldest period during the so-called 'Little Ice Age', when Europe experienced a much colder climate with severe winters (image **C**).

C A 'Frost Fair' on the River Thames during the 'Little Ice Age'

Volcanic activity

Violent volcanic eruptions blast huge quantities of ash, gases and liquids into the atmosphere.

- Volcanic ash can block out the Sun, reducing temperatures on the Earth. This tends to be a short-term impact.
- The fine droplets that result from the conversion of sulphur dioxide to sulphuric acid act like tiny mirrors reflecting radiation from the Sun. This can last a lot longer and can affect the climate for many years.

The cooling of the lower atmosphere and reduction of surface temperatures is called a *volcanic winter*.

> **Eruption of Mount Tambora, 1815**
>
> In 1815 there was a massive volcanic eruption of Mount Tambora in Indonesia (image **D**). It was the most powerful eruption in the world for 1600 years! Ash and sulphuric acid caused average global temperatures to fall by 0.4–0.7 °C and 1816 became known as 'The year without a summer'.
>
> Across the world harvests failed. There were major food shortages throughout North America and western Europe, including the UK. Food prices rose sharply and there were riots and looting in European cities. It was the worst famine in Europe in the nineteenth century, resulting in an estimated 200 000 deaths.

D Artist's impression of the eruption of Mount Tambora in 1815

Stretch yourself

Carry out some research about 1816, 'The year without a summer'.
Find more information about the impacts of the eruption of Mount Tambora. Could this happen again in the future?

Practice question

Use the example of Mount Tambora to explain how and why volcanic activity can affect global climate. *(4 marks)*

ACTIVITIES

1. Use diagram **A** to answer the following questions.
   a. Which of the Milankovich cycles takes 41 000 years to complete?
   b. Explain the eccentricity cycle.
   c. What is the evidence that the eccentricity cycle has affected global climates?
   d. Describe the precession cycle.
2. Describe how sunspot activity can have an effect on global climates.

4.3 What are the human causes of climate change?

On this spread you will find out about the human causes of climate change

Human causes of climate change

Many scientists believe that human activities are at least partly to blame for the rapid rise in temperatures – known as global warming – since the 1970s. To understand how this is possible you need to understand a natural feature of the atmosphere called the *greenhouse effect*.

What is the greenhouse effect?

You probably know that a greenhouse is a small building entirely made of glass and used by gardeners to create warm conditions to grow plants. So how does it work?

Glass allows radiation (heat) from the Sun to enter the greenhouse (diagram **A**). However, this heat cannot escape through the glass. As a result, the greenhouse becomes warmer than the air outside and is ideal for growing tomatoes and vegetables which need constant warm conditions.

Like a greenhouse, the atmosphere allows most of the heat from the Sun (short-wave radiation) to pass straight through it to warm up the Earth's surface (diagram **B**). However, when the Earth gives off heat in the form of long-wave radiation, some gases such as carbon dioxide (CO_2) and methane are able to absorb it. These gases are called *greenhouse gases*.

In the same way that glass traps heat inside a greenhouse, the greenhouse effect keeps the Earth warm. Without this 'blanketing' effect it would be far too cold for life to exist on Earth.

> **Think about it**
> Think about your own **carbon footprint**. How do you as an individual contribute to the production of greenhouse gases in your everyday life?

A The greenhouse effect

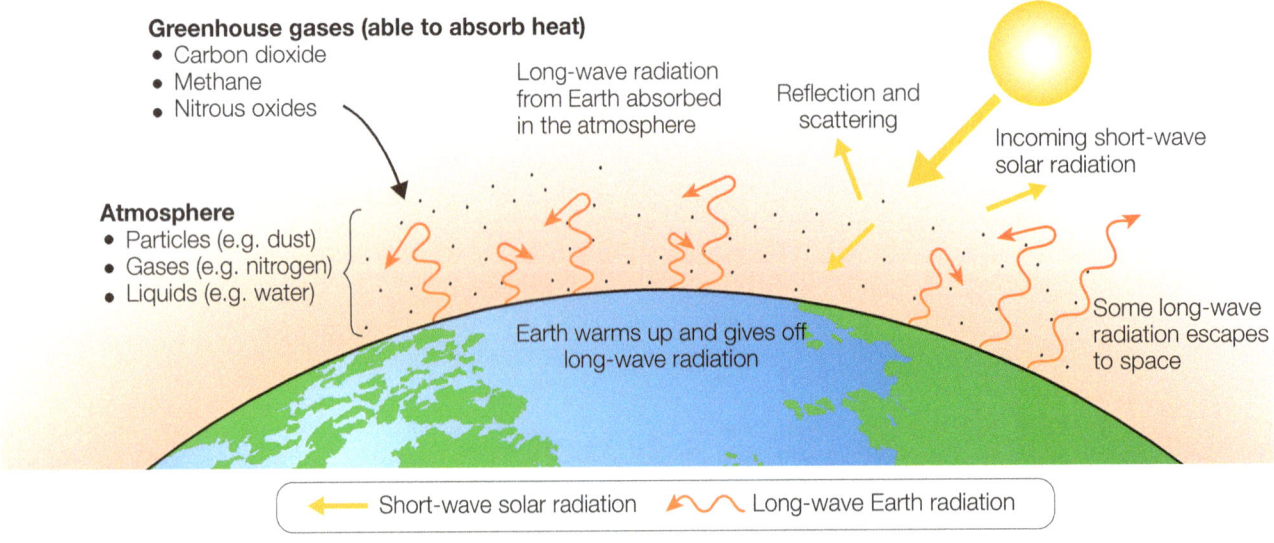

B How the greenhouse effect works

Climate change

The human impact

In recent years, the amounts of greenhouse gases in the atmosphere have increased. Scientists believe that this is due to human activities (diagram **C**).

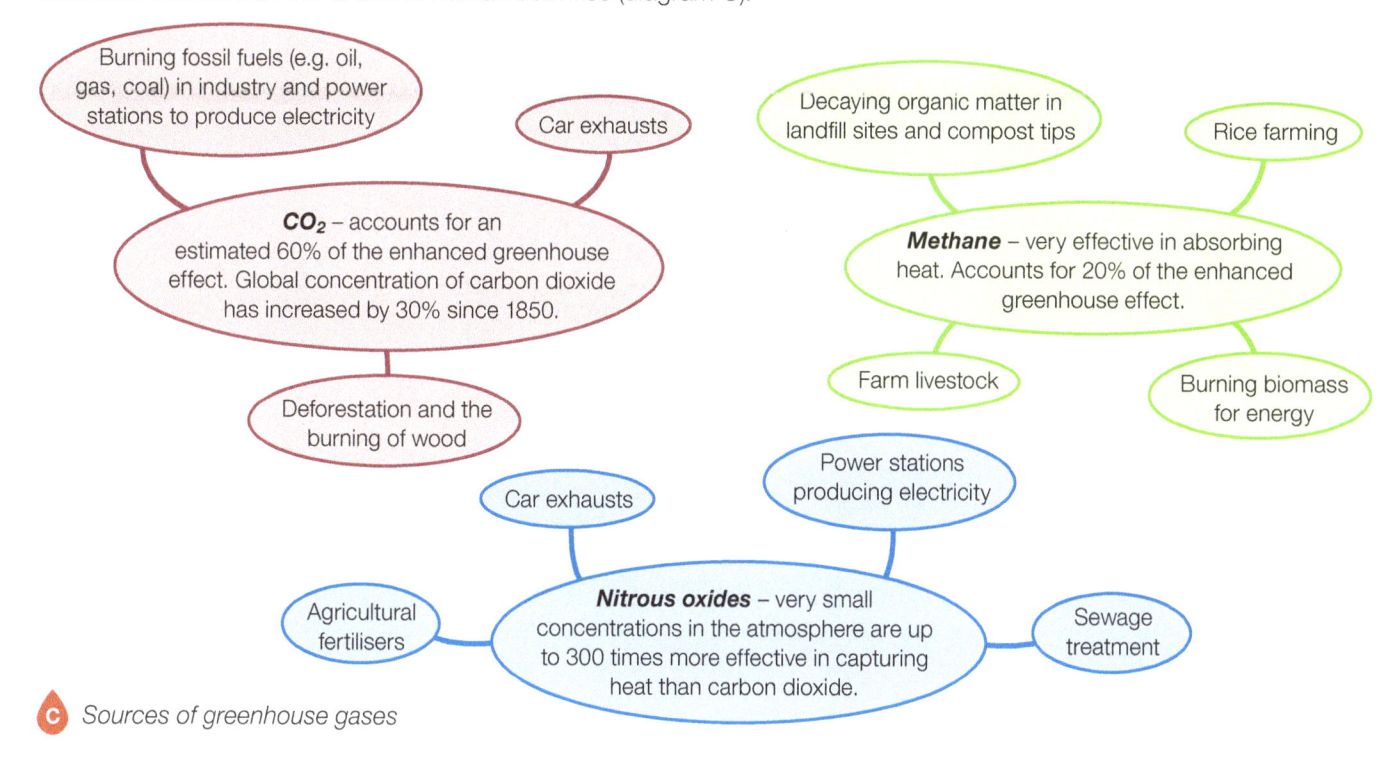

- Burning fossil fuels (e.g. oil, gas, coal) in industry and power stations to produce electricity
- Car exhausts
- **CO₂** – accounts for an estimated 60% of the enhanced greenhouse effect. Global concentration of carbon dioxide has increased by 30% since 1850.
- Deforestation and the burning of wood

- Decaying organic matter in landfill sites and compost tips
- Rice farming
- **Methane** – very effective in absorbing heat. Accounts for 20% of the enhanced greenhouse effect.
- Farm livestock
- Burning biomass for energy

- Car exhausts
- Power stations producing electricity
- Agricultural fertilisers
- **Nitrous oxides** – very small concentrations in the atmosphere are up to 300 times more effective in capturing heat than carbon dioxide.
- Sewage treatment

C Sources of greenhouse gases

Graph **D** shows the recorded changes in carbon dioxide since the 1960s. The trend of this graph is identical to that of average global temperatures. Many scientists believe that this provides clear evidence that human activities are affecting global climates.

It is the increased effectiveness of the greenhouse effect – the so-called *enhanced greenhouse effect* – that scientists believe is causing recent global warming. For the first time in history, human activities appear to be affecting the atmosphere with potentially dramatic effects on the world's climate. By the end of the century average global temperatures could rise by 1.8–4 °C. This could lead to a rise in sea level of 28–43 cm.

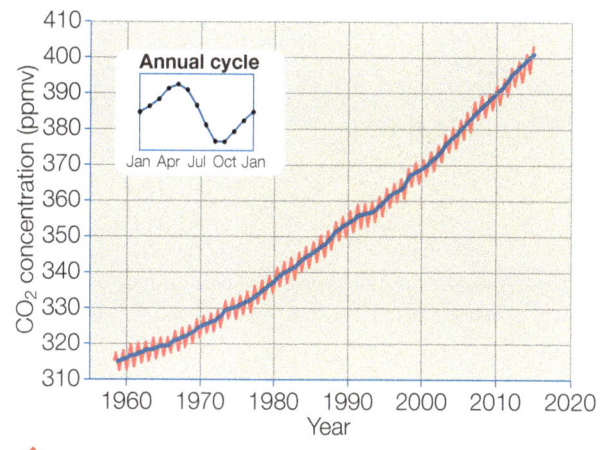

D Increase in CO_2 obtained from direct readings at the Mauna Loa Observatory, Hawaii

ACTIVITIES

1. Make a large copy of diagram **B**. Add the main sources of greenhouse gases (diagram **C**) using simple sketches.
2. a Describe the trend of CO_2 concentration in the atmosphere (graph **D**).
   b Can you suggest why CO_2 in the atmosphere increases in the winter but decreases in the summer? (Hint: think about plants.)
   c Does the graph support the suggestion that human activities may be contributing to global warming? Explain your answer.
3. Explain the enhanced greenhouse effect.

Stretch yourself

Research more information about the sources of greenhouse gases resulting from human activities. Focus your research on carbon emissions and find out which countries are the highest contributors.

Practice question

Outline two reasons why human activities effect the concentration of CO_2 in the atmosphere. *(4 marks)*

4.4 Managing the impacts of climate change (1)

On this spread you will find out how the causes of climate change can be managed (mitigated)

How can climate change be managed?

Alternative energy sources

The burning of **fossil fuels** (coal, oil and gas) to produce electricity, fuel vehicles and power industry contributes 87 per cent of all human-produced CO_2 emissions. The rest comes from land-use changes – mostly deforestation (9 per cent) and industrial processes such as making cement (4 per cent).

To help reduce carbon emissions many countries are turning to alternative sources of energy such as:

- hydro-electricity
- nuclear power
- solar, wind and tidal.

These do not emit large amounts of CO_2. Some are also renewable and will last into the future. Nuclear power uses uranium to generate electricity but does not emit CO_2 as a by-product.

The UK aims to produce 15 per cent of its energy from renewable sources by 2020. There has been investment in renewable energy projects such as wind power. Power companies are encouraged to use renewable sources. A new nuclear reactor is being built at Hinkley Point in Somerset (photo **A**).

A Artist's impression of the new Hinkley Point nuclear reactor. China General Nuclear Power Corp (CGN) is investing US$8.4 billion in Hinkley Point

Carbon capture

Coal is the most polluting of all fossil fuels. China gets 80 per cent of its electricity from burning coal, India 70 per cent and the USA 50 per cent. How can coal continue to be used in a less damaging way?

Carbon capture and storage (CCS) uses technology to capture CO_2 produced from the use of fossil fuels in electricity generation and industrial processes. It is possible to capture up to 90 per cent of the CO_2 that would otherwise enter the atmosphere.

Diagram **B** shows how carbon capture works. Once captured, the carbon gas is compressed and transported by pipeline to an injection well. It is injected as a liquid into the ground to be stored in suitable geological reservoirs.

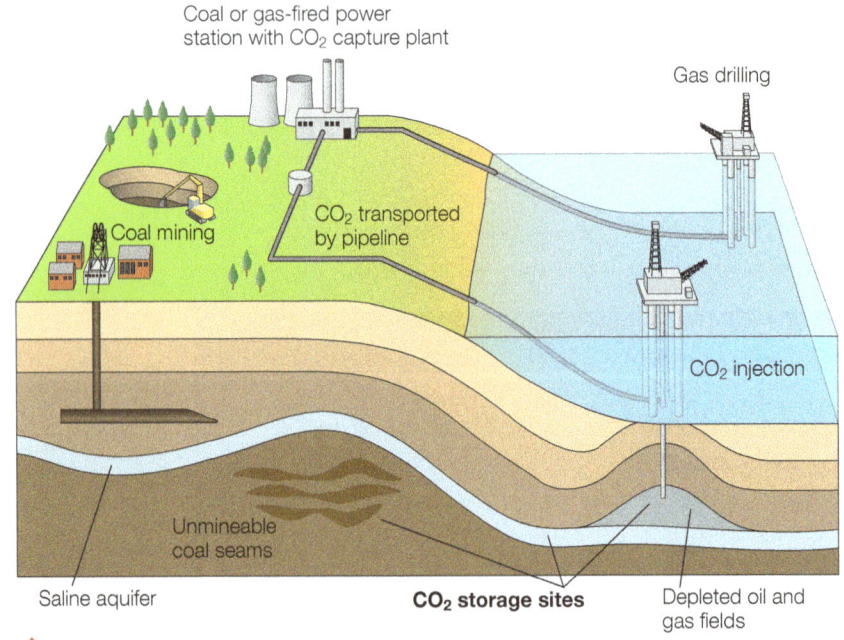

B Carbon capture and storage

Climate change

Planting trees

Trees act as carbon sinks, removing CO_2 from the atmosphere by the process of *photosynthesis*. They also release moisture into the atmosphere. This has a cooling effect by producing more cloud, reducing incoming solar radiation.

Tree planting is well established in many parts of the world. Plantation forests can absorb CO_2 at a faster rate than natural forests and can do so effectively for up to 50 years.

International agreements

Climate change is a global issue and requires global solutions. Carbon emissions spread across the world and affect everyone (figure **C**).

What are the global impacts of climate change?
- Stronger tropical storms
- Higher global temperatures affect food production and water supply
- More heat-related illness and disease, such as malaria
- **Environmental impacts**, such as desertification
- Increased risk of natural hazards, such as droughts and floods
- Wildlife at risk as habitats and ecosystems change
- **Economic impacts**, such as lower crop yields and damage to infrastructure
- Rising sea levels threaten low-lying coastal areas

C Global impacts of climate change

2005
The Kyoto Protocol – the first international treaty – became law. Over 170 countries agreed to reduce carbon emissions by an average of 5.2 per cent below their 1990 levels by 2012. Of the major greenhouse gas emitters, only the USA and Australia refused to sign the treaty.

2009
World leaders met in Copenhagen to consider international agreements on tackling climate change beyond 2012. The outcome was the Copenhagen Accord. It pledged to reduce emissions with financial support for developing nations to help them cope with the impacts of climate change. But there was no legally binding agreement.

2015
Paris Agreement 2015 – 195 countries adopted the first-ever universal and legally binding global climate deal.
- To peak greenhouse gas emissions as soon as possible and achieve a balance between sources and sinks of greenhouse gases in the second half of this century.
- To keep global temperature increase below 2°C and limited to 1.5°C above pre-industrial levels.
- To review progress every five years.
- US$100 billion a year to support climate change initiatives in developing countries by 2020, with further finance in the future.

There have been criticisms that many of these agreements are 'promises' or aims and not firm commitments.

ACTIVITIES

1. How can alternative sources of energy address the problem of carbon dioxide emissions?
2. Make a copy of diagram **B**. Use detailed annotations to describe how carbon capture and storage works.
3. Why are forests described as 'carbon sinks'?
4. Do you think international agreements will help to solve the problems associated with climate change? Explain your answer.

Stretch yourself

Find out more about carbon capture and storage.
- What are the benefits of this mitigation option?
- What problems and issues need to be overcome for it to be widely used in the future?

Maths skills

Draw a pie chart to show changes to human-produced CO_2 emissions: burning fossil fuels, land use and industrial processes. (Don't forget to multiply the percentages by 3.6 to convert them into degrees.)

Practice question

'International agreements are critical in the challenge to reduce global carbon emissions.' Use evidence to support this statement. *(6 marks)*

4.5 Managing the impacts of climate change (2)

On this spread you will find out how climate change can be managed by adapting to changes

How can we adapt to climate change?

Scientists believe that climate change will have a huge impact on agricultural systems across the world.

- Patterns of rainfall and temperature will change.
- Extreme weather events such as heatwaves, droughts and floods will become more common.
- The distribution of pests and diseases will change.

Farmers will need to adapt to these changes.

Agricultural adaptation in low latitudes

Scientists think that the greatest changes to agriculture will occur in low latitudes. Southern Africa's maize crop could fall by 30 per cent by 2030 and the production of rice in south Asia could fall by 10 per cent.

There are several adaptations that can be made (photo **A**).

Agricultural adaptation in middle latitudes

A warmer climate in Europe and North America could lead to an increase in production of certain crops such as wheat. In the UK, Mediterranean crops such as vines (photo **B**) and olives may thrive.

Introducing drought-resistant strains of crops

Educating farmers in water harvesting techniques

New irrigation systems

Shade trees can be planted to protect seedlings from strong sunshine

New cropping patterns can be introduced, e.g. changing planting/sowing dates

A *A farmer using a drip irrigation system to grow organic vegetables in Thailand*

B *Vineyards such as this one in Surrey may become more widespread in the UK*

Managing water supply

Climate change is already causing more severe and more frequent droughts and floods. Unreliable rainfall and periods of water shortage require careful management. Future climate change will affect the current patterns of water supply, impacting on the quantity and quality of our water. It is the most vulnerable, particularly in rural parts of poorer countries, who are likely to be affected the most.

Climate change

Managing water supply in the Himalayas

Millions of people in Asia depend on rivers fed by snow and glacial melt for their domestic and agricultural water supply. In the Himalayas most of the 16 000 glaciers are receding rapidly due to global warming. This threatens the long-term security of water supply in the region.

Photo **C** shows an artificial glacier project that will supply water to villages in Ladakh, India. Water is collected in winter through a system of diversion canals and embankments and it freezes. When the 'glacier' melts in spring it will provide water for the local villages.

C *Creating artificial glaciers to provide water for villages*

Reducing risk from rising sea levels

Did you know that average sea levels have risen by 20 cm since 1900? By 2100 sea levels are expected to rise by a further 26–82 cm. This will flood important agricultural land in countries such as Bangladesh, India and Vietnam.

As sea levels rise, rates of coastal erosion will increase. Fresh water supplies will become contaminated by saltwater and coastal areas will be prone to damage from storm surges.

Managing rising sea levels in the Maldives

The Maldives are a group of tiny islands in the Indian Ocean some 500 km south-west of India. The highest point on the islands is just 2.4 m. Some climate models suggest that the islands may be uninhabitable by 2030 and submerged by 2070.

The 380 000 inhabitants have a very uncertain future as sea levels rise.

- Construction of sea walls – a 3 m sea wall is being constructed around the capital Male with sandbags used elsewhere (as in this photo)
- Building houses that are raised off the ground on stilts
- Restoration of coastal mangrove forests – their tangled roots trap sediment and offer protection from storm waves
- Ultimately the entire population could be relocated to Sri Lanka or India
- Construction of artificial islands up to 3 m high so that people most at risk could be relocated

D *How can the Maldives manage sea-level rise?*

ACTIVITIES

1. How can farmers adapt to the possible impacts of climate change?
2. a What do you think the people in photo **C** are doing?
   b How does this system of water harvesting work?
   c Why is it important that local communities in remote areas start taking action to secure their water supply?
3. How might rising sea levels affect coastal communities?
4. How is the Maldives managing sea-level rise?

Stretch yourself

Research more information about water harvesting techniques. Find out, for example, how water droplets in fog can be harvested from the air to support people living in the Atacama Desert in Chile.

Practice question

Choose *either* the risk of reduced water supply *or* rising sea levels. For the issue chosen, describe examples of strategies used to manage them. *(6 marks)*

37

Unit 1 Living with the physical environment

Section B The living world

Amazon rainforest in the north-western basin of South America

Unit 1 Living with the physical environment is about physical processes and systems, how they change, and how people interact with them at a range of scales and in a range of places. It is split into three sections.

Section B The living world includes:

- ecosystems
- tropical rainforests
- hot deserts.

You have to study ecosystems, tropical rainforests and hot deserts.

What if...

1. the Sun stopped shining?
2. all the world's rainforests were cut down?
3. the world turned to desert?
4. the Antarctic was fully industrialised?

Unit 1 Section B

Specification key ideas	Pages in this book
5 Ecosystems	**40–5**
• Ecosystems exist at a range of scales and involve the interaction between biotic and abiotic components.	40–5
6 Tropical rainforests	**46–55**
• Tropical rainforests have a range of distinctive characteristics.	46–7
• Deforestation has economic and environmental impacts.	48–51
• Tropical rainforests need to be managed to be sustainable.	52–5
7 Hot deserts	**56–61**
• Hot desert ecosystems have a range of distinctive environmental characteristics.	56–7
• Areas on the fringe of hot deserts are at risk of desertification.	58–61

Your key skills

To be a good geographer, you need to develop important geographical skills – in this section you will learn the following skills:

- Drawing labelled maps and diagrams.
- Drawing a climate graph.
- Literacy – writing a news report.
- Finding evidence from photos.
- Describing patterns from maps and data.
- Using numerical data.
- Carrying out personal research.

Your key words

As you go through the chapters in this section, make sure you know and understand the key words shown in bold. Definitions are provided in the Glossary on page 354. To be a good geographer you need to use good subject terminology.

Your exam

Section B makes up part of Paper 1 – a one and a half hour written exam worth 34 per cent of your GCSE.

5 Ecosystems

5.1 Introducing a small-scale ecosystem

On this spread you will find out about the components of a small-scale ecosystem in the UK

Example

What is an ecosystem?

An **ecosystem** is a natural system made up of plants, animals and the environment. There are often complex interrelationships (links) between the living and non-living components of an ecosystem. *Biotic* components are the living features of an ecosystem such as plants and fish. *Abiotic* components are non-living environmental factors such as climate (temperature and rainfall), soil, water temperature and light.

Ecosystems can be identified at different scales:

- a local small-scale ecosystem can be a pond (photo **A**), hedgerow or woodland
- a global-scale ecosystem can be a tropical rainforest or deciduous woodland. These global ecosystems are called biomes.

A freshwater pond ecosystem

Freshwater ponds provide a variety of habitats (homes) for plants and animals. There are big variations in the amount of light, water and oxygen available in different parts of a pond.

Diagram **B** shows how different habitats suit certain plants, insects and animals.

Here are some terms that you need to understand.

A *Each of these environments is an important habitat and forms part of the pond ecosystem*

Plants such as reeds grow in the water around the edge of the pond.

On the banks grow grasses, bushes and trees.

At the edges of the pond, the water is shallow and there will be plants such as water lilies.

On the surface are ducks and small insects such as water boatman.

At the centre the water is deeper and there will be fish.

Term	Definition
Producers	Producers convert energy from the environment (mainly sunlight) into sugars (glucose). The most obvious producers are plants that convert energy from the Sun by photosynthesis.
Consumers	Consumers get energy from the sugars produced by the producers. A pond snail is a good example of a consumer because it eats plants.
Decomposers	Decomposers break down plant and animal material and return the nutrients to the soil. Bacteria and fungi are good examples of decomposers.
Food chain	A food chain shows the direct links (hence the term 'chain') between producers and consumers in the form of a simple line (diagram **C**).
Food web	A food web shows all the connections between producers and consumers in a rather more complex way (hence the term 'web' rather than 'chain') (diagram **D**).
Nutrient cycling	Nutrients are foods that are used by plants or animals to grow. There are two main sources of nutrients: • rainwater washes chemicals out of the atmosphere • weathered rock releases nutrients into the soil. When plants or animals die, the decomposers help to recycle the nutrients making them available once again for the growth of plants or animals. This is the nutrient cycle.

40

Ecosystems

B *A freshwater pond ecosystem*

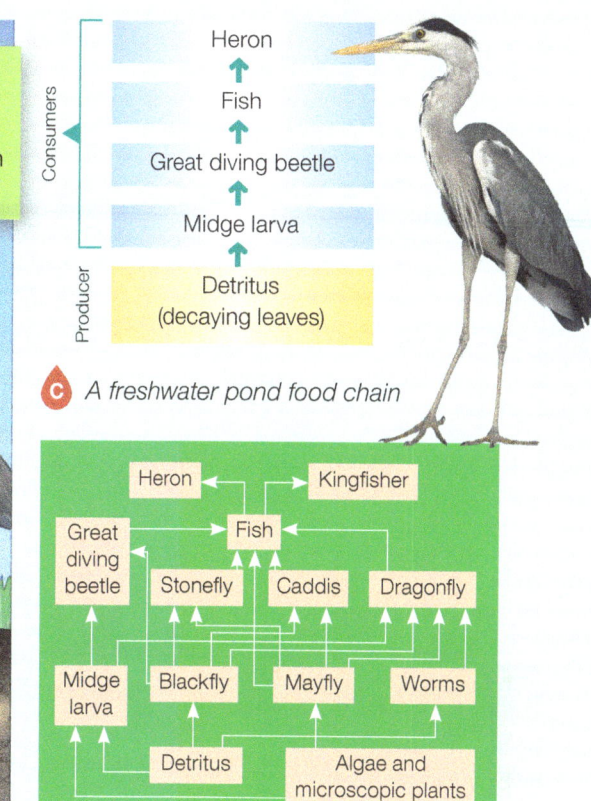

Energy from the Sun

Pond surface – plenty of oxygen and light here. Animals breathe through their gills, lungs or skin.

Pond margin – plenty of oxygen and light here. Plenty of shelter for the plants and insects, which small animals eat.

Above the pond surface – birds and animals breathe oxygen. Food is found in or on the water, or in the margins.

Kingfisher, Dragonfly, Heron, Reed mace (bulrush), Marsh marigold, Water boatman, Waterlily, Algae, Duck, Midge larvae, Tadpoles, Frog, Great diving beetle, Small fish (e.g. stickleback), Predatory fish (e.g. perch), Pond snail, Dragonfly nymph, Waterworm, Water flea, Rat-tailed maggot

Mid-water – animals breathe through gills or skin. Fish are the main predators. Food is found on the surface or in the pond.

Pond bottom – little oxygen or light. Plenty of shelter (rotting plants and stones) and food. Decomposers and scavengers live here.

Consumers: Heron ← Fish ← Great diving beetle ← Midge larva

Producer: Detritus (decaying leaves)

C *A freshwater pond food chain*

Food web: Heron, Kingfisher, Great diving beetle, Fish, Stonefly, Caddis, Dragonfly, Midge larva, Blackfly, Mayfly, Worms, Detritus, Algae and microscopic plants

D *Freshwater pond food web*

Species	Energy source
Frog tadpole	Microscopic plants, algae, midge larvae
Algae	Sunlight
Sticklebacks	Tadpoles, young fish, water fleas, beetles
Heron	Fish, frogs and tadpoles, larger insects
Perch	Small fish (e.g. sticklebacks), beetles, water fleas

E *Freshwater pond species and energy sources*

ACTIVITIES

1. a Describe the pond ecosystem in photo **A**.
   b Identify a producer.
   c Why are ducks good examples of consumers?
   d Imagine that the pond became polluted. How would this impact on the ecosystem?
2. a Where do most decomposers live in the pond ecosystem?
   b Why are decomposers important in nutrient recycling?
3. Look at table **E**. The organisms in the table form a food chain, but they are not in the correct order! Place them in the correct order – you have to decide who is eating who!

Practice question

Explain and describe the features of a small-scale ecosystem in the UK. *(4 marks)*

Stretch yourself

Find a food web diagram for a different small-scale ecosystem in the UK, such as a hedgerow or deciduous woodland.

- Identify the producers in your food web.
- Use a colour or highlighter to show a food chain within the food web.

41

5.2 How does change affect ecosystems?

On this spread you will find out how changes to the ecosystem affect its components

What are the impacts of change on an ecosystem?

Ecosystems can take hundreds if not thousands of years to develop. If an ecosystem is to be sustainable it needs to be in balance. If there is a change to one of the components it may well have knock-on effects for the rest of the ecosystem.

What causes change to ecosystems?

Changes to an ecosystem can occur naturally or result from human activities. Change can take place on different scales:

- global-scale changes, such as climate change
- local-scale changes, such as changes to a habitat – for example, when a hedge is removed.

Natural changes

Ecosystems can adapt to slow natural changes with few harmful effects. But rapid changes can have serious impacts. Extreme weather events such as droughts can be devastating to ponds and lakes. They could dry up in places, which changes the edge-of-pond environment (photo **A**). Plants will dry out and die. Fish, starved of oxygen, might not survive.

Changes due to human activities

Human activity can have many impacts on ecosystems (diagram **B**). Once a component has been changed it can have serious knock-on effects on the ecosystem.

A *Pond in Brighton, England, affected by drought, after a period of dry weather*

B *The impact of human changes on small-scale ecosystems*

Agricultural fertilisers can lead to eutrophication: nitrates increase growth of algae, which will deplete oxygen and fish may die.

Ponds may be drained to use for farming. Aquatic plants will die, as will fish and other pond life.

Woods cut down, destroying habitats for birds and affecting the nutrient cycle.

Hedgerows removed to increase size of fields. Habitats will be destroyed, altering the plant/animal balance.

42

Ecosystems

How can changes affect the pond ecosystem?

Look back to diagram **B** on page 41. What if the pond owner added some perch, a predator, to the ecosystem?

| The perch will eat more of the smaller fish and small animals, such as frogs. | → | This will reduce the amount of food for creatures further up the food chain, such as herons. | → | With fewer frogs, there will be an increase of creatures below frogs in the food chain, such as slugs. |

Avington Park lake, Winchester, Hampshire

Avington Park is a country estate close to Winchester in Hampshire. The lake in the grounds of the estate is of historical and ecological importance. Lack of maintenance in recent years resulted in the accumulation of silt and the growth of vegetation. This created an excellent habitat for birds, but the impressive view of the lake from the house had been lost.

Restoration of the lake was carried out in 2014 (photo **C**). The aim was to restore the lake as part of the landscape, and to preserve and improve its function as a habitat for birds. Restoration involved desilting and redefining the lake and creating new waterside habitats to attract nesting birds and waterfowl. Following its restoration, the lake can again be seen from the house, and has become a healthy ecosystem for a diverse range of wildlife.

C Avington Park lake restoration

ACTIVITIES

1. a What evidence can you find in photo **A** that the pond has been affected by drought?
   b Suggest the effects of the drought on the pond margin. How could this affect the pond ecosystem?
   c If the pond dried up completely, what effect would this have on the ecosystem?
2. a Select one change in diagram **B**. Describe how it could affect the ecosystem.
   b Imagine the landowner cut down all the vegetation at the side of the pond to create a wooden deck for fishing. How might this affect the ecosystem?
3. a What were the changes that caused the Avington Park lake's poor condition?
   b How has the lake been restored?

Stretch yourself

Frogs are an important part of the pond ecosystem. Imagine that disease wipes out all the frogs in a pond. Find out how this would affect the ecosystem in the short term and the long term.

Practice question

Using a named example, explain how change can have short-term and long-term effects on an ecosystem. (6 marks)

Think about it

Consider a pond near to where you live or close to school. To what extent is the pond a thriving and healthy ecosystem?

43

5.3 Introducing global ecosystems

On this spread you will find out about the distribution and characteristics of global ecosystems

The distribution of global ecosystems

Large-scale ecosystems are known as **global ecosystems (or biomes)**. These are defined mainly by the dominant type of vegetation that grows in the region, such as tropical rainforest or **tundra**.

Global ecosystems form broad belts across the world from west to east, parallel to the lines of latitude (map **A**). This is because the climate and characteristics of ecosystems are determined by global atmospheric circulation (pages 18–19).

Variations in these west-to-east belts of vegetation are due to factors such as:

- ocean currents
- winds
- the distribution of land and sea.

These factors produce small variations in temperature and moisture, which in turn affect the ecosystems. For example, the Mediterranean region – with its dry, hot summers and warm, wet winters – has its own global ecosystem.

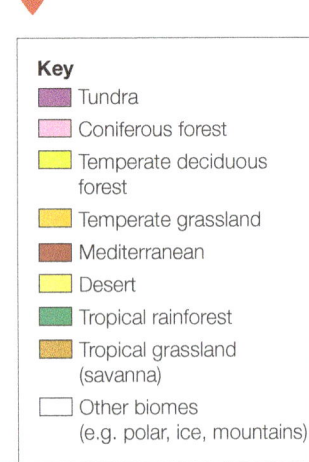

A *Global ecosystems*

Key
- Tundra
- Coniferous forest
- Temperate deciduous forest
- Temperate grassland
- Mediterranean
- Desert
- Tropical rainforest
- Tropical grassland (savanna)
- Other biomes (e.g. polar, ice, mountains)

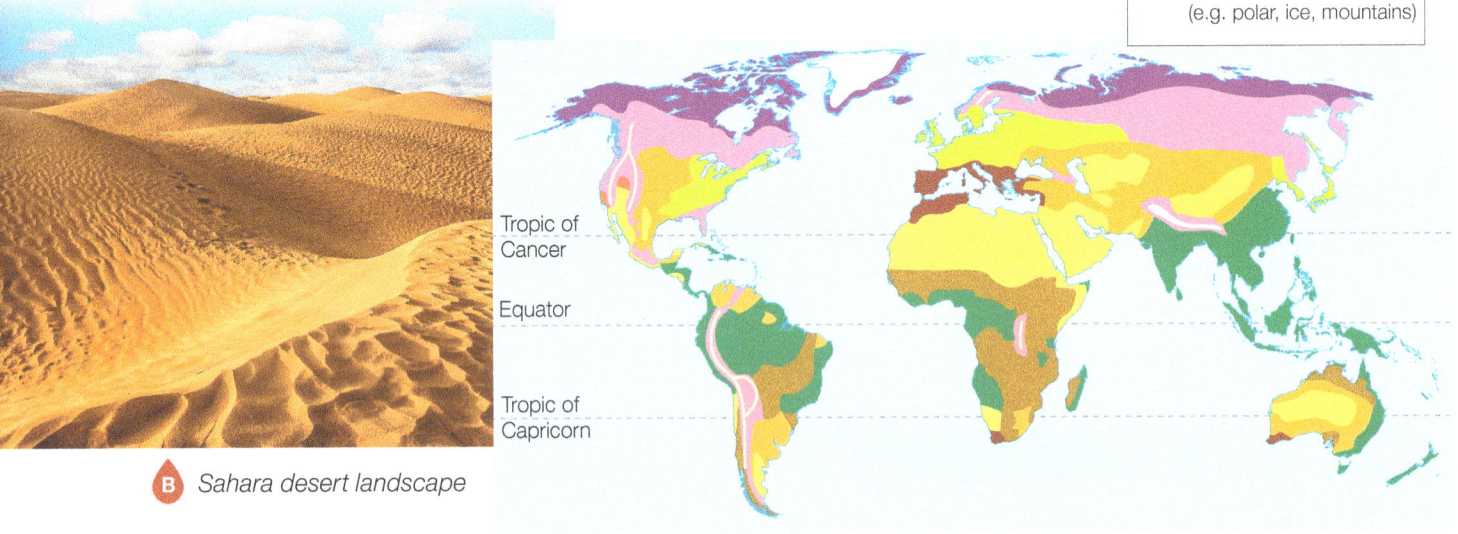

B *Sahara desert landscape*

C *Coniferous forest, Russia*

D *Tropical savanna, Kenya*

E *Alpine tundra, Peru*

44

Ecosystems

The characteristics of global ecosystems

Global ecosystem	Location	Characteristics
Tropical rainforest	Close to the Equator	High temperatures and heavy rainfall associated with equatorial low-pressure belt creates ideal conditions for plants to grow. Rainforests cover 6 per cent of the Earth's land surface. More than half the world's species of plants and animals live in this global ecosystem. A quarter of all medicines come from rainforest plants.
Desert	Roughly 30° north and south of the Equator	Deserts cover one fifth of the world's land surface. Hot deserts are associated with the sub-tropical high-pressure belts. Sinking air stops clouds from forming, resulting in high daytime temperatures, low night-time temperatures and low rainfall. Plants and animals have to be well adapted to survive in these conditions.
Polar	Arctic/Antarctic	Cold air sinks at the North and South Poles, resulting in very low temperatures and dry conditions. The main polar regions are Antarctica and Greenland where temperatures can fall below −50°C.
Deciduous and coniferous forests	Roughly 50–60° north of the Equator	Deciduous trees shed their leaves in winter to retain moisture. Coniferous trees are cone-bearing evergreens, retaining their leaves to maximise photosynthesis during the brief summer months. The UK's natural vegetation is deciduous forest. Further north, for example in Canada and Scandinavia, coniferous forests dominate as they are better suited to colder climates.
Temperate grassland	Roughly 30–40° north and south of the Equator. Inland away from coasts, with hot summers and cold winters.	This includes the vast areas of grassland in North America (prairies) and eastern Europe (steppes). These areas experience warm, dry summers and cold winters. Grasses can tolerate these conditions and this land is mainly used for grazing animals.
Mediterranean	Roughly 40–45° north of the Equator. Also isolated locations south of the Equator (South Africa, Western Australia).	Countries around the Mediterranean enjoy hot, sunny and dry summers, with mild winters. This is due to the pressure belts migrating slightly north and south during the year. Mediterranean vegetation includes olive trees and fruit trees, such as lemons and oranges. Other parts of the world have a similar climate, for example California (USA), South Africa and parts of Australia.
Tropical grassland (savanna)	Between 15–30° north and south of the Equator	The tropical climate in these low latitudes is characterised by distinct wet and dry seasons. The dry season can be very hot and wild fires can break out. Violent thunderstorms can occur during the wet season. Large herds of animals graze on these grasslands, along with predators such as lions and leopards.
Tundra	From the Arctic Circle to about 60–70° north (e.g. Canada, northern Europe). There are only very small areas of tundra in the southern hemisphere due to the lack of land at these latitudes.	Tundra is characterised by low-growing plants adapted to retain heat and moisture in the cold, windy and dry conditions. These regions are found in northern Canada and across northern Europe. It is a fragile ecosystem, easily damaged by humans and threatened by developments such as oil exploitation and tourism. Animals such as reindeer are adapted to survive the cold.

ACTIVITIES

1 Describe the pattern of global ecosystems (biomes) in North America.
2 Why do most global ecosystems form broad latitudinal belts across the world?
3 Why is the Mediterranean popular with northern Europeans in both the summer and the winter?

Stretch yourself

Do some research to compare deciduous and coniferous forests. What are the characteristics of each ecosystem and how have plants and animals adapted?

Practice question

Describe the global pattern of the tundra ecosystem.
(4 marks)

45

6 Tropical rainforests

6.1 Environmental characteristics of rainforests

On this spread you will find out about the environmental characteristics of tropical rainforests

If you were to enter a tropical rainforest you would need a torch and strong shoes, as it is dark and damp. It is also very noisy with the clicks, howls and whistles of insects and animals. You would have difficulty moving about because the vegetation is very lush and dense (photo **A**).

- The trees grow very tall, often up to 45 m high.
- There is a great variety of wildlife – often up to 100 species in a single hectare!

Where are tropical rainforests found?

Tropical rainforests are found in a broad belt through the tropics in:

- Central and South America
- central Africa
- south-east Asia
- northern Australia.

(You can see these areas on map **A** on page 44.)

What is the climate like?

Tropical rainforests thrive in warm and wet conditions. The equatorial zone where they are found is characterised by high rainfall (over 2000 mm a year) and high temperatures (averaging about 27 °C) throughout the year.

Look at table **B**. It provides climatic information for the weather station at Manaus, in the Amazonian rainforest in Brazil.

- *The temperature is high and constant throughout the year.* This is because the powerful Sun is overhead for most of the time.
- *The rainfall is high.* This is because the global atmospheric circulation causes an area of low pressure to form at the Equator. The rising air creates clouds and triggers heavy rain.
- *Rainfall varies throughout the year*, with a distinct wet season lasting about six months. This is due to a period of intense rainfall when the equatorial low-pressure area is directly overhead.

A *Tribal groups such as the Achuar live sustainably in tropical rainforests. The plants, animals and fish provide shelter, food and medicines*

Maths skills

Use the data in table **B** to draw a climate graph for Manaus showing temperature and rainfall.
- Shade the gap between the average minimum and maximum temperature lines. This is the *temperature range*.
- How will you show humidity and sunshine information on your graph?

Month	Temperature (°C) Max.	Temperature (°C) Min.	Rainfall (mm)	Relative humidity (%)	Sunshine (average hours per day)
January	31	24	249	89	4
February	31	24	231	89	4
March	31	24	262	89	4
April	31	24	221	90	4
May	31	24	170	89	5
June	31	24	84	87	7
July	32	24	58	87	8
August	33	24	38	85	8
September	33	24	46	84	8
October	33	24	107	85	7
November	33	24	142	86	6
December	32	24	203	88	5

B *Climate data for Manaus, Brazil*

What are the soils like?

Tropical rainforest soils are surprisingly infertile. Most nutrients are found at the surface, where dead leaves decompose rapidly in the hot and humid conditions. Many trees and plants have shallow roots to absorb these nutrients. Fungi growing on the roots transfer nutrients straight from the air. This is a good example of *nutrient cycling*.

Heavy rainfall can quickly dissolve and carry away nutrients. This is called *leaching*. It leaves behind an infertile red, iron-rich soil called *latosol*.

What plants and animals are there?

Tropical rainforests support the largest number of species of any biome. Over half of all plant and animal species on the planet live on just 7 per cent of the land surface. Tropical rainforests have a huge **biodiversity**, providing habitats for an enormous range of species.

- Birds live in the canopy (branches) feeding on nectar from flowers.
- Mammals, such as monkeys and sloths, are well adapted to living in the trees.
- Animals such as deer and rodents live on the forest floor.

How have they adapted to rainforests?

A tropical rainforest is made up of layers (diagram **C**). The majority of plant and animal species are found in the canopy where there is most light. Small animals, including monkeys, birds, snakes and frogs are common in the tropical rainforest. Many never set foot on the ground, using the trees and canopy for shelter, to hide from predators and as a source of food. A rainforest is a very fragile ecosystem. Plants and animals (biotic factors), along with fungi and bacteria on the forest floor, enjoy a close but fragile relationship with the abiotic factors such as soils, temperature and moisture. Small changes to biotic or abiotic factors, such as deforestation or water pollution, can have serious knock-on effects on the entire ecosystem.

Fast-growing trees such as kapok out-compete other trees to reach sunlight – such trees are called emergents

Many leaves have flexible bases so that they can turn to face the Sun

Water drips off leaves

Many leaves have a 'drip tip' to allow the heavy rain to drip off the leaf

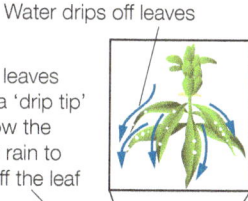

Thin, smooth bark on trees to allow water to flow down easily

Buttresses – massive ridges help support the base of the tall trees and help transport water. May also help oxygen/carbon dioxide exchange by increasing the surface area

Plants called epiphytes can live on branches high in the canopy to seek sunlight – they obtain nutrients from water and air rather than soil

Lianas – woody creepers rooted to the ground but carried by trees into the canopy where they have their leaves and flowers

C *Stratification and vegetation **adaptations** in a tropical rainforest*

Stretch yourself

Imagine you are a conservationist working in a tropical rainforest. Give a two-minute presentation on the importance of soil in the tropical rainforest biome.

Practice question

Describe and explain the main plant adaptations in a tropical rainforest environment. *(6 marks)*

ACTIVITIES

1. **a** Draw the areas of tropical rainforest (map **A**, page 44) onto a blank outline map of the world. Use an atlas to label the countries or regions (e.g. Ecuador, the Amazon, etc.) where tropical rainforests are found.

   b Write a paragraph describing the distribution of tropical rainforests. Link their distribution to global atmospheric circulation (diagram **B** on page 18).

2. Select *three* species of plants or trees from diagram **C**. Describe how each has special adaptations so that it can thrive in this environment.

6.2 Causes of deforestation in Malaysia

On this spread you will find out about the causes of deforestation in Malaysia

Case study

About Malaysia
- Malaysia is a country in south-east Asia.
- It is made up of Peninsular Malaysia and East Malaysia, which is part of the island of Borneo
- The natural vegetation in Malaysia is tropical rainforest.
- 67 per cent of Malaysia's land is covered by rainforest.

A The location of Malaysia

Deforestation in Malaysia

'Orang-utan' means 'person of the forest'. These great apes are losing their natural habitat. As natural rainforest in Malaysia is destroyed, many young orang-utans are killed or orphaned (photo **B**).

Deforestation is the cutting down of trees, often on a very large scale. The timber is a highly valued export. Deforestation means the land can be used for other profit-making enterprises, such as cattle ranching, commercial farming, the production of rubber and palm oil.

The rate of deforestation in Malaysia is increasing faster than in any tropical country in the world. Between 2000 and 2013, Malaysia's total forest loss was an area larger than Taiwan!

B A young orphaned orang-utan at the Semenggoh Wildlife Rehabilitation Centre, Malaysia

Did you know?
Between 1990 and 2004 orang-utans in Borneo lost habitat twice the size of Fiji.

ACTIVITIES

1. Complete a spider diagram to show the causes of deforestation in Malaysia. Use photos to illustrate your diagram.
2. Write a two-minute news report about deforestation in Malaysia. Focus on where it is, why it's important and how it has been destroyed.

Stretch yourself

Investigate commercial oil palm farming in Malaysia.
1. What is oil palm used for?
2. How is rainforest cleared to make way for this type of farming?
3. What damage is done to habitats and the natural environment?

Practice question

Photo **D** shows a hydroelectric dam in Sarawak, Malaysia. Evaluate *two* possible environmental impacts of developments such as the Bakun Dam. *(4 marks)*

Tropical rainforests

What are the threats to Malaysia's rainforests?

Logging

Malaysia became the world's largest exporter of tropical wood in the 1980s. Clear felling, where all trees are chopped down in an area, was common. This led to the total destruction of forest habitats.

Recently, clear felling has largely been replaced by **selective logging**, where only fully grown trees are cut down. Trees that have important ecological value are left unharmed.

Road building

Roads are constructed to provide access to mining areas, new settlements and energy projects.

Logging requires road construction to bring in machinery and take away the timber.

C Road construction and logging in Sarawak, East Malaysia

Energy development

In 2011, after five decades of delays, the controversial Bakun Dam in Sarawak started to generate electricity.

The Bakun Dam (205 m) is Asia's highest dam outside China.

Several more dams are planned to boost Malaysia's electricity supplies.

D The Bakun Dam

The dam supplies energy for industrialised Peninsular Malaysia.

The dam's reservoir flooded over 700 km² of forests and farmland.

E Slash and burn

Mineral extraction

Mining (mainly tin and smelting) is common in Peninsular Malaysia. Rainforest has been cleared for mining and road construction. Drilling for oil and gas has recently started on Borneo.

Population pressure

In the past, poor urban people were encouraged by the government to move into the countryside from the rapidly growing cities. This is called transmigration. Between 1956 and the 1980s, about 15 000 hectares of rainforest was felled for the settlers. Many then set up plantations.

Commercial farming

Malaysia is the largest exporter of palm oil in the world. During the 1970s, large areas of land were converted to palm oil plantations. Plantation owners receive 10-year tax incentives, so increasing amounts of land have been converted to plantations.

Subsistence farming

Tribal people living in the rainforest practise subsistence farming. Traditionally, local communities would hunt and gather food from the forest and grow some food crops in cleared pockets of forest. This type of farming is small scale and sustainable.

One method of clearing land is 'slash and burn' (photo **E**). This involves the use of fire to clear the land. The burning creates valuable nutrients that help plants to grow. However, these fires can grow out of control, destroying large areas of forest.

49

6.3 Impacts of deforestation in Malaysia

On this spread you will find out about the impacts of deforestation in Malaysia

Case study

Impacts of deforestation in Malaysia

Photo **C** shows a rainforest landscape devastated by deforestation. Imagine all the habitats that have been destroyed. Notice that the trees have been reduced to stumps. The hillslopes have been stripped of vegetation, exposing the soil to erosion by rain and wind. Chart **A** shows the impact of deforestation on the area covered by Malaysia's rainforest.

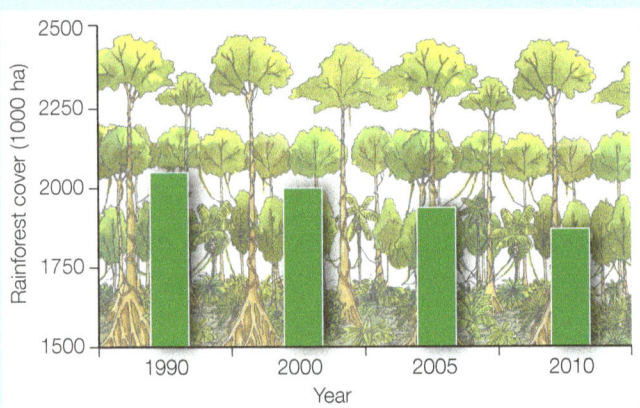

Soil erosion

Soil takes thousands of years to form – but it can be stripped away in a matter of hours. Removal of soil by wind and rain is called **soil erosion**. The roots of trees and plants bind the soil together. So deforestation means that soil can easily become loose and erode away.

Loss of biodiversity

Biodiversity is a measure of the variety of plants and animals in a particular ecosystem. Rainforests are the most biodiverse ecosystem in the world. Deforestation destroys the ecosystem and the many habitats that exist on the ground and in the trees. This reduces the biodiversity.

A *The size of Malaysia's rainforest, 1990–2010*

Biodiversity in the Main Range, Peninsular Malaysia

The Main Range is an upland region stretching for 500 km along the backbone of Peninsular Malaysia. This region is important because:

- it is the largest area of continuous forest left in Peninsular Malaysia (photo **B**)
- the forests are particularly rich in their biodiversity, with over 600 species
- the highland forests are home to over 25 per cent of all plant species found in Malaysia
- there are still many undiscovered plants that have medicinal qualities that could provide cures for diseases.

B *Main Range Mountains, Peninsular Malaysia*

C *Deforestation in Malaysia*

Contribution to climate change

Deforestation can have an impact on local and global climates. During photosynthesis, trees absorb CO_2 and emit oxygen. CO_2 is a greenhouse gas that is partly responsible for global warming. By absorbing CO_2, trees store the carbon and help to reduce the rate of global warming.

So, deforestation can affect climate because:

- trees give off moisture by the process of transpiration; deforestation reduces the moisture in the air resulting in a drier climate
- the process of evaporation uses up heat and cools the air; if trees are cut down, this cooling ceases and temperatures rise.

Tropical rainforests

Economic development

Deforestation in many parts of the world is driven by profit. However, while deforestation may result in short-term economic gains, it may lead to long-term losses.

D *Mining in the Malaysian rainforest*

Economic gains

- Development of land for mining, farming and energy will lead to jobs both directly (construction, farming) and indirectly (supply and support industries).
- Companies will pay taxes to the government, which can be used to improve public services, such as education and water supply.
- Improved transport **infrastructure** opens up new areas for industrial development and tourism.
- Products such as oil palm and rubber provide raw materials for processing industries.
- Hydro-electric power will provide cheap and plentiful energy.
- Minerals such as gold are very valuable.

Economic losses

- Pollution of water sources and an increasingly dry climate may result in water shortages.
- Fires can cause harmful pollution. They can burn out of control, destroying vast areas of valuable forest.
- Rising temperatures could devastate some forms of farming such as growing tea, fruit and flowers.
- Plants that could bring huge medical benefits and high profits may become extinct.
- Climate change could have economic costs as people have to adapt to living in a warmer world.
- The number of tourists attracted by rainforests could decrease.

ACTIVITIES

1. Study photo **C**.
    a. Describe the environment in the foreground.
    b. Are there signs of slash and burn farming? What are they?
    c. How might soil erosion become a problem in the future?
    d. How do you think this forest clearance will have affected the species living in the forest?
2. Describe and explain the effects of deforestation on climate change.
3. Make a poster with a photo showing deforestation in Malaysia. Add a series of colour-coded text boxes explaining possible economic gains and losses.

Stretch yourself

Write a report about the Main Range in Peninsular Malaysia.
- What are the characteristics of its biodiversity?
- Why is it considered to be a special area?

Illustrate your account with labelled photos.

Practice question

Explain, with reference to an example, why it is important to retain biodiversity. *(4 marks)*

6.4 Managing tropical rainforests

On this spread you will find out about rates of deforestation and why rainforests need to be protected

What are the rates of deforestation?

Tropical rainforests are perhaps the most endangered ecosystem on Earth. Every two seconds an area of rainforest the size of a football field (about one hectare) is being destroyed. That's over 1500 hectares an hour!

- Tropical rainforests once covered over 15.5 million km². The figure is now just over 6.2 million km².
- An area of rainforest the size of China has been lost.

Look at graph **A**. The fastest rates of deforestation are in Brazil and Indonesia. These countries account for over 40 per cent of the world's deforestation. But deforestation in Brazil is decreasing, and in Indonesia it is increasing.

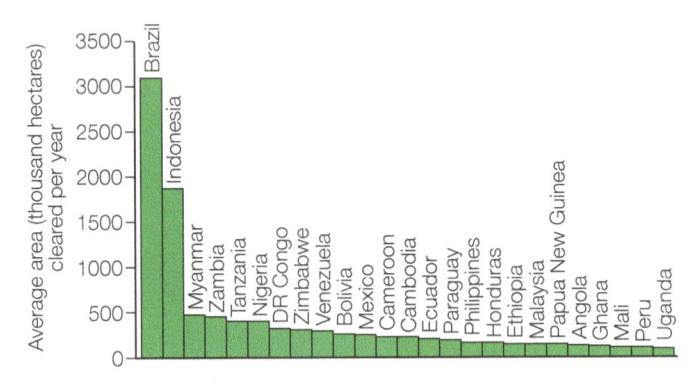

A Rates of tropical deforestation, 2010–15

Deforestation in Brazil

The rates of deforestation in Brazil have varied a lot since 1988 (graph **B**). Historically, small-scale farming was largely responsible for deforestation in Brazil.

However, most deforestation now involves large landowners and big companies. Most rainforest has been cleared for cattle ranching.

Since 2004, the rate of deforestation in Brazil has fallen by nearly 80 per cent to the lowest levels on record. There are several reasons for this:

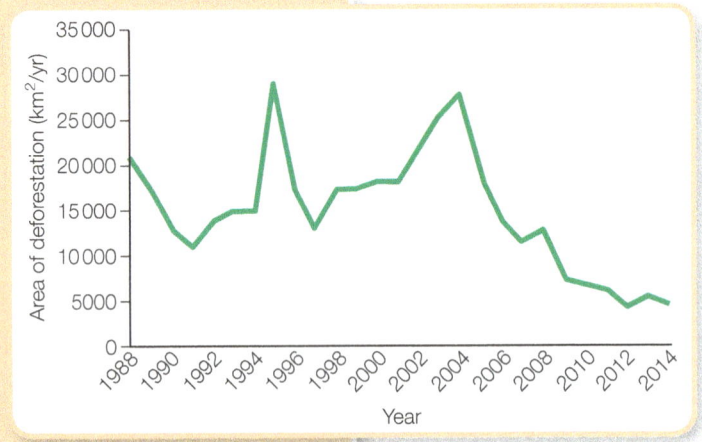

- the Brazilian government has cracked down on illegal deforestation
- Brazil is leading the world in **conservation** – over half of the Amazon is now protected
- Brazil is committed to reducing carbon emissions to tackle climate change
- consumer pressure not to use products from deforested areas has led to a decline in cattle ranching.

B Deforestation in the Brazilian Amazon, 1988–2014

Maths skills

Use the information on the right to draw a pie chart. (Remember: To calculate degrees, multiply each percentage by 3.6.)
- Shade each segment a different colour.
- Write the name of the country and the percentage alongside each segment.

Share of tropical deforestation, 2010–15 (%)

Brazil	27	Tanzania	4	Zimbabwe	3
Indonesia	17	Nigeria	4	Venezuela	3
Myanmar	4	DR Congo	3	Other tropical countries	31
Zambia	4				

Tropical rainforests

Why should tropical rainforests be protected?

There are several reasons why tropical rainforests should be protected from further deforestation.

Biodiversity
Tropical rainforests contain half of all the plants and animals in the world. They are home to thousands of different species. Some plants may become extinct before they have even been discovered!

Climate change
Rainforests absorb and store carbon dioxide, a gas that is partly responsible for climate change.

Climate
Known as the 'lungs of the world', 28 per cent of the world's oxygen comes from the rainforests. They prevent the climate from becoming too hot and dry.

Medicine
Around 25 per cent of all medicines come from rainforest plants. More than 2000 tropical forest plants have anti-cancer properties.

Resources
Tropical rainforest trees provide valuable hardwoods as well as nuts, fruit and rubber.

Water
Rainforests are important sources for clean water – 20 per cent of the world's fresh water comes from the Amazon Basin.

People
Indigenous tribes live in harmony in the world's rainforests making use of the forest's resources without causing any long-term harm.

The Achuar people in the Peruvian Amazon

The Achuar are a primitive tribe of about 11 000 people. They live in small communities and rely on the resources of the rainforest for their buildings, food and fuel (photo **C**). They treat the rainforest with respect as their lives depend upon it.

There are rich reserves of oil in this region. Oil companies want permission to explore and drill for oil. If this happens the Achuar will lose some of their traditional lands, and may see their environment damaged by oil pollution.

The Achuar are resistant to oil exploration. They have had success in defending their land. In 2012, the oil company Talisman Energy stopped their oil exploration in the region.

C *A traditional Achuar hut*

ACTIVITIES

1 Study graph **A**. Why do you think that most deforestation happens in Brazil and Indonesia?
2 Study graph **B**.
   a Describe the trend in deforestation since 2005.
   b Why do you think the rate of deforestation has decreased recently?
3 Outline reasons why rainforests should be protected.

Stretch yourself

Find out about the Achuar people.
- What effect is deforestation having on the tribe?
- What are the main threats to their continued life in the Peruvian rainforest?

Practice question

'The rainforest is more valuable when left intact than when destroyed.' Using a case study, use examples to support or challenge this view. *(9 marks)*

6.5 Sustainable management of tropical rainforests

On this spread you will find out about different strategies for managing rainforests sustainably

How can rainforests be managed sustainably?

To protect the world's tropical rainforests they need to be managed **sustainably**. There are two main reasons for this:

- to ensure that rainforests remain a lasting resource for future generations
- to allow valuable rainforest resources to be used without causing long-term damage to the environment.

Tribes such as the Achuar (see page 53) have been managing rainforests sustainably. It is the large companies, wealthy landowners and illegal loggers whose drive for profit can result in unsustainable practices.

Selective logging and replanting

The most damaging form of deforestation is *clear felling*. All trees, big and small, are chopped down in the area being cleared. This completely destroys the ecosystem.

- **2 years before felling:** Pre-felling study to identify what is there.
- **1 year before felling:** Trees marked for felling. Arrows painted on trees to indicate direction of felling to avoid damaging other valuable trees.
- **Felling:** Trees felled by licence-holders.
- **3–6 months after felling:** Survey to check what has been felled. Prosecution may result from illegal felling.
- **2 years after felling:** Treatment plan drawn up to restore forest.
- **5–10 years after felling:** Remedial and regeneration work by state forestry officials. Replacement trees planted.
- **30–40 years after felling:** Cycle begins again.

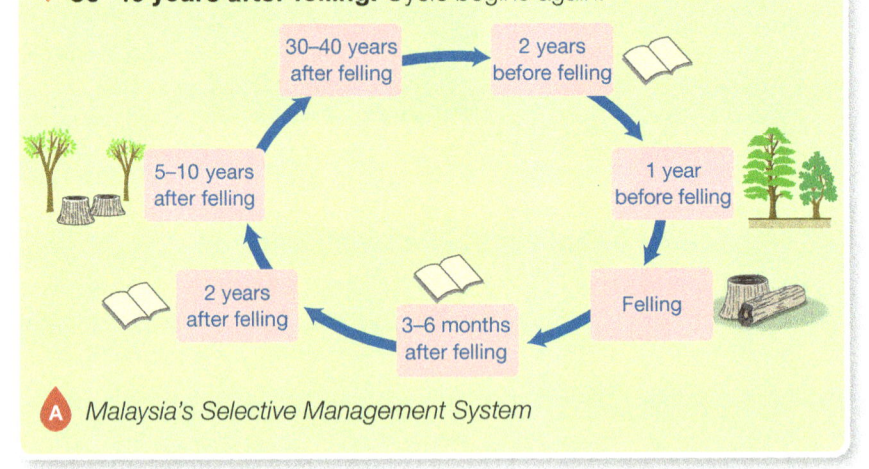

A *Malaysia's Selective Management System*

A more sustainable approach to logging involves *selective logging* (diagram **A**). Managed carefully, this technique – which was introduced in Malaysia in 1977 – is completely sustainable.

Conservation and education

Rainforest can be preserved in conservation areas, such as national parks or nature reserves. These areas can be used for education, scientific research and tourism.

Recently, large international businesses have supported conservation projects in exchange for carrying out scientific research or the provision of raw materials.

B *Tonka beans*

Givaudan

Givaudan is a Swiss perfume company. It works with Conservation International, and aims to protect 148 000 hectares of rainforest in the Caura Basin, Venezuela. Local Aripao people are encouraged to harvest and market tonka beans (photo **B**), which have a caramel-like smell. A warehouse where beans can be dried and stored was built in 2012. This improves their quality and increases their value.

Ecotourism

Countries like Costa Rica, Belize and Malaysia have promoted their forests for **ecotourism**. Ecotourism aims to introduce people to the natural world, to benefit local communities and protect the environment for the future. Through income generated by ecotourism, local people and governments benefit from retaining and protecting their rainforest trees. This is a more sustainable option than cutting them down for short-term profit.

International agreements

Rainforests are now understood to be of global importance. They absorb carbon dioxide from the atmosphere, releasing oxygen and maintaining levels of humidity. International agreements have been made to help protect rainforests.

Hardwood forestry

The Forest Stewardship Council (FSC) is an international organisation that promotes sustainable forestry. Products sourced from sustainably managed forests carry the FSC label.

The FSC tries to educate manufacturers and consumers about the need to buy sustainable hardwood such as mahogany. It aims to reduce demand for the rare and valuable hardwoods.

Debt reduction

Some countries have borrowed money to fund developments. To pay off these debts some have raised money from massive deforestation programmes. Recently, some donor countries and organisations have reduced debts in return for agreement that rainforests will not be deforested. This has become known as 'debt-for-nature swapping'.

C Tourist accommodation in an eco-lodge, Costa Rica

Carbon sinks

In 2008, the Gola Forest on Sierra Leone's southern border with Liberia became a protected national park (photo **D**).

The park plays a significant role in reducing global warming. It acts as a carbon sink by absorbing carbon dioxide from the air.

D Scientists in Sierra Leone's Gola Forest

ACTIVITIES

1 Why is Malaysia's Selective Management System a good example of sustainable management?
2 How can encouraging people to make commercial use of forest products such as the tonka bean (photo **B**) help conserve rainforests?
3 How can we, as consumers, help to conserve rainforests?

Stretch yourself

Find out more about the Gola Forest National Park and its rainforest conservation projects. What do you think its donors get out of the deal? Is it a 'win-win' situation?

Practice question

Describe and explain *two* benefits of international cooperation in sustainably managing tropical rainforests. *(4 marks)*

7 Hot deserts

7.1 Environmental characteristics of hot deserts

On this spread you will find out about the characteristics of hot deserts

What are hot deserts like?

A desert is an area that receives less than 250 mm of rainfall per year. The resulting dryness or aridity is the main factor controlling life in the desert (photo **A**). Did you know that there are both hot and cold deserts? Parts of the Arctic and Antarctic are as dry as some of the desert areas in Africa.

Where are hot deserts found?

Map **B** shows the locations of the world's hot deserts. Notice that they are mostly found in dry continental interiors, away from coasts, in a belt at approximately 30°N and 30°S. There are some coastal deserts too, for example, the Atacama Desert in South America.

What is the climate like?

The location of the hot deserts can be largely explained by the global atmospheric circulation (see page 18). At these latitudes air that has risen at the Equator descends forming a persistent belt of high pressure. This explains the lack of cloud and rain and the very high daytime temperatures. It also explains why, with the lack of cloud cover, temperatures can plummet to below freezing at night during the winter. Graph **C** describes the climate of In Salah, a weather station in the middle of the Sahara Desert in Algeria.

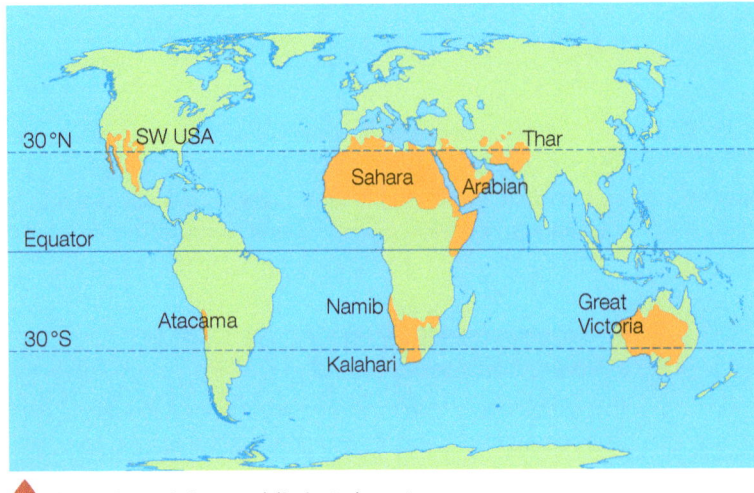

A Jordan – a hot desert environment

What are desert soils like?

Desert soils tend to be sandy or stony, with little organic matter due to the general lack of leafy vegetation. They are dry but can soak up water rapidly after rainfall. Evaporation draws salts to the surface, often leaving a white powder on the ground. Desert soils are not very fertile.

Who lives in hot deserts?

Many people live in hot desert areas. They have adapted by wearing clothes that shade them from the Sun but provide warmth at night when temperatures drop. Many keep animals and depend on them for all their needs. They are very skilled at surviving the harsh conditions by hunting and foraging for food crops.

B Location of the world's hot deserts

C A hot desert climate – In Salah, Algeria

Hot deserts

What plants and animals are found in a hot desert?

Hot deserts are home to a surprising diversity of plants and animals. In all but the driest areas, plants and animals find ways of surviving the hostile conditions. Plants tend to have very thin leaves or spines to reduce water loss and some have very long roots to reach deep underground water. For example, the cactus is a common desert plant.

How have plants and animals adapted?

With the lack of water, vegetation is low-growing and sparse. Plants have developed several adaptations to enable them to cope with the environment (diagram **E**).

Many rodents are nocturnal, surviving the extremely high daytime temperatures by living in burrows underground and only venturing out during the cooler nights (photo **D**). Snakes and lizards retain water by having a waterproof skin and producing only tiny amounts of urine. Camels – the 'ships of the desert' – are well adapted to cope with many days without water.

D A desert jerboa

Some plants have horizontal root systems, just below the surface

Seeds can stay dormant for years, but can germinate quickly when it rains

Some plants store water in their roots, stems, leaves or fruit (these are called succulents)

Small leaves, spines, glossy and waxy leaves all help reduce water loss

E Plant adaptations to hot desert climate

Some plants have long taproots (7–10 m deep) to reach groundwater

Think about it
Most people who live in the Sahara Desert are nomads who move from place to place. How does this lifestyle suit living in a hot desert?

ACTIVITIES

1. **a** Describe the characteristics of the hot desert shown in photo **A**.
   b Why is this landscape a hostile environment for plants and animals?
2. **a** Make a copy of map **B** to show the location of the world's hot deserts. Use an atlas or the internet to find the names of the hot deserts and label them on your map.
   b Describe the pattern of hot deserts.
   c Explain the cloudless conditions shown in photo **A**.
   d How do these cloudless conditions account for the high daytime temperatures and low night-time temperatures?
3. **a** Describe the pattern of temperatures for In Salah (graph **C**).
   b The total annual rainfall in London is about 600 mm. How does this compare with the rainfall for In Salah?
   c How do plants cope with very low rainfall (diagram **E**).

Stretch yourself
Find out about plants called succulents and how they have special adaptations for living in hot deserts.

Practice question
Use diagram **E** to explain how plants have adapted to the hostile conditions in hot deserts. *(4 marks)*

57

7.2 Causes of desertification in hot deserts

On this spread you will find out about the causes of desertification

What is desertification?

Desertification happens where land is gradually turned into a desert (photo **A**), usually on the edges of an existing desert. This can occur when land is **overgrazed** by livestock or stripped of vegetation by people collecting firewood. Once exposed to the weather, it will crack and break up. It will then be eroded by wind and water.

Where is desertification a problem?

Most of the areas at risk from desertification are on the borders of existing deserts, for example the Sahara Desert in Africa (map **B**). An estimated one billion people live in the areas at risk. Desertification affects rich countries as well as poorer ones. It is a significant problem in parts of the USA, Europe (especially Spain) and Australia.

What causes desertification?

Desertification can be caused by natural events, such as droughts, as well as poor land management. The areas close to deserts are ecologically very fragile. Slight changes in temperature and rainfall associated with climate change can have serious impacts. This makes these semi-desert areas even more prone to overgrazing or over-cultivation.

In Australia over 40 per cent of the 5 million km² of desert and semi-desert land has been affected by desertification. This is caused mainly by the pressure of grazing on fragile land affected by drought.

A Oryx grazing alongside the Namib Desert, Namibia

Did you know?
A heavy storm can erode soil that has taken thousands of years to form. Half of the topsoil on Earth has been lost in the last 150 years!

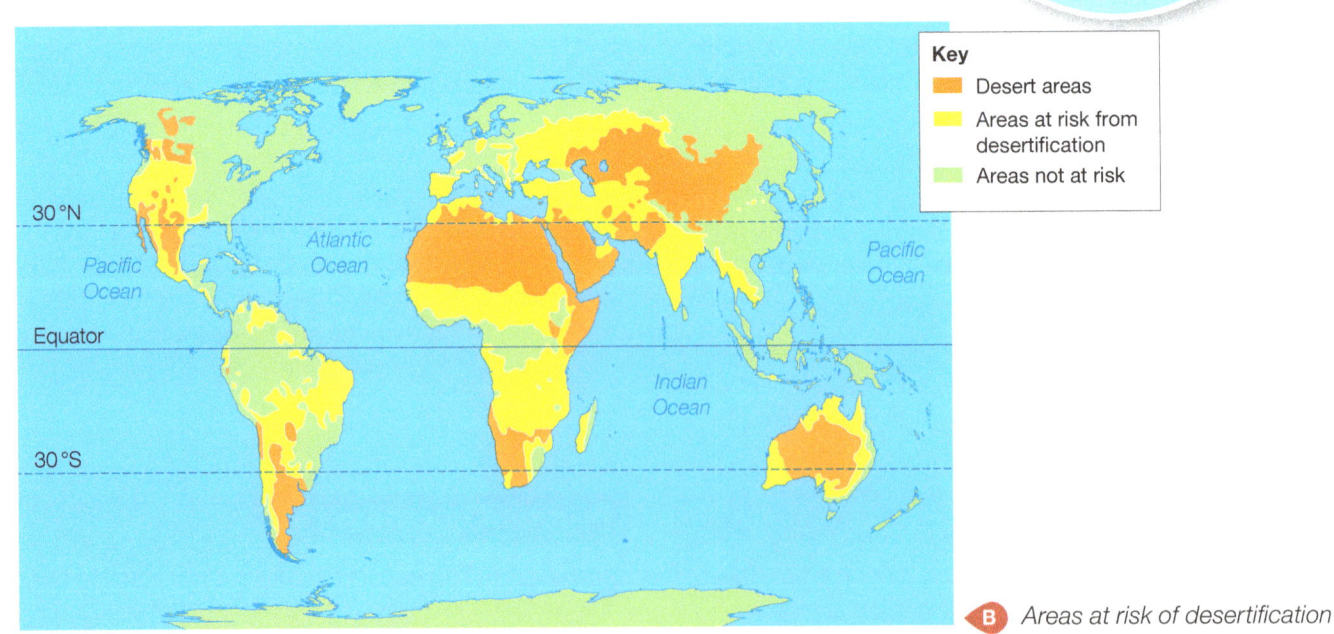

B Areas at risk of desertification

Key:
- Desert areas
- Areas at risk from desertification
- Areas not at risk

Hot deserts

In some desert regions, such as the Sahel on the southern fringes of the Sahara Desert, *climate change* is resulting in drier conditions and unreliable rainfall. On average it now rains less than it did 50 years ago.

Population pressure can result in land close to existing deserts being overgrazed. This means that there are too many animals to be supported by the limited vegetation. When the vegetation has been destroyed the land will turn to desert.

Soil erosion is often linked to desertification. When vegetation has been destroyed the soil is exposed to the wind and the rain making it vulnerable to erosion.

Over-cultivation resulting from the need to produce more food can lead to the soil becoming exhausted. It will turn to dust and become infertile.

Population growth is also increasing the demand for *fuelwood*. Trees are stripped of their branches and eventually die.

C Causes of desertification

Desertification in the Badia, Jordan

The Badia is a dry rocky desert in eastern Jordan. Its average annual rainfall is less than 150 mm and summer temperatures exceed 40 °C. The lack of water in this region is a major problem affecting the people who live there.

Much of the land has been traditionally grazed by the nomadic Bedouin who herd sheep, goats and camels on the rough shrubby grassland. An influx of sheep from Iraq following the 1991 Gulf War led to overgrazing and desertification.

Desertification made the land unproductive and people moved away from the area. Without vegetation, soil erosion became a major problem too.

D Location of the Badia

ACTIVITIES

1. a Describe the landscape in photo **A**.
   b Can you see any evidence that this area is suffering from desertification?
2. Use map **B** to describe the pattern of areas 'at risk' from desertification.
3. a How does population pressure increase the risk of land becoming desert (photo **C**)?
   b What human activities can lead to soil erosion?
   c Is soil erosion an environmental disaster?
4. What caused desertification to occur in the Badia region in Jordan?

Stretch yourself

Investigate desertification in a high-income country (HIC), such as the USA, Spain or Australia.
- What are the impacts and causes?
- What forms of management are being used to address the issue?

Practice question

'Desertification is largely caused by poor land management.' Use evidence to discuss this statement. *(6 marks)*

59

7.3 Reducing desertification in hot deserts

On this spread you will find out about how desertification can be reduced in hot desert environments

Holding back the desert

Land at risk of desertification needs to be managed sustainably so that people can live and prosper without damaging the environment.

Water and soil management

Commercial farming in hot deserts often involves **irrigation**. Water from underground sources or from rivers and canals can be sprayed onto crops or used to flood fields. But too much irrigation can cause problems leading to a process called *salinisation* (diagram **A**). The high rate of evaporation in hot deserts leads to a build-up of salts on the surface. This reduces soil fertility and kills plants.

Water management is at the centre of attempts to combat desertification in Australia. Local farmers are encouraged to use the following methods to prevent soil erosion.

- Ponding banks – areas of land enclosed by low walls to store water.
- Contour traps – embankments built along the contours of slopes to prevent soil from being washed down during heavy rainfall.

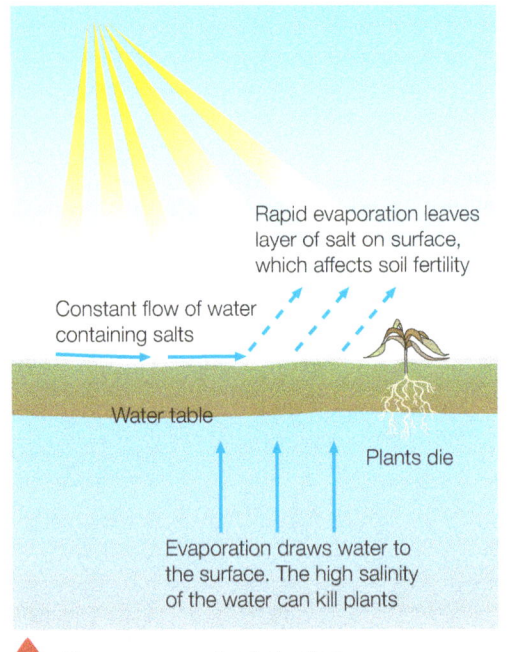

A *The process of salinisation*

Water and soil management in the Badia, Jordan

The Tal Rimah Rangeland Rehabilitation Project aims to reverse the desertification caused by overgrazing in the 1990s.

- Local people have built low stone walls to stop water running down slopes after heavy rainfall.
- This water is used to irrigate newly planted *Atriplex* shrubs that are well adapted to semi-desert environments (photo **B**).
- *Atriplex* hold the soil together and provide grazing for sheep and goats.
- As soil conditions improve, plants have started to grow, attracting birds and butterflies to the area.

B *Atriplex shrubs growing in shallow ditches in the Badia*

National parks

In some parts of the world, hot desert areas at risk of desertification have been protected by making them into national parks.

- The Desert National Park in the Thar Desert, India was created in 1992 to protect some 3000 km^2 of desert and reduce the risk of desertification.
- The Zion National Park (photo **C**) is one of four desert national parks in the USA. It was established in 1919 to protect a desert canyon near Las Vegas.

C *Zion National Park*

Hot deserts

Tree planting in the Thar Desert, India

Tree planting is an important way of reducing erosion. Tree roots bind the soil together and the leaves and branches provide shade, grazing for animals and fuelwood.

The most important tree in the Thar Desert is the *Prosopis cineraria* (photo **D**). It is well adapted to the hostile desert conditions and has many uses.

The *Prosopis cineraria* provides:
- plenty of foliage and seed pods for animals to eat
- good quality firewood
- strong wood for building material
- shade and moist growing conditions for plants
- roots to stabilise sand dunes.

Appropriate technology

Many people living on the edges of deserts are poor. **Appropriate technology** involves using methods and materials that are appropriate to their level of development. They may not have access to expensive machinery. Sustainable approaches have to be practical and appropriate.

'Magic stones' in Burkina Faso, West Africa

In rural parts of Burkina Faso lines of stones have been used to reduce soil erosion. Using basic tools and trucks to transport the stones, local people have built low stone walls between 0.5 m and 1.5 m high along the contours of slopes (photo **E**). When rain washes down the hillside, the walls trap water and soil. This has helped to increase crops by up to 50 per cent and reduce desertification.

D Prosopis cineraria *in the Thar Desert*

E *Building a wall with 'magic stones'*

ACTIVITIES

1. What is salinisation and how is it caused (diagram **A**)?
2. a Why do you think the *Atriplex* shrubs in photo **B** are planted in shallow trenches?
   b How have these plants benefited local people and the natural environment?
3. What are the sustainable qualities of the *Prosopis cineraria* tree (figure **D**)?
4. a How do 'magic stones' use appropriate technology to help solve the problem of desertification?
   b What Australian management scheme is similar to the use of 'magic stones'?
   c Make a simple sketch to show how 'magic stones' work.

Stretch yourself

Carry out your own research about *one* of the four desert national parks in the USA:
- Grand Canyon
- Zion
- Arches
- Canyonlands.

How are the authorities in your chosen park managing the environment to reduce desertification?

Practice question

Explain how the effects of salinisation shown in diagram **A** can lead to desertification and how they can be reduced. *(6 marks)*

Unit 1 Living with the physical environment

Section C Physical landscapes

Estuaries and strait on Ko Lanta Island, Thailand

Unit 1 Living with the physical environment is about physical processes and systems, how they change, and how people interact with them at a range of scales and in a range of places. It is split into three sections.

Section C Physical landscapes includes:

- an overview of Middle and Far East landscapes
- coastal landscapes
- hot desert landscapes
- river landscapes.

You have to study Middle and Far East landscapes and coastal landscapes. You must also study one of the other two types of landscapes.

What if...

1. the landscape of China was completely flat?
2. all our cliffs collapsed?
3. India had droughts every year?
4. the world entered a new Ice Age?

Unit 1 Section C

Specification key ideas	Pages in this book
8 Physical landscapes in the Middle and Far East	**64–5**
• The Middle and Far East have a range of diverse landscapes.	64–5
9 Coastal landscapes	**66–83**
• The coast is shaped by a number of physical processes.	66–71
• Distinctive coastal landforms are the result of rock type, structure and physical processes.	72–9
• Different management strategies can be used to protect coastlines from the effects of physical processes.	80–3
10 Hot desert landscapes	**84–97**
• Hot deserts are shaped by a number of physical processes.	84–7
• Distinctive landforms result from different physical processes in hot deserts.	88–93
• Development of hot desert environments creates opportunities and challenges.	94–7
11 River landscapes	**98–113**
• The shape of river valleys changes as rivers flow downstream.	98–9
• Distinctive fluvial landforms result from different physical processes.	100–5
• Different management strategies can be used to protect river landscapes from the effects of flooding.	106–13

Your key skills

To be a good geographer, you need to develop important geographical skills – in this section you will learn the following skills:

- Drawing cross-sections.
- Drawing labelled sketches and diagrams.
- Drawing sketches from photos.
- Using and describing information in photos.
- Using maps.
- Literacy – describing landforms and processes.

Your key words

As you go through the chapters in this section, make sure you know and understand the key words shown in bold. Definitions are provided in the Glossary on page 354. To be a good geographer you need to use good subject terminology.

Your exam

Section C makes up part of Paper 1 – a one and a half-hour written exam worth 34 per cent of your GCSE.

8 Physical landscapes in the Middle and Far East

8.1 The Middle and Far East

In this spread you will find out about the relief and landscapes found in the Middle and Far East

What is relief?

Relief is a term used by geographers to describe the physical features of the landscape. This includes:

- height above sea level, usually measured in metres
- steepness of slopes
- shapes of landscape features.

The relief of an area is determined mainly by its geology – the rocks that form the landscape. Tough, resistant rocks such as limestone, granite and slate form upland areas, whereas weaker sands and clays form lowland plains.

The landscapes of the Middle and Far East

A landscape is an area whose character is the result of the action and interaction of natural and human factors. Map **B** shows the relief of the Middle and Far East. Some of the main landscape features of the region:

- The Himalayas – an extensive mountain range stretching through western China, Nepal, northern India and Pakistan. Formed by the collision of two huge tectonic plates (the African plate and the Eurasian plate), the Himalayas represent a destructive (collision) margin. The tough sedimentary and metamorphic rocks have been crumpled and uplifted to form some of the world's highest mountain peaks, including Mount Everest (8848 m).

- Plateaus – these extensive, largely flat landscapes at high elevations include the Iranian Plateau, which covers most of Iran, Afghanistan and Pakistan. Rising to just over 5000 m, the Iranian Plateau is not entirely flat, with mountains and river basins. It contains two deserts. Other plateaus include the Deccan Plateau in southern India (rising to 500 m) and the Tibetan Plateau, known as the 'Rooftop of the World' (rising to over 5000 m).

- Plains, steppes and deserts – these low-lying flat regions extend over vast areas and include the West Siberian Plain, Mongolia and the Rub' al Khali desert, which extends across Saudi Arabia, Oman, the United Arab Emirates and Yemen. Virtually inhospitable to people, it is known as the 'Empty Quarter'.

- Alluvial plains – several huge river systems have formed extensive coastal alluvial deltas such as the River Ganges in Bangladesh and the Yellow River in China, which forms the vast North China Plain.

A *Views of Chukhung Glacier and Mount Ama Dablam from Chukhung Valley, Himalayas, Nepal*

Physical landscapes in the Middle and Far East

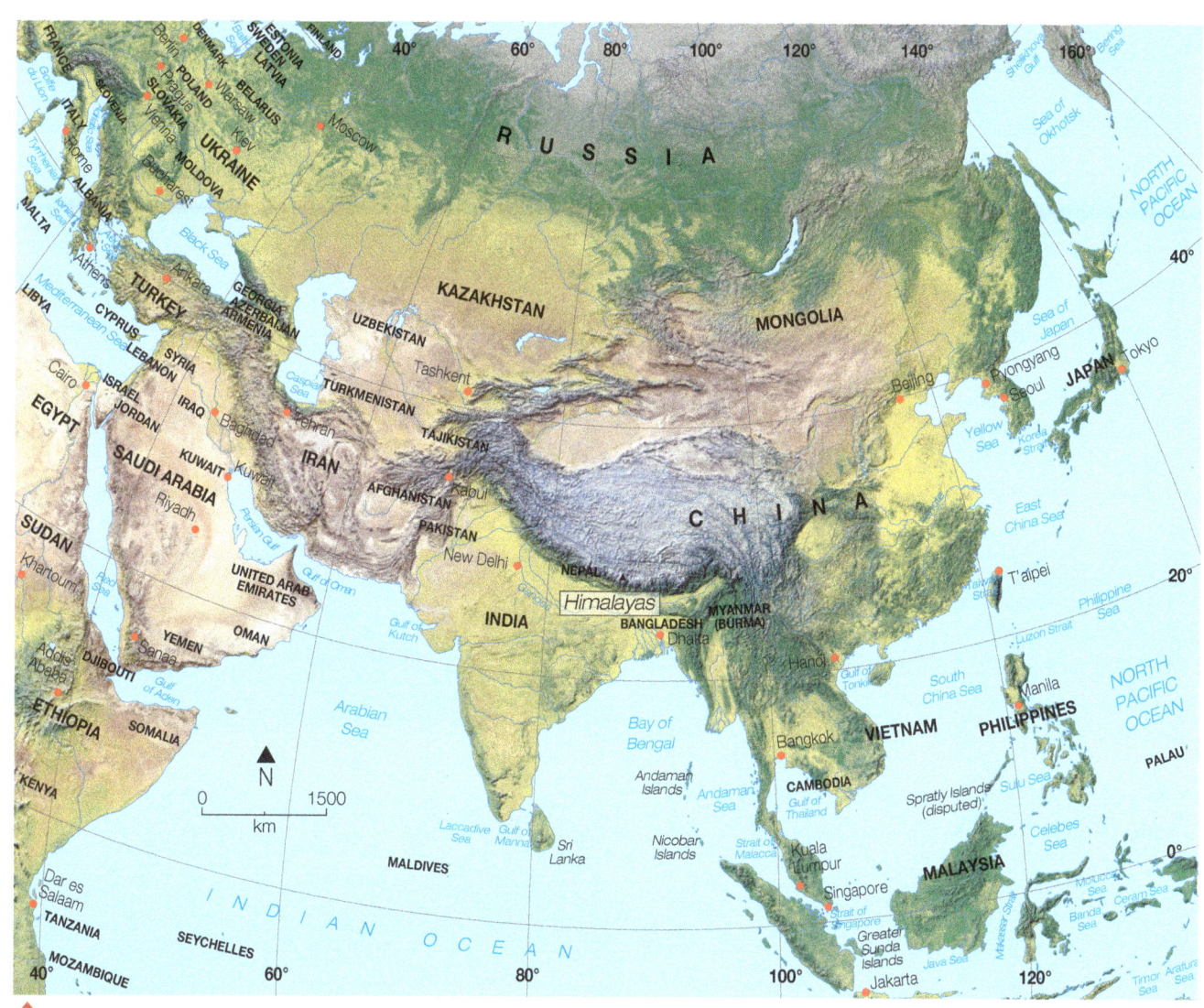

B *The relief of the Middle and Far East*

ACTIVITIES

1. Study photo **A**. Describe the Himalayan landscape shown.
2. Study map **B**, an atlas map showing the relief of the Middle and Far East.
   a. Locate the Himalayas and Mount Everest. What is the height of Mount Everest?
   b. What is the name of the plateau to the north of Mount Everest?
   c. Locate Mongolia. What is the name of the desert in this remote region?
   d. Describe the relief of Iran.
   e. Name two cities located on the River Ganges' alluvial plain.
   f. What common landscape feature is prefixed by the following: Siberian, Mongolian and Deccan?

Stretch yourself

Use the internet to find a photo to illustrate each of the following landscapes: plateau, desert and alluvial plain. Annotate each photo to describe the main landscape features.

Practice question

To what extent does relief affect the location of major settlements in the Middle and Far East? *(6 marks)*

9 Coastal landscapes

9.1 Wave types and their characteristics

On this spread you will find out about the formation and characteristics of waves

How do waves form?

Waves are formed by the wind blowing over the sea. Friction with the surface of the water causes ripples to form and these develop into waves. The distance the wind blows across the water is called the *fetch*. The longer the *fetch*, the more powerful the wave.

Waves can also be formed more dramatically when earthquakes or volcanic eruptions shake the seabed. These waves are called *tsunami*. In March 2011 a wall of water up to 40m high crashed into the Japanese coast north of Tokyo destroying several coastal settlements and killing over 20 000 people (photo **B**).

What happens when waves reach the coast?

In the open sea, despite the wavy surface, there is little horizontal movement of water. Only when the waves approach the shore is there forward movement of water as waves break and surge up the beach (diagram **C**).

The seabed interrupts the circular movement of the water. As the water becomes shallower, the circular motion becomes more elliptical. This causes the crest of the wave to rise up and eventually to collapse onto the beach. The water that rushes up the beach is called the *swash*. The water that flows back towards the sea is called the backwash.

A *Surfers at Lombok Island, Indonesia*

B *Tsunami waves hit the coast of Japan*

C *Waves approaching the coast*

Circular orbit in open water | Friction with the seabed distorts the circular orbital motion | Top of wave moves faster | Increasingly elliptical orbit | Wave begins to break | Water from previous wave returns | Water rushes up the beach | Shelving seabed (beach)

66

Coastal landscapes

Wave types

It is possible to identify two types of wave at the coast.

Constructive waves

These are low waves that surge up the beach and 'spill' with a powerful swash (diagram **D**). They carry and deposit large amounts of sand and pebbles and 'construct' the beach making it more extensive. Surfers prefer constructive waves because they give longer rides (photo **A**)! These waves are formed by storms often hundreds of kilometres away.

D Constructive waves

Destructive waves

These are formed by local storms close to the coast, and they can 'destroy' the beach – hence their name. They are closely spaced and often interfere with each other producing a chaotic swirling mass of water. They become high and steep before plunging down onto the beach (diagram **E**). There is little forward motion (swash) when a destructive wave breaks but a powerful backwash. This explains the removal of sand and pebbles and the gradual destruction of the beach.

E Destructive waves

ACTIVITIES

1. **a** Copy diagram **C** and draw an arrow to show the direction of the waves.
   b Add the labels *swash* and *backwash* in the correct places.
   c What causes the waves to rise up and break on the beach?
   d When waves break on a sandy or pebbly beach the amount of backwash is often less than the amount of swash. Why do you think this is?
   e Larger pebbles are found at the top of the beach with smaller ones near the bottom. Use your answer to **d** to suggest reasons why.
2. Why do surfers prefer constructive waves to destructive waves?
3. Outline the characteristics of constructive and destructive waves. Complete a copy of the table below.

Wave characteristic	Constructive wave	Destructive wave
Wave height		
Wave length		
Type of wave break (spilling or plunging)		
Strength of swash		
Strength of backwash		
Net beach sediment (gain or loss)		

Stretch yourself

Carry out some research about the tsunami waves that struck Japan in March 2011.
- Why were the waves so high and so powerful?
- What were the impacts on people and human activities?
- What effect did the waves have on the physical geography of the coast of Japan?

Practice question

Compare the characteristics of constructive and destructive waves. *(4 marks)*

67

9.2 Weathering and mass movement

On this spread you will find out about processes of weathering and mass movement at the coast

Rockfalls at Praia de Luz

Photo **A** shows a dramatic rockfall at Praia da Luz in the Algarve, Portugal. The area is characterised by frequent rockfalls and collapses, more common in the winter and after rainfall. In both August 2009 and October 2014 huge rockfalls took place, collapsing into the sea. Processes such as this combine with the action of the waves to shape the coastline.

What causes cliffs to collapse?

Cliffs collapse because of different types of weathering. This is the weakening or decay of rocks in their original place on, or close to, the ground surface. It is mostly caused by weather factors such as rainfall and changes in temperature.

There are three types of weathering:

- **Mechanical (physical) weathering** – the disintegration (break-up) of rocks. Where this happens, piles of rock fragments called *scree* can be found at the foot of cliffs.

- **Chemical weathering** – caused by chemical changes. Rainwater, which is slightly acidic, very slowly dissolves certain types of rocks and minerals.

- *Biological weathering* – due to the actions of flora and fauna. Plant roots grow in cracks in the rocks. Animals such as rabbits burrow into weak rocks such as sands.

A Rockfall with coastal erosion Praia de Luz, Portugal

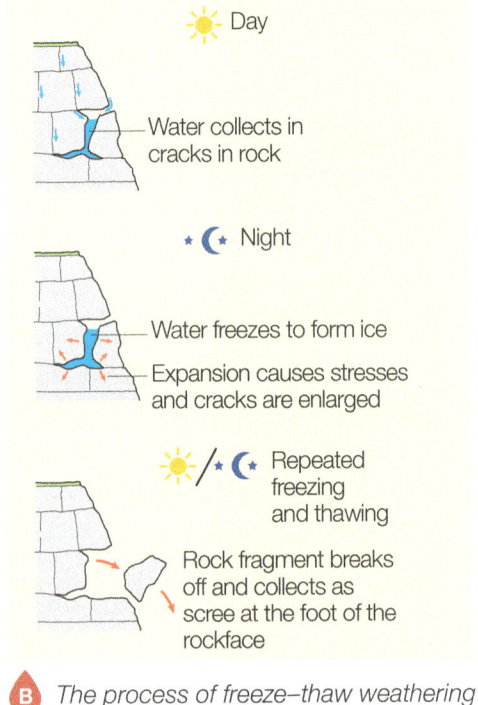

B The process of freeze–thaw weathering

C Landslide in the mountains in Camiguin Island, Philippines

Coastal landscapes

Weathering process	Description
Freeze–thaw (mechanical)	Look at diagram **B**. • Water collects in cracks or holes (pores) in the rock. • At night this water freezes and expands and makes cracks in the rock bigger. • When the temperature rises and the ice thaws, water will seep deeper into the rock. • After repeated freezing and thawing, fragments of rock may break off and fall to the foot of the cliff (scree).
Salt weathering (mechanical)	• Seawater contains salt. When the water evaporates it leaves behind salt crystals. • In cracks and holes these salt crystals grow and expand. • This puts pressure on the rocks and flakes may eventually break off.
Carbonation (chemical)	• Rainwater absorbs CO_2 from the air and becomes slightly acidic. • Contact with alkaline rocks such as chalk and limestone produces a chemical reaction causing the rocks to slowly dissolve.

What are the processes of mass movement?

Mass movement is the downward movement or **sliding** of material under the influence of gravity. In 2001, the tropical storm Lingling hit the southern island of Camiguin in the Philippines. The subsequent landslide of mud and boulders flattened hundreds of houses, killing as many as 234 people.

Diagram **D** describes some of the common types of mass movement found at the coast. Both mass movement and weathering provide an input of material to the coastal system. Much of this material is carried away by waves and deposited further along the coast.

D Types of mass movement at the coast

a Rockfall – fragments of rock break away from the cliff face, often due to freeze–thaw weathering
- Cliff face
- Scree

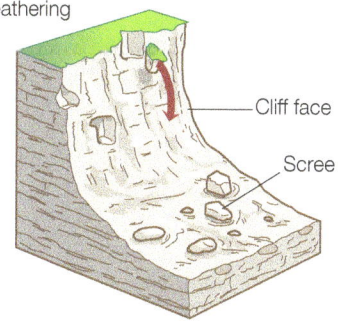

b Landslide – blocks of rock slide downhill
- Slide plane
- Detached rock
- Bedding of rocks

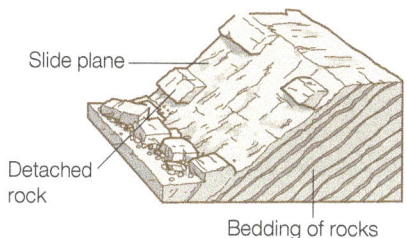

c Mudflow – saturated soil and weak rock flows down a slope
- Soil
- Stream
- Lobe
- Saturated soil and rock debris
- Bedrock

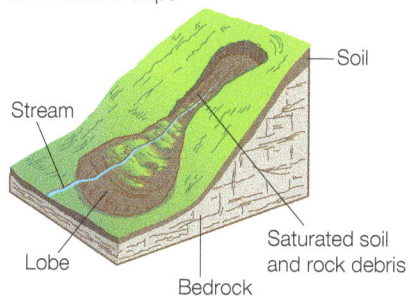

d Rotational slip – slump of saturated soil and weak rock along a curved surface
- Head
- Scarp
- Foot
- Curved slip plane
- Toe

ACTIVITIES

1. **a** Draw a simple sketch of the coastline in photo **A**. Label the rockfall, the chalk cliffs and the rocky beach.
   b Do you think freeze–thaw is active here?
   c What is scree? Label this feature on your sketch.
   d How might rockfalls be a hazard to people?
2. Make a copy of diagram **B** and add detailed annotations to describe the process of freeze–thaw weathering.
3. Describe the process of mass movement in photo **C** and suggest the causes.

Stretch yourself

Investigate the Beachy Head rockfall in 2001.
- Which weathering and mass movement processes were responsible?
- What impact did the rockfalls have on the shape of the coast?
- Find out how and why the Belle Tout lighthouse had to be moved.

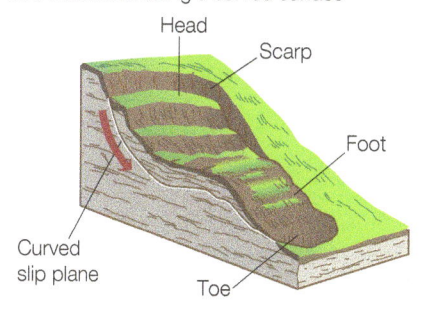

Practice question

Describe the effects of weathering and mass movement on a cliffed coastline. *(6 marks)*

69

9.3 Coastal erosion processes

On this spread you will find out about the processes of erosion and deposition

Coastal erosion
Erosion involves the removal of material and the shaping of landforms. There are several different processes of coastal erosion.

A *Processes of erosion*

Solution
The dissolving of soluble chemicals in rocks, e.g. limestone.

Corrasion
Fragments of rock are picked up and hurled by the sea at a cliff. The rocks act like tools scraping and gouging to erode the rock.

Hydraulic power
This is the power of the waves as they smash onto a cliff. Trapped air is forced into holes and cracks in the rock eventually causing the rock to break apart. The explosive force of trapped air operating in a crack is called *cavitation*.

Abrasion
This is the 'sandpapering' effect of pebbles grinding over a rocky platform often causing it to become smooth.

Attrition
Rock fragments carried by the sea knock against one another causing them to become smaller and more rounded.

Coastal transportation
Sediment of different sizes can be transported in four different ways. (diagram **B**):

- solution
- suspension
- saltation
- traction.

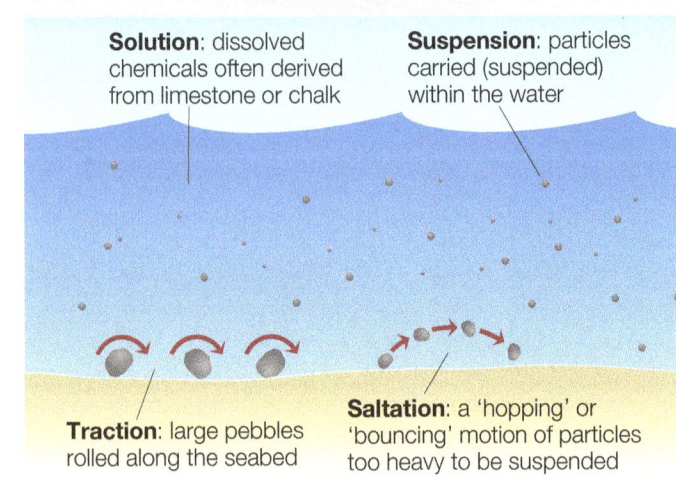

Solution: dissolved chemicals often derived from limestone or chalk

Suspension: particles carried (suspended) within the water

Traction: large pebbles rolled along the seabed

Saltation: a 'hopping' or 'bouncing' motion of particles too heavy to be suspended

B *Types of coastal transportation*

Coastal landscapes

Longshore drift

The movement of sediment on a beach depends on the direction that waves approach the coast (diagram **C**). Where waves approach 'head on', sediment is simply moved up and down the beach. But if waves approach at an angle, sediment will be moved *along* the beach in a 'zigzag' pattern. This is called **longshore drift**.

Longshore drift is responsible for a number of important coastal landforms including beaches and spits (pages 74–5).

Coastal deposition

Coastal **deposition** takes place in areas where the flow of water slows down. Waves lose energy in sheltered bays and where water is protected by spits or bars (see page 75). Here sediment can no longer be carried or moved and is therefore deposited. This explains why beaches are found in bays, where the energy of the waves is reduced. This is called *wave refraction* (diagram **D**).

Mudflats and saltmarshes are often found in sheltered estuaries behind spits where there is very little flow of water.

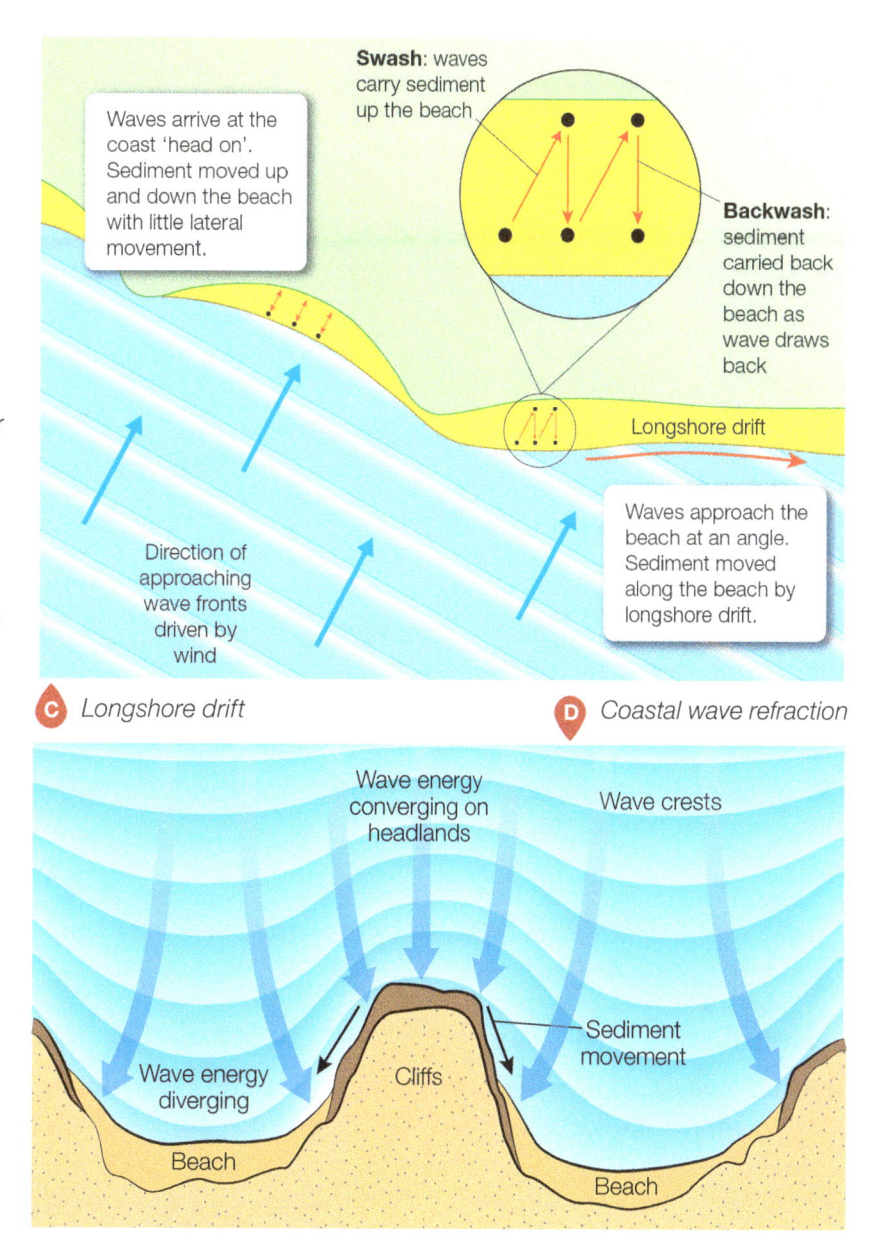

C Longshore drift

D Coastal wave refraction

ACTIVITIES

1. **a** Draw an annotated diagram similar to **B** to show the processes of *erosion*. Show a wave breaking against the foot of a cliff.
   b Add detailed labels to describe the *five* processes of erosion.
2. **a** What is meant by the term 'longshore drift' (diagram **C**)?
   b Why does this only occur on some beaches?
   c Draw a diagram to show the process of longshore drift. Add labels to describe what is happening.
   d Imagine you are doing a fieldwork investigation for evidence of longshore drift along a stretch of coast. What evidence would you look for and why?

Stretch yourself

Find out more about the coastal locations where deposition occurs.
- Focus on a stretch of coastline near to your school or one that you have visited.
- Use maps and satellite images to zoom in on locations where deposition has happened. Describe the material that has been deposited and suggest reasons why.

Practice question

What factors affect the processes operating along a stretch of coastline? *(6 marks)*

9.4 Coastal erosion landforms

On this spread you will find out about the characteristics and formation of coastal landforms

What is a landform?

You will come across the term 'landform' all the time in physical geography. A landform is a feature of the landscape that has been formed or sculpted by processes of:

- erosion
- transportation
- deposition.

What factors influence coastal landforms?

Some rocks are tougher and more resistant than others. Rocks such as granite, limestone and chalk form impressive cliffs and headlands because they are more resistant to erosion. Softer rocks, clays and sands are more easily eroded to form bays or low-lying stretches of coastline.

Geological structure includes the way that layers of rocks are folded or tilted. This can be an important factor in the shape of cliffs. Faults are cracks in rocks. Enormous tectonic pressures can cause rocks to 'snap' rather than fold (bend) and movement (or *displacement*) happens on either side of the fault. Faults form lines of weakness in rocks, easily carved out by the sea.

A *The formation of headlands and bays*

Headlands and bays

Different types of rock at the coastline will be eroded at different rates. Weaker bands of rock (such as clay) erode more easily to form *bays*. As the bays are sheltered, deposition takes place and a sandy beach forms (diagram **A**).

The tougher, more-resistant bands of rock (such as limestone or sandstone) are eroded much more slowly. They stick out into the sea to form **headlands**. Erosion dominates in these high-energy environments, which explains why there are no beaches. Most *erosional* landforms are found at headlands.

B *Wave-cut platform and beach near Beachy Head, UK*

Cliffs and wave-cut platforms

When waves break against a **cliff**, erosion close to the high tide line will wear away the cliff to form a wave-cut notch. Over a long period of time – usually hundreds of years – the notch will get deeper and deeper, undercutting the cliff. Eventually the overlying cliff can no longer support its own weight and it collapses.

Through a continual sequence of wave-cut notch formation and cliff collapse, the cliff will gradually retreat. In its place will be a gently sloping rocky platform called a **wave-cut platform** (photo **B**). A wave-cut platform is typically quite smooth due to the process of abrasion. However, in some places it may be scarred with rock pools.

Coastal landscapes

Caves, arches and stacks

Lines of weakness in a headland, such *as faults*, are particularly vulnerable to erosion. The energy of the waves wears away the rock along a line of weakness to form a **cave** (diagram **C**). Over time, erosion may lead to two back-to-back caves breaking through a headland to form an **arch**. Gradually the arch is enlarged by erosion at the base and by weathering processes (such as freeze–thaw) acting on the roof. Eventually the roof will be worn away and collapse to form an isolated pillar of rock known as a **stack**.

> **Remember!**
> - A cliff, a river meander or a delta *are* all landforms.
> - A process such as longshore drift is *not* a landform.
> - A geological feature such as a joint in a rock outcrop is *not* a landform.
>
> If you are in any doubt, check with your teacher!

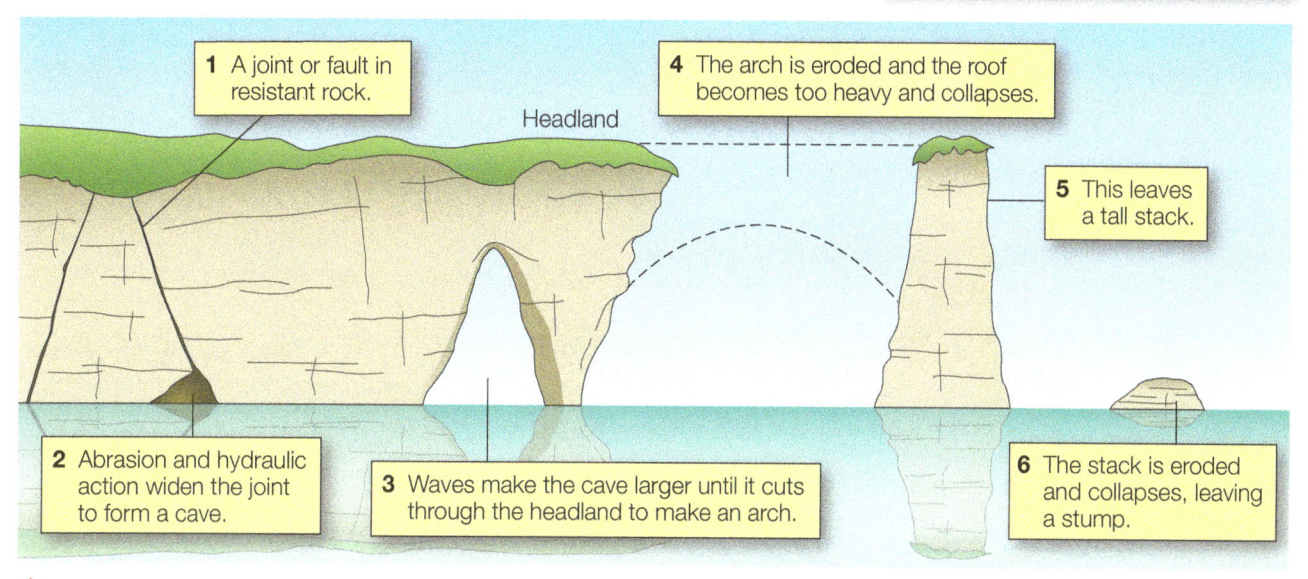

1. A joint or fault in resistant rock.
2. Abrasion and hydraulic action widen the joint to form a cave.
3. Waves make the cave larger until it cuts through the headland to make an arch.
4. The arch is eroded and the roof becomes too heavy and collapses.
5. This leaves a tall stack.
6. The stack is eroded and collapses, leaving a stump.

C How caves, arches and stacks are formed

Ko Tapu, Thailand

Ko Tapu (photo **D**) is a limestone sea stack about 20 m in height. It lies to the west from the northern part of Khao Phing Kan. It is characterised by having a narrow base and a broad top. This reflects active erosion by waves between the high and low tide lines.

D Sea stacks in Ko Tapu, Thailand

Stretch yourself

Find an example of a coastline with headlands and bays. This could be a stretch of coastline near to where you live or one that you have visited.
- Search for a map or satellite photo and add labels to describe the main features.
- Find out about the different types of rock.

Practice question

Use one distinctive coastal landform to illustrate the erosive power of the sea. *(6 marks)*

ACTIVITIES

1. Draw a sequence of diagrams to show the formation of headlands and bays. To test your understanding, draw your coast facing a different direction to diagram **A**.
2. Draw a sequence of labelled diagrams to show how a cliff is undercut by the sea and then collapses to form a wave-cut platform. Use your labels to explain the processes and landforms.
3. Use a sequence of diagrams to explain the formation of a stack (diagram **C**).

9.5 Coastal deposition landforms

On this spread you will find out about the characteristics and formation of coastal deposition landforms

Beaches

Beaches are deposits of sand and shingle (pebbles) at the coast. Sandy beaches are mainly found in sheltered bays (photo **A**). The waves entering the bay are *constructive* waves (see page 67). They have a strong swash and build up the beach.

Not all beaches are made of sand. Much of the south coast of England has pebble beaches. These high-energy environments wash away the finer sand and leave behind the larger pebbles. These come from nearby eroded cliffs or are deposited onshore from vast accumulations out to sea.

Diagram **B** shows the profile of a typical sandy beach. Notice the clear ridges called *berms*. One of these marks the high tide line where seaweed and rubbish get washed up onto the beach.

Sand dunes

At the back of the beach in photo **A**, sand deposited on the beach has been blown inland by onshore winds to form *dunes*. Diagram **C** shows how dunes change in form and appearance the further inland.

Embryo dunes form around deposited obstacles such as pieces of wood or rocks.

↓

These develop and become stabilised by vegetation to form *fore dunes* and tall *yellow dunes*. Marram grass is adapted to the windy, exposed conditions and has long roots to find water. These roots help bind the sand together and stabilise the dunes.

↓

In time, rotting vegetation adds organic matter to the sand making it more fertile. A much greater range of plants colonise these 'back' dunes.

↓

Wind can form depressions in the sand called *dune slacks*, in which ponds may form.

C *Development of sand dunes*

A *Sandy beach in Sri Lanka*

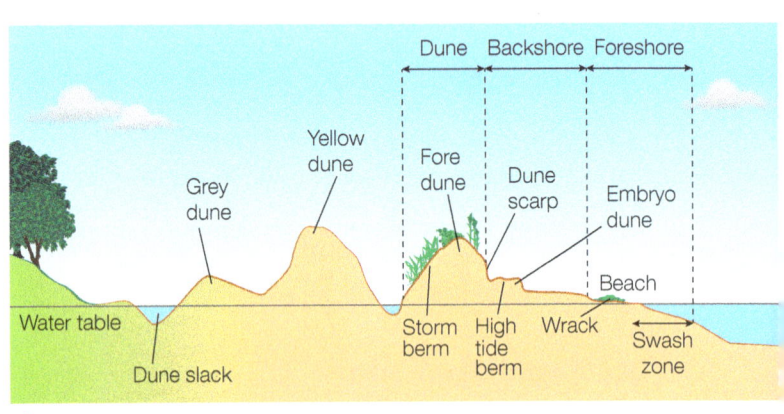

B *Cross-section through beach and sand dunes*

D *Sidney Spit, Vancouver Island, British Columbia, Canada*

Coastal landscapes

Spits

A **spit** is a long, narrow finger of sand or shingle jutting out into the sea from the land (photo **D**).

Spits form on coasts where there is significant longshore drift. If the coastline changes orientation and bends sharply, sediment is then deposited out to sea (diagram **E**). As it builds up, it starts to form an extension from the land. This process continues with the spit gradually growing further out into the sea. Strong winds or tidal currents can cause the end of the spit to become curved to form a feature called a *recurved end* (photo **D**). There may be a number of recurved ends marking previous positions of the spit.

In the sheltered water behind the spit, deposits of mud have built up. An extensive saltmarsh has formed as vegetation has started to grow in the emerging muddy islands. Saltmarshes are extremely important wildlife habitats and over-wintering grounds for migrating birds.

Bars

Longshore drift may cause a spit to grow right across a bay, trapping a freshwater lake (or *lagoon*) behind it. This feature is called a **bar** (photo **F**).

An offshore bar forms further out to sea. Waves approaching a gently sloping coast deposit sediment due to friction with the seabed. The build-up of sediment offshore causes waves to break at some distance from the coast.

In the UK some offshore bars have been driven onshore by rising sea levels following ice melt at the end of the last glacial period some 8000 years ago. This type of feature is called a *barrier beach*. Chesil Beach in Dorset is one of the best examples of this feature in the UK.

ACTIVITIES

1 Describe the processes responsible for the formation of the beach and the sand dunes in photo **A**.
2 Draw a sketch of Hurst Castle Spit. Add labels to describe the characteristic features and the processes responsible for the spit's formation.
3 Describe the characteristics and possible formation of the bar in photo **F**.

Stretch yourself

Investigate the characteristics and formation of sand dunes.
- Why do they only form in certain places on the coast?
- Research 'sand dune succession' to find out the sequence of events in the formation of sand dunes.
- What are the characteristics of marram grass and why does it thrive on sand dunes?

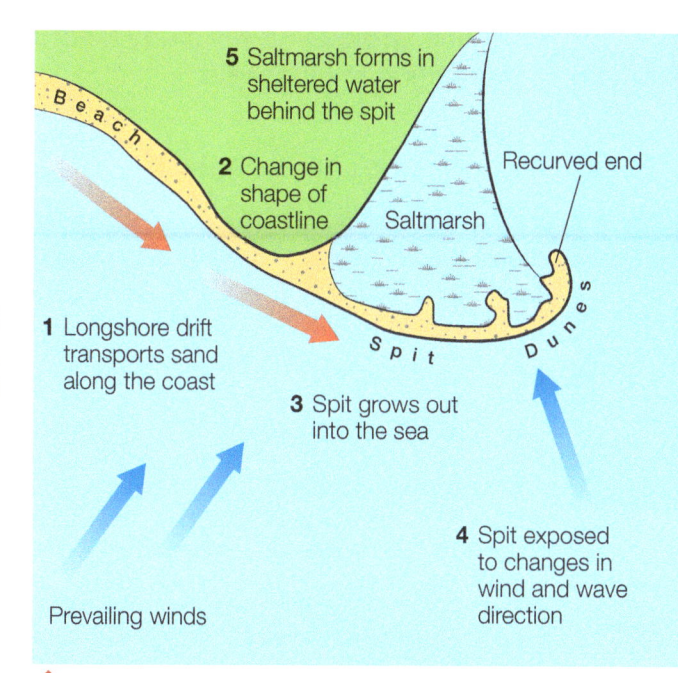

E The formation of a spit

F Bar at Miyazu Bay in Kyoto, Japan

Practice question

How do the processes of deposition lead to the formation of distinctive landforms?
(6 marks)

75

9.6 Coastal landforms in Indonesia (1)

Example

On this spread you will study landforms of erosion and deposition in Indonesia

The Indonesian coastal environment

Indonesia, consisting of about 18 000 islands, has a complex coastline whose length has been estimated as just over 80 000 km (map **A**). The islands show a huge diversity of landforms, reflecting tectonic activity, marine processes aand changes in sea level.

Marine processes are important in shaping Indonesia's coastal landforms, particularly along the exposed south coast of Sumatra and Java.

- During the winter (in the southern hemisphere), the moderate south-easterly trade winds drive relatively high-energy waves onto the southern coasts. This is the dry season.

- During the summer, the winds switch to come from a westerly direction. These lighter winds create less-powerful waves but are responsible for the heavy rains of the wet season.

Indonesia's humid tropical climate has promoted intense chemical weathering and formation of deep soils. Following heavy rainfall in the wet season, rivers wash huge quantities of sediment to the coast where it forms extensive beach deposits. The main coastal landforms in Indonesia are beaches, mangroves, cliffs and coral reefs.

A *The islands of Indonesia*

Beaches

Beaches of sand and gravel are extensive around the coasts of Indonesia, especially near the mouths of rivers and along shorelines to the lee of fringing coral reefs. Sandy beaches are typically backed by swash ridges or berms. Near Yogyakarta in southern Java, extensive sand deposits are backed by vegetated sand dunes (photo **B**).

Along much of the Indonesian coast, beach ridges and dunes have been colonised by natural woodland species, such as Casuarina, together with planted or self-seeded coconut palms. Many beaches show evidence of erosion with the formation of low cliffs and undercutting of vegetation. However, this is not the case where there is a plentiful supply of fluvial sediment.

B *Parangtritis beach, 20 km south of Yogyakarta, Central Java, Indonesia*

Mangroves

Depositional coastlines are typically sandy or swampy. In the humid tropics, swampy sectors are usually occupied by mangroves, which colonise the upper part of the intertidal zone. Once established, mangroves can protect the coast from wave action and encourage the build-up of sediment, which then becomes trapped in the tangle of roots. In this way, shorelines can extend seawards.

Coastal landscapes

Cliffs

Coastal cliffs are relatively rare in the humid tropics. There are several reasons for this:

- Extensive deposition of fluvial sediment has resulted in the formation of wide deltas and extensive beaches in front of hills and mountains, protecting them from the direct action of waves.

- Fringing and barrier reefs of coral shelter exposed stretches of coastline from waves.

- The general absence of strong wind and wave action in these environments.

C *Coastal landforms at Nguyahan beach, Yogyakarta, Java, Indonesia*

Where uplands reach the coast, they tend to form steep, vegetated slopes extending almost to the water's edge. Wave action may undercut the base of the slope, removing weathered material to expose rocky outcrops or accumulations of boulders on the shore. Landslides occur frequently on steep coastal slopes that have been undercut by the sea.

Steep coastal slopes are extensive in Indonesia, especially around Sulawesi and the islands to the east. Elsewhere, strong wave action on the southern coasts of Sumatra and Java has formed dramatic cliffs where resistant rocks such as sandstone and limestone have been eroded to form wave-cut notches and caves (photo **C**). In places, rocky platforms have developed at the foot of cliffs, pitted by the action of weathering, wave action and wind scour.

Coral reefs

Reefs, built up by coral and other marine organisms, occur extensively in Indonesian waters, especially in the Flores Sea and Banda Sea. The warm, clear, saline water in the seas around Indonesia is ideal for the growth of coral. The only exceptions are close to river mouths, where salinity is diluted by river water, and the presence of silt reduces water clarity and sunlight penetration. This accounts for the limited development of coral reefs in the shallow, often muddy, seas south and west of Kalimantan, and in the sediment-laden waters off the deltaic coastline of northern Java.

Changes in sea level associated with tectonic activity have created many complex coral reef landforms along Indonesia's coastline, including the formation of coral atolls.

ACTIVITIES

1. Draw an outline sketch of the island of Java (map **A**).
   a. Use labelled arrows to show the direction of the prevailing south-easterly trade winds, which approach the south coast of the island during the winter (dry season).
   b. Draw a labelled arrow to show the direction of longshore drift along the south coast of Java during the winter.
   c. Suggest why the south coast of Java is likely to exhibit more-developed coastal landforms than the north coast.
2. Study photo **B**.
   a. Describe the sand dunes in the photo.
   b. Suggest reasons for the development of sand dunes on this stretch of coastline. Consider the supply of sand and the prevailing wind direction.

Stretch yourself

Use the internet to find a photo of the Indonesian coast at Yogyakarta, similar to photo **C**. Add labels to identify the main coastal landforms on your photo.

Practice question

Using photo **C**, suggest reasons for the development of the coastal landforms on this stretch of limestone coast in southern Java. *(6 marks)*

9.7 Coastal landforms in Indonesia (2)

On this spread you will use map and photo evidence to study landforms of erosion and deposition in Indonesia

Indonesian coastal examples

Krakatoa Islands

Krakatoa, a volcanic island in the Sunda Strait, erupted violently in 1883 leaving behind the residual islands of Sertung, Panjang and Rakata (map **A**). By 1927, a new volcanic island, Anak Krakatoa, had formed within the caldera. This has grown steadily and is now over 230 m high.

The relatively soft pumice rock that forms the residual islands has been extensively eroded by the sea to form cliffs up to 250 m in height. These cliffs are receding rapidly. Sand deposited have built up in sheltered locations and a spit has formed on the northern tip of Sertung.

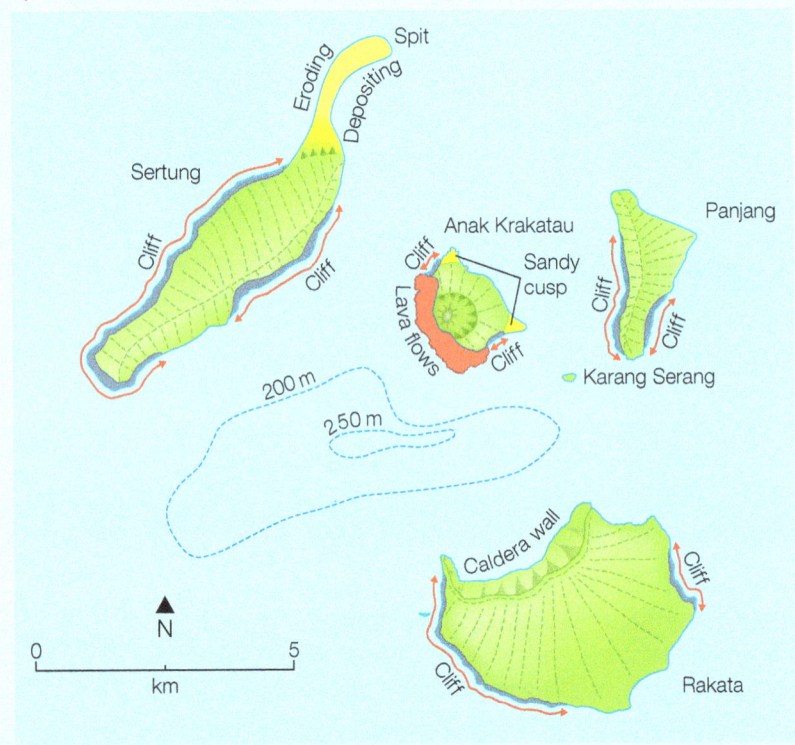

A *The islands of Indonesia*

B *View from Anak Krakatoa looking towards the south-east*

Coastal landscapes

Mahakam Delta, Kalimantan, Indonesia

The densely vegetated Mahakam Delta is located on the east coast of Kalimantan (map **C**). It is an actively growing delta system, forming under conditions of relatively high tides, low wave energy and large inputs of fluvial sediment.

The extensive delta is broadly bow-shaped but characterised at high tide by numerous mudflats extending out to sea either side of small distributary channels. The distribution of these mudflats and estuarine channels is largely controlled by tidal processes.

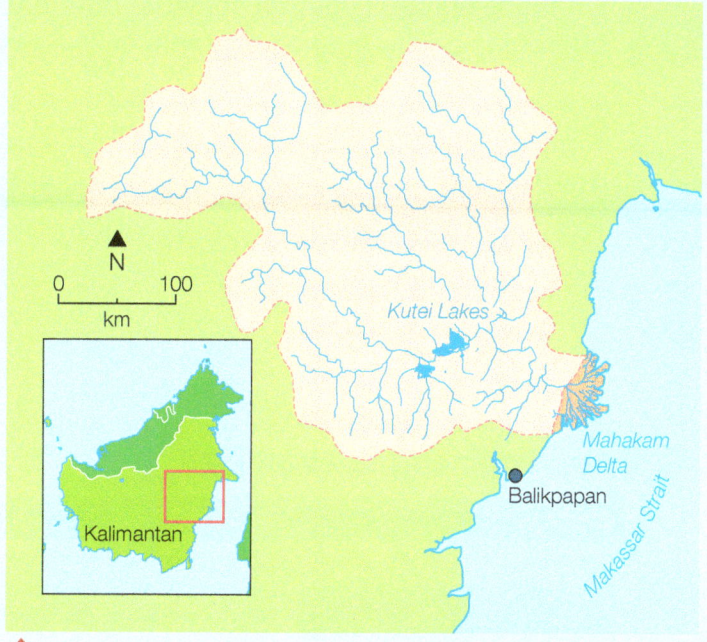

ACTIVITIES

1. Study diagram **A**.
   a. Identify the landforms of coastal erosion and deposition.
   b. Explain the formation of the spit on the island of Sertung.
   c. Why are there extensive cliffs on the islands?
   d. Suggest why sandy cusps (small sandy beaches) have formed at the two locations on Anak Krakatoa. (Think about the wind directions and the location of the neighbouring islands.)

2. Study map **A** and photo **B**.
   a. What is the name of the island in the distance?
   b. Suggest why the island has a very dramatic cliff.
   c. What is the evidence that the lava flow that extends down to the sea has been formed relatively recently?
   d. Suggest why there are some localised sand deposits at the edge of the lava flow.

3. Study map **C**.
   a. Describe the shape of the delta at high tide.
   b. What are distributaries and how are they important in shaping the delta?
   c. What other factors and processes affect the shape of the delta?
   d. If sea level rises in the future, how might this affect the shape and extent of the delta?

C Location of Mahakam Delta, Kalimantan, Indonesia

D Mahakam Delta

E Segara Anakan, a mangrove-fringed lagoon, Java, Indonesia

Practice question

Describe and explain the characteristic features of the Mahakam Delta, Indonesia. *(4 marks)*

Stretch yourself

Carry out some research using the internet to find out more about the characteristics and formation of Mahakam Delta. Illustrate your account with annotated photos. Find out how people use the resources of the delta and how human activity is affecting the landform.

9.8 Coastal management strategies

On these spreads you will consider different coastal management strategies and look at an example of Mactan Island, Philippines

There are three different management strategies for defending the coast.

- **Hard engineering** – this involves using artificial structures such as sea walls to control natural processes.
- **Soft engineering** – this involves less intrusive, more environmentally friendly methods that work with natural processes to protect the coast.
- **Managed retreat** – this increasingly popular option enables the controlled retreat of the coastline, often allowing flooding to occur over low-lying land.

Hard engineering strategies

Strategy	Description	Advantages	Disadvantages
Sea wall	Concrete or rock barrier to the sea placed at the foot of cliffs or at the top of a beach. Has a curved face to reflect the waves back into the sea. Cost: US$7000–US$14 000 per metre	Effective at stopping the sea. Often has a walkway or promenade for people to walk along.	Can be obtrusive and unnatural to look at. Very expensive and has high maintenance costs.
Groynes	Timber or rock structures built out to sea from the coast. They trap sediment being moved by longshore drift, thereby enlarging the beach. The wider beach acts as a buffer to the incoming waves, reducing wave attack. Cost: timber groynes US$200 000 each (at every 200 m)	Results in a wider beach, which can be popular with tourists. Provides useful structures for people interested in fishing. Not too expensive.	In interrupting longshore drift, they starve beaches down drift, often leading to increased rates of erosion elsewhere. The problem is not so much solved as shifted. Groynes are unnatural and rock groynes in particular can be unattractive.
Rock armour	Piles of large boulders dumped at the foot of a cliff. The rocks force waves to break, absorbing their energy and protecting the cliffs. The rocks are usually brought in by barge to the coast. Cost: US$135 000–US$400 000 per 100 m	Relatively cheap and easy to maintain. Can provide interest to the coast. Often used for fishing.	Rocks are usually from other parts of the coastline or even abroad. Can be expensive to transport. They do not fit in with the local geology. Can be very obtrusive.
Gabions	Wire cages filled with rocks that can be built up like bricks to support a cliff or provide a buffer to the sea. Cost: up to US$80 000 per 100 m	Very cheap to produce and flexible in the final design. Can improve drainage of cliffs. They will eventually become vegetated and will merge into the landscape.	For a while they look very unattractive. The cages only last 5–10 years as they rust.

Coastal landscapes

Soft engineering strategies

Strategy	Description	Advantages	Disadvantages
Beach nourishment and re-profiling	The addition of sand or shingle to an existing beach to make it higher or wider. The sediment is usually obtained locally so that it blends in with the existing beach material. Bulldozers are used to re-profile the beach, steepening it to increase protection. Usually brought onshore by barge. Cost: up to US$800 000 per 100 m	Relatively cheap and easy to maintain. Blends in with existing beach. Increases tourist potential by creating a bigger beach.	Needs constant maintenance unless structures are built to retain the beach.
Dune regeneration	Sand dunes are effective buffers to the sea yet they are easily damaged and destroyed especially by trampling. Marram grass can be planted to stabilise the dunes and help them to develop. Areas can be fenced to keep people off newly planted dunes. Cost: US$300–US$3000 per 100 m	Maintains a natural coastal environment that is popular with people and wildlife. Relatively cheap.	Time-consuming to plant the marram grass and fence off areas. People do not always respond well to being prohibited from accessing certain areas. Can be damaged by storms.
Planting mangroves	A dense network of mangrove trees helps to stabilise mud and sand deposits, providing a natural buffer to stormy seas and storm surges. Cost: about US$1000 per hectare	Maintains a natural coastal environment that is popular with people and wildlife (important breeding ground for fish). Relatively cheap to plant seedlings and maintain.	Prone to damage by storms before they become established. Has limited economic potential unlike coastal tourist developments, so faces competition for land development.

Managed retreat

Strategy	Description	Advantages	Disadvantages
Managed retreat (coastal realignment)	A deliberate policy of allowing the sea to flood or erode an area of relatively low-value land. It is a form of soft engineering as it allows natural processes to take place and does not intervene in the way that hard engineering does. Cost: highly variable, but commonly several million US dollars, depending on the scale	It is a more sustainable option than hard engineering. As sea levels continue to rise, it is likely to become increasingly popular. Creates natural environments such as saltmarshes, which are disappearing elsewhere.	Floods areas of land previously used as farmland. May lead to habitat loss when areas are inundated by seawater.

Coastal management strategies

Example

Coastal management at Mactan Island, Philippines

Mactan is a densely populated island located a few kilometres from Cebu Island in the Philippines. It is a low-lying coral island characterised by a low, rocky shoreline with small beaches. Rising to just 6m above sea level it is vulnerable to the effects of monsoon winds and waves, storm surges associated with tropical cyclones and, in the long term, sea level rise. The island has several industrial enterprises but has recently been developed as a high-class tourist destination. Most developments have taken place on the island's south-eastern coastline (map **A**).

How has the coastline been managed?

It is possible to identify three phases of modification to Mactan's south-east coast since the 1970s:

1. Early modification involving retaining the small sandy bays with small-scale construction of sea walls.

2. Use of a variety of structures to retain beaches, including groynes and breakwaters, together with **beach nourishment**.

3. Excavation of rocky beach and creation of new and artificial beaches.

Shangri-La's Mactan Resort was the first to opt for rock excavation and the creation of an artificial beach (photo **B**). Initially, rocks were excavated from a 350m stretch of coastline to create a large bay. Two large rock outcrops were left in place to help shelter the new beach and retain the sand. Two large groynes were constructed at either end of the bay, also to help retain the sand. Sand was placed just offshore for the waves to carry it into the bay. Eventually three foreshore beaches were established, joined by a continuous backshore beach.

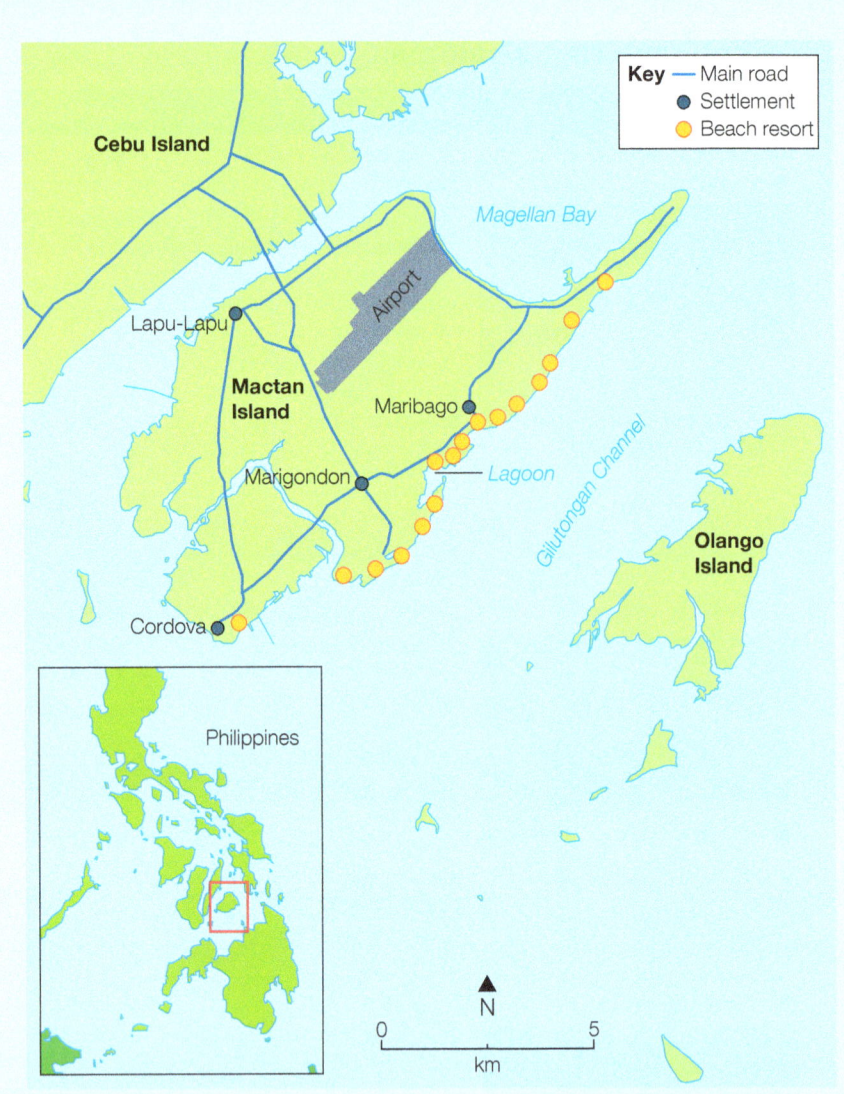

A Beach resort location on the south-eastern coast of Mactan Island, Philippines

B The artificial beach at Shangri-La's Mactan Resort

Coastal landscapes

What have been the effects of management?

While these recent tourist developments have brought considerable economic benefits, they have modified the coast considerably, creating an environment that is artificial, expensive to maintain, harmful to ecosystems and potentially damaging to other stretches of coastline. Some of the negative impacts include:

- Beaches artificially retained in one place starved beaches further along the coast. This in turn led to a greater reliance of imported sand (often unsustainable) from elsewhere.
- To retain beaches, more and more structures such as groynes were built, which impacted on natural tidal and marine processes.
- Sand has been mined illegally from other places to feed Mactan's artificial beaches.
- Extensive stretches of coast no longer have a natural coastline.

As diagram **C** shows, these modifications have potentially significant impacts on coastal processes such as longshore drift, landforms and ecosystems. Scientists are concerned that the artificial coastal developments will be expensive to maintain and may not hold up to the threats posed by sea level rise, monsoon wind and waves, and tropical cyclones.

C Modifications of Mactan's rocky coast for tourist developments

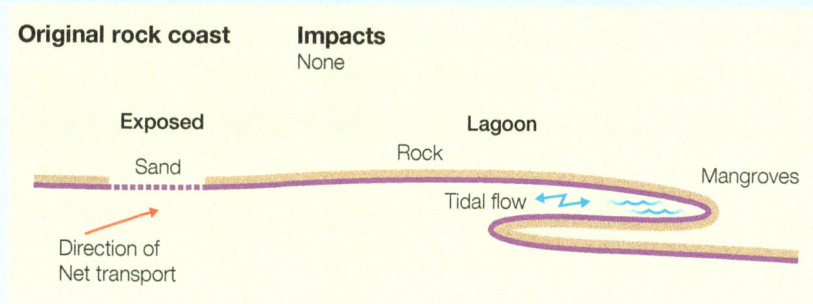

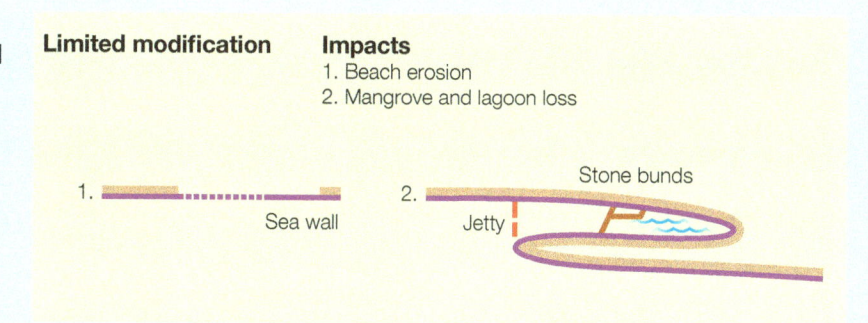

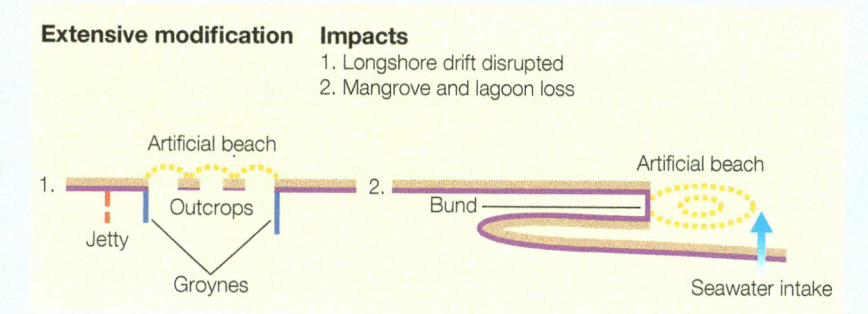

Original rock coast — Impacts: None
- Exposed: Sand; Direction of Net transport
- Lagoon: Rock, Mangroves, Tidal flow

Limited modification — Impacts:
1. Beach erosion
2. Mangrove and lagoon loss
- 1. Sea wall
- 2. Jetty, Stone bunds

Extensive modification — Impacts:
1. Longshore drift disrupted
2. Mangrove and lagoon loss
- 1. Jetty, Outcrops, Groynes, Artificial beach
- 2. Bund, Artificial beach, Seawater intake

ACTIVITIES

1. Outline the reasons for modifying the coastline on Mactan Island.
2. Study photo **B**.
   a. Draw a simple sketch to show the coastal modifications. Use annotated labels to describe the purpose of the modifications.
   b. Suggest possible harmful impacts on natural coastal processes and the environment.
3. Study diagram **C**.
   a. Make a large copy of the original rock coast and add detailed annotations to describe the natural coastal landforms and ecosystems.
   b. For either limited modification or extensive modification, describe the changes to the coastline and suggest how these changes might impact on coastal processes and ecosystems.

Stretch yourself

Use the internet to find one or more photos showing coastal defences at Mactan Island in the Philippines. Annotate your photo(s) to describe and explain the purpose of the coastal defences shown.

Practice question

Discuss the advantages and disadvantages of a named coastal management scheme.
(6 marks)

10 Hot desert landscapes

10.1 Aeolian (wind) processes

On this spread you will find out about the role of wind in hot desert environments

What are the processes of wind action in hot deserts?

Hot deserts are affected by both seasonal and local winds. Wind action – erosion, transportation and deposition – is active in sandy deserts, where the loose sand and finer particles can be picked up by the wind. Particles carried by wind become very rounded, even spherical, due to the process of attrition. This is a distinguishing characteristic of wind-blown sand.

Wind erosion

There are two main types of erosion by wind: abrasion and deflation.

Abrasion

Abrasion is sometimes referred to as the 'sandpaper effect' but in the case of deserts it is better described as 'sand blasting'! It involves wind-blown sand being driven against rock surfaces, carving or sculpting them into a variety of shapes. Much of this erosion occurs within a metre of the desert floor, which is where the bulk of sand transportation occurs. The concentration of abrasion close to the ground surface can result in the formation of strange mushroom-shaped features (photo **A**).

Several factors affect the intensity of abrasion including the strength, duration and direction of the wind, the nature of the wind-blown sand (rock type, angularity) and the lithology and vulnerability of the exposed rock outcrops.

Deflation

Deflation involves the removal of loose material from the desert floor, often resulting in the exposure of the underlying bedrock. Over time, the desert surface is lowered and often starts to resemble a cobble pavement, as only the larger stones are left behind (photo **B**).

Strong eddies or localised winds can hollow-out the desert surface to produce a deflation hollow. These can be very extensive, covering thousands of square kilometres.

A *Mushroom rock carved by abrasion, Wadi Rum, Jordan*

B *The impact of deflation on a desert surface*

Hot desert landscapes

Wind transportation

Look at diagram **C**. It shows the three main ways that sand will be transported by the wind.

1. **Surface creep** – larger particles are rolled along the desert floor.
2. **Saltation** – sand particles move in a series of leaps as they are picked up by a gust of wind before being dropped again a few centimetres downwind.
3. **Suspension** – fine sands and clays are picked up and carried by the wind for considerable distances, sometimes way beyond the margins of the desert itself. Sand from the Sahara has been transported to northern Europe and even Florida in the USA, over 8000 km away. Suspension is particularly common when high-velocity winds create sandstorms.

Wind deposition

Deposition of sand will take place when wind velocity falls. The larger sand grains will be deposited first as the velocity starts to drop, followed by the smaller grains. Sand will most commonly be deposited in sheltered areas protected from the wind, for example on the leeward side of exposed rock formations.

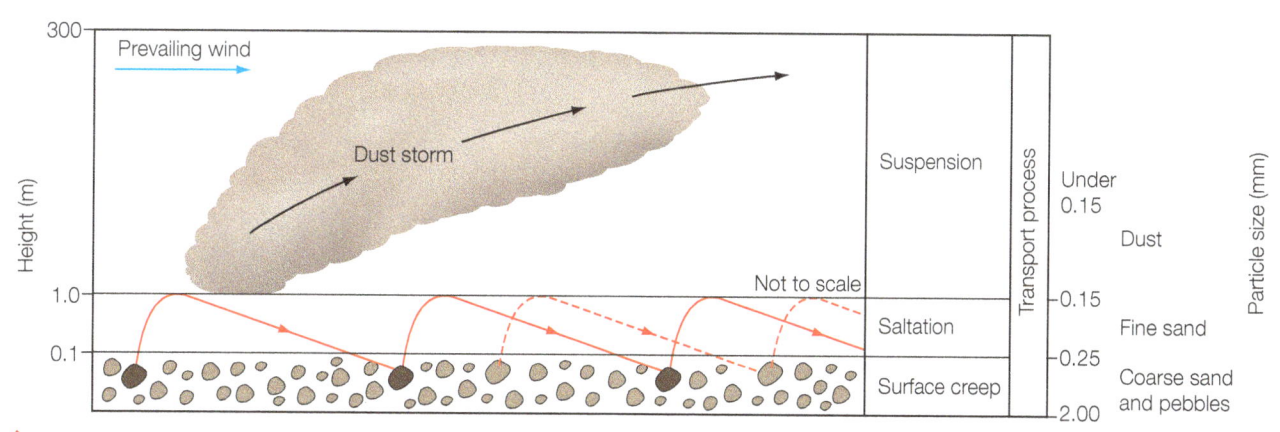

C The processes of wind transportation

ACTIVITIES

1. Study photo **A** and diagram **C**.
    a. Describe the mushroom rock in photo **A**.
    b. What forms of wind transportation are most likely to have been responsible for the erosion of this landform? Justify your answer by using diagram **C**.
2. Study photo **B**.
    a. What is the evidence that wind deflation has been operating on this desert surface?
    b. Is there any evidence of abrasion?
3. Under what conditions does wind deposition occur?

Stretch yourself

Use the internet to find out more about wind deposition. See what you can find out about an extensive deposit of wind-blown sand and dust called loess.

Practice question

Outline the processes of wind transportation. *(4 marks)*

10.2 Water processes

On this spread you will find out about the role of water in hot desert environments

What are the water processes in hot deserts?

You may be surprised to learn that water action is considered to be the dominant process in most of the world's deserts. In mountain ranges, erosion dominates following storm events or periods of snowmelt. On the lowland desert plains, deposition is the main process. Water action can involve rivers that may flow permanently or temporarily through hot deserts, or sheets of water (called sheetflow) that wash over mountain slopes following torrential rainstorms.

Look at photo **A**. It shows an **alluvial fan**. This is a depositional feature formed by water flowing out of a mountain range onto the flat desert plain. The sediment has been eroded from the mountains and then transported along a river channel before being deposited on the edge of the desert plain.

It is worth remembering that in the past the climate of the low latitudes was wetter than it is today and many present-day landscapes reflect evidence of this more actively erosive period.

A *Alluvial fan, Death Valley, USA*

Hot desert landscapes

Water erosion

There are two main types of erosion by water: abrasion and hydraulic power.

Abrasion

Abrasion is sometimes referred to as the 'sandpaper effect'. As rock fragments are carried by water, they become abraded as they scrape against the underlying bedrock. High-impact collisions between rock fragments can chip away sharp edges – this process is known as attrition. Together, abrasion and attrition cause angular rock fragments to become more rounded as they are carried downstream by a river.

Hydraulic power

Hydraulic power is the sheer power of a body of water as it is forced against the banks and bed of a river or as it surges down a mountain slope. Hydraulic power is most effective when rock material has been previously weakened by weathering (such as freeze–thaw or insolation) so that it is loose and crumbly.

Water transportation

Look at diagram **B**. It shows the ways that sediment can be transported by water. **Traction**, **saltation** and **suspension** are responsible for the physical transport of sediment. Whereas the process of **solution** involves the dissolving of chemicals, for example when rivers flow over soluble limestone.

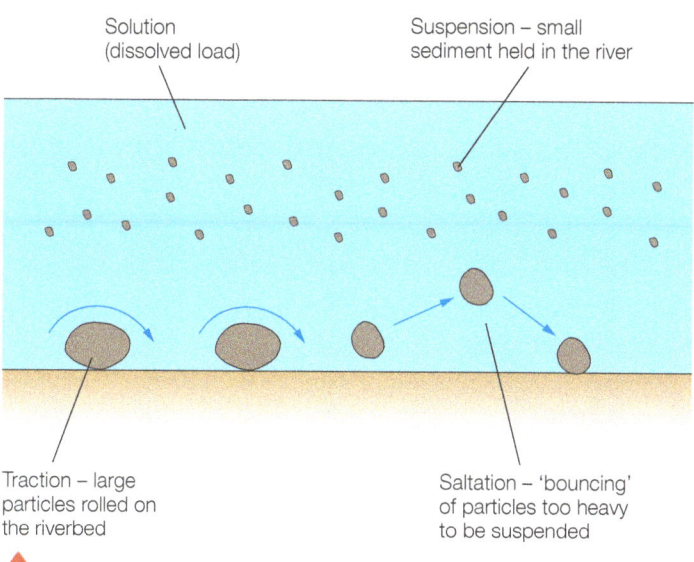

B *The processes of water transportation*

- Solution (dissolved load)
- Suspension – small sediment held in the river
- Traction – large particles rolled on the riverbed
- Saltation – 'bouncing' of particles too heavy to be suspended

Water deposition

Deposition of water-transported sediment occurs when the velocity (speed of flow) falls. This can take place in several different environments, for example close to the banks of a river or on the inside bend of a meander. In hot deserts many rivers are seasonal. This means that they are very effective at eroding and transporting sediment in periods of high flow (for example after snow melt) but then deposit sediment as flows fall in the summer. Summer storms can flush out huge quantities of sediment from mountains, depositing it to form vast alluvial fans (photo **A**).

ACTIVITIES

1. Study photo **A**.
   a. Draw a sketch of the photo to show the alluvial fan in relation to the mountains in the background and the flat desert plain in the foreground. Add labels to describe the main features in the photo.
   b. What evidence would you look for in the field to suggest that the alluvial fan was deposited by water?
2. Draw a diagram to show the processes of abrasion and hydraulic power. Add detailed labels to describe the processes.

Stretch yourself

Use the internet to find your own photo of a desert alluvial fan. Add labels to show its main features.

Practice question

Outline the main processes by which water can transport sediment in hot deserts. *(4 marks)*

10.3 Wind landforms

On this spread you will find out about the characteristics and formation of landforms resulting from the effects of wind

How does wind affect the characteristics and formation of landforms?

Wind is responsible for the formation of a number of distinctive landforms. Some are extremely extensive, covering thousands of square kilometres, whereas others are very small indeed, such as the sculpting of individual rock fragments (photo **A**).

Yardangs

Yardings are elongated ridges separated by deep grooves cut into the desert surface. They look like the hulls of upturned ships! They can vary in size from just a few centimetres in height and length to several kilometres in length and hundreds of metres in height.

A *A ventifact – a rock sculpted by wind abrasion*

B *Yardangs developed in white limestone near Dakhla, Egypt*

Look at photo **B**. It is an aerial photo showing eroded white limestone yardangs (ridges) in Egypt. Notice that these landforms cover an extensive area.

Yardangs are commonly formed in areas of alternating, vertically bedded, hard and soft rocks (diagram **C**). The weaker rocks are eroded by abrasion to form deep troughs, whereas the tougher rocks are left upstanding. It is these more-resistant rocks that form the yardangs. In order for yardangs to form, the winds need to blow from the same direction. They do not develop in regions where the winds are multi-directional.

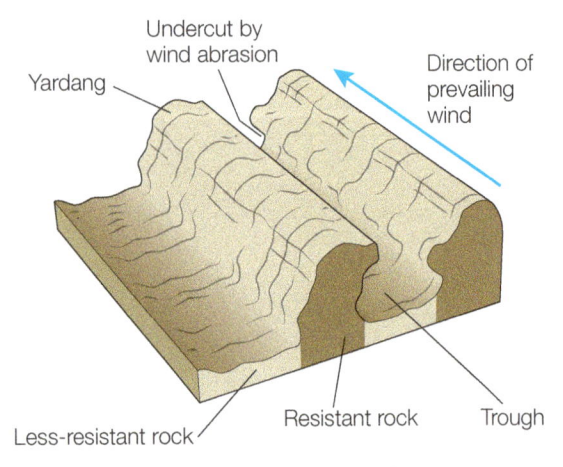

C *Characteristics and formation of yardangs*

Hot desert landscapes

Zeugen

Zeugen are similar to yardangs in that they also form ridges, in some cases up to 30 m high. The key difference is that zeugen develop in horizontally layered rocks rather than vertical rocks. This gives them a pedestal-like shape, with a flat-topped 'cap rock' protecting the less-resistant underlying layers. Look at photo **D**. Notice the horizontal layering of the rock and the presence of a darker, tougher 'cap rock' on the top of the landform.

The main process responsible for the formation of zeugen is abrasion. With most abrasion being concentrated within few metres of the desert surface, zeugen often have a slightly narrower, more eroded lower portion. You can see this in photo **D** where abrasion has eroded a noticeable notch in the weaker lighter-coloured rock.

Diagram **E** describes the formation of zeugen. Notice that the rocks are horizontal and that abrasion cuts down to develop deep grooves into the layer of weaker rock. While wind abrasion is considered to be the dominant process, it seems likely that other processes, such as water erosion and weathering (the concentration of moisture in the form of dew), may affect the development of zeugen.

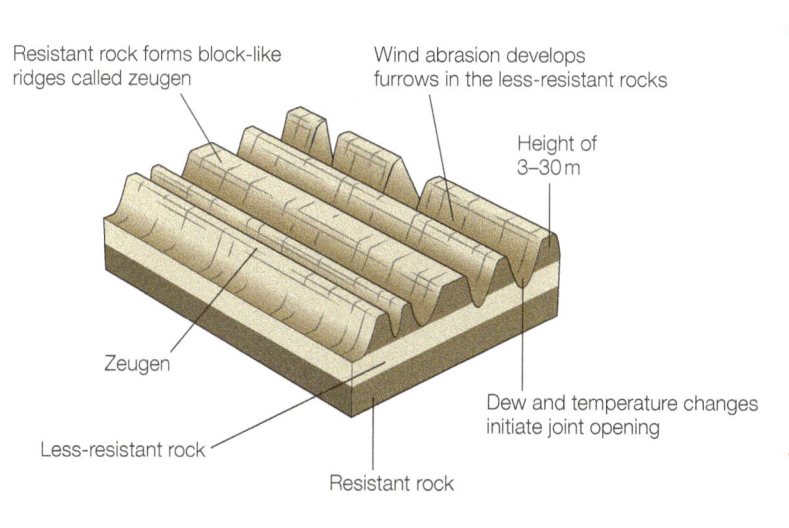

D *Zeugen rock formation near Mazara, Oman*

E *Characteristics and formation of zeugen*

Wind landforms

Sand dunes

In sandy deserts the wind can form vast and beautiful **sand dunes**. Desert sand dunes usually start with deposition on the leeward side of an obstacle, such as a rock. As more and more sand is deposited it becomes increasingly shaped by the wind to form linear or crescent-shaped dunes. While sand dunes are rare features of the deserts in the USA, they form extensively in the Sahara, the Middle East and in Australia.

There are two common forms of sand dune: barchans and sief dunes.

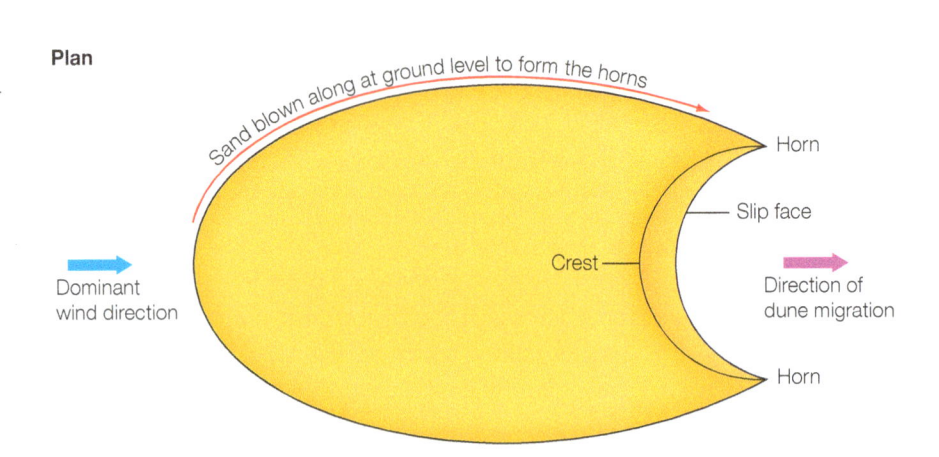

Barchans

Barchans are crescent-shaped sand dunes, which are often found in isolation in deserts where there is a relatively limited supply of sand but a strongly dominant wind direction (diagram **F**). They are transverse sand dunes, forming at right angles to the prevailing winds.

Look at diagram **F**. Notice that sand is blown up the gentle windward side of a barchan before sliding down the steeper sheltered side, which has highly mobile extending 'horns'. Over time, the feature moves forward several metres a year. Barchans are common on the edge of El Kharga Oasis in Egypt and in parts of the Atacama Desert.

Seif dunes

Seif dunes are elongated linear sand dunes that are commonly found in extensive areas of sand called sand seas, such as in the Sahara Desert (photo **G**). In places, they may stretch for several hundred metres forming parallel to the prevailing wind direction. It is possible that they may develop from barchan sand dunes, as explained in diagram **H**.

F The formation of a barchan sand dune

G Seif sand dunes in the Sahara Desert

Hot desert landscapes

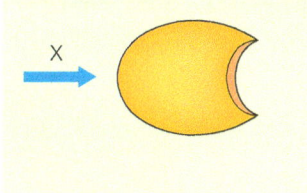

A A barchan develops under the influence of a dominant wind blowing constantly from direction X.

B Then the wind changes direction and blows from Y. This causes one of the horns to lengthen.

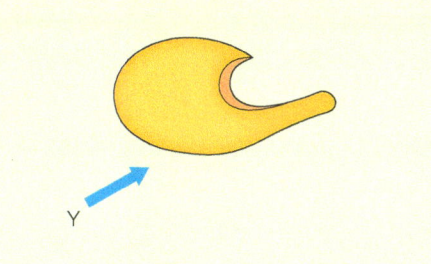

C Over a period of time, the wind alternates between X and Y. The horn becomes considerably longer.

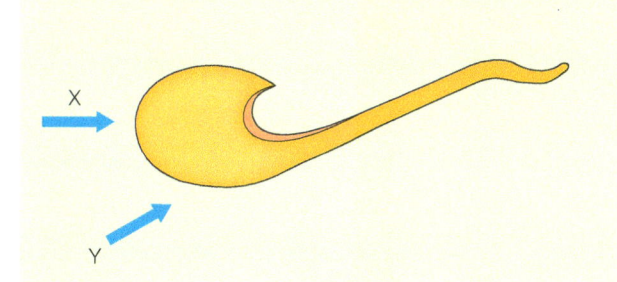

D As the wind direction continues to alternate, the dune is steadily transformed into a longitudinal or seif dune. Other slip faces may develop as well.

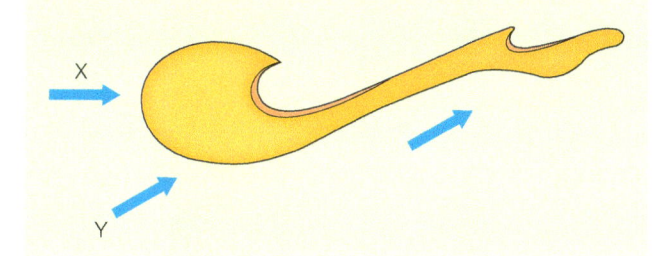

H *The development of a seif dune from a barchan dune*

ACTIVITIES

1. The following statements apply to yardangs and zeugen. Decide which is which.
   a Commonly formed in horizontal rocks.
   b Commonly formed in vertical rocks.
   c Often have a resistant flat-topped 'cap rock'.
   d Often have deep grooves formed by abrasion.
   e Often resemble the hull of an upturned ship.
   f May be hundreds of metres in height and extend for several kilometres in length.
2. Draw a sketch of photo **D**. Add labels to describe the main characteristics of the landform.
3. Draw two simple diagrams to contrast the formation of yardangs and zeugen.
4. Use diagrams to describe the formation of barchans and seif dunes.

Stretch yourself

Use the internet to find your own photos of barchans and seif dunes. Use diagrams **F** and **H** to help you add labels to your chosen photos.

Practice questions

1. Describe the characteristics of yardangs. *(4 marks)*
2. Discuss the importance of rock type and geological structure in the characteristics and formation of zeugen. *(6 marks)*
3. Evaluate the importance of wind direction in the formation of sand dunes. *(6 marks)*

91

10.4 Water landforms

On this spread you will find out about the characteristics and formation of landforms resulting from the effects of water

How does water affect the characteristics and formation of landforms?

Water erosion and deposition are responsible for the formation of a wide variety of landforms in hot deserts. Look at diagram **A**. It shows a typical hot desert landscape with many landforms associated with erosion, transportation and deposition by water. Some of these features, such as wadis and canyons, are still being actively formed by erosion. Others, such as mesas and buttes, are gradually being diminished by a combination of erosion, weathering and mass movement.

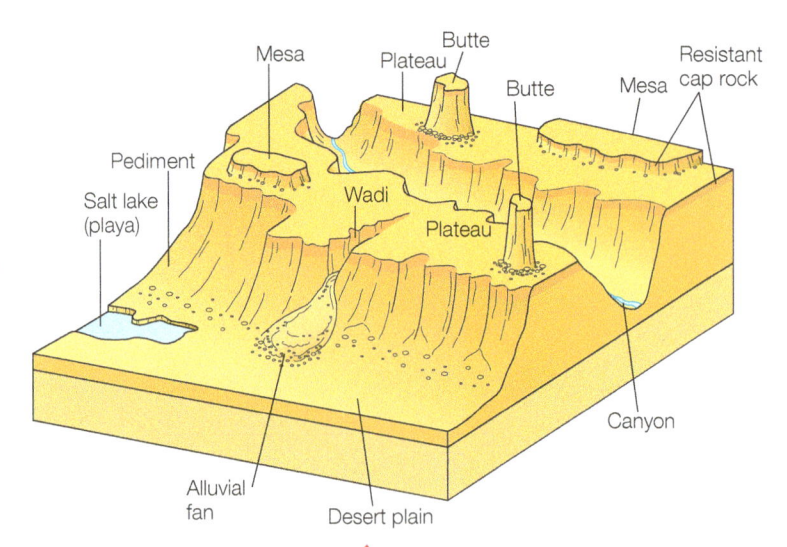

A Landforms created by water action in hot deserts

Badlands

Look at photo **B**. This spectacular desert landscape is known as **badlands**. Rising steeply from the desert floor are isolated landforms called mesas and buttes, some of which have been deeply incised by rivers to form narrow canyons. Badlands are typically formed from weak, horizontally bedded, sedimentary rocks that have been easily eroded by water to form dramatic features of the landscape. Badlands are found extensively in parts of Canada and the USA – Badlands National Park in South Dakota takes its name from this type of landscape.

- Mesas – large plateau-like features often bordered by steep wadis or canyons. The word 'mesa' comes from the Spanish word meaning 'table'.
- Buttes – smaller pinnacles of rock and represent a more-advanced stage of erosion. They are usually surrounded by flatter desert plains.
- Canyons – steep-sided gorges, mostly associated with rapid down-cutting into plateaus.

Both mesas and buttes have extensive scree slopes formed by mass movement (rockfalls) and mechanical weathering.

B Badlands, Monument Valley, Arizona

Wadis

A **wadi** is a dry riverbed, most commonly cut into a plateau (photo **C**).

- Wadis typically have steep sides and sharp plateau edges as a result of severe downward erosion by water.
- They have flat boulder-strewn bottoms, in-filled with coarse sediment, carried by fast-flowing rivers.
- Extending out in front of wadis are extensive gravel and sand deposits washed out by the water or subsequently eroded by wind. You can see the extensive deposits at the bottom of Wadi Rum in photo **C**.
- Riverbeds often exhibit braiding, where many channels split and re-join to form complex patterns, typical of the 'flashy' nature of rivers in a hot desert environment.

C Wadi Rum, Jordan

Hot desert landscapes

Alluvial fans

At the edge of a mountain range, the sediment washed out through a wadi or canyon is deposited to form a delta-like **alluvial fan** (photo **A** page 86). As the river water spreads from the mountain front, energy is lost and sediment is deposited rapidly.

Over time, as water re-works this vast store of sediment, the alluvial fan displays clear layering and sorting. Coarser sediment becomes concentrated closest to the mountain range as the finer sediment is washed out onto the desert plain. Alluvial fans can extend for several kilometres away from the mountain edge and can reach thicknesses of up to 300m.

Salt lake (playa)

A **salt lake** (or **playa**) is an enclosed desert lake, recharged by surface rivers that may only flow intermittently. There is no outflow. Salt lakes are extremely flat and any remaining water will be very shallow. The large surface area will encourage evaporation and a white salty crust will often form around their edges. In some deserts, the accumulation of salt is sufficient to enable it to be exploited commercially, for example in the Chott el Djerid in southern Tunisia.

D Chott el Djerid, a salt lake in southern Tunisia

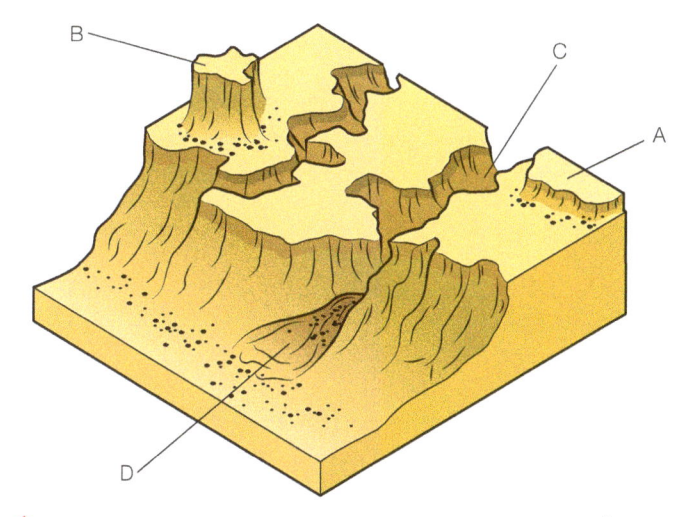

E Typical desert landscape formed by water

ACTIVITIES

1. Study diagram **E**, which shows a typical desert landscape formed by water processes.
   a. Describe the layering of the rocks.
   b. Do the rock layers affect the shape of the landforms?
   c. Identify the names of the desert landforms at A, B, C, and D.
   d. Describe, in no more than 100 words, how water has formed this landscape.

2. Study photo **C**.
   a. Describe the characteristics of Wadi Rum.
   b. Is there evidence that this landscape is being actively eroded by water?
   c. What evidence would you expect to see in the floor of a wadi if the water table was close to the surface?
   d. Why are wadis potentially dangerous places to travel or camp?

Practice questions

1. Study photo **B**. What are the main characteristics of a mesa? *(4 marks)*
2. Describe the hot desert landforms resulting from water deposition. *(4 marks)*
3. 'Water erosion is more important than deposition in the formation of hot desert landforms.' To what extent do you agree with this statement? *(6 marks)*

Stretch yourself

Use the internet to find out more about desert water-formed landforms in Badlands National Park, South Dakota, USA. Include annotated photos and sketches in your study.

93

10.5 Opportunities for development in hot deserts

On this spread you will find out about how people use hot desert environments

Case study

Where is the Thar Desert?

The Thar Desert is one of the major hot deserts of the world. It stretches across north-west India and into Pakistan (map **A**). The desert covers an area of some 200 000 km² mostly in the Indian state of Rajasthan. It is the most densely populated desert in the world.

A Location of the Thar Desert

Did you know?
The Thar Desert is just slightly smaller than the whole of the UK!

The landscape is mainly sandy hills with extensive mobile sand dunes and clumps of thorn forest vegetation – a mixture of small trees, shrubs and grasses.

Rainfall is low, between 100 and 240 mm per year, and summer temperatures in July can reach 53 °C.

Soils are sandy and not very fertile, with little organic matter to enrich them. They drain very quickly so there is little surface water.

What are the opportunities for development?

Despite the hostile conditions, the Thar Desert offers a number of opportunities for human activity and economic development.

B The desert environment near Jaisalmer

Mineral extraction

The desert region has valuable reserves of minerals which are used all over India and exported across the world. The most important minerals are:

- gypsum (used in making plaster for the construction industry and in making cement)
- feldspar (used to make ceramics)
- phosphorite (used for making fertiliser)
- kaolin (used as a whitener in paper).

There are also valuable reserves of stone in the region. At Jaisalmer the Sanu limestone is the main source of limestone for India's steel industry. Valuable reserves of marble are quarried near Jodhpur, to be used in the construction industry.

Tourism

In recent years the Thar Desert, with its beautiful landscapes, has become a popular tourist destination. Tens of thousands visit the desert each year, many from neighbouring Pakistan.

Desert safaris on camels, based at Jaisalmer, have become particularly popular with foreigners as well as wealthy Indians from elsewhere in the country. An annual Desert Festival held each winter is a popular attraction. Local people benefit by providing food and accommodation and by acting as guides or rearing and looking after the camels.

Hot desert landscapes

Energy

The Thar Desert is a rich energy source.

- *Coal* – there are extensive lignite coal deposits in parts of the Thar Desert and a thermal energy plant has been constructed at Giral (map **A**).
- *Oil* – a large oilfield has been discovered in the Barmer district, which could transform the local economy.
- *Wind* – recently there has been a focus on developing wind power, a renewable form of energy. The Jaisalmer Wind Park was constructed in 2001 (photo **C**). This is India's largest wind farm.
- *Solar* – with its sunny, cloudless skies, the Thar Desert offers ideal conditions for solar power generation. At Bhaleri, solar power is used in water treatment.

C The Jaisalmer Wind Park

Farming

Most of the people living in the desert are involved in subsistence farming. They survive in the hot and dry conditions by grazing animals on the grassy areas and cultivating vegetables and fruit trees.

Commercial farming, which has grown in recent decades, has been made possible by irrigation. The construction of the Indira Gandhi Canal in 1958 (see page 97) has revolutionised farming, and crops such as wheat and cotton now thrive in an area that used to be scrubby desert (photo **D**). Other crops grown under irrigation include pulses, sesame, maize and mustard.

D Growing wheat on irrigated land in the desert

ACTIVITIES

1. a Describe the natural environment of the Thar Desert in photo **B**.
   b What are the challenges of this environment for the local people?
   c What are the animals in the photo?
   d Why is this traditional form of farming appropriate to the environment?
2. a Why is the Thar Desert a good location for a large wind farm?
   b Why do you think the Indian government is keen to develop wind and solar energy in the Thar Desert?
3. How has irrigation led to improvements in farming?
4. Design a poster describing how people can make use of the Thar Desert.

Stretch yourself

Find out more about the Carbon Neutral Company's Thar Desert Wind Farm.
- What is the potential for renewable energy projects in the Thar Desert?
- Why is it important to develop 'carbon neutral' energy in the future?

Practice question

Explain how hot deserts such as the Thar Desert can provide opportunities for development.
(6 marks)

10.6 Challenges of development in hot deserts

On this spread you will find out about how people use hot desert environments

Case study

Challenges for development in the Thar Desert

Extreme temperatures

The Thar Desert suffers from extremely high temperatures (graph **A**), sometimes exceeding 50°C in the summer. This presents challenges for people, animals and plants living in this environment.

- Working outside in the heat of the day can be very hard, especially for farmers.
- High rates of evaporation lead to water shortages, which affect people as well as plants and animals.
- Plants and animals have to adapt to survive in the extreme heat. Some animals are nocturnal, hibernating in the cooler ground during the daytime. Livestock, such as cattle and goats, need shade to protect them from the intense Sun.

Water supply

Why are there water shortages?

Water supply has become a serious issue in the Thar Desert. As the population has grown and farming and industry have developed, demand for water has increased. Water in this region is a scarce resource.

The desert has low annual rainfall, high temperatures and strong winds. This causes high rates of evaporation.

What are the sources of water?

There are several sources of water in the Thar Desert.

- Traditionally, drinking water for people and animals is stored in ponds, some of which are natural (*tobas* – photo **B**) and others are artificial (*johads*).
- There are a few rivers and streams that flow through the desert, such as the River Luni which feeds a marshy area called the Rann. But these are intermittent, and flow only after rainfall. Most settlements are found alongside these rivers.
- Some water can be obtained from underground sources (aquifers) using wells but this water is salty and not very good quality.

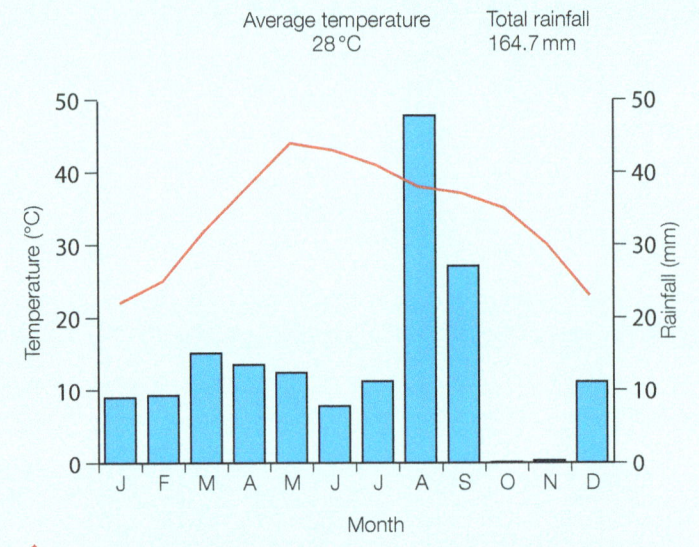

Average temperature 28°C   Total rainfall 164.7 mm

A Average temperature and rainfall in Sukkur, near the Thar Desert, 2005–15

B A pond in the Thar Desert

Hot desert landscapes

The Indira Gandhi Canal

The main form of irrigation in the desert is the Indira Gandhi (Rajasthan) Canal (photo **C**). This source of freshwater has transformed an extensive area of the desert and has revolutionised farming.

Commercial farming, growing crops such as wheat and cotton, now flourishes in an area that used to be scrub desert.

Two of the main areas to benefit from the canal are centred on the cities of Jodhpur and Jaisalmer, where over 3500 km² of land is under irrigation.

The canal provides drinking water to many people in the desert.

Constructed in 1958 the canal has a total length of 650 km.

C *The Indira Gandhi Canal*

Accessibility

Due to the very extreme weather and the presence of vast barren areas there is a very limited road network across the Thar Desert. The high temperatures can cause the tarmac to melt and the strong winds often blow sand over the roads.

Many places are accessible only by camel, which is a traditional form of transport in the region. Public transport often involves seriously overladen buses (photo **D**).

ACTIVITIES

1. **a** What is the source of water shown in photo **B**?
   b What do you think the quality of the water is like? Explain your answer.
   c The rivers and streams in the desert are 'intermittent'. What does this mean and why is it a problem for water supply?
2. Why do you think the Rann is a protected area in the Thar Desert?
3. How has the Indira Gandhi Canal brought benefits to the region?
4. Why do the high temperatures and the limited road network in the Thar Desert present challenges for development?

Practice question

Suggest two reasons why irrigation is important for future human development of the Thar Desert. *(4 marks)*

D *Public transport in the Thar Desert*

Stretch yourself

Carry out some research about the Indira Gandhi Canal.
- Search for a detailed map to show its route through the desert.
- Investigate how it has 'revolutionised' farming in the region. Illustrate your work with captioned or annotated photos.
- Do you think another canal should be constructed and, if so, where?

11 River landscapes

11.1 Changes in rivers and their valleys

On this spread you will find out how rivers and their valleys change with distance downstream

What is a drainage basin?

Diagram **A** shows a typical *drainage basin*, an area of land drained by a river and its tributaries. Make sure you are familiar with the key terms on this diagram, as you will need to remember them.

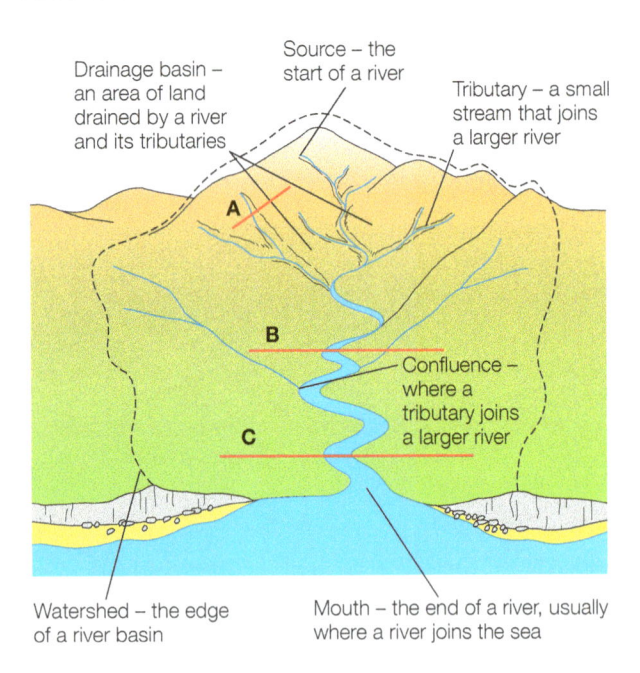

- Drainage basin – an area of land drained by a river and its tributaries
- Source – the start of a river
- Tributary – a small stream that joins a larger river
- Confluence – where a tributary joins a larger river
- Watershed – the edge of a river basin
- Mouth – the end of a river, usually where a river joins the sea

A V-shaped valley
Valley: steep-sided, V-shaped
River: narrow, shallow, turbulent

B Floodplain
Valley: wider, flat floor
River: wider and deeper

C Levees
Valley: very wide and flat
River: wide, deep, with large sediment load

A *Drainage basin*

How does the long profile of a river change downstream?

Imagine that you were on a raft floating down the river in diagram **A**.

- In the mountains your speed (velocity) would vary considerably. Where the water is shallow and turbulent there is friction with the bed and banks, slowing the rate of flow. But if you encounter rapids, where the channel narrows and the river becomes deeper, you would move much faster!

- Further downstream, the river's channel is much deeper due to the tributaries bringing additional water. Now less water is in contact with the bed and banks and the velocity increases, even though the gradient is less steep than in the mountains. You would now be floating faster!

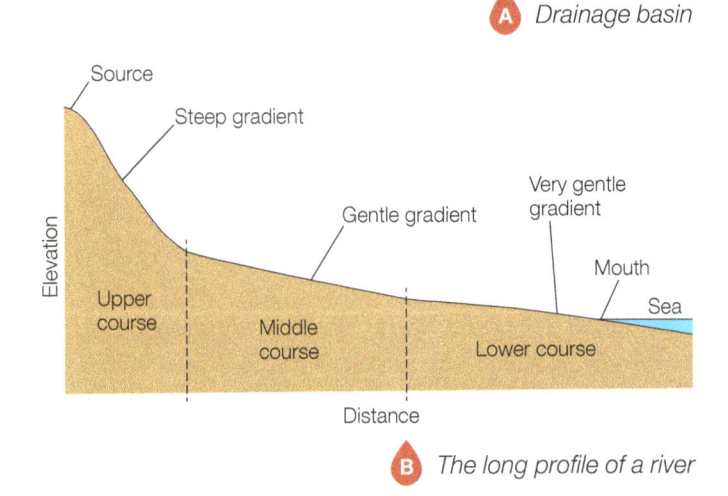

Source – Steep gradient – Gentle gradient – Very gentle gradient – Mouth – Sea
Upper course | Middle course | Lower course
Elevation / Distance

B *The long profile of a river*

River landscapes

If you plotted your journey as a line graph it would look like diagram **B**. This is called the long profile of a river. Notice that the river has a steep gradient in its upper course and a much gentler gradient in its lower course. This concave shape is an ideal profile. In most cases, a river's long profile will vary because, for example, of the river crossing bands of tough and weak rock. A waterfall, for example, creates a step in the long profile of a river.

C *A river running through Himachal Pradesh, India*

How does the cross profile of a river and its valley change downstream?

A **cross profile** is an imaginary 'slice' across a river channel and its valley at a particular point. Diagram **A** shows the cross profile of both a river and its valley downstream. The river channel becomes wider and deeper, with the river valley becoming wider and flatter. Its sides are less steep compared with its V-shaped appearance further upstream.

In reality there will be variations in places. For example, river management can alter the shape of a river channel, and different types of rock or human activities such as quarrying can affect the cross profile of a valley.

These changes downstream are due to the amount of water flowing in the river. As tributaries bring water from other parts of the drainage basin the river becomes bigger. With more water and more energy it is able to erode its channel, making it wider and deeper.

The changes to the valley cross profile are mainly due to channel erosion broadening and flattening the base of the valley. Together with weathering and mass movement, these processes make the sides of the valley less steep.

Did you know?
The longest river in the world is the Amazon, at 6992 km. This is followed by the River Nile (6853 km) and the Yangtze (6300 km).

ACTIVITIES

1. **a** Copy the long profile (diagram **B**).
   b Locate the three cross profiles shown in diagram **A** on your diagram. Draw each cross profile and add labels to describe the valley and the river.
   c Describe how a river and its valley change with distance downstream.
2. Photo **C** shows a river in the hills of Himachal Pradesh, India.
   a Describe the river. Comment on its width, depth and type of flow (turbulent or smooth).
   b Describe the shape of the valley.
   c Suggest where in the long profile of the river this photo was taken. Explain your answer.

Stretch yourself

Investigate the changes in a river close to your home or school. Use a map or photos to show how the river and its valley change with distance downstream.

Practice question

Describe how the shape of a river valley changes downstream.
(4 marks)

11.2 Fluvial (river) processes

On this spread you will find out how rivers erode, transport and deposit material

What are the processes of erosion?

Photo **A** shows a small stream in near Xijiang, Guizhou Province, China. There is very little water in the river and very little is happening! It is like this for much of the year. The river is using all its energy to overcome friction and just transport water downstream.

It is only after heavy rainfall that the river has enough energy to erode and enlarge its channel and the river valley. It is possible to identify two types of erosion:

- **vertical erosion** (downwards)
- **lateral erosion** (sideways).

These combine to cause the downstream changes to the river channel and the river valley described on pages 102–3.

A A small stream at low flow near Xijiang, Guizhou Province, China

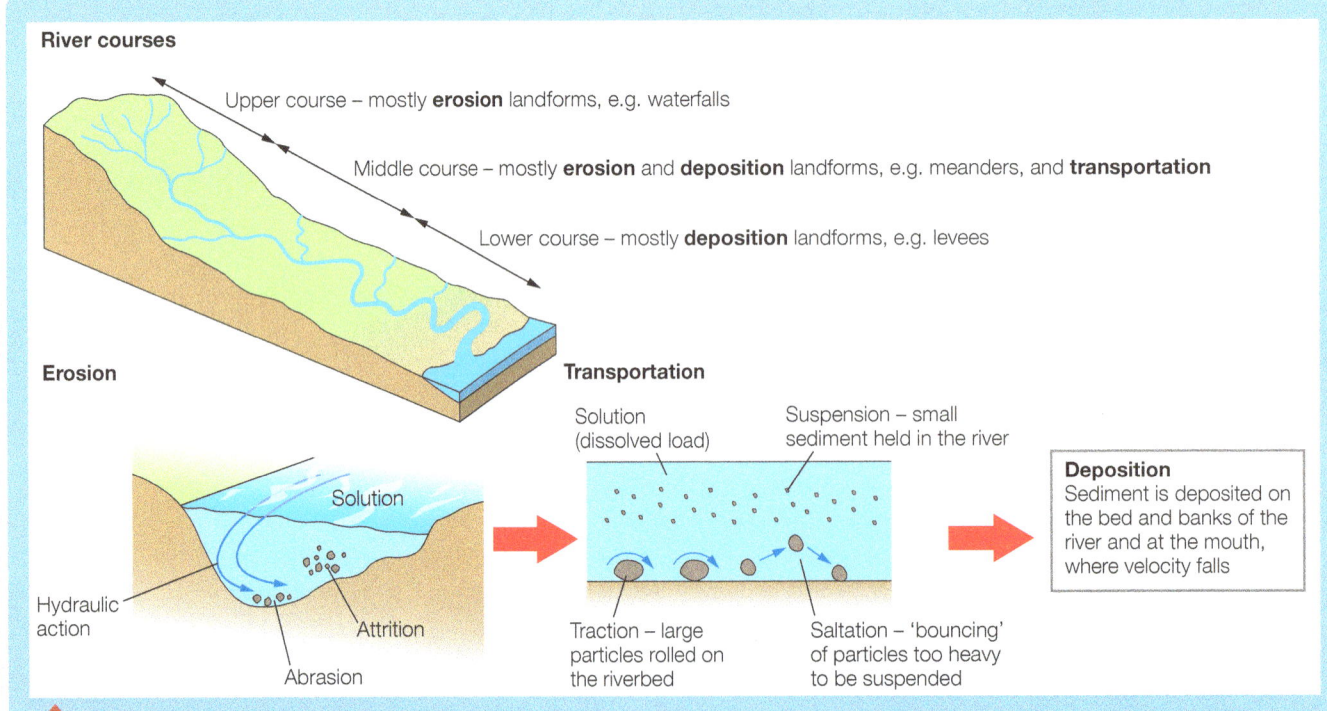

River courses

Upper course – mostly **erosion** landforms, e.g. waterfalls

Middle course – mostly **erosion** and **deposition** landforms, e.g. meanders, and **transportation**

Lower course – mostly **deposition** landforms, e.g. levees

Erosion
- Solution
- Hydraulic action
- Attrition
- Abrasion

Transportation
- Solution (dissolved load)
- Suspension – small sediment held in the river
- Traction – large particles rolled on the riverbed
- Saltation – 'bouncing' of particles too heavy to be suspended

Deposition
Sediment is deposited on the bed and banks of the river and at the mouth, where velocity falls

B River courses and fluvial processes

Diagram **B** shows the four processes of erosion that take place in a river:

- **Hydraulic action** – the force of the water hitting the riverbed and banks. This is most effective when the water is moving fast and when there is a lot of it.

- **Abrasion** – when the load carried by the river repeatedly hits the bed or banks dislodging particles into the flow of the river.

- **Attrition** – when stones carried by the river knock against each other, gradually making the stones smaller and more rounded.

- **Solution** – when the river flows over limestone or chalk, the rock is slowly dissolved. This is because it is soluble in mildly acidic river water.

River landscapes

What are the processes of transportation?

The material transported by a river is called its *load*. Diagram **B** shows the four main types of *transportation* that occur in a river:

- traction
- saltation
- suspension
- solution.

The size and total amount of load that can be carried will depend on the river's rate of flow – its *velocity*. After a rainstorm, rivers often look very muddy because they are flowing fast and transporting a large amount of sediment (photo **C**). At low flow, when rivers are clear, very little sediment is being transported (photo **A**).

C A river in high flow

When does deposition take place?

Deposition occurs when the velocity of a river decreases. It no longer has enough energy to transport its sediment so it is deposited.

- Larger rocks tend to be deposited in the upper course of a river. They are only transported for very short distances, mostly by *traction*, during periods of very high flow.

- Finer sediment is carried further downstream, mostly held in *suspension*. This material will be deposited on the riverbed or banks, where velocity is slowed by *friction*.

- A large amount of deposition occurs at the river mouth, where the interaction with tides, along with the very gentle gradient, greatly reduces the river's velocity.

ACTIVITIES

1. **a** What is the evidence in photo **A** that this river is experiencing low flow conditions?
   b Do you think the river is transporting any load? Explain your answer.
   c What evidence is there that erosion and deposition take place in this river?
   d Under what conditions would you expect active erosion to take place?
2. Use diagram **B** to draw a labelled diagram describing the processes of river erosion.
3. How do the size of the sediment and the velocity of the river affect the processes of river transportation?
4. Where and when does deposition take place in a river?

Stretch yourself

1. Investigate how velocity affects the processes of erosion, transportation and deposition.
2. Find out about the Hjulstrom Curve and make a simple copy of the graph. Add annotations to describe what it shows.

Practice question

To what extent is the size and shape of a river valley the result of the work of the river under flood conditions? *(9 marks)*

101

11.3 River erosion landforms

On this spread you will find out how rivers erode their valleys to form distinctive landforms

What are the distinctive river landforms?

Diagram **A** shows a typical river from source to mouth and its distinctive landforms.

- In the river's upper course, erosion dominates to form landforms such as *interlocking spurs*, *waterfalls* and *gorges*.

- Further downstream, erosion and deposition combine to form *meanders* and *ox-bow lakes*.

- As the river nears the sea, deposition dominates to form a *floodplain*, *levees* and the river estuary. You need to be able to recognise these features and describe how they form.

Of course, not all rivers are 'typical' and it's possible to find landforms of erosion and deposition at various points along the course of a river.

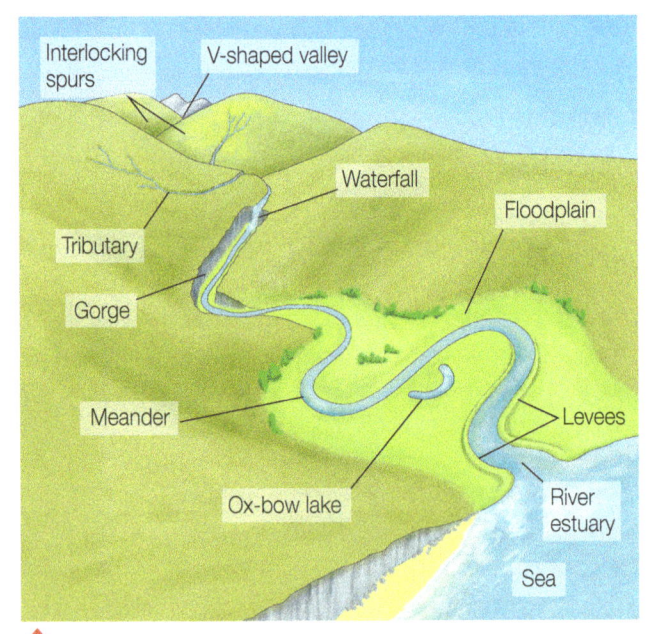

A River landforms from source to mouth

Distinctive river erosion landforms

Interlocking spurs

Notice in photo **B** how a small mountain stream in the foothills of the Himalayas weaves its way through the V-shaped valley and around the 'fingers' of land that jut out. These are called *interlocking spurs*. The river is near its source, and is not powerful enough to cut through the 'spurs' of land, so has to flow around them.

B Interlocking spurs formed by a Himalayan mountain stream, Nepal

River landscapes

Waterfalls

As it makes its way from source to mouth, a river often flows over a variety of different rock types. Tougher, more-resistant rocks are less easily eroded than weaker rocks and they will form 'steps' in the long profile of a river. These steps form waterfalls (diagram **C**).

Waterfalls are most commonly formed when a river flows over a relatively resistant band of hard rock. When the river plunges over a waterfall it forms a deep and turbulent *plunge pool*. Here the processes of erosion, particularly hydraulic action and abrasion, are active and they combine to undercut the waterfall. Eventually the overhanging rock collapses and the waterfall retreats upstream. Over many years the retreating waterfall will leave behind a steep-sided gorge (diagram **A**).

Waterfalls can also form when a drop in sea level causes a river to cut down into its bed creating a step in the long profile of a river. This step is called a *knick point* and it is marked by the presence of a waterfall. Waterfalls can also be found in glacial hanging valleys.

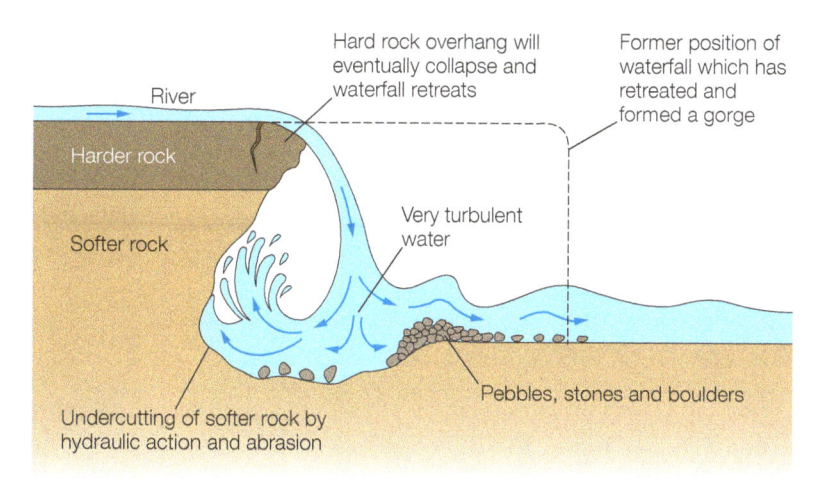

C Formation of a waterfall

Gorges

A gorge is a narrow steep-sided valley that is usually found immediately downstream of a waterfall. It is formed by the gradual retreat of a waterfall over hundreds or even thousands of years (diagram **D**).

Gorges may sometimes form in other ways. At the end of the last glacial period, around 8000 years ago, huge quantities of water from melting glaciers poured off upland areas to form gorges such as Cheddar Gorge in the UK. More rarely, some gorges form on limestone as a result of the collapse of underground caverns.

D Formation of a gorge

ACTIVITIES

1 Draw a sketch of the river and its valley in photo **B**. Label the interlocking spurs and the V-shaped valley. Add labels to describe the valley sides and the river channel. Is it high or low flow?

2 Make a copy of diagram **C**. Add another diagram to show what happens when the overhanging rock collapses.

3 With the aid of diagrams explain how a gorge is formed as a waterfall retreats.

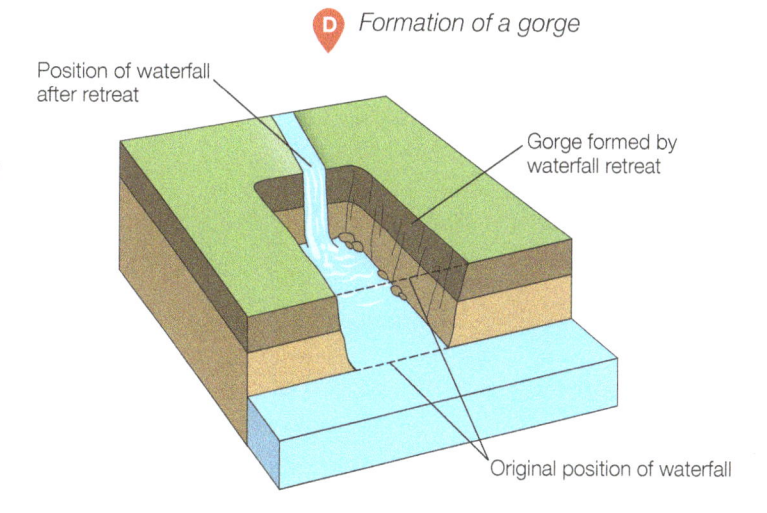

Stretch yourself

1 Search online for a photo to show each of the three landforms described on this spread.

2 Add detailed labels to describe the main characteristics of each landform.

Practice question

Explain why a waterfall is only a temporary feature on a river's course. *(4 marks)*

11.4 River erosion and deposition landforms

On this spread you will find out about river landforms created by deposition and erosion

River landforms

Meanders

Meanders are the wide bends of a river commonly associated with flat plains (photo **A**). They are the most efficient channel for a heavily laden river as it flows over fine sediment on very gentle slopes. Meanders are constantly changing their shape and position. This is a result of the processes of **lateral (sideways) erosion** and deposition in the river channel.

Diagram **B** shows the main features and processes taking place in a meandering river. The *thalweg* is the line of fastest flow (velocity) within the river. It swings from side to side causing erosion on the *outside* bend and deposition on the *inside* bend. Over time this process of erosion and deposition causes meanders to migrate across the valley floor.

A A river meandering among the high grasslands of Rourgai, Sichuan, China

Pools and riffles

Meandering streams carrying coarse sediment may develop alternating deep sections (called *pools*) and shallow sections (called *riffles*). Pools are usually found on the outside bends of meanders where, during periods of high flow, the faster flow erodes a deep channel.

Riffles result from the deposition of coarse sediment, also at times of high flow, and are characterised by more turbulent slower-flowing water. During low-flow conditions, however, water tends to flow more slowly through a pool section, depositing fine muddy sediment. Under these low-flow conditions, water may flow slightly faster in a riffle section, accounting for the lack of fine sediment here. This is what you are most likely to see when conducting fieldwork.

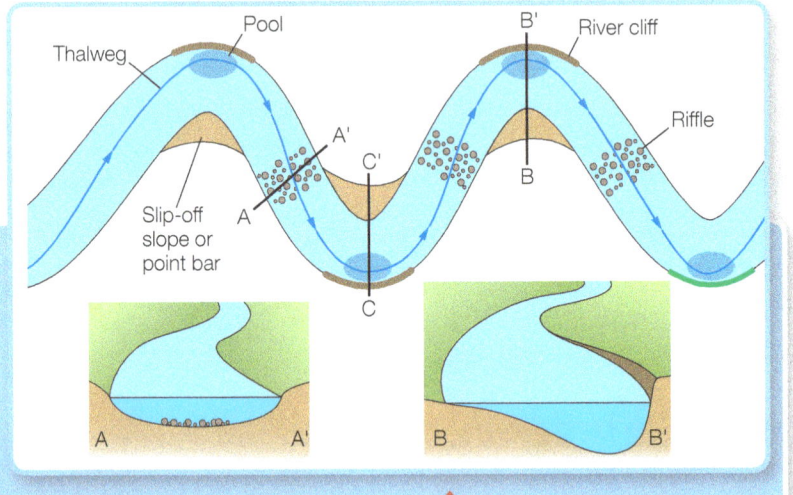

B Processes and landforms of a meandering river

Ox-bow lakes

Over time, as meanders migrate across the valley floor, they may start to erode towards each other (diagram **C**). Gradually the neck of the meander narrows until it is completely broken through (usually during a flood) to form a new straighter channel. The old meander loop is cut off by deposition to form an ox-bow lake.

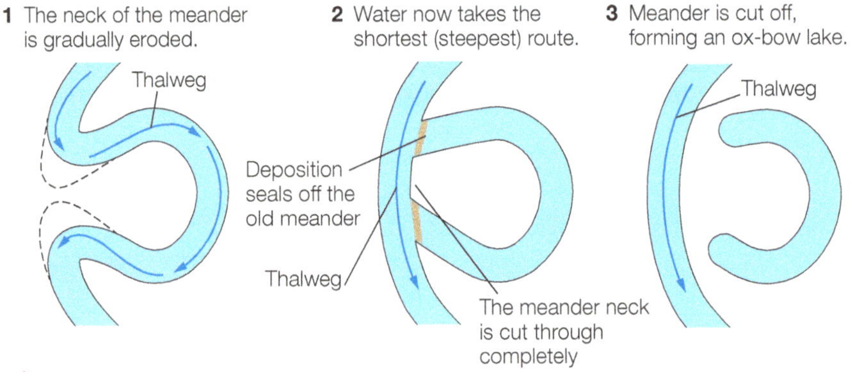

1 The neck of the meander is gradually eroded.

2 Water now takes the shortest (steepest) route.

3 Meander is cut off, forming an ox-bow lake.

C Stages in the formation of an ox-bow lake

River landscapes

River deposition landforms

Floodplains and levees

A floodplain is a wide, flat area of marshy land on either side of a river, and found in the middle and lower courses. Floodplains are made of *alluvium*, a sediment (*silt*) deposited by a river when it floods. Floodplains are used for farming as the soils are very fertile.

There are two processes responsible for the formation of a floodplain (diagram **D**).

◆ Meanders migrate across the floodplain due to lateral erosion. When they reach the edge of the floodplain they erode the valley side (bluff). This explains why floodplains are very wide.

◆ When the river floods it deposits silt, creating a very flat floodplain. Layer upon layer builds up over many years to form a thick deposit of fertile alluvium.

A levee is a raised river bed (*levé* in French means 'rise') found alongside a river in its lower course (diagram **D**). It is formed by flooding over many years. A ridge of sediment is deposited naturally to build up the levee.

During low-flow conditions deposition takes place, raising the riverbed and reducing the capacity of the channel. When flooding occurs, water flows over the sides of the channel. Here the velocity of the river decreases rapidly leading to deposition of sediment on the riverbanks. First the coarser sands are deposited and then the finer silt and mud. Gradually after many floods the height of the banks can be raised by as much as 2 m.

Estuaries

Estuaries are *transitional zones* between river and coastal environments (photo **E**) and are affected by wave action as well as river processes. The main process operating in estuaries is deposition. During a rising tide, river water is unable to be discharged into the sea. The river's velocity falls and sediment is deposited. At low tide these fine deposits form extensive *mudflats*. Over time, mudflats develop into important natural habitats called *saltmarshes*.

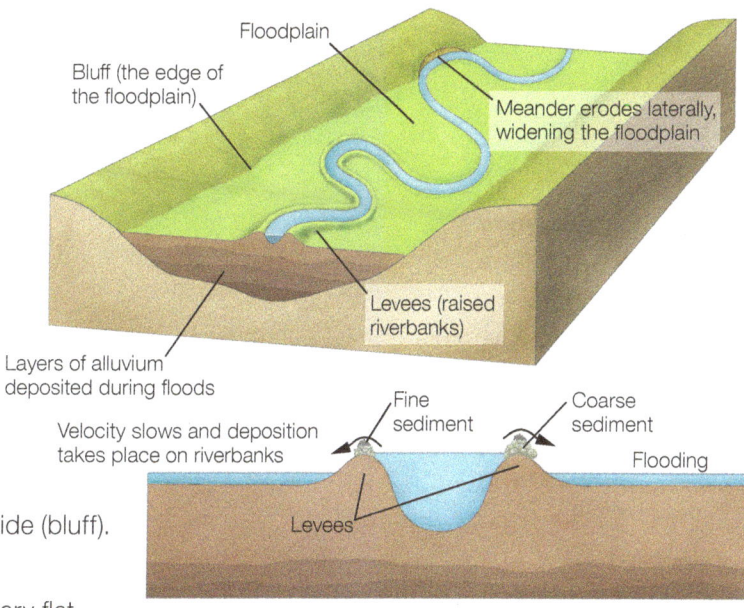

D The formation of floodplains and levees

E Pahang River estuary, Malaysia

ACTIVITIES

1. **a** Sketch a cross-section of the meander C–C' in diagram **B**.
   b Draw and label the following: thalweg, deposition, lateral erosion, river cliff, slip-off slope (or point bar).
2. Draw a sequence of labelled diagrams to show how an ox-bow lake forms. Make sure you show the importance of both erosion and deposition in this process.
3. Describe with the aid of a diagram how a levee is formed.

Stretch yourself

Search for an aerial photograph of a floodplain. Make sure it shows meanders, ox-bow lakes, a floodplain and levees.
- Label these features on your photo.
- Describe how the land is used.

Practice question

The gradient of the River Mississippi drops, on average, only 10 cm/km for the last 1000 km of its course to the Gulf of Mexico. Consider how this can result in the river changing course.
(4 marks)

11.5 Factors increasing flood risk

On this spread you will find out about how physical and human factors can increase the risk of flooding

What is flooding?

On 19 November 2009 a remote mountain weather station at Seathwaite in the Lake District, UK, recorded an astonishing 314.4 mm of rain in just 24 hours. This was the wettest day ever recorded in the UK. It unleashed a devastating flood that tore through valleys, washing away bridges and inundating the small town of Cockermouth (photo **A**).

Flooding is where land that is not normally underwater becomes inundated. A river **flood** occurs when a river channel can no longer hold the amount of water flowing in it. Water overtops the banks and floods the adjacent land – the floodplain.

What causes flooding?

River floods usually occur after a long period of rainfall, often during the winter. The volume of water steadily increases causing river levels to rise. Eventually the river may overtop its banks to cause a flood.

Sudden floods can occur following torrential storms. These are called *flash floods*. They are more often associated with heavy rainstorms that occur in the summer.

We can identify both physical and human factors that increase *flood risk*.

A *Cockermouth floods, 2009*

Physical factors

- **Precipitation** – torrential rainstorms can lead to sudden flash floods as river channels cannot contain the sheer volume of water flowing into them. Steady rainfall over several days can also lead to flooding in lowland river basins.

- **Geology (rock type)** – impermeable rocks (rocks that do not allow water to pass through them) such as shales and clays encourage water to flow overland and into river channels. This speeds up water flow and makes flooding more likely.

- **Steep slopes** – in mountain environments steep slopes encourage a rapid transfer of water towards river channels. This increases the risk of flooding.

Human factors (land use)

- **Urbanisation** – building on a floodplain creates impermeable surfaces such as tarmac roads, concrete driveways and slate roofs. Water is transferred quickly to drains and sewers and then into urban river channels. This rapid movement of water makes flooding more likely.

- **Deforestation** – much of the water that falls on trees is evaporated or stored temporarily on leaves and branches. Trees also use up water as they grow. When trees are removed much more water is suddenly available and transferred rapidly to river channels, increasing the flood risk.

- **Agriculture** – in arable farming, soil is left unused and exposed to the elements for periods of time. This can lead to more surface runoff. This is increased if the land is ploughed up and down steep slopes, as water can flow quickly along the furrows.

River landscapes

What is a hydrograph?

The volume of water flowing along a river is its **discharge**. It is measured in *cumecs* – cubic metres per second. A **hydrograph** is a graph that plots river discharge after a storm (graph **B**). It shows how discharge rises after a storm, reaches its peak and then returns to the normal rate of flow.

One of the most important aspects of a hydrograph is the *lag time*. This is the time in hours between the highest rainfall and the highest (peak) discharge. This shows how quickly water is transferred into a river channel and is a key factor in the flood risk. The shorter the time lag the greater the risk of flooding.

B *A flood hydrograph*

What affects the shape of a hydrograph?

The shape of a hydrograph is affected by rainfall and by drainage basin characteristics (table **C**).

C *Factors affecting the shape of a hydrograph*

Drainage basin and precipitation characteristics	'Flashy' hydrograph with a short lag time and high peak	Low, flat hydrograph with a low peak
Basin size	Small basins often lead to a rapid water transfer.	Large basins result in a relatively slow water transfer.
Drainage density	A high density speeds up water transfer.	A low density leads to a slower transfer.
Rock type	Impermeable rocks encourage rapid overland flow.	Permeable rocks encourage a slow transfer by groundwater flow.
Land use	Urbanisation encourages rapid water transfer.	Forests slow down water transfer, because of interception.
Relief	Steep slopes lead to rapid water transfer.	Gentle slopes slow down water transfer.
Soil moisture	Saturated soil results in rapid overland flow.	Dry soil soaks up water and slows down its transfer.
Rainfall intensity	Heavy rain may exceed the infiltration capacity of vegetation and lead to rapid overland flow.	Light rain will transfer slowly and most will soak into the soil.

ACTIVITIES

1 Describe the effects of the flooding in Cockermouth (photo **A**). Consider the social, economic and environmental impacts.
2 What is the difference between a normal river flood and a flash flood?
3 What features of the urban environment increase the risk of flooding? Give reasons for your answer.
4 What physical and human factors are likely to produce a hydrograph (table **C**) with a short time lag and a high peak?

Stretch yourself

Research online about the Cockermouth flood of 2009.
- What were the main physical and human causes of the flood?
- What were the impacts?
- What has been done since 2009 to reduce the likelihood of future flooding?
- How successful were the post-2009 defences in coping with the extreme rainfall in December 2015?

Practice question

'River flooding is a natural phenomenon.'
To what extent do you consider this statement to be correct? *(9 marks)*

11.6 Managing floods – hard engineering

On this spread you will find out about the costs and benefits of hard engineering to manage river flooding

What is hard engineering?

Hard engineering involves using man-made structures to prevent or control natural processes from taking place. This form of flood management is usually very expensive – individual projects can cost several million pounds. But this is the preferred option for protecting expensive property or land, such as housing estates, railways and water treatment works. The costs have to be weighed against the benefits.

- **Costs** – the financial cost of the scheme, and any negative impacts on the environment and on people's lives
- **Benefits** – financial savings made by preventing flooding, along with any environmental improvements

Diagram **A** shows a drainage basin with hard and soft engineering options.

Dams and reservoirs

Dams and reservoirs are widely used around the world to regulate river flow and reduce the risk of flooding. Most dam projects are multi-purpose, having several functions, for example:

- flood prevention
- hydro-electric power generation
- irrigation
- recreation.
- water supply

Dams can be very effective in regulating water flow. During periods of high rainfall, water can be stored in the reservoir. It can then be released when rainfall is low. But the construction of dams can be very controversial. They cost huge amounts of money and the reservoir often floods large areas of land. Many people may have to be moved from their homes.

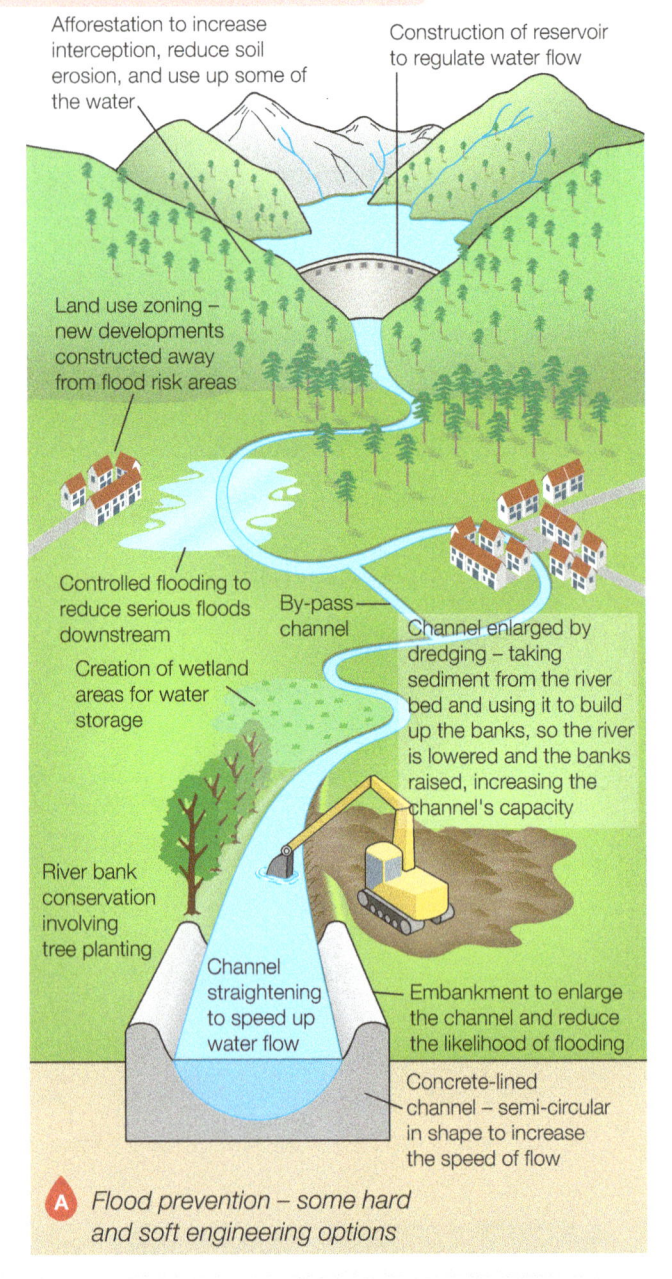

A Flood prevention – some hard and soft engineering options

Labels in diagram:
- Afforestation to increase interception, reduce soil erosion, and use up some of the water
- Construction of reservoir to regulate water flow
- Land use zoning – new developments constructed away from flood risk areas
- Controlled flooding to reduce serious floods downstream
- Creation of wetland areas for water storage
- By-pass channel
- Channel enlarged by dredging – taking sediment from the river bed and using it to build up the banks, so the river is lowered and the banks raised, increasing the channel's capacity
- River bank conservation involving tree planting
- Channel straightening to speed up water flow
- Embankment to enlarge the channel and reduce the likelihood of flooding
- Concrete-lined channel – semi-circular in shape to increase the speed of flow

Clywedog reservoir, Llanidloes, Wales

The Clywedog reservoir (photo **B**) was constructed in the 1960s to help prevent flooding of the River Severn. Its concrete dam is over 70 m high and 230 m wide and the reservoir stretches for nearly 10 km. It has been in continuous use since 1967, filling up in the winter and gradually releasing water in the summer to retain a constant flow. Although some flooding has continued to affect settlements further downstream, Clywedog has undoubtedly prevented catastrophic floods.

B The Clywedog dam and reservoir

River landscapes

Channel straightening

River straightening involves cutting through meanders to create a straight channel. This speeds up the flow of water along the river. Whilst river straightening may protect a vulnerable location from flooding, it may increase the flood risk further downstream. The problem is not really solved but shifted somewhere else!

In some places straightened sections of river are lined with concrete. This speeds up the flow and prevents the banks from collapsing, which can cause the channel to silt up. But the concrete channels create a very unattractive and unnatural river environment and can damage wildlife habitats.

Embankments

An embankment is a raised riverbank. Raising the level of a riverbank allows the river channel to hold more water before flooding occurs.

Hard engineering structures involving concrete walls or blocks of stone are frequently used in towns or cities to prevent flooding of valuable property. Sometimes mud dredged from the river may be used. This is cheaper and more sustainable and looks more natural.

Flood relief channels

A flood relief channel is a man-made river channel constructed to by-pass an urban area.

During times of high flow, sluice gates can be opened to allow excess water to flow away into the flood relief channel and reduce the threat of flooding.

The Jubilee River, Maidenhead

In the UK a flood relief channel, named the Jubilee River, has been constructed on the River Thames near Maidenhead in Berkshire (map **C**). The 11 km channel was opened in 2002. It cost £110 million to construct and with a length of nearly 12 km is the longest man-made channel in the UK. As well as reducing the risk of flooding for over 3000 properties, the Jubilee River has had a positive impact on the environment by creating new wetlands. It is also popular for recreational activities such as walking and fishing.

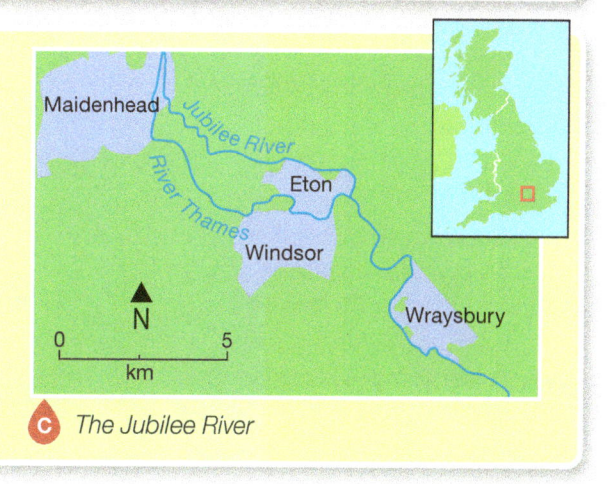

C The Jubilee River

ACTIVITIES

1. Draw a diagram in the style of diagram **A** to illustrate the different types of hard engineering described on this spread.
2. Consider the costs (disadvantages) and benefits (advantages) of dams and reservoirs such as at Clywedog.
3. Construct a summary table to describe the costs and benefits of the following hard engineering options:
   - channel straightening
   - embankments
   - flood relief channels.

Stretch yourself

Search online for more information about the Jubilee River flood relief channel.
- Why was it built? (Had there been some serious floods in the past?)
- What have been the environmental and social benefits of the flood relief channel?
- Try to assess the costs and benefits of the Jubilee River.

Practice question

To what extent are hard engineering schemes sustainable? *(9 marks)*

11.7 Managing floods – soft engineering

On this spread you will find out about the costs and benefits of managing river flooding using soft engineering

What is soft engineering?

Soft engineering involves working with natural river processes to manage the flood risk. Unlike hard engineering it does not involve building artificial structures or trying to stop natural processes. It aims to reduce and slow the movement of water into a river channel to help prevent flooding. In common with all forms of management there are costs (disadvantages) and benefits (advantages).

Planting trees to establish a woodland or forest is called *afforestation*. Trees obstruct the flow of water and slow down the transfer to river channels. Water is soaked up by the trees or evaporated from leaves and branches. Tree planting is relatively cheap and has environmental benefits.

Wetlands and flood storage areas

Wetland environments on river floodplains are very efficient in storing water (photo **A**). Wetlands are deliberately allowed to flood to form flood storage areas. Water can be stored to reduce the risk of flooding further downstream.

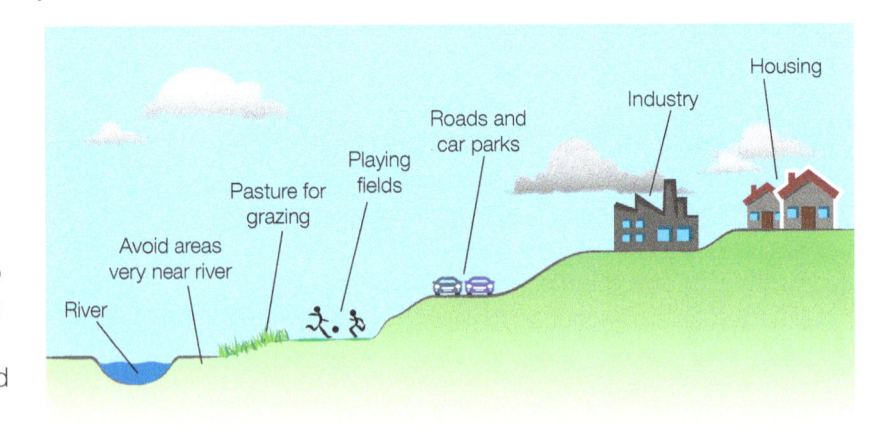

A *Flood storage area, near Rye, UK*

Floodplain zoning

Floodplain zoning restricts different land uses to certain locations on the floodplain (diagram **B**). Areas close to the river and at risk from flooding can be kept clear of high-value land uses such as housing and industry. Instead these areas can be used for pasture, parkland or playing fields. Floodplain zoning can reduce overall losses caused by flood damage. But it can be difficult to implement on floodplains that have already been developed and can cause land prices to fall.

B *Floodplain zoning*

River restoration

Where the course of a river has been changed artificially, river restoration can return it to its original course. River restoration uses the natural processes and features of a river, such as meanders and wetlands to slow down river flow and reduce the likelihood of a major flood downstream (photo **C**).

C *Restoration of the River Glaven, Norfolk, UK*

River landscapes

Preparing for floods

Rivers and river basins are monitored remotely using satellites and computer technology. Instruments are used to measure rainfall and to check river levels. Computer models can then be used to predict discharges and identify areas at risk from flooding.

In England and Wales the Environment Agency issues **flood warnings** if flooding is likely. Warnings are sent to the emergency services and the public using social media, text and email. There are three levels of warning:

- *Flood watch* – flooding of low-lying land and roads is expected. People should be prepared and watch river levels.

- *Flood warning* – there is a threat to homes and businesses. People should move items of value to upper floors and turn off electricity and water.

- *Severe flood warning* – extreme danger to life and property is expected. People should stay in an upper level of their home or leave the property.

The UK Environment Agency makes maps identifying areas at risk from flooding. People living in these areas are encouraged to plan for floods. This might include:

- planning what to do if there is a flood warning (e.g. moving valuable items upstairs)
- using flood gates to prevent floodwater from damaging property (photo **D**)
- using sandbags to keep floodwater away from buildings.

Local authorities and emergency services use these maps to plan responses to floods. For example, installing temporary flood barriers, evacuating people, closing roads and securing buildings and services.

Flood prediction is based on probability and one of the 'costs' is that places can become blighted by being 'at risk' from flooding. This can cause property values to drop and insurance premiums to increase.

> **Think about it**
>
> Is your town, city or village at risk from flooding? What defences are in place to protect the area from floods?

D Flood gate protecting property from the rising River Severn, Deerhurst, Gloucestershire

ACTIVITIES

1. What is the purpose of a flood storage area (photo **A**).
2. a What is the evidence in photo **C** that this river channel and its floodplain have been modified?
   b Suggest *three* reasons why these changes may lead to a reduction in the flood risk further downstream.
3. Suggest why some river engineers and local people prefer soft rather than hard engineering schemes.

Stretch yourself

Imagine a builder has submitted a planning application to build new houses on the area labelled 'Playing fields' on diagram **B**. Explain why, as the planner considering the proposal, you have rejected the scheme. Propose a better option.

Practice question

Use an example of one soft engineering river flood management strategy to show how it has a limited effect on the environment. *(4 marks)*

111

11.8 Managing floods in the Huai River Basin, China

Example

On this spread you will find out about the flood management scheme in the Huai River Basin in China

Where is the Huai River Basin?

The Huai River is a major river in China located roughly midway between the Yellow River and the Yangtze – China's two largest rivers. It is a major tributary of the Yangtze River (map **A**). The source of the river is in the Tongbai Mountains.

Historically, the course of the river has changed significantly. It used to flow directly into the Yellow Sea but now joins the Yangtze via Lake Hongze.

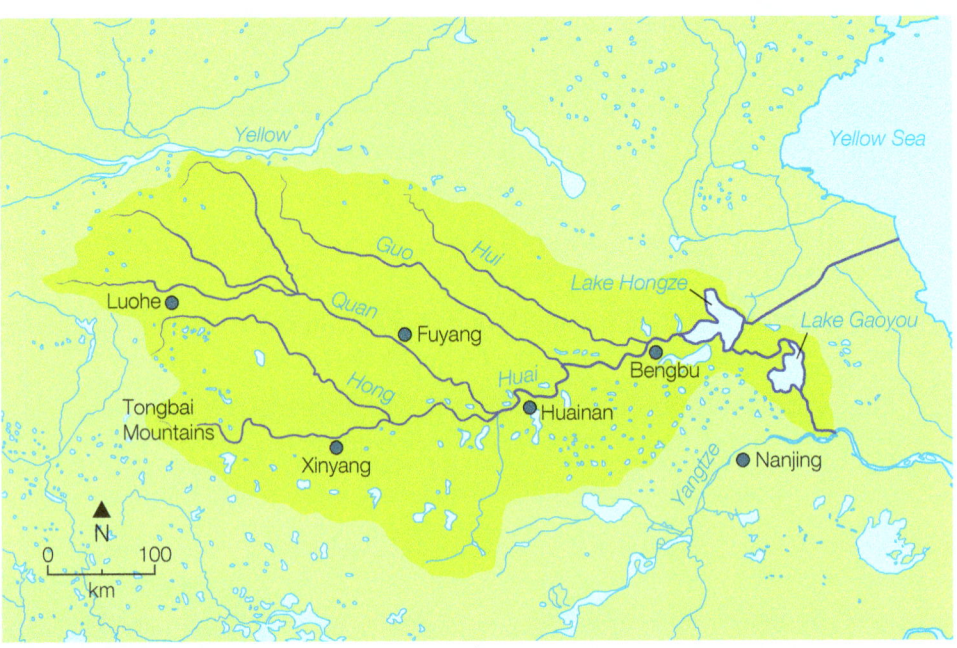

A The location of Huai River Basin

What is the flood risk?

Flooding has long been a problem in the Huai River Basin. Over the last 450 years, flooding has occurred nearly 100 times a century, killing hundreds of people and destroying agricultural land.

In 1931 China suffered a series of devastating floods, considered to be the deadliest natural disaster ever recorded. As many as 4 million people may have been killed when floods tore through the Yangtze, Yellow and Huai river basins, as snowmelt combined with heavy monsoon rains and typhoons to unleash devastating amounts of water in the region. The city of Nanjing (map **A**) was devastated by the floods and millions are thought to have drowned or starved in the aftermath of the event.

In 2003 serious flooding in the Huai River Basin left thousands homeless and caused economic losses of US$4.5 billion. In 2016 heavy rains led to severe flooding in the Huai/Yangtze River Basin region (photo **B**). Over 100 people were killed, thousands were left homeless and vast areas of agricultural land were inundated.

How has the Huai River Basin been managed to reduce flooding?

Following the catastrophic floods of 1931, part of the Huai River was dredged to remove silt and increase the capacity of the river channels. An artificial channel (the Subei Canal) protected by flood barrages was constructed from Lake Hongze

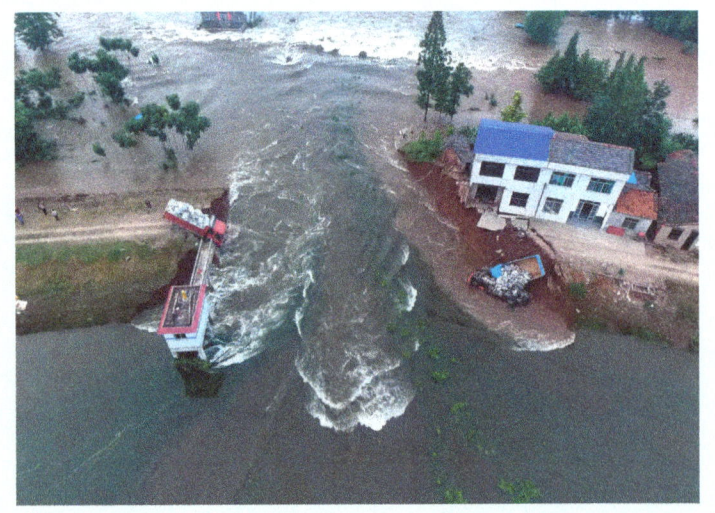

B Flooding caused by heavy rain, July 2016

to the Yellow Sea (map **A**). However, during the Second World War, deliberate flooding to slow down the Japanese invasion disrupted the river system and destroyed the new artificial channel.

In 1951 work began on a comprehensive water conservancy project aimed at controlling water flows to support agriculture and reduce the flood risk.

- Dykes destroyed during the war were repaired and the Subei Canal was reconstructed.
- In places, the river was returned to its original course (river restoration), enabling small-scale flooding of wetlands to occur, thereby preventing larger, more-damaging floods downstream.
- **Dams** were constructed in the river's headwaters, in the Tongbai Mountains.
- In the 1960s and 1970s the northern tributaries were joined to the newly constructed Bian Canal to control flooding in the northern Huai plain.

C *The Wanfu floodgate, near Yangzhou*

The Huai River Basin Flood Management and Drainage Improvement Project (2010)

In 2010 the Huai River Basin Flood Management and Drainage Improvement Project was launched. Costing US$600 million and supported by the World Bank, the ambitious project aims to provide more secure protection from flooding and increase agricultural productivity in some of the poorest rural districts in the river basin. The project involves a combination of structural and behavioural approaches to reducing the flood risk.

Structural approaches

The flood prevention measures include the strengthening of dykes, river dredging and new channel excavation, riverbank reinforcement and stabilisation, and the construction of flood control works such as pumping stations, sluice gates and bridges (photo **C**).

Behavioural approaches

In addition, the project has considered improvements to disaster assessment such as river modelling and data collection. This enables accurate flood forecasting, enabling people to receive warnings and take action. People have been encouraged to develop emergency preparedness plans to improve their resilience to flooding.

ACTIVITIES

1. Describe the causes and effects of the 1931 floods in China. See if you can find any photos on the internet to support your answer.
2. Study photo **B**. Suggest the social, economic and environmental effects of the flood.
3. Use a table to identify the hard engineering and soft engineering approaches that have been adopted to reduce the risk of flooding in the Huai River Basin.
4. Study photo **C**.
   a. Is this an example of hard or soft engineering?
   b. What is the purpose of a floodgate?
   c. Apart from flood prevention, what other benefit has this construction brought for local people?

Stretch yourself

Access the World Bank report 'China flood control project: a bigger role for farmers and a better alert system' at www.worldbank.org to find out more about the impact of the Huai River Basin Flood Management and Drainage Improvement Project on individual people, and discover how local farmers play an important role in reducing flood risk.

Practice question

With reference to an example, discuss the importance of combining hard and soft engineering in reducing the flood risk.

Unit 2 Challenges in the human environment

Section A Urban issues and challenges

Ha Dong District, Hanoi, Vietnam

Unit 2 Challenges in the human environment is about human processes and systems, how they change both spatially and temporally. They are studied in a range of places, at a variety of scales and include places in various states of development. It is split into three sections.

Section A Urban issues and challenges includes:

- global patterns of urban change
- urban growth in a city in a newly emerging economy
- opportunities and challenges in world cities.

You need to study all the topics in Section A – in your final exam you will have to answer questions on all of them.

What if…

1 we all lived to be 100?
2 there was no countryside?
3 no-one migrated?

Unit 2 Section A

Specification key ideas	Pages in this book
12 The urban world	**116–19**
• A growing percentage of the world's population lives in urban areas.	116–19
13 Urban growth	**120–39**
• Urban growth creates opportunities and challenges for cities in lower-income countries (LICs) and newly emerging economies (NEEs).	120–39
14 World cities	**140–75**
• World cities have global importance as centres for finance, business and trade, as well as culture and politics. These, like others, face a variety of social, economic and environmental opportunities and challenges.	140–75

Your key skills

To be a good geographer, you need to develop important geographical skills – in this section you will learn the following skills:

- Using numerical data.
- Finding evidence from photos.
- Describing population trends from graphs.
- Using a variety of graphic techniques to present data.
- Literacy skills – describing information in photos and preparing a presentation.

Your key words

As you go through the chapters in this section, make sure you know and understand the key words shown in bold. Definitions are provided in the Glossary on page 354. To be a good geographer you need to use good subject terminology.

Your exam

Section A makes up part of Paper 2 – a one and a half-hour written exam worth 34 per cent of your GCSE.

12 The urban world

12.1 An increasingly urban world

On this spread you will find out how the world's cities are growing

What is urbanisation?

By 1804 global population had doubled from half a billion to one billion in 300 years. By 1999 the total had doubled from 3 billion to 6 billion in just 39 years! The bigger the global population, the faster it grows (graph **A**).

Urbanisation – the increase in the proportion of the world's population who live in cities – is also growing. It is the result of the natural increase of a population (births minus deaths) plus **migration**. Urban growth is the increase in the area covered by cities.

Urbanisation has taken place at different times and at different speeds in different parts of the world. The UK was one of the first countries in the world to become urbanised.

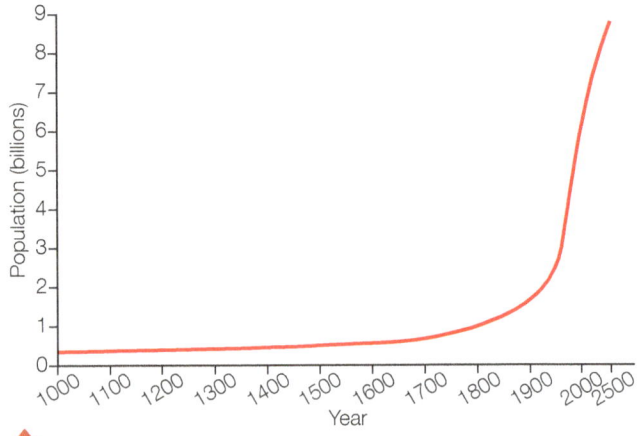

A Global population growth since the year 1000

How does urbanisation vary around the world?

The proportion of people living in towns and cities varies in different parts of the world (table **B**).

- In most of the world's richer countries over 60 per cent of the population live in cities.
- In south and south-east Asia around half the population live in towns and cities.
- All but nine countries in Africa have urban populations of more than 24 per cent. The average is almost 40 per cent.

In different regions of the world the urban population is growing at different rates (graph **C**).

Did you know? More than half the world's population now live in towns and cities.

B Global urban population, 2014

Percentage of population in urban areas (%)	Country
	Key: North America, Central and South America, Africa, Europe, Asia, Oceania
75–100	Canada, Mexico, USA, Argentina, Brazil, Chile, Colombia, Cuba, Guyana, Panama, Peru, Venezuela, Uruguay, Gabon, Libya, Belarus, Denmark, Estonia, Finland, France, Norway, Spain, Sweden, UK, Armenia, Azerbaijan, Georgia, Japan, Jordan, Kuwait, Lebanon, Saudi Arabia, Pakistan, Qatar, South Korea, Turkey, UAE, Australia, New Zealand
50–74	Bolivia, Costa Rica, Dominican Republic, Ecuador, Honduras, Nicaragua, Paraguay, Puerto Rico, Suriname, Algeria, Angola, Botswana, Cameroon, Cote d'Ivoire, Ghana, Morocco, Republic of the Congo, South Africa, Tunisia, Albania, Algeria, Andorra, Austria, Belgium, Bosnia and Herzegovina, Bulgaria, Croatia, Czech Republic, Germany, Greece, Hungary, Iceland, Ireland, Italy, Kosovo, Latvia, Liechtenstein, Lithuania, Luxembourg, Malta, Moldova, Monaco, Montenegro, Netherlands, North Macedonia, Poland, Portugal, Romania, San Marino, Serbia, Slovakia, Slovenia, Switzerland, Tunisia, Ukraine, China, Cyprus, Indonesia, Israel, Kazakhstan, Malaysia, Mongolia, North Korea, Oman, Russia, Singapore, Sri Lanka, Syria, Uzbekistan
25–49	Guatemala, Benin, Central African Republic, Democratic Republic of Congo, Djibouti, Egypt, Equatorial Guinea, Guinea, Guinea-Bissau, Lesotho, Liberia, Madagascar, Malawi, Mali, Mauritania, Mozambique, Namibia, Nigeria, Senegal, Sierra Leone, Somalia, South Sudan, Sudan, Swaziland, Tanzania, Togo, Zambia, Zimbabwe, Bangladesh, Bhutan, Cambodia, India, Kyrgyzstan, Laos, Myanmar, Philippines, Tajikistan, Turkmenistan, Vietnam, Yemen
0–24	Burkina Faso, Burundi, Chad, Eritrea, Ethiopia, Niger, Kenya, Rwanda, Uganda, Afghanistan, Nepal, Thailand, Papua New Guinea

116

The urban world

The distribution of the world's urban population

Different rates of urbanisation around the world have changed the distribution of the world's urban population. The projected changes between 1950 and 2050 are shown in graph **D**.

- The largest growth in urban population by 2050 will take place in India, China and Nigeria.
- These three countries will account for 37 per cent of the projected growth of the world's urban population between 2014 and 2050.
- By 2050, India is projected to add 404 million urban dwellers, China 292 million and Nigeria 212 million.

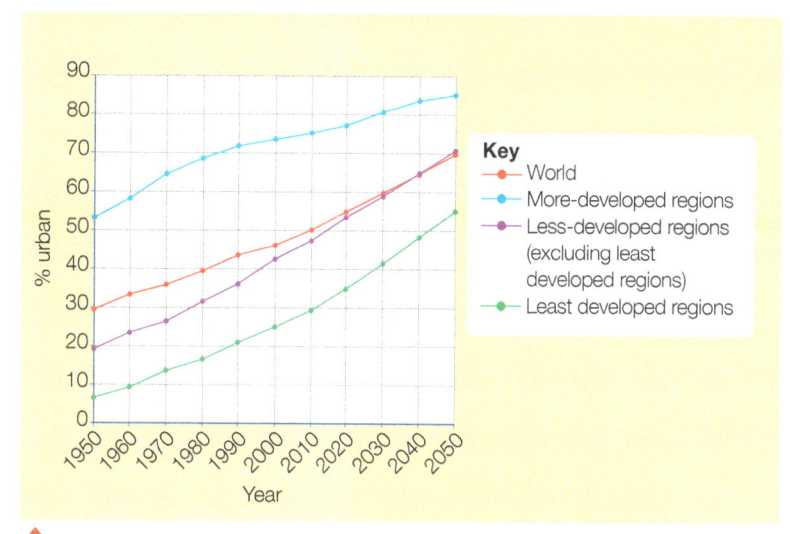

C Urban population, 1950–2050

Maths skills

1. Complete a copy of the table by filling in the missing values.

2. Use bar graph **D** to state which continent will have the biggest change in its share of world urban population by 2050.

Type of country	Country	% urban population, 1950	% urban population, 2050 (estimated)	% change in urban population 1950–2050
HIC	UK	79		+9
NEE	Nigeria		75	+65
LIC	Botswana	3	81	

ACTIVITIES

1. **a** Name the continent outside Europe, North America and Oceania which has the highest percentage of its population living in urban areas (table **B**).

   b With the aid of an atlas, name one country in Central Africa with an urban population of less than 49 per cent.

2. Describe the trends shown by each of the lines on graph **C**. Support your answer with evidence from the graph.

3. Suggest why Asian countries such as India and China are likely to have a higher urban population percentage in 2050 than in 2000.

4. Give examples of how the process of urbanisation has happened at different times and speeds.

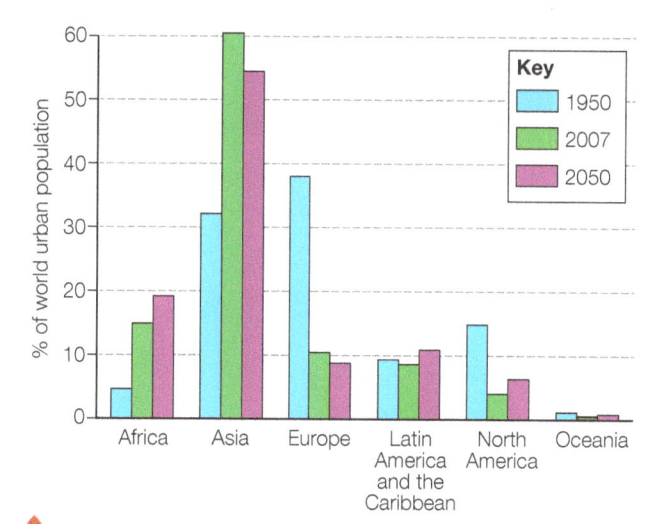

D Distribution of the world's urban population in 1950, 2007 and 2050 (estimated)

Stretch yourself

Produce a presentation (five slides maximum) to illustrate urban trends in different parts of the world.

Practice question

Suggest why there is such a low rate of urbanisation in rich countries and why some show evidence of counter-urbanisation. *(6 marks)*

117

12.2 The emergence of megacities

On this spread you will find out what factors make cities grow

Why do cities grow?

More than half the world's population now live in urban areas, and cities all over the world are continuing to grow. There are two main reasons why cities are getting bigger.

- *Rural–urban migration* – the movement of people from the countryside into towns and cities.
- **Natural increase** – where the birth rate is higher than the death rate.

A natural increase in population occurs when there is high proportion of young adults aged 18–35. Therefore, more children will be born. The smaller proportion of older people means the death rate is lower. Improvements to health care, particularly in urban areas of poorer countries, can also result in a lower death rate. Natural increase therefore tends to be higher in LICs (such as Cambodia) and in some NEEs (such as India).

Rural–urban migration is caused by *push* and *pull* factors. These are the real or imagined disadvantages of living in a rural area and advantages of living in a town or city (diagram **B**).

Sunita's story

My name is Sunita. Two years ago my parents, my brother Rakesh and I came to live in Mumbai, in an area called Dharavi. Everyone here is poor. Our house only has two rooms, but we have electricity. My father says at least we have work. One day maybe my brother and I will be rich!

Dharavi is crowded, noisy and very busy. Outside our house people wash laundry, sew clothes and bash dents out of oil cans to recycle them. There are 15 000 small workshops here.

It is very smelly, with open sewers. I like to walk to the biscuit factory because it smells nicer there!

I go to school every morning and learn maths and literacy. In the afternoon I help my mother clean the house. Then I go rag picking with my friends to earn some money.

A Dharavi, Mumbai

'Push' factors

People want to leave the countryside because:

- farming is hard and poorly paid
- desertification and soil erosion make farming difficult
- drought and other climate hazards reduce crop yields
- farming is often at subsistence level, producing only enough food for the family, leaving nothing to sell
- poor harvests may lead to malnutrition or famine
- there are few doctors or hospitals
- schools provide only a very basic education
- rural areas are isolated due to poor roads.

'Pull' factors

People are attracted to the city because:

- there are more well-paid jobs
- a higher standard of living is possible
- they have friends and family already living there
- there is a better chance of getting an education
- public transport is better
- a range of entertainments are available
- there are better medical facilities.

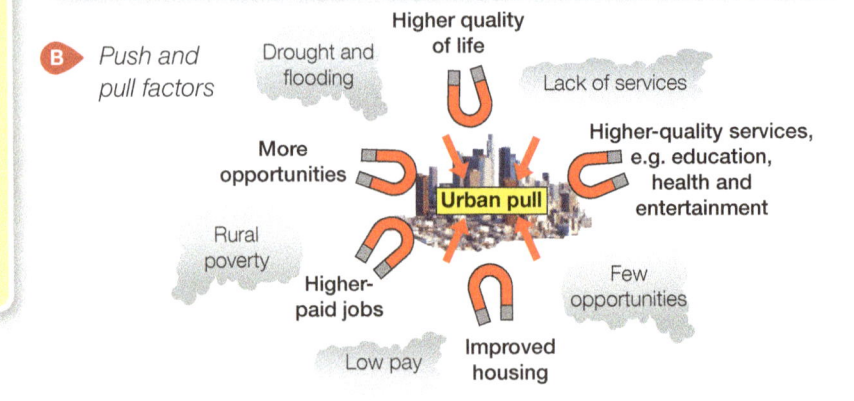

B Push and pull factors

Drought and flooding · Higher quality of life · Lack of services · More opportunities · Higher-quality services, e.g. education, health and entertainment · Rural poverty · Urban pull · Higher-paid jobs · Few opportunities · Low pay · Improved housing

118

The urban world

What are megacities?

These are cities with a population of over 10 million. In 2015 there were 28 of these megacities (map **C**), and the United Nations estimates that by 2050 there may be as many as 50. There are three types of megacities.

Slow-growing

Where?
South-east Asia, Europe and North America

Features
Population at 70%+ urban
No squatter settlements

Examples
Osaka-Kobe
Tokyo
Moscow
Los Angeles

Growing

Where?
South America and south-east Asia

Features
Population 40–50% urban
Under 20% in squatter settlement

Examples
Beijing
Rio de Janeiro
Shanghai
Mexico City

Rapid-growing

Where?
South/south-east Asia and Africa

Features
Population under 50% urban
Over 20% in squatter settlements

Examples
Jakarta
Lagos
Mumbai
Manila

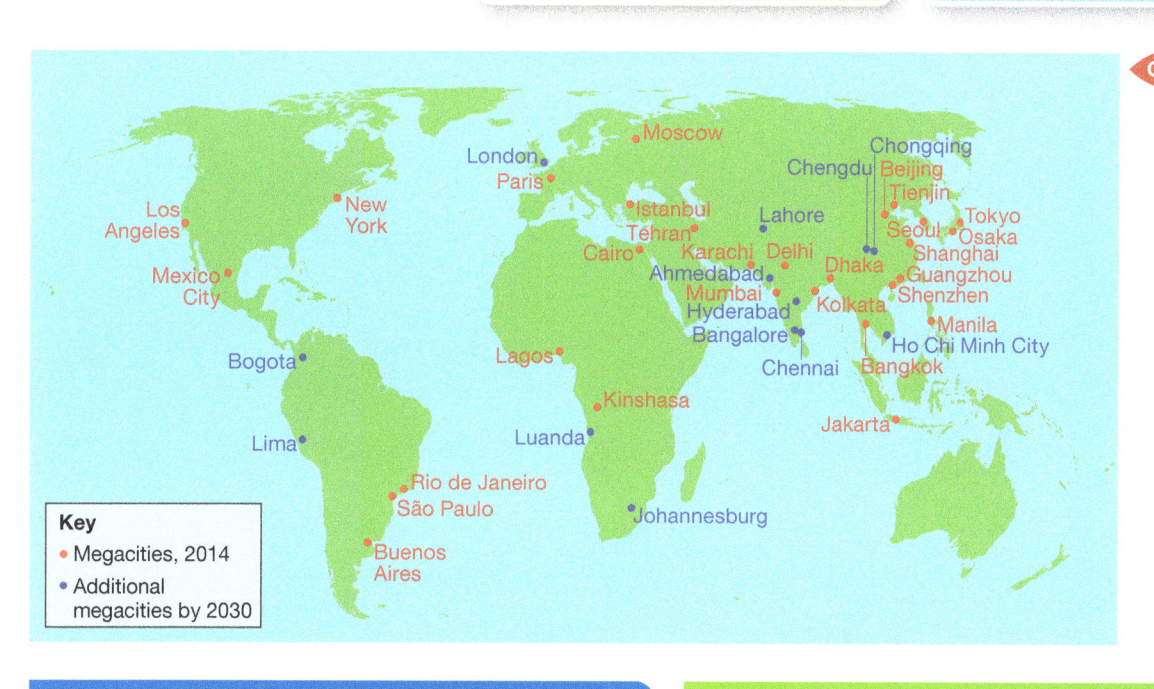

C The distribution of megacities in 2014 and 2030 (projected)

ACTIVITIES

1. **a** Give three factors which might explain why Sunita's family moved to Mumbai.
   b Explain whether these are push or pull factors.
2. Draw a table with three columns headed Social, Economic and Environmental. List each of the push and pull factors listed in diagram **B** under the correct heading.
3. Describe how the three types of megacities are different from each other.

Stretch yourself

Using population data, calculate the rate of natural increase of Malawi, the Philippines, and Colombia. Is there a pattern between these countries?

Practice question

Use map **C** to describe the changes in the distribution of megacities between 2014 and 2030. *(6 marks)*

119

13 Urban growth

13.1 Introducing Mumbai

On this spread you will find out about Mumbai's location and its global and regional importance

Example

Location and geographical features

- Mumbai is India's leading commercial city. It is located in the state of Maharashtra, bordering the Arabian Sea.
- Mumbai experiences a hot tropical climate, with monsoon rains between June and September. Its water supply depends on the seasonal rains. Annual rainfall is over 2400 mm.
- Originally, Mumbai consisted of seven islands surrounded by swamps, but by 1845 these were combined into a single island by a large-scale land reclamation scheme. The city centre is on a small peninsula at the southern tip of the island.
- Mumbai has a large and deep natural harbour. It is on a major shipping route through the Mediterranean Sea via the Suez Canal, along with other shipping routes connecting to Europe, Africa and south-east Asia.
- The city has road, air and railway links to all the major industrial cities in India and air transport connections all over the world.
- Mumbai has a wide river estuary to the east, protecting the ships from waves in the Indian Ocean when in dock.

Did you know? Mumbai has a coastline of about 150 km.

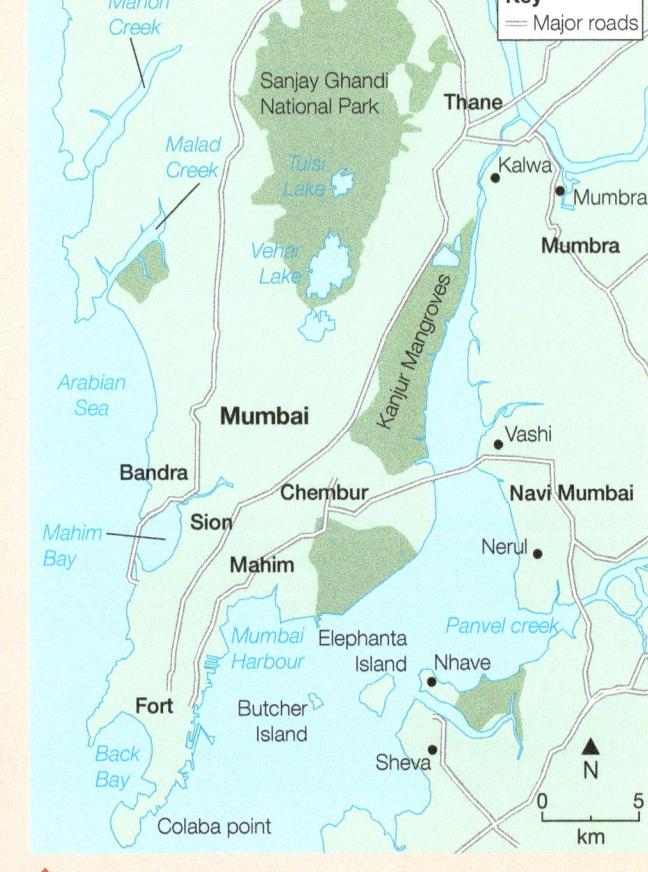

A The location of Mumbai

B Mumbai City District

120

Urban growth

Reasons for importance

It is India's biggest city and the fourth largest in the world. In 2017, the population of Mumbai was 21.6 million.

Mumbai expanded rapidly during the British colonial period as its trade links with the rest of the world grew.

Until the 1970s, much of Mumbai's wealth was the result of the cotton trade and the large number of textile mills. Most of these have now closed down.

Over the past 30 years the city has experienced an economic boom. It is now graded as an 'alpha' world city due to its economic importance.

Mumbai is by far the most globalised city in south Asia – a region with 1.5 billion people – and the main destination for foreign investment.

Its airport records the most international passengers in south Asia.

Mumbai handles over 40 per cent of India's foreign trade and produces almost 25 per cent of its industrial goods.

The headquarters of 20 of India's top 50 companies are based in Mumbai. Many transnational corporations (TNCs) have become established here, including Tata, the State Bank of India and Reliance.

The city is the centre of many service industries, especially banking, insurance and finance, as well as being a focus for India's hi-tech companies.

C *Mumbai city centre*

Despite Mumbai's wealth (the city is the richest in India and has many billionaires), over 9 million people live in slums or informal housing.

Dharavi is India's largest and most densely populated slum area, with up to 1 million people living in an area of just over 2 km^2, close to the city centre.

The Bollywood and Marathi cinema industries, based in Mumbai, produce more movies than anywhere else in the world.

International hotels attract business people and tourists from all over the world.

India's main television companies, news organisations and publishers all have headquarters there.

ACTIVITIES

1. Describe the location of Mumbai and explain why its position helped the city to grow.
2. On an outline map of India, mark the following:
   - a Mumbai
   - b New Delhi (the capital city)
   - c Arabian Sea
   - d Bay of Bengal
   - e Indian Ocean
   - f Maharashtra state
3. Using maps **A** and **B** and photo **C**, explain the limitations and advantages of the site of Mumbai.
4. How does photo **C** show differences of land use in Mumbai?

Stretch yourself

Research the changes that took place in Mumbai during British colonial rule. How long did this period last? What effects did it have? Which industries and trading links developed during this time?

Practice question

Suggest why the physical geography of the Mumbai area helped the city to develop.
(4 marks)

121

13.2 Mumbai: a growing city

On this spread you will find out about the causes of the growth of Mumbai

Example

What caused Mumbai to grow into one of the world's largest cities?

Migration

Mumbai developed as a settlement when British colonists used the area for industry and as a seaport. More recently, the city has grown for reasons that are typical throughout many low-income countries (LICs) and newly emerging economies (NEEs). Rural–urban **migration** has contributed to the rise in Mumbai's population, which has doubled in size over the past 20 years. A minority of wealthier residents live in suburbs such as New Mumbai, while more than half live in the city's slums and squatter settlements.

Young people migrate to Mumbai because job opportunities are limited in rural areas. Most migrants to Mumbai come from Maharashtra state (70 per cent), with a smaller proportion from other Indian states such as Bihar and Madhya Pradesh. The average age of migrants is 21 and almost two thirds are male. Increased use of machinery in farming has meant fewer workers are needed, and changes to farming practices have forced small farms to sell up to larger landowners. Some migrants come to Mumbai alone, but many move to join relatives and friends who are already established in the city.

Most foreign migrants come from other south Asian countries, particularly Pakistan and Bangladesh, searching for work. A small proportion come from western countries, including the UK and USA, working mainly in the finance sector or in large TNCs.

Recently, the pace of population growth has slowed. (Between 1971 and 1981 the population of Mumbai grew by 38.1 per cent, whereas between 2001 and 2011 the population grew by only 4.7 per cent.) The city is not providing enough employment opportunities and the government has invested money in rural projects to persuade young people to stay in their home areas.

> Working on the farm has become very difficult. There have been several droughts over the past few years and there has not been enough for my family to eat. I don't have much land and I can't afford to buy fertilisers or machinery. My children have to walk a long way to school and there are no doctors or hospitals in the area.

> I came here with my family because I thought there would be more chances to get a job that pays well. I believed that we would have a better house with electricity and running water. My children would have a good education and we would get access to proper health care.

A *Reasons why people move to Mumbai from the countryside in Maharashtra*

Natural increase

Mumbai's population has also grown because of **natural increase**. The people that migrate into Mumbai are young, so are more likely to have children. Falling death rates, due to improved medical care, means that more babies are being born than people are dying, further increasing the urban population.

Natural increase is still rapid in most parts of Mumbai, particularly among the poorer sectors of the population. Natural increase in the migrant population has traditionally been low, though many are of childbearing age. However, some family planning programmes in India have had some success, so family size is steadily being reduced.

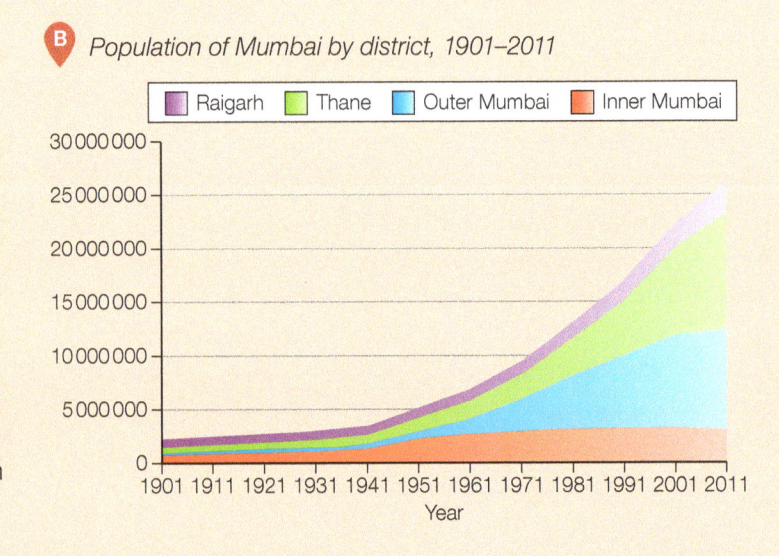

B *Population of Mumbai by district, 1901–2011*

Legend: Raigarh, Thane, Outer Mumbai, Inner Mumbai

Urban growth

Population distribution and diversity

The historic core of inner Mumbai now contains only 12 per cent of the total population, compared with 45 per cent in 1941. Areas of recent growth have been the outer regions of Thane and Raigarh as the city has expanded into the countryside – a process known as **urban sprawl**. The city centre has become one of the most densely populated areas in the world, with approximately 25 000 people per square kilometre.

There is a mix of religious groups in Mumbai, reflecting the many cultural backgrounds and places people come from (table **C**).

Mumbai's sex ratio is skewed – for every 1000 boys, there are just 848 girls. This is blamed partly on sex-selective abortions, as well as the male-dominated nature of migration.

C *Religious diversity in Mumbai*

Religion	Population (%)
Hindu	67.4
Muslim	18.5
Buddhist	5.2
Jain	4.0
Christian	4.2
Sikh	0.6
Parsi, Jew and other religious minorities	0.1

Maths skills

Draw a divided bar graph to show the various religious groups in Mumbai. Explain why there is such a mix of religions in Mumbai.

ACTIVITIES

1. How has the economy of Mumbai changed since the end of Britain's colonial rule?
2. Explain why Mumbai is now recognised as a 'world city'.
3. Describe the changes in population of Mumbai since 1900. Why has the growth of population slowed down in some parts of the city?
4. On a copy of the population graph for Mumbai add suitable annotations. For example:
   a. After the Second World War, the partition of India and the formation of Pakistan causes the largest human mass migration in history. Many Hindu refugees settle in Mumbai where the Indian government gives them asylum.
   b. Mumbai becomes a megacity as its population reaches 10 million.
   c. The Green Revolution (a government programme to improve agriculture, started in the 1960s) reduces farm work in rural areas and only large farms can afford the chemicals and machinery. Farm workers move to the city to look for a better quality of life.
   d. Natural increase (higher birth rate than death rate) causes a faster rate of increase than migration at the end of the last century.
5. Decide whether these are rural push or urban pull factors affecting migration into Mumbai from the surrounding rural areas.
   a. Difficult living conditions due to unreliability of monsoon rains.
   b. Affordable accommodation in Dharavi.
   c. Unemployment due to mechanisation of agriculture.
   d. Improved economic prospects.
   e. Better access to schools and hospitals.
   f. Extreme poverty.
   g. No job opportunities.
   h. Presence of family and friends in central Mumbai.
   i. Cinemas, museums, theatres and concert halls.
   j. Poor educational opportunities.
   k. Modern computer-based companies.
   l. Lack of clean water and electricity.
   m. Relations have moved to the city already.
6. Explain the role of migration and natural increase as factors in Mumbai's changing population.

Stretch yourself

Draw a table with three columns, headed: social factors, economic factors, environmental factors. List examples of push and pull factors under each heading. Which factors are most important in explaining rural–urban migration into Mumbai?

Practice question

Explain why Mumbai's population has more than doubled in size since 1991. *(4 marks)*

13.3 Social opportunities

On this spread you will find out how urban growth has created social opportunities in Mumbai

Social opportunities

Mumbai is renowned for its cultural activities and restaurants specialising in most types of cuisine. Its nightlife is a big attraction, particularly for young people, and includes a vibrant music scene, hundreds of cinemas, nightclubs and theatres.

Shops

There are many high-class shopping districts in Mumbai, often aimed at the large tourist market as well as the growing middle class. Mumbai is well known for its high-end stores selling internationally branded goods, but it also has hundreds of small shopping centres, traditional bazaars and roadside stalls targeting the local population.

A number of large shopping malls have opened in recent years. The Palladium Mall, which opened in 2008, houses about 100 stores, spread across four levels. It includes major, international brands encompassing designer labels, high fashion, cosmetics and jewellery. The mall also has a range of cafes, fine dining restaurants, a stand-up comedy venue, spas and salons. These facilities have helped to attract employment, improve the environment, and provide a safe and secure shopping experience under one roof.

A The Palladium Mall

Did you know?
Bollywood produced almost 2000 films in 2017, more than any other film industry in the world.

Did you know?
Mumbai is famous for the biggest street festival celebrated in India. Ganesh Chaturthi brings the whole city onto the streets.

Leisure

Mumbai has countless local, cultural and religious festivals, such as Elephanta, Banganga and Ganesh Chaturthi, all of which are attended by huge crowds (photo **B**). Diwali, the Hindu festival of light, takes place in October and is particularly popular with both locals and visitors.

Sports are universally popular, particularly cricket but also soccer, field hockey and kabaddi (a traditional Indian team sport). Many residents use the local beaches for swimming, such as Juju Beach, although these can be highly polluted at times. The migrant population has also introduced a wide range of interests, cuisine, films, theatre, music and entertainment to Mumbai, enhancing the city's rich and diverse mix of cultural activities. Bollywood music is extremely popular, heard throughout the city's shops, taxis and streets.

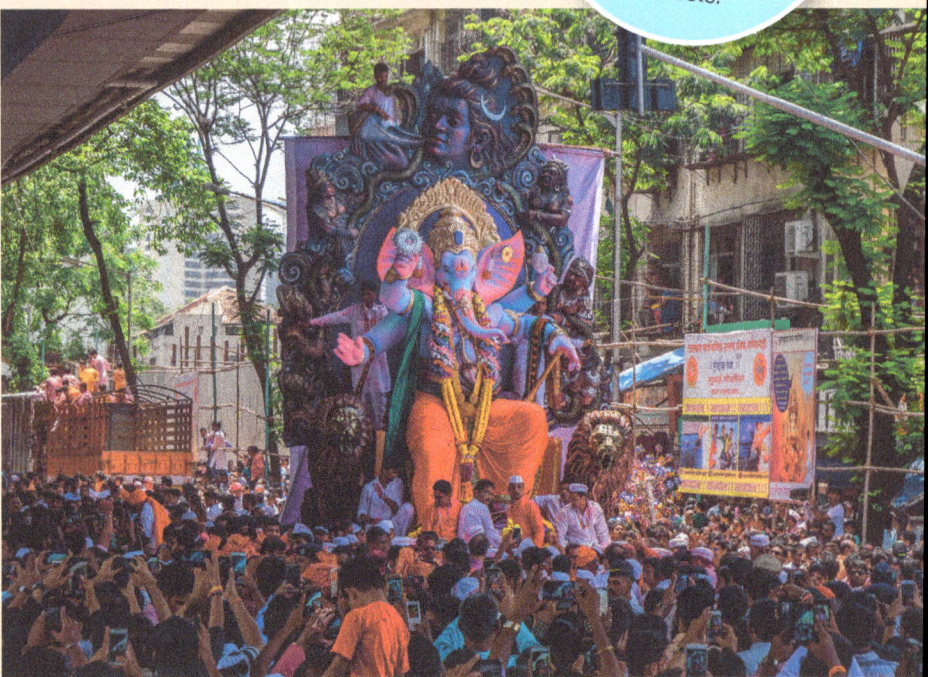

A Ganesh Chaturthi festival, Mumbai

Health

Public services are easier to fund in densely populated areas. Mumbai, therefore, has better health facilities than the surrounding rural areas of Maharashtra. It is much easier to reach hospitals and clinics quickly in a city, and specialist equipment is more readily available. In the event of an emergency, response times are quicker and survival rates much higher as a result. Education about general health care is also more accessible in a city, including information about family planning and birth control.

Mumbai has India's best public health infrastructure (with over 400 public hospitals and clinics), but its medical personnel and health facilities are inadequate to serve its population properly. Some government-run hospitals provide basic health care free of charge or for a small fee, but these are insufficient to meet the growing demand. Wealthier residents tend to use private hospitals.

Education

The authorities have built more than 1000 primary and secondary schools in Mumbai. Government schools are free, but parents are expected to pay for textbooks and school uniforms. Literacy rates in Mumbai are high compared with surrounding rural parts of Maharashtra.

Inadequate resources and declining standards in government schools means many families choose to pay for their children to attend the city's private secondary schools.

Mumbai is also a major centre of higher education, although standards vary enormously. Some wealthier families send their children abroad for higher education. The University of Mumbai was founded in 1857 and there are numerous other colleges and universities, such as SNDT Women's University, the Indian Institute of Technology (IIT), and the National Centre for Software Technology (NCST). The Haffkine Institute is an important research centre for medicine and other sciences.

Water supply

Access to a clean and reliable water supply is variable in Mumbai. Most of the water comes from six dammed lakes in the Thane district. In the Dharavi slum, the water pipes are in use for only two hours a day, leading to queues for this water. However, this is at least clean drinking water, which often is not available in poorer rural areas or involves a long walk to the local well. Having the opportunity to drink water without the risk of bacteria causing cholera, typhoid or dysentery is a significant advantage for the people of Mumbai.

Energy supply

There is one electricity provider for Mumbai. It obtains most of its power from Tata Power, which produces most of its electricity from thermal (oil and coal) power plants. Although there are frequent power cuts, electricity is generally available across most parts of Mumbai.

ACTIVITIES

1. Why do you think that Mumbai is a popular tourist destination?
2. Several large shopping malls have been opened in Mumbai in the past 10 years. Why have they become popular with many people in Mumbai? Why are they not welcomed by all?
3. How has migration into Mumbai influenced the range of leisure activities available in the city?
4. Explain why Mumbai's health and educational facilities may be superior to those found in rural areas of India.
5. Why is it essential to provide both a good quantity and good quality of water in a city such as Mumbai?

Stretch yourself

Contrast social conditions in Mumbai with those of the surrounding countryside in Maharashtra. In what ways are social facilities better in the city of Mumbai?

Practice question

To what extent do urban areas of LICs or NEEs provide social opportunities for people? Use a case study to support your answer. *(6 marks)*

13.4 Economic opportunities

On this spread you will find out how urban growth has created economic opportunities in Mumbai

Economic opportunities

Mumbai's economy is expanding rapidly, offering a wide range of employment opportunities. Almost all of India's major companies have offices in the city, which is sometimes known as the 'Gateway to India'. The city accounts for 7 per cent of India's GDP and 40 per cent of its foreign trade. It has earned the reputation of being an enterprising city where people are prepared to do anything to make a living. Mumbai has one of the highest incomes per head in the country, with a growing number of jobs provided by service industries such as finance.

Did you know? The world's most expensive house is in Mumbai. Antilia, a 27-story skyscraper, is valued at over US$1 billion.

Investment has been greatest in…
- Manufacturing (food processing, textiles, engineering, jewellery, computers and electronic equipment)
- Services (banking, ICT and call centres)
- Construction (housing, factories and offices)
- Shipbuilding and salvaging
- Oil refining and petrochemicals
- Entertainment and leisure (Bollywood, hotels and restaurants)
- Aerospace industries
- Advertising and publishing
- Medical research and optical engineering
- Renewable energy

Manufacturing and services

Mumbai's port and the city's numerous manufacturing companies generate many employment opportunities. As new services are required, investment has grown, rapidly increasing the number of jobs and resulting in economic development.

Foreign TNCs	Bank of America, Bayer, Citigroup, GlaxoSmithKline, Johnson & Johnson, Pfizer, Volkswagen, Walt Disney
Indian companies	Cipla, CRISIL, Educomp, Future Group, Hindustan Unilever, Lupin, Piramal, Tata

A Leading Indian and international companies with regional headquarters in Mumbai

Did you know? Mumbai has the highest number of billionaires and millionaires of any city in India.

The financial sector

Mumbai has been the financial hub of India and a major trade and business centre since the mid-nineteenth century. The headquarters of large financial institutions are now based in South Mumbai, including two stock exchanges, the Reserve Bank of India and the Mint. Photo **B** shows the rapid development of the Mumbai skyline with the financial cluster and concentration of TNC headquarters.

B Mumbai financial sector

Urban growth

The informal sector

The booming economy has benefited millions of people living in Mumbai, but approximately two thirds of the workforce are forced to find jobs in the **informal sector**, making a living however they can. The majority of these workers are poorly paid and have no formal employment contract. Many are without any insurance cover or unemployment benefit. They do not contribute any taxes to the **formal economy** and the government receives no income from them. Sometimes they work in dangerous and unregulated conditions. Jobs include street vending, rag picking (searching through waste heaps for useful materials), breaking up and recycling old electronic products, recycling waste, making pottery, driving, welding, hairdressing, labouring, working in construction and selling food and drink.

Did you know?
Did you know that there are more than 250 000 street vendors in Mumbai?

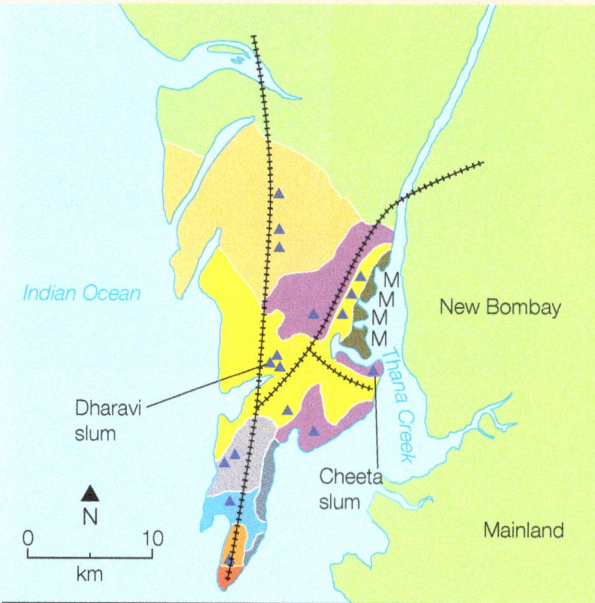

C Street vendor in Mumbai

ACTIVITIES

1. Examine photo **C**.
    a. What do you think the vendor is selling?
    b. What might be the advantages and disadvantages for street vendors of working in the informal economy?
    c. Why are the authorities clamping down on street vendors in some areas of Mumbai?
2. Contrast the main features of the formal and informal economy in Mumbai.
3. Which types of employment have grown and which have declined in Mumbai in recent years? Explain these changes.
4. Study table **A**. Find out the main products or services associated with at least three foreign and three domestic companies. What do you notice about them?
5. Using map **D**, describe and explain the pattern of land use in Mumbai.

Stretch yourself

Investigate the activities of one TNC based in Mumbai. Explain why the company chose to place its regional headquarters in the city. Why is the Indian government keen to attract TNCs?

Practice question

Assess the importance of the informal sector of Mumbai's economy. *(4 marks)*

D Mumbai's land use zones

Key:
- M Marshes and salt pans
- Defence area
- Port
- CBD
- European town and area of former colonial development
- Old industry and chawls
- Twentieth century industrial expansion
- Inner suburbs
- Outer suburbs
- ▲ Slums
- ┼┼┼ Railway

127

13.5 Managing urban growth

On this spread you will find out about the challenges of managing urban growth in Mumbai

Example

Slums and squatter settlements

The UN defines slums as 'informal settlements that lack one or more of the following five conditions: access to clean water, access to improved sanitation, sufficient living area that is not overcrowded, durable housing and secure tenure'.

When migrants arrive in Mumbai, they often find that life is different to how they imagined. There is an acute shortage of housing, so poorer people live in squatter settlements and slums. **Squatter settlements** are residential areas where people have illegally built homes on land they do not own. They are areas of great social deprivation, associated with poverty, unemployment, poor health care and inadequate educational facilities. Housing is cramped, overcrowded and poorly constructed, and is often a long distance from places of employment. Many homes lack basic amenities such as gas, electricity, running water or a sewage system. Up to 55 per cent of the population live in slums in Mumbai, compared with 20 per cent in both Rio de Janeiro and Delhi. Slums occupy almost a quarter of the available building land in the city.

There are hundreds of slum areas in Mumbai. Many are in the suburbs and in outer parts of the city, often on waste ground or land that is poorly drained or unsuitable for housing. Some, such as Dharavi, are close to the city centre. The authorities are keen to clear these to make the area more attractive to businesses and tourists.

Challenges of living in Dharavi, a slum area in Mumbai

Construction
Some houses are poorly constructed, as they were built with basic materials such as iron, broken bricks and plastic sheets. However, many are now built with bricks and some have a piped water supply. Residents live in very small homes (e.g. 2.5 m^2), often with large families. Ownership is insecure as landowners can remove them without any compensation.

Services
Many homes do not have running water, some have no electricity and a high proportion have no sewage connections. Some homes use illegal connections to electricity pylons. Sewers are often open drains that lead to Mahim Creek – a small stream that has become highly polluted, causing the spread of contagious diseases. Drinking water is rationed – it is generally obtained from public standpipes, which come on at 6 am for just two hours a day. Many people are forced to purchase over-priced water from street vendors. However, there have been some improvements in the availability of essential services, especially power supply, schools and health facilities.

A *Slum area in Dharavi, Mumbai*

Health
Population density is high, with over 250 000 people per square kilometre. Infant mortality rates are 40 per 1000. Waste cannot always be disposed of and builds up in the street, increasing the chances of disease. Burning rubbish often creates a fire risk to homes and the smoke is harmful to health. There is poor sanitation and a lack of toilet facilities (one toilet for every 1500 people). Air pollution is a serious problem, leading to a higher risk of lung cancer, asthma and tuberculosis. Life expectancy is only 50 years, on average.

Community life

Some residents have lived in Dharavi for 50 years or more – in this time there have been improvements to housing and local amenities. Most homes have a gas stove and some have electricity, so residents may have access to a TV and use of a computer or tablet. Schools have been built and there are local community groups where people help each other. Shops can be found throughout the settlement and most items can be purchased locally. Crime rates are quite low. Despite the negative portrayal of the slum areas, some people appreciate the community spirit and like living in Dharavi, particularly where they are well established and they have made improvements to their homes. Rents are usually very low (as low as US$2.90 per month), which makes housing affordable in an otherwise very expensive city.

B *Inside Dharavi*

Economic activity

Unemployment rates are high. Much employment is poorly paid irregular jobs in the informal sector. Average incomes may be less than US$60 a month. The settlement is located close to downtown Mumbai and lies between Mumbai's two main suburban rail lines, so people can commute easily to work. However, Dharavi also has thousands of small industries that provide services and goods to local residents. Some products, such as leather goods, pottery and recycled plastic, are sold more widely and in certain cases are exported abroad. There is a large-scale recycling industry, based on the reprocessing of waste from landfill sites in Mumbai and other parts of the world. Virtually nothing is wasted – Mumbai has a recycling rate of over 80 per cent. Unfortunately, working conditions are hazardous, with workers handling toxic waste, which can affect health and life expectancy.

ACTIVITIES

1. Suggest why the number of people living in slums in Mumbai continues to increase.
2. Imagine you are a newly arrived migrant from a rural area in western India.
   a. What would please you?
   b. What would disappoint you?
3. With the help of photos **A** and **B**, outline the main problems of day-to-day living in Dharavi. Explain how the conditions shown are a risk to human health.
4. Explain why Dharavi has sometimes been described as a 'slum of hope and opportunity'.
5. Why are some people reluctant to leave the slum areas, despite the possibility of living in much better homes?

> Crime is a major problem. Children don't go to school. The family lives on top of each other and there is no privacy. Disease is rife and day-to-day life for us is a real struggle for survival.

> There is a real community spirit here and my neighbours are helping us to improve our house. I work part-time as a cleaner and my husband has a stall in downtown Mumbai. People here are welcoming and proud of where they live.

C *Different views of Dharavi*

Stretch yourself

Research everyday life for the people of Dharavi. Focus on the challenges facing the residents living there. How do people manage to overcome these problems?

Practice question

Using an example, assess the extent to which urban growth puts pressure on basic services such as housing, water, sanitation and health systems. *(6 marks)*

13.6 Providing basic resources and services

On this spread you will find out about the challenges of providing basic resources and services in Mumbai

Example

Water and sanitation – problems and solutions

Among the common sights in Mumbai are water vendors on the street selling water in containers. It is often difficult for residents of some slums to obtain drinking water from any other source.

Almost 90 per cent of the population in Mumbai has a piped water supply that has been treated and purified at source. By contrast, the average for rural parts of India is only 16 per cent. In most slum areas people rely on standpipes that might be working for only a few hours a day or water vendors. Water from the streams is not suitable for drinking because it is so polluted.

Even though Mumbai has reported tremendous progress towards achieving access to water for all, this does not mean continuous and safe access to water, or affordable water. The water infrastructure in Mumbai is more than 100 years old and is poorly constructed. Due to its age, there are regular bacterial infections so disease can spread easily. The city is only supplied with water for six hours a day. Much water is lost due to leakage and the insufficient supply does not keep up with the demand. Where the leaks occur, bacteria and other harmful contaminants such as lead and arsenic gather and eventually enter the water supply. This can lead to serious diseases including typhoid, cholera and dysentery.

To help solve these problems it is proposed to create another dam in the Vaitarna River, introduce rainharvesting devices, repair leaks and construct more small-scale water recycling/treatment plants.

A *Water supply issues in Mumbai*

Urban growth

B *Solar-powered lights at Hanging Garden Malabar Hill, Mumbai*

Energy supply – problems and solutions

Like most cities in India, Mumbai depends on fossil fuels to produce the bulk (70 per cent) of its electricity, and much of the gas and coal needed is imported from abroad. Two new coal-fired power stations are planned, to reduce the city's electricity shortage and light the streets at night. However, the country is also investing in a major renewable and nuclear energy programme, with the aim of reducing its dependence on fossil fuels and meeting climate change targets. India is already the world's fifth largest producer of wind power and is rapidly developing its solar energy provision – by 2020 the Indian government hopes to increase solar power capacity by 100 000 megawatts. Despite environmental objections, the country's nuclear power programme is being stepped up and is expected to double in capacity by 2040, contributing almost 10 per cent of the country's total electricity. By 2025, 23 reactors are due to be constructed, making India the second largest producer of nuclear power in the world. Some of the electricity generated will be fed into the network to supply the increasing demands for power in Mumbai.

The frequent power cuts in Mumbai are both costly to businesses as well as being inconvenient. Many offices, factories and wealthy residents depend on their own generators when power is cut.

The cost of petrol and diesel is high in India, so more people are gradually turning to electrically powered and hybrid vehicles for transport. The Indian government has an ambitious target of moving completely to electric vehicles by 2030 to help reduce its carbon emissions by almost 40 per cent.

Various strategies are in place to save energy in homes and businesses. All new buildings must conform to strict energy conservation regulations, and appliances have to show energy performance and consumption data. From 2006 onwards, all energy companies have had to supply at least 6 per cent of electricity through renewable schemes. In Mumbai, solar power is produced in places such as parks and other public places (photos **B** and **C**). By 2030 it is intended that at least 40 per cent of energy will be from renewable or sustainable sources.

C *Solar-powered traffic lights in Mumbai*

Providing basic resources and services

Providing access to health care

The principal health problems in Mumbai are linked with infectious disease. In the summer monsoon months, malaria and dengue fever are rife as the rain and high humidity allow mosquitoes to flourish (photo **D**). Diarrhoea and typhoid outbreaks occur frequently in poorer parts of Mumbai, caused by people eating contaminated food and water. Tuberculosis is spread from person to person through the air, and other respiratory diseases are caused by chronic air pollution. Health issues also common to western cities include hypertension (caused by stress, smoking and high alcohol consumption) and diabetes (often aggravated by obesity, and high sugar and alcohol intake).

India spends only 1.4 per cent of GDP on its health care system – one of the lowest rates in the world. Seven per cent of children die before they reach the age of five (compared with 0.7 per cent in the USA). In theory, medical treatment is free for everyone, but with a rapidly growing population it is difficult to meet the demand for proper health care. Private hospitals are used by people who can afford to pay (approximately 25 per cent of the population). The remainder make use of the 17 public hospitals, as well as the clinics supported by non-governmental organisations (NGOs) or charities, but these are understaffed and lack funding for equipment and medicines. Many people rely on basic health care or traditional remedies.

D *The* Aedes aegypti *mosquito carries and spreads malaria and dengue fever*

Providing access to education

Access to education is much better in Mumbai compared with the surrounding rural areas. Theoretically, education in India is compulsory between the ages of six and 14, but this is not always achieved because:

- many students drop out of school, especially from poorer families where children might be needed to earn money
- girls sometimes have fewer educational opportunities than boys
- there are not enough school places or teachers.

Over half of all children end formal schooling by the age of 12, and around one in 10 do not attend school at all.

Up to 30 per cent of people send their children to private schools because of smaller class sizes and better resources, although these schools can be quite expensive. Across the city there are more than 10 universities and several advanced research and education institutes.

C *Girls attending a small, private primary school operating from a one-room flat in Mumbai*

Urban growth

Reducing unemployment and crime

Unemployment in Mumbai is officially only 5.5 per cent of the total population, but only about 30 per cent are employed *formally*, with written contracts of employment, paid holiday, pension entitlement and social security provision. The rest work in the *informal* economy, which is often unpredictable, insecure and poorly paid. People create their own jobs such as couriers, cleaners and cooks, or by selling items, making and repairing things on a small scale, taking in laundry or reprocessing waste products instead of throwing them away.

To reduce unemployment levels in Mumbai the government has adopted a number of strategies:

- Greater focus on vocational training, with emphasis on providing practical skills needed by modern industry.
- Developing small-scale cottage industries in rural areas, aimed at stemming the flow of migrants from the countryside into Mumbai.
- Providing incentives to foreign companies to establish headquarters and branches in Mumbai.
- Introducing self-employment opportunities for educated urban youths, supported by some government funding.

Many businesses require skilled workers. However, migrants who arrive from rural areas are often unskilled, so opportunities for work are limited. Housing is overcrowded and living conditions are poor. In some instances this can lead to higher crime rates, as people turn to illegal activities in order to survive. Violent crime, against women as well as men, has escalated in recent years.

In 2015 the city recorded 42 940 cases of serious crime, increasing from 40 361 cases in 2014. Cyber crime rose by 50.1 per cent, with most cases related to credit card fraud. Kidnapping and abduction rose by an enormous 192 per cent in Mumbai in 2015, with the national increase being only 7.5 per cent.

Mumbai has also been subject to terrorism. In November 2008, a major attack took place over four days in the commercial heart of Mumbai. Altogether, 173 people were killed and over 300 were injured as a result of shootings and bombings at a railway station, a cafe, a theatre, two hospitals and two hotels.

Crime-prevention strategies have been introduced, including digitising criminal records, strict gun control measures, CCTV cameras, forensic laboratories, police vehicles and improved training. Nevertheless, police services are under pressure.

ACTIVITIES

1. Explain why Mumbai often has a shortage of drinking water despite being surrounded by water.
2. Describe how water and energy are supplied to Mumbai.
3. Study photo compilation **A**. Identify the problem or issue being illustrated in each image.
4. Outline ways in which water supply and energy supply are being improved in Mumbai.
5. Compare the principal health problems affecting people living in Mumbai with those of a city in a high-income country (HIC) such as the USA or Japan. Explain the differences.
6. What measures are being taken to reduce crime in Mumbai?

Stretch yourself

Find out more about how dirty water can lead to serious diseases. To what extent have these diseases been reduced or eliminated in India?

Practice question

To what extent have attempts to improve access to basic services such as health and education been successful in Mumbai?
(6 marks)

133

13.7 Managing waste, recycling and pollution

On this spread you will find out how environmental issues in Mumbai are being managed

As a result of Mumbai's size and high growth rate, urban sprawl, traffic congestion, waste disposal and pollution pose serious threats to the quality of life in the city.

Waste disposal and recycling

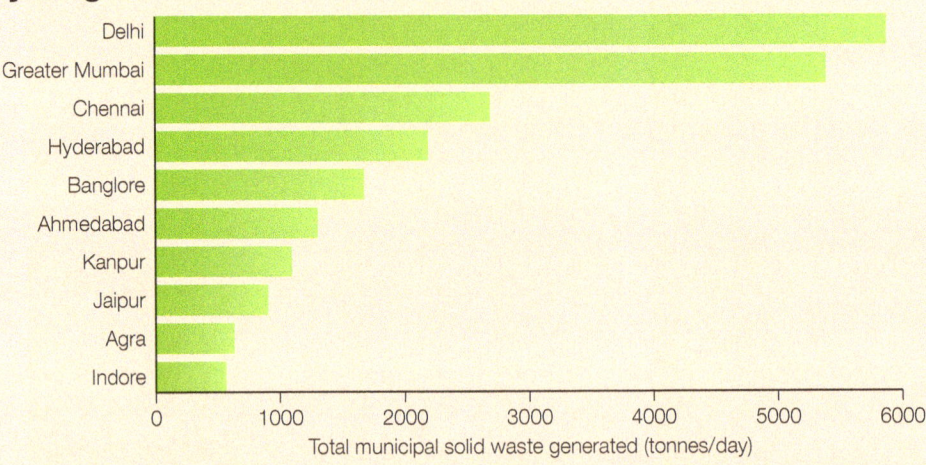

Dealing with increasing amounts of waste from industry and from people's homes is expensive, and the city lacks the infrastructure to cope with the huge volumes involved. Lack of sanitation systems means that rubbish and sewage is often disposed of in streams and in the sea. Mumbai has only three dumping grounds to handle the 9600 metric tonnes of waste generated daily. The major landfill at Deonar is about 90 years old and is on the verge of collapsing. The rubbish heaps are over 20 m high, as tall as a five- or six-storey building. More than 70 per cent of collected urban waste is dumped straight into the landfills, which produce toxins and greenhouse gases. Toxins produced by waste leach into the soil and groundwater, and become environmental hazards for many years.

A Top 10 cities in India that generate the highest municipal waste

Mumbai also generates an estimated 120 000 tonnes of electronic waste (e-waste) annually – the highest in India (chart **B**). This comprises discarded electronic appliances such as mobile phones, computers and televisions. In areas such as Dhavari, people break down this e-waste, boiling, crushing or burning parts in order to extract valuable materials such as gold or platinum. However, the toxic chemicals inside such as cadmium and lead can pose serious health risks. Mumbai's hospitals are starting to see patients with 10 times the expected level of lead in their blood.

There have been some recent improvements in waste management. Mumbai is now ranked at number 10 among the 15 cleanest cities in India. Investment in more effective solid waste collection and waste treatment plants that harness energy have made a difference, although the authorities admit that over 20 per cent of all waste is still not collected. In 2016 a new centre was opened for the collection of hazardous e-waste and its disposal in an environmentally friendly manner.

B E-waste generation in cities of India

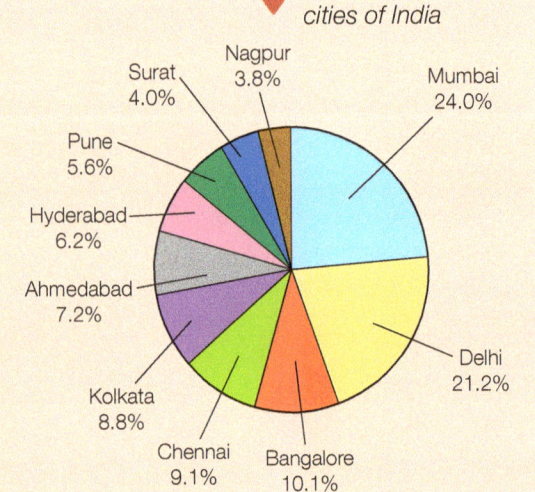

Ragpickers are people who search through waste to find materials that might be salvageable and recycled to make useful products. They mainly look for glass, metals and plastic, which are then sold to scrap merchants who sell it onto small workshops and factories. In Mumbai there are over 250 000 ragpickers – at least 100 000 of whom are under the age of 14. They typically work from 5 am until 8 pm or 9 pm, and may earn just $2 per day.

Air and water pollution

Air pollution is a significant health issue in Mumbai and across India as a whole. It is responsible for more deaths (1.85 million in 2015) than in any other country. Major causes include the burning of fuel in homes and businesses, vehicle exhaust fumes and factory emissions. Average nitric oxide and nitrogen oxide levels have been recorded at 250 micrograms per cubic metre (mcg/m^3), more than three times the recommended safe limit of 80 mcg/m^3. Air pollution is directly or partially responsible for respiratory illness, lung diseases, pneumonia, asthma, lung cancer, heart disease and even damage to internal organs such as the brain, liver and kidney. It is particularly damaging to the lungs of young children. In 2015 an air quality index was introduced to monitor and improve air quality in Mumbai. Suggestions for air quality improvements included using LPG instead of burning coal, introducing a low benzene petrol, reducing diesel use, replacing traditional cooking stoves, restricting open burning of biomass, improving public transport, and charging higher road tax on older vehicles. The government recognises the need to encourage new technologies that can reduce emissions of sulphur dioxide and nitrogen oxide but limits also need to be set and enforced on emissions.

Water pollution is also a serious problem, causing a major threat to public health and damaging the local fishing industry – commercial catches have dropped by over 50 per cent in the past 10 years. It has also affected the nearby beaches, causing damage to tourism and the local economy. It can result in epidemics of disease such as typhoid and diarrhoea.

Sources of water pollution:

- The dumping of domestic waste and organic waste heavily pollute rivers flowing into the Arabian Sea.
- Runoff from open sewers in the slums and squatter settlements pollute rivers, such as the Mithi.
- Illegal activities such as washing boats, cleaning oil drums and discharging toxic and hazardous waste into the rivers.
- Tonnes of raw sewage pour into the estuaries and sea each day.
- Tonnes of industrial waste enter the sea each day.
- Oil spills from local oil refineries.
- Ships have been known to empty their fuel tanks in the sea because there are no facilities to dispose of the fuel properly.

To help reduce water pollution, new sewage treatment plants have been built, fines have been imposed for illegal dumping of pollutants, and new flush latrines and sewers have been introduced in some slums and squatter settlements.

C *One of Dharavi's recycling 'slumdog entrepreneurs'*

ACTIVITIES

1. Most of Mumbai's waste goes to landfill. Explain the environmental problems associated with landfill sites. How could waste disposal in Mumbai be made more sustainable?
2. Explain why so much e-waste has to be disposed of in Mumbai.
3. What do the charts **A** and **B** show about waste disposal in Mumbai?
4. How do ragpickers make a living? What are the hazards of this work?
5. Explain the main causes and effects of air and water pollution in Mumbai.

Stretch yourself

Investigate the types of products that are recycled in Dharavi. Why are recycling rates so high in Mumbai? How do these rates compare with your home city or area?

Practice question

Explain why air pollution is a major problem for people who live in Mumbai. *(4 marks)*

13.8 Managing traffic congestion

On this spread you will find out about the challenges of traffic congestion in Mumbai

Example

Traffic problems

Mumbai is one of the most congested cities in India (photo **A**). This is the result of rapid population increase, economic growth and the expansion of motorised transport. Traffic congestion increases stress and air pollution levels, and wastes time for commuters and businesses. This additional time has economic effects, as more needs to be spent on fuel and drivers working for commercial companies. Not surprisingly, a large proportion of people rely on walking or make use of two-wheelers and auto rickshaws for their journeys (chart **B**).

The number of cars increased by over 57 per cent between 2009 and 2017, while the use of buses increased by 23 per cent. There are 430 vehicles per kilometre in Mumbai – the highest density of any city in India (Kolkata has the second highest with 308 vehicles per kilometre). Journeys, especially during peak rush hour periods, are subject to lengthy delays and local buses are often dangerously overcrowded.

Train journeys make up almost a quarter of all journeys in Mumbai (chart **B**). The colonial-era train network is the main method of public transport, but the trains invariably carry up to four times more passengers than their seating capacity allows (photo **C**). Over 3500 people die on Mumbai's railways each year. Most deaths are caused by passengers crossing tracks, sitting on train roofs and being electrocuted by overhead cables, or hanging from doors and windows.

Did you know?
Mumbai railways carry 2.2 billion passengers every year.

A *Congested roads in Mumbai*

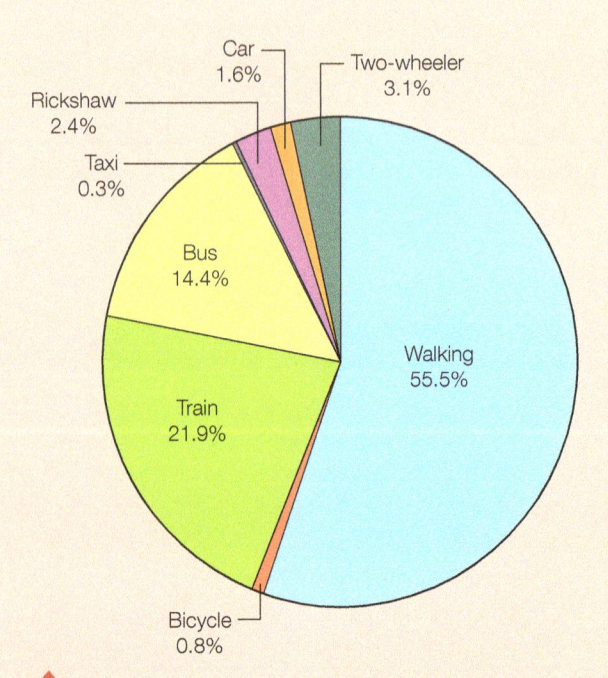

Mode of transport for journeys in Mumbai:
- Walking 55.5%
- Train 21.9%
- Bus 14.4%
- Two-wheeler 3.1%
- Rickshaw 2.4%
- Car 1.6%
- Bicycle 0.8%
- Taxi 0.3%

B *Mode of transport for journeys in Mumbai*

C *Mumbai's overcrowded trains*

Urban growth

Traffic solutions

A number of improvements have been aimed at reducing traffic congestion and improving air quality:

- Over 40 new roads are planned by 2020, aiming to make traffic movement more efficient and help cut down on journey times.

- The Western Freeway, an ambitious coastal link road project, is under construction. It will connect the central business district in South Mumbai to Kandivali in the north – a distance of almost 30 km.

- The first phase of the link road project, the Bandra–Worli Sea Link bridge, cost US$250 million and was completed in 2010 (photo **D**). It provides an improved connection between the city and the western suburbs, helping to reduce travel time from over an hour to around 20–30 minutes.

- A 5 km tunnel under the Sanjay Gandhi National Park is also planned.

- An expansion of the metro is underway, as well as a new monorail system (photo **E**).

- New toll roads are proposed for certain roads leading into the city centre to reduce congestion.

D *Bandra–Worli Sea Link*

E *Mumbai's new monorail system*

ACTIVITIES

1. What impacts does traffic congestion have on the people of Mumbai? Classify these into economic, social and environmental impacts.
2. What are the main types of transport used in Mumbai?
3. Explain why public transport in Mumbai is under so much pressure.
4. Describe efforts being made to reduce traffic congestion in Mumbai. Are these schemes likely to be successful? Explain your answer.

Stretch yourself

Research the activities of Brihanmumbai Electric Supply and Transport (BEST), the company responsible for supplying public transport and energy in Mumbai. What are the main issues it faces in providing public transport?

Practice question

Using an example of a city in an LIC or NEE, explain the issues resulting from traffic congestion and how they might be resolved. *(6 marks)*

13.9 Improving the quality of life for the urban poor

On this spread you will find out how urban planning is improving the quality of life in the Dharavi slum settlement in Mumbai

Example

Previous plans for Dharavi

The Dhavari **slum** is located close to the central business district of Mumbai (map **A**). The land is valuable and there have been many attempts to redevelop the area, but with limited success. Plans have included:

- clearing illegally constructed buildings and rebuilding in their place – though often people simply set up another **squatter settlement** elsewhere
- leasing slum land to community groups and giving loans for improvements
- privatising slum development, allowing commercial companies to improve the settlement – though many people could not afford the prices charged by the private companies
- community action, known as bottom-up development, where local people decided what was needed and worked with local organisations.

Current plans for redevelopment

Mumbai's Slum Rehabilitation Authority is now responsible for developing better housing on squatter sites or relocating residents to alternative accommodation. The scheme plans to:

- provide shopping centres, hospitals, schools, a piped water supply, electricity, roads and decent housing for local residents
- give land to commercial companies for **redevelopment**, on the condition that they build basic affordable housing for the slum residents
- divide Dharavi into 10 sectors, with each one developed by a different company
- build a number of high-rise tower blocks
- allocate each family a self-contained, carpeted dwelling of approximately 20 m², free of cost.

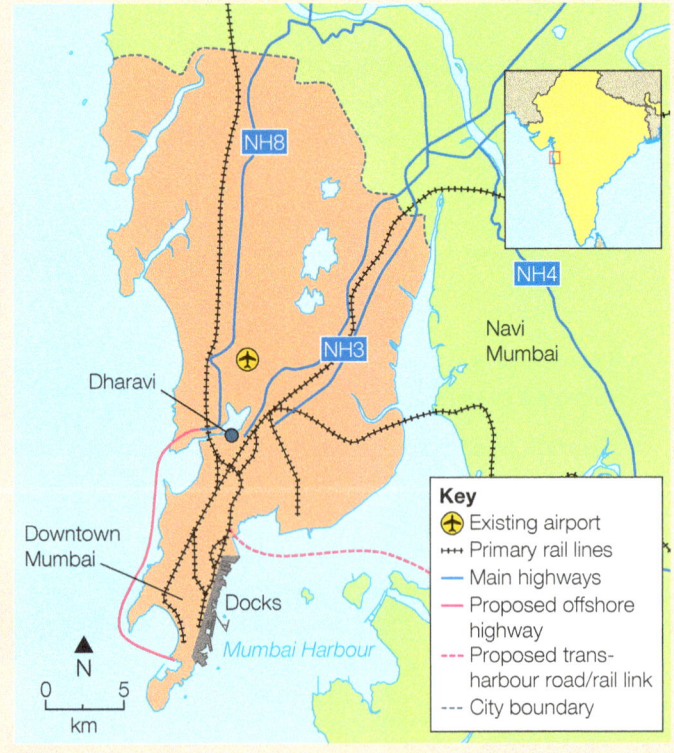

A Location of Dharavi

B Plan for Dharavi slum redevelopment

Urban growth

Problems with the scheme

- The guarantee of housing only applies to people who have lived in the slum from before 2000. Unfortunately, over 65 per cent of slum dwellers have arrived since then, so they are in danger of being evicted and moved elsewhere, usually to the edge of the city where there are few opportunities for employment. They then have to commute long distances.
- It has been difficult to persuade commercial businesses to invest in the project.
- Many people work in the informal sector, either in Dhavari or in downtown Mumbai, so they are reluctant to move.
- The demand for housing is much greater than the supply. By 2017, only 160 000 homes had been built for the residents of slums in Mumbai.
- Redevelopment of Dhavari is likely to destroy the huge number of small businesses (up to 20 000) in the slum areas, which are part of a thriving economy. Over 200 000 people work in the recycling industry – much of this industry would be wiped out. The government is only prepared to legalise and relocate industries that are not 'polluting'.
- Commercial developers are keen to make a profit from selling luxury apartments and building shopping complexes. These are inaccessible to the poor residents of Dhavari.

Other projects

Communal land trust: In 2017, it was proposed some land is given to a communal land trust, which would consult with the local community to build homes for almost 60 000 families. This project is likely to cost US$2.4 billion. The challenge for the planners is to improve conditions for the urban poor but at the same time protect the local social communities.

Slum Sanitation Project: This project has started to improve sanitation facilities for up to 1 million slum dwellers. Over 400 community toilet blocks have been introduced with approximately 6000 individual toilets.

Mumbai Electrification Project: So far, this has provided over 10 000 slum residents with new electricity connections.

ACTIVITIES

1. There have been many suggestions of ways to improve the quality of life for the residents of Dharavi. Suggest the possible advantages and disadvantages of each method listed below.
   a. Provide building materials so residents can build stronger, safer houses.
   b. Provide a clean, safe water supply.
   c. Give residents a free, one-room flat in a tower block to make space for luxury high-rise homes.
   d. Install hygienic toilets to replace the filthy, broken toilet blocks.
   e. Upgrade streets and storm drains so residents can improve their homes and work spaces.
   f. Allow access to credit to allow residents to improve their homes.
   g. Construct community buildings so that residents have a social centre.
   h. Provide a legal and safe electricity supply to all slum homes.
   i. Build paved and formally named roads.
   j. Charge tourists to take a guided tour of the slum area.
   k. Invest in a new police unit patrolling the community to reduce crime.
   l. Make 'Dharavi' a brand name to help market and sell all the products produced in the slum.
2. Explain why many local people have been opposed to Mumbai's Slum Rehabilitation Authority plans.
3. What difficulties have there been in attempts to improve the slum housing in Mumbai?
4. How have recent strategies for slum improvement in Dharavi attempted to involve local people?
5. With a partner, discuss whether Dharavi should be demolished or improved.
6. Explain how an urban planning scheme in Mumbai has had a positive effect on local residents.

Stretch yourself

Research the Dharavi redevelopment plans in more detail. Find out the main changes proposed for the area and consider the advantages and disadvantages for the local people.

Practice question

Evaluate the impacts of an urban planning scheme in a named LIC or NEE city. *(9 marks)*

14 World cities

14.1 What is a world city?

In this spread you will find out what a world city is and where they are

A **world city** is an important multinational city, having a large influence over the whole world. It has a large and diverse population. A **megacity** has a population of over 10 million, but not all have all the characteristics of a world city. A world city is generally considered to be a focal point in the global economy, such as London, New York and Tokyo. It is ranked by the importance of its global trade, politics, culture, science and the degree to which it is connected with the global economic system (table **A**). They tend to have similar characteristics, as shown in diagram **C**.

A++	London, New York
A+	Paris, Hong Kong
A	Moscow, Mumbai
A–	Zurich, Johannesburg

A Ratings of world cities

Distribution of world cities

The majority of world cities are situated in higher-income countries (HICs). These cities are not necessarily the largest in population or area, but they exert a powerful economic, cultural and political influence, both regionally and globally. They tend to have strong connections with other parts of the world. A significant number of world cities are located in Europe (e.g. London, Paris, Amsterdam, Brussels). Several are found in the USA (e.g. New York, Chicago, Los Angeles). Another cluster is concentrated in south and east Asia (e.g. Tokyo, Shanghai, Beijing, Hong Kong, Mumbai, Singapore). São Paulo, Buenos Aires, Sydney and Johannesburg can be considered world cities, though there are relatively few in the southern hemisphere.

B Current and future megacities, 2015–2030 (population figures represent those of the wider metropolitan area for each city)

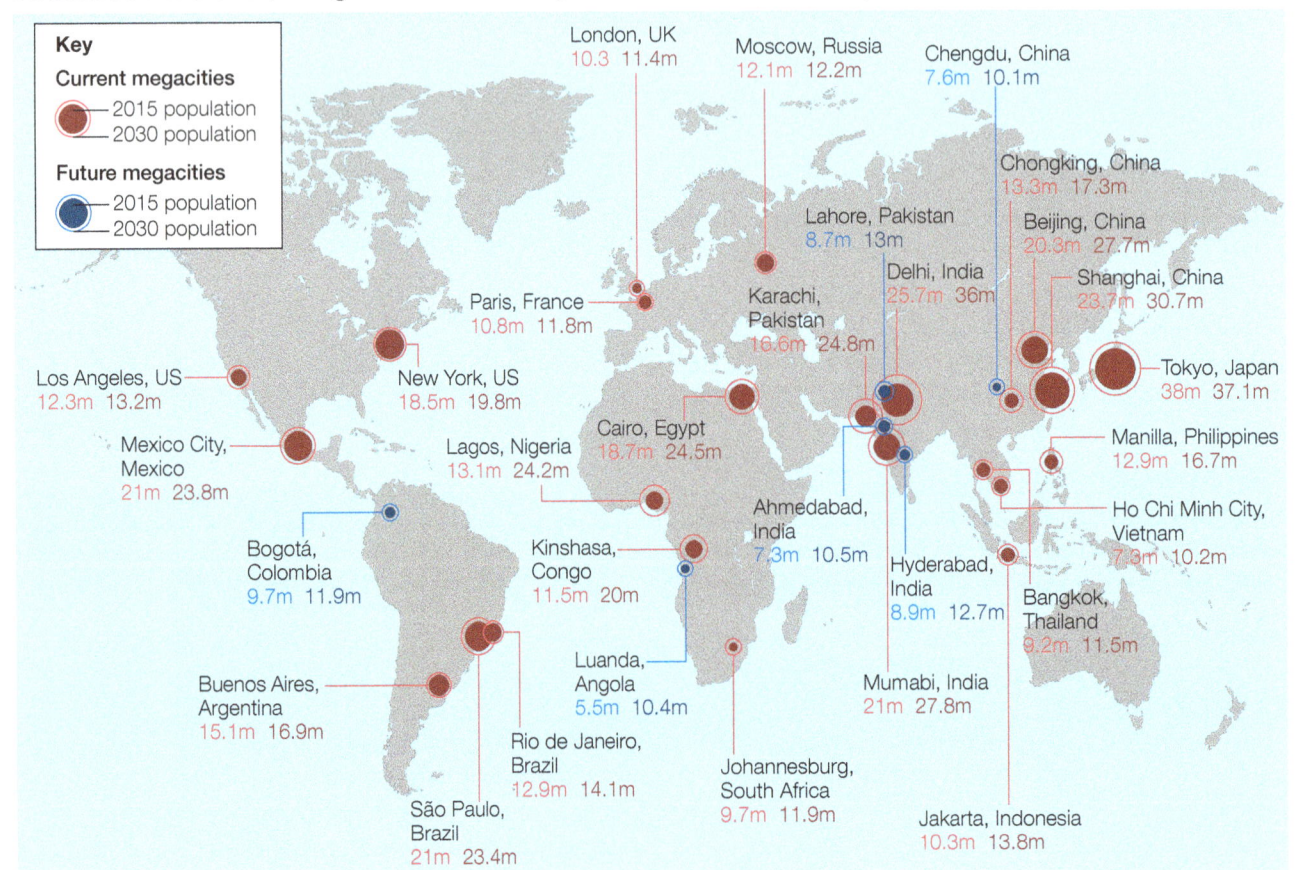

Key
Current megacities
- 2015 population
- 2030 population

Future megacities
- 2015 population
- 2030 population

London, UK 10.3 11.4m
Moscow, Russia 12.1m 12.2m
Chengdu, China 7.6m 10.1m
Chongking, China 13.3m 17.3m
Lahore, Pakistan 8.7m 13m
Beijing, China 20.3m 27.7m
Paris, France 10.8m 11.8m
Delhi, India 25.7m 36m
Shanghai, China 23.7m 30.7m
Karachi, Pakistan 16.6m 24.8m
Los Angeles, US 12.3m 13.2m
New York, US 18.5m 19.8m
Tokyo, Japan 38m 37.1m
Mexico City, Mexico 21m 23.8m
Cairo, Egypt 18.7m 24.5m
Manilla, Philippines 12.9m 16.7m
Lagos, Nigeria 13.1m 24.2m
Ahmedabad, India 7.3m 10.5m
Ho Chi Minh City, Vietnam 7.3m 10.2m
Bogotá, Colombia 9.7m 11.9m
Kinshasa, Congo 11.5m 20m
Hyderabad, India 8.9m 12.7m
Bangkok, Thailand 9.2m 11.5m
Buenos Aires, Argentina 15.1m 16.9m
Luanda, Angola 5.5m 10.4m
Mumbai, India 21m 27.8m
Rio de Janeiro, Brazil 12.9m 14.1m
Johannesburg, South Africa 9.7m 11.9m
Jakarta, Indonesia 10.3m 13.8m
São Paulo, Brazil 21m 23.4m

World cities

Economic features
- Headquarters of several transnational corporations (TNCs)
- International financial institutions
- Stock exchange with international influence
- Major centre for finance with large banks, investment institutions, insurance companies, accountancy firms

Political features
- Major political centre, having powerful influence on international events and world affairs
- Large and diverse population

What does a world city look like?

Transport features
- Large mass transport networks such as metro and rail
- Important international airport(s)

Cultural features
- Established cultural institutions, including well-known museums, theatres, opera companies, orchestras and art galleries
- Influential media/news outlets providing for global networks
- Renowned legal, sporting, medical and entertainment facilities
- Internationally recognised, high-performing universities, known for advanced research
- International tourist attractions

C Characteristics of world cities

ACTIVITIES

1. Outline the differences between a megacity and a world city.
2. Explain how world cities are connected.
3. On a world map, plot the locations of the following world cities (as defined by the Globalization and World Cities Research Network). Use different colours for the three types. Describe the distribution of these cities. Which parts of the world do not appear to have many world cities?

    Alpha++: London, New York, Tokyo

    Alpha+: Hong Kong, Paris, Singapore, Shanghai, Dubai, Sydney, Beijing

    Alpha: Milan, Toronto, São Paulo, Madrid, Chicago, Mumbai, Los Angeles, Moscow, Frankfurt, Mexico City, Amsterdam, Kuala Lumpur, Brussels

4. Explain why some large megacities have not become world cities.

Maths skills

1. Count up the number of megacities found in each continent shown in map **B**. Which continent has the greatest number? In which continents are the future megacities?
2. Which cities show the greatest increase in population between 2015 and 2030 (projected)?
3. Work out the percentage population growth rates for 2015–2030 in Lagos, Delhi and London. Try to explain the differences in growth rates.

Stretch yourself

Research the growth of 'millionaire' cities (cities with a population of over 1 million). How many were there in 1900, 1950, 2000 and 2018? How has the distribution of these cities changed over time?

Practice question

Outline the distinctive features of world cities. *(4 marks)*

141

14.2 London: a world city

On this spread you will find out about London's location and its population

Example

For over 200 years London has been a city of both national and international importance. It is by far the largest city in the UK and dominates the economic activity of the country. London has worldwide connections and has become the pre-eminent global financial centre. More international tourists visit London than any other city and London has become renowned for its cultural life, shopping, fashion and entertainment. It is home to more universities and other higher education facilities than anywhere else in Europe.

Location and development

The original site of London was selected because it was a piece of fairly dry land near a fording point (and eventually a bridging point) across the River Thames. The city was built initially on the north bank of the Thames but then developed on both banks. London is situated in south-east England, approximately 50km inland from the North Sea, at the meeting point of several routeways. It lies in a clay basin, with the chalk hills of the North and South Downs to the south and the Chiltern Hills to the north-west. When new bridges were built in the eighteenth century, the city spread into the surrounding countryside in a process of rapid urban sprawl.

A London's location in England, UK

By 1940 the population had reached 8.3 million but, following the Second World War, it decreased to 6.3 million by 1991. Since then the number of inhabitants has grown rapidly to over 8.8 million (2018), with both Inner and Outer London growing in size. This total represents 14 per cent of the UK population on just 0.6 per cent of the land area. London's population is projected to reach 11.5 million by 2050 (chart **B**). The wider city region, covering much of the south-east, has a population of approximately 23 million. Greater London covers an area of almost 1600 km^2. It measures 60 km west to east, 50 km north to south and has a population density in excess of 5000 people per square kilometre.

Did you know?
London reached a population of 1 million by 1811 – the first city in the world to do so. It remained the most populated city until Tokyo's population surpassed it in 1957.

B London's changing population

142

World cities

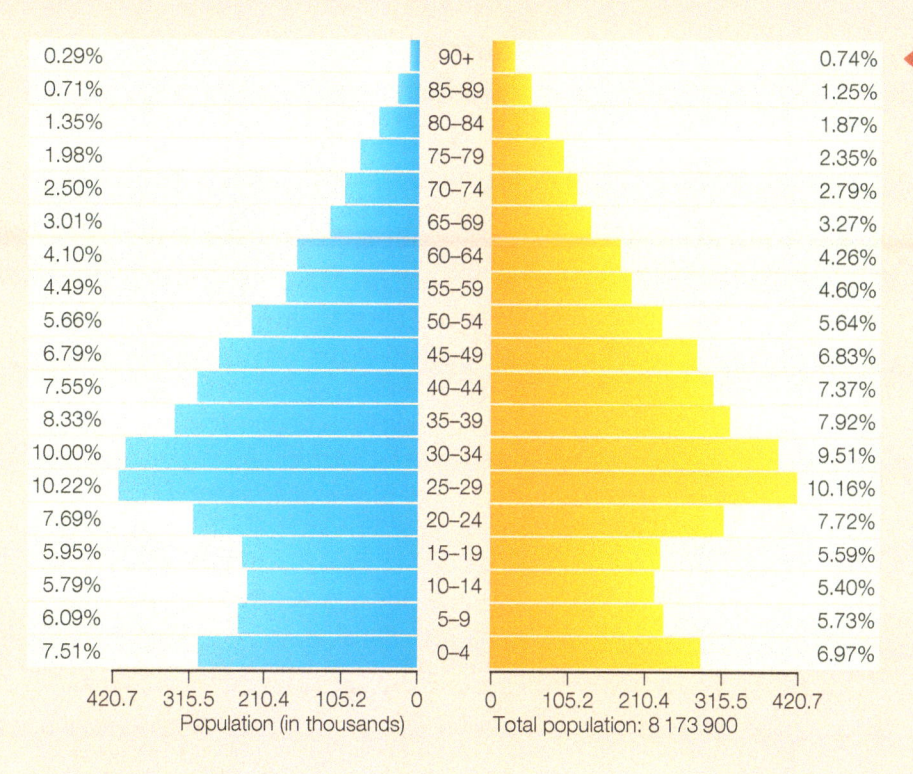

Male	Age	Female
0.29%	90+	0.74%
0.71%	85–89	1.25%
1.35%	80–84	1.87%
1.98%	75–79	2.35%
2.50%	70–74	2.79%
3.01%	65–69	3.27%
4.10%	60–64	4.26%
4.49%	55–59	4.60%
5.66%	50–54	5.64%
6.79%	45–49	6.83%
7.55%	40–44	7.37%
8.33%	35–39	7.92%
10.00%	30–34	9.51%
10.22%	25–29	10.16%
7.69%	20–24	7.72%
5.95%	15–19	5.59%
5.79%	10–14	5.40%
6.09%	5–9	5.73%
7.51%	0–4	6.97%

Population (in thousands)
Total population: 8 173 900

C London's population by age and sex, 2011

Within Europe, London has strong economic connections with other major cities, such as Paris, Geneva, Milan and Frankfurt, and is integral to the economic core of the region. However, its relationship with Europe is uncertain as the UK prepares to leave the European Union in 2019.

Chart **C** shows that a significant proportion of London's population is aged 20–34 (more than 20 per cent). The increasing number of 0–4 year olds suggests a rising birth rate and, typical of many large cities, there are relatively few in the older age groups.

D London is classed as a A++ world city

London: a world city

43	Romans create the settlement of Londinium at a bridging point across the River Thames. A defensive wall is built to protect the settlement from invasion (photo **F**)
260	London is a flourishing town. Population 45 000
410	London is mostly abandoned after the Roman period ends
600–900	London grows slowly. Population 10 000
1348	The Black Death spreads quickly, killing up to half the population
1500	Population 75 000. Several outbreaks of the plague
1600	Population 200 000
1666	The Great Fire of London. Most of London is destroyed
1714	Population 630 000
1801	Population 1 million
1840	Population 2 million. London is the largest and most influential city in the world
1900	Population 6 million
1906	The world's first underground railway service opens
1921	Population 7.5 million
1940	The Blitz (German bombing) causes widespread destruction. Population 8.3 million
1946	Heathrow Airport opens
1961	Population 8 million
1981	Population 6.7 million
1982	The Thames Barrier is built (to protect London from tidal floods)
1986	The M25, the world's longest orbital motorway, is completed around London
1991	Population 6.3 million
1994	The Eurostar high-speed rail link to Paris via the Channel Tunnel opens
2000	New landmarks are built to celebrate the Millennium, e.g. the London Eye, the Millennium Dome
2001	Population 7.2 million
2012	London hosts the Summer Olympics
2017	Population 8.8 million

E London's population timeline

National and international migration

Graph **G** shows that since 1998 domestic (within the UK) migration has been negative; that is, the number of people moving out of London has been greater than the number of UK residents moving in. International net migration has always been positive during the time period shown, so there have always been more foreign-born people moving into London than out of it. Since 2001, the number of foreign-born residents has shown a substantial increase, rising by 1.3 million (over 60 per cent). Many migrants are in their 20s and 30s and are of child-bearing age, so the rate of natural increase has gone up.

International migration has changed the character of London. It is genuinely one of the most multicultural places on the planet, with many different races, cultures and languages in evidence throughout the city. Many wealthy migrants from HICs (e.g. USA and EU countries) characteristically stay a few years to make money and then return to their home countries. Poorer migrants from lower-income countries (LICs) (e.g. India, Pakistan, Jamaica and Nigeria) more often stay permanently. In 2017, figures indicate 37 per cent of Londoners were born abroad.

F Ruins of an Ancient Roman wall, built to protect Londinium from invasion – this is now the edge of the square mile of the City

World cities

Key
- Domestic emigration
- Domestic immigration
- International immigration
- International emigration
- Difference (net migration)

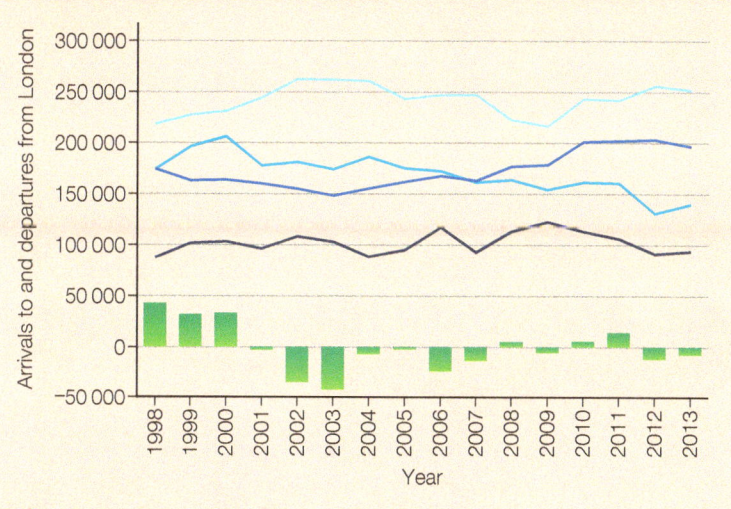

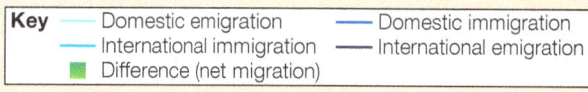

G People moving into and out of London

Did you know?
Over 300 languages are spoken in London – more than in any other city in the world. The most established of these include Gujarati, Bengali, Mandarin, Punjabi, Hokkien and Cantonese.

Impacts of international migration to London

Positive impacts

- *Migrants make money*: between 2000 and 2017, migrants have contributed more than US$28 billion to UK finances.
- *Migrants bring skills*: these would have cost the government US$9.6 billion if they were educated in the UK.
- *Migrants pay taxes*: they tend to stay employed and most migrants are less reliant on benefits than UK-born workers (they are 43 per cent less likely to receive state benefits than UK-born residents).
- *Migrants bring diversity*: new cultures bring new talents, foods, music and entertainment.

Negative impacts

- *Housing shortages* due to population pressures in London.
- *Increased birth rates,* putting pressure on schools and health services.
- *Lower wages*: new immigrants may accept lower-paid jobs than London locals, which can drive down wages.
- *Unaffordable housing*: money from wealthy foreign investors and wealthy migrants can push up house prices, reducing the supply of affordable housing.

ACTIVITIES

1. Explain why London is considered to be a world city. Give three reasons why London is influential worldwide and three reasons why it is influential in the UK.
2. Using timeline **E**, construct a line graph to shown London's changing population. This can be done from AD43, or from 1801 to show more recent trends. Annotate the timeline to show reasons for increases and decreases in population.
3. Describe how the population of London has changed since 1801. Explain the changes shown in graph **B**. What do you think will happen to the population of London in the future? Explain why.
4. What does population pyramid **C** show about age distribution in London? (Which age groups are largest and smallest?)
5. Make a list of the advantages and disadvantages of migration for London. What problems might occur if many recent migrants returned to their home countries?

Stretch yourself

Research the proportion of different nationalities that now live in London. Explain why these different groups have come to London and what contribution they make to London's life.

Practice question

Using an example of a city in an HIC, explain why national and international migrants are attracted to large cities. (6 marks)

14.3 The importance of London as a world city

In this spread you will find out about London's national and global importance

Example

A Panorama of some of London's important buildings and attractions

Finance

London is the most influential financial centre worldwide. It is a world leader in the global insurance industry, foreign exchange, banking transactions and trade on the stock market. Londoners earn 23 per cent more than the UK average wage and, therefore, have greater purchasing power. The financial sector is a large contributor to the UK economy, generating 22 per cent of the country's GDP, and employs investors and managers from many parts of the world. Foreign investment in property has increased dramatically, causing a significant rise in property prices. Some skyscrapers such as the Shard have been purchased by foreign investors, as have some famous football teams.

Business

There has been growth in most sectors in recent years. The number of businesses per 1000 people is greater than in the rest of the UK. London has a workforce of over 5 million and is home to the headquarters of many large companies, including TNCs. The number of jobs in London has been rising almost continuously since 1990 and at least 1.3 million workers commute into central London each day. The City of London (the financial district) has a resident population of 6000, which increases to almost 400 000 on a typical working day.

Even the recession after 2007 did not really slow the rise in employment. Graph **B** shows that the biggest growth in jobs was in services, especially professional, scientific, technical and real estate activities. The biggest decline in was in manufacturing – London has very few factories left.

Did you know? London has 215 museums and over 800 art galleries. In 2017, 47 million people visited London museums.

B Employment changes in London, 1996–2014

Primary and utilities
Manufacturing
Construction
Wholesale and motor trades
Retail
Transportation and storage
Accommodation and food service activities
Information and communication
Financial and insurance activities
Real estate
Professional, scientific and technical
Administrative and support service activities
Public administration and defence, compulory social security
Education
Human health and social work activities
Arts, entertainment and recreation
Other service activities
All industries

% change between 1996 and 2014

World cities

Culture

Increasing global interconnections and migrations mean that large cities such as London, especially in HICs, have huge numbers of people of different races, religions and cultures. A significant proportion of London's population are migrants who were born abroad. This has strongly influenced the entertainment, cuisine, sport and lifestyle of the city, including its food (Indian, Chinese and Thai), fashion (French, Italian), music (American, African), films (Bollywood) and festivals (Notting Hill Carnival). London has one of the highest concentrations of museums and art galleries of any city and is home to one of the most diverse range of entertainment venues in the world.

Politics

The UK Parliament, based in London, is made up of government ministers elected to the House of Commons every five years and peers nominated to the House of Lords by the government. The monarch, currently Queen Elizabeth II, resides at Buckingham Palace and has a largely ceremonial role. In the past, the UK was one of the world's superpowers, with an extensive empire in the Americas, Africa and the Asian Pacific. Nowadays, the UK is still an influential member of important international organisations such as the G8, NATO and the UN Security Council. It also has strong links with Commonwealth countries – a voluntary group of 53 countries, many of which were once British colonies.

Greater London has a directly elected mayor and its own local government, which makes many political decisions.

Trade

London has trade links with many parts of the world, as well as within the UK. It has a trade surplus (exports exceed imports) of approximately US$41 billion per year (diagram **C**). Service exports in particular are important, with London contributing over 50 per cent of the total for the UK. Its principal links are with the EU, which operates a single market, whereby goods can be traded between member states without tariffs or taxes. The USA is also an important trading partner and there has been a recent growth in trade with China. The internet is becoming more significant for trade, for example in finance, communications and the creative industries – all of which are well represented in London.

Television is one of the UK's most successful media exports to English-speaking countries, accounting for over US$1.33 billion of export earnings in 2016.

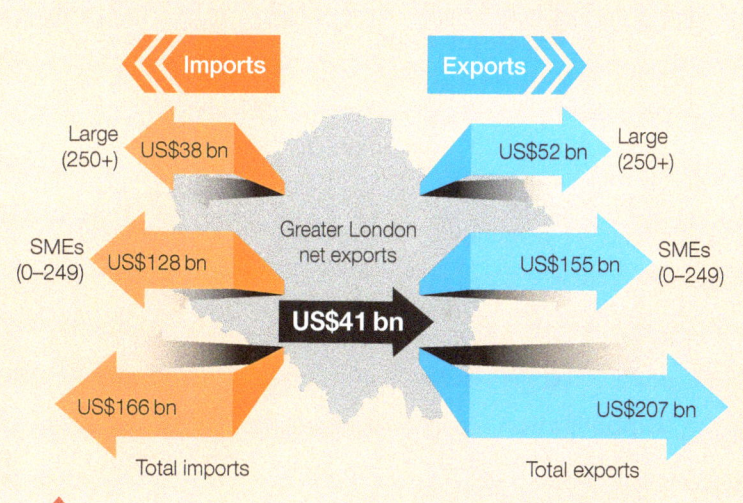

C London's international trade in 12 months, 2013–14

	Imports	Exports	
Large (250+)	US$38 bn	US$52 bn	Large (250+)
SMEs (0–249)	US$128 bn	US$155 bn	SMEs (0–249)
Total imports	US$166 bn	US$207 bn	Total exports

Greater London net exports: US$41 bn

ACTIVITIES

1. Explain why the financial sector is so important to London and to the whole UK.
2. Describe recent changes in employment in London. What types of jobs have shown the greatest percentage increase, and which have decreased in importance?
3. Study photo **A**. Try to identify the landmarks shown. Explain why London has become such a popular city for international tourists.
4. London's trade surplus with the rest of the world was US$41 billion in 2014. Explain what this means.
5. What might be the benefits and problems of living in a large city such as London?

Stretch yourself

Find out more about the cultural connections between London and the rest of the world. This includes fashion, music, sport, film and other entertainment. Use logos and photos to illustrate your work.

Practice question

Explain how London has maintained its position as a world city. *(6 marks)*

14.4 London's economic, social and environmental opportunities

In this spread you will find out about London's economic, social and environmental opportunities

Example

Economic: employment

In the past few decades, employment patterns have changed in London and the rest of the UK. Manufacturing has declined because:

- technology has replaced many human roles in modern industries, such as car production
- other countries, such as China, Malaysia and Indonesia, can produce cheaper goods as labour there is less expensive
- lack of investment, high labour costs and outdated machinery made UK products too expensive.

There has been a big shift from the manufacturing sector to the service (tertiary) sector – health care, office work, financial services and retail. Today, the service sector contributes over 81 per cent to the UK's economic output, compared with 46 per cent in 1948.

Most recently, the quaternary sector has developed, creating jobs in research, information technology and the media. London is now a world centre for financial services (banking, insurance, securities dealing and fund management), media, information and communication, research and the creative industries.

Globalisation has been partly responsible for the explosion of the quaternary sector in London, with many people now working on global brands and products. It has also boosted world trade and enabled more products to be imported to the UK.

However, unemployment is slightly higher in London than in other parts of the UK (5.6 per cent compared with 4.4 per cent for the UK in 2017 – see graph **A**). Map **B** illustrates that unemployment varies considerably between London boroughs.

Environmental: urban greening

Urban greening means to increase the amount and proportion of green spaces within a city. These green spaces are essential for people's quality of life.

Almost 48 per cent of London can be classified as open or green space (map **C**). With 8 million trees in London (roughly one per person), it is the world's largest 'urban forest'. Parks, woodlands and even domestic gardens

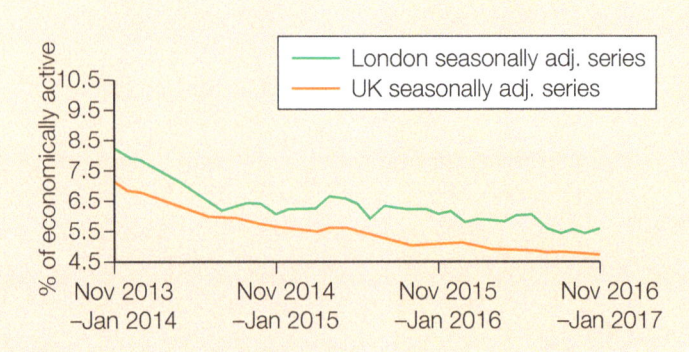

A Unemployment rate in London and the UK, 2013–17

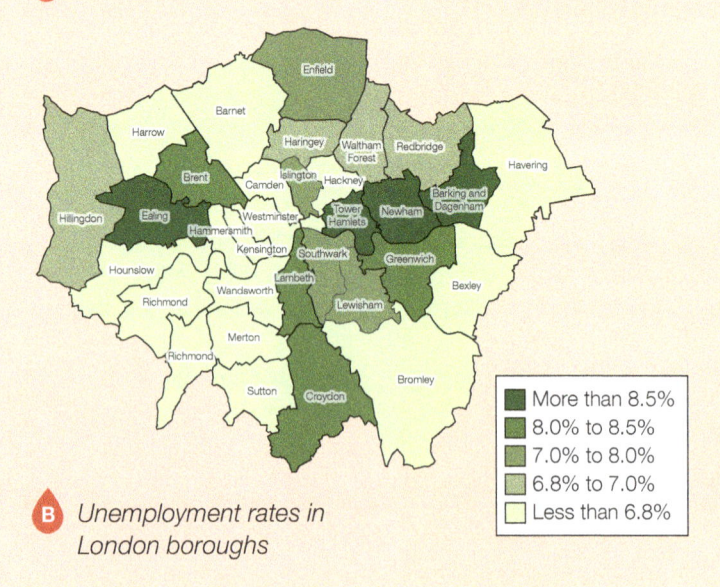

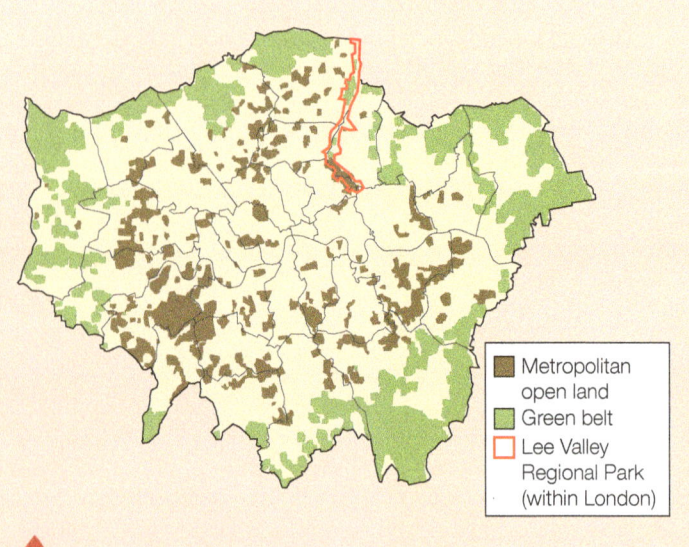

B Unemployment rates in London boroughs

- More than 8.5%
- 8.0 to 8.5%
- 7.0 to 8.0%
- 6.8 to 7.0%
- Less than 6.8%

C Areas of green space in London

- Metropolitan open land
- Green belt
- Lee Valley Regional Park (within London)

148

provide a habitat for wildlife, including birds, insects and mammals. There are 13 000 wildlife species in London. Londoners utilise 30 000 allotments (shared open spaces where people grow their own food).

Strategies to offer green spaces within London's urban area:

- A wide range of green spaces for public use, including Hampstead Heath, Burnham Beeches, Queens Park and Stoke Common, provide a mix of open space, wildlife habitat and recreational areas. London has more big parks than many cities. They include royal parks, such as Hyde Park, which once belonged to the royal family.

- Ecological conservation areas, designed to encourage wildlife back into the city, make cheap use of an otherwise derelict areas, reintroduce species and reduce maintenance costs.

- Rooftop green spaces – the Greater London Authority has produced a map of around 700 green roofs in central London alone, covering an area of 17.5 hectares (around 25 football pitches). These roofs are used as recreational spaces and spaces to grow plants.

- Canals, rivers and river jetties provide significant water bird breeding roosts.

- Major new building projects take into consideration urban green spaces, including the Olympic Village.

Social: recreation and entertainment

Being a large city with a diverse population, London has a huge range of recreational and entertainment venues as well as many cultural attractions.

300 music venues, nightclubs and comedy clubs (e.g. Wembley Arena, O2, Brixton Academy, Ministry of Sound, The Comedy Store)	'Theatreland', mainly concentrated in the West End, with over 200 shows a day and 15 million attendances per year	240 museums (e.g. British Museum, Victoria and Albert, Natural History, Science, Imperial War)
World-class dance and ballet (e.g. Royal Opera House, Coliseum, Sadlers Wells)	Over 20% of the UK's cinema screens are located in London (800)	850 art galleries (e.g. Tate Galleries, National Gallery)
Tourist attractions (e.g. Buckingham Palace and the Changing of the Guard, Big Ben and the Houses of Parliament, St Paul's Cathedral, Piccadilly Circus, Trafalgar Square), including four UNESCO world heritage sites: Tower of London, Maritime Greenwich, Westminster Palace and Kew's Royal Botanic Gardens. London is the most visited city in the world, with over 19 million overseas visitors per year	Over 300 festivals and carnivals a year (e.g. Notting Hill Carnival, Carnaval Del Pueblo, Thames Festival)	London is the world's third busiest film production centre
	World-famous sports venues (e.g. Premier League football clubs, cricket at Lords and the Oval, Rugby Union at Twickenham, rowing on the Thames, athletics at the London Stadium)	Classical music venues (e.g. Barbican Centre, Royal Albert Hall, Royal Festival Hall)

ACTIVITIES

1. a Study graph **A**. Compare unemployment rates between London and the whole UK between 2013 and 2017.
   b Study map **B**. Describe the distribution of unemployment rates across London.
2. a Estimate the percentage area of green or open space in London.
   b Describe where the different types of open space are found in London.
3. a What are the advantages of green or open space in a city?
   b Why is it sometimes difficult to keep areas of open space intact?

Stretch yourself

Give a short presentation on the social and environmental opportunities offered in London to one of the following: a teenager; the parent of a young family; or a pensioner.

Practice question

Assess the extent to which a named world city provides economic and social opportunities for the local population.
(9 marks)

14.5 London's economic and social challenges

Example

On this spread you will find out how change has created economic and social challenges in London

Urban deprivation

Urban deprivation in London is surprisingly high considering London is one of the world's wealthiest cities. There are great inequalities in housing, education, health and employment. It is estimated that over 20 per cent of adults are living in poverty, and this figure doubles for children. Some ethnic groups experience higher than average levels of poverty (e.g. some Asian and Afro-Caribbean communities).

Average earnings in London are higher than in the rest of the UK but the cost of living is high and many people earn low wages. There is a significant gap between rich and poor. The richest 10 per cent of Londoners own 60 per cent of all asset wealth in London, while the poorest 80 per cent of the population share just 20 per cent of the assets. These huge differences in wealth result in big differences in people's access to housing, education and health.

Levels of poverty are measured by the index of multiple deprivation (IMD). This is a measure that takes into account employment figures, educational attainment, health and access to housing. Some parts of London record low IMD levels, particularly certain boroughs in east and north London such as Tower Hamlets, Barking, Dagenham and Haringey. Some of these are in the 5 per cent most deprived areas in the UK. By contrast, many outer, suburban areas of London are among the least deprived in the country. Even within the same borough there are huge contrasts in wealth and poverty. For instance, Kensington and Chelsea contains some of the wealthiest and poorest citizens in London, as does Tower Hamlets.

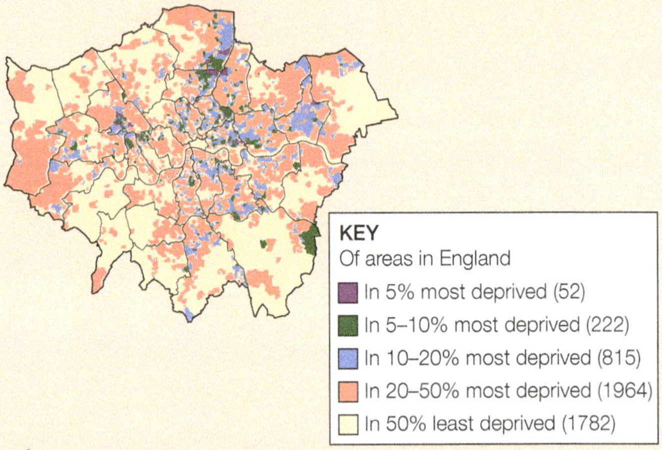

KEY
Of areas in England
- In 5% most deprived (52)
- In 5–10% most deprived (222)
- In 10–20% most deprived (815)
- In 20–50% most deprived (1964)
- In 50% least deprived (1782)

A *Index of multiple deprivation (IMD), 2015, London*

Housing

London is currently experiencing a severe housing crisis. More and more people are living alone, partly because of increasing levels of divorce. Higher net levels of immigration contribute to pressures on housing, as does an ageing population. At the same time, the population is increasing by up to 120 000 people per year, yet fewer than 25 000 homes are being built per year. This increased demand means prices have risen significantly and many Londoners are priced out of the housing market. In 2017, the average price of a home in central London, the most expensive area, was US$2.3 million, and in east London, the cheapest area, it was US$650 000. Buying a house in London costs roughly 14 times average earnings, which is the highest level on record.

Rents are also higher in London than in any other part of the country. More people in London rent than own their home and those that rent pay more than half their weekly pay on rent. While some live in poor-quality, small, rented accommodation, others live in some of the most expensive properties in the world. Finding they cannot afford to live in London, many workers are forced to commute increasing distances to work. Graph **B** shows the relative rise in prices for housing and rented accommodation.

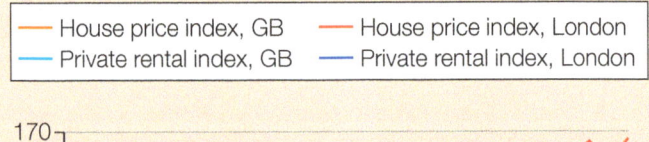

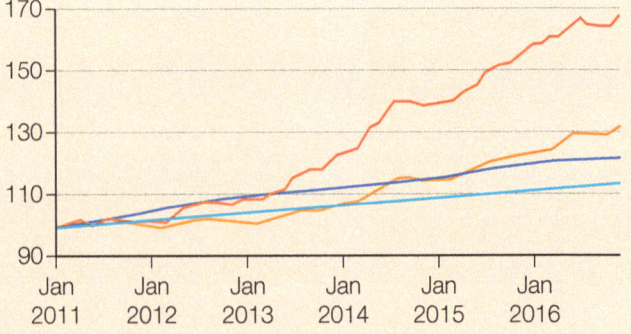

- House price index, GB
- House price index, London
- Private rental index, GB
- Private rental index, London

B *London's over-heated housing market*

World cities

Education

London is home to several prestigious universities. London University itself has approximately 20 colleges and educates over 125 000 students every year. This includes record numbers of overseas students – higher than in any other city in the world.

While there are great inequalities in children's education achievement across the city, some of the poorest boroughs have some of fastest-improving schools in the country. Greater London has the highest proportion of students achieving high grades compared with all other regions in England (chart **C**).

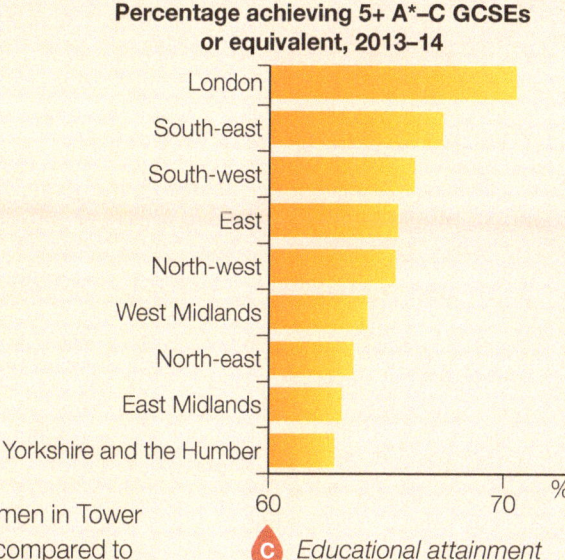

Percentage achieving 5+ A*–C GCSEs or equivalent, 2013–14

(Bar chart showing, from highest to lowest: London, South-east, South-west, East, North-west, West Midlands, North-east, East Midlands, Yorkshire and the Humber; x-axis 60–70%)

C *Educational attainment in England, by region*

Health

Health inequalities in London are among the worst in the UK. Women in Tower Hamlets, for instance, can expect to live for 30 years in ill health, compared to under 12 years for men in Enfield. Out of the 32 London boroughs, people living in Kensington and Chelsea, one of the wealthiest areas in the capital, have the longest life expectancy. Women in the borough live to an average age of 86.4 years, while men live to 83.4 years. Other London boroughs with high life expectancies include Bromley, Sutton, Bexley, Richmond on Thames, Harrow and Kingston on Thames. By contrast, Barking and Dagenham has the shortest life expectancy, where men live for 77.5 years and women live 81.8 years, on average. Greenwich, Newham, Islington, Lambeth, Brent and Tower Hamlets also recorded lower life expectancies. The inequalities are mostly the result of differences in people's homes, education, local environment, jobs and access to public services. There is a clear relationship between wealth and health – the poor are more likely to suffer from an avoidable illness or condition, lack social support, have higher levels of disability at an earlier age, and may have lower mental well-being.

ACTIVITIES

1. **a** What is meant by deprivation?
   b Study map **A**. Explain differences in levels of deprivation in London, as shown by the IMD.
2. **a** Study graph **B**. Describe changes in the house price index for London and the rest of the UK since 2011.
   b Explain why these changes have happened.
   c What are the effects of these changes on people purchasing homes for the first time?
   d What does it mean for people who wish to work in London?
   e By what percentage has rent on private houses increased in London and elsewhere in the UK since 2011?
3. Study graph **C**. Compare educational attainment of students in London with those in the rest of England.
4. Suggest why life expectancy in Barking and Dagenham is lower than in Kensington and Chelsea.
5. **a** On a map of London boroughs, plot the places that have the lowest and highest life expectancies.
   b Describe the pattern shown.

Stretch yourself

Research the cost of housing in London. Which areas are the most and least expensive? How do prices compare with the rest of the UK? Why is housing so expensive in London?

Practice question

Assess the extent of social and economic inequalities in London. *(6 marks)*

151

14.6 London's environmental challenges

On this spread you will find out about the issues of dereliction, building on brownfield and greenfield sites and the impact of urban sprawl

Example

Brownfield and greenfield sites

One possible answer to the housing shortage in London is to build on **greenfield sites** (photo **A**). These are usually agricultural land or woodland around the edge of the city that have never been built on. However, this can lead to **urban sprawl** and is not popular with people living in the countryside.

An alternative is to build on **brownfield sites** in the city (photo **B**). These are areas of previously developed land that may be derelict now and have potential for redevelopment. **Dereliction** may occur when people leave urban areas, abandoning buildings and houses. Often this land has been used for industry and the ground may be contaminated by chemicals. There are many sites like this in London due to the decline of the manufacturing industry. Recent government figures show that there are over 250 hectares of brownfield sites that are not in line for development of any sort. Developing the Olympic Park for the 2012 Olympics is a good example of how derelict land can be brought back into use (see 14.8). UK government policy is to encourage brownfield site development wherever possible. Future housing projects involve targets to develop 60 per cent brownfield sites and 40 per cent greenfield sites.

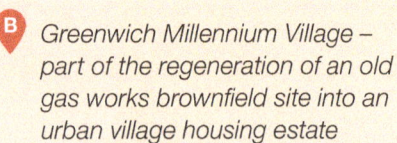

A New housing built on green belt land

B Greenwich Millennium Village – part of the regeneration of an old gas works brownfield site into an urban village housing estate

Developing brownfield sites

Advantages	Disadvantages
Helps to keep farmland from development by reusing existing sites. Close to bus and train routes in city centre, so less car use. Prevents urban sprawl as countryside is not built on. Redevelops old industrial sites that have fallen into disuse. Easier to get planning permission as councils want to use brownfield sites. Contaminated and unattractive sites are cleaned up. Near to facilities in towns such as shops, entertainment, hospitals and other services. Can make use of existing infrastructure such as electricity, gas and water supplies.	Tends to be costly as old buildings need to be demolished and the land cleared. Cost of land may be high in areas close to city centre. Some areas may be congested with traffic and not very accessible. Air and water pollution levels may be higher on old industrial sites. Locations may be in rundown parts of the inner city, so sites are often less desirable for housing.

Developing greenfield sites

Advantages	Disadvantages
More space for gardens as plots are larger. Some shops and business parks on the outskirts provide local facilities. Land may be cheaper in outer suburban and rural areas. Fewer problems of air and water pollution. Land is less likely to be contaminated. Possible to develop the site without considering existing buildings and layout. The environment may be healthier in outer suburban and semi-rural areas.	Noise and light pollution may increase as development occurs in rural–urban fringe. High-quality agricultural land may be built on, and recreational land is lost. Public transport is worse in rural areas, so more need for cars. People may have to commute long distances for employment. Rapid urban sprawl may cause the loss of vegetation and therefore wildlife habitats.

152

World cities

Urban sprawl

Urban sprawl involves the expansion of urban settlements into the surrounding rural areas. This has social, economic and environmental impacts:

- More people means that more cars are used, increasing traffic, air pollution and accidents.
- Higher taxes are needed to pay for infrastructure such as roads and water works to allow building developments to go ahead.
- People in sprawling communities may live further from their friends and family, leading to social isolation.
- Sprawling cities consume green spaces, affecting wildlife habitats as well as reducing available farmland and recreational space.

Should London's green belt be protected?

Around many cities in the UK, including London, is a **green belt** (map **C**). Established in 1947 to prevent further urban sprawl, green belt land is protected by strict planning controls. Since then, it has helped to maintain farmland, woodland and parkland around London. The purposes of the green belt around London were to stop the unrestricted growth of London into the countryside, to prevent urban settlements merging into each other, to protect rural areas, to preserve the character of historic towns and to encourage the recycling of derelict and other urban land. There is a great deal of opposition from local people to building houses on green belt land.

Now, with the pressure for more housing in London, people are questioning whether we can afford to keep the green belt. They suggest that less valuable areas of green belt land could be used for building new homes on greenfield sites. They argue that many sites have already been redeveloped and that the remaining brownfield land is insufficient to house London's growing population. A national shortage of new housing has meant that recent government policy has allowed the use of greenfield sites, despite fierce opposition by many existing residents.

Did you know? The number of households in London is expected to increase by 500 000 by 2030.

C London's green belt

ACTIVITIES

1. Explain why it is often preferable to build on former brownfield sites. What are the disadvantages of doing this?
2. Why are many people concerned about the spread of London into the surrounding rural areas?
3. Measure the width of the green belt around London in five places. What is the average width?
4. Is the green belt around London likely to survive? Give reasons for your answer.
5. Describe the differences between the homes shown in photos **A** and **B**. Which social groups are they targeted at?

Stretch yourself

Debate the case for and against development of the green belt around London. Consider the views of different interest groups such as: commuters who work in London; property developers; environmental campaigners; people who live on the edge of the green belt; Londoners trying to purchase their first home; the government department responsible for housing.

Practice question

Explain the housing issues affecting people living in London and how these issues might be resolved.
(6 marks)

14.7 Managing London's resources

On these spreads you will find out about London's challenges with food supply, traffic congestion, waste disposal and water and energy conservation

Food supply

By 2035, the population of London is expected to rise to over 10 million (from 8.3 million in 2017). This will increase the future demand for food. Despite its efficient and productive farming sector, the UK is not self-sufficient for food supplies. In fact, London imports about 48 per cent of the total food consumed and this proportion is increasing, partly because of London's multicultural population and the demand for foods from across the world.

Why London imports so much food:

- UK-produced food can be expensive due to poor harvests and the price of animal feed.
- Supermarkets, competing for low prices, can source cheaper food from abroad.
- Demand for greater choice and more exotic foods is increasing.
- The UK climate is unsuitable for the production of some foods, such as cocoa, tea and bananas.
- There is demand for seasonal produce all year round, such as strawberries and tomatoes.

While the majority of imports are from Europe, up to 150 countries supply food for London's population, including countries in Asia, Africa and South America.

Transporting food by air is very expensive, although much is also transported by boat. There is concern about the UK's dependency on foreign food imports and the need for greater food security. This has led to a growing interest in sourcing food locally to reduce carbon emissions. People are being encouraged to eat seasonal foods produced in the UK.

Keeping the city moving

London is one of the most congested cities in Europe. The average speed of traffic is just 23 km/h, falling to only 10.5 km/h in central London. A car journey during rush hour may take 50 per cent longer than at other times of the day. The city is a major hub for transport, with many railway services and major roads radiating from the capital. Transport for London (TfL) controls public transport and is responsible for the provision of underground trains (tubes), buses, river transport and the local rail network. There are several airports that serve London, including Heathrow and Gatwick – the two busiest airports in the UK.

London has a well-developed, integrated transport system, meaning that all forms of transport can link to one another. London also serves a transport network hub for the whole of the UK – many UK motorways converge on London's orbital ring road, the M25. Trains link the UK together at stations such as Kings Cross and connect to Europe via the Eurostar from St Pancras.

London also has an integrated cycle network. New cycle superhighways (photo **C**) encourage more people to cycle in an effort to reduce traffic and harmful emissions from vehicles. Over the past 50 years, cyclists have increased from 1 per cent to 15 per cent of road users in London.

Did you know?
London's Heathrow Airport has more international passengers per year than any other airport in the world.

A Traffic congestion in London

As people demand greater mobility and accessibility, the number of vehicles has increased, as has the problem of traffic congestion. Greater wealth has meant that 60 per cent of households in London have access to a car and 15 per cent have more than one car. Commercial transport is largely done by road and the development of online shopping has increased the number of delivery vehicles. Traffic congestion causes problems for:

- the environment – air pollution from vehicles, including nitrogen oxide and fine particulates; discolouration of buildings; noise pollution from heavy vehicles

- people's health – respiratory diseases such as asthma; stress caused by lengthy delays

- the economy – delays from late deliveries; drivers' wages (approximately US$8.5 billion in 2017).

Strategies to reduce traffic congestion

Congestion charging

Drivers pay US$20 to enter central London during the day. This policy was introduced in 2003 to cut down the number of vehicles, reduce the levels of traffic congestion and air pollution, encourage greater use of public transport, reduce accident rates and allow certain vehicles (e.g. taxis, buses and delivery vehicles) to operate more efficiently. If drivers fail to pay the congestion charge they are fined US$185 (electric cars are exempt from payment). The policy has had some success: the total number of vehicles has decreased by 10 per cent in the central zone; per mile crash rates are down 22 per cent; and carbon dioxide emissions have decreased 16 per cent. However, over two thirds of businesses in the central charging zone found that their sales and revenue decreased, and over a quarter of businesses have considered relocating outside the charging zone.

Encouraging bicycles

A bicycle hire scheme has operated in central London since 2010, and there are plans to extend the scheme into outer suburban areas soon. There are over 13 000 bikes available from 800 docking stations. Aimed at commuters as well as tourists and visitors, the project hopes to reduce congestion and pollution. Bike lanes on most major roads and 'cycle superhighways' have been created to encourage more people to cycle.

Improvements to public transport

Crossrail is a new, east–west rail route across London, linking Shenfield and Abbey Wood in the east with Reading and Heathrow in the west. It tunnels under the city centre, reducing journey times and increasing the total number of passenger journeys in London. It is hoped Crossrail 2, a similar project on a north–south route across London, will open in 2030. The schemes will improve the integrated transport system in London by providing more interchanges with the Underground network.

B *Central London Congestion Charge zone*

Did you know?
Covering 188 km, the M25 motorway is the world's longest orbital road around a city.

C *Cyclists using the new east–west cycle superhighway on the Embankment in the City of Westminster*

155

Managing London's resources

Waste disposal, reducing and recycling

Not surprisingly, a city the size of London produces vast amounts of waste. A mix of methods are used to deal with this waste, including recycling, landfill (where the waste is buried in the ground) and incineration (where the waste is burned, often to produce electricity). A quarter of London's waste is still transported to landfill sites outside London.

However, it is now understood that landfill waste contributes to wider environmental problems, such as the production of methane, which adds to the greenhouse gases in the atmosphere. So more of London's waste is now recycled (currently around 30 per cent) or incinerated (46 per cent).

London's future targets:

- Zero waste to go to landfill by 2025.
- Reduce domestic waste per household from 1000 kg in 2010 to 800 kg by 2030.
- Generate more energy from organic and non-recycled waste (40 per cent total waste).
- Increase the amount of waste recycling to over 50 per cent (currently, London's recycling rates are fairly low compared with other cities).

Although London's population has grown, the amount of household waste has reduced by 10 per cent between 2013 and 2018. This has been achieved by:

- introducing specialised kerbside collections and facilities for recycling different types of household waste
- agreeing higher targets with contractors who handle waste
- making technological improvements in recycling
- educating students in schools and the general public about recycling
- introducing extra charges for households that produce more waste.

D *Truck delivers waste to London's Mucking Marshes Landfill site*

E *Edmonton Solid Waste Incineration Plant. Waste that cannot be recycled is burned here, producing energy, which is used to generate electricity*

Energy conservation

Energy is supplied to businesses and homes in London in the form of electricity and gas for buildings, and petrol and diesel for transport. Current energy consumption in London mainly consists of gas (45 per cent), electricity (30 per cent) and petrol, diesel and aviation fuel (23 per cent).

A third of London's buildings have the worst energy performance ratings, wasting a large proportion of their energy. Over 300 000 London households are considered to be fuel-poor, which means they cannot afford to keep their homes warm due to low incomes and high energy costs. Some improvements to the efficiency of London's buildings have been made in recent years:

- Energy efficiency programmes have helped to insulate 350 000 lofts and 257 000 cavity walls in London's houses. Around 800 000 energy-efficient boilers have been installed.

- Many households have taken up low-carbon heating, and others have installed solar (photovoltaic) panels.

- The amount of energy used by London businesses has declined by 40 per cent and overall energy consumption has fallen by 16 per cent since 2005.

Water conservation

The south-east of England has less water available per person than some desert countries, so there are great pressures on London's water supplies. The average Londoner uses an average of 160 litres of water in a day and London businesses consume over 130 million cubic metres of water per year.

To fulfil future demand, a number of large-scale water transfer schemes are proposed. One huge scheme intends to transport water from Kielder Reservoir (Northumberland) to restock London reservoirs – a distance of around 480 km.

Savings are being be made by the use of water meters, increasing the use of recycled water, introducing more-efficient domestic appliances and using waste (grey) water to irrigate plants.

ACTIVITIES

1. What are the arguments for and against sourcing London's food supplies as locally as possible?
2. Give two economic and two environmental problems caused by traffic congestion.
3. Describe different ways that public transport can be used to reduce traffic congestion in urban areas.
4. Explain how Crossrail will:
    a reduce journey times in London
    b increase the number of passenger journeys
    c improve integrated transport in London.
5. Explain the advantages and disadvantages of London's Congestion Charge scheme.
6. a Do you think cycling should be part of a sustainable transport strategy? Give reasons.
    b Suggest how the benefits from cycling can be social, economic and environmental.
7. Explain how waste recycling can help to make cities more sustainable.

Stretch yourself

Research the different ways that waste is disposed of in London. Summarise the advantages and disadvantages of
a incineration
b landfill
c recycling as a means of waste disposal.

Practice question

Assess the effectiveness of strategies to reduce traffic congestion in London. *(6 marks)*

14.8 London Olympic Park: an urban regeneration project

On these spreads you will find out about the large-scale regeneration of London's Olympic Park

The Lower Lea Valley was chosen as the site for the London Olympic Games in 2007. Over a period of five years the site was transformed in preparation for the Games. It was also intended to leave a long-term legacy for the whole area, in terms of social, economic and environmental improvements. A total of US$13.5 billion was spent on the project.

Why the Lea Valley area needed regeneration

A number of issues in the area meant Lea Valley was well suited for regeneration:

- One of the poorest and most deprived areas in London
- High levels of unemployment
- High crime rates
- Poor public health
- Lower than average educational attainment
- Previous lack of investment in the area
- Lack of infrastructure
- Environmental degradation and dereliction
- Problems of fly tipping and water pollution
- Decline in traditional industries

Population fact file

Population: Local borough of Newham has a population of 275 000 residents.

Ethnicity: 46% Asian/Asian British; 27% white; 18% black/black British; 5% mixed/multiple ethnic group; 4% other ethnic groups.

Fertility rate: 2.8, making it one of the highest in the UK.

Age range: 25% are under 18 years; 68% are 18 to 64 years; only 7% are aged 65 years and older (mid-2015). The average age is 30 years.

Deprivation: In 2010, Newham was the second most deprived local authority in England; by 2015 it was ranked 25.

A *Olympic Park site: before redevelopment*

World cities

Main features of the Olympic Park project

The Olympic Park site was transformed between 2007 and 2012:

- The land was purchased by the government.
- Old factories and housing were demolished.
- Heavily polluted land was cleaned up as were the many waterways that crossed the area.
- Overhead electricity pylons were removed and placed underground.
- Much of the area was converted into a park with a mix of wildlife habitats and tourist attractions.
- Several sports venues and associated buildings were constructed including the main athletics stadium, velodrome and Athletes' Village, in readiness for the Olympic Games.
- Following the Games, the London Legacy Development Corporation (LLDC) was set up to ensure that there were many long-term economic, social and environmental benefits from the huge investment. The process of regeneration will not be complete until 2030.

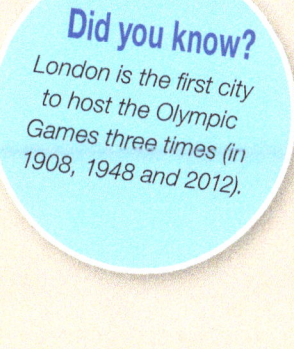

Did you know? London is the first city to host the Olympic Games three times (in 1908, 1948 and 2012).

B Olympic Park site: after redevelopment

Impacts of the Olympics Park project

Social

- Almost 500 homes and a large church were knocked down.
- Over 9000 homes will be available as affordable housing. Some of these will be allocated to specific workers such as teachers, nurses and other medical staff.
- Housing prices in the area generally increased but most became unaffordable to local people.
- Several of the Olympic sports venues have been made available to use for the local residents.
- The Olympic athletics stadium has been converted into a football stadium (West Ham Football Club) but is still used for athletics in the summer.
- Five new residential neighbourhoods are being created. Some are being sold privately and others are allocated for social housing.
- A new school has been built to fulfil the demand for extra places. This is educating 2000 students between the ages of four and 18.

London Olympic Park: an urban regeneration project

Economic

- The total cost of the scheme was much higher than expected. The original estimate was US$5.7 billion, but the final cost exceeded US$12.8 billion.
- Londoners had to pay over US$1.4 billion towards the cost of the scheme through local council taxes.
- There was significant financial investment in new infrastructure and local businesses.
- The money spent and the jobs created in construction, commerce and tourism have resulted in a multiplier effect for the local economy.
- The benefits of the Olympics to the wider economy are estimated to be in excess of US$14.2 billion.
- The buildings and venues are all being used or have been sold to developers.
- Although not a part of the Olympic Park, the centre of Stratford now has a large retail and business complex, providing employment for over 10 000 people.
- In the Olympic Park, 12 000 new permanent jobs have been created, many of which are skilled and highly paid.
- Much of the employment was short term and local residents did not benefit as most jobs went to people from outside the area.
- There have been considerable improvements to transport, making Stratford a major transport hub. Developments include a new Underground station, two new lines, a high-speed rail service to Kings Cross station and a possible stopping point for the Eurostar service from London to Paris.
- Despite the huge investment, the area remains one of the poorest and most deprived in the country.

C *Location and land usage of the Olympic Park in 2012 and 2015*

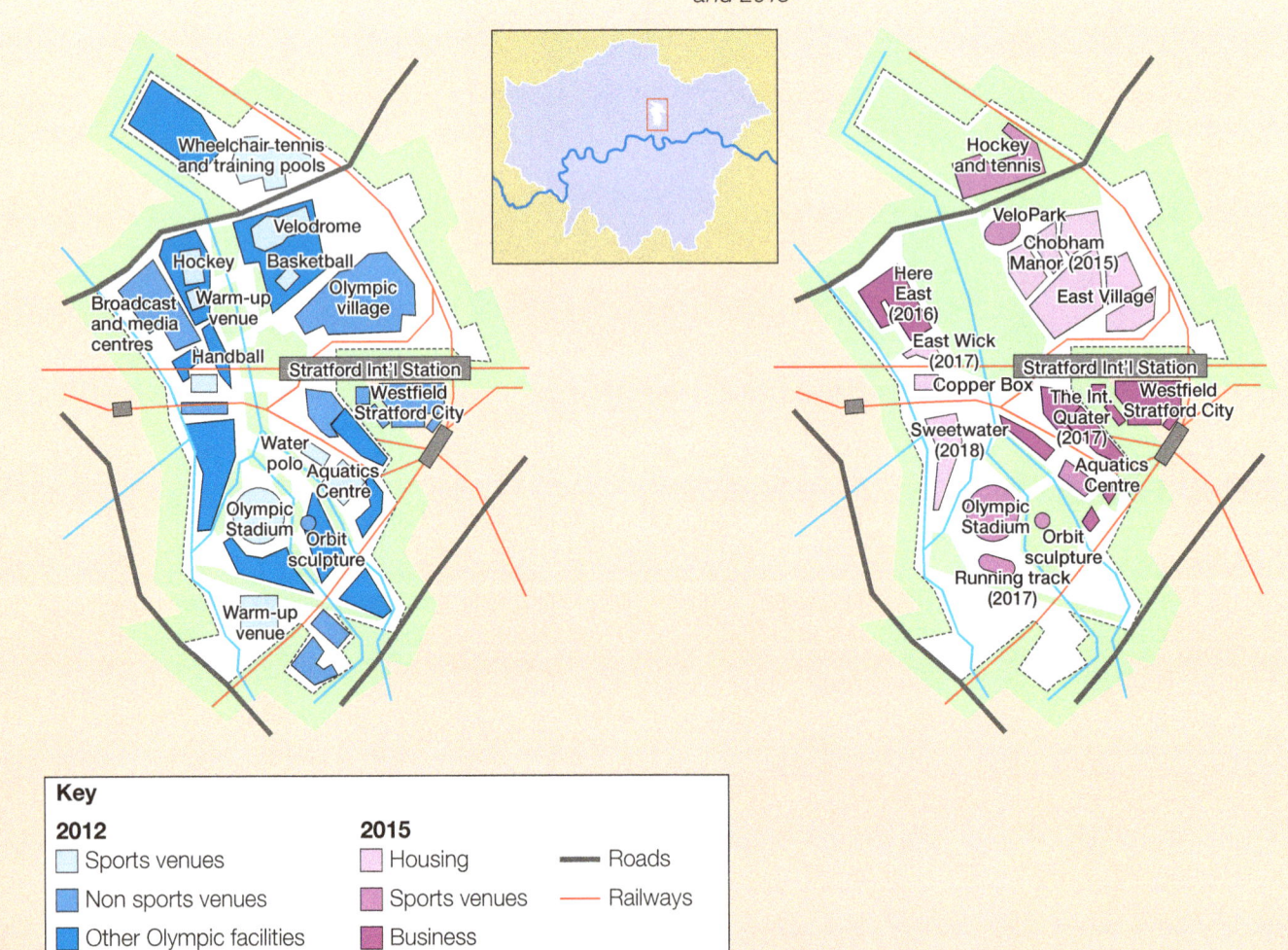

Key

2012
- Sports venues
- Non sports venues
- Other Olympic facilities

2015
- Housing
- Sports venues
- Business

— Roads
— Railways

World cities

Environmental

- Over 200 hectares of former brownfield land have been converted into a large urban park and recreational area.
- Almost 100 allotments were lost.
- The area has been replanted with a diverse mix of vegetation including 5000 trees and 400 000 other plants. There is a variety of woodland, parkland and wetland environments.
- The old Lea Valley canals and rivers have been cleaned up and are no longer polluted. New wildlife habitats have been created. Some wildlife was carefully transferred to other locations.
- Some of the buildings were constructed from recycled materials, but much had to be imported from abroad.
- Several walking and cycling routes have been created.
- Many of the homes being constructed are water and energy efficient.

D *Walking and cycling routes have been created alongside the newly cleaned Lea Valley canals*

ACTIVITIES

1. Describe the location of the Queen Elizabeth Olympic Park in London.
2. Explain why east London and the Lower Lea Valley were in need of regeneration. Why was this important for London's bid for the Olympic Games?
3. Why were some local people against the development of the Olympic site?
4. Assess the economic costs and benefits of urban regeneration in the Olympic Park/Stratford area.
5. Study maps **C**. Identify five changes in function that have occurred.

Stretch yourself

Evaluate each of these statements about regeneration in the Stratford/Olympic Park area, using evidence from the text and your own research.

- The positive effects of urban regeneration have been greater than the negative effects.
- Regeneration has improved the economy of the local area.
- The environmental impact of regeneration is entirely positive.

Practice question

For an urban regeneration project you have studied, to what extent has the local area been improved?
(9 marks)

161

14.9 New York: a world city

On these spreads you will find out about New York's location and population

Example

New York is a major world city with a population of 8.6 million. (The wider city region has a population in excess of 18 million.) Like London, it is a one of the world's most significant financial and commercial centres. The city is situated on the eastern seaboard of the USA and is part of a huge urban agglomeration that stretches from Boston in the north to Washington in the south.

A *New York City skyline*

Location and growth of the city

The city of New York was originally located at the southern end of Manhattan Island in the early 1600s, when settlers established a trading post. The location at the mouth of the River Hudson was ideal for gaining access to inland parts of the country. The site provided a large and deep natural harbour, so trade developed rapidly. The city was first named New Amsterdam, but later, in 1664, the British captured the port and renamed the city New York.

B *New York City and New York State*

World cities

C The five districts of New York

Did you know?
The city of 'New Amsterdam' was given to the Duke of York in 1664 as an 18th birthday present from his father. He renamed the city 'New York'.

Did you know?
The island of Manhattan was purchased from a Native American tribe in 1626 for the equivalent of about US$1000 in modern currency.

Subsequently, New York became the port of entry for millions of immigrants, arriving from Europe mainly. Almost 18 million migrants entered the USA via Ellis Island between 1890 and 1955, searching for a new life in a country that symbolised greater freedom and democracy. Over half the goods entering the USA at this time came through the docks in New York harbour. Today, the city covers an area of over 1500 km² and has extended across Staten Island, the Bronx, Manhattan, Brooklyn, Queens and part of New Jersey (map **C**).

Maths skills

Examine table **E**.

a Draw a line graph to show the changing population of the city of New York between 1870 and 2014.
b When were the periods of greatest percentage increase?
c When did population decline?
d Give reasons for the changes shown on your graph.

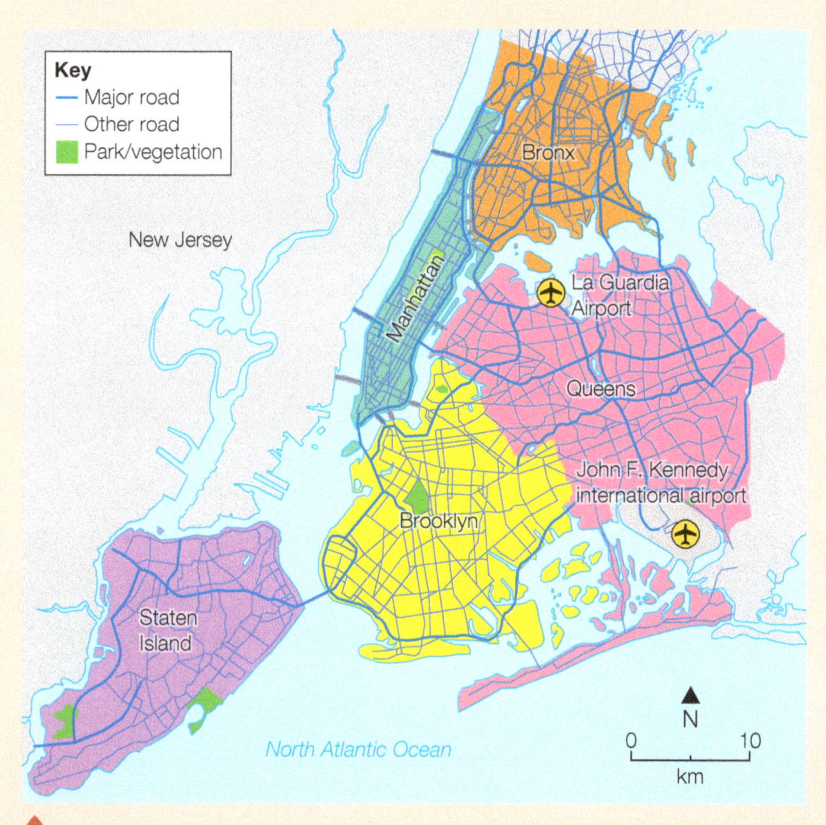

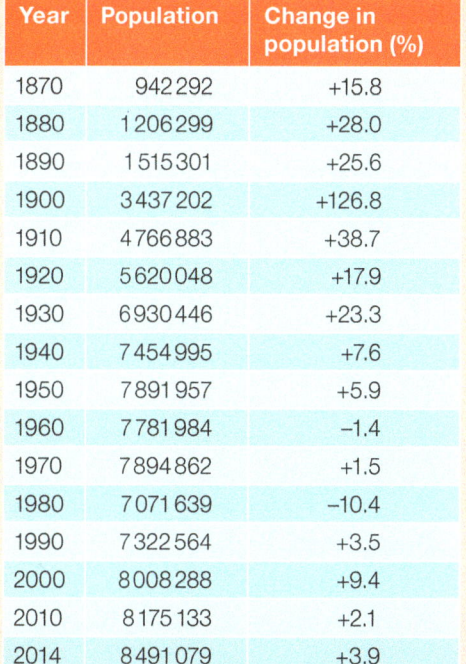

D Map of New York City

Year	Population	Change in population (%)
1870	942 292	+15.8
1880	1 206 299	+28.0
1890	1 515 301	+25.6
1900	3 437 202	+126.8
1910	4 766 883	+38.7
1920	5 620 048	+17.9
1930	6 930 446	+23.3
1940	7 454 995	+7.6
1950	7 891 957	+5.9
1960	7 781 984	−1.4
1970	7 894 862	+1.5
1980	7 071 639	−10.4
1990	7 322 564	+3.5
2000	8 008 288	+9.4
2010	8 175 133	+2.1
2014	8 491 079	+3.9

E Population of New York City, 1870–2014

New York: a world city

Impacts of national and international migration

New York has one of the most international and cosmopolitan populations in the world. The USA is often called a 'melting pot' because it is home to immigrants from all over the world. New York is traditionally regarded as the 'gateway to the USA', as the vast majority of migrants entered the country through the city. Many settled in New York as it was a major centre of business and employment. Over 800 languages are spoken in New York and there are enclaves of different nationalities throughout the city. Even now, the city contains an estimated 3 million people who were born abroad.

- There are more Chinese people in New York than in any other city outside Asia.
- More Italians live in New York than in any other city outside Italy.
- There are more Jewish people in New York than in any city outside Israel.
- More West Indians live in the city than anywhere else in the world beyond the West Indies.
- There are more Puerto Ricans than in any other city in the world.
- There are more people from the Dominican Republic in New York than in any other city, apart from Santo Domingo.
- Over 2 million people of Spanish origin live in New York.
- The first language of over half of New York's population is not English.
- The black population of New York is almost 2 million – double the number of any other American city.

There is also a great deal of internal or national migration, which affects the population of New York. For several decades the process of counter-urbanisation has taken place, whereby residents move beyond the city limits to live in smaller settlements in the commuter zone. However, some younger migrants have returned in recent years to live and work in the core of the city in a process known as reurbanisation. Many are young ambitious professionals working in Manhattan and other central areas.

Chart **F** shows how migration into New York is continuing to take place on a large scale, which helps to limit the population decline from central parts of New York, as well as stimulating the economy by providing a source of labour and new businesses. Table **G** shows the proportion of immigrants in different types of work.

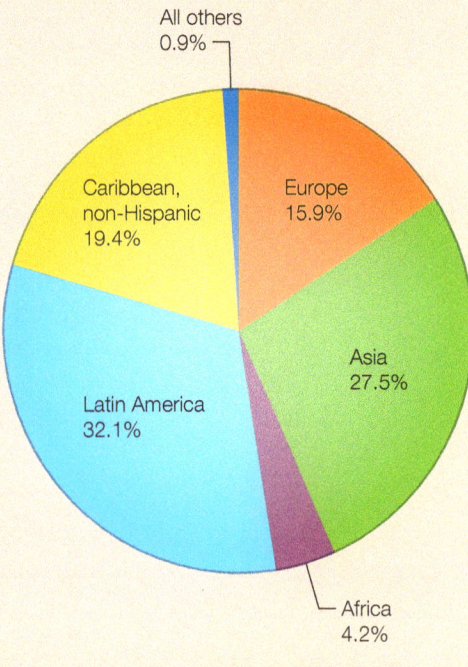

All others 0.9%
Caribbean, non-Hispanic 19.4%
Europe 15.9%
Asia 27.5%
Latin America 32.1%
Africa 4.2%

Foreign-born population = 3 066 599

F *Areas of origin of the foreign-born population of New York, 2011*

Occupation category	Immigrant share (%) (of all workers in occupation)
Health care support	49.1
Building and grounds cleaning and maintenance	43.2
Construction and extraction	37.8
Personal care and service	35.4
Transportation and material moving	34.7

Analysis of the US Census Bureau's 2015 American Community Survey 1-year PUMS data by the American Immigration Council.

G *Occupations of immigrant workers in New York*

Advantages of migration

◆ Immigrant households in New York pay large amounts of tax, contributing to federal, state and local taxation. The total is estimated to be over US$42 billion per year (2015).

◆ Migrants have a sizeable income to spend on goods and services, which stimulates the local economy (over US$100 billion per year).

◆ Migrants own over a half of all small businesses in New York and account for over US$7 billion of income per year. For example, nine out of 10 laundries are owned by immigrants, as are eight out of every 10 grocery stores.

◆ Immigrants have brought a wide range of cuisines, styles of music and other cultural activities to New York.

◆ The arrival of younger migrants has helped to balance the structure of the population. Most are of working age and many have children who are enrolled in local schools.

Arguments against continued immigration

◆ Immigrants may not understand English so it is difficult for them to integrate into American society.

◆ There are cultural differences that sometimes lead to prejudice and conflict.

◆ Some American citizens feel that immigrants undercut wages because they are prepared to work for lower incomes.

G Manhattan's Chinatown is home to the highest concentration of Chinese people outside Asia

ACTIVITIES

1. Describe the site and location of New York.
2. Suggest reasons for the early growth of New York.
3. Study map **D**. How far is it across the city from west to east and from north to south?
4. Outline the advantages of migration for a world city such as New York.

Stretch yourself

Find out further details of the site of New York (the land on which the city is built), its situation (its location in the wider region) and the reasons for the city's growth. You could produce an annotated map to show the main features.

Practice question

Explain how migration has been responsible for the growth and structure of New York's population. *(6 marks)*

14.10 The importance of New York as a world city

On this spread you will find out about New York's national and global importance

Example

The city of New York has many different functions – it is important as a centre for:

- commercial and business activity
- the financial sector
- international politics and diplomatic activity
- creative industries, including fashion, art and advertising
- culture and entertainment, including the media
- education, research and technology
- the manufacturing industry
- air, rail and road transport
- shipping and international trade.

The economic core of New York is focused on Manhattan Island. Many of the buildings there are tall skyscrapers, reflecting the high cost of land. Wall Street (the finance district of New York) is located in Downtown Manhattan. The tourist district and hotels, Fifth Avenue (shopping), Broadway (theatre), the Empire State Building and United Nations Buildings are all in Midtown Manhattan.

Did you know?
The Federal Reserve Bank of New York has the largest gold storage in the world. The vault is 24 m below street level and contains US$90 billion in gold (25 per cent of the world's reserves).

Business and finance

Until the mid-twentieth century, New York was a pre-eminent manufacturing centre, producing goods for national and international markets. However, from the 1960s manufacturing went into long-term decline as a result of foreign competition, the relatively high cost of labour and land, and a lack of investment. Some foreign competitors had modern, more-efficient factories and the newly industrialising countries, such as Malaysia, had a cheaper labour force.

As the manufacturing industry declined, so the financial sector flourished and New York became a world leader, alongside London and Tokyo, in investment banking, insurance, hedge funds and foreign exchange dealing. The two New York stock exchanges combined have the largest daily trading volumes in the world.

New York has also become a world leader in the creative sector. Over a quarter of American fashion designers locate their offices there – other parts of the sector are also flourishing, including film, television, advertising and performing arts. New York is the third largest film-producing city in the world, after Los Angeles and Mumbai.

Trade

New York has the largest oil-importing port in the USA and the third largest container terminal. Nearby is Port Newark Container Terminal, the busiest on the east coast of the USA. China is the source of the greatest value of imports to New York, whereas Canada takes the greatest value of New York's exports (graph **B**). Overall, imports far exceed exports, so New York has a trade deficit of around US$55 billion. Approximately 6 per cent of all American imports and 5.5 per cent of exports go through the port of New York. Imports include oil, vehicles, electronics, gold, aluminium, plastics and pharmaceuticals. Exports include diamonds (worked), jewellery, artwork, aircraft parts and vaccines. Trade of lighter and more valuable cargoes is largely by air, through the three main airports: JFK, LaGuardia and Newark.

A *Manhattan Island, central New York – Wall Street is in the foreground*

World cities

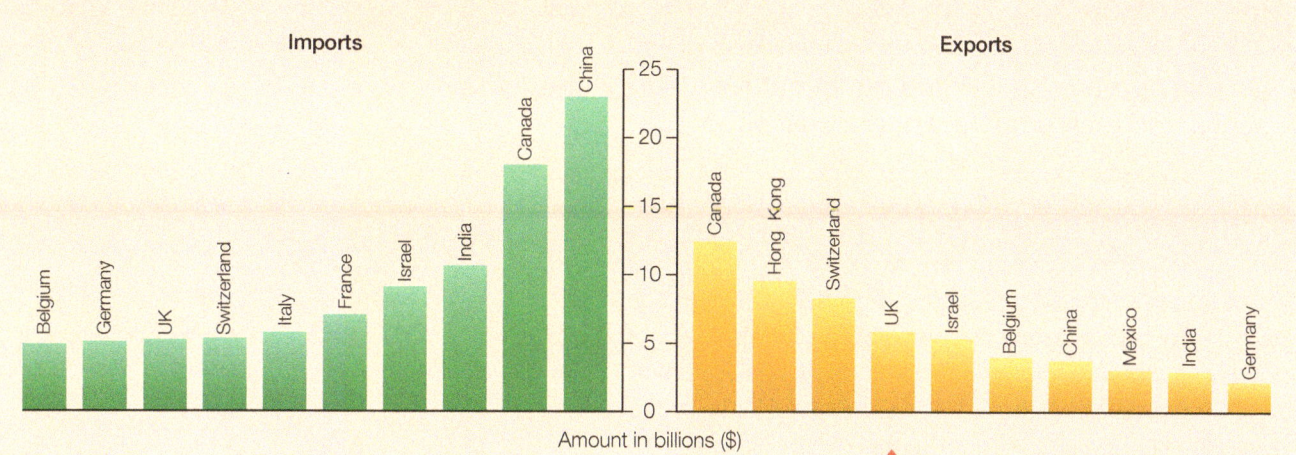

B Top 10 countries New York imported from and exported to in 2015

Imports (in billions $): Belgium, Germany, UK, Switzerland, Italy, France, Israel ~9, India ~11, Canada ~18, China ~23

Exports (in billions $): Canada ~12.5, Hong Kong ~9.5, Switzerland ~8.5, UK ~6, Israel ~5, Belgium ~4, China ~3.5, Mexico ~3, India ~2.5, Germany ~2

Culture

With almost 40 per cent of its population born outside the USA and from 200 ethnic groups, New York is one of the most diverse cities in the world. Its demographic variety has led to a rich variety of cultural activities.

- Diverse cultural heritages and ancestries: contrasting places of worship, celebration of religious festivals, specialty shops and services, specialist language newspapers and media services

- Famous tourist venues, both historical and contemporary (e.g. Ellis Island, Statue of Liberty, Empire State Building, Times Square, One World Trade Centre)

- Varied art and music genres (e.g. jazz in Harlem, hip-hop in the Bronx, Pop Art in East Village)

- Over 500 art galleries and museums (e.g. Metropolitan Museum of Art, Museum of Modern Art, Whitney and Guggenheim museums)

- World famous universities, many with a high percentage of overseas students (e.g. Columbia University)

- Theatres (Broadway), opera, ballet and classical music (e.g. New York Philharmonic, New York City Ballet), concerts (e.g. Carnegie Hall)

- Professional sports (e.g. Yankees baseball, New York Mets, American football, basketball, hockey, soccer, championship boxing matches in Madison Square Garden)

Politics

New York has an international political presence in the form of the United Nations Building and its various agencies, such as UNICEF (United Nations Children's Fund). These are located in Manhattan.

New York City is administered by a mayor, who chooses senior staff and criminal court justices, and prepares the annual budget – in 2017 this was over US$80 billion. City government is dominated by the Democratic Party.

ACTIVITIES

1. Using map **D** (14.9) and photo **A**, work out which direction the photographer was facing when the picture was taken. Name the bridges on the right of the photo. What are the names of the rivers that run to the west and east of Manhattan Island? Describe the area of Lower Manhattan shown in the picture, comparing it with the area immediately behind.
2. Assess the importance of New York as an international financial centre.
3. On a world map, locate the main countries that trade with New York (distinguish between the source countries for imports and the destination countries for exports). What are the main imports into and exports out of New York?
4. Explain why New York exerts considerable influence as a political centre even though it is not the capital city.
5. Give reasons why New York attracts large number of tourists both from within the USA and also from across the world.

Stretch yourself

Research the main purposes of the UN, its history and the role of the organisation in New York. In which other cities does the UN have buildings and activities?

Practice question

Explain why New York is considered to be an important world city. *(4 marks)*

14.11 New York's economic, social and environmental opportunities

On this spread you will find out about New York's economic, social and environmental opportunities

Example

Economic: employment

As with most post-industrial cities, New York has undergone considerable changes in its employment structure in recent years. The rapid decline of the manufacturing industry caused economic and environmental problems, but service industries have since grown, such as computing, shopping, entertainment, finance, advertising and information.

Features of employment in New York:

- The largest sources of employment are in the financial sector, high-tech, property (real estate) and health care.
- The city is the most important centre for mass media, journalism and publishing in the USA.
- An increasing share of employment is in creative industries such as advertising, fashion, design and architecture.
- New York has become a centre for ICT and digital industries. Many new businesses are directly involved with IT, manufacturing hardware and designing software. Part of New York is nicknamed 'Silicon Alley' because it is a hub for telecommunications and computer technology, including biotechnology.
- Manufacturing has suffered long-term decline but has recently shown signs of stabilising. With 78 000 jobs, employment in manufacturing represented just 2 per cent of the city's economy in 2015, down from almost 33 per cent in 1950.
- Financial services account for more than 35 per cent of the city's employment income and employ 450 000 people.
- Accommodation and food services, professional services and health care accounted for 54 per cent of private jobs in 2010–15.

The city's economy is large and diverse and has fully recovered job losses from the last recession. Employment is growing rapidly and has outpaced the rest of the USA. Growth has occurred in most types of employment, although services have grown most rapidly.

Unemployment rates vary, as shown in graph **B**, but the trend since the last recession (in 2008–09) has been sharply downwards to around 5 per cent.

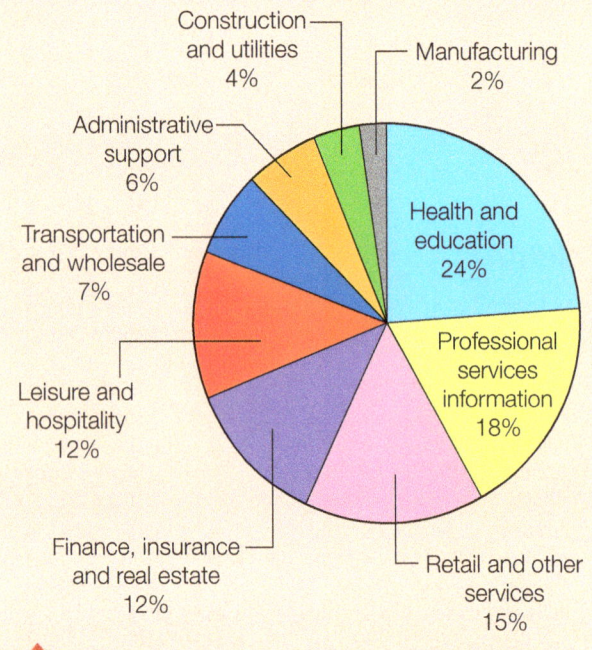

A Average annual employment by major sectors, New York, 2015

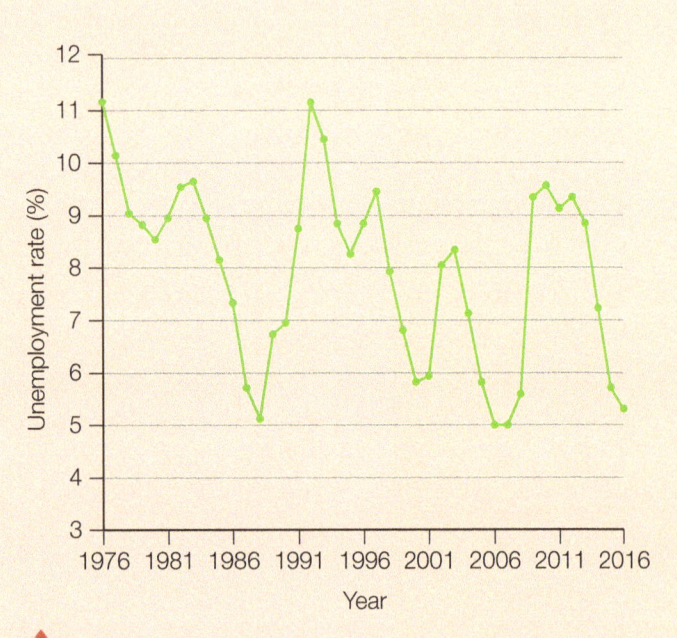

- Construction and utilities 4%
- Manufacturing 2%
- Administrative support 6%
- Health and education 24%
- Transportation and wholesale 7%
- Professional services information 18%
- Leisure and hospitality 12%
- Finance, insurance and real estate 12%
- Retail and other services 15%

B Average annual unemployment rate, New York, 1976–2016

168

Social: recreation and entertainment

New York provides a huge array of entertainment and events for tourists as well as locals. For example:

- The Museum of Modern Art
- Coney Island beach and amusements
- The Rockefeller Centre
- The New York City ballet
- The New York Philharmonic orchestra
- The Billie Jean King National Tennis Center
- Central Park
- Live bands at Brooklyn Bowl
- A Staten Island Yankees baseball match
- A literary reading at Brooklyn Public Library
- A meal in Chinatown

C The High Line Park, Manhattan

Environmental: urban greening

Just under a third of New York is made up of open space and a large proportion of the population live within 500m of parkland or waterways. There is over 113 km^2 of parkland in New York and 22 km of public beaches. Green spaces provide a natural and free recreational resource as well as a habitat for wildlife.

There have been a number of green initiatives for the city:

- New York City's Green Infrastructure Program aims to use water more sustainably and support high levels of biodiversity in urban ecosystems. Public and private buildings are adapted to have roof gardens, with facilities for rainwater harvesting and wastewater recycling.
- The Comprehensive Waterfront Plan helps to protect and maintain the natural features of the estuaries and riverside habitats covering the 900 km of waterways around New York.
- The New York City open space network of green corridors connects different parts of the city, with plans to complete 500 km of bicycle and footpaths.
- Over 1000 neighbourhood parks and community gardens are maintained by community stewardship groups, partly funded by the local government.
- The High Line (photo **C**) is a disused elevated railway track through the industrial heart of the city, now converted into a public park.

ACTIVITIES

1. Describe the pattern of employment in New York.
2. Explain why manufacturing has become less important in New York than it was in the past.
3. Describe the trend in unemployment in New York since the 1970s. Explain why the rate of unemployment varies so much.
4. a Classify the examples of recreation activities in New York into categories such as: sporting events; eating out; museums and galleries; concerts; theatre and ballet; nightlife; outdoors.
   b Research online to find other things to do in New York. Add these to your lists.
5. Using photo **C**, describe the features of the High Line Park in New York.
6. Explain what is meant by urban greening. Outline how environmental improvement can improve the quality of life for the people of New York.

Stretch yourself

Explain what is meant by urban sustainability. How does involving local people in decision-making make urban greening initiatives more successful?

Practice question

Explain the changes in employment in New York over the past 50 years.
(6 marks)

14.12 New York's economic and social challenges

On this spread you will find out about some of New York's economic and social challenges

Example

Urban deprivation and inequality

Inequality in incomes is very pronounced in New York. In 2017, the highest earning 1 per cent of the workforce earned almost 50 times the average salary for all employees. Over 21 per cent were living below the poverty line (less than US$23 000 per year for a family with two children). Meanwhile, the upper 5 per cent of Manhattan residents earned more than US$860 000 on average in 2014.

High- and extreme-poverty neighbourhoods have three times as much violent crime as low-poverty neighbourhoods. Extreme-poverty neighbourhoods had five times the rate of serious rent arrears, and a 20 per cent lower employment rate. Around 1 million citizens receive welfare support due to unemployment or low incomes. Differences in income levels are reflected in social and health statistics. For example, life expectancy in some of the poorest boroughs of Brooklyn and parts of the Bronx is as low as 74 years, whereas in the wealthier parts of the city such as downtown Manhattan it is greater than 85 years – a difference of 11 years.

A Income inequality in New York City, 2012

Share of income:
- 32.9% — Top 1%
- 24.1% — Next 9%
- 17.6% — Next 15%
- 15.9% — Next 25%
- 9.9% — Bottom 50%

Did you know?
There are four times as many abandoned houses as there are homeless people in New York.

Deprivation in Morrisania and Crotona, the Bronx

Parts of the Bronx area of New York are among the most deprived areas of the USA. Local residents face problems with crime, drug use, poor environment, unemployment and poor health.

- 44% of the population live below the official poverty level – the highest rate in the city
- 20% of residents aged 16 or older are unemployed – the highest rate in the city
- High levels of air pollution and environmental degradation
- Low participation in active sport and creative activities
- Rates of smoking, obesity, diabetes and drug use are all among the highest in the city
- Life expectancy is 74 years – city average is 79 years
- Poor quality of local housing and shops; poor access to shops selling fresh fruit and vegetables for a healthy diet
- Death rates due to drugs, homicide and HIV are more than twice those of the city as a whole
- Teenage birth rate is twice the city average (43 births per 1000 girls aged 15–19, compared to 23 for the city as a whole)
- Death rates from cancer and heart disease are above the city average
- Highest rates of alcohol-related hospital visits in the city (2367 per 100 000 people)
- Poor educational outcomes – almost 38 per cent of adults do not finish high school
- Highest level of adults going to prison in New York (370 per 100 000 people) – four times the city average. Residents are twice as likely to be assaulted in Morrisania and Crotona than in the rest of the city

B Housing in Morrisania, the Bronx

Housing inequality

The growing population has led to a shortage of affordable housing in New York. Wages have risen much more slowly than house prices, so many people are priced out of the market. Rental prices have risen by over 40 per cent in the past 20 years, whereas wages have increased by less than 10 per cent. It is not unusual for up to a half of total income to be spent on rent, often for a small apartment.

In a reversal of previous trends, more people now wish to live in New York than leave it. This includes existing residents as well as migrants from within the USA and from abroad. Previously unfashionable neighbourhoods in Brooklyn and the Bronx have become popular areas in which to live, even among people with young families, and the rush to the suburbs appears to have slowed. Manhattan contains nine of the 10 most affluent and highly priced neighbourhoods in New York. Here, the average price of a home is almost US$2 million. Beyond the city boundary in Connecticut and Long Island are some of the most expensive and palatial houses, occupied by many of the most wealthy residents.

Housing shortages and high rents have led to increased levels of homelessness, with over 60 000 sleeping in homeless shelters every night. As a result, the city mayor has developed a new housing strategy which prioritises the building of over 200 000 affordable homes. So far, over 70 000 have been built and purchased or rented, mainly by low- and middle-income residents. Many are aimed at groups such as hotel workers, teachers, police, fire fighters and health workers, so that they can continue to live in the city.

ACTIVITIES

1. Compare the two urban environments shown in photos **B** and **C**. Comment on the likely social and economic inequalities.
2. Explain how social deprivation may affect life expectancy.
3. Describe the distribution of income groups in New York.
4. Describe the social conditions of people living in Morrisania and Crotona in the Bronx.
5. What is the difference between the supply of and demand for rented homes among the poorest in New York? What are the implications of this?

Wealth and low social deprivation in Brooklyn Heights, Brooklyn

Brooklyn Heights is a much more affluent area of central New York, with a population of 52 000. It is situated directly across the East River from Manhattan. The average household income is US$147 000 (2017). Three quarters of the workforce are in 'white collar' or professional occupations. Many are young professionals who wish to live close to the city centre. Much of the housing is owner-occupied and less than 4 per cent of the population is unemployed. Life expectancy is 83 years on average. Educational outcomes are high, with almost 80 per cent of the adult population educated to degree level or equivalent. Less than 8 per cent are below the poverty line.

C Housing in Brooklyn Heights, Brooklyn

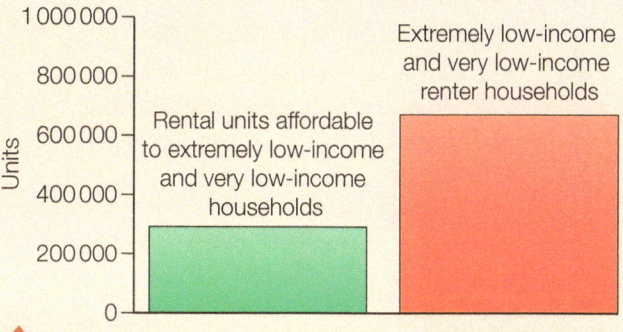

D Supply and demand among extremely low-income and very low-income renter households

Stretch yourself

Research differences in house prices, education and health between two contrasting parts of New York. For example, you could compare a wealthy part of Manhattan with a poorer district such as Coney Island in Brooklyn or Mott Haven in the Bronx.

Practice question

Assess the consequences of social inequality in New York. *(6 marks)*

14.13 New York's environmental challenges

On these spreads you will find out about some of New York's environmental challenges

Example

Transport in New York

New York's transport system includes:

- one of the world's most extensive subway networks, covering most parts of the city 24 hours a day
- a more limited commuter rail system
- an extensive bus system throughout the five boroughs, also operating 24 hours a day
- a taxi service, widely available in all parts of the city
- extensive ferry services connecting the islands and districts of the city
- three international airports and several smaller airports providing regional and global services
- an aerial tramway service (photo **A**).

The public transport company, New York City Transit Authority, transports between 5.5 and 7.5 million passengers per day for less than US$3 per person. Because of the widespread availability and reliability of public transport, only about 50 per cent of households own a car. As a result of this reliance on public transport systems, New York has a lower carbon footprint than most other American cities. Traffic congestion is still a problem, however, as there are too many vehicles for existing roads, with bottlenecks at bridges and tunnels linking New York islands (photo **B**).

A Aerial tramcar, connecting Roosevelt Island to Manhattan

B Heavy traffic on the Williamsburg Bridge during rush hour in New York City. The bridge connects Lower Manhattan with the borough of Brooklyn

Maths skills

Using the data below, draw a graph to show how New Yorkers commute into the city.

Subway	42%
Drive alone	25%
Bus	13%
Walk	10%
Carpool	5%
Commuter rail	3%
Taxi	1%
Bicycle	0.8%
Ferry	0.2%

C A parking place for electric vehicles in Central Park, New York

172

Strategies to reduce congestion and air pollution

Traffic congestion can lead to air pollution. There are also the negative economic effects of increased journey times, higher fuel consumption and greater risk of accidents.

To improve New York's environmental sustainability, there are a number of plans to develop the efficiency of the transport network and encourage greater use of public transport:

- Using rapid bus transit services to connect outer parts of the city with the central core.
- Reopening underground stations that were closed in the 1970s and 1980s.
- Establishing new commuter rail routes to the outer suburbs.
- Expanding the number and range of all-year commuter ferry routes.
- Introducing bicycle lanes and providing better access for pedestrians.
- Experimenting with a congestion pricing zone at the southern end of Manhattan Island.
- Fitting catalytic converters to exhausts of diesel city buses.
- Developing a biodiesel plant in Brooklyn to distribute biodiesel to filling stations in the city.
- Extending the availability of charging stations throughout the city for electric cars (photo **C**).

Urban sprawl

Urban sprawl is the spread of the city into the surrounding rural areas. Until recently, the middle class tended to move to the outer areas and the inner city population declined. Due to population growth, businesses relocated to suburbs for cheaper land and better accessibility. The city of New York experienced major economic and social problems in the 1970s and 1980s and nearly went bankrupt, which hastened the movement of richer people to the suburbs. This, in turn, meant house building encroached into former rural areas and was accompanied by transport developments, out-of-town shopping, businesses and leisure complexes. Since 2010, however, the rural–urban fringe and outer suburbs have experienced either slow growth or slight decline, as more people are choosing to live in areas close to the city centre.

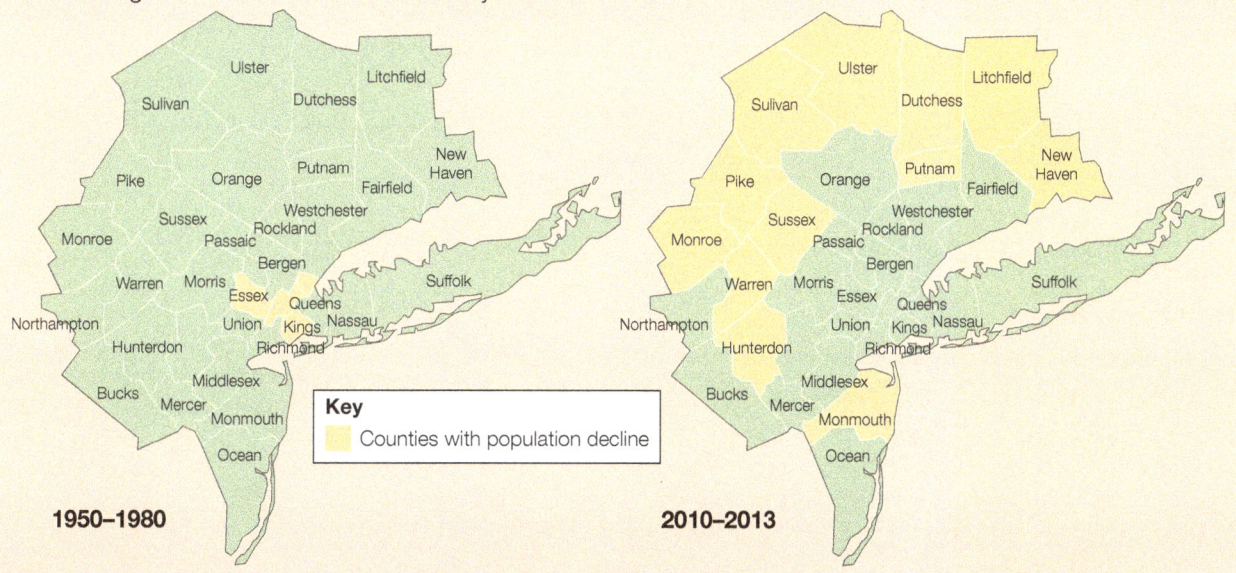

D *New York State counties with population decline, 1950–80 and 2010–13*

New York's environmental challenges

Food, energy, water

Food supply

New York's food supply for its 8 million inhabitants is sourced predominantly from domestic suppliers, but with its increasingly international population a sizeable proportion is now imported from abroad. Consumers are keen to access exotic food all year round. Almost 6 million tonnes of food are consumed per year and it is estimated that the equivalent of 6 million hectares of land is needed to produce this food. Up to 95 per cent of the city's fresh food is transported from outer suburban depots by lorry into the city centre. The principal depot is Hunts Point Terminal Produce Market in the Bronx, the largest wholesale produce market in the world.

Trends in the supply of food for New York include:

- the increasing supply of organic produce – this is more intensive than conventional farming because no chemical fertilisers or herbicides are used
- sourcing of local and regional food – smaller, independent food stores and farmers' markets promote fresher produce, reduce food miles and help to boost the local economy
- increasing use of technology and capital investment – agribusiness is intensive farming aimed at maximising the amount of food produced, where farms are run as commercial businesses.

Did you know?
Starting in 2015, all New York residents must recycle their old electronics, such as computers and TVs, or face a US$100 fine.

Energy conservation

Despite increasing demand for electricity in New York, energy consumption has fallen in recent years. This is due to the decline of heavy industry and improved energy conservation, such as low-energy appliances, better building insulation and fuel-efficient vehicles. New York's energy mix has also changed considerably in the past 25 years. In 1995 most of New York's energy came from coal, oil and gas (fossil fuels). Since 2005, the proportion of energy from renewable sources has increased – in 2016 this represented 25 per cent of the total electricity generated (chart **E**). There has been a huge investment in solar and wind energy – by 2030 over half of New York's electricity will be produced from renewables. The remaining electricity comes from a combination of oil, gas and nuclear-fuelled power stations. To help reduce air pollution, New York State became the first north-eastern state to demand that all heating oil be ultra-low sulphur diesel.

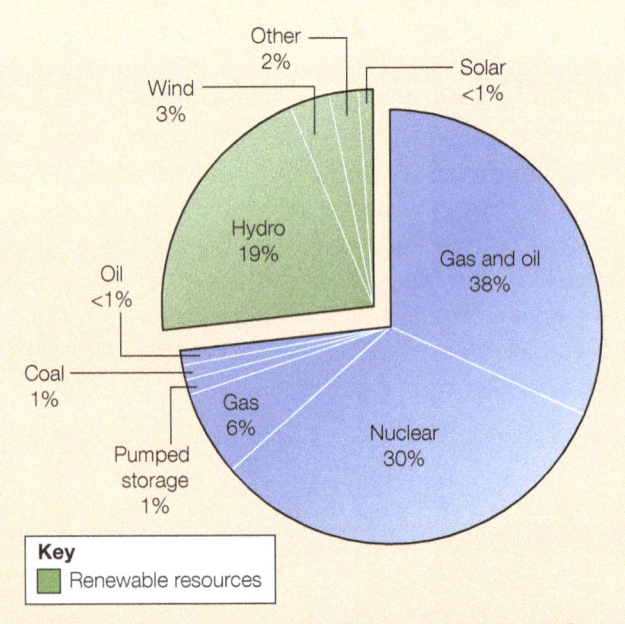

E *Energy sources for New York's electric power supply, 2016*

Source: New York Independent System Operator. Note: Sum may not total 100% due to rounding.

Pie chart values: Other 2%, Wind 3%, Solar <1%, Hydro 19%, Oil <1%, Coal 1%, Pumped storage 1%, Gas 6%, Gas and oil 38%, Nuclear 30%. Key: Renewable resources.

Water conservation

New York consumes almost 5 million cubic metres of water per day, for domestic and industrial/commercial purposes. The main source of this water is from the Catskill Mountains (New York State) where there are several major reservoirs with aqueducts and tunnels leading southwards to the city (photo **F**). The water moves mainly under gravity from watershed areas that are protected from pollution and contamination. Occasional droughts occur but in general the supply is reliable all year round. In 2018, the city decided to invest over US$1 billion in various measures to ensure that this quality of water supply would be maintained in the future. This includes modernising filtration plants, carrying out extensive repairs of leaks and constructing a new long-distance tunnel from the Catskills.

Water conservation measures have included fixing leaking reservoirs and pipes to reduce water waste, irrigating farmland using precise drip pipes and sprays, fixing homes and businesses with water meters and educating the public about water conservation in the home.

Dealing with waste

Urban waste in New York includes domestic rubbish as well as waste from industrial and commercial activities and institutional waste schools, universities and hospitals (some of which is hazardous to public health and the environment). It is estimated that New York produces more waste than any other city in the world (well over 160 000 tonnes per week) – 80 per cent of New York products are used once and then thrown away.

F *An artificial lake in the Catskill Mountains holds water for New York City residents*

Some waste is incinerated, but the majority is disposed of at landfill sites. Incineration requires less land than landfill sites and can produce energy from burning solid waste, but it produces particulates and carbon dioxide emissions that need managing. Much of Manhattan's waste is incinerated across the Hudson River, in New Jersey. Landfill sites can be cost-effective and, when reaching capacity, can be sealed and landscaped. However, they attract vermin, flies and scavenging birds, are unsightly and unhealthy, and produce methane (a powerful greenhouse gas).

Many of the landfill sites in New York have exceeded their capacity so much of the rubbish is taken by barge and lorry to landfill sites beyond the city to nearby states. Some is dumped over 400 km away in states as far afield as Virginia and Ohio.

Recycling rates in New York are surprisingly low. They have dropped from 23 per cent in 2001 to just 15 per cent in 2016. There is a 20-year plan that focuses on waste reduction and improved recycling. Composting, resource and energy targets have been established and in 2016 the ambitious target of zero waste by 2030 was set. Commercial companies, which produce 75 per cent of the waste, will be required to recycle materials – this has been optional until now.

Did you know?
The New York State disposes of nearly 23 million tonnes of rubbish each year. New York City alone sends a 15 km-long fleet of rubbish trucks each day to sites up to 400 km away.

ACTIVITIES

1. Describe changes in rate of urban sprawl around the edges of New York.
2. Explain how water is supplied to the people of New York. As the population increases, outline how water consumption can be made more sustainable.
3. Suggest why recycling rates are still quite low in New York. How is it possible to increase the level of recycling in a big city?
4. Why is it important for a city the size of New York to have a well-organised public transport system?

Stretch yourself

Outline the environmental and economic arguments for reducing landfill and incineration but increasing recycling and waste reduction.

Practice question

Compare the approaches taken by London and New York authorities in tackling the challenges of traffic congestion and waste disposal. *(6 marks)*

Unit 2 Challenges in the human environment

Section B The changing economic world

Nigeria's Minister of Transport tightens the last screw of the country's first standard gauge railway modernisation project linking the capital city Abuja and the north-western state of Kaduna

Unit 2 Challenges in the human environment is about human processes and systems, how they change both spatially and temporally. They are studied in a range of places, at a variety of scales and include places in various states of development. It is split into three sections.

Section B The changing economic world includes:

- the global development gap
- rapid economic development in Nigeria.

You need to study all the topics in Section B – in your final exam, you will have to answer questions on all of them.

What if...

1. no one went on holiday?
2. there was no international aid?
3. everything was made in China?

Unit 2 Section B

Specification key ideas	Pages in this book
16 The development gap	**178–201**
• There are global variations in economic development and quality of life.	178–91
• Various strategies exist for reducing the global development gap.	192–201
17 Nigeria: a newly emerging economy	**201–17**
• Some LICs and NEEs are experiencing rapid economic development, which leads to significant social, environmental and cultural change.	201–17

Your key skills

To be a good geographer, you need to develop important geographical skills – in this section you will learn the following skills:

- Comparing countries using a range of social and economic measures of development
- Interpreting population pyramids
- Using numerical data
- Finding information from photos
- Describing patterns of distribution
- Presenting data using different graphical techniques.

Your key words

As you go through the chapters in this section, make sure you know and understand the key words shown in bold. Definitions are provided in the Glossary on page 354. To be a good geographer, you need to use good subject terminology.

Your exam

Section B makes up part of Paper 2 – a one and a half hour written exam worth 34% of your GCSE.

15 The development gap

15.1 Our unequal world

On this spread you will find out about global variations in economic development and quality of life

What is development?

Development means positive change that makes things better. As a country develops it usually means that people's standard of living and quality of life will improve. Different factors affect a country's level and speed of development.

- *Environmental* factors such as natural hazards, e.g. earthquakes
- *Economic* factors such as **trade** and debt
- *Social* factors such as access to safe water and education
- *Political* factors such as stable government or civil war

The **development gap** is the difference in standards of living between the world's richest and poorest countries.

A Does this family enjoy a good quality of life?

Measuring development

Gross national income (GNI)

Wealth and income can be used to describe a country's level of economic development. A common measure used by the World Bank is **gross national income (GNI)**.

GNI is the total value of goods and services produced by a country, plus money earned from, and paid to, other countries. It is expressed per head (per capita) of the population.

The World Bank uses four different levels of income to divide the countries of the world into: high, upper-middle, lower-middle and low.

The UK, most of Europe, North America and Australia, Argentina and Japan are all **high-income countries (HICs)** (map **B**). Most, but not all, **low-income countries (LICs)** are in Africa.

This *economic* indicator is one way of showing development. Some countries may seem to have a high GNI as they are relatively wealthy and have a small population. But this does not always mean that their citizens enjoy a good quality of life. Equally, some people in LICs are well off and enjoy a high standard of living.

Some countries have begun to experience higher rates of economic development, with a rapid growth of industry. These are known as **newly emerging economies (NEEs)**, for example, Brazil, Russia, India, China and South Africa (the BRICS countries) and the MINT countries (Malaysia, Indonesia, Nigeria and Turkey).

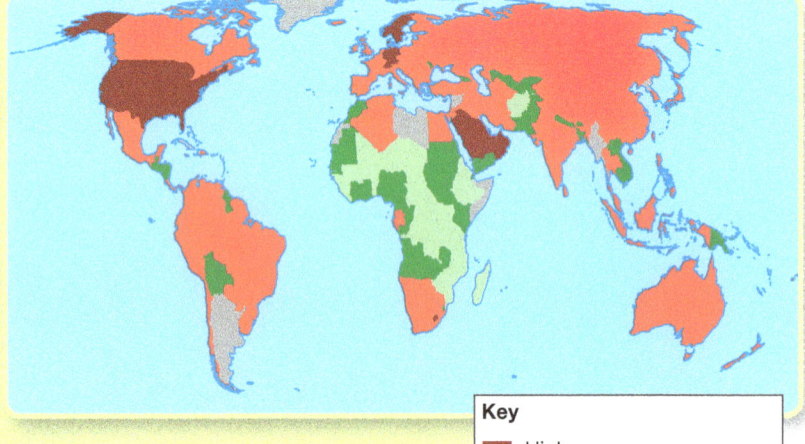

Key
- High
- Higher-middle
- Lower-middle
- Low
- No data

PPP (purchasing power parity) – adjustment made to income to equate what can be purchased for the same amount in different countries

B GNI per capita in PPP terms, 2013

The development gap

Human development index (HDI)

Devised by the United Nations (UN), HDI links wealth to health and education. It aims to show how far people are benefiting from a country's economic growth. It is a *social* measure. Measures used to produce the HDI are:

- **life expectancy** at birth
- **number of years of education**
- **GNI per head.**

The HDI is expressed in values 0–1, where 1 is the highest. This enables countries to be ranked. The highest-ranked country in 2014 was Norway (0.944), followed by Australia (0.935) and Switzerland (0.930). The lowest-ranked country in 2014 was Niger (188th) with an HDI of 0.348. The lowest 10 countries were all in Africa.

Table **C** lists various countries according to their HDI, using four categories of development.

HDI score	Country
	Key: North America, Central and South America, Africa, Europe, Asia, Oceania
Very high	Canada, USA Argentina, Chile Norway, France, Germany, Poland, Portugal, Spain, Switzerland, UK Saudi Arabia, UAE Australia, New Zealand
High	Mexico Brazil, Peru, Columbia, Venezuela Algeria, Libya Romania, Ukraine Russia, China, Kazakhstan, Thailand
Medium	Morocco, South Africa, Namibia India, Mongolia
Low	Mali, Niger, Chad, Sudan, Angola Myanmar, Pakistan

C HDI scores of various countries, 2014

How can we measure quality of life?

Economic and social measures use broad statistics to measure standard of living for whole countries. But they cannot give an accurate measure of an individual's quality of life.

A good quality of life will mean different things in different countries. Consider, for example, safety and security, freedom and the right to vote, women's rights and … happiness!

The strange-looking map (map **D**) is called a *topological* map. Instead of using true scale, it has been drawn to show the size of each country in proportion to the number of people living on US$10 a day or less.

D Topological map showing the number of people living on US$10 a day or less

ACTIVITIES

1. What factors affect the quality of life of the family in photo **A**?
2. Describe the pattern of high and low income countries (map **B**).
3. a Describe the global pattern of HDI (table **C**).
   b What are the advantages of HDI as a measure of development?
4. Comment on the usefulness of map **D** in classifying people's quality of life.

Stretch yourself

Investigate other ways of subdividing the world, for example the PQLI (page 180), world peace or gender equality.

Practice question

To what extent is the HDI the most effective measure of development? *(6 marks)*

15.2 Measuring development

On this spread you will find out about the economic and social indicators of development

What are the measures of development?

There are many economic and social measures of development. For example:

- gross national income (GNI), used by the World Bank to measure economic development
- the united nation's human development index (HDI), involving both economic and social factors.

Table **A** identifies several economic and social measures of development and lists examples from selected countries. You will study Nigeria in Chapter 16.

A *Measures of development for selected countries*

Country	GNI per head (US$)	HDI	Birth rate (per 1000 per year)	Death rate (per 1000 per year)	Infant mortality (per 1000 live births per year)	Number of doctors (per 1000 people)	Literacy rate (%)	% of population with access to safe water
USA	55 200	0.915	12.49	9.35	5.87	2.5	99.0	99
Japan	42 000	0.891	7.93	9.51	2.08	2.3	99.0	100
UK	43 430	0.907	12.17	9.35	4.38	2.8	99.0	100
Brazil	11 530	0.755	14.46	6.58	18.60	1.9	92.6	98
Turkey	10 830	0.761	16.33	5.88	18.87	1.70	95.0	100
China	7 400	0.727	12.49	7.53	12.44	1.90	96.4	95
Nigeria	**2970**	**0.514**	**37.64**	**12.90**	**72.70**	**0.40**	**59.6**	**69**
Ivory Coast	1 450	0.462	28.67	9.55	58.70	0.01	43.1	82
Bangladesh	1 080	0.570	21.14	5.61	44.09	0.40	61.5	87
Zimbabwe	840	0.509	32.26	10.13	26.11	0.10	86.5	77

How useful are the measures of development?

Some of the measures shown in table **A** are more useful than others.

- **Birth rate** is a reliable measure. As a country develops, women are likely to become educated and want a career rather than staying at home. They marry later and have fewer children.
- **Death rate** is a less reliable measure. Developed countries such as the UK, Germany and Japan tend to have older populations and death rates will be high. In less developed countries, such as the Ivory Coast or Bangladesh, death rate may be lower because there are proportionally more young people.
- **Infant mortality** rate is a useful measure of a county's health care system.
- The number of doctors per 1000 people indicates how much money a country has for medical services.
- A high **literacy rate** shows a country has a good education system.
- A high percentage of access to clean water shows a country has modern infrastructure, such as dams, reservoirs and water treatment plants.

An indicator with several variables, such as the human development index (HDI) or the physical quality of life index (PQLI), combines social and economic factors. These indicators are generally more useful.

The development gap

What are the limitations of economic and social measures?

A single measure of development can give a false picture, as it gives the *average* for the whole country. Both photos in **B** were taken in an Arab country with a high GNI. But these two people clearly have a very different quality of life.

Other factors may limit the usefulness of economic and social measures of development:

- Data could be out of date or hard to collect.
- Data may be unreliable (the level of infant mortality is well above the figures given by some countries).
- They focus on certain aspects of development and may not take into account subsistence or informal economies, which are important in many countries.
- Government corruption may mean that data are unreliable.

In many countries the top 10 per cent of the population may own 80 per cent of the wealth. It may also be concentrated in cities while rural areas remain very poor.

How can we compare people's quality of life?

People in different countries have very different ideas of what affects their quality of life. Consider refugees fleeing war-torn Syria in 2016 to seek sanctuary in Europe. They have virtually nothing but they are at least relatively safe. This is why it is very difficult to use social indicators to compare different countries' level of development.

B *Variations in development within a rich country.*

Maths skills

Studying correlation (relationship) between data sets

Graph **C** is called a scattergraph (see page 346). It shows the relationship between HDI and birth rate. You might expect that the higher the level of development (HDI) the lower the birth rate. This is shown by the negative relationship indicated by the 'best fit' line.

1. Draw a scattergraph to show the correlation between HDI and *one* of the other measures in table **A**. Describe the relationship (if there is one) and draw a best fit line.
2. Use the data in the table to do the same to show the correlation between a *social* index and an *economic* one.

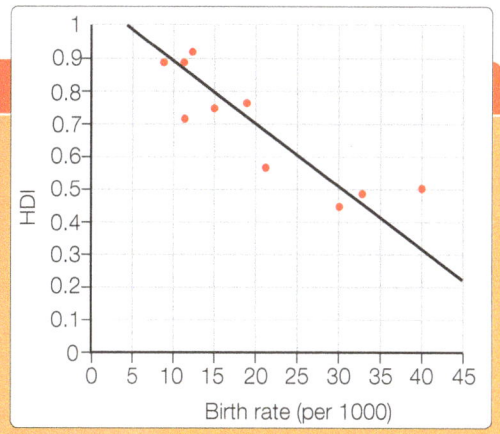

C *Correlation between HDI and birth rate*

ACTIVITIES

1. Study table **A**.
    a. List the measures where a higher figure indicates a higher level of development.
    b. List the measures where a lower figure indicates a higher level of development.
    c. Which figures for Turkey appear to be anomalies (exceptions)?
    d. Why is death rate a poor measure of development?
2. Suggest why there are such clear differences in the quality of life of the two people in the photos in **B**.

Stretch yourself

Why is it so difficult to give a true picture of the level of development in many Arab countries?

Practice question

Use a range of development indicators to explain the difference between standard of living and quality of life.
(6 marks)

15.3 The demographic transition model

On this spread you will find out how levels of development can be linked to the demographic transition model

What is the demographic transition model?

The demographic transition model (DTM) (diagram **A**) shows changes over time in the population of a country. It is based on the changes that took place in western countries such as the UK.

The gap between birth rate and death rate is called *natural change*. This usually shows a natural increase in population but in Stages 1 and 5 a *natural decrease* happens.

The total population of a country responds to variations in birth and death rates (natural change). It will also be affected by migration, both *immigration* (people moving in) and *emigration* (people moving out). This is not shown in the DTM.

What links the DTM with development?

As a country becomes more developed its *population characteristics* change. Graph **A** shows the general increase in level of development from Stage 1 to Stage 5.

A *The demographic transition model*

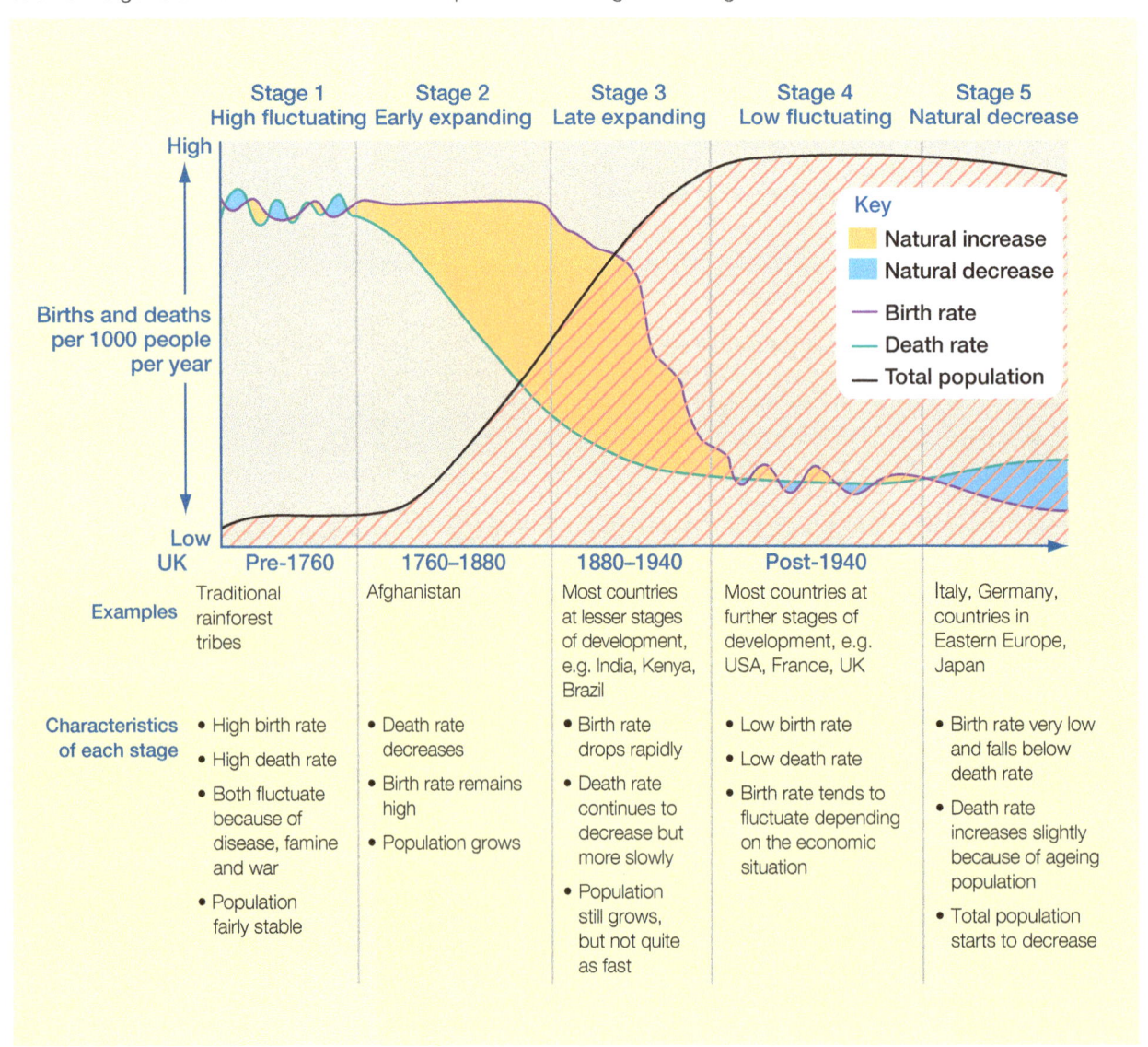

	Stage 1 High fluctuating	Stage 2 Early expanding	Stage 3 Late expanding	Stage 4 Low fluctuating	Stage 5 Natural decrease
UK	Pre-1760	1760–1880	1880–1940	Post-1940	
Examples	Traditional rainforest tribes	Afghanistan	Most countries at lesser stages of development, e.g. India, Kenya, Brazil	Most countries at further stages of development, e.g. USA, France, UK	Italy, Germany, countries in Eastern Europe, Japan
Characteristics of each stage	• High birth rate • High death rate • Both fluctuate because of disease, famine and war • Population fairly stable	• Death rate decreases • Birth rate remains high • Population grows	• Birth rate drops rapidly • Death rate continues to decrease but more slowly • Population still grows, but not quite as fast	• Low birth rate • Low death rate • Birth rate tends to fluctuate depending on the economic situation	• Birth rate very low and falls below death rate • Death rate increases slightly because of ageing population • Total population starts to decrease

Key:
- Natural increase
- Natural decrease
- Birth rate
- Death rate
- Total population

Births and deaths per 1000 people per year

The development gap

Countries at different stages of development

Stage 1: Traditional rainforest tribes
In parts of Indonesia, Brazil and Malaysia, small groups of people live separately with little contact with the outside world. They have high birth and death rates (photo **B**).

Stage 2: Afghanistan
Afghanistan is one of the poorest and least developed countries in the world. Its birth rate is 39 per 1000 and its death rate is 14 per 1000. About 80 per cent of the population are farmers who need children to support them in the fields and tending livestock.

B *Rainforest tribe*

C *Germany's ageing population*

Stage 3: Nigeria
Nigeria is a newly emerging economy (NEE) experiencing economic growth. The death rate is much lower than birth rate (see page 204). The country's population is growing rapidly.

Stage 4: USA
The USA is one of the most developed countries in the world. Good-quality health care means death rates are low (8 per 1000). Women tend to have small families, choosing to study and follow careers. Therefore, birth rate is low (13 per 1000). Population growth is due mainly to immigration.

Stage 5: Germany
Germany is a well-developed country experiencing population decline as death rate exceeds birth rate. The birth rate is 8.2 per 1000 – the lowest in the world. Women have careers and have few children. With an ageing population, Germany's death rate (11.2 per 1000) will continue to rise (photo **C**).

ACTIVITIES

1. Draw a sketch to show the DTM. Indicate on your sketch the links with economic development.
2. How does a falling birth rate reflect increased economic development?
3. How can an increasing death rate reflect high levels of development?
4. Consider the possible impacts for Germany of being in Stage 5 of the DTM. How might it have a negative effect on development?

Stretch yourself

Investigate the population and developmental characteristics of Afghanistan. Do you agree that it is in Stage 2 with a low level of development?

Practice question

Evaluate how far economic development can be linked to the DTM. *(6 marks)*

15.4 Changing population structures

On this spread you will find out how the population structures of two contrasting countries are changing

Population pyramids

Geographers don't only look at total population numbers – they also look at the *structure* of a population. That means thinking about how many babies are being born and how many people are dying – and how the number of people in different age groups is changing. This is done using graphs called *population pyramids*.

A population pyramid is a type of graph which shows the percentage, or number, of males and females in each age group – how many aged 0–4 years, 5–9 years, and so on.

Understanding population pyramids

It is important to know how to 'read' a population pyramid.

- *Understanding the overall* shape. For example, if the pyramid is wide at the bottom – like those for Mexico in graph **A** – it means that there is a high proportion of young people in the population.
- *Interpreting details* – for example, bars that are longer or shorter than those above and below them. Shorter bars could indicate high death rates in those age groups – perhaps through war or famine.

The dependency ratio

The *dependency ratio* is the proportion of people below (aged 0–14) and above (over 65) normal working age. This is calculated by adding together the numbers for both groups, then dividing by the number aged 15–64 (the 'working population'), and multiplying by 100.

The lower the number, the greater the number of people who work and are less dependent. The higher the number, the greater the number who are dependent on the working population. Low dependency ratios are more common in HICs than NEEs and LICs.

Dependency ratios change as a country develops.

Why is Mexico's population structure changing?

Mexico has a large proportion of young people. Under-15s currently make up 28 per cent of the population, and just over 7 per cent are over 65. The average age is 27. But Mexico's population structure is slowly changing:

- Death rate is falling – just 5 deaths per 1000. More babies are being born and people are living longer, due to an increase in childhood vaccination and improved health care.
- Birth rate is 19 per 1000 and falling rapidly. Even if people have fewer children than their parents, the population of Mexico will continue to rise for some time to come.

It is expected to be at least 50 years before Mexico's population levels out. Today's young people will then be moving into old age.

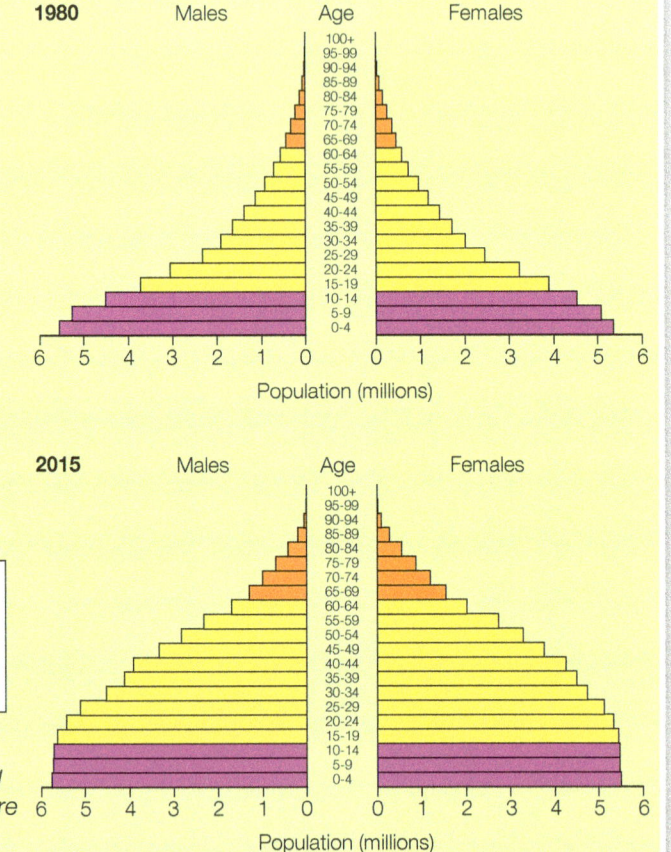

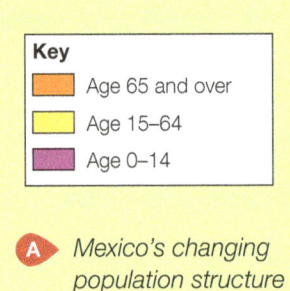

Key
- Age 65 and over
- Age 15–64
- Age 0–14

A Mexico's changing population structure

The development gap

How is Japan's population structure changing?

By contrast with Mexico, Japan has an ageing population which is getting smaller (graph **B**). Japan has the oldest population in the world – 27 per cent of the population are over 65 (with under-15s just 13.1 per cent). The average age is 46. Japan's population structure is also changing:

- People are living longer. Death rate is 10 per 1000. Average life expectancy in Japan is 80 for men and 87 for women, due to a healthy diet (low in fat and salt) and a good quality of life. Japan is one of the richest countries in the world and has good health care and welfare systems. There are 230 doctors for every 100 000 people (compared with 207 in Mexico).

- Birth rate in Japan is 8 per 1000 and has been falling since 1975. The average age when women have their first child rose from 26 in 1970 to 30 in 2012. The number of couples getting married has fallen and the age at which they get married has increased.

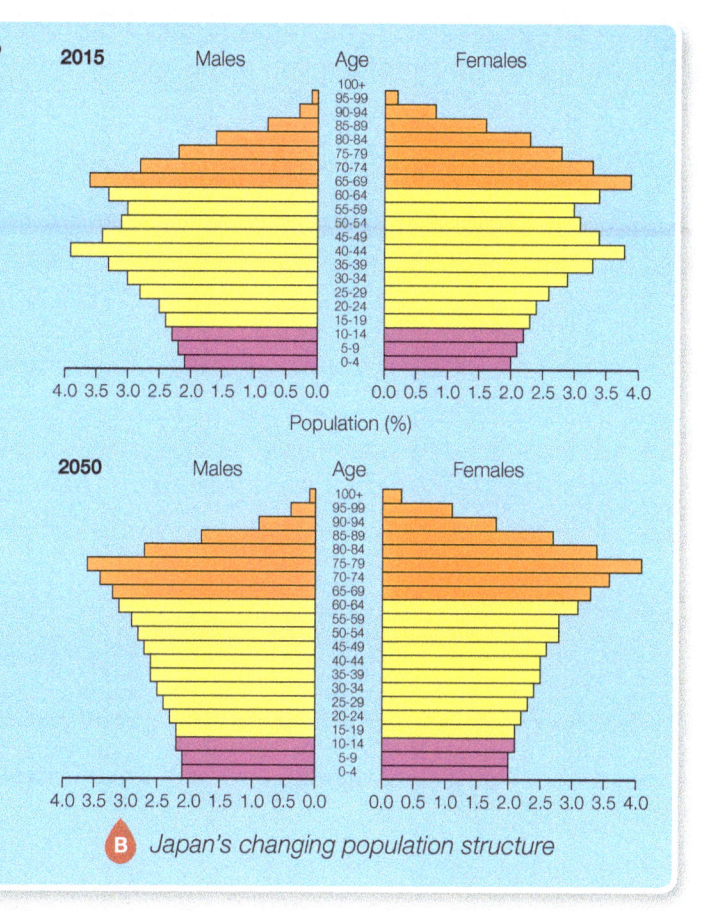

B *Japan's changing population structure*

Population pyramids and the DTM

Countries at different stages of the DTM have different-shaped population pyramids. If you can recognise the different basic shapes, and understand what they're showing, then you can tell which stage of the model a country has reached (diagram **C**).

C *Population pyramid shapes for the stages of the DTM*

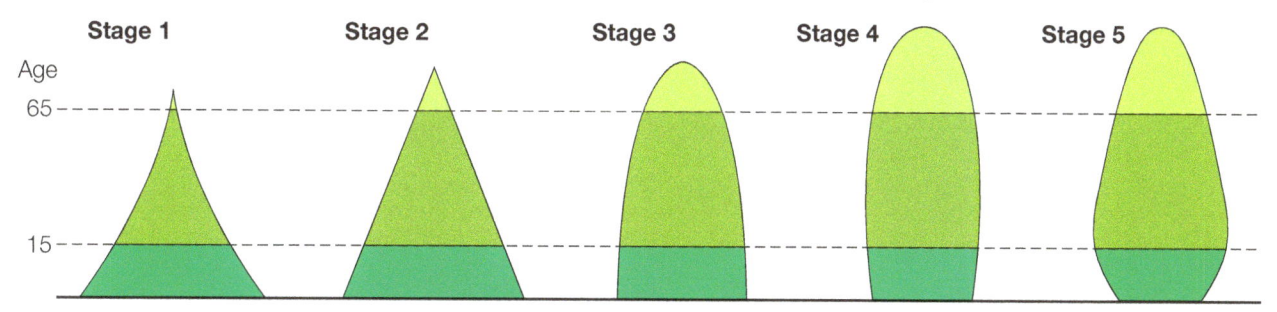

ACTIVITIES

1. Explain what population pyramids show.
2. Look at the two population pyramids for Mexico (graph **A**).
   a. Describe the shape of the pyramid in 1980.
   b. What changes took place between 1980 and 2015?
   c. Suggest reasons for the changes you have identified.

Stretch yourself

Use the population pyramids for Japan (graph **B**) to explain why the country's population is getting older and is declining.

Practice question

Compare the population structure of an LIC or NEE with one for an HIC. *(6 marks)*

185

15.5 Causes of uneven development

On this spread you will find out about the physical, economic and historical causes of uneven development

Physical causes of uneven development

The physical geography of some countries can make development difficult. For example:

- The most landlocked countries on Earth are in Africa. This means a country is only bordered by land. With no access to the seas, a country is cut off from seaborne trade, which is important for economic growth.

- Tropical Africa, South America and Asia have more climate-related diseases and pests than cooler parts of the world (such as mosquitoes, which can spread malaria). Disease affects the ability of the population to stay healthy enough to work.

- Extreme weather events, such as cyclones, droughts and floods, often hit tropical regions – Africa in particular is badly affected (photo **A**). An extreme weather season can slow development and it can be costly to repair damaged infrastructure.

- The lack of adequate supplies of safer water is a barrier to economic development.

A *Sheep that have fallen victim to drought in Somalia*

Clean water is essential to ensure good health and enable people to work effectively

Drought affects many of the world's poorer countries, particularly in Africa

Poor irrigation limits the development of commercial farming

People can waste several hours a day walking to collect water

Many countries lack the money to develop water storage and distribution systems

B *Filling water containers to carry back to the village in Kenya*

Economic causes

It can be said that poverty causes poverty. Low life expectancy, frequent illness and the lack of a nutritious diet make economic development hard to achieve.

Trade

North America and Europe dominate world trade (graph **C**). The importance of Asia is growing as it includes Japan and the emerging economies of India and China. Most of the world's trade is between richer countries.

Rich countries and large international companies have a lot of power. They want to pay as little as possible for their raw materials, many of which come from LICs. There is often more supply than demand for raw materials, which keeps prices low. Processing, which adds value, takes place in the richer developed countries. In this way, the rich countries get richer and the poorer countries are not able to develop.

C *Percentage of world trade by region*

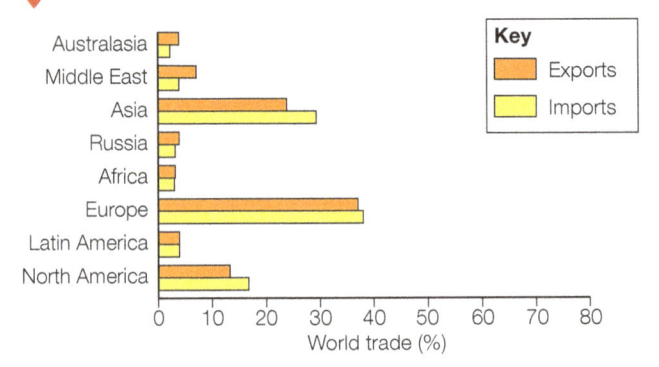

The development gap

LICs and NEEs have traditionally exported *primary products* such as minerals and agricultural products. In the last 20 years many of these countries have developed manufacturing. Manufactured products now make up about 80 per cent of the exports of NEEs. Some countries have trade surpluses, while others have trade deficits. This often leads to a 'debt trap', which makes further development difficult.

Copper in Zambia

In Zambia copper accounts for over 60 per cent of the total value of exports. Its other exports include sugar, tobacco, gemstones and cotton. Its main trading partner is Switzerland (45 per cent of total exports). The price for copper has fluctuated a lot since 2000 (graph **D**). With an HDI of 0.39, Zambia is described as having 'low human development'.

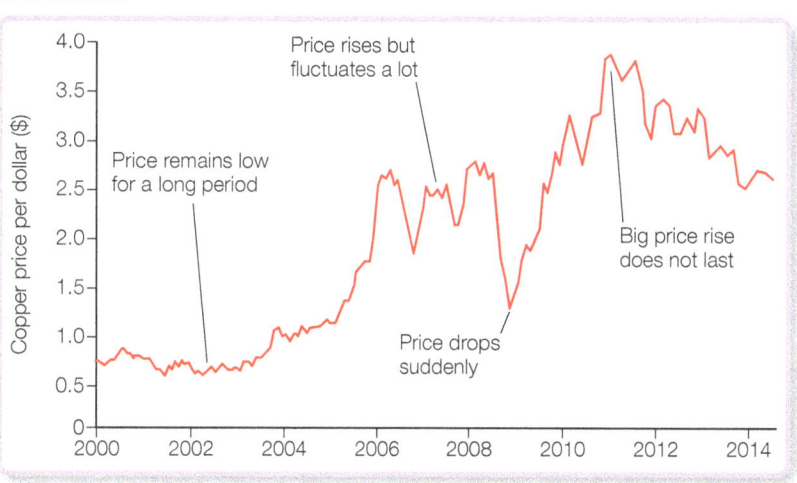

D World price for copper, 2000–14

Historical causes

Many richer countries have a long history of industrial and economic development. While some countries, particularly in Asia and South America (e.g. China, Malaysia and Mexico) have recently emerged as industrialised nations, many other countries have yet to experience any significant economic growth.

Colonialism

From around 1400, European explorers set out to control new territories, often seeking mineral wealth such as gold. From 1650 to 1900 over 10 million people were transported from Africa to North America to work as slaves on plantations. Almost all of the wealth produced in this period went to European powers.

By the end of the nineteenth century much of Africa and parts of South America and Asia had been divided up between the European superpowers. Countries such as the UK, Germany, Spain and France had powerful empires and colonies. Since 1950 former European colonies have gained independence. In many cases this has been a difficult process, resulting in civil wars and political struggles for power. Money has been spent on armaments and some governments have been corrupt. This political instability has held back development.

Think about it

What are the economic risks when a country is dependent on a single export?

ACTIVITIES

1. What are the main physical causes of unequal global development? Try to expand the list given.
2. What are the issues with water supply in photo **B**?
3. a What percentage of world trade shown in graph **C** was 'exports from Europe'?
   b What percentage of world trade was 'imports to Asia'?
4. a Describe the trends in the world price for copper (graph **D**).
   b What impact does this have on the Zambian economy?

Stretch yourself

Investigate the impact of colonialism in Kenya and the difficulties associated with independence.

Practice question

Explain the link between trade and the development gap. *(6 marks)*

15.6 Uneven development – wealth and health

On this spread you will find out how uneven development leads to inequalities of wealth and health

What is the imbalance between rich and poor?

There is a global imbalance between rich and poor. Some countries, particularly in Africa and parts of the Middle East, have lower levels of development and a poorer quality of life than richer western countries.

Imbalances also exist within countries. Areas of considerable poverty can be found in parts of the UK and USA, and great wealth in some of the world's poorest countries. Inequalities exist at all scales and in all countries.

How does uneven development lead to disparities in wealth?

There is a clear link between a country's development and the wealth of its people. The most developed countries enjoy the greatest wealth. Wealth, in the form of **gross national income (GNI)** is often used as a measure of levels of development (map **B** page 178).

There are significant differences between the wealth of different global regions (graph **B**).

- In 2014 the fastest growth in wealth was in North America, which now holds 35 per cent of total global wealth. This wealth is held by just over 5 per cent of the world's adult population!
- The USA is not the world's wealthiest country (that is Qatar), but it is the world's most important economic 'engine of growth'.
- Of the NEEs, China has recorded the highest growth since 2000. Personal wealth in India and China has quadrupled since 2000, yet its global share of wealth is still well below that of its population.
- Africa's share of global wealth is very small (about 1 per cent).

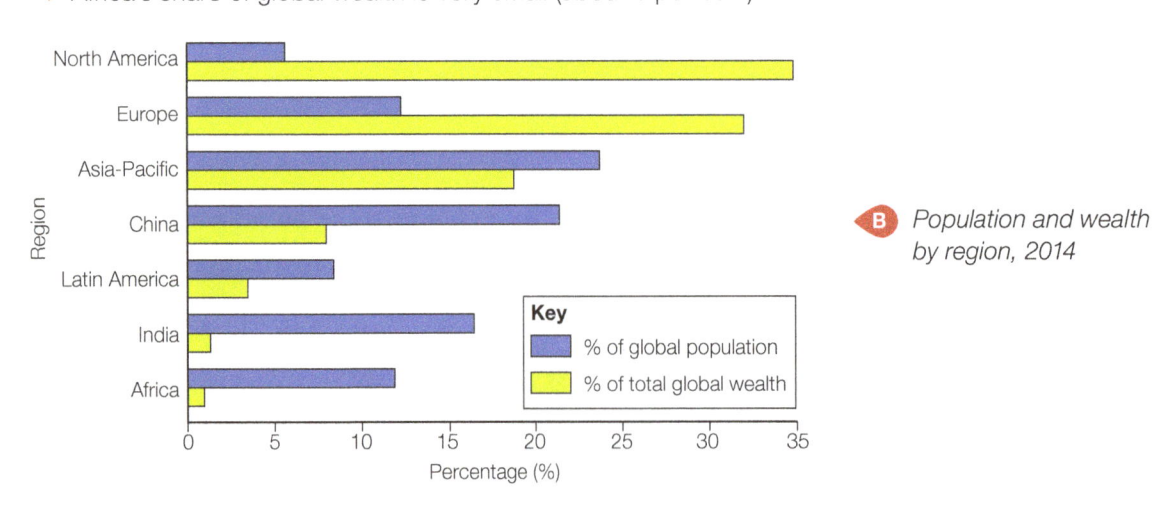

Did you know?
The wealthiest 1 per cent now possesses more than half of total global wealth.

A A cartoon highlighting global inequalities

B Population and wealth by region, 2014

Key
- % of global population
- % of total global wealth

The development gap

Disparities in health

Levels of development are closely linked to health. LICs are unable to invest in good-quality health care. In the world's poorest countries health care is often very patchy. There is a wide disparity between causes of death in HICs and LICs.

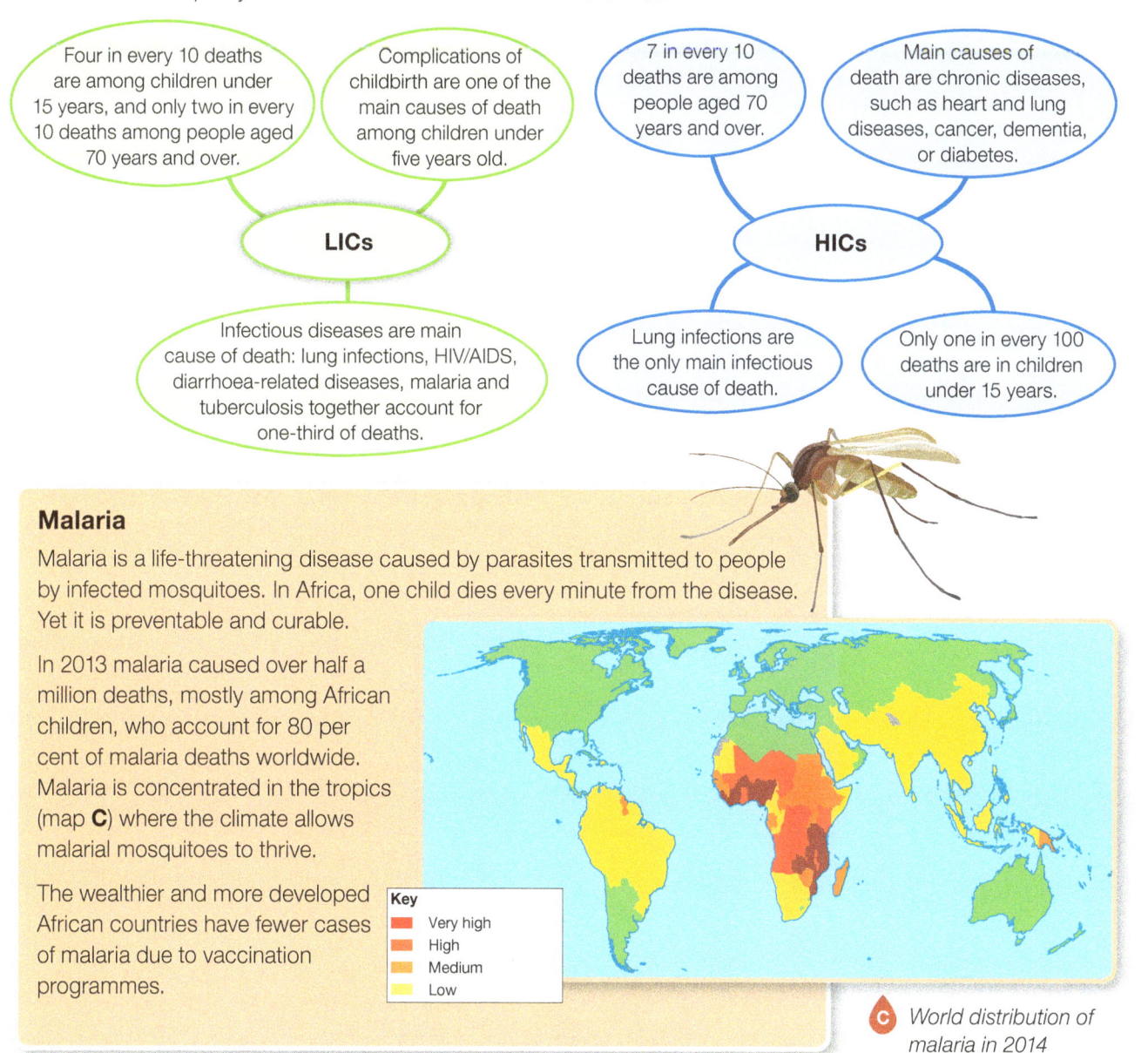

LICs
- Four in every 10 deaths are among children under 15 years, and only two in every 10 deaths among people aged 70 years and over.
- Complications of childbirth are one of the main causes of death among children under five years old.
- Infectious diseases are main cause of death: lung infections, HIV/AIDS, diarrhoea-related diseases, malaria and tuberculosis together account for one-third of deaths.

HICs
- 7 in every 10 deaths are among people aged 70 years and over.
- Main causes of death are chronic diseases, such as heart and lung diseases, cancer, dementia, or diabetes.
- Lung infections are the only main infectious cause of death.
- Only one in every 100 deaths are in children under 15 years.

Malaria

Malaria is a life-threatening disease caused by parasites transmitted to people by infected mosquitoes. In Africa, one child dies every minute from the disease. Yet it is preventable and curable.

In 2013 malaria caused over half a million deaths, mostly among African children, who account for 80 per cent of malaria deaths worldwide. Malaria is concentrated in the tropics (map **C**) where the climate allows malarial mosquitoes to thrive.

The wealthier and more developed African countries have fewer cases of malaria due to vaccination programmes.

Key
- Very high
- High
- Medium
- Low

C World distribution of malaria in 2014

ACTIVITIES

1. How does cartoon **A** show the causes and effects of global disparities of wealth?
2. a Which two regions in graph **B** have a higher share of global wealth than their share of the world's population?
   b Which region has the greatest disparity between wealth and population?
3. Describe and suggest reasons for the pattern of malaria cases (map **C**).
4. To what extent is malaria a disease of poverty?

Stretch yourself

Investigate why malaria is such a devastating disease in Africa. What factors will influence its future eradication from the continent?

Practice question

How does uneven development lead to disparities of global wealth? *(4 marks)*

15.7 Uneven development – migration

On this spread you will find out how uneven development leads to international migration

What are the different types of migration?

Photo **A** shows a group of migrants fleeing from poverty, war and persecution in Afghanistan and Syria. They are seeking safety and the chance of a better life in Europe. International migration is one of the main consequences of uneven development, as people seek to improve the quality of their lives.

Migration is the movement of people from place to place. It can be voluntary, where people consider the advantages and disadvantages of moving. Or it can be forced, where people have little or no choice to escape natural disasters, wars or persecution. It is important to make sure you understand the following terms.

- **Immigrant** – a person who moves into a country.
- **Emigrant** – a person who moves out of a country.
- **Economic migrant** – a person who moves voluntarily to seek a better life, such as a better-paid job or benefits like education and health care.
- **Refugee** – a person forced to move from their country of origin often as a result of civil war or a natural disaster such as an earthquake.
- **Displaced person** – a person forced to move from their home but who stays in their country of origin.

A Afghan and Syrian migrants in a temporary shelter in Greece, 2015

Middle East refugee crisis, 2015

In the last few years hundreds of thousands of desperate refugees have fled their homes in Syria, Afghanistan and Iraq in search of a better life in Europe. They are responding to uneven levels of development.

In Syria a civil war has raged since 2011. In five years the war has claimed 470 000 lives, and 11.5 per cent of Syria's population has been killed or injured. Four million have fled the country to temporary camps in Turkey, Jordan and Lebanon. Here there are no jobs and few prospects of a better life.

Thousands have made the dangerous journey across the Mediterranean in overcrowded and unsafe boats. Some of these have capsized and many lives have been lost. Some people made the long journey by land through Turkey and into eastern Europe (map **B**).

B Main migration routes from Syria into Europe

190

The development gap

In August 2015 Germany announced that it would process asylum claims for anyone who reached Germany. This sparked a mass exodus across Europe (photo **C**). Many more people left Syria to escape the war.

It's estimated that 1.1 million migrants entered Germany in 2015. German Chancellor Angela Merkel came under pressure to slow the number of arrivals. In March 2016, the EU and Turkey signed a deal to give Turkey political and financial benefits in return for taking back refugees and migrants.

Many refugees have also travelled to Sweden and through France towards the UK. The UK government has pledged to accept 20 000 refugees.

In January 2016, Sweden announced it was going to deport 80 000 migrants.

C *Syrian refugees walking through Europe to Germany*

Economic migration to the UK

The UK has a long history of accepting migrants from all over the world. The country is known for its tolerant approach and many parts of the UK benefit from being multicultural.

Since 2004 over 1.5 million economic migrants have moved to the UK, two-thirds of whom are Polish. The unemployment rate in Poland is over 10 per cent, and workers can earn up to five times as much in the UK. Money is often sent home to friends and relatives.

Most migrants pay tax, which is good for the UK economy. They are prepared to work hard, often doing manual jobs such as working on farms (photo **D**). However, they do put additional pressure on services such as health and education.

D *Migrant workers on a Lincolnshire farm*

ACTIVITIES

1. What is the difference between an economic migrant and a refugee?
2. a Describe and suggest reasons for the routes taken by Syrians fleeing their country (map **B**).
   b Why was there a surge in migration to Europe in August 2015?
3. What are the arguments for and against the UK accepting economic migrants?

Stretch yourself

Investigate the migration crisis involving people from Syria, Afghanistan and Iraq. What are the latest trends? Try to find some statistics to support your research.

Practice question

How does uneven development cause international migration? *(4 marks)*

5.8 Reducing the gap

On this spread you will find out how investment, industrial development and tourism can reduce the development gap

What strategies can reduce the development gap?

Reducing the development gap can involve a range of strategies that aim to improve a country's economy and the quality of life of its people.

Investment

Many countries and TNCs choose to invest money and expertise in LICs to increase their profits. Investment can involve:

- the development of infrastructure such as water, roads and electricity
- the construction of dams to provide electricity
- improvements to harbours and ports
- the development of new industries.

Investment can support a country's development by providing employment and income from abroad. As economies grow, poverty decreases and education improves. People become more politically involved, leading to better government. Investment is not the same as a loan, which is simply the provision of money with agreed terms of repayment.

Industrial development

Industrial development brings employment, higher incomes and opportunities to invest in housing, education and **infrastructure**. This is called the *multiplier effect* (diagram **A**). Countries such as Malaysia, Brazil, Mexico and China have all followed programmes of industrialisation to achieve their current levels of development.

A factory creates employment for its workers and money (taxes) for the government.

Money can be invested in schools, roads and services such as water and health care.

The population becomes better educated and healthier.

Opportunities for new investments such as supply industries, shops and community facilities.

A *The multiplier effect*

Foreign investment in Africa

China has now become Africa's most important trading partner, overtaking the USA. However, in recent years a number of American companies have invested in the continent (map **B**).

More than 2000 Chinese companies have invested billions of dollars in Africa, mainly in energy, mining, construction and manufacturing. They have invested in a power plant in Zimbabwe, hydroelectricity in Madagascar and railway construction in Sudan.

Chinese investment has led to new roads, bridges, stadiums and other projects being built all over Africa. The building of the new headquarters of the African Union was funded entirely by China, at a cost of $US200 million.

Overall, there are many benefits to Chinese investment in Africa for all countries involved.

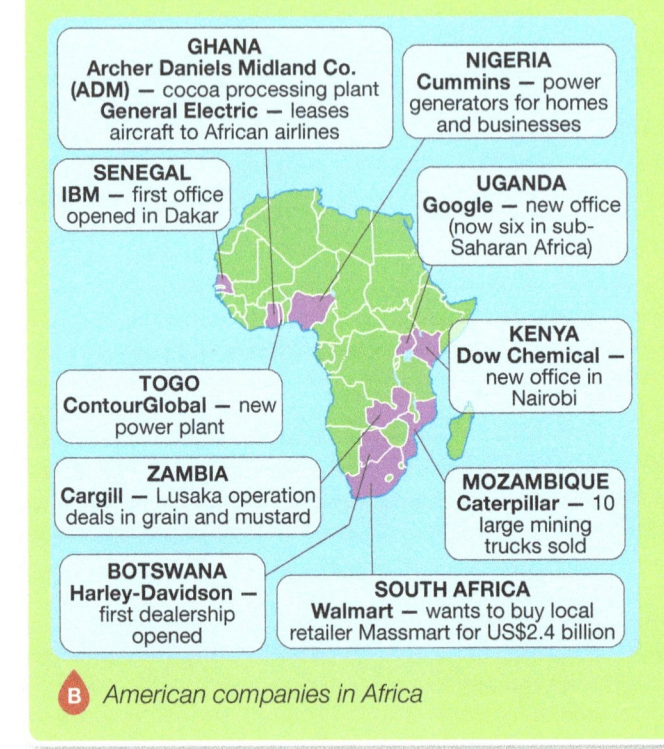

GHANA — Archer Daniels Midland Co. (ADM) — cocoa processing plant; General Electric — leases aircraft to African airlines

NIGERIA — Cummins — power generators for homes and businesses

SENEGAL — IBM — first office opened in Dakar

UGANDA — Google — new office (now six in sub-Saharan Africa)

TOGO — ContourGlobal — new power plant

KENYA — Dow Chemical — new office in Nairobi

ZAMBIA — Cargill — Lusaka operation deals in grain and mustard

MOZAMBIQUE — Caterpillar — 10 large mining trucks sold

BOTSWANA — Harley-Davidson — first dealership opened

SOUTH AFRICA — Walmart — wants to buy local retailer Massmart for US$2.4 billion

B *American companies in Africa*

The development gap

Industrial development in Malaysia

Malaysia is one of the richest countries in south-east Asia. Since the 1970s it has seen a dramatic growth in its wealth and the quality of life of its population. This is due to the development of its natural resources such as oil and gas, palm oil and rubber. It has made use of foreign investment to exploit these resources and develop a thriving manufacturing sector. One of Malaysia's leading products is the Proton car (photo **C**).

Today, Malaysia has a highly developed mixed economy with growing financial and service sectors (table **D**) and flourishing trade links with the rest of the world.

C Proton automated car assembly line

D Malaysia's economic profile

Sector	Average % annual growth rate 2011–15	% share of GDP in 2015
Services	7.2	58.3
Manufacturing	5.7	26.3
Construction	3.7	2.9
Agriculture	3.3	6.6
Mining	1.1	5.9

Tourism

For some countries, tourism has helped to reduce the development gap. Countries with tropical beaches, spectacular landscapes or abundant wildlife have become tourist destinations. This has led to investment and increased income from abroad, which can be used for improving education, infrastructure and housing.

Several countries in the Caribbean, such as the Bahamas and the British Virgin Islands, and Indian Ocean islands such as the Seychelles (photo **E**) and the Maldives have become highly dependent on tourism. This can be an advantage and a disadvantage. Tourism can generate a lot of income but is vulnerable in times of economic recession.

E A tourist village in the Seychelles

ACTIVITIES

1. What is the difference between an investment and a loan?
2. Why do countries such as China and the USA choose to invest in Africa? What are the advantages and disadvantages of foreign investment for African countries?
3. What is the multiplier effect and how can it help to reduce the development gap (diagram **B**)?
4. How can tourism help to close the development gap (photo **E**)?

Stretch yourself

Use the internet to research Chinese and American investment in Africa. Use labels to locate examples of these investments on an outline map of Africa.

Maths skills

Draw two appropriate graphs to display the data in table **D**.

Practice question

How can industrial development reduce the development gap? *(4 marks)*

193

15.9 Reducing the gap – aid and intermediate technology

On this spread you will find out how aid and intermediate technology can reduce the development gap

What is aid?

Aid is when a country or non-governmental organisation (NGO) such as Oxfam donates resources to another country to help it develop or improve people's lives. Aid can take the form of:

- money (grants or loans)
- emergency supplies (tents, medicines, water, etc.)
- food such as rice or wheat, technology (tools or machinery)
- skills (people with special skills such as doctors or engineers).

There are different types of aid, in different circumstances and sometimes with specific conditions attached (diagram **A**).

Short-term – emergency help usually in response to a natural disaster, such as a flood or earthquake

Long-term – sustainable aid that seeks to improve resilience, e.g. wells to reduce the effects of drought, or improvements in agriculture

Bilateral – aid from one country to another (which is often tied)

Types of aid

Tied – aid may be given with certain conditions, e.g. that the recipient has to spend the aid money on the donor country's products

Multilateral – richer governments give money to an international organisation such as the World Bank, which then redistributes the money as aid to poorer countries

Voluntary – money donated by the general public in richer countries and distributed by NGOs such as Oxfam

A *Different types of aid*

How can aid reduce the development gap?

Only long-term aid that is freely given can really address the development gap. Aid can enable countries to invest in development projects such as roads, electricity and water management, which can bring long-term benefits. On a local scale, aid can help improve people's quality of life if it focuses on health care, education and services.

UK aid

The UK currently spends 0.7 per cent of its gross domestic product (GDP – the measure of the wealth of a country) on overseas aid – the target set by the UN. In 2013 the top three recipients of UK Official Development Assistance (ODA) were Pakistan (US$477 million), Ethiopia (US$464 million), and Bangladesh (US$384 million).

B *Tearfund, a UK charity, providing health and hygiene education in Pakistan*

UK aid to Pakistan

Pakistan receives more aid from the UK than any other country (photo **B**). There are currently 66 million people in Pakistan living in poverty, equivalent to the entire population of the UK. The population is set to rise by 50 per cent in less than 40 years. In 2013 aid was spent mainly in the education sector and to reduce hunger and poverty.

The development gap

Goat Aid from Oxfam

Goat Aid Oxfam is a project set up to help families in African countries such as Malawi. The money donated is used to buy a family a goat. This has many advantages for the family and the local community, because:

- goats are an excellent food source, providing both milk and meat
- manure can be used as a crop fertiliser
- milk can be sold as a source of income to pay for food and education
- goats can be bred easily and the kids sold at market or given to other families
- care of the goats builds community spirit.

This helps to improve people's quality of life and to raise the level of development.

C *Goat Aid provides money to buy school uniforms*

What is intermediate technology?

Intermediate technology is sustainable technology that is appropriate to the needs, skills, knowledge and wealth of local people. It must be suitable for the local environment and must not put people out of work.

How can intermediate technology reduce the development gap?

Intermediate technology takes the form of small-scale projects often associated with agriculture, water or health. These involve local communities, and can make a real difference to the quality of people's lives.

Irrigation at Adis Nifas, Ethiopia

The village of Adis Nifas is in northern Ethiopia, north Africa. Here, a small dam (about 15 m high and 300 m long) was built to create a reservoir close to the village's fields. Appropriate machinery and money were given and the village provided the labour.

Each family has been given an area of irrigated land with fruit trees. Elephant grass is grown to divide the fields and help prevent soil erosion. The irrigated land is now providing a permanent food supply for the villagers.

The project made use of intermediate technology to build and run the dam scheme (photo **D**).

- Employment for local people
- Local tools and knowledge
- Local materials such as stones and sand
- Treadle pumps used to lift water to the fields
- Reduction in soil erosion stops the reservoir silting up

D *Taking water from the Adis Nifas dam*

ACTIVITIES

1. Outline the different types of aid and suggest which are most appropriate in reducing the development gap.
2. **a** To what extent is Oxfam's Goat Aid project sustainable?
   b Can you suggest any problems with the scheme?
3. What evidence is there that the Adis Nifas project is sustainable?
4. Write a paragraph arguing the case for the use of aid to fund intermediate technology projects.

Stretch yourself

Find out more about the Tekeze Dam in Ethiopia. Will the dam help Ethiopia's development needs?

Practice question

Explain why the use of aid must be sustainable if it is to be effective in raising a poor country's level of development.
(6 marks)

195

15.10 Reducing the gap – Fairtrade

On this spread you will find out how Fairtrade can reduce the development gap

Is trade fair?

Richer countries benefit more from world trade than poorer countries. This explains why in some cases the development gap is widening. Rich countries are powerful enough to protect their trade using two main systems.

- *Tariffs* are taxes paid on imports. They make imported goods more expensive and less attractive than home-produced goods.
- *Quotas* are limits on the quantity of goods that can be imported. They are usually applied to primary products so they affect mainly poorer countries.

What is free trade?

Free trade is when countries do not charge tariffs and quotas to restrict trade with each other. This has the potential to benefit the world's poorest countries and help reduce the development gap.

The World Trade Organization (WTO) aims to make trade easier and remove barriers. One of the main barriers to trade is *agricultural subsidy*. This is financial support from governments to help their farmers. Rich countries can afford to pay subsidies and so their products are cheaper than those produced by poorer countries. This goes against free trade.

Trading groups are countries that have grouped together to increase the level of trade between them by cutting tariffs and discouraging trade with non-members. The European Union (EU) is an example.

There are advantages for poor countries in joining a trading group.

- It encourages trade between member countries.
- Richer countries cannot shop around for cheaper prices.
- Members can command a greater share of the market.
- Members are able to get higher prices for their goods.

Cocoa from Ghana

Ghana in West Africa is the world's largest producer of cocoa beans (photo **A**). Most of the processing and packaging of the cocoa is done in Europe. The EU charges 7.7 per cent import tariff on cocoa powder and 15 per cent on chocolate. But no tariff is charged on raw cocoa beans. So Ghana is forced to export the beans rather than develop its own industry making chocolate, which would be more valuable.

A *Cocoa farmer in Ghana*

Key
- Major trade group
- Loose-knit trade group
- Smaller trade group of HICs
- Smaller trade group of LICs
- OPEC countries

B *Global trading groups*

The development gap

Poorer countries have formed trading groups (map **B**), such as CARICOM (Caribbean Community), UEMOA (West African Economic and Monetary Union) and ECOWAS (Economic Community of West African States – see page 206).

Fairtrade

You may have seen the **Fairtrade** logo (image **C**). Fairtrade sets standards for trade with poorer countries. It seeks to reduce the development gap by improving the quality of life for ordinary farmers. Fairtrade is an international movement. It helps to ensure that producers in poor countries get a fair deal.

- The farmer gets all the money from the sale of their crop.
- It guarantees the farmer a fair price.
- Part of the price is invested in local community development projects.
- In return, the farmer must agree to farm in an environmentally friendly way.
- The product gains a stronger position in the global market.

C *The Fairtrade logo*

D *A Gumutindo farmer from Uganda*

Ugandan coffee farmers

Over 90 per cent of small coffee farmers in eastern Uganda have joined the Gumutindo Coffee Cooperative to gain economies of scale. This means making savings by buying and selling larger amounts of coffee. The farmers also earn extra income from the Fairtrade Premium. This would not be possible if individual farmers tried to sell their coffee.

The first stage of processing the coffee beans is done on the farm. The semi-processed beans are worth more to the farmer than unprocessed beans. They are then sent to a nearby warehouse for milling, before being packed for export abroad, where the final roasting takes place. The processing of the coffee beans adds value to the product and increases the farmer's income.

Last year the money from the Fairtrade Premium helped pay my son's school fees. Other farmers have tried to copy what we are doing and the quality of the coffee is getting better!

ACTIVITIES

1. Describe how the cocoa farmer in photo **A** harvests his crop.
2. a What is the difference between tariffs and quotas?
   b What effect do EU tariffs have on Ghanaian farmers?
3. Which countries are members of the following trading groups: EU; NAFTA; OPEC (map **B**)?
4. a Write a paragraph explaining how Fairtrade benefits poorer countries.
   b How does it help reduce the development gap?

Stretch yourself

Investigate whether there are any disadvantages of the Fairtrade scheme.

Practice question

Discuss whether trade or aid is the best way for poorer countries to develop. *(9 marks)*

15.11 Reducing the gap – debt relief

On this spread you will find out how debt relief and microfinance loans can help reduce the development gap

Loans and debt

One country may borrow money from another country, or from an international organisation such as the World Bank, in order to invest in development projects. This loan has to be repaid with interest.

How have poor countries built up debt?

Many of the world's poorest countries built up debt in the 1970s and 1980s. This led to a **debt crisis**. Many poor countries borrowed money to develop their economies by investing in industry, manufacturing and infrastructure. Low commodity prices reduced the value of their exports and high oil prices increased the price of imports. Both these factors increased the debt of poor countries.

The highly indebted poor countries (HIPCs) are the 39 countries with the highest level of poverty and debt (map **A**). They are unable to repay their debt and the high level of interest.

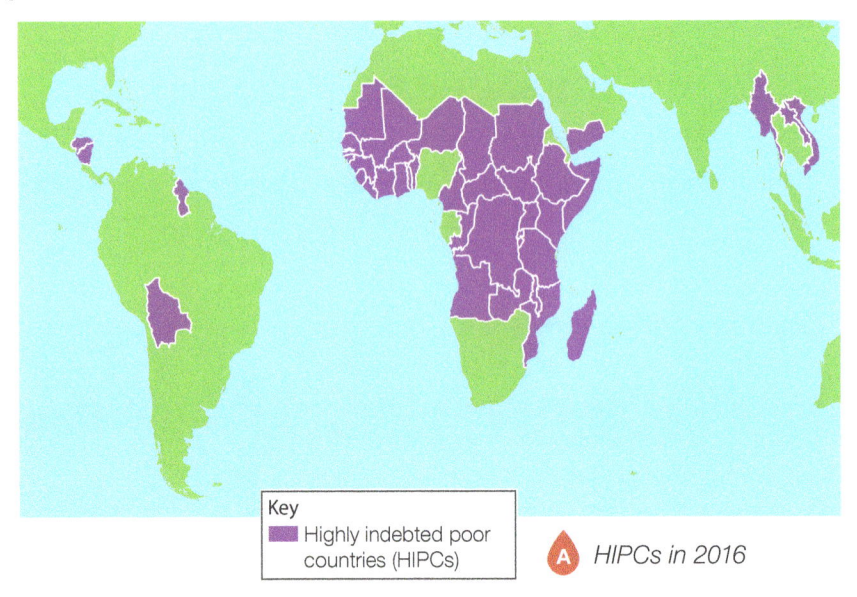

A HIPCs in 2016

Key: Highly indebted poor countries (HIPCs)

Debt relief

At their meeting in 2005, the world's richest countries (known as the 'G8') agreed to cancel the debts of many of the HIPCs (text **B**). To qualify for debt relief, countries had to:

- demonstrate they could manage their own finances
- show there was no corruption in their government
- agree to spend the saved debt money on education, health care and reducing poverty.

> On 6 January 2006, the IMF cancelled the debts owed to it by 19 of the world's poorest countries. This will change the lives of millions of people. In Ghana the money saved is being used for basic infrastructure, including rural feeder roads, as well as increased expenditure on education and health care. In Tanzania, the government is using the money saved to import vital food supplies for those affected by drought. Across Africa, lifting the burden of debt is allowing millions of dollars to be directed to fighting poverty instead of repaying rich countries.

B Announcement by the IMF in 2006

By 2015, 36 of the HIPCs had met these conditions and were receiving full debt relief from the International Monetary Fund (IMF). The total amount of debt relief for all HIPCs is around US$75 billion. The three countries yet to satisfy the terms for debt relief are Eritrea, Somalia and Sudan.

Despite the debt relief, African countries still have debt of over US$300 billion and are unlikely to ever be able to repay it.

The development gap

How can debt relief reduce the development gap?

Debt relief can help poor countries invest money in development projects, such as industry, resources or infrastructure. By cancelling their debts, some countries have used the money saved to improve the quality of life for their people. For example, in Tanzania free education is now available, resulting in a 66 per cent increase in attendance. In Uganda the government has spent money to provide safe water to over 2 million people.

However, debt relief can also lead to problems.

- Countries may get into further debt, expecting that this will also be written off in the future.
- Corrupt governments may keep the money rather than use it to help the poor.

What is microfinance?

Microfinance is small-scale financial support available directly from banks set up especially to help the poor. Small **microfinance loans** enable individuals or families to start up small businesses and helps them to become self-sufficient. Many borrowers are women. As small businesses thrive, employment opportunities increase and incomes rise.

Did you know?
The world's poorest countries pay more than US$1.5 billion a day in interest repayments.

Grameen Bank, Bangladesh

This bank was set up in Bangladesh in 1976. The name comes from the Sanskrit word for 'village'. The bank was founded to help local people, especially women, use their skills to develop small businesses. Borrowers have a share in the ownership of the bank, so there is a good rate of repayment. Loans are often less than US$100 with low interest. The bank has so far lent over US$11 billion to 7 million members.

The bank lends US$200 to village women to buy a mobile phone. Other villagers then pay the women to use the phones. The loan can then be repaid and the borrower makes a small profit. The phones help people to check prices before they go to market, keep in touch with relatives who have moved to the city and receive health advice. Halima Khatun owns 15 hens and sells their eggs for a living. She uses the village phone to try to get a better price (photo **C**).

C Using the village phone

Last week, they wanted to pay me 12 taka per hali [four eggs]. I checked the prices using the village phone. The price was 14 taka in nearby markets. We agreed to buy and sell at 13 taka per hali.

ACTIVITIES

1. a Which continent has the most HIPCs (map **A**)?
   b Use an atlas to name two HIPCs from this continent and one from each of two other continents.
2. Do you think debt relief for HIPCs benefits richer countries? Give your reasons.
3. Explain how the use of a mobile phone has helped Halima Khatun and her egg business. Can you suggest other ways that she might use the phone to support her business?

Stretch yourself

Investigate the 'Make Poverty History' movement. What are its links with debt relief?

Practice question

How can debt relief help to improve the status of women? *(4 marks)*

15.12 Reducing the gap – tourism

On this spread you will find out how tourism in Jamaica can help reduce the development gap

Example

What is the state of Jamaica's economy?

Jamaica is one of the largest islands in the West Indies. Its population is 2.7 million, just over a third of the size of London. Its economy is based upon a range of minerals (such as bauxite and oil), agricultural products (sugar and rum) and some manufacturing. It is classed as an 'upper middle-income country', but has suffered from slow growth, debt and high unemployment over a long period.

How has tourism contributed to Jamaica's development?

Tourism, along with bauxite and energy, is one of the few growth sectors of Jamaica's economy. The country has become a popular tourist destination (map **B**), offering beautiful beaches (photo **A**), a warm sunny climate and rich cultural heritage. Jamaica enjoys good international air communications and is a hub for cruise ships.

Tourism is important to the Jamaican economy, generating taxes, employment and income. Over the last few decades it has helped raise the level of development in Jamaica and reduce the development gap.

A *Turtle Beach, Ocho Rios, Jamaica*

B *Tourist attractions in Jamaica*

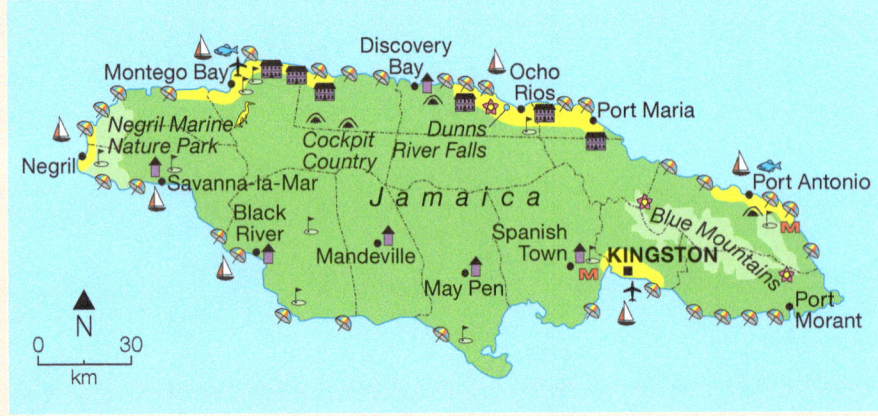

Key
- Main tourist areas
- Hotels outside main tourist areas
- Beach/bathing areas
- Watersports
- Deep-sea fishing
- Caves
- Botanic garden
- Golf course
- Museum
- Bird sanctuary/wildlife reserve
- National Park
- Parish boundary
- Airport
- Plantation house

Economy

In 2014 tourism contributed 24 per cent of Jamaica's GDP – one of the highest proportions of any country in the world. This is expected to rise to 32 per cent by 2024. Income from tourism is US$2 billion each year and taxes paid to the government contribute further to the development of the country (graph **C**). This in turn helps to reduce the development gap.

The increase in tourism from cruises has brought many benefits. However, the annual 1.1 million cruise passengers only spend an average US$70 per day. This compares with an average US$120 per day spent by the 2.5 million other visitors.

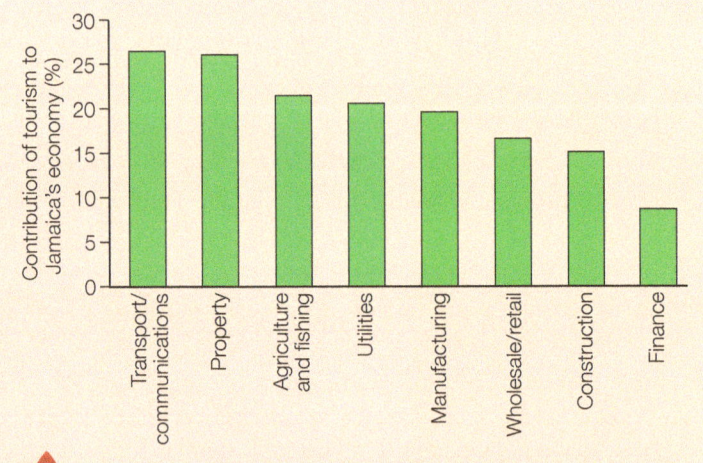

C *How tourism contributes to Jamaica's economy by sector*

200

The development gap

Employment

Tourism is the main source of employment in Jamaica. It provides jobs for 200 000 people, either directly in hotels, transport and tourist attractions or indirectly in shops, manufacturing and banking. These are mainly in or around the main tourist towns.

Employment in tourism provides income which helps to further boost the local economy as people spend money in shops and on services and recreation (photo **D**). Those in employment learn new skills which can improve their prospects of better-paid jobs in the future. The quality of life for many people has improved.

Infrastructure

Tourism has led to a high level of investment on the north coast where much of the country's tourism is centred. New port and cruise-liner facilities have been built at Trelawny together with new hotel accommodation. However, improvements in roads and airports have been slower and some parts of the island remain isolated.

D *Tourism boosts the local economy*

Quality of life

In the northern tourist areas of Montego Bay and Ocho Rios, wealthy Jamaicans live in high-quality housing with a high standard of living. These areas have benefited from the tourist industry. However, large numbers of people live nearby in poor housing with limited food supply and inadequate access to fresh water, health care and education.

Think about it
What disadvantages might tourism bring to countries like Jamaica?

The environment

Mass tourism can create environmental problems such as footpath erosion, excessive waste and harmful emissions. It can also bring environmental benefits. Conservation and landscaping projects provide job opportunities and encourage people to visit the island.

Montego Bay on the north coast has been improved by landscaping, and a new water treatment plant at Logwood has reduced pollution from hotels. The Negril Marine Park attracts many tourists and brings direct and indirect income. Community tourism and sustainable **ecotourism** is expanding in more isolated regions, with people running small-scale guesthouses or acting as guides.

ACTIVITIES

1. **a** Describe the distribution of the main tourist areas of Jamaica (map **B**).
   b What are Jamaica's main tourist attractions?
2. **a** Name the two sectors which benefit most from tourism (graph **C**). Give the percentages.
   b Suggest why these sectors benefit so much.
3. How can tourism boost the economy of local communities (photo **D**)?
4. How will improvements to infrastructure and the environment help to increase tourism and boost the economy?

Stretch yourself
Investigate how increased tourism at resorts such as Ocho Rios and Montego Bay can have a multiplier effect on Jamaica's development.

Practice question
Explain why the Jamaican government sees tourism as a way to reduce the development gap. *(4 marks)*

16 Nigeria: a newly emerging economy

16.1 Exploring Nigeria (1)

On this spread you will find out about Nigeria's location and its global and regional importance

Where is Nigeria?

Nigeria is a country in West Africa. Nigeria borders Benin, Niger, Chad and Cameroon (map **A**).

At latitude 4°14', Nigeria extends from the Gulf of Guinea in the south to the Sahel in the north. It has a tropical climate with variable rainy and dry seasons in different parts of the country. It is hot and wet most of the year in the south, but inland there is a long, dry season.

What is the global importance of Nigeria?

Nigeria is a newly emerging economy (NEE) (see page 178). This means that it is one of a number of countries experiencing a period of rapid economic development. In 2014, Nigeria became the world's 21st largest economy – by 2050 it should be in the top 20. Nigeria is predicted to have the world's highest average GDP growth for 2010–15.

Nigeria supplies 2.7 per cent of the world's oil – the 12th largest producer. Much of the country's economic growth has been based on oil revenues. But it has also developed a very diverse economy, which now includes financial services, telecommunications and the media. In common with cities around the world, the centre of Lagos is a thriving global economic hub (photo **B**).

Politically, Nigeria has a significant global role. It currently ranks as the fifth largest contributor to UN peacekeeping missions around the world (photo **C**).

A The location of Nigeria

Did you know?
Lagos is the fourth most densely populated city in the world, with a population of 13.5 million and 18 150 people per km².

B The city business skyline in Lagos

C A Nigerian peacekeeper in Liberia

202

Nigeria: a newly emerging economy

Year	Population	Annual change (%)	Fertility rate	Urban population (%)	Urban population	% of world population
1990	95 617 345	2.65	6.6	29.70	28 379 229	1.97
1995	108 424 822	2.55	6.37	32.20	34 918 670	2.04
2000	122 876 723	2.53	6.17	34.80	42 810 252	2.14
2005	139 611 303	2.59	6.05	39.10	54 541 496	2.28
2010	159 424 742	2.69	5.91	43.60	69 440 943	2.45
2015	182 201 962	2.71	5.74	48.10	87 680 500	2.63

D *How has Nigeria developed in 25 years?*

Maths skills

Use table **D** to answer the following questions.
1 By what percentage did Nigeria's total population increase between 1990 and 2015?
2 By what percentage did Nigeria's urban population increase in this period?
3 By how much did the percentage of urban population increase?
4 By what percentage did Nigeria's share of world population increase?

Nigeria's importance in Africa

Nigeria has one of the fastest-growing economies in Africa. In 2014 it had the highest GDP in the continent and the third largest manufacturing sector. With a population of more than 182 million people, it has the largest population of any African country.

Nigeria has low levels of productivity and there are widespread issues over land ownership. But it still has the highest farm output in Africa. About 70 per cent of the population are employed in agriculture. Most are subsistence farmers growing food crops, such as yams, cassava, sorghum and millet, or keeping livestock. Nigeria has over 19 million cattle, the largest number in Africa (photo **E**).

Nigeria could lead the way in Africa's future development. Despite its problems with internal corruption and lack of infrastructure – with poor roads and frequent power cuts – the country has huge potential. US President Barack Obama said Nigeria is 'critical to the rest of the continent and if Nigeria does not get it right, Africa will really not make more progress'.

E *Cattle herding in Nigeria*

ACTIVITIES

1 Describe the location of Nigeria (map **A**).
2 Give reasons for the global importance of Nigeria.
3 a Work in pairs to find out more about Nigeria. Start by writing out some questions, such as 'How large is Nigeria compared to the UK?' or 'Who are Nigeria's famous sportspeople?'
   b Do some online research to answer your questions.
   c Present your findings as a poster display, and add some data and photos you find interesting.
4 Do you agree with US President Obama that 'if Nigeria does not get it right, Africa will really not make more progress'?

Stretch yourself

Find out more about the international role of Nigeria. How are the country and its people having a global impact?

Practice question

Discuss how Nigeria has a growing influence in Africa. *(6 marks)*

203

16.2 Exploring Nigeria (2)

On this spread you will find out about political, social, cultural and environmental aspects of Nigeria

Political context

The political map of Africa was drawn by a small group of powerful European countries at the Berlin Conference in 1883. These countries literally carved up control of Africa between them. This explains why many country borders are straight lines. Europeans exploited Africa's resources, including its people, who were traded as slaves.

In the 1960s many African countries gained their independence. Nigeria became fully independent from the UK in 1960. However, bitter power struggles resulted in a series of dictatorships and a civil war between 1967 and 1970. Lack of political stability affected Nigeria's development and led to widespread corruption. It is only since 1999 that the country has had a stable government. Recent elections in 2011 and 2015 were seen as free and fair.

Several countries are now starting to invest in Nigeria.

- China is making major investments in construction and technology (photo **A**).
- South Africa is investing in businesses and banking.
- American companies such as General Electric are investing in new power plants.
- American corporations such as Walmart, and IT giants IBM, Microsoft and Oracle are operating in Nigeria.

Social context

Nigeria is a multi-ethnic, multifaith country. Ethnic groups in Nigeria include the Yoruba (21 per cent of the population), Hausa and the Fulani (29 per cent), and Igbo (18 per cent) as well as many smaller groups. Christianity, Islam and traditional African religions are practised widely. This social diversity is one of Nigeria's great strengths, but has also been a source of conflict.

In 1967 the Igbo-dominated south-east tried to separate from Nigeria to become the Republic of Biafra. As a result, the country was torn by civil war until the Biafrans were defeated in 1970.

More recently, economic inequality between the north and south of Nigeria has created new religious and ethnic tensions, with the rise of the Islamic fundamentalist group Boko Haram. This has created an unstable situation in the country, and has had a negative impact on the economy, with a reduction in investment from abroad and a rise in unemployment.

Table **B** compares some key social indicators with those for the UK.

A In 2016, Huawei opened the Innovation and Experience Centre at the University of Lagos as a training platform to nurture ICT talent

B Key facts: Nigeria and the UK compared

Fact	Nigeria	UK
Land area	924 000 km^2	244 000 km^2
Population (millions)	182 (largest in Africa)	65
Population growth rate (% per year)	2.4	0.6
Birth rate (per 1000)	38	12
Death rate (per 1000)	13	9
Infant mortality rate (per 1000 live births)	73	4
Life expectancy (years)	52	81
Literacy rate (%)	61	99
GNI per head (US$)	2970	43 430
Capital	Abuja (2 million)	London (8.6 million)
Largest city	Lagos (11 million)	London
Internet users (%)	38	90
Percentage in poverty	70	15

Nigeria: a newly emerging economy

Regional variations

There are huge variations in levels of wealth and development within Nigeria. Urban areas have a greater share of public services and facilities. For example, 60 per cent of children in urban areas attend secondary school, but only 36 per cent in rural areas. This encourages widespread rural–urban migration.

GDP per person varies greatly across the country. GDP is generally higher in the south, which benefits from physical features such as the Niger Delta, higher rainfall and access to oil reserves. GDP is lower in the semi-arid north, where drought, desertification and lack of resources all make life harder. Also, the growing threat from the militant Islamist group Boko Haram is limiting economic growth in the north.

C 'Nollywood' – Nigeria's thriving film industry

Cultural context

With such a diverse population, Nigeria enjoys a rich and varied culture.

- Nigerian music is enjoyed across the continent and beyond. Have you heard of Fela Kuti?
- Nigerian cinema – known as 'Nollywood' – is the second largest film industry in the world, ahead of the USA and behind India (photo **C**).
- In literature, well-known Nigerian writers include Wole Soyinka, Chinua Achebe, Chimamanda Ngozi Adichie and Nnedi Okorafor.
- In sport, the Nigerian football team has won the African Cup of Nations three times, most recently in 2013. Several Nigerian football players have played for Premier League sides including Victor Moses, John Obi Mikel, Jay-Jay Okocha and Nwankwo Kanu.

D Nigeria's natural environments

Northern Nigeria – the far north-east of the country is semi-desert. Further south, tropical grassland (savanna) dominates, mainly used for grazing cattle. Crops such as cotton, millet and groundnuts.

Jos Plateau – this upland region, centred on the city of Jos, is wetter and cooler than surrounding savanna. Densely populated farmland with some woodland.

Southern Nigeria – high temperatures and high annual rainfall. Much of this area is forest, with crops such as cocoa, oil palm and rubber. Hard to keep cattle here because of the tsetse fly. Unique to Africa, this pest transmits a parasite that can be lethal to livestock.

Environmental context

Nigeria's natural environments form a series of bands across the country (map **D**). This reflects the decreasing rainfall towards the north in West Africa. These environmental regions extend to the east and west of Nigeria. To the north is the Sahel and the Sahara Desert.

ACTIVITIES

1. How important is political stability to the development of Nigeria's economy?
2. Working in pairs, carry out some research into Nigeria's diverse culture (music, film, books and sport). What role has Nigeria's culture played in its recent economic development?
3. Describe the challenges and opportunities of Nigeria's natural environment for promoting economic growth.
4. Suggest reasons for the variations in wealth (GDP) across Nigeria.

Stretch yourself

How have social and political conflict affected development in Nigeria in recent years?

Practice question

Describe briefly how politics has shaped Nigeria's economic development. *(4 marks)*

16.3 Nigeria in the wider world

On this spread you will find out about Nigeria's changing relationships with the wider world

How have Nigeria's political links changed?

Until 1960 Nigeria was part of the British Empire. Its political links were with the UK and other members of the Empire. Since becoming independent in 1960, Nigeria has become a member of the British **Commonwealth** (photo **A**). It now has equal status with all countries including the UK. Although Nigeria is a republic, it recognises the British Queen as the Head of the Commonwealth.

Nigeria's political role has changed in recent decades. It has become a leading member of African political and economic groups as well as international organisations such as the UN (figure **B**).

A The Nigeria team at the 2014 Commonwealth Games

B Nigeria's political links

African Union – economic planning and peacekeeping group. Nigeria is in alliance with Niger, Chad, Benin and Cameroon to provide troops.

ECOWAS (Economic Community of West African States) – trading group made up of the countries of West Africa with headquarters in Abuja.

CEN-SAD (Community of Sahel-Saharan States) – has similar aims to ECOWAS, and also seeks to develop sporting links.

United Nations – in 2013 Nigeria contributed the fifth largest number of troops to the UN peacekeeping force. In 2014–15 it was a temporary member of the UN Security Council.

OPEC (Organisation of Petroleum Exporting Countries) – aims to stabilise the price of oil and to ensure a regular supply.

Nigeria's political links

What are Nigeria's global trading relationships?

Nigeria is a major global trading nation (chart **C**). Its main exports are crude and refined petroleum, natural gas, rubber, cocoa and cotton. Its main imports are refined petroleum from the EU and the USA, cars from Brazil and the USA, telephones, rice and wheat.

One of the fastest-growing imports is telephones. Imported from China, these are in demand from Nigeria's growing population and emerging middle class. Nigeria ranks seventh in the world for the number of mobile phones used.

Imports Key: China, EU, USA, India, Japan, South Africa, UAE, Ivory Coast

Exports Key: EU, USA, India, Indonesia, Brazil, South Africa, Japan, Ivory Coast

Total trade Key: EU, USA, India, China, Brazil, South Africa, Japan, South Korea

C Nigeria's trading relationships

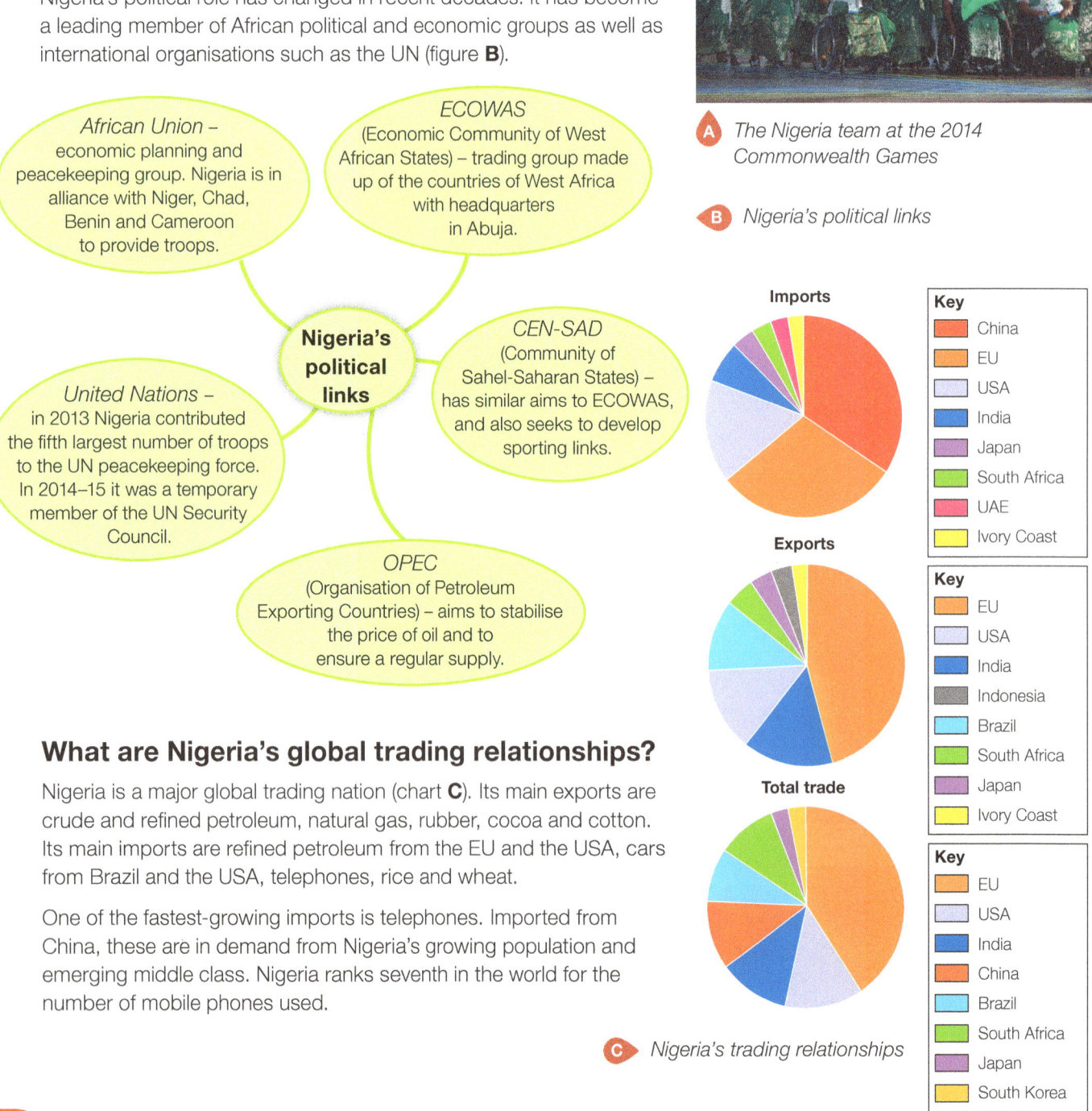

Nigeria: a newly emerging economy

Crude oil

Crude oil dominates Nigeria's exports. Until 2013, the USA was Nigeria's biggest customer. Nigeria's oil is described as 'sweet oil' – oil with less than 42 per cent sulphur. It is higher quality than oil from the Middle East, and suitable for refining into gasoline (fuel).

Until recently, the greatest demand for Nigerian oil was from the USA. However, with the recent development of shale oil in the USA, demand for Nigerian oil has fallen. India is now Nigeria's biggest customer. Between 2013 and 2014 exports of crude oil to India, China, Japan and South Korea increased by 40 per cent.

Agriculture

The reliance on crude petroleum has reduced the importance of agricultural products, although 40 per cent of the population is employed in this sector. Australia (30 per cent) followed by Indonesia (15 per cent) are the biggest customers for Nigerian cotton (photo **D**). Cocoa and rubber exports are low, with most exported to the West Indian island of Barbados for processing.

Despite Nigeria's membership of the two African trading groups, ECOWAS and CEN-SAD, only two other countries in West Africa are significant trading partners – Ghana and Ivory Coast.

D Picking cotton for export

Maths skills

Present the data in table **E** in the form of two flow line maps (see page 349). Use arrows of different thicknesses (proportional to the percentages) to show the export of crude oil from Nigeria. How have the destinations changed between 2010 and 2014? Explain the possible reasons for these changes.

E Nigerian crude oil exports (%)

	2010	2014
USA	43	3
Brazil	8	10
Canada	2	n/a
Americas (other)	n/a	2
India	14	18
Indonesia	n/a	4
Asia (other)	3	6
France	3	n/a
Netherlands	4	10
Germany	3	n/a
Spain	5	9
Europe (other)	5	25
South Africa	3	7
Africa (other)	3	6
Australia	1	n/a

ACTIVITIES

1. **a** Approximately what percentage of Nigeria's total trade is with the EU (chart **C**)?
   b Which country is the top importer into Nigeria? Can you suggest why?
   c Why do you think the EU is the main destination for Nigeria's exports?
   d Suggest why there are only two African countries among Nigeria's top trading partners.
2. What is the meaning of 'sweet oil'? Why is Nigeria fortunate in having large reserves of 'sweet oil'?
3. 'Nigeria has an important role to play both regionally and internationally.' Do you agree with this statement?

Stretch yourself

Oil accounts for 80–90 per cent of Nigeria's foreign revenues. Investigate how the global fall in oil prices in 2015–16 affected Nigeria's economy.

Practice question

Explain how political and economic factors have influenced Nigeria's changing relationships with other parts of the world. *(6 marks)*

16.4 Balancing a changing industrial structure

On this spread you will find out how Nigeria's economy is changing

Nigeria's sources of income

Traditionally, primary products were Nigeria's main source of income. Agricultural products such as cocoa, timber, oil palm, groundnuts and cotton were its main exports.

The discovery of oil in the Niger Delta in the 1950s led to a big change in Nigeria's economy. Today, oil accounts for about 14 per cent of the country's GDP and 98 per cent of its export earnings. Nigeria has the world's 10th highest level of oil reserves. At the present rate of production it has around 50 years' supply left.

A *Oil production in the Niger Delta*

B *Changes in Nigeria's employment structure, 1999–2012*

Does Nigeria have a balanced economy?

The economy of a country is divided into sectors (e.g. retail, tourism, finance, public services). Graph **B** shows recent changes in the structure of Nigeria's economy. Since 1999 there have been major changes in the country's **industrial structure**.

- Employment in agriculture (*primary* sector) has fallen, due to increasing use of farm machinery and better pay and conditions in other sectors of the economy.

- Industrialisation and economic growth (*secondary* sector) under a stable government has increased employment in oil production, manufacturing and industries such as construction, motor manufacturing, sugar refining, paper and pharmaceuticals.

- The growth of communications, retail and finance in the service (*tertiary*) sector.

These changes mean that Nigeria now has a more *balanced* economy, with a more even balance between the different sectors.

Key
- Agriculture
- Industry
- Services

Why is Nigeria's economy developing?

- Rapid advances in technology.
- Investment in science and technology training – Nigeria's huge population is seen as a potential asset for the country.
- Greater concern for the environment.
- Information technology is beginning to drive the economy rather than oil.
- Many people speak English, giving potential for growth in telecommunications.
- Increased use of telecommunications – Nigeria is able to benefit from global finance and trade.

C *Factors in Nigeria's developing economy*

Nigeria: a newly emerging economy

Nigeria's growing manufacturing sector

Manufacturing involves making products from raw materials. In the past, growth in manufacturing was hindered by Nigeria's dependence on the export of raw materials, particularly agricultural produce. Processing was mostly done abroad.

Today, manufacturing accounts for 10 per cent of Nigeria's GDP. It is currently growing faster than the telecommunications, oil and gas or agricultural sectors. Goods produced include:

- processed foods
- leather items
- textiles
- soaps and detergents.

With its growing home market, relatively cheap labour force and improving infrastructure, the manufacturing sector seems likely to increase in the future and become even more diverse.

Maths skills

Use an appropriate form of presentation to show the following data.

Nigeria's employment structure 2014

Agriculture	40%
Oil	25%
Manufacturing	10%
Wholesale and retailing	10%
Transport and communications	8%
Finance and business	7%

How is manufacturing affecting economic development?

The growth of manufacturing in Nigeria has stimulated economic development in several ways.

- Regular paid work gives people a more secure income and provides an ever-larger home market for purchasing products such as cars, clothes and electrical appliances.
- Manufacturing industries stimulate growth through close links with each other, for example, companies supplying parts for making cars (photo **D**).
- As industries grow, more people are employed, and revenue from taxes increases.
- A thriving industrial sector attracts foreign investment, which stimulates further economic growth.
- Oil processing has created chemical by-products. This has led to the growth of a huge range of chemical industries, including soaps, detergents and plastics.

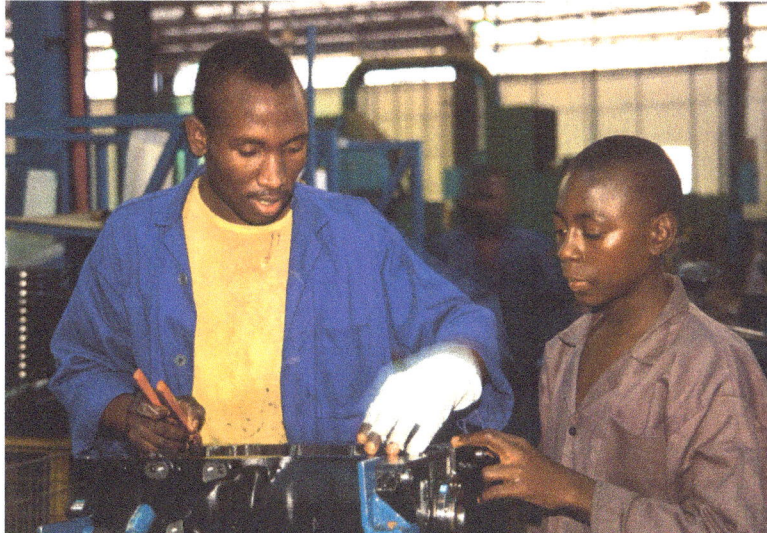

D *Peugeot car factory in Kaduna, Nigeria*

ACTIVITIES

1. How has oil transformed Nigeria's economy?
2. a Approximately what percentage were employed in agriculture in 1999 (chart **B**)?
   b By approximately how much had the percentage employed in agriculture declined by 2012?
   c Describe how the employment structure changed between 1999 and 2012.
3. Choose *three* examples of manufacturing in Nigeria. For each one, describe how it can stimulate wider economic development (the multiplier effect – see page 192).

Stretch yourself

Find out about the Innoson Vehicle Manufacturing Company, which started to manufacture cars at its Nnewi factory in 2010. How has this company stimulated economic development in Nigeria?

Practice question

How can the growth of manufacturing in Nigeria stimulate economic development? *(4 marks)*

16.5 The impacts of transnational corporations

On this spread you will find out about the role of TNCs in Nigeria's development

What is a transnational corporation?

A **transnational corporation (TNC)** is a large company that operates in several countries. A TNC usually has its headquarters in one country with production plants in several others. TNCs locate in foreign countries in order to take advantage of:

- tax incentives
- laxer environmental laws
- cheaper labour
- access to a wider market.

TNCs in Nigeria

About 40 TNCs operate in Nigeria. The majority have their headquarters in the UK, USA or in Europe. Those based in the UK include KFC (fast food) and Unilever (food and home care). Transnational operations bring advantages and disadvantages for Nigeria (photo **A**).

Advantages
- Companies provide employment and the development of new skills.
- More money is spent in the economy.
- Investment by companies in local infrastructure and education.
- Other local companies benefit from increased orders.
- Valuable export revenues are earned.

Disadvantages
- Local workers are sometimes poorly paid.
- Working conditions are sometimes very poor.
- Management jobs often go to foreign employees brought in by the TNC.
- Much of the profit generated goes abroad.
- Grants and subsidies used to attract TNCs could have been used to invest in Nigerian industry.

A Advantages and disadvantages of TNCs for Nigeria

Unilever in Nigeria

Unilever is an Anglo-Dutch TNC with joint headquarters in London and Rotterdam. It produces a range of foods, drinks and items for the home.

Unilever's operations in Nigeria started in 1923 with the manufacture of soap using locally produced palm oil. Since then the company has diversified to include manufacture of foods, non-soap detergents and personal care items. It currently employs about 1500 people.

Unilever's products are aimed at the growing Nigerian market and the development of brands to improve people's quality of life. It works with local cultures and markets to develop new products and aims at high standards of employment and environmental stewardship. The company claims that all of its palm oil comes from sustainable sources.

It has promoted improvements in health care (photo **B**), education and water supply as part of its social responsibility programme in Nigerian communities. In 2014 Unilever was voted the second best place to work in Nigeria!

B The Global Vice President of Oral Care at Unilever (second from left) joins the Nigerian Minister for Health (right) to demonstrate to how to brush teeth during World Oral Health Day (organised by Pepsodent, Unilever)

Nigeria: a newly emerging economy

Mining and oil extraction

Mining and extraction of precious metals (photo **C**) and raw materials – particularly oil – can lead to serious pollution. These can damage ecosystems and affect people's jobs.

- Tin mining led to soil erosion. Local water supplies were also polluted with toxic chemicals.

- Many oil spills in the Niger Delta have had disastrous impacts on freshwater and marine ecosystems. Oil spills can cause fires, sending CO_2 and other harmful gases into the atmosphere. They cause *acid rain*, which harms plants and aquatic ecosystems.

- Some economic developments in the Niger Delta have caused violent conflicts with local people.

C Mining for gold in Nigeria

Another view
Shell claims that theft of crude oil, sabotage and illegal refining are the main sources of oil pollution. Do you agree with Shell? Why might it say this?

Bodo oil spills (2008/09)

In 2008 and 2009 two large oil spills devastated the livelihoods of thousands of farmers and fishermen living in the swamps around the town of Bodo in the Niger Delta (photo **D**). Leaks in a major pipeline caused 11 million gallons of crude oil to spill over a 20 km² area of creeks and swamps.

In 2015, Shell agreed to pay US$78 million compensation to individuals and to the community of Bodo. The money will be used to build health clinics and improve schools. This is the largest compensation paid by an oil company to a local community affected by environmental damage. Shell has also agreed to clean up the swamps and fishing grounds.

D An oil-polluted fish farm in Bodo

ACTIVITIES

1. **a** How has rapid industrial development harmed the environment in Nigeria (photo **A**)?
   b What measures could be introduced to reduce damage to the environment?
2. **a** Describe the waste that has been dumped in photo **B**.
   b What problems might arise from this waste dump?
   c Why has waste been dumped here and what could be done to solve the problem in the future?
3. What are the environmental problems associated with oil spills?

Stretch yourself

Make a detailed study of either the Bodo or the Bonga oil spills.

- Find out what happened and the impacts on people and the environment.
- What has been done to clean up the area and compensate the people?
- How can oil spills be prevented?

Practice question

Explain how Nigeria's rapid economic growth can have harmful impacts on the environment. *(6 marks)*

16.8 Quality of life in Nigeria

On this spread you will find out how economic development has affected the quality of life for people in Nigeria

Quality of life

As a country's economy develops, ordinary people will usually see some benefits. Their quality of life should improve (photo **A**).

- Reliable, better-paid jobs in manufacturing industries or services (for example, health care and education)
- Higher disposable income to spend on schooling, home improvements, food, clothes and recreation
- Improvements to infrastructure such as roads
- Better access to safe water and sanitation
- Improved access to a better diet means higher productivity at work and in school
- Reliable electricity supplies providing lighting and heating – easier to go out at night, and for children to do homework
- Better-quality health care, with more doctors and better-equipped hospitals

A The benefits of economic development

Have all Nigerians benefited from economic development?

Quality of life is commonly measured by the UN's HDI (human development index) (see page 179). Nigeria's HDI has been increasing steadily since 2005 (graph **B**). This trend is expected to continue.

- In 2000, Nigeria was placed among the 'least developed nations' in terms of wealth and education.
- In 2011, Nigeria had one of the highest average HDI improvements in the world over the past decade.

Most indicators show an improving trend (table **C**). This suggests that economic development since 1990 has improved the quality of people's lives. Remember, when looking at the use of mobile phone and the internet, that these have only become available recently!

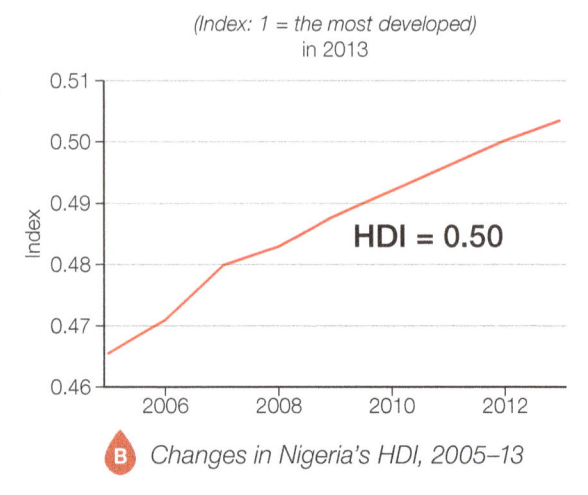

(Index: 1 = the most developed) in 2013

HDI = 0.50

B Changes in Nigeria's HDI, 2005–13

Has it all been good news?

Despite the clear improvements, many people in Nigeria are still poor. Limited access to services such as safe water, sanitation and reliable electricity is still a problem.

Thirty years ago, Nigeria was at a similar stage of development to Malaysia and Singapore. Since then, these two countries have moved far ahead of Nigeria, despite Nigeria's huge oil revenues. Its oil wealth has not been used effectively, and the gap between rich and poor has become wider.

Nigeria: a newly emerging economy

Indicator	1990	2000	2005	2010	2013
Life expectancy at birth	46	47	49	51	52
Births attended by skilled health staff (%)	31	–	–	44	38
Mortality rate (per 1000)	213	188	159	131	117
Sanitation facilities (% of population with access)	37	33	31	29	28
Safe water (% of population with access)	46	55	59	63	64
Secondary school enrolment (%)	25	24	35	44	–
Mobile phone subscriptions (per 100 people)	0	0	13	55	73
Internet users (per 100 people)	0	0	4	24	38

C Changes in Nigeria's quality of life, 1990–2013   Source: World Bank

D Protests in London following the capture of 200 schoolgirls by the militants Boko Haram

Corruption has been a major factor and the oil wealth was not used to diversify the economy. Now the price of oil has fallen and technology is leading to developments of shale oil elsewhere. Therefore, Nigeria's over-dependence on oil could become a problem in the future.

Will people's quality of life continue to improve?

Sixty per cent of Nigeria's population live in poverty. Improvement in their lives depends on the country coping with a number of challenges.

- *Political* – the need for a continuing stable government to encourage inward investment.

- *Environmental* – the pollution of the Niger Delta by oil spills has devastated the lives of the local Ogeni people. Pests like the tsetse fly restrict commercial livestock farming. Parts of the far north are under threat from desertification.

- *Social* – historical distrust remains between several tribal groups, such as the Yoruba and Igbo. There is also the religious divide between the predominantly Christian south and the Muslim north. Recent kidnappings by the militant group Boko Haram spread fear among Nigerians and potential investors (photo **D**).

ACTIVITIES

1. **a** What is the evidence from photo **A** that this family enjoys a reasonably good quality of life?
   b What other information would you need to know?
   c Imagine that a similar photo was taken in five years' time. How might they show signs of further improvement in the quality of their lives?
2. Describe the trend in Nigeria's HDI between 2005 and 2013 (graph **B**).
3. **a** What is the evidence that people's quality of life is improving (table **C**)?
   b Suggest reasons for the trend in 'sanitation facilities'.
   c Do you think these indicators accurately reflect people's quality of life?

Think about it

What factors affect your own quality of life? Are they different from those that affect quality of life in Nigeria?

Stretch yourself

Investigate Nigeria's electricity supply.
- To what extent has it improved over the last 20 years?
- What are the challenges faced by the industry?
- Why is a reliable and efficient electricity supply essential if a country is to develop?

Practice question

Evaluate to what extent economic development has improved the quality of people's lives in Nigeria. *(6 marks)*

217

Unit 2 Challenges in the urban environment

Section C Global issues

Bangkok, Thailand

Unit 2 Challenges in the urban environment is about human processes and systems, how they change both spatially and temporally. They are studied in a range of places, at a variety of scales and include places in various states of development. It is split into three sections.

Section C Global issues includes:

- water
- energy
- population
- communication.

You are required to study either 'water and energy resources' or 'population and communication' in Section C – in your final exam, you will have to answer one question from a choice of two.

What if...

1. all countries were equal?
2. we only ate genetically modified food?
3. everyone had clean water to drink?
4. all power was renewable?

Unit 2 Section C

Specification key ideas	Pages in this book
17 Water	**218–31**
• Demand for water resources is rising globally but supply can be insecure, which may lead to conflict.	218–23
• Different strategies can be used to increase water supply.	224–31
18 Energy	**232–43**
• Demand for energy resources is rising globally but supply can be insecure, which may lead to conflict.	232–5
• Different strategies can be used to increase energy supply.	236–43
19 Population	**244–75**
• Global population is increasing for a variety of reasons with significant impacts; strategies are in place to manage this.	244–63
• There are a number of reasons for international migration and significant impacts result from the process.	264–75
20 Communication	**276–313**
• Developments in ocean ports and airports offer many opportunities for growth and development, as well as presenting many challenges.	276–95
• The development of ICT has led to many worldwide opportunities for development.	296–313

Your key skills

To be a good geographer, you need to develop important geographical skills – in this section you will learn the following skills:

- Describing patterns of distribution in maps and graphs.
- Carrying out research.
- Using numerical data.
- Presenting data using different graphical techniques.
- Drawing and labelling diagrams.

Your key words

As you go through the chapters in this section, make sure you know and understand the key words shown in bold. Definitions are provided in the Glossary on page 354. To be a good geographer you need to use good subject terminology.

Your exam

Section C makes up part of Paper 2 – a one and a half-hour written exam worth 34 per cent of your GCSE.

17 Water

17.1 Global water supply

On this spread you will find out that demand for water is rising globally but supply is not spread evenly across the world

Water surplus and deficit

Map **A** shows global patterns of **water surplus** and **water deficit**. Regions with a water surplus have a plentiful supply of water with supply exceeding demand. These regions include North America, Europe and parts of Asia. Other regions have a water deficit, where demand exceeds supply and supplies are under pressure.

Regions with high rainfall usually have a water surplus. Areas with low rainfall, such as hot deserts, are more likely to have a water deficit.

Areas of high population density and high concentrations of industry have the highest demand for water. Without sufficient water supply these areas may experience a water deficit. Areas with low rainfall but a lower demand may have a water surplus!

Water security/insecurity

Water security means having access to enough clean water to sustain well-being, good health and economic development. Regions which do not have access to sufficient safe water supplies are described as being in a situation of **water insecurity**.

Water security is very important for improving quality of life because it:

- reduces poverty
- helps to improve education
- increases living standards.

What is water stress?

Many countries face high water stress (table **B**). This means that more than 80 per cent of available water is used every year, leaving the threat of water scarcity.

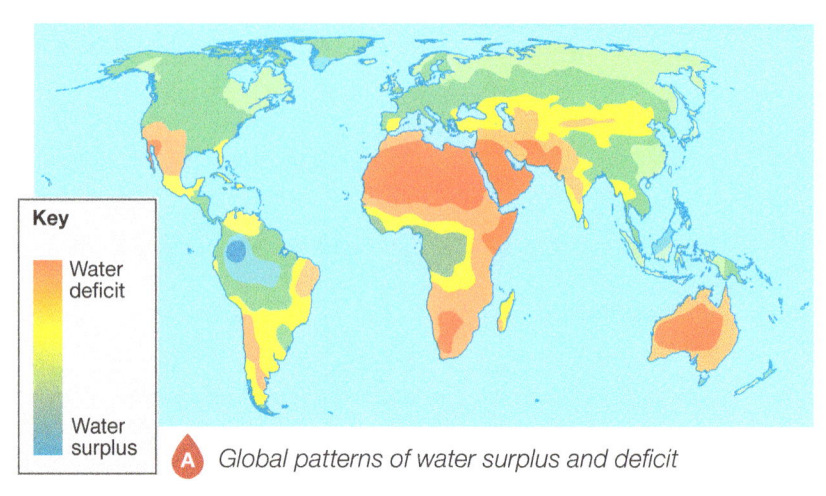

A Global patterns of water surplus and deficit

Key: Water deficit / Water surplus

Ratio of water withdrawal to supply (%)	Country
	Key: North America, Central and South America, Africa, Europe, Asia, Oceania
Extremely high (80+)	Kazakhstan, Mongolia, Iran, Oman, Saudi Arabia, Yemen
High (40–79)	Mexico, Chile, Peru, Turkey, India, South Africa, Australia
Medium–high (20–39)	USA, Argentina, China, New Zealand
Low–medium (10–19)	Canada, Russia
Low (<10)	Bolivia, Brazil, Guatemala, Honduras, Paraguay Central African Republic, Chad, Ghana, Nigeria, Democratic Republic of Congo, Sierra Leone, Zimbabwe Papua New Guinea

B Water stress on countries around the world

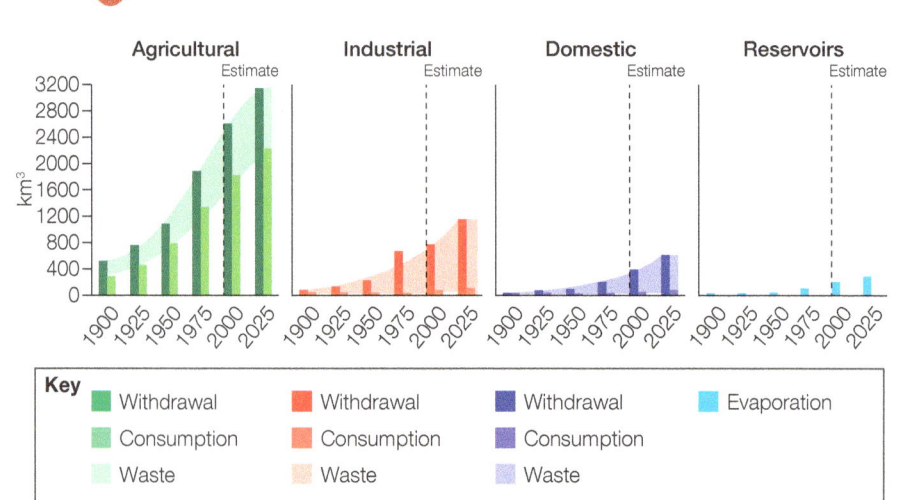

C Global water consumption since 1900

Key: Withdrawal / Consumption / Waste / Evaporation (Agricultural, Industrial, Domestic, Reservoirs)

Countries begin to experience water stress when less than 1700 m³ is available per person per year. Below 1000 m³, water stress may damage economic development – and human health and well-being. Regions with high water stress include several Caribbean islands, Bahrain, Cyprus, Malta and the Middle East.

Why is water consumption increasing?

The steady growth of the world's population, by roughly 80 million each year, means that more water is needed. Water consumption is increasing because economic development results in greater demand (figure **C**).

There are other reasons why we are all using more water.

- Changes in lifestyle and eating habits have increased the average use of water per head.
- Global demand for food is expected to increase by 70 per cent by 2050 – water is used to irrigate crops and in food processing.
- All sources of energy require water in their production. Global energy consumption is expected to increase by 50 per cent by 2035.
- As urbanisation increases, more water is needed for drinking, sanitation and drainage.

What is water stress?

Water stress takes into account several physical factors that are related to water resources. These include:

- water scarcity
- water quality
- accessibility of water
- environmental flows (the quality, quantity and timing of water flow needed to maintain healthy ecosystems in streams, rivers, and the estuaries they feed).

Water availability

There are a number of factors affecting the availability of water supplies.

Geology – infiltration of water (as in the Sahara Desert) through permeable rock builds up important groundwater supplies. Much of London's water comes from the chalk underlying the city.

Climate – regions with high rainfall usually have surplus water. Those with drier climates have less water available.

Over-abstraction – pumping water out of the ground faster than it is replaced by rainfall. This can cause wells to dry up, sinking water tables and higher pumping costs. Lower water tables mean that rivers are not fed by springs in the dry season.

Pollution – increasing amounts of waste and growing use of chemicals in farming have led to higher levels of pollution. In some low-income countries (LICs) and newly emerging economies (NEEs) water sources are often used as open sewers leading to **waterborne diseases**.

Limited infrastructure – poorer countries may lack the infrastructure for transporting water to areas of need (for example, pumping stations and pipes).

Poverty – many poorer communities lack mains water or only have access to shared water supplies.

D What affects the availability of water?

ACTIVITIES

1. **a** Define the meaning of 'water surplus' and 'water deficit'.
   b Which continent has the highest water deficit (map **A**)?
   c Which are the main areas of water surplus?
   d Explain the different patterns of water surplus and deficit.
2. Describe and suggest reasons for the pattern of global water stress (table **B**).
3. **a** Describe the trends in each of the four graphs in figure **C**.
   b Which shows the most waste? Why?
4. 'Poverty is the main factor affecting water supply.' To what extent do you agree with this statement?

Stretch yourself

Explain how access to safe water can improve people's standard of living.

Practice question

Explain how both physical and human factors can influence the availability of water. (*6 marks*)

17.2 The impact of water insecurity

On this spread you will find out about the impacts of water insecurity

What are the impacts of water insecurity?

Water insecurity can cause social, economic and environmental problems. It is experienced in some richer, more developed countries, as well as LICs.

Waterborne disease and water pollution

In countries where water supply infrastructure is limited, there may be little or no sanitation. There may be open sewers and high levels of pollution in rivers and other water sources. Contaminated drinking water can cause outbreaks of life-threatening disease such as cholera and dysentery.

With a shortage of clean water, people may have to queue for a long time to obtain a supply from standpipes (photo **A**). This wastes time and reduces levels of productivity.

A Queuing for water at a standpipe

Water pollution: the River Ganges, India

The River Ganga (Ganges) is 2520 km long and flows through northern India and Bangladesh. It is the most polluted river in the world, with both human and industrial waste.

- Over 1 billion litres of raw sewage enter the river each day from the cities, towns and villages along its banks.
- Every day hundreds of factories discharge 260 million litres of untreated wastewater into the river.
- The major polluting industry along the Ganges is the leather industry, because toxic chemicals leak into the river.
- Runoff from pesticides and fertilisers is another major source of pollution.

Pollution of the Ganges has become so serious that bathing in the river and drinking its water have become very dangerous.

Food production

Agriculture uses 70 per cent of global water supply and suffers the most from water insecurity. Drier regions of the world with unreliable rainfall are most at risk. The USA supplies 30 per cent of the world's wheat, maize and rice. Droughts and water shortages are serious issues across much of the USA (graph **B**) and can have a global impact on food production and supply.

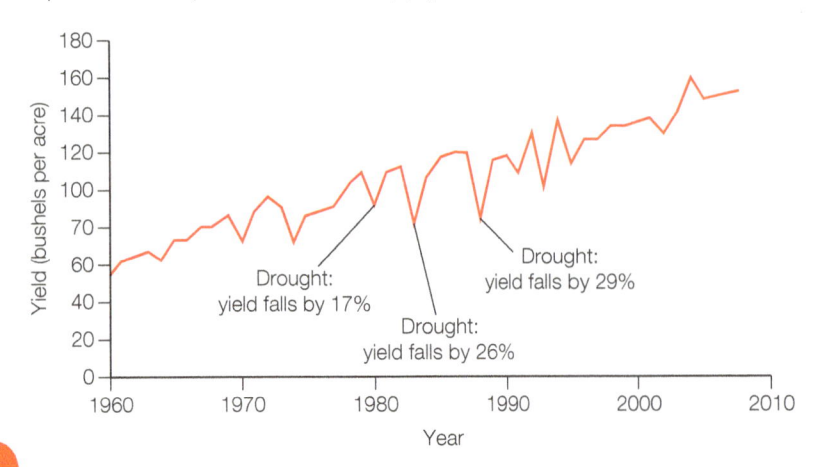

Water shortages in Egypt

Shortage of water is affecting Egypt's food security. The River Nile is Egypt's primary source of water. Climate change and the demands of countries upstream are expected to reduce its flow by 90 per cent by the end of the century. Although 80 per cent of Egypt's water supply is used in agriculture, food production is likely to decline by 30 per cent over the next 30 years. Egypt currently has to import 60 per cent of its food.

B Crop yields in the USA

Water

Industrial output

Growth of the manufacturing industry, particularly in NEEs, is making increasing demands on water supplies.

Water conflict

In the past, wars were fought over oil supplies – in the future, they may be fought over water. This is because water sources, such as rivers and groundwater aquifers, cross national and political borders. Many of the world's great rivers, such as the Nile and Danube, flow through several countries. Issues such as reservoir construction and pollution can impact on more than one country, and create conflict (map **C**).

Did you know?
About one fifth of the world's population live where there is not enough water to meet demand.

Chinese industry
By 2030 Chinese industry will use 33 per cent of the country's available water. Water shortages cost China US$40 billion in lower industrial production. Some factories have closed temporarily due to water shortages. Also, China depends on its coal resources to drive its economic growth. Coal mining and power stations use 20 per cent of China's water.

Turkey built a large number of dams on the Tigris and Euphrates rivers, causing an angry response from Iraq and Syria. Water is sold from the Manavgat River.

The River Jordan flows through Jordan and Israel. Israel draws water from the Sea of Galilee. Groundwater is polluted and in short supply. Israel buys water from Turkey.

Lake Chad has shrunk to 5% of its previous size, due to climate and over-abstraction. This affects the whole population.

Egypt's population of 160 million relies on the Nile for its water. The river flows through seven other countries. Egypt will not allow those countries to do anything to affect its flow (for example, to build dams). This causes great tension in the region.

The River Ganges flows through Northern India and Bangladesh. India has built barriers to control the flow, and this affects the water supply to Bangladesh.

C The world's potential water conflict zones

The Rogun Dam, Tajikistan

Several rivers flow from mountainous Tajikistan to Uzbekistan in the west. In 2014 the World Bank agreed to finance the Rogun Dam Project on the Vakhsh River (map **D**). The construction of the dam has been hit by economic and political problems. Once completed, electricity generated by the dam will support industrial development in Tajikistan.

The project is very controversial in neighbouring Uzbekistan, which suffers from a water deficit. Irrigated cotton is Uzbekistan's main export and there is concern about the impact of reduced water supplies on its economy. The Nurek Dam (map **D**), built in the 1970s, already affects the flow of the river. The new dam could lead to further tensions.

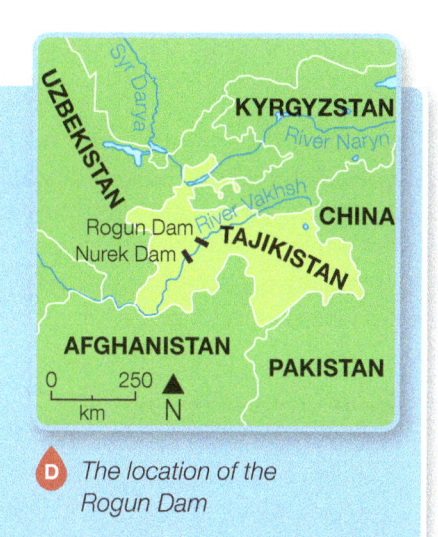

D The location of the Rogun Dam

ACTIVITIES

1. Suggest the social and economic impacts of polluted water supplies in LICs.
2. a Study graph **B**. In which year was the greatest fall in yields due to drought?
   b Which decade saw the worst drought?
3. What are the causes of the potential conflicts identified on map **C**?

Stretch yourself
Research more information on one of the potential conflicts in map **C**. Do you agree that future wars may be fought over water resources? Why?

Practice question
Explain how human actions can contribute to water insecurity. *(6 marks)*

223

17.3 How can water supply be increased?

On this spread you will find out about strategies to increase water supply

The amount of water available is limited. To make more water available means finding new sources or moving it from areas of surplus to areas of deficit.

Diverting supplies and increasing storage

Water supplies can be artificially diverted and stored for use over longer periods. For example, in some parts of the world surface water evaporates rapidly and is lost. This water can be stored in deep reservoirs or in permeable rocks (aquifers) underground.

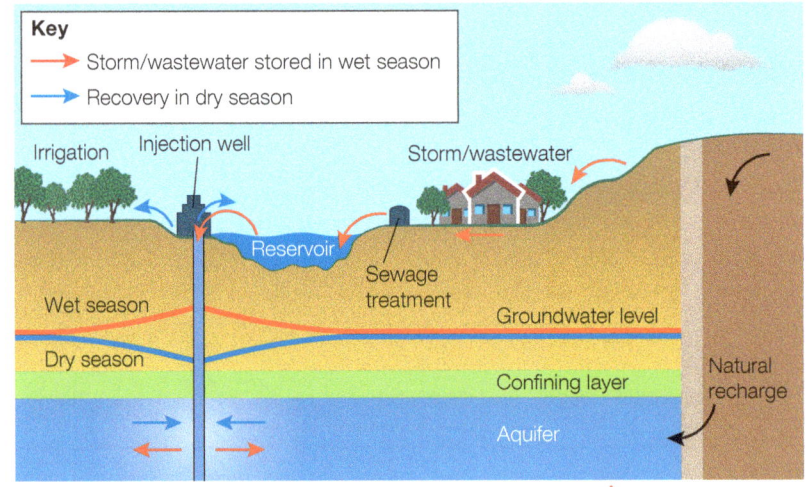

A Aquifer storage and recovery

In Oklahoma, USA, rainfall is infrequent but heavy. Surface water quickly evaporates. So it is collected and diverted into underlying alluvial soils where it can be stored (diagram **A**). Alluvial soils are loose at the surface with good water-holding capacity.

Dams and reservoirs

Dams control water flow in rivers by storing water in reservoirs. Rainfall can be collected and stored when it is plentiful and then released gradually during drier periods. The control of water flow enables it to be transported and used for irrigation. It helps to prevent flooding.

Dams range widely in size. There are huge, multi-purpose dams such as the Three Gorges Dam in China. Small earth or cement dams a few metres high are common in sub-Saharan Africa. Large dams are expensive to construct and maintain. They can lead to the displacement of large numbers of people. Also, they may reduce the flow of water downstream. In hot and arid regions, reservoirs with a large surface area can lose a lot of water through evaporation.

Kielder Water, Northumberland, UK

Kielder Water is the UK's largest reservoir in terms of its storage capacity (photo **B**). The dam, 1.2 km long and 50 m high, was built in the late 1970s at North Tyne Valley near Falstone. The valley is relatively narrow, reducing the cost of building. The 10 km-long reservoir took two years to fill.

The reservoir regulates flow in the North Tyne River, making up for water abstracted (taken) further downstream. Water is also used to generate electricity.

B Kielder Water

Water

Water transfers

Water transfer schemes aim to redistribute water from areas of water surplus to areas of water deficit. They often involve elaborate systems of canals and pipelines to take water from one river basin to another. In the UK, the Kielder transfer scheme carries water south to the rivers Wear and Tees.

China's south–north water transfer scheme

China is spending over US$79 billion on an ambitious project to transfer water from the Yangtze River in the south to the Yellow River Basin in the arid north (map **C**). The water will be transferred through three canal systems. The eastern and central routes were completed in 2015. The western route is due for completion by 2020.

The western route involves building several dams and hundreds of tunnels through the Bayankela Mountains. The entire project could take 50 years. However, it is still uncertain whether the scheme will actually be completed.

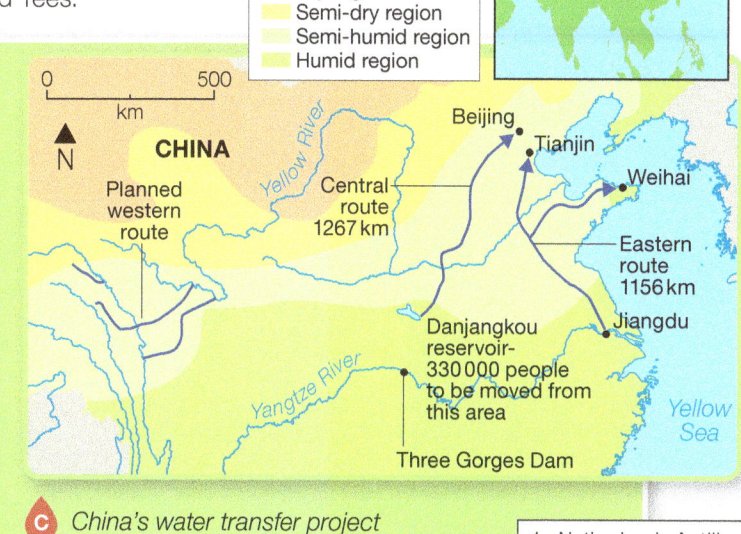

C China's water transfer project

Desalination

Desalination involves removing salt from seawater to produce fresh water. This is a very expensive process. It is used only where there is a serious shortage of water with few alternatives to increase water supply. Both Saudi Arabia and UAE have developed desalination plants.

There are several issues linked with the process of desalination, such as:

◆ environmental impacts on ecosystems when salt waste is dumped back into the sea

◆ the vast amount of energy required, adding to carbon emissions

◆ the high cost of transporting the desalinated water to inland areas.

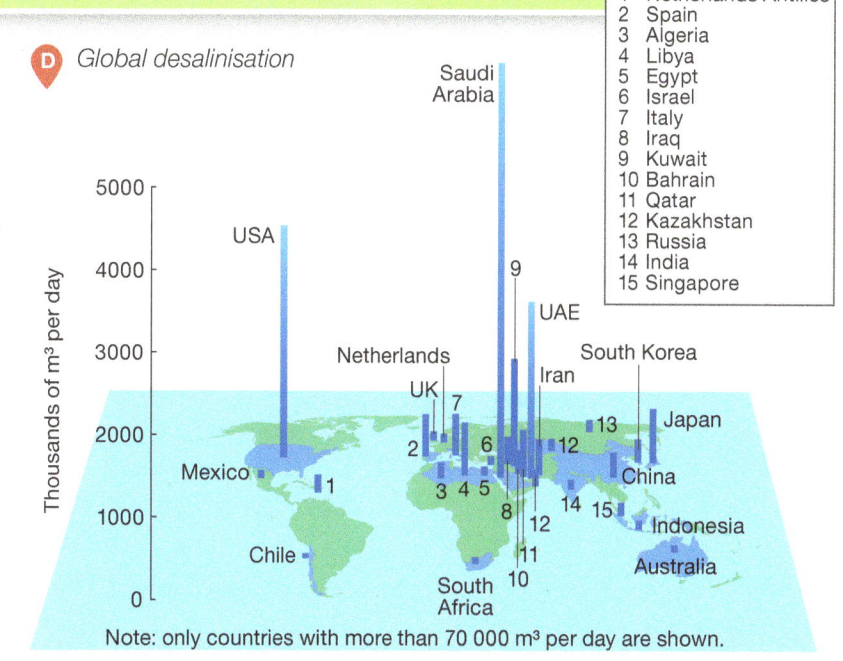

Future technological improvements may reduce costs and make this process more economically viable for NEEs or even LICs.

D Global desalinisation

1 Netherlands Antilles
2 Spain
3 Algeria
4 Libya
5 Egypt
6 Israel
7 Italy
8 Iraq
9 Kuwait
10 Bahrain
11 Qatar
12 Kazakhstan
13 Russia
14 India
15 Singapore

Note: only countries with more than 70 000 m³ per day are shown.

ACTIVITIES

1 Copy diagram **A** and add labels to describe how water can be collected and stored underground for future use.
2 What are the advantages and disadvantages of creating reservoirs such as Kielder Water (photo **B**)?
3 Explain how China's climate has influenced the Chinese plan to transfer water (map **C**).
4 Describe the distribution of the countries where large amounts of water are desalinised (diagram **D**).

Stretch yourself

Imagine you're a journalist sent to investigate the western route of China's south–north water transfer scheme. Investigate the advantages and disadvantages of this route. Write a front-page report for tomorrow's paper.

Practice question

Explain the costs and benefits involved in strategies to increase water supply. (6 marks)

17.4 The Lesotho Highland Water Project

On this spread you will find out about a large-scale water transfer scheme in Lesotho

Example

Lesotho is a highland country in southern Africa surrounded by the country of South Africa (map **A**). It has few resources, high levels of poverty, and is unable to feed its growing population. Most farms are for subsistence and productivity is low. Lesotho is heavily dependent economically on South Africa.

Despite experiencing food insecurity, Lesotho has a water surplus. The mountains receive high rainfall (graph **B**) and the demand for water is low.

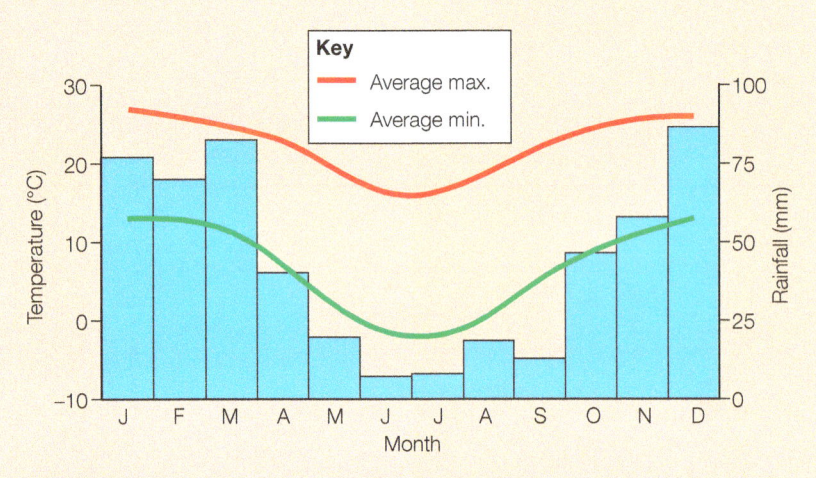

A *Location map of Lesotho*

B *The climate of Lesotho*

What is the Lesotho Highland Water Project?

The Lesotho Highland Water Project is a huge water transfer scheme aimed to help solve the water shortage in South Africa. On completion, 40 per cent of the water from the Segu (Orange) River in Lesotho will be transferred to the River Vaal in South Africa. It is a massive scheme involving the construction of dams, reservoirs and pipelines as well as roads, bridges and other infrastructure developments (map **C**). It will take 30 years to complete.

The main features of the scheme:

- The Katse and Mohale Dams (completed in 1998 and 2002) store water that is transferred through a tunnel to the Mohale Reservoir.
- Water is then transferred to South Africa via a 32 km tunnel enabling hydroelectric power (HEP) to be produced at the Muela plant.
- The Polihali Dam will hold 2.2 billion m^3 of water with a 38 km transfer tunnel.
- The Tsoelike Dam will be built at the confluence of the Tsoelike and Senqu rivers. It will have a storage capacity of 2223 million m^3 and a pumping station.
- The Ntoahae Dam and pumping station will be built 40 km downstream from Tsoelike Dam on the Senqu River.

By 2020 there will be 200 km of tunnels and 2000 million m^3 of water will be transferred to South Africa each year.

C *Map of the project*

Water

What are the advantages and disadvantages of the scheme?

Advantages for Lesotho
- Provides 75% of its GDP.
- Income from the scheme helps development and to improve standard of living.
- Supplies the country with all its HEP requirements.
- Improvements to transport infrastructure with access roads built to the construction sites.
- Water supply will reach 90% of the population of the capital, Maseru.
- Sanitation coverage will increase from 15 to 20%.

Advantages for South Africa
- Provides water to an area with an uneven rainfall pattern and regular droughts.
- Provides safe water for the 10% of the population without access to a safe water supply.
- Freshwater reduces the acidity of the Vaal River Reservoir. Water pollution from industry, gold mines and sewage was destroying the local ecosystem.
- The influx of water from Lesotho is restoring the balance.

D The Katse Dam

Disadvantages for Lesotho
- Building of the first two dams meant 30 000 people had to move from their land.
- Destruction of a unique wetland ecosystem due to control of regular flooding downstream of the dams.
- Corruption has prevented money and investment reaching those affected by the construction.
- Construction of the Polihali Dam will displace 17 villages and reduce agricultural land for 71 villages.

Disadvantages for South Africa
- Costs are likely to reach US$4 billion.
- 40% of water is lost through leakages.
- Increased water tariffs to pay for the scheme are too high for the poorest people.
- Corruption has plagued the whole project.

ACTIVITIES

1. Describe the location of Lesotho (map **A**).
2. a How can you work out from graph **B** that Lesotho is in the southern hemisphere?
   b Describe the seasonal distribution of rainfall.
   c During which months would you expect there to be a water surplus?
3. Using photo **D**, draw an annotated field sketch of the Katse Dam.
4. Discuss in pairs the advantages and disadvantages of this scheme. Who are the winners and losers?

Maths skills
Use climate graph **B** to estimate the total annual rainfall for Lesotho.

Stretch yourself
Use the internet to research the impact of the scheme on the people of Lesotho.

Practice question
Evaluate whether the Lesotho Highland Water Project is worth the enormous costs involved. (*6 marks*)

17.5 Sustainable water supplies

On this spread you will find out about strategies for a sustainable water supply

What is sustainable water supply?

Population growth and economic development will lead to greater demand for water in the future. In 2005 the UN began a 10-year 'Water for Life' campaign worldwide. The aim was to ensure that water resources are managed in a sustainable way in the long term.

Sustainable approaches to water supply focus on the careful management of water resources and the need to reduce waste and excessive demand.

Water conservation

Conserving water is about reducing waste and unnecessary use. This can include strategies such as:

- reducing leakages (25–30 per cent of global water supply is lost through leakage)
- monitoring illegal and unmetered connections
- water tariffs, with charges increasing sharply after a certain level of usage
- improving public awareness of the importance of saving water
- water meters to encourage people to use water wisely
- preventing **pollution**.

> **Did you know?**
> Turning the tap off while you brush your teeth saves 6 litres of water per minute!

A How to use water sustainably

How can you save water at home?
- Plant drought-tolerant plants
- Wash vegetables in a container, not under a running tap
- Only use washing machines and dishwashers for a full load
- Live with a dirty car rather than washing it frequently
- Install low-flow shower heads
- Collect rainwater for use in the garden
- Water gardens early morning or late evening to reduce water loss
- Install a twin-flush toilet system
- Turn off tap when brushing teeth

Groundwater management

Groundwater stored in underground aquifers has to be managed to maintain the **water quality** and quantity. To ensure supplies are sustainable, water abstraction (loss) must be balanced by recharge (gain). If groundwater levels fall, water can become contaminated, making expensive water treatment necessary.

In many LICs individual families or groups own wells. National laws are ineffective and often ignored. So effective community-based management is needed.

B Repairs to a well in Sierra Leone

Recycling

Water recycling involves re-using treated domestic or industrial wastewater for useful purposes such as irrigation and industrial processes. For example:

- Large quantities of recycled water are used for cooling in electricity-generating and steel-making plants. In some Australian power stations, recycled water replaces enough freshwater to fill an Olympic-sized swimming pool.
- In Kolkata, India, sewage water is re-used for fish farming and agriculture. Sewage is pumped into shallow lagoons where sunlight helps algae to photosynthesise. This oxygenates the water so that it can be re-used.
- Some nuclear power plants, such as the Palo Verde Nuclear Generating Station in Arizona, USA, use recycled water for cooling (photo **C**).

Using grey water

Grey water is taken from bathroom sinks, baths, showers and washing machines. It may contain traces of dirt, food, grease, hair and some cleaning products. If used within 24 hours it contains valuable fertiliser for plants. Water from toilets is considered to be 'black' water and cannot be used in the same way.

Grey water is mainly used for irrigation and watering gardens (diagram **D**). In Jordan, 70 per cent of the water used for irrigation and gardens is grey water.

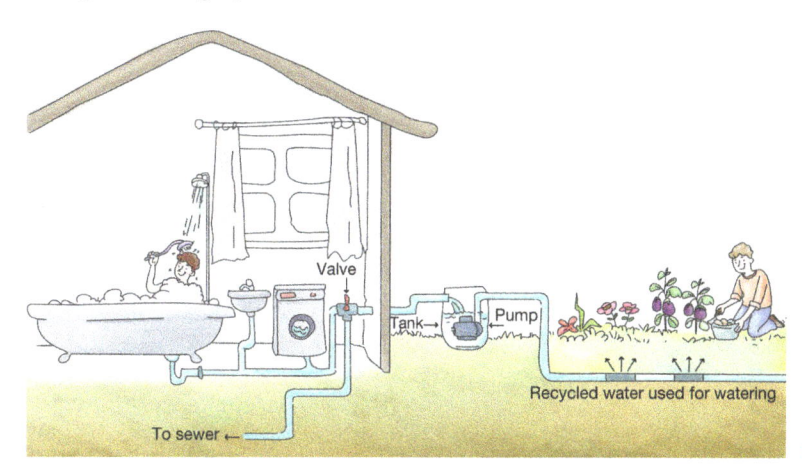

Participatory Groundwater Management (PGM), India

In rural India, 50 per cent of water for irrigation and 85 per cent of drinking water is groundwater. Communities are encouraged to conserve water from their wells through the PGM scheme. Without careful management, the future of some rural communities is at risk. The PGM scheme involves:

- training local people to record rainfall and to monitor groundwater levels and water abstraction
- helping farmers to plan when and how much water to use for irrigation
- encouraging farmers to plant crops to fit in with annual periods when water is available.

Through PGM, rural communities have used scientific monitoring to balance water supply and demand using sustainable practices.

C Palo Verde Nuclear Generating Station

D Re-using grey water

ACTIVITIES

1. Explain whether you think your household makes sustainable use of water (diagram **A**).
2. Why is the involvement of local communities so important in the sustainable management of groundwater in rural areas?
3. What is the difference between 'grey' water and 'black' water?

Stretch yourself

Investigate why it is not only in areas of low rainfall where sustainable use of water is needed.

Practice question

Use examples to explain why both demand and supply affect the sustainable use of water. (*6 marks*)

17.6 The Wakel River Basin project

On this spread you find out about a local scheme to increase sustainable water supply

Case study

Rajasthan is a region in north-west India (map **A**). It is the driest and poorest part of India, and largely covered by the Thar Desert (see page 94). Summer temperatures can reach 53°C. Rainfall is less than 250 mm per year with 96 per cent between June and September. There is little surface water, as rain quickly soaks away or evaporates.

What are the issues with water supply?

Water management in the region has been poor. Over-use of water for irrigation has led to waterlogging and salinisation. Over-abstraction from unregulated pumps has resulted in falling water tables in aquifers and some wells have dried up. With access to wells controlled by households or villages, there has been little coordination of water management.

The Wakel River Basin Project

The Wakel river basin is located in the south of Rajasthan. The United States Agency for International Development has funded a project called the Global Water for Sustainability Program (2004–14). This non-government organisation (NGO) has been working with local people in the Wakel river basin to improve their water security and overcome the problems of water shortages. Local people needed to be actively involved in the decision-making process to make the water management successful.

The two main aims of the scheme are to:

- increase water supply and storage using appropriate local solutions
- raise awareness in local communities of the need for effective water management.

A *Location map of Rajasthan*

Did you know?
Each taanka can hold 20 000 litres – enough to supply a family for several months.

Increasing water supply

The project has encouraged greater use of rainwater harvesting techniques to collect and store water. This benefits villages and individual families. The methods used include the following:

- *Taankas* – underground storage systems about 3 m in diameter and 3–4 m deep (photo **B**). They collect surface water from roofs.
- *Johed* – small earth dams to capture rainwater. These have helped to raise water tables by up to 6 m. Five rivers that used to dry up following the monsoon now flow throughout the year.
- *Pats* – irrigation channels that transfer water to the fields.

B *Collecting water from a concrete taanka*

Water

How does the *pat* system work?

In the *pat* system, a small dam called a bund diverts water from the stream towards the fields. Bunds are made of stones and lined with leaves to make them waterproof.

Villagers take turns to irrigate their fields using water controlled in this way. The irrigation channels need regular maintenance to avoid them breaking or silting up. This is done by the villager whose turn it is to receive the water.

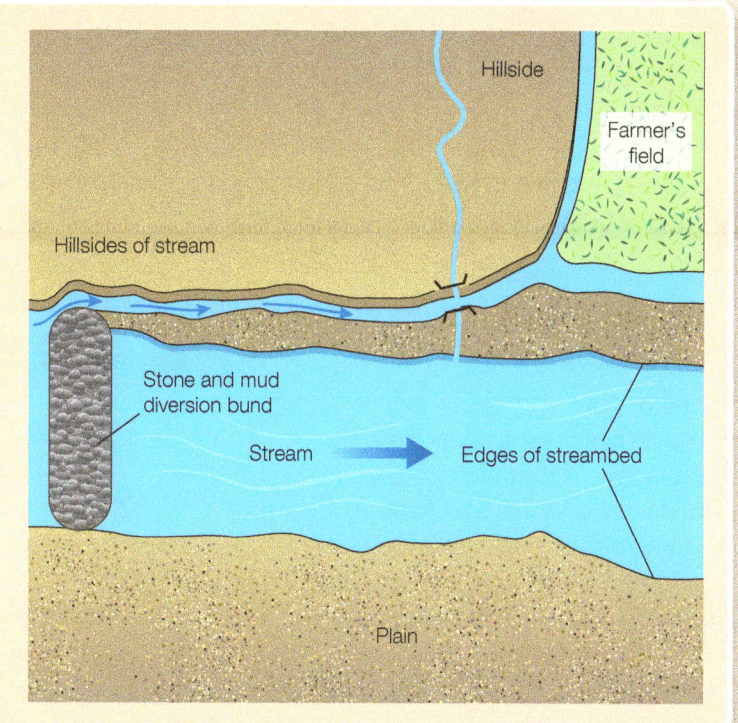

C The *pat* irrigation system

Increasing public awareness

Education is used to increase awareness of the need for communities to work together to conserve water (photo **D**). By conserving water, water security is increased and problems such as soil erosion, desertification and groundwater pollution are reduced.

D A cycle campaign to spread the message about the importance of water conservation

ACTIVITIES

1. Summarise the physical and human factors causing water insecurity in the region.
2. **a** What are the key design features of a *taanka* (photo **B**)?
   b How does this form of water harvesting benefit local communities?
3. **a** Copy diagram **C** and add labels to describe how the *pat* system works.
   b How does this system demonstrate the importance of communities working together to improve water security?

Stretch yourself

Give reasons for working at a local rather than a national level when developing an effective sustainable water scheme.

Practice question

Evaluate the success of a local scheme for increasing sustainable water supplies. *(4 marks)*

18 Energy

18.1 Global energy supply and demand

On this spread you find out that global demand for energy is rising but supply is not evenly distributed

Global energy consumption and supply

Energy consumption per person is very high in countries such as the USA, Canada, Australia, much of Europe and parts of the Middle East (table **A**). It is low across most of Africa and parts of south-east Asia. In regions of high energy consumption there is a growing demand for industry, transport and domestic use.

Some regions have energy resources such as coal, oil or gas. Some areas are also able to produce electricity (table **B**), for example by using nuclear power.

The balance between energy supply (production) and demand (consumption) determines the level of **energy security**. If supply exceeds demand then a country has an *energy surplus*. If demand exceeds production, there is an energy deficit and the country suffers from *energy insecurity* (table **C**).

Energy consumption per person (kg of oil equivalent)	Country
	Key: North America, Central and South America, Africa, Europe, Asia, Oceania
>10000	Iceland
5001–10000	Canada, USA, Saudi Arabia, Australia
2501–5000	France, Germany, Italy, Portugal, Ukraine, Russia, New Zealand
1001–2500	Argentina, Brazil, Chile, Belarus, Poland, Sweden, China, Japan, Mongolia, Thailand
501–1000	Colombia, Ecuador, Peru, Egypt, Namibia, India
0–500	Chad, Mali, Mauritania, Niger, Tanzania, Cambodia, Myanmar, Philippines

A *Examples of global energy consumption*

Energy production in MTOES (millions of tonnes of oil equivalent)	Country
	Key: North America, Central and South America, Africa, Europe, Asia, Oceania
>1000	USA, Chile, China, Japan, Russia
200–999	Canada, Brazil, France, Germany, Iceland, India, Saudi Arabia, Australia, New Zealand
100–199	Portugal, Sweden, Colombia
50–99	Argentina, Egypt, Belarus, Poland, Ukraine, Thailand
<50	Ecuador, Peru, Chad, Mali, Mauritania, Namibia, Niger, Tanzania, Italy, Cambodia, Mongolia, Myanmar, Philippines

B *Examples of global energy supply (production)*

C *Energy security status, by region*

Region	Energy security	Energy sources
Russia and Eastern Europe	Energy surplus	• Large reserves of natural gas and oil • Uranium resources which can be used for nuclear energy
Western Europe	Energy insecurity (deficit)	• Dependent on energy imports, particularly oil and gas • Low energy efficiency
Middle East	Energy surplus	• Large oil reserves • Unstable political regimes affect fuel supply
North America	Energy insecurity	• Large coal reserves • Opportunity to exploit oil reserves in sensitive areas such as the Arctic • Huge energy consumption • Deficit in energy until technological advances allowed exploitation of oil shale
Asia	Energy insecurity	• Large coal and uranium deposits • Rapidly increasing demand outstrips supply
Sub-Saharan Africa	Energy insecurity	• Depends on foreign TNCs to exploit reserves, for example Nigerian oil • Limited energy supplies with rising rates of consumption

What factors affect energy supply?

Costs of exploitation and production
Some energy sources are costly to exploit. Oil rigs and pipelines require huge investment. Nuclear power stations are expensive to build.

Physical factors
The geology of an area determines the location and availability of **fossil fuels**. Coal is formed from vegetation laid down and altered by pressure and heat over millions of years. Natural gas and oil is trapped in folded layers of rocks. **Geothermal energy** is produced in areas of tectonic activity such as Iceland and the Pacific Rim.

Technology
Technological advances have allowed energy sources in remote or difficult environments, such as the North Sea and the Arctic, to be exploited. They can also reduce costs. Technology has made possible the exploitation of shale gas by fracking.

Political factors
Political factors affect decisions about which energy sources to exploit and from which countries energy can be obtained.

- Political instability in the Middle East has meant that many oil-consuming countries are looking for alternative sources of energy.
- Some Western countries and Israel currently want to stop Iran developing nuclear power. They fear it will be used for non-peaceful purposes.
- The German government is planning to stop generating nuclear power by 2020.
- The UK government has decided to cut subsidies for renewable energy such as solar and wind.

Climate
The amount of sunshine and wind influence the availability of **solar energy** and **wind energy**. Tidal power needs a large tidal range in order to be effective. Hydroelectric power (HEP) needs a suitable dam site, often in sparsely populated mountainous areas with high rainfall.

Why is energy consumption increasing?

Economic development
As countries develop, their demand for energy supplies rises. By 2035, newly emerging economies (NEEs) will account for more than 90 per cent of the growth in demand for energy. Recent growth in Asia's energy demand has been led by China, but this has now started to slow down. Greater energy demand is expected to accompany rapid economic growth in India and other parts of south-east Asia. This is due to industrialisation and greater wealth.

Rising population and technology
In 2015 the world's population was 7.5 billion. By 2050 it is predicted to rise to 9 billion. All these extra people will use more energy. Many will grow up in an increasingly energy-thirsty world.

The increasing use of technology, such as computers and other electrical equipment, means a greater demand for energy. As quality of life improves and prosperity increases, the demand for vehicles, lighting and heating also increases.

ACTIVITIES

1. a Describe the pattern of energy consumption (shown in table **A**).
   b Compare tables **A** and **B**. What are the main similarities and differences?
2. What are the reasons for the growth in global energy consumption?
3. How have technological advances affected the consumption and supply of energy?

Stretch yourself
Investigate the rising energy demand in Nigeria. Why is its demand for energy increasing?

Practice question
Explain why many countries are experiencing energy insecurity. (6 marks)

18.2 Impacts of energy insecurity

On this spread you will find out about the costs and impacts associated with energy insecurity

What can be done about energy insecurity?

Many countries experience energy insecurity. In order to secure their future energy needs, they must consider a range of options. To increase its energy supply, a country may:

- try to further exploit its own energy sources
- reach agreements with other countries to import energy
- reduce its energy consumption through new technologies or greater energy saving.

Energy insecurity can have **economic, social and environmental impacts**.

Exploiting resources in difficult and sensitive areas

In the past, energy resources were relatively easy to exploit. For example, coal seams have been exposed at the Earth's surface. Today, complex techniques and expensive equipment are needed to extract oil and gas reserves in sensitive areas, such as deep below the North Sea.

Energy resources exist in some of the world's most hostile, dangerous and environmentally sensitive regions. These include the Amazon and Antarctica. Exploiting these resources in the future will depend on:

- the development of technologies that make exploitation cost-effective
- the environmental implications of **energy exploitation** in areas that are extremely sensitive and could easily be damaged.

Exploiting energy resources in the Arctic

Map **A** shows energy resources in the Arctic. This region holds an estimated 13 per cent (90 billion barrels) of the world's undiscovered oil resources and 30 per cent of its unexploited natural gas.

This region has great potential to supply energy in the future, but exploitation is difficult and expensive. The environmental consequences of an oil spill, for example, would be catastrophic for the fragile Arctic ecosystem. Recovery from damage would be slow given the low temperatures and short growing season.

To exploit energy resources in the Arctic, several economic and environmental factors need to be addressed (figure **B**).

A Oil and natural gas resources in the Arctic (yellow shading)

B Economic and environmental costs of oil and gas exploitation in the Arctic

- People demand higher wages to work there
- Drilling equipment may sink during the summer thaw
- Political issues develop because the territory north of the Arctic Circle is claimed by eight countries
- Strict environmental controls are needed to prevent damage
- Long distances and limited transportation increases transport costs
- Special equipment is needed to withstand the extreme temperatures

Impacts of energy insecurity on food production

Food production uses 30 per cent of global energy. Energy is used to power farm machinery, store farm produce and manufacture fertilisers and chemicals.

Agriculture is also an energy generator. Use of biofuels has increased in response to concerns about carbon dioxide emissions. Use of biofuels such as maize and sugar cane have contributed significantly to increased food prices. In addition, biofuels are often grown on land previously used for growing food crops (image **C**).

In some low-income countries (LICs) such as Tanzania and Mali firewood is the main source of energy. Instead of working on the land, people – often women – have to spend hours walking to collect the wood. This impacts on food production in regions with high food insecurity.

Impacts of energy insecurity on industry

Energy is essential for industry as a source of power and a raw material. Oil, for example, has many uses in manufacturing chemicals, fuels, plastics and pharmaceuticals.

Some countries suffer from shortfalls in electricity production, resulting in frequent power cuts. In Pakistan, regular power cuts can last for 20 hours a day. This costs the country an estimated 4 per cent of its GDP. Energy shortages have led to the closure of more than 500 companies in the industrial city of Faisalabad alone. Pakistan relies heavily on imported oil, which makes energy expensive as well as insecure.

Potential for conflict

Shortages of energy can lead to political conflict when one state holds a bigger share of an energy resource. For example, Russia controls 25 per cent of the world's natural gas supplies. It could put pressure on its customers – mostly in western Europe – by raising prices or even cutting off supplies.

The Middle East produces 40 per cent of the world's gas and 56 per cent of its oil. The Gulf and Iraq wars in the 1990s and 2000s were driven by the West's fear of a global oil shortage and rising prices.

There are flashpoints where the transport of oil is at risk from political conflicts, terrorism, hijack or collision (map **D**).

C ActionAid's 'Food not fuel' campaign

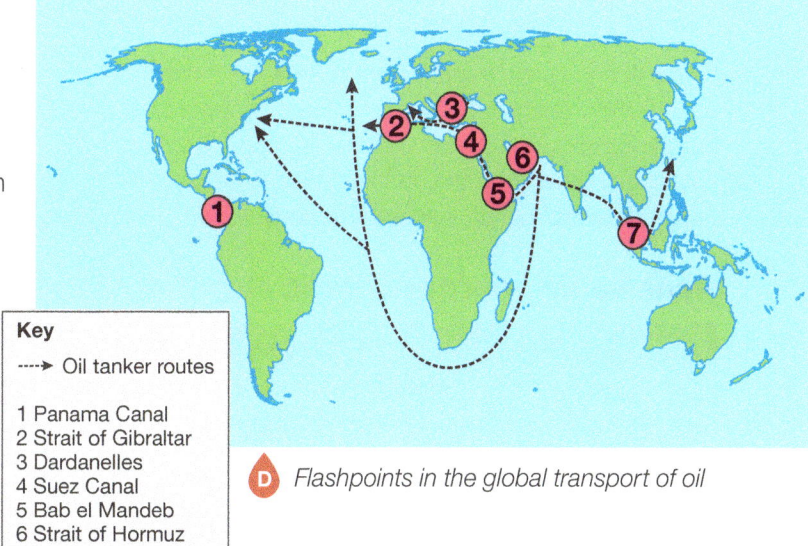

Key
----→ Oil tanker routes

1 Panama Canal
2 Strait of Gibraltar
3 Dardanelles
4 Suez Canal
5 Bab el Mandeb
6 Strait of Hormuz
7 Strait of Malacca

D Flashpoints in the global transport of oil

ACTIVITIES

1. **a** What are the main economic and environmental costs and impacts associated with exploiting oil and gas from the Arctic (figure **B**)?
   b Do you think the Arctic should be exploited for energy resources? Justify your answer.
2. What are the benefits and costs of growing crops for fuel (image **C**)?
3. Which flashpoints on map **D** do you think are the most vulnerable and why?

Stretch yourself

Investigate recent international incidents which have been linked to energy insecurity.

Practice question

Explain how physical and human factors can contribute to energy insecurity. (6 marks)

18.3 Strategies to increase energy supply

On this spread you will find out about how energy supplies can be increased

What are the options for increasing energy supplies?

There are two main options for increasing energy supplies.

♦ Develop and increase the use of renewable (sustainable) sources of energy, such as **wind**, **solar** and **hydroelectric power (HEP)**.

♦ Continue to exploit non-renewable fossil fuels such as oil and gas and develop the use of nuclear power.

Graph **A** shows the trend for global energy sources up to 2035. Notice the balance between renewables, including HEP and non-renewables. To achieve a sustainable **energy mix** countries need to develop the use of renewable energy sources (map **B**).

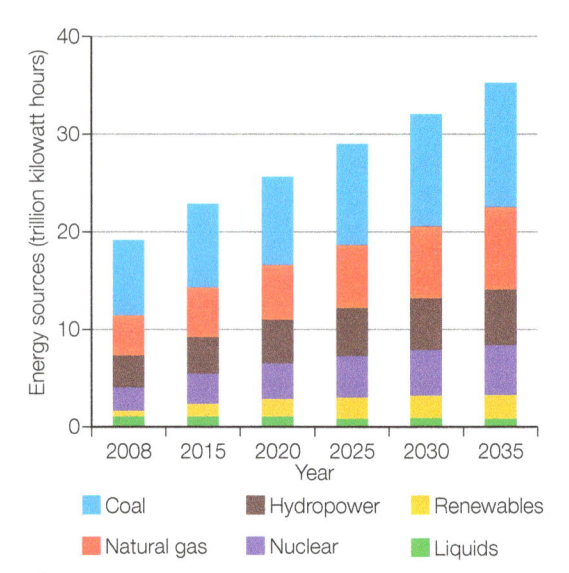

A *Global energy sources for electricity production*

Renewable energy sources

Renewable energy source	How does it work?	Can it increase energy supplies?
Biomass	Energy produced from organic matter includes: • burning dung or plant matter • the production of biofuels, by processing specially grown plants such as sugar cane.	• Using land to grow biofuels rather than food crops is very controversial. • Burning organic matter can create smoky unhealthy conditions. • Fuelwood supplies are limited.
Wind	Turbines on land or at sea are turned by the wind to generate electricity.	• In 2014, wind power met 10% of the UK's electricity demand. • Unpopular, but considerable potential.
Hydro (HEP)	Large-scale dams and smaller micro-dams create enough water to turn turbines and generate electricity.	• Large dams are expensive and controversial. • Micro-dams are becoming popular options at the local level. • An important energy source in several countries. It currently contributes 85% of global renewable electricity.
Tidal	Turbines within barrages (dams) built across river estuaries use rising and falling tides to generate electricity.	There are few tidal barrages (the largest is the Rance in France) due to high costs and environmental concerns.
Geothermal	Water heated underground in contact with hot rocks creates steam that drives turbines to generate electricity.	Limited to tectonically active countries: • the USA has the most geothermal plants (77) • Iceland provides 30% of the country's energy • the Philippines and New Zealand.
Wave	Waves force air into a chamber where it turns a turbine linked to a generator.	• Portugal has built the world's first wave farm, which started generating electricity in 2008. • There are many experimental wave farms but costs are high and there are environmental concerns.
Solar	Photovoltaic cells mounted on solar panels convert sunlight into electricity.	• Energy production is seasonal. • Solar panel 'farms' need a lot of space. • Great potential in some LICs with high levels of sunshine.

Non-renewable energy sources

Non-renewable energy resources are unsustainable. At some point the economic and environmental costs of these resources will become too high. Or they will run out.

Fossil fuels

Fossil fuels are sources of energy formed from organic matter millions of years ago. They include coal, gas and oil. Although limited, there are still plenty of resources left in the world. Despite high carbon dioxide emissions they remain important for electricity production. Carbon capture techniques (page 34) can help overcome the environmental impact.

Nuclear power

Nuclear power stations are very expensive to build. However, the cost of the raw material, uranium, is relatively low because small amounts are used.

The main problem with nuclear power is disposal of the radioactive waste. It can remain dangerous for longer than 100 years. Despite the good safety record, there is considerable opposition. There is fear of further accidents like those at Chernobyl or Fukushima after the Japanese tsunami in 2011.

ACTIVITIES

1. a How much electricity will be produced from coal in 2020 (graph **A**)?
   b Describe the pattern shown on the graph.
2. Describe and suggest reasons for global variations in hydroelectricity potential (map **B**).
3. a Which form of renewable energy has the most potential as an energy source?
   b Suggest advantages and disadvantages of focusing on this form of renewable energy.

Stretch yourself

Produce a case study of one type of renewable energy in your country. Outline its location, when it started and the short-term and long-term advantages and disadvantages. Do you think your choice is a viable option for the future?

Maths skills

Use an appropriate presentation to show the global use of energy, using these figures:
- 78% fossil fuels
- 19% renewables (of which traditional biomass 13%; hydro 3%; rest 3%)
- 3% nuclear

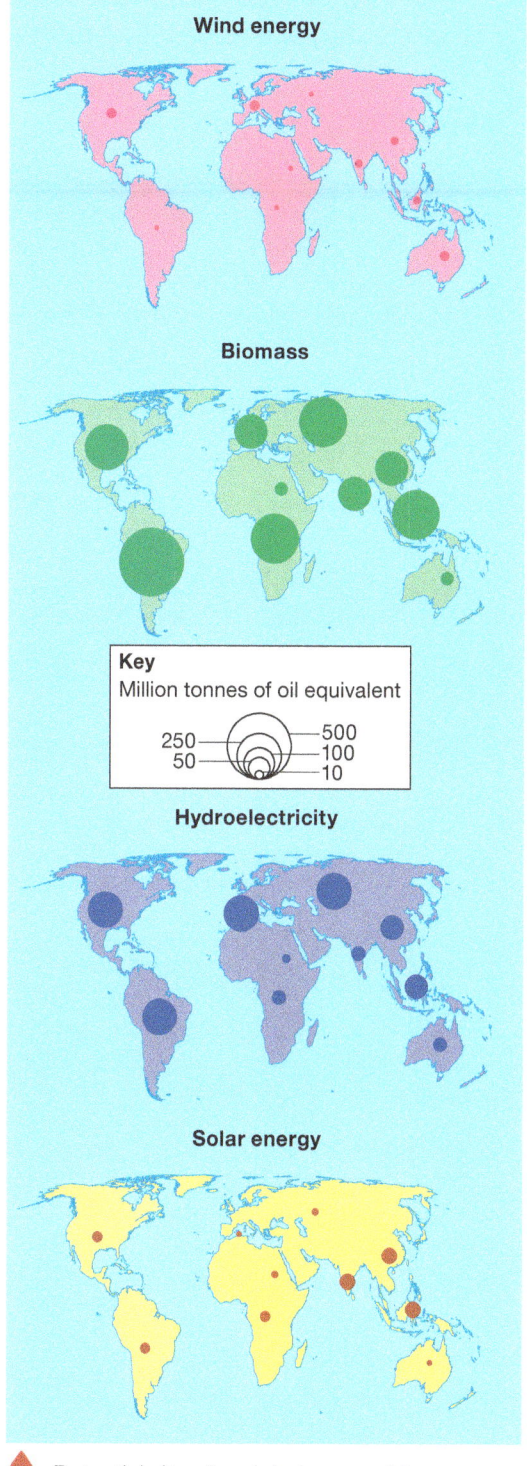

B Potential sites for global renewable energy production

Practice question

Explain why the contribution of renewable energy to world energy production is likely to remain less than fossil fuel production. *(6 marks)*

237

18.4 Gas – a non-renewable resource

Example

On this spread you will find out about the advantages and disadvantages of extracting a fossil fuel

What is natural gas?

Natural gas is a hydrocarbon. Like oil, natural gas forms from the decomposition of organisms deposited on the seabed millions of years ago (diagram **A**). This is why it is called a *fossil* fuel. The organic matter was buried by layers of sediment and heated by compression. Lack of oxygen produced thermal reactions that converted the organic material into hydrocarbons.

The colourless and odourless natural gas rises up through cracks and pores (holes) in the overlying rocks. It then collects in concentrations called reservoirs. It is from these reservoirs that natural gas is extracted.

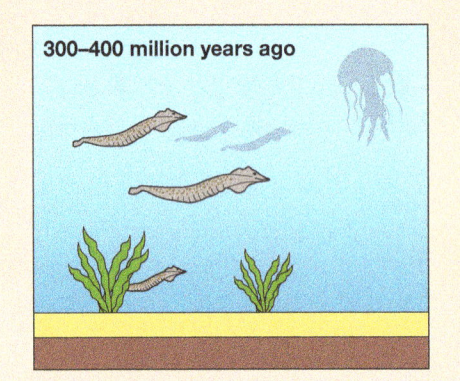

A *The formation of oil and natural gas*

300–400 million years ago
Remains of tiny sea plants and animals buried on ocean floor. Over time these are covered by sand and sediment.

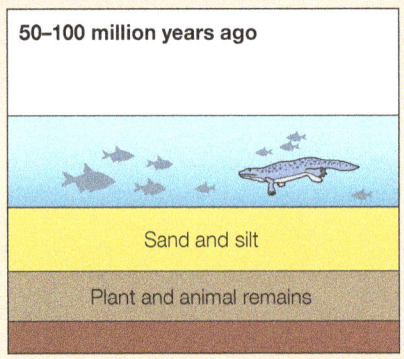

50–100 million years ago
Over millions of years the remains are buried deeper. Enormous pressure and heat turns them into hydrocarbons (oil and gas).

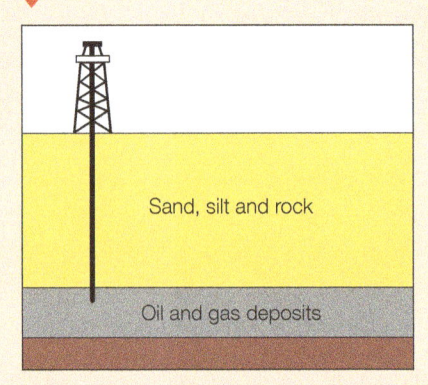

Today, oil and gas deposits are reached by drilling down through layers of sand, silt and rock.

Where is natural gas found?

Nearly 60 per cent of known natural gas reserves are in Russia, Iran and Qatar (table **B**). These reserves are sufficient to last for the next 54 years at the current rate of production.

Recently technology has allowed **shale gas** to be extracted (table **C**). Shales are black sedimentary rocks formed from the same organic matter that is the source of oil and gas. To extract shale gas, the rock is broken up by a process called fracking. This process is very controversial and there is a lot of opposition.

Country	Production in million m^3
Russia	48.0
Iran	36.0
Qatar	25.0
Saudi Arabia	9.0
Turkmenistan	8.0
United Arab Emirates	7.0
Venezuela	6.0
Nigeria	5.5
Réunion Island	5.5
China	4.5

B *The top 10 gas-producing countries in 2015*

Country	Biggest reserves (trillion m^3)
China	36.1
USA	24.4
Argentina	21.9
Mexico	19.3
South Africa	13.7
Australia	11.2
Canada	11.0
Libya	8.2
Algeria	6.5
Brazil	6.4
Poland	5.3

C *Global shale gas deposits*

Energy

Extracting natural gas

Advantages

- Cleanest of the fossil fuels with 45% less CO_2 emissions than other non-renewable sources and less toxic chemicals such as NO and SO_2.
- Less risk of environmental accidents than oil.
- Provides employment for 1.2 million people.
- Can be transported in a variety of ways, i.e. through pipelines or by tankers over land and sea.
- Relatively abundant compared to other fuels. This is increasing as technology makes exploitation of shale gas more economic.

D A gas pipeline

Provides electricity during peak demand periods. Unlike nuclear and HEP, gas-fired power stations can be shut off and turned back on as required.

Disadvantages

- Dangerous if handled or transported carelessly.
- Some gas reserves are in countries that are politically unstable or prepared to use gas supply as a political weapon.
- Contributes to global warming by producing CO_2 and methane emissions.
- Fracking is controversial. Lots of water is needed. Wastewater and chemicals could contaminate groundwater and minor earthquakes are possible.
- Pipelines are expensive to build and maintain.

Extracting natural gas in the Amazon

The Camisea Gas Project began in 2004 to exploit a huge gas field in the Amazonian region of Peru. The project has brought both advantages and disadvantages for Peru.

Advantages
- It could save Peru up to US$4 billion in energy costs.
- Peru could make several billion dollars in gas exports – up to US$34 billion over the 30-year life of the project.
- It provides employment opportunities and helps boost local economies.
- Improved infrastructure could bring benefits to local people. Agriculture could become more productive.

Disadvantages
- Deforestation associated with the pipeline and other developments will affect natural habitats.
- The project could impact on the lives of several indigenous tribes, affecting their traditional way of life and their food and water supplies.
- Local people have no immunity to diseases introduced into the area by developers.
- Clearing routes for pipelines has led to landslides and pollution of streams resulting in decline of fish stocks.

ACTIVITIES

1. Using diagram **A**, describe the formation of natural gas.
2. a. Why is fracking an important technological development?
   b. Describe the global distribution of shale gas basins (table **C**).
   c. Why is fracking such a controversial process?
3. Suggest advantages and disadvantages of transporting gas by pipeline (figure **D**).

Maths skills

Present the figures in table **B** as bars or proportional circles on an outline map of the world. Take care to work out an appropriate scale. Use a single colour to shade the bars or circles.

Stretch yourself

Evaluate the importance of shale gas in the natural gas market. Present your findings as a news report.

Practice question

'The advantages of exploiting natural gas outweigh the disadvantages.' Do you agree with this statement? Justify your decision. *(9 marks)*

239

18.5 Sustainable energy use

On this spread you will find out how it is possible to move towards a sustainable energy supply

What is a sustainable energy supply?

A sustainable energy supply involves balancing supply and demand. It also involves reducing waste and inefficiency. Moving towards a more sustainable future needs individual actions and decisions made by businesses, councils and national governments.

To increase energy supply, renewable sources of energy can be developed and fossil fuels can be exploited more efficiently. Energy demand can be reduced by increasing **energy conservation** and designing more energy-efficient homes and workplaces (diagram **A**). Reducing the use of fossil fuels and increasing efficiency will help reduce carbon dioxide emissions and our **carbon footprint**.

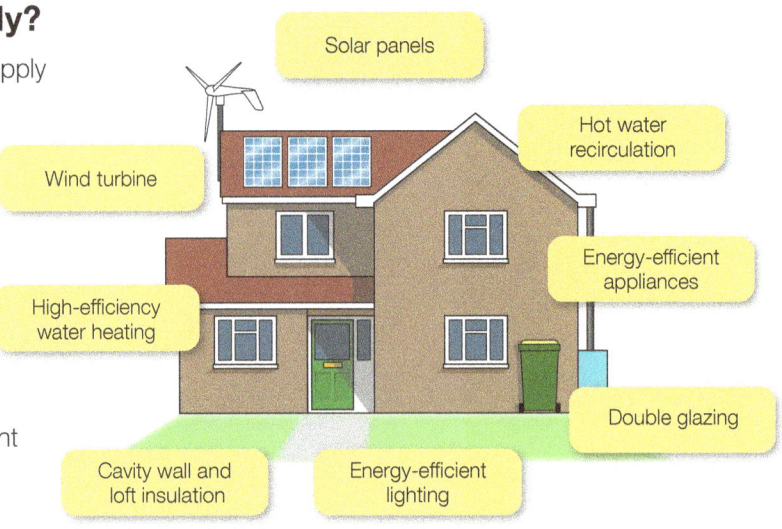

A Energy conservation in the home

Labels: Solar panels, Hot water recirculation, Wind turbine, Energy-efficient appliances, High-efficiency water heating, Double glazing, Cavity wall and loft insulation, Energy-efficient lighting

Sustainable energy developments in Malmo, Sweden

To improve energy conservation, we need to consider sustainable approaches to the design of homes, workplaces and transport systems. These can be seen in innovations in Malmo, an industrial city of about 300 000 people on Sweden's west coast.

Malmo's Western Harbour (figure **B**) is one of the best examples of sustainable urban redevelopment in the world. The houses have been designed to generate and conserve energy and the transport system aims to reduce car usage.

- Creation of green spaces and roof gardens.
- All 1000 buildings in the district use 100% renewable energy.
- From 2019, all buses will run on a mixture of biogas and natural gas.
- Solar tubes on the outside of buildings produce hot water, which can be stored in aquifers 90 m below ground and used to heat buildings during the winter. The water is pumped using electricity from wind power.
- Cyclists have priority at crossroads. A sensor system turns lights green when a cyclist approaches.
- Energy comes from photovoltaic panels on the roofs of houses and workplaces, a 2 MW wind turbine and biogas from local sewage and rubbish.
- Frequent buses and water taxis offer public transport options for local people. This has reduced car usage and people's carbon footprint. A car share scheme has also been introduced.

B Malmo's Western Harbour

Reducing energy demand

There are several ways of reducing energy demand. These can include:

- financial incentives
- raising awareness of the need to save and use energy more efficiently
- greater use of off-peak energy tariffs
- using less hot water for domestic appliances.

How can technology increase efficiency of fossil fuels?

Vehicle manufacturers are using technology to design more fuel-efficient cars to reduce oil consumption and their carbon footprint. These developments include the use of carbon fibre, which is lighter than conventional steel, improved engines and aerodynamic designs to increase fuel efficiency.

The recent development of electric and hybrid cars will increase the efficient use of fossil fuels (photo **D**). In the USA the growth in the use of electric cars could reduce the use of oil for transport by up to 95 per cent.

The development of biofuel technology in car engines can reduce the use of oil. Brazil has reduced its petrol consumption by 40 per cent since 1993 by using sugar cane ethanol (photo **E**). Around 90 per cent of all new cars in Brazil can run on both ethanol and petrol. Brazilians are increasingly choosing environmentally friendly ethanol because it is cheaper than petrol. However, growing biofuels rather than food crops is a controversial issue in Brazil.

Reducing energy demand at Marriott hotels

The chain of Marriott hotels in the UK and Europe spends US$85 million a year on energy. An automated system places the hotel chain on energy-saving standby if the national electricity supply grid needs to reduce demand.

Everything from air conditioning to ice coolers in the corridors can be turned down at a moment's notice without customers noticing. Not only will this reduce energy demand but the hotel chain is paid a supplement for reducing its energy use.

C *An energy-saving Marriot hotel*

D *An electric car*

E *Ethanol fuel at a gas station in São Paulo, Brazil*

ACTIVITIES

1. **a** In what ways is your own home energy-efficient?
   b What are the least energy-efficient aspects of your home?
2. How is Malmo's Western Harbour a model for sustainable urban development?
3. Choose a new model *either* of a car *or* aircraft. State how the manufacturers have designed it to be more energy efficient.

Stretch yourself

Investigate how energy ratings on electrical appliances contribute to energy sustainability.

Practice question

Evaluate why changes in individuals' actions and in the built environment are necessary if energy use is to become sustainable. (*6 marks*)

18.6 The Chambamontera micro-hydro scheme

Example

On this spread you will find out about a local sustainable energy scheme

Where is Chambamontera?

Chambamontera is an isolated community in the Andes Mountains of Peru (map **A**). It is more than two hours' drive on a rough track from Jaén, the nearest town.

Why does Chambamontera need a sustainable energy scheme?

Most people in the area are dependent on subsistence farming with some small-scale coffee growing and rearing of livestock (photo **B**). Development has been severely restricted by a lack of electricity for heat, light and power. Despite farming being efficient, nearly half the population survive on just US$2 a day.

The steep slopes rise to 1700m and the rough roads are impassable in winter. This makes Chambamontera a very isolated community. Due to the low population density it was uneconomic to build an electricity grid to serve the area.

What is the Chambamontera micro-hydro scheme?

The solution to Chambamontera's energy deficit involved the construction of a micro-hydro scheme supported by the charity Practical Action. The high rainfall, steep slopes and fast-flowing rivers make this area ideal for exploiting water power as a renewable source of energy (diagram **C**).

The total cost of the micro-hydro scheme was US$51 000. There was some government money and investment from Japan, but the community had to pay part of the cost. The average cost per family was US$750. Credit facilities were made available to pay for this.

A Location map of Chambamontera

B Agriculture in the Andes

C How the scheme works

Population

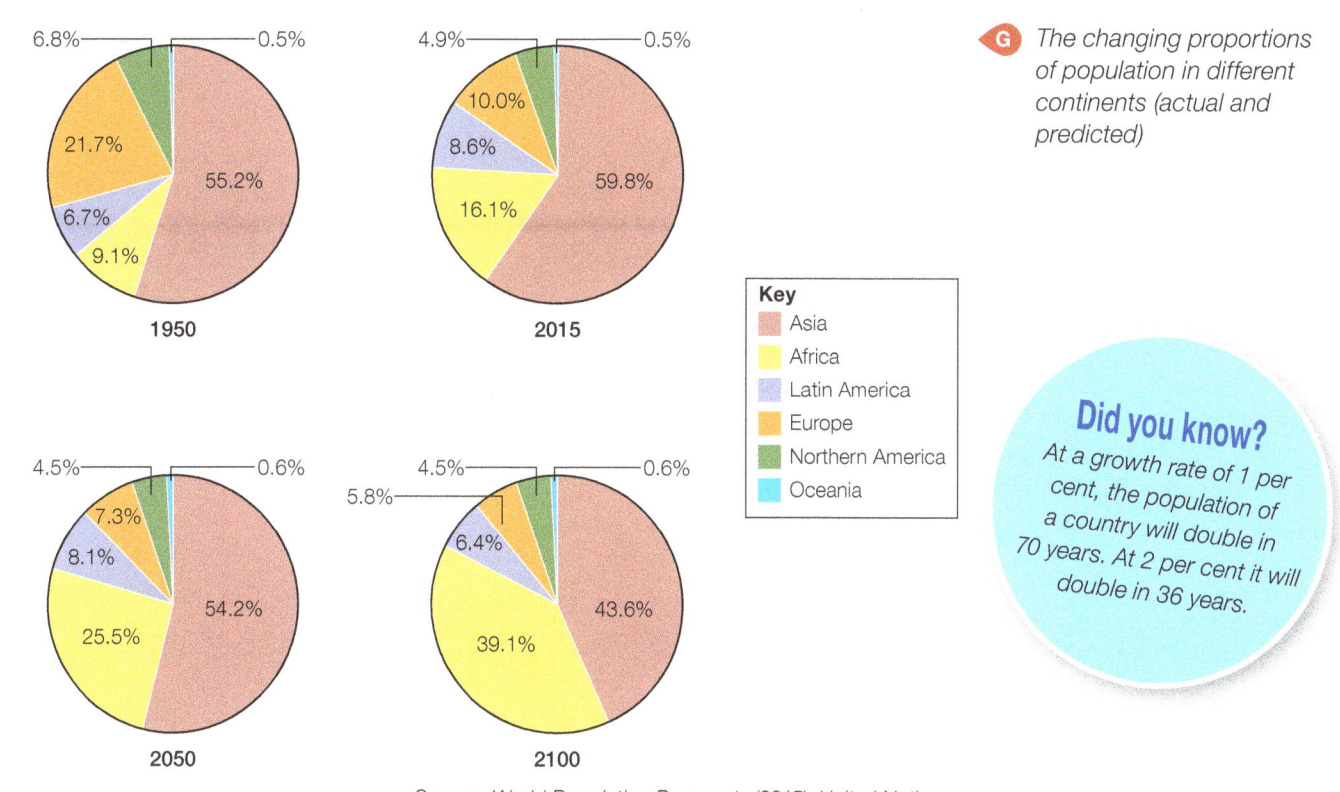

1950
- 55.2%
- 9.1%
- 6.7%
- 21.7%
- 6.8%
- 0.5%

2015
- 59.8%
- 16.1%
- 8.6%
- 10.0%
- 4.9%
- 0.5%

2050
- 54.2%
- 25.5%
- 8.1%
- 7.3%
- 4.5%
- 0.6%

2100
- 43.6%
- 39.1%
- 6.4%
- 5.8%
- 4.5%
- 0.6%

Key
- Asia
- Africa
- Latin America
- Europe
- Northern America
- Oceania

G The changing proportions of population in different continents (actual and predicted)

Source: *World Population Prospects* (2015), United Nations.

Did you know?
At a growth rate of 1 per cent, the population of a country will double in 70 years. At 2 per cent it will double in 36 years.

Did you know?
Just over 100 billion people have lived on the Earth. About 7.5 per cent of the people ever born are alive today.

ACTIVITIES

1. Look up a world population clock to see the estimated total for today. How much has it changed since March 2018?
2. **a** Draw a graph to show the data table **C**. (Be careful to ensure that the horizontal axis in years is plotted accurately.)
   b What does the graph illustrate? Give details of the graph's shape and quote figures from the graph to support your answer. Use key terms such as exponential, J-shaped, S-shaped, levelling off, zero growth.
3. Explain why population growth has been very rapid at certain times.
4. Give reasons why it is very difficult to make accurate forecasts about future world population totals.
5. **a** Explain why there is much concern about increases in global population.
   b Do future population trends give any cause for optimism?

Stretch yourself

Produce a presentation (up to 10 slides) to illustrate and explain world population trends in the past and future (estimated). Explain why there is such an increasing divergence in forecasts of population size for the end of the century.

Practice question

With the help of table **C**, explain global population trends from 1800 to the present day. *(6 marks)*

247

19.2 Why is the world population increasing?

On these spreads you will find out about the causes of the increase in global population

Today, **birth rates** vary at between 5 per 1000 people per year and 40 per 1000 people per year, depending on the country. Generally, **death rates** lie between 5 per 1000 people per year and 20 per 1000 people per year – unless there is an epidemic, famine or war, which will increase levels significantly.

Natural change (the difference between birth and death rates) helps to indicate whether a country's population is increasing or decreasing (although migration can also be a factor). Until recently, all countries have been in a situation of **natural increase**, except in periods of epidemic, famine or war. In Europe, between 1347 and 1353, the Black Death killed about a third of the population. Today, some countries have reduced their birth rates so much that they are now experiencing **natural decrease** and population is declining. For example, many countries in eastern Europe, such as Bulgaria, Ukraine and Serbia, have declining populations.

Did you know?
Average life expectancy worldwide increased from 67 to 71 years between 2000 and 2015.

Maths skills

Country	Continent	Birth rate (per 1000)	Death rate (per 1000)
Angola	Africa	44	9
Afghanistan	Asia	38	13
Ghana	Africa	30	7
Bolivia	South America	22	6
Brazil	South America	14	7
UK	Europe	12	9
Japan	Asia	8	10
Bulgaria	Europe	8	15

A *Birth rates for selected countries, 2017*

1. Work out the natural change in population for the eight countries listed in table **A** (birth rate minus death rate per 1000).
2. Which country shows
   a. the highest population growth rate
   b. the highest negative population change?
3. Which areas of the world appear to have the most rapid population growth?
4. What do you notice about the countries with higher death rates? Explain why death rates are higher in these countries.

B *Average life expectancy is increasing worldwide*

Population

Infant mortality rate (per 1000 live births)	Country
	Key: North America, Central and South America, Africa, Europe, Asia, Oceania
<11	Canada, USA
	Chile, Costa Rica, Cuba, Uruguay
11–30	Mexico
	Argentina, Brazil, Colombia, Ecuador, Guatemala, Honduras, Nicaragua, Panama, Paraguay, Peru, Suriname, Venezuela
	Botswana, Egypt, Libya, Morocco, Zimbabwe
	Albania, Algeria, Andorra, Austria, Belarus, Belgium, Bosnia and Herzegovina, Bulgaria, Croatia, Czech Republic, Denmark, Estonia, Finland, France, Germany, Greece, Hungary, Iceland, Ireland, Italy, Kosovo, Latvia, Liechtenstein, Lithuania, Luxembourg, Malta, Moldova, Monaco, Montenegro, Netherlands, North Macedonia, Norway, Poland, Portugal, Romania, San Marino, Serbia, Slovakia, Slovenia, Spain, Sweden, Switzerland, Tunisia, Ukraine, UK
	Armenia, Cambodia, China, Cyprus, Georgia, Indonesia, Israel, Japan, Jordan, Kazakhstan, Kyrgyzstan, Lebanon, Malaysia, North Korea, Oman, Philippines, Russia, Saudi Arabia, Singapore, South Korea, Sri Lanka, Tajikistan, Thailand, Turkey, UAE, Uzbekistan, Vietnam
	Australia, New Zealand
31–90	Bolivia, Guyana
	Benin, Burkina Faso, Burundi, Cameroon, Cote d'Ivoire, Democratic Republic of Congo, Djibouti, Equatorial Guinea, Eritrea, Ethiopia, Gabon, Ghana, Guinea, Guinea-Bissau, Kenya, Lesotho, Liberia, Madagascar, Malawi, Mauritania, Mozambique, Namibia, Republic of the Congo, Rwanda, Senegal, Sierra Leone, South Africa, South Sudan, Sudan, Syria, Swaziland, Tanzania, Togo, Uganda, Zambia
	Azerbaijan, Bangladesh, Bhutan, India, Laos, Mongolia, Myanmar, Nepal, Pakistan, Thailand, Turkmenistan, Yemen
	Papua New Guinea
91–120	Dominican Republic
	Central African Republic, Chad, Mali, Niger, Nigeria, Somalia
>120	Angola
	Afghanistan

C *Global infant mortality rates, 2011*

Factors explaining population change

Improved medical care

Improvements in medical care, greater access to penicillin and other life-saving drugs have had a huge impact on survival rates, with the result that life expectancies in many low-income countries (LICs) have risen rapidly. Greater numbers of doctors, nurses and hospitals have made a substantial difference to mortality rates in many parts of the world. Fewer babies die at birth so birth rates may be reduced as more children survive to adulthood. However, there is still a great deal of regional variation – table **C** shows that **infant mortality** rates are lowest in North America, most of Europe, Japan and Australasia – all areas with higher standards of medical care.

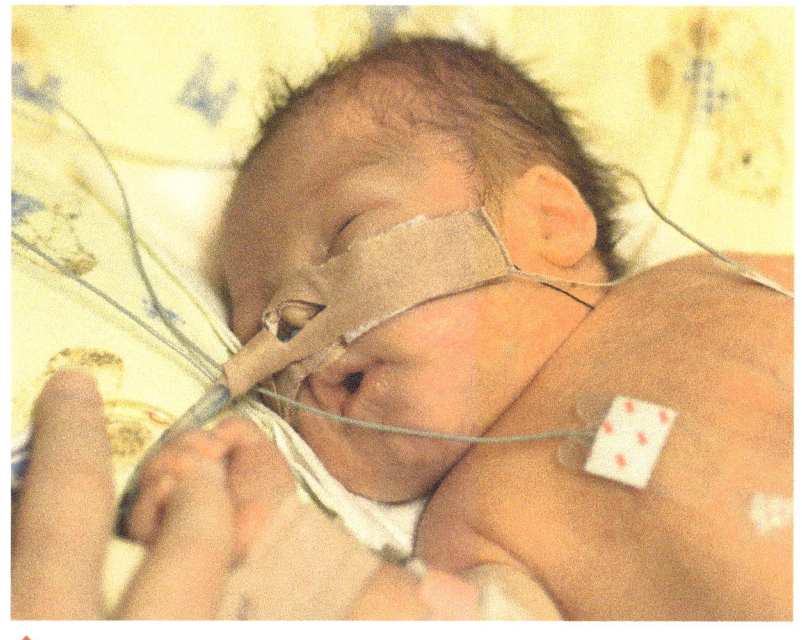

D *Improved medical care increases chances of survival at birth*

Why is the world population increasing?

Improved sanitation

Sanitation concerns public health facilities, particularly the provision of high-quality drinking water and the maintenance of hygiene through the safe disposal of human excreta (sewage) and refuse. Poor sanitation is one of the most common causes of diseases, such as diarrhoea, dysentery, cholera and typhoid. Improvements in the provision of clean water and toilets are known to have a significant impact on death rates and, by implication, life expectancy. The United Nations (UN) and World Health Organization (WHO) claim that approximately 1.6 million children under five die each year from drinking unclean water. As many as 2.6 billion people worldwide, over one third of the world's population, have little or no access to proper toilet facilities. Not surprisingly, many countries are unable to invest in sewage facilities for their entire population and around 90 per cent of wastewater is untreated and allowed to be discharged directly into rivers and oceans. Table **E** shows that access to improved sanitation is particularly poor in countries in intertropical Africa and parts of east and south Asia.

> **Did you know?**
> Three children in the world die per minute due to poor sanitation.

E Proportion of populations with access to improved sanitation, 2015

Proportion of population (%)	Country
	Key: North America, Central and South America, Africa, Europe, Asia, Oceania
<50	Dominican Republic, Madagascar, Benin, Burkina Faso, Cameroon, Central African Republic, Chad, Cote d'Ivoire, Democratic Republic of Congo, Djibouti, Equatorial Guinea, Eritrea, Ethiopia, Gabon, Ghana, Guinea, Guinea-Bissau, Kenya, Lesotho, Liberia, Malawi, Mali, Mauritania, Mozambique, Namibia, Niger, Nigeria, Republic of the Congo, Senegal, Sierra Leone, Swaziland, Tanzania, The Gambia, Togo, Zambia, Zimbabwe, Afghanistan, Bhutan, Cambodia, India, Nepal, Papua New Guinea
50–75	Bolivia, Guatemala, Nicaragua, Panama, Angola, Botswana, South Africa, Indonesia, Laos, Malaysia, Mongolia, Pakistan, Philippines, Russia
76–90	Mexico, Brazil, Colombia, Ecuador, Guyana, Paraguay, Peru, Puerto Rico, Suriname, Uruguay, Algeria, Morocco, Bulgaria, Romania, Armenia, Azerbaijan, Myanmar, China, Georgia, Iran, Iraq, Syria, Vietnam
>90	USA, Canada, Argentina, Chile, Costa Rica, Cuba, Venezuela, Egypt, Libya, Andorra, Austria, Belarus, Belgium, Bosnia and Herzegovina, Croatia, Czech Republic, Denmark, Estonia, Finland, France, Germany, Greece, Hungary, Ireland, Italy, Latvia, Lithuania, Moldova, Netherlands, Norway, Poland, Portugal, San Marino, Serbia, Slovakia, Slovenia, Spain, Switzerland, Sweden, Tunisia, Ukraine, UK, Cyprus, Israel, Japan, Jordan, Kazakhstan, Kyrgyzstan, Lebanon, Malaysia, Oman, Saudi Arabia, Sri Lanka, Tajikistan, Thailand, Turkey, UAE, Uzbekistan, Australia
No data	Somalia, South Sudan, Sudan, Yemen, New Zealand

F Providing high-quality drinking water significantly improves life expectancy

> **Did you know?**
> A tenth of the world's population do not have access to clean drinking water.

Role of foreign aid

Aid is any help or assistance given to improve the quality of life of people in the receiving country. It includes money, equipment, goods, staff, training and technical advice. It can be provided as short-term aid or long-term aid. Short-term aid (emergency relief) usually follows a natural disaster or a political crisis and serves to keep people alive. By contrast, long-term aid (development aid) is provided to improve standards of living and quality of life over a longer period. Improvements to water and sanitation in squatter settlements and programmes to increase agricultural productivity are both good examples.

Bilateral aid, where one country gives to another, is the most common method. Alternatively, aid can be channelled through international organisations, such as the United Nations Children's Fund (UNICEF), and non-governmental organisations (NGOs), including charities. Money spent on health programmes and economic development can help to support local populations: it may help to increase life expectancies and reduce infant mortality rates, as well as improve wealth prospects and standards of living. Ethiopia is one of several countries in Africa that has achieved the UN Millennium Development Goal of reducing its child mortality rates by over two-thirds (photo **G**).

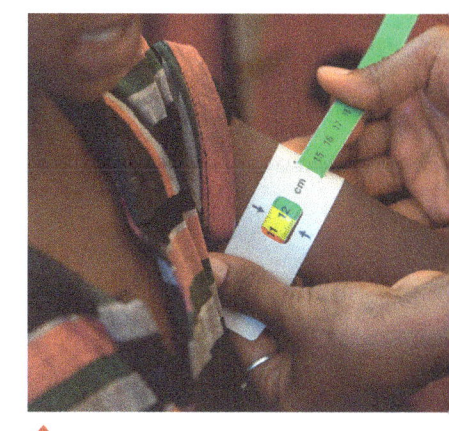

G Measuring the arm circumference of a child, Ethiopia

Religion

Religious and cultural beliefs can affect population growth in several ways:

- In some cultures having a large family is a sign of status and virility.

- For certain religions, such as Judaism and Roman Catholicism, high birth rates are beneficial to maintain or increase the number of followers and ensure the religion survives.

- Several faiths are strongly opposed to abortions and/or contraception. Roman Catholics are officially against the use of any artificial means of birth control, although many catholic countries have seen a considerable drop in birth rates in recent years.

- Some religions may attempt to stop women from pursuing a career and encourage them to have large families.

Graph **I** shows data for selected religions and **fertility rates** in different continents. It shows that Muslim women tend to have a slightly larger number of children than the average in each continent or region. However, it also shows that local culture is a more significant factor. For instance, Christians in sub-Saharan Africa are still having many more children than Muslims in Europe.

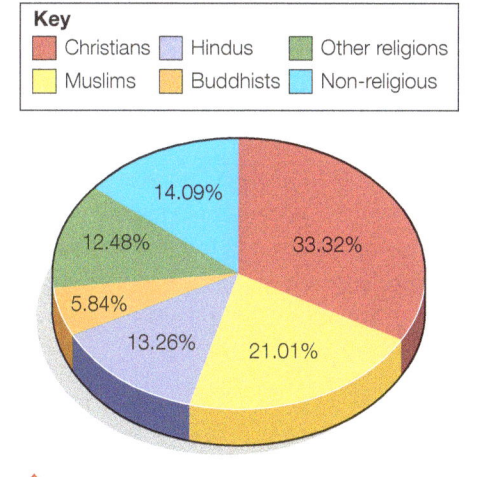

H The proportions of major world religions

I Total fertility rates by region and religion, 2010–15

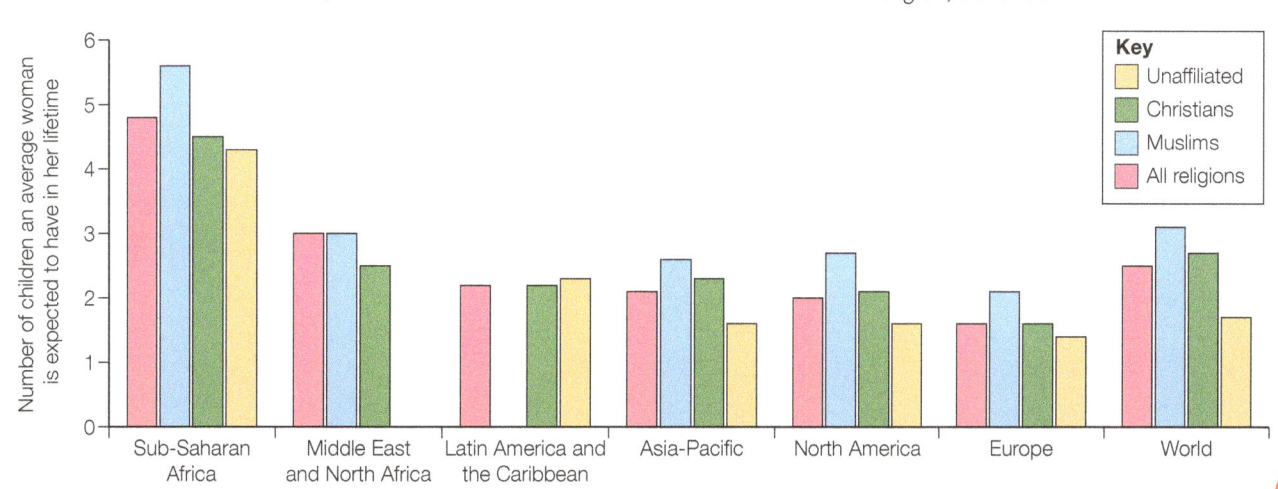

Why is the world population increasing?

Status of women

Several countries, such as Germany and Norway, have introduced legal quotas to ensure that women are well represented in business and senior management roles. Improvements in the status and education of women, leading to lower birth rates, may slow down the rate of population growth. A proportion of women deliberately choose not to have children or delay starting a family to pursue a career. In most high-income countries (HICs) a higher percentage of women remain childless than previous generations – in the UK, for instance, this is currently 25 per cent, compared to 10 per cent in the previous generation. A further consideration is the cost of childcare, which can be prohibitively high.

> As economies develop and education improves, opportunities for women increase alongside those for men.

> A larger workforce is required so women must participate more in paid work outside the home. Reaching a good standard of living in a household often requires two incomes.

> Over time, prejudice against women holding more senior positions at work reduces. Equality increases and is perceived not only as acceptable but also desirable.

J *Women's evolving role in society and the workforce*

Role of children

In some traditional societies, it is important to have a large family to ensure that children are available to work, perhaps on a farm or in a family business. Where infant mortality rates are high, family size tends to be larger to ensure that some children survive.

When a country becomes more urbanised, family size tends to decrease and the rate of population growth decreases, possibly because child labour is less important. In many HICs, family size is also smaller, maybe due to the expense of raising children, including the cost of transport, entertainment, education, food and accommodation. Fewer children means parents have more money to spend on each one, giving them better future opportunities.

Education

Increased educational opportunities tend to result in lower rates of population growth. Education about sanitation and health care can help to reduce death rates. Educating more women, including female literacy programmes, often increases awareness of family planning and contraception, resulting in a drop of birth rates. Women who are educated may also take up career opportunities and join the workforce, rather than having children at an earlier age. Graph **K** shows a clear link between female attendance at secondary school (and therefore female literacy) and fertility rate.

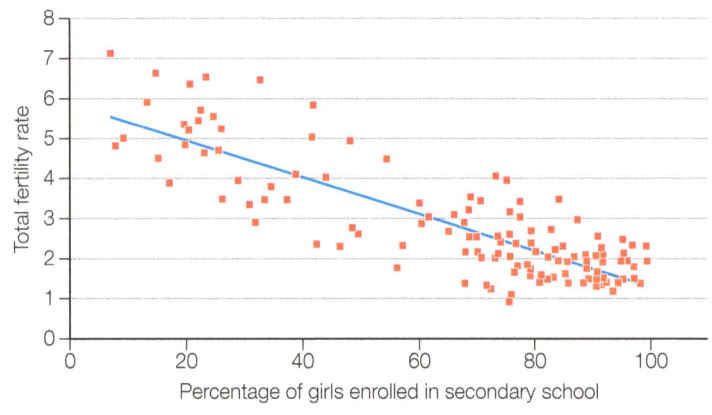

Source: Earth Policy Institute from UNESCO.

K *Female secondary education and total fertility rates, 2011*

Population

Age structure

Population structure refers to the proportions of different age groups of a population. A population pyramid is a type of bar graph used to show the **age structure** and **gender structure** of a country, city or area. The horizontal axis is divided into either total number or percentage of the population. The central vertical axis shows age categories, e.g. every 10 years, every five years or every year. The lower part of the pyramid shows the younger section of the population; the upper part, or apex, shows the elderly. Interpreting population pyramids reveals a great deal about a population, such as birth rates, death rates (to a lesser extent), life expectancy and the level of economic development.

Population structure is changing in many parts of the world. Some countries have a youthful population, whereas others have an ageing population. If the pyramid is steep with a large base it means the birth rate is high and life expectancy is probably low. The composition of the population is important because it helps planners to forecast how many services and facilities, such as schools and hospitals, may be needed in the future.

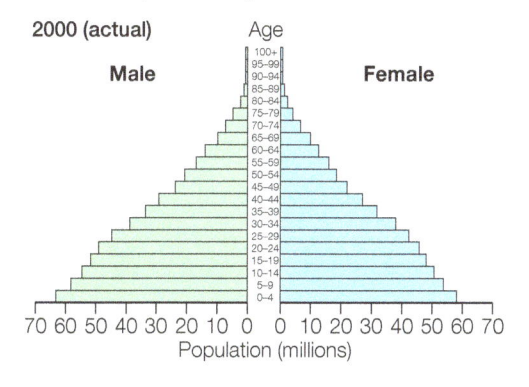

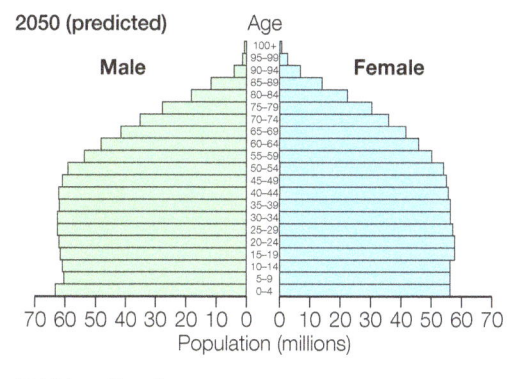

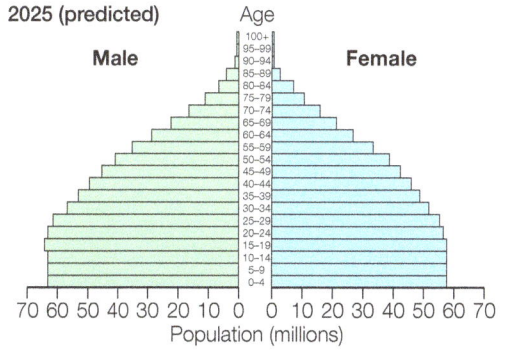

ACTIVITIES

1. Why might people in HICs such as Germany and Japan have very small families?
2. Explain why some LICs still have high birth rates.
3. Study table **C**. Describe the pattern of infant mortality rates globally. Explain why there is so much variation.
4. Study table **E**. In which parts of the world is there limited access to improved sanitation? Explain why access to sanitation may be an important factor affecting population growth rates.
5. How do these factors affect population change:
   a religion
   b the changing status of women?
6. Study graph **K**. Describe the link between the percentage of girls in secondary school and total fertility rates. Explain this link.
7. Study graphs **L**.
   a Describe the shapes of the three population pyramids for India. Be clear about the similarities and differences.
   b Explain in your own words how India's population pyramids are likely to reflect economic changes over this period of time.
8. 'We didn't start breeding like rabbits, we stopped dying like flies.' Why does this statement summarise the population growth of the past 200 years.

Stretch yourself

Investigate the age structure of several contrasting countries by describing the population pyramids of these countries. When describing them, divide each population pyramid into three distinct age groups (cohorts): 0–15 or the young; 16–65 or the working age; and 65+ or the retired.

Practice question

Assess the importance of different factors in explaining the global increase in population over the past 100 years. *(6 marks)*

L Population structure for India (actual and predicted)

253

19.3 Environmental and economic impacts of population change

On these spreads you will find out about environmental and economic impacts of population change

Population and resource balance

Environment and population are tightly connected – many environmental problems are caused or made worse by overpopulation. Overpopulation exists when there are too many people in an area in relation to the available resources, putting pressure on those resources. It means that a continued increase in population will reduce the average standard of living for all.

Evidence of unsustainable resource use can be seen around the world:

- Topsoil is being eroded up to 50 times quicker than it is being formed. Feeding over 7 billion people is becoming increasingly difficult.
- There are serious problems of overfishing worldwide, which means that the main source of protein for billions of people is in jeopardy.
- Pumping water from aquifers (underground water sources) is taking place so fast that they are at risk of drying out. Today, more than 2 billion people live in over 50 countries that are experiencing water stress or scarcity.
- It is estimated that up to 50 per cent of vertebrate animals have become extinct in the past 50 years.
- Pressures from climate change are affecting the balance between population and resources. In some parts of the world there is evidence of reduced yields of staple foodstuffs such as wheat and rice. It may be that some people will be forced to move as 'climate refugees', leading to further conflict over resource availability.
- Increasing wealth in richer countries results in greater consumption of resources. Fewer than one in 25 of the world's people live in the USA but they consume roughly a quarter of the world's resources.

Did you know? A glass bottle made today will take 5000 years to properly decompose.

Economic development

If population growth takes place rapidly, or a country becomes overpopulated, standards of living will often stagnate or even fall. Bangladesh and Somalia are both overpopulated as they have insufficient food and materials. They suffer from natural disasters such as flooding, drought and famine, and are characterised by low incomes, poverty, malnutrition, high infant and **child mortality**, poor living conditions and high levels of **migration** – all of which contribute to slow or negative economic growth.

However, higher rates of population growth do not always imply low rates of economic growth. A steadily increasing population can mean an increase in the number of workers and therefore economic development. It can mean a growing market for most goods and services, resulting in more investment in capital goods and machinery, creating further income and employment. For example, the rapid economic growth of the USA in the twentieth and early twenty-first centuries may be due partly to high levels of immigration and the high fertility rates of some ethnic groups.

In a country with abundant resources and money, population growth can contribute to economic development. However, in a country with limited resources and poor infrastructure, a rapidly growing population puts pressures on the resources that do exist. More people means more mouths to feed, more health care and more education services to provide, stunting economic growth.

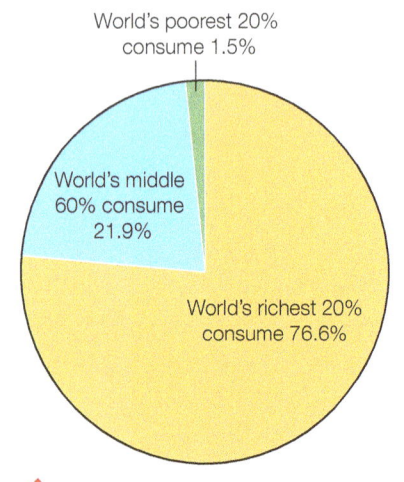

World's poorest 20% consume 1.5%
World's middle 60% consume 21.9%
World's richest 20% consume 76.6%

A World consumption of resources

Did you know? The plastic that is being put into seas and oceans kills up to 1 million sea creatures every year.

Population

Age structure

Population change caused by variations in birth and death rates, as well as migration, can affect the age structure of a country's population.

Youthful population

A youthful population occurs when the average age of the population is reduced. This may happen if the birth rate rises and the death rate remains quite high. Countries such as Bangladesh and Uganda have a large proportion under 15 years old but a small proportion over 65. The population pyramid has a wide base, reflecting the high birth rate, and a narrow peak, reflecting the relatively small percentage of elderly people (graph **B**). Issues that arise from this include the need to supply additional resources for dependent children, including educational provision and health care. This puts even greater pressure on the country's strained economy.

Ageing population

An ageing population occurs when the average age of the population increases. This may happen if both birth and death rates decrease. Countries such as Japan and the UK have a small proportion under 15 years old but a larger proportion between 15 and 64 and over 65. The population pyramid has a narrower base, reflecting the low birth rate, and a wider peak, reflecting the relatively large percentage of elderly people and prolonged life expectancy (graph **C**). Overall, the population pyramid is straighter in shape.

Issues that arise from this:

- Increased demand for health care because more illness occurs in old age. The government has to find more funding to support older people and this comes from taxation of present workers.
- Increased demand for other services such as nursing homes, daycare centres and people to help them care for themselves at home.
- A pensions crisis. As there are more elderly people and the proportion of working people is decreasing, so the taxes must increase to pay the pensions bill.

> **Did you know?**
> One in seven of the world's population have to survive on less than US$1 per day.

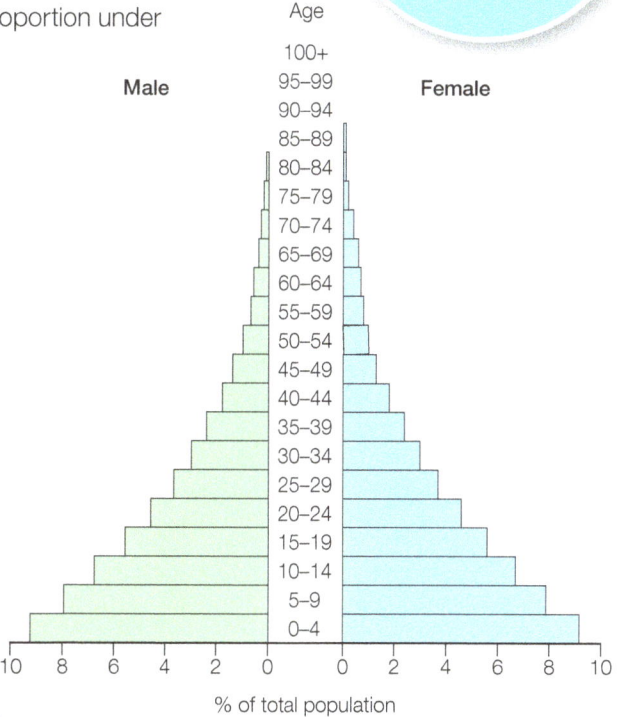

B Population pyramid for Uganda, 2016

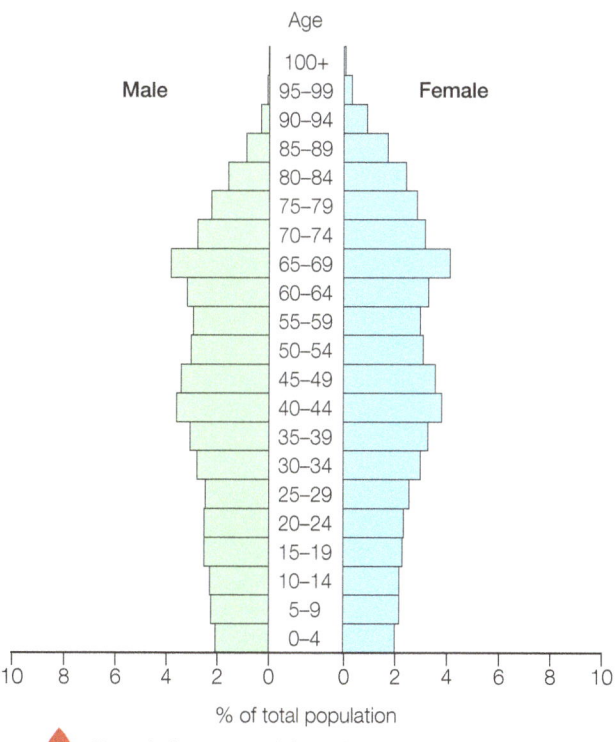

C Population pyramid for Japan, 2016

Maths skills

Using graphs **B** and **C**, work out the percentage of the population aged under 15, the percentage between ages 15 and 64, and the percentage aged 65 and over for both Uganda and Japan. Compare the figures for the two countries. What issues might these two countries be facing as a result?

Environmental and economic impacts of population change

Food supply

Globally, there is sufficient food to feed the world's population. However, food supply is unevenly distributed and the level of food consumption varies across the world. North America and Europe consume the most, with an average daily intake of over 3400 calories. Most countries consume closer to the recommended daily 2000–2400 calories. However, in some parts of world such as sub-Saharan Africa, daily calorie intake per head is below this level (map **D**).

The key question is: how can the world feed more than 10 billion people by 2055 in a way that allows economic growth but also reduces pressure on resources and the environment? Diagram **F** shows how three different needs must be met at the same time.

Global food consumption is increasing for several reasons:

- Increasing levels of development and higher standards of living mean that people can afford to buy more food.
- Populations are growing, particularly in India, Indonesia, China and much of Africa.
- There is greater availability of food due to improved transport and storage.

The term 'food security' means having access to enough safe, affordable and nutritious food to maintain a healthy and active life. The highest concentration of countries at risk of food insecurity is in sub-Saharan Africa. Other countries with food insecurity include Afghanistan, Haiti and Bangladesh. Food insecurity may lead to problems of under-nutrition and malnutrition, famine, soil erosion, social unrest and higher death rates.

As the world's population grows, traditional methods and modern technology are being used to increase food production. These include the use of higher yielding varieties of plants, greater use of biotechnology or genetically modified crops, more effective fertilisers and herbicides, irrigation and soil conservation. As farming techniques improve, crop yields rise, more land is placed under cultivation and food supplies increase in many parts of the world.

Daily calorie intake per head Recommended daily calorie intake: 2000–2400	Country Key: North America, Central and South America, Africa, Europe, Asia, Oceania
3480–3770	Canada, USA, France, Germany, Italy
3270–3479	Poland, Iceland
2850–3269	Argentina, Brazil, Chile, Egypt, Belarus, Portugal, Sweden, Ukraine, China, Russia, Saudi Arabia, Australia, New Zealand
2390–2849	Colombia, Peru, Mali, Mauritania, Cambodia, Japan, Myanmar, Philippines, Thailand
<2390	Ecuador, Chad, Namibia, Niger, Tanzania, India, Mongolia

D *Food consumption (in calories) in countries around the world*

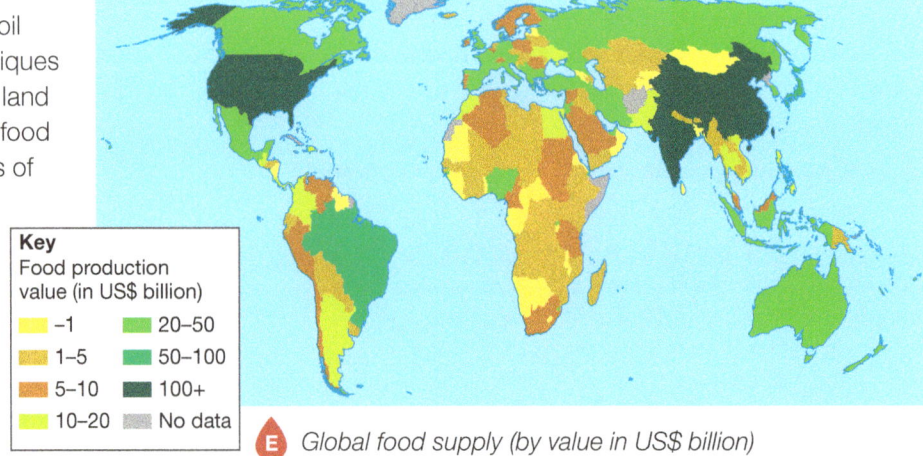

Key
Food production value (in US$ billion)
- –1
- 1–5
- 5–10
- 10–20
- 20–50
- 50–100
- 100+
- No data

E *Global food supply (by value in US$ billion)*

Environmental degradation

Population growth has significant effects on the natural environment, often causing **environmental degradation**.

- The destruction of habitats and threats to biodiversity – up to 100 species a day are being permanently lost from the tropical rainforests and up to 80 per cent of this global ecosystem has been cleared since 1950. Fragile ecosystems such as coral reefs and estuaries are particularly threatened by human activity.
- Over-exploitation of resources both on land and in the sea due to intensive farming methods leads to soil erosion and degradation, waterlogging and salination. Soil erosion can cause the silting up of reservoirs and the blocking of rivers.
- Climatic change associated with the accumulation of greenhouse gases, caused by deforestation, industrial activity, burning of fossil fuels and intensive farming.
- Toxic pollutants result in contamination of both land and water resources. Excessive amounts of nitrates and phosphates can cause algae blooms that are consumed by fish and may cause death and disease as well as being passed up the food chain. Acid rain destroys forests and lakes and ozone depletion, caused by the release of chlorofluorocarbons, is mainly caused by manufacturing processes.

Deforestation in Brazil

Brazil has the highest annual loss of natural forest in the world, and records the third highest rate of natural habitat destruction globally. Much of the deforestation is associated with land clearance for commercial ranching, large-scale mining schemes and exploitation of forest resources. Monoculture in the form of soya and cocoa crops, as well as cattle ranching, have caused soils to become quickly degraded. Some of the world's most varied and valuable ecosystems have been converted into fast-growing plantations (mostly eucalyptus) producing paper pulp.

Closing the food gap

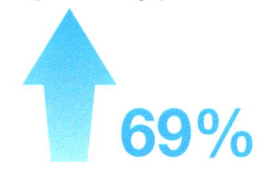

69%

Required increase in food calories to feed 9.6 billion people by 2050

Supporting economic development

28%

Global population directly or indirectly employed by agriculture

Reducing environmental impact

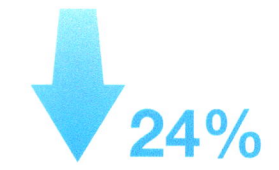

24%

Global greenhouse gas emissions from agriculture and land use change

F The 'great balancing act': to sustainably feed 9.6 billion people by 2050, these three needs must be met at the same time

Did you know?
Up to 50 per cent of all land-based plants and animals could be wiped out by 2050 by climate change.

ACTIVITIES

1. Explain how population growth may put pressure on essential resources.
2. 'Rapid population growth is essential for economic development.' Do you agree? Explain your view.
3. Compare the population structure of Uganda with that of Japan (graphs **B** and **C**). Contrast the economic issues facing both countries as a result of their population structures.
4. Why must the world achieve a 'great balancing act' to sustainably feed a world population of 9.6 billion by 2050?
5. Explain the term 'environmental degradation'. Using two examples, explain the causes and effects of environmental degradation.

Stretch yourself

Research two contrasting ideas about population growth and its link with resources: e.g. those proposed by Malthus and Boserup. Compare their ideas and assess whether their views are still valid today.

Practice question

To what extent does the global increase in population put pressure on the natural environment? *(6 marks)*

19.4 Strategies to manage population growth

On these spreads you will find out about strategies to manage population growth, including contrasting approaches to reducing the birth rate

Example

India

India has a population of 1.35 billion (in 2018), making it second only to China, which has 1.41 billion people. India's population currently represents almost 18 per cent of global population, which means one out of six people in the world live there. By 2030, India's population is almost certain to overtake that of China (graph **A**). The birth rate is 19 per 1000, while the death rate is 7 per 1000 per year. Over half of India's population is below the age of 25 and almost two thirds are below the age of 35. While India's population increases more than any other country in the world each year, its population growth rates are now decreasing.

Population policies

- India started its family planning programme in 1951 and became the first country in the world to have a government-sponsored population policy. This included family planning and contraceptive services but also involved many social changes.

- From the 1970s onwards, India used a mix of enforcement and persuasion to carry out policies of population control, including compulsory sterilisation. In the mid-1970s the Indian government introduced a campaign to sterilise poorer men. Between June 1975 and March 1977, an estimated 11 million men and women were sterilised, usually in operating theatres in makeshift camps. Often there was no follow-up medical care and many people died from infections. The policy was very unpopular and not long afterwards the government was voted out of office.

- India made abortion legal in 1972 and raised the minimum age of marriage to 18 for females and 21 for males. However, this age limit is difficult to enforce, especially in rural areas.

- India now has one of the world's highest rates of female sterilisation, with about 37 per cent of women undergoing sterilisation, according to the UN. Only a tiny fraction (around 1 per cent) of men choose to have vasectomies. In some parts of India, women may receive about 1400 rupees (US$20) to be sterilised, equivalent to nearly two weeks' wages for a manual worker.

- The current National Population Policy aims to achieve a stable population by 2045. Objectives of the policy include making contraception available even in the most remote districts, providing proper health care nationwide, and reducing the fertility rate to replacement levels in all areas of India.

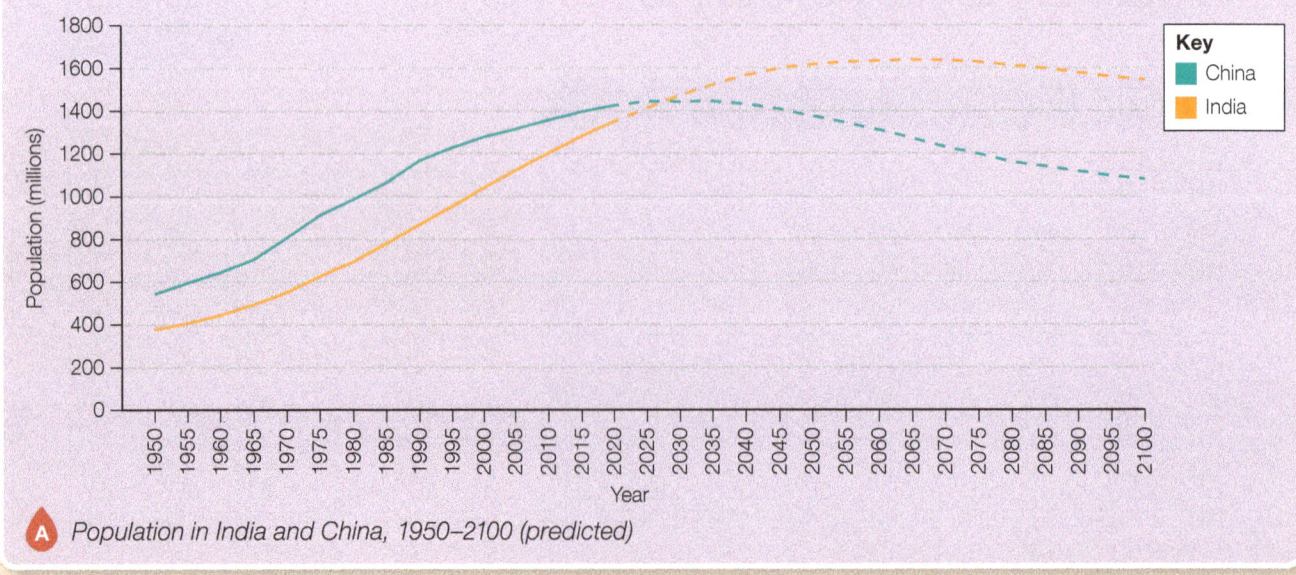

A *Population in India and China, 1950–2100 (predicted)*

Population

India's birth rate has dropped by more than half in 35 years – from 5.7 children per woman in the mid-1960s to 2.4 in 2017. Fertility is, therefore, only just above replacement level. However, this varies considerably across the country (map **B**). Another concern is gender imbalance, arising from the selective abortion of girls. In some communities there are fewer than eight women for every 10 men.

Population pyramids **C** show that the ages of India's population are becoming more balanced, partly as a result of population policy. In the pyramids for 2017 and 2057, a higher proportion of people are of working age, which is better for the country's economy. The pyramids show that life expectancy is increasing and birth rates are decreasing.

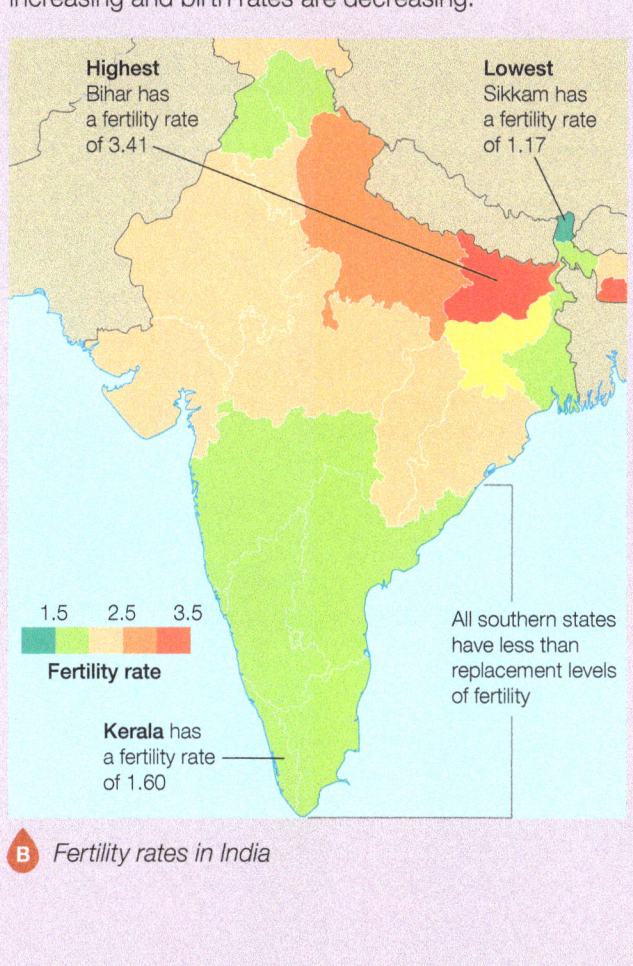

Highest Bihar has a fertility rate of 3.41

Lowest Sikkam has a fertility rate of 1.17

Fertility rate: 1.5 – 2.5 – 3.5

Kerala has a fertility rate of 1.60

All southern states have less than replacement levels of fertility

B Fertility rates in India

1970 — Population 553 943 226

2017 — Population 1 342 512 705

2057 (predicted) — Population 1 736 685 152

C Population pyramids for India, 1970, 2017 and 2057 (predicted)

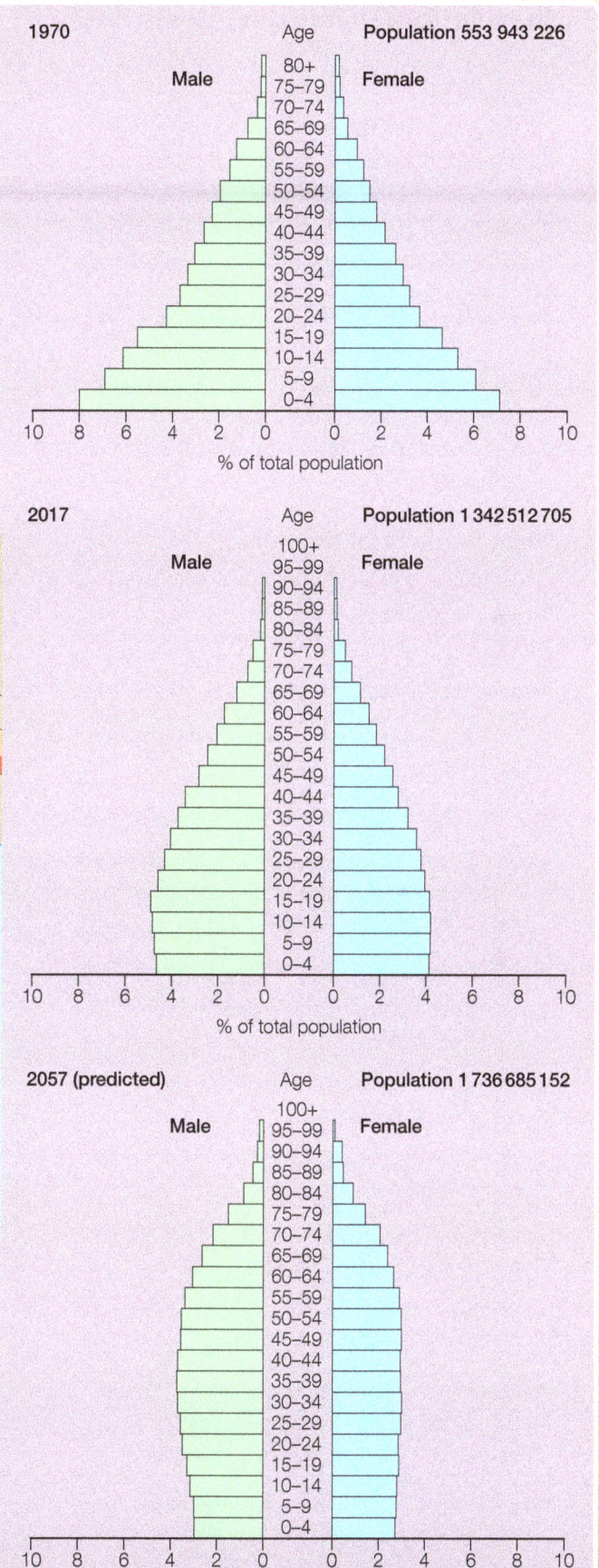

259

Strategies to manage population growth

Population policies in Kerala, India

Kerala, a state in south-west India (map **B**), has managed to control its population growth by investing in healthcare and education, while still allowing people the freedom to choose their own family size.

Why was a population policy needed?

Kerala is densely populated and, in the 1950s and 1960s, was one of the poorest parts of India. Population growth was rapid and this put a great deal of pressure on the limited resources available. Repeated births were seen as insurance against multiple infant and child deaths. Basic health care and family planning services were not available in rural villages.

Main features of the policy

- Education for couples about the advantages of having smaller families.
- Free advice on family planning and contraception made widely available.
- Female literacy is encouraged and boys and girls are treated equally in education.
- Free education for all, up to the age of 14.
- Promotion of delayed marriage for girls, with the earliest allowed at age 18. Strict enforcement of the Child Marriage Restraint Act.
- Improved health services, including vaccination programmes, to lower infant mortality rates.
- Registration of all births to improve access to health care for all.
- Provision of maternity leave only for the first two babies.
- Improved facilities for safe abortion, making them more widely available.
- Strong promotion of having a small family, i.e. two children per woman.
- Ownership of land in Kerala was changed so that no family could have more than 8 hectares, including the largest families.
- Food programmes for the poor focus on mothers and children, using ration cards and free school lunches.

Population	33 million, 3.5% of India's population
Population density	819 people per km^2 (3 × the Indian average)
Overall literacy rate (2011)	94%
Female literacy rate	92% (India: 65%)
Average age of marriage for women	22 years (India: 17 years)
Birth rate (per 1000)	14 (India: 22)
Death rate (per 1000)	6 (India: 7)
Fertility rate in 1951–1961	5.6 children
Fertility rate in 2017	1.6 children (replacement rate is 2.05) (India: 2.4)
Proportion of couples using modern family planning/contraception	60%
Infant mortality rate (IMR) in 1961–1971	66 per 1000 live births
Infant mortality rate (IMR) in 2017	11 per 1000 (India: 46 per 1000)
Gender ratio	1058 females for every 1000 males (India: 940 per 1000 males)
Life expectancy at birth	76 years (India: 66 years)
Percentage aged over 60	12.9% (India: 8.5%)

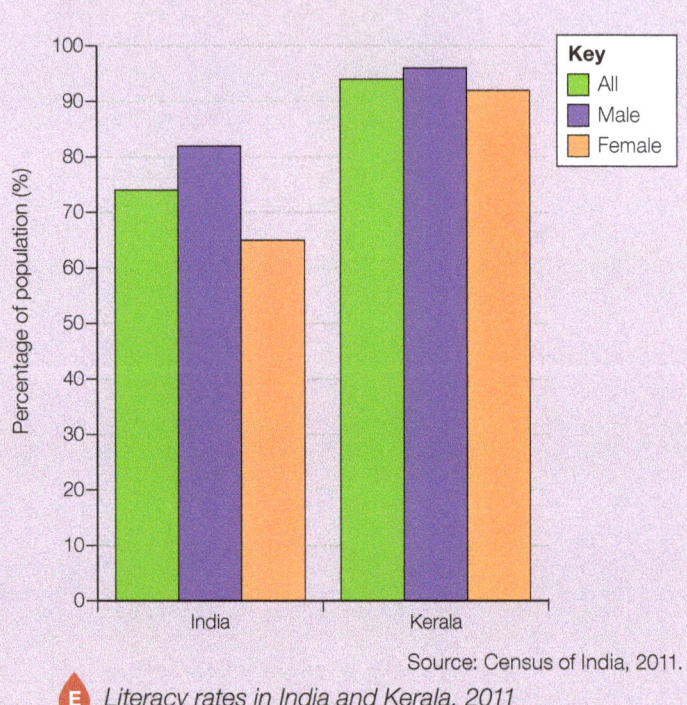

D *Kerala fact file*

E *Literacy rates in India and Kerala, 2011*
Source: Census of India, 2011.

Population

Incentives used

- Those who have smaller families receive higher pensions and other financial benefits.
- Cash payments are given to mothers who have their first child after they are 19 and then register the birth officially.
- Some financial rewards are given for women who have abortions after they have had two children.
- Women who become sterilised after having two children qualify for discounted or even free health insurance and personal accident cover.
- Childcare and nursery centres have been opened in rural areas and city slums to enable women to go to paid jobs and have a career.

Benefits of the policy

- Kerala now has the slowest population growth rate in India (below replacement level) (graph **F**).
- University attendance is now greater for females than males.
- Literacy rates have risen rapidly to become the highest in India, especially among women.
- On average, women in Kerala marry five years later and have their first child six years later than the average for the country.
- Kerala leads the country in women's education. Better-educated women are more likely to delay marriage and keep their children healthy, so infant mortality rates have declined. This has also led to a drop in birth rates because, if children are surviving, families no longer need to have additional children to replace those that die young.
- The policy has worked because people have seen the benefits of small family size without the need to use much government regulation.
- Kerala has some of the highest economic and social development indicators in the whole of India.

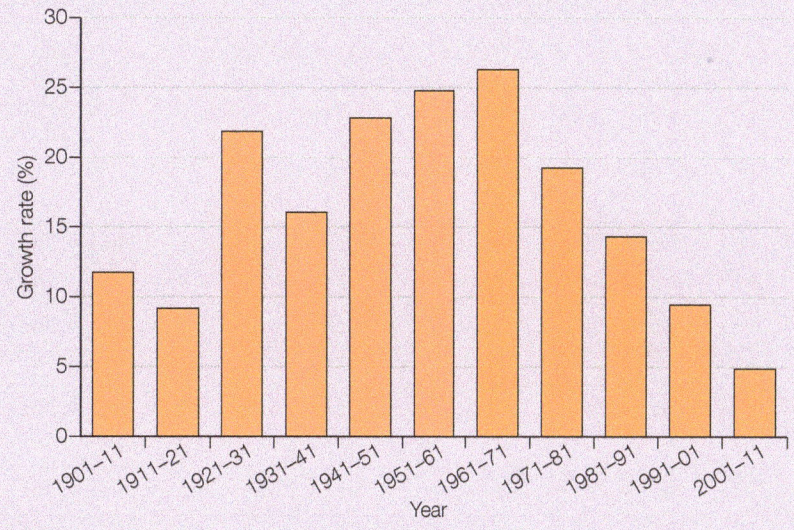

F *Population growth rate of Kerala, 1901–2011*

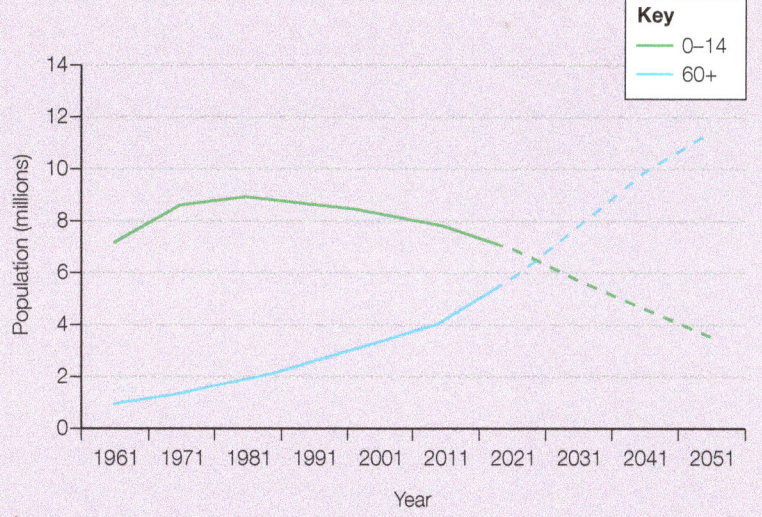

G *Changes in population structure in Kerala, 1961–2051 (predicted)*

Problems with the policy

The fertility rate has dropped below the replacement rate, resulting in a smaller number of young people but an increasing number of older people (graph **G**). Kerala could have an ageing population with low fertility and low death rates by 2025. This could create economic problems for the government because the elderly do not contribute much tax revenue and it is costly to provide care in hospitals and medical centres. It would also mean that the cost of pensions would rise, yet there would be a smaller workforce to pay for this.

Strategies to manage population growth

Thailand

The fall in Thailand's birth rate has been partly the result of the National Family Planning Programme run by the Ministry of Public Health since 1970. Thailand's population in the early 1970s was rising rapidly (table **H**). The birth rate was almost 40 per 1000, while the death rate was only 10 per 1000 – population growth was 3 per cent per year.

Main features of the policy

- Public information programmes to increase awareness of contraception.
- Free provision of contraception, made available widely including in bars, restaurants, workplaces and public transport, in both urban and rural areas.
- Targeting of contraceptive pills specifically at mothers. Micro-credit schemes were only available to women using contraception.
- Free vasectomies and contraceptive injections offered, along with family planning.
- Sterilisations made available and accessible to women.
- Posters advertising the benefits of having no more than two children.
- Health centres established across the country.
- Training paramedics or 'barefoot doctors' and midwives, often from local villages – they were known and trusted by their local communities. Most areas of the country were covered, including many remote rural communities.
- Clear links made between family planning, economic development and an improved quality of life.

Benefits of the policy

Table **H** illustrates the effectiveness of the policy while it was in place.

- The annual population growth rate dropped from 3.3 per cent in the mid-1970s to 0.6 per cent in 2005, and just 0.3 per cent in 2017.
- Since 1971, income per capita has increased enormously. The government has changed people's attitudes from 'we need more field hands' to 'fewer children mean a better quality of life'. As people participated in family planning, a scheme allowed them to borrow animals such as pigs and buffalo to help with farming. They could then sell them on and keep any profit.
- AIDS was a special cause for concern in Thailand prior to the campaign. By promoting the widespread use of contraception (condoms) this problem was reduced (from 2 per cent prevalence in 1997 to 1.1 per cent in 2017).

Did you know? Buddhist scripture says 'many children make you poor' – 95 per cent of the Thai population is Buddhist.

Criticisms of the policy

A reduced birth rate leads to an ageing of population, which in turn means fewer people of working age and a greater need for support for the elderly. In 2017, 13 per cent of the population was over 60 and this could rise to 25 per cent by 2030.

	Growth rate (%)	Fertility rate	Contraceptive usage (%)	Total population (million)	GNP per capita (US$)
1970	3.2	6.5	15	35.38	110
1990	1.4	2.2	68	47.37	1220
1999	0.8	1.7	72	61.62	1950
2016	0.3	1.4	82	68.80	5995

H *Changes in Thailand's population and economy, 1970–2016*

Population

Changes to the policy

After the success of the campaign, fertility rates dropped below replacement levels in the early 2000s, so the policy was adjusted to 'maintain fertility rates at replacement levels'.

In some parts of the country, free family planning was withdrawn because fertility rates had fallen, particularly in the northern and central regions. By contrast, it was still promoted in the southern and north-eastern areas, where birth rates were still high.

Current government policy is to prevent further drops in fertility rates. In a complete reversal of previous strategies, married couples are encouraged to have children with special incentives, such as tax reductions and child benefits, and greater emphasis is given to the quality of medical care for newborn infants.

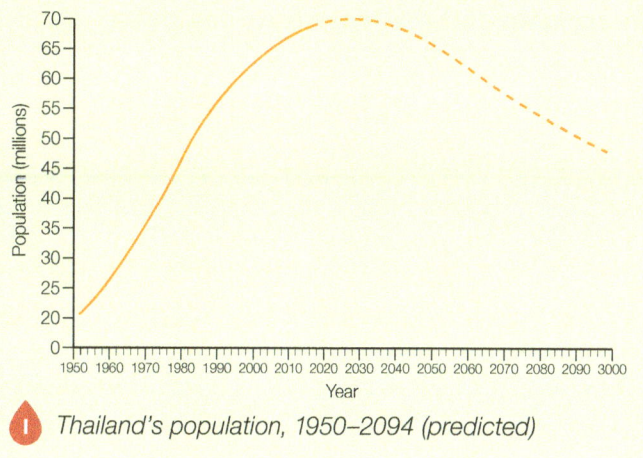

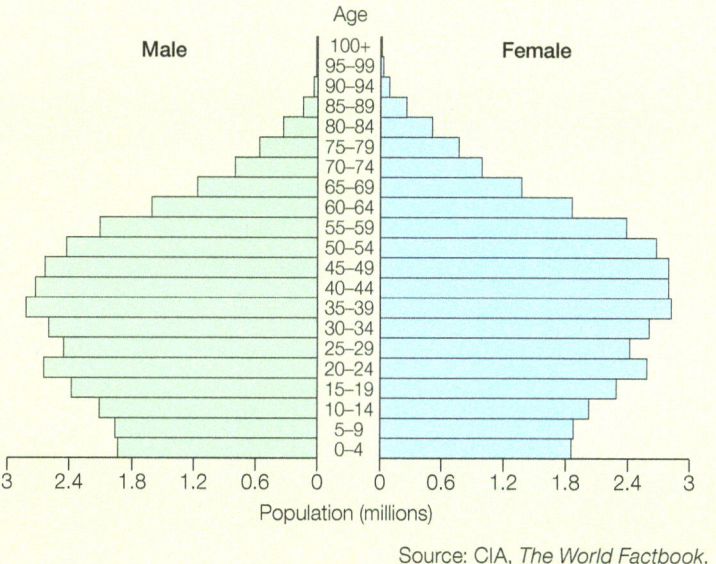

I Thailand's population, 1950–2094 (predicted)

J Thailand's population structure, 2016

Source: CIA, *The World Factbook*.

ACTIVITIES

1. Explain why the government has made attempts to control population growth in India. Why do you think that population policies have not always worked?
2. Describe the projected changes in population in India and China from the present day to 2100. Explain the trends shown in graph **A**.
3. Using population pyramids **C**, outline the changes in India's population pyramids between 1970 and 2057. Why are these changes likely to take place?
4. Compare the population characteristics of Kerala with the whole of India. Produce some simple graphs to highlight the differences.
5. Select four of the strategies used in Kerala to manage population change. Explain why they were introduced.
6. To what extent has Kerala's population policy been successful?
7. Explain why female literacy is so important as part of an effective population policy.
8. Using graph **I**, explain why population trends in Kerala may create problems in the future.

Stretch yourself

Find out what other countries are doing (or have done) to cope with rapid population increase. For example, research population policies in China and/or Kenya. Give reasons why it is difficult for governments of many poorer countries to achieve a reduction in the rate of population growth.

Practice question

For one named country, assess the successes and failures of its population policies. *(8 marks)*

263

19.5 International migration

On these spreads you will find out about reasons for international migration, its impacts and the features of major international migrations in the twenty-first century

Reasons for international migration

International **migration** is running at record levels and is predicted to increase further. However, as a proportion of total population, only 0.8 per cent of the world's population moved country between 2010 and 2015 – a smaller proportion than during some of the large-scale migrations of the late nineteenth and early twentieth centuries.

People move home for many different reasons. Every individual's decision to move is the result of push and pull factors. Negative aspects of a person's home area push them away from it and make them look for somewhere better. Positive characteristics of new places, which attract people to move there, are called pull factors.

Push factors include events that *force* people to move, such as:
- war, conflict and political instability
- ethnic and religious persecution
- natural disasters and crises, such as earthquakes, tsunamis, drought and famines.

Social and economic push factors include:
- unemployment
- low wages or poor working conditions
- shortage of food
- poor access to essential services
- inadequate educational opportunities.

Pull factors include:
- a better quality of life and standard of living
- varied employment opportunities
- higher wages
- improved health care
- access to education services
- political stability
- more freedom.

A combination of war, religious and ethnic persecution, and poverty is causing the movement of **refugees** and **economic migrants** on a global scale. UN figures claim that one in every 110 people in the world is either a refugee, a displaced person or is seeking asylum. In 2016, UN figures suggested that wars and conflicts across the globe had forced over 20 million migrants to flee their homes and that number is expected to increase over the next few years.

A *Syrian, Afghan and African refugees arriving in Greece in a dinghy boat from Turkey*

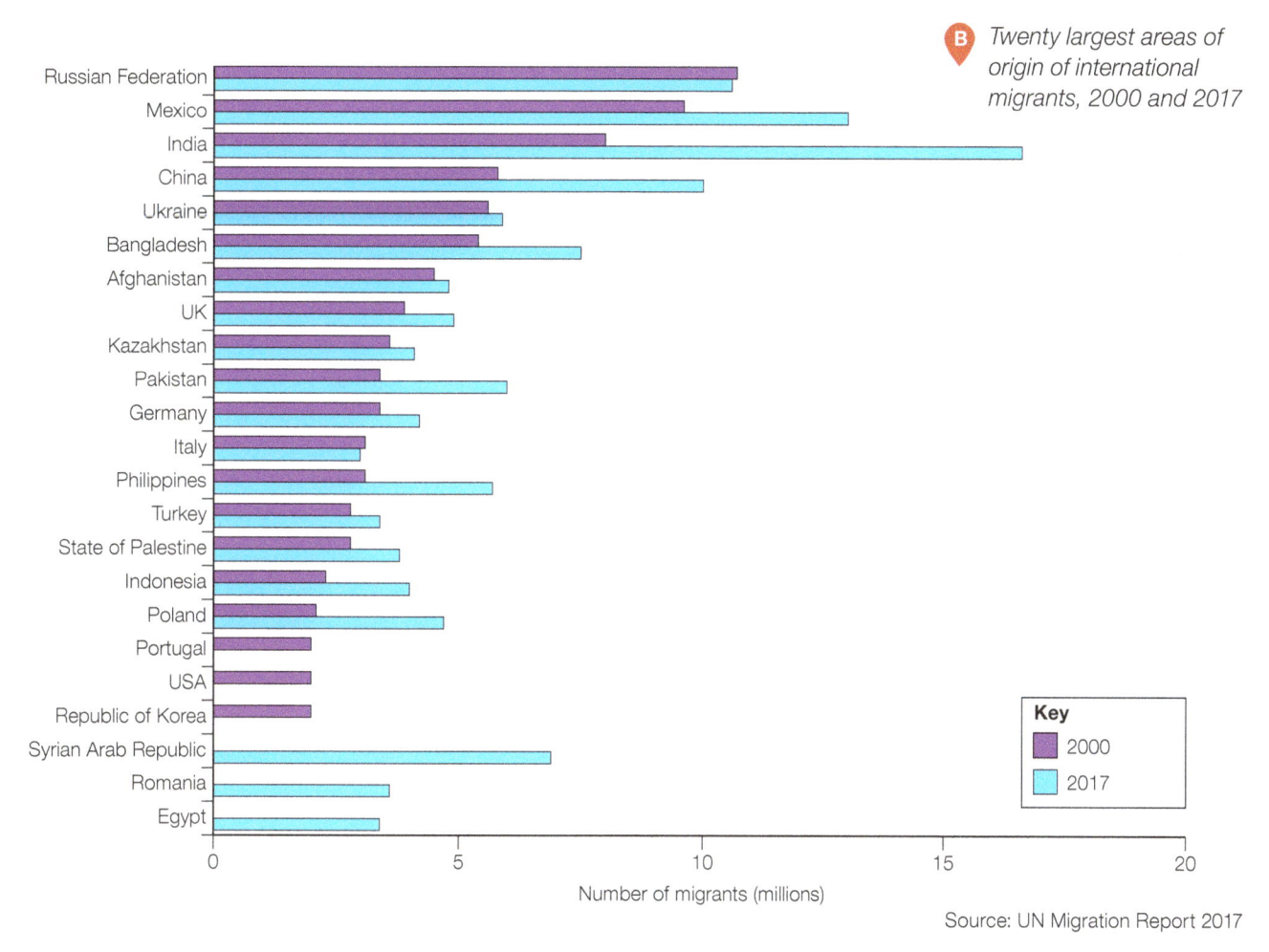

Population

B *Twenty largest areas of origin of international migrants, 2000 and 2017*

Bar chart showing number of migrants (millions) for 2000 and 2017:

- Russian Federation: ~11 (2000), ~11 (2017)
- Mexico: ~10 (2000), ~13 (2017)
- India: ~8 (2000), ~17 (2017)
- China: ~6 (2000), ~10 (2017)
- Ukraine: ~6 (2000), ~6 (2017)
- Bangladesh: ~5.5 (2000), ~7.5 (2017)
- Afghanistan: ~4.5 (2000), ~5 (2017)
- UK: ~4 (2000), ~5 (2017)
- Kazakhstan: ~3.5 (2000), ~4 (2017)
- Pakistan: ~3.5 (2000), ~6 (2017)
- Germany: ~3.5 (2000), ~4 (2017)
- Italy: ~3 (2000), ~3 (2017)
- Philippines: ~3 (2000), ~5.5 (2017)
- Turkey: ~3 (2000), ~3.5 (2017)
- State of Palestine: ~3 (2000), ~3.5 (2017)
- Indonesia: ~2.5 (2000), ~4 (2017)
- Poland: ~2 (2000), ~4.5 (2017)
- Portugal: ~2 (2000)
- USA: ~2 (2000)
- Republic of Korea: ~2 (2000)
- Syrian Arab Republic: ~7 (2017)
- Romania: ~3.5 (2017)
- Egypt: ~3.5 (2017)

Number of migrants (millions)

Key
- 2000
- 2017

Source: UN Migration Report 2017

Impacts of international migration

The impacts of migration on the **country of origin** and the **host country** can be positive or negative (table **C**).

C *Various impacts of international migration*

A large number of women may be left in the country of origin. The structure of this population becomes unbalanced.	Migrants earn enough money to send some home. The country of origin can benefit enormously.	Marriage rates may fall and family structures break down.	Money leaves the host economy as remittances are sent home.
There is often a growth of new providers of local services and an expansion of ethnic retailing.	Too many migrants can be perceived to be a burden on health and social services.	Added pressures on housing. Insufficient accommodation often leads to increased rental costs and house prices.	Mixing between different cultures can lead to greater understanding and integration.
Educational, health and social services in the country of origin may decline as there are fewer people.	When migrants return to their home country they may take back useful skills. This can help economic development.	Schools taking many immigrant children may be under pressure, particularly if there are language difficulties.	Migration brings labour and skills, taxes are paid, and the economy grows as a result.
The population density is reduced and the birth rate decreases. There are workforce shortages.	Migrant workers may be exploited and not earn as much as they had expected.	The average age rises, so the dependant population increases.	Farming may decline in the country of origin and rural land is abandoned.
There may be a loss of cultural leadership and tradition.	There may be racial prejudice and tensions if migrants are perceived as a threat to jobs and communities.	The loss of many enterprising younger people means a reduction in skills and possibly a slowdown in the economy.	Increased calls for government controls on immigration and a rise of anti-immigration political parties.

265

International migration

Major international migrations in the twenty-first century

Recent migrations have included the following types:

- *voluntary*, e.g. Mexicans moving to the USA
- *forced*, e.g. Syrians escaping war to Turkey and parts of Europe
- *temporary*, e.g. Americans employed by oil companies in the Middle East
- *permanent*, e.g. British migrants settling in Australia and New Zealand.

Migrants may move for different reasons. They can be classed as:

- **economic migrants**: people who are trying to improve their standard of living and who move voluntarily to seek employment
- **asylum seekers**: people who believe that their lives are at risk if they remain in their home country and who seek to settle in another (safe) country
- **refugees**: people who have proven to the authorities that their lives would be at risk if they were forced to return home, have had their claim for asylum accepted by the authorities and can now stay in the destination country. Legally, a refugee is an asylum seeker with a successful asylum claim.

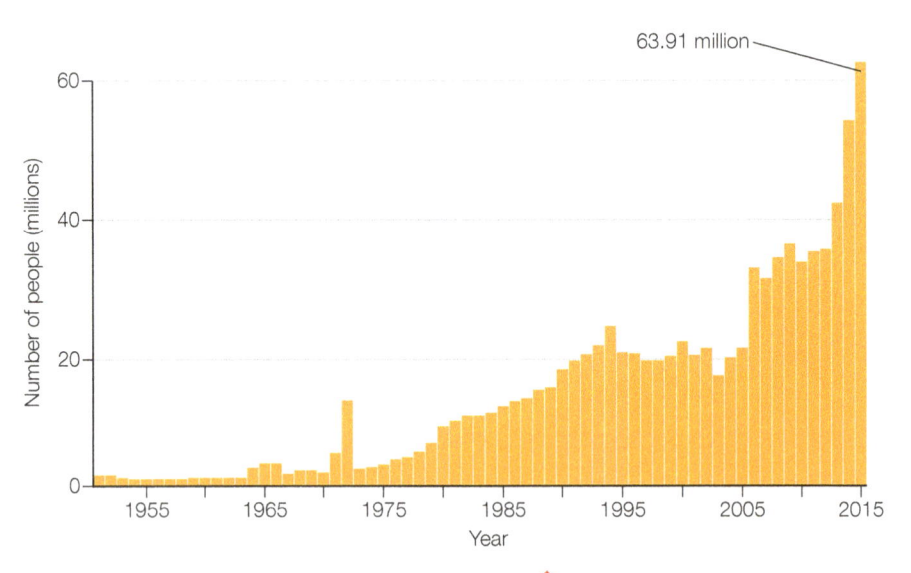

Refugee migrations have increased steadily during the twenty-first century, mainly because of armed conflict in several parts of the world (graph **D**). By early 2018, there were over 65 million refugees worldwide, escaping from wars and natural disasters in places such as Syria and South Sudan. Some refugees left their homes many years ago, unable to return because conditions have not improved, including many from Afghanistan and Pakistan.

D *Persons of concern, including refugees, asylum seekers, internally displaced persons, and others, 1950–2015*

Examples of international migrations

Forced migrations occur because people have no choice. They either move or they stay and face extreme hardship, persecution or even death. This happens when there is a war or natural disaster.

Refugee migrations

Sub-Saharan Africa

Sub-Saharan Africa accounts for more than a quarter of the world's refugee population – approximately 18 million people. Numbers have grown exponentially in the past decade, as wars have broken out or become worse in many countries, including Nigeria, Somalia, Central African Republic, South Sudan and Burundi.

In Nigeria, more than 2 million people have been forced from their homes, including those who have escaped from the violence and intimidation of the militant group Boko Haram. Many have crossed international borders to find sanctuary in neighbouring countries, including Niger, Chad and Cameroon.

Ethiopia hosts nearly 740 000 refugees, mostly from Somalia, Eritrea, Sudan and South Sudan – the largest refugee population in a single African country. The country maintains an open-door policy that welcomes refugees and allows humanitarian access and protection.

Population

Myanmar (Burma)

The Rohingya people are predominantly Muslim. They are a small ethnic group comprising just over 1 million people, living in western Myanmar. An escalation of violence in Myanmar's Rakhine State from August 2017 onwards led to vast numbers of people fleeing across the border into Bangladesh, in a desperate search for safety. Most of the refugees are women, children and small babies.

According to the UN, between 25 August 2017 and January 2018, 688 000 new arrivals had been registered. They were staying in host communities, existing refugee camps, new makeshift settlements or camps, or just wherever they could find space. Nearly 100 000 refugees, including children, were suffering from fever and diarrhoeal diseases. Many were traumatised and some had arrived with injuries caused by gunshots, shrapnel, fire and landmines. According to many of the arriving migrants, villages had been burned down and parents or relatives had been killed as a result of ethnic violence.

E *Hungry Rohingya children reaching for bread, Bangladesh*

ACTIVITIES

1. Classify the factors below into either push or pull factors. Can they be split further into economic, environmental and social factors?

   job prospects
   political or social unrest
   attractive environments
   improved housing
   high standard of living
   high-quality health care
   low income
   soil exhaustion
   greater religious/political freedom
   educational opportunities
   high wages
   racial/religious tolerance
   high unemployment
   racial intolerance
   housing shortages
   natural disasters
   poverty
   a warmer climate

2. Classify the statements in table **C** into economic, social, demographic (population) or political impacts. Then subdivide them into positive and negative impacts, and decide whether the impacts affect the country of origin or host (destination) country. Set them out in a table as follows:

Impacts	Economic	Social	Demographic	Political
Positive for country of origin				
Negative for country of origin				
Positive for host country				
Negative for host country				

3. a Who are 'asylum seekers' and how do they differ from economic migrants?
   b Why do wars often produce large numbers of asylum seekers?

4. Study graph **D**. Describe trends in the number of asylum seekers and refugees between 1950 and 2015. Explain the changes that have taken place from 2005.

5. Outline the push factors prompting high levels of migration from:
   a Myanmar (Burma)
   b Afghanistan.

Stretch yourself

Use the internet to make your own study into asylum seekers associated with a recent and/or ongoing world conflict, such as civil war in Somalia, Yemen, South Sudan or Myanmar. Research the causes of this conflict and its implications for asylum seekers and refugees.

Practice question

The advantages of migration outweigh the disadvantages. Do you agree? Explain your answer. *(6 marks)*

19.6 Causes and impacts of forced migration

On these spreads you will find out about causes and impacts of the refugee migration from Syria and types of migration into Europe

Example

Refugee migration from Syria

The Syrian crisis is caused by an armed conflict in Syria between government and opposition forces. In 2017 alone, it was estimated that the number of deaths from this war exceeded 500 000. In a single week in February 2018, more than 500 civilians were killed in bombing raids in opposition-held areas of Damascus, the capital city. More than 10 million Syrians, 45 per cent of the country's population, have been displaced as a result of this civil war, which started in 2011. Of these, 6.5 million were displaced within Syria and approximately 4 million sought refuge in other countries.

More than 1 million went to neighbouring Lebanon, a small and relatively poor country – one in four of its current population are now refugees, many located in camps established by the UN. Over 2 million Syrian refugees have also crossed the border into neighbouring Turkey (map **A**). In both cases, these destinations may be temporary transit points as migrants seek a further move into European countries (map **B**).

Map A – Destinations of Syrian refugees displaced by civil war:
- Turkey: 2 910 000
- Internal displacement: 6 300 000 (equals to one-third of its population)
- Lebanon: 1 011 000
- Iraq: 233 000
- Jordan: 656 000
- Egypt: 118 000

A *Destination of Syrian refugees displaced by civil war*

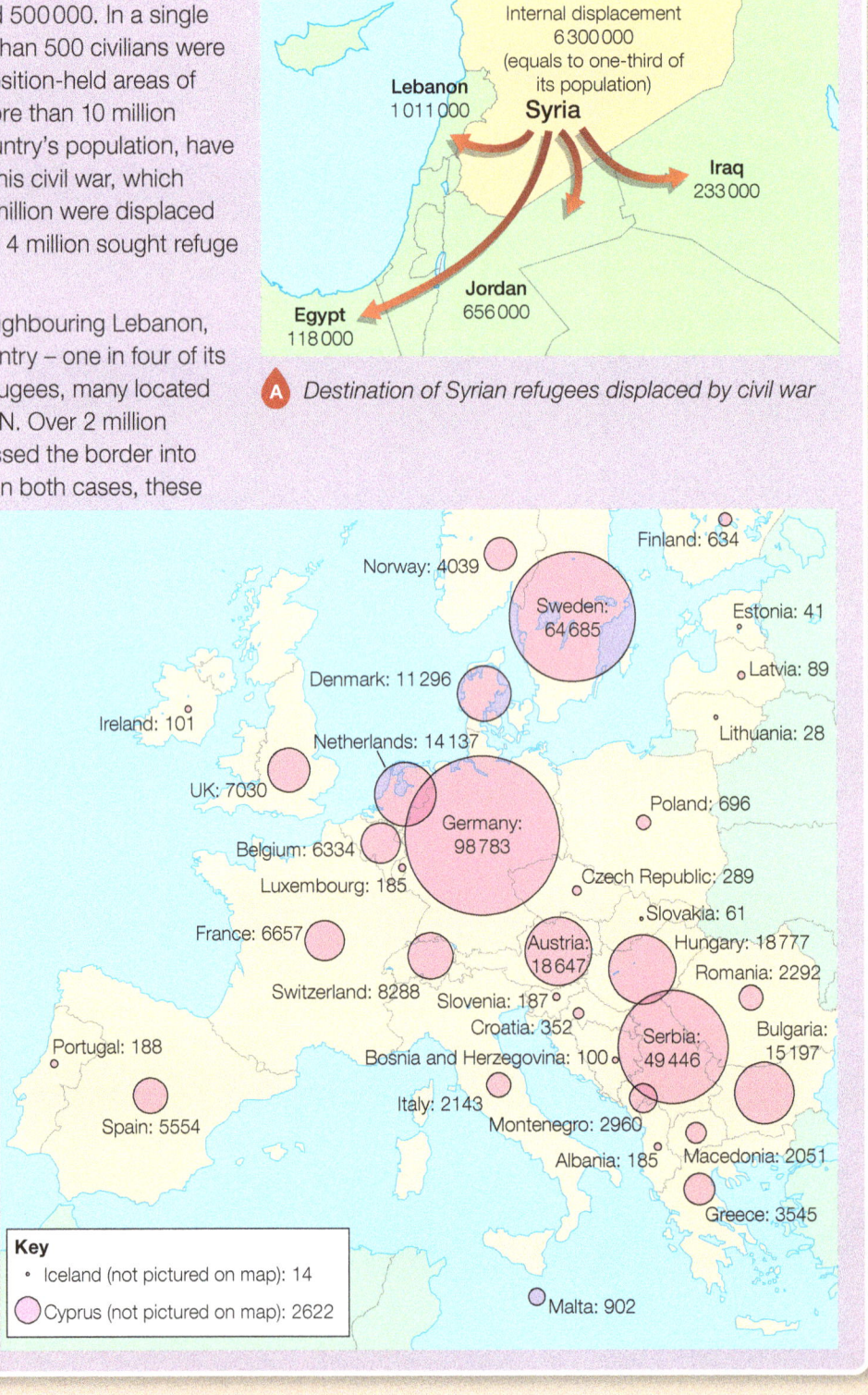

Did you know?
Roughly 76 million people or (1 per cent of the world's population) have been forced from their homes because of natural disasters or armed conflict. This is the highest number since the early 1950s.

Map B – Syrian asylum applications to European countries (as of July 2015):
- Finland: 634
- Norway: 4039
- Sweden: 64 685
- Estonia: 41
- Denmark: 11 296
- Latvia: 89
- Ireland: 101
- Netherlands: 14 137
- Lithuania: 28
- UK: 7030
- Germany: 98 783
- Poland: 696
- Belgium: 6334
- Czech Republic: 289
- Luxembourg: 185
- Slovakia: 61
- France: 6657
- Austria: 18 647
- Hungary: 18 777
- Switzerland: 8288
- Romania: 2292
- Slovenia: 187
- Croatia: 352
- Serbia: 49 446
- Bulgaria: 15 197
- Portugal: 188
- Bosnia and Herzegovina: 100
- Italy: 2143
- Montenegro: 2960
- Spain: 5554
- Albania: 185
- Macedonia: 2051
- Greece: 3545
- Malta: 902

Key
- Iceland (not pictured on map): 14
- Cyprus (not pictured on map): 2622

B *Syrian asylum applications to European countries (as of July 2015)*

Population

...nding host countries ...social impacts. These ...educational services. ...tended school for ...le to understand. ...n feel left out because ...ers give to the Syrian children. ...insufficient teachers, so the school day ...ded in half and children can only attend for the morning or afternoon.

There is also a perception that Syrians are willing to work for less money, so local people feel that wages are being undercut and their living standards decline. There have been stresses on infrastructure such as electricity, water and sanitation. Electricity supplies are now available for less than 16 hours per day, and much less in rural areas. Public water services are restricted to just three days per week in most areas. The need to dispose of huge amounts of rubbish has also become a major issue.

Migration into Europe – refugees, asylum seekers and economic migrants

Syrian refugees are not the only people wishing to migrate to Europe. During the summers of 2015–17, the migrant crisis and its effects appeared across TV news screens nearly every day. In 2016, a total of over 600 000 migrants entered Europe from North Africa and the Middle East, through Italy (via Libya) and several of the Greek islands. **Squatter settlements** sprung up around national borders across central and western Europe. News reports showed migrants crossing the Mediterranean Sea on overcrowded, makeshift boats supplied by smugglers. Many refugees were known to have drowned or died in the cramped conditions on board. EU governments were torn between their desire to save lives and offer sanctuary and pressure from their home populations, wary of admitting more migrants into overcrowded countries.

Causes

There are many reasons why migrants are prepared to make what is often a dangerous and lengthy trip to Europe.

- The strongest push factor is armed conflict or terrorism, not just in Syria, but also, for example, in Somalia, Libya, Eritrea, Chad, Afghanistan and Iraq. Roughly 55 per cent of those making the journey to Europe originate from countries affected by war or generalised violence, or having repressive governments.

- Several countries in Africa have rapid population growth rates, are overpopulated, have high unemployment rates and, in some cases, are experiencing severe drought, such as Sudan, Ethiopia, Somalia and Kenya.

- Some countries, such as Libya, have gone through periods of political instability, have little control of their borders and are unable to provide security or full economic support for their citizens.

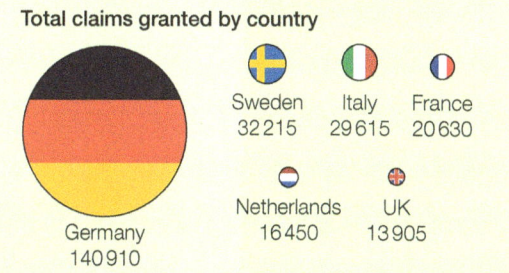

Main nationalities granted asylum
1 Syria 2 Eritrea 3 Iran 4 Afghanistan 5 Iraq

Whole EU 292 540

Total claims granted by country

Germany 140 910
Sweden 32 215
Italy 29 615
France 20 630
Netherlands 16 450
UK 13 905

C Approved asylum applications in EU countries, 2015

- The opportunity to secure higher living standards in Europe is a strong pull factor. Many of those seeking residence in Europe are economic migrants drawn by the prospect of employment, as well as safety and security.

- With slow or zero growth rates, western European countries have fewer people of working age and an increasingly elderly population. The demand for labour means that some European countries are prepared to admit a managed number of migrants from outside the EU.

Maths skills

Study diagram **C**. What percentage of total asylum applications in the EU were granted in each of the six countries shown? Compare Germany's total with that of the UK.

269

Causes and impacts of forced migration

Impacts

There is no doubt that western Europe is an attractive destination for migrants. Over 2 million migrants move to Europe each year – this is greater than any other part of the world (although it is only a small proportion of the total population of 740 million). This leads to some changes in the population structure, gender balance and ethnic make-up of many European countries. Roughly 10 per cent of people living in Europe were born outside Europe, a figure that has increased rapidly in recent years.

The flow of migrants has caused controversy and political debate in EU countries. Many EU citizens would like to see a reduction in numbers but this is unlikely, as predictions suggest further significant increases (up to 50 per cent in the next decade). While Europe needs a certain number of additional workers, problems have arisen because migrants have tended to settle in countries close to the point of entry, particularly Italy and Spain. The cost of rescuing migrants and accommodating them is over 200 million Euros per year, for Italy alone. There is some evidence that the severe crisis of 2015–17 has eased temporarily (there were 70 per cent fewer entries into Italy by boat in 2017 compared with 2016). However, this may also be the result of a combination of:

D *Activists protest against Belgium's asylum and migration policy, 2018*

- tighter immigration controls, especially in eastern European countries
- a managed quota system for refugees throughout Europe
- arrangements with Turkey and other countries to return illegal migrants (photo **D**)
- investment in refugee and economic migrant accommodation in countries outside the EU
- an information campaign designed to deter dangerous sea crossings.

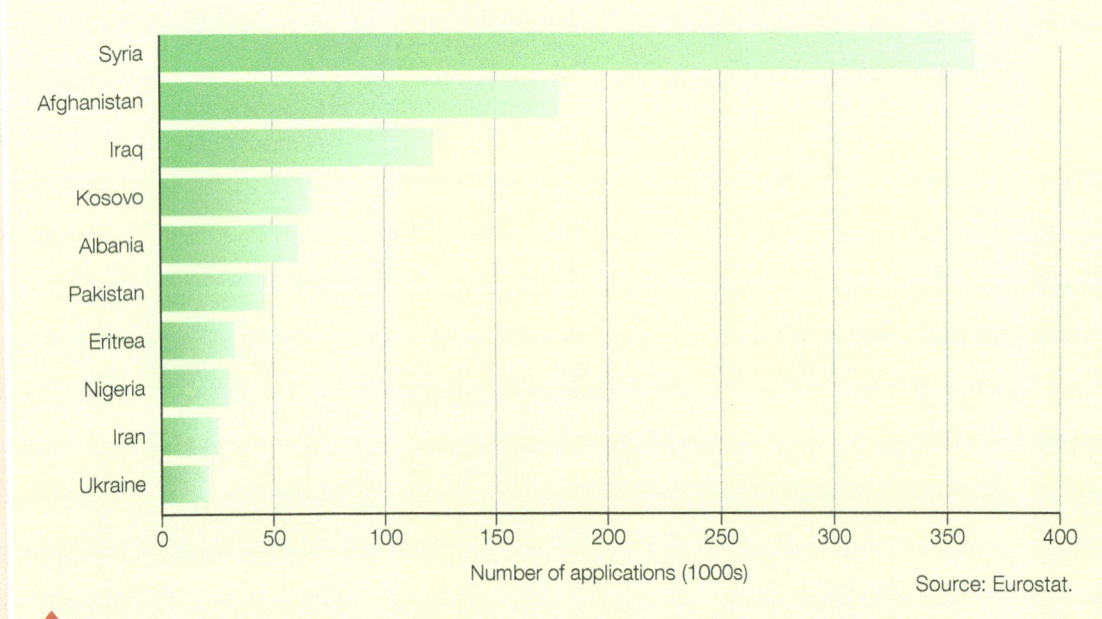

E *Top 10 origins of people applying for asylum in the EU (first-time applications in 2015)*

Source: Eurostat.

Population

Freedom of movement within the EU

There are also substantial migrations of people within Europe who are allowed to move freely under the rules of the EU. Wealthier countries usually receive **immigrants** searching for work and a better lifestyle. In general, since the EU was enlarged to 28 countries, there has been a movement of people from eastern Europe (e.g. Poland, Hungary, Romania, Bulgaria) to northern and western Europe.

ACTIVITIES

1. Study table **F**.
   a. The father is keen to move but the mother wants to stay. Suggest reasons for each opinion.
   b. Identify the push and pull factors affecting the children.
   c. If the family moves to the EU, how might the individual members benefit?
   d. Suggest any possible problems or issues that the family might face in travelling to the EU and once they arrive.

Family member	Situation
Father	Subsistence farmer – crops unpredictable due to frequent drought. Part-time fisherman – catches are reducing because of overfishing.
Mother	Housewife with limited primary education. Wider extended family lives nearby.
Adult son	Secondary education completed. Would like the chance to go to university or obtain an interesting job. Currently unemployed, apart from occasional farm work.
Daughters	Partway through school. Want to get as well qualified as possible. School resources are sometimes in short supply.

F *Factors affecting a family in east Africa who are considering moving to the EU*

2. Large groups of asylum seekers have migrated to Europe since 2014.
   a. What specific issues do the various groups face in their attempts to get to Europe?
   b. What factors make European nations an attractive destination?
   c. How are destination countries reacting to the asylum seekers?

3. Using map **A**, draw a graph to show the number of refugees from Syria internally displaced and in the surrounding countries. What are the causes of the Syrian refugee crisis? What impact has this crisis had on surrounding countries?

4. Using map **B** describe the distribution of European countries with large numbers of asylum applications from Syria. Explain why some countries have received far more applications than others.

5. Map the top 10 origins of people applying for asylum in the EU as shown in graph **E**. Draw proportional bars to represent the numbers from each country. What do many of these countries have in common?

6. What might be the consequences of large-scale migration on the host countries of the EU?

Stretch yourself

Research the origins of Europe's migrant crisis, which involves the movement of migrants (both economic migrants and asylum seekers) from North Africa and the Middle East to western Europe. Find out about the push and pull factors, the routes taken, the reaction of EU governments and the impacts on the host countries.

Practice question

The number of refugees has increased in the past few years. Using an example, assess the challenges faced by both the refugees and the destination country. *(9 marks)*

19.7 Causes and impacts of voluntary migration

On these spreads you will find out about economic migration and its impacts

Example

Voluntary migration is when people move of their own free will. They are usually in search of a higher standard of living, although they may be moving for social reasons as well, such as gaining access to a good education or obtaining reliable health care.

Mexican migration to the USA

Mexico and the USA are geographically close but also significantly different in many ways (table **A**).

The data in table **A** show marked differences in economic and social indicators. Income levels are four times higher in the USA compared with Mexico and the proportion of inhabitants below the poverty line three times lower. Not surprisingly, many Mexicans decide to migrate for economic reasons to the USA. Indeed, Mexico has the highest percentage of **emigrants** of any country in the world (11.5 per cent).

	USA	Mexico
Population (millions)	327	124
GDP per capita (US$)	57 600	18 500
Average wage (US$)	60 154	15 300
Internet access (%)	74	46
Population below poverty line (%)	15	47
Birth rate (per 1000)	12.5	18.3
Death rate (per 1000)	8.3	5.3
Population under 15 years (%)	18	27
Median age (years)	38.5	28.1
Infant mortality (per 1000)	5.8	11.6
Access to improved sanitation (%)	100	85

A Economic and social data for the USA and Mexico

B The Rio Grande River flowing through Hot Springs Canyon along the Mexican border in Big Bend National Park

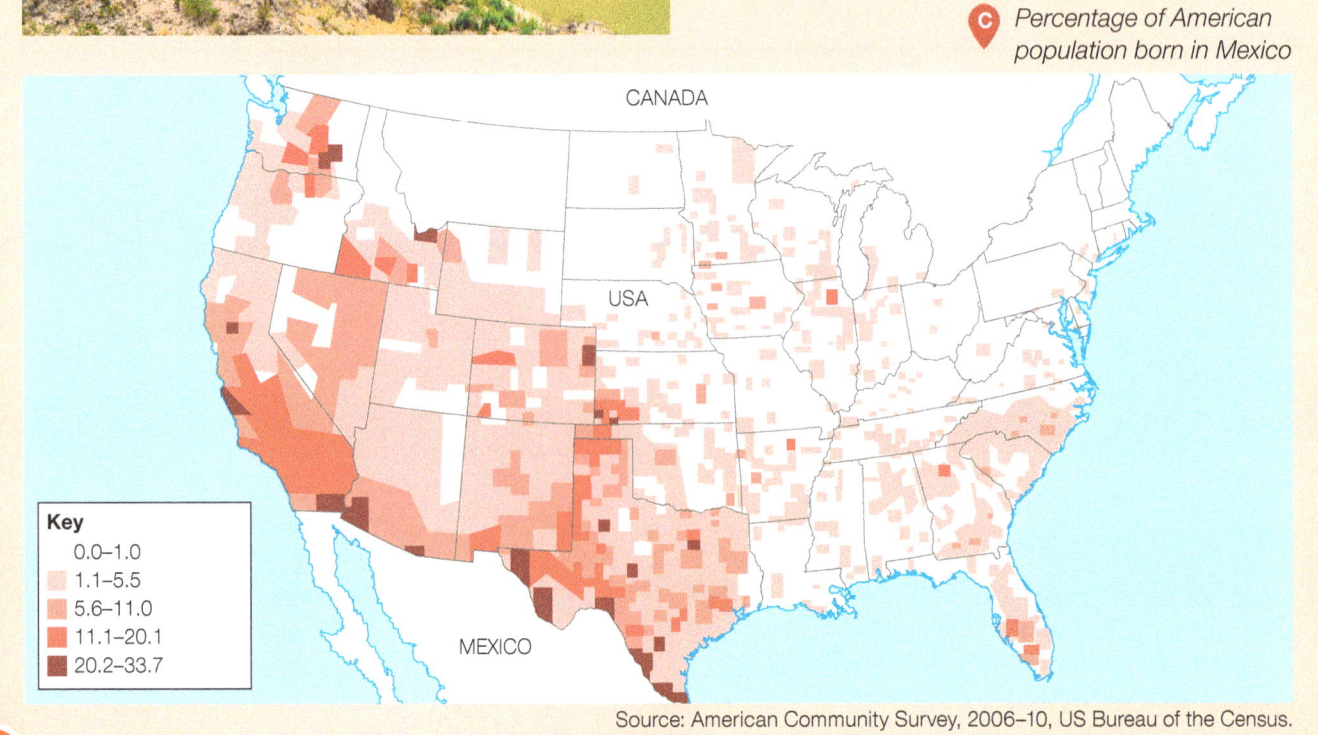

C Percentage of American population born in Mexico

Key
- 0.0–1.0
- 1.1–5.5
- 5.6–11.0
- 11.1–20.1
- 20.2–33.7

Source: American Community Survey, 2006–10, US Bureau of the Census.

Fifty years ago, almost all migration from Mexico to the USA was seasonal, and largely focused on agricultural workers living close to the border. Today, the level of migration (both temporary and permanent) is on a much greater scale. Approximately half the migrants have a visa to live and work in the USA (around 500 000), but the remainder enter the country illegally. The majority are men, many of whom send money back to their families in Mexico. Altogether, there are 6 570 000 illegal Mexican migrants in the USA – 57 per cent of all illegal migrants. The journey into the USA can be dangerous as a large desert covers much of the border area and migrants also have to cross the Rio Grande River (photo **B**). Many migrants have died from drowning and exposure in trying to reach the USA (approximately 10 000 in the past 20 years). US Border Patrol tries to prevent illegal immigrants from entering the country and up to half are deported. The Patrol uses heat sensors, night-vision telescopes and aircraft including Black Hawk helicopters. A large proportion of migrants find their way to Texas and California (map **C**), where they tend to work in low-paid jobs in catering, construction, agriculture, manufacturing and truck driving. Economic inequality, rural poverty and significantly lower wages have played a role in pushing Mexicans to migrate to the US.

Recent changes

Since the recession starting in 2008, there have been fewer migrants from Mexico (graph **E**). Reasons for this include:

- poorer employment prospects in the USA
- more effective border controls by law enforcement in the USA (photo **F**)
- long-term decline in Mexico's fertility rates
- improving economic conditions in Mexico
- the difficulty of accessing education and medical care in the USA
- the dangerous and violent conditions in the border region, associated with drug crime
- antagonism towards potential migrants, including the threat to build a security wall along the border.

There has been a drop in the proportion of Mexicans as a share of all immigrants entering the USA from almost 30 per cent in 2000 to 27.5 per cent in 2014. However, this is still a significant total and the number of illegal migrants from Mexico remains at half a million per year.

Push factors	Pull factors
Poorly paid jobs	Well-paid jobs
Poor health care provision	Good health care provision
Poorer education prospects	Better education prospects
Lower literacy rates	Higher literacy rates
Lower life expectancy	Higher life expectancy
High unemployment rates	Low unemployment rates
Very high crime rates	Moderate crime rates
High proportion living under the poverty line	Low percentage living under the poverty line
Water shortages, even in the more developed areas of Mexico	Few water shortages
Natural disasters including volcanoes, earthquakes, hurricanes and tsunamis	Existing migrant communities in states such as Texas and California make it easier for people to settle once moved. People are also enticed to move in order to be with their families

D What causes Mexicans to migrate to the USA?

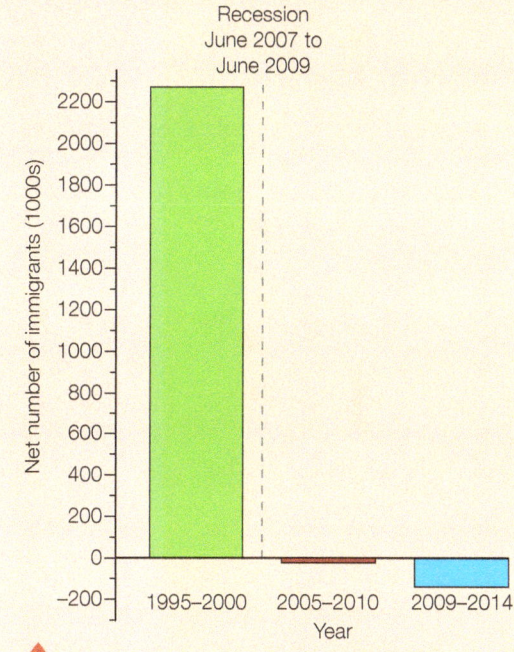

E Net migration to the USA from Mexico

F US Customs and Immigration agent with an illegal immigrant handcuffed at the Tijuana Mexico US San Diego California border crossing

Causes and impacts of voluntary migration

Remittances sent back by migrants to families in Mexico (up to US$16 billion per year) are not spent on goods and services in the USA, so are lost to the American economy.

Perceived threats to jobs and undercutting of wages have led to ethnic tensions between Mexican migrants and local working class Americans. Vigilante groups have sprung up along borders and in larger settlements, aimed at tracking down illegal migrants.

The money that is returned to Mexico provides a boost to the local economy there. It is worth more than tourism and is now the second most important contributor to the economy after the oil industry.

As farmworkers leave the land in Mexico there are insufficient workers on farms to cultivate crops, leading to potential food shortages and increased imports. Farmland may be abandoned.

Language barriers can be a problem particularly if Mexicans remain in closed communities with other Mexicans. Migrants become segregated into certain areas.

Some Mexicans may be bringing drugs into the USA, causing a spike in crime.

Working Mexican migrants pay taxes, spend money and help to overcome skill shortages in the USA.

There are some cultural advantages associated with foods, music and fashions of the immigrant population.

The birth rate drops, people of childbearing age leave and an ageing population remains. Gradually there are fewer workers to pay taxes and support those left behind.

Not all Mexicans have integrated with American communities. Many cannot speak fluent English, largely due to living in closed communities with other Mexican immigrants.

A gender imbalance results from the migration of young men from Mexican villages to the USA. They often stay permanently so families are disrupted and there is a shortage of marriage partners for women in Mexico.

Because some Mexican migrants are prepared to work for low wages, local companies sometimes reduce their wage offers to local Americans, which causes resentment.

There is reduced pressure on health care, education, social services and employment in parts of Mexico as migrants leave for the USA.

Qualified and skilled workers, such as doctors, teachers and engineers leave, which means a critical shortage of essential workers.

G *Impacts of Mexican migration*

Population

H Illegal immigrants on the roof of the 'death train' through Mexico to the USA

Did you know?
Between 2009 and 2013, approximately 8 million illegal migrants arrived in the USA.

ACTIVITIES

1. Give reasons why so many Mexicans have chosen to migrate to the USA.
2. What difficulties are faced by migrants who try to enter the USA illegally?
3. Describe changes in the number of Mexicans seeking to migrate to the USA in recent years. Explain these changes.
4. Study map **C**. Describe and account for the distribution of areas with a high percentage of people born in Mexico.
5. a Study diagram **G**. Decide whether the impacts are:
    - i   advantages to the USA
    - ii disadvantages to the USA
    - iii advantages to Mexico
    - iv disadvantages to Mexico.
   b Give one example of an economic impact, a demographic impact, a social impact and a political impact.

Stretch yourself

Write a newspaper article (around 300 words) about one migration that is in the news. Include a map if possible. Explain why people have become migrants, where they are travelling to, what is happening to them and the impacts they have on the host country.

Maths skills

In 2015, 1 051 031 people were granted lawful permanent residence in the USA. The top countries of origin of these 'green card' recipients were:

- Mexico: 158 619 (15 per cent)
- China: 74 558 (7 per cent)
- India: 64 116 (6.1 per cent)
- Philippines: 56 478 (5.4 per cent)
- Cuba: 54 396 (5.2 per cent)

The Department of Homeland Security (USA) estimated that there were 11.4 million unauthorised (illegal) immigrants living in the USA in 2015. The top countries of origin were:

- Mexico (59 per cent)
- El Salvador (6 per cent)
- Guatemala (5 per cent)
- Honduras (3 per cent)
- Philippines (3 per cent)

Construct appropriate graphs to show these statistics. Find out the names of other source countries that produce a significant number of migrants to the USA.

Practice question

Using an example, evaluate the impacts of one voluntary international migration on the source country, the host country and the migrants themselves. *(9 marks)*

275

20 Communication

20.1 Development of ocean shipping and ports

On these spreads you will find out about the development of ocean shipping and ports

The need for ocean shipping

Transport by sea has happened throughout recorded history, for both passengers and cargo. Many ports in western Europe and eastern North America developed either by trading with each other across the Atlantic or by importing raw materials from colonies and exporting manufactured goods in return. Ocean travel has declined in importance for passengers because of the speed and relatively low price of air transport, but it is still popular for short journeys and leisure cruises.

Shipping of goods has grown as countries across the world trade with each other. Countries have become increasingly interdependent – depending on each other for goods and services. The volume and flow patterns of ocean shipping reflect the locations of raw materials, processed products and manufactured goods. The value of exported goods as a share of global GDP rose from 15 per cent in 1990 to 25 per cent in 2016. The world's major ports (map **A**) have benefited from these growing international trading links, and many have seen a faster increase in economic activity than cities located further inland.

The importance of ocean shipping

It is estimated that up to 90 per cent of world trade, as measured by weight of cargoes, is transported on water. The main reason is that the cost of shipping is relatively cheap. For example, a television set transported from south-east Asia to Europe incurs a transport charge of only US$1.5. The volume of shipping globally is now in excess of 11 billion tonnes per year. This represents an increase of 100 per cent since the 1990s.

Water transport is particularly used for large bulky cargoes, such as metals, minerals (e.g. iron ore and bauxite), coal, fertilisers, animal feed and cereals (e.g. wheat and maize). Apart from these dry cargoes, it is also suited to liquid cargoes, such as crude oil. Perishable commodities, such as fresh flowers, are more likely to be transported quickly to markets by air.

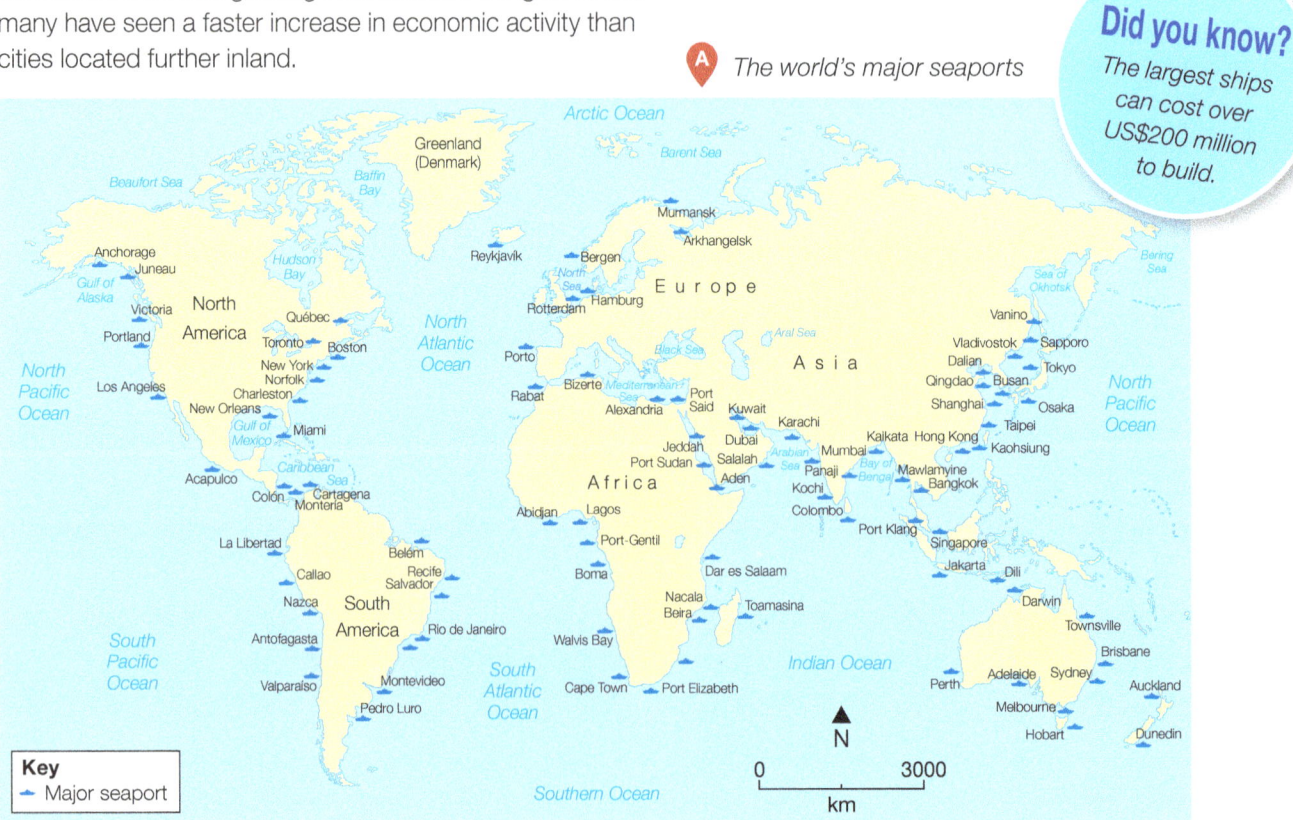

A The world's major seaports

Did you know? The largest ships can cost over US$200 million to build.

276

Communication

Types of vessel

Prior to 1900 ocean-going ships had similar characteristics. They carried all cargoes in the hold of the ship and it took a great deal of time to load and unload the goods. Nowadays, ships have specific purposes and are specifically designed to carry particular goods:

- **Bulk carriers** carry bulk dry cargoes such as foodstuffs (e.g. rice and cereals) and ores (e.g. iron ore and bauxite for aluminium).

- **Tankers** transport liquid cargoes, such as crude oil, petroleum, some chemicals, fruit juices and wine. Specialist tankers carry liquid petroleum gas (LPG) and liquefied natural gas (LNG) at a low temperature.

- **Refrigerated ships** or reefers carry perishable goods at precise temperatures, including fresh meats and fish, fruit and vegetables.

- **Container ships** carry goods in containers of standard size, usually 20-foot units (or twenty-foot equivalent units – TEUs). Much of the handling is done mechanically and loading is very quick.

- **Roll-on/roll-off (Ro-Ro) ships** transport road vehicles with their loads. Vehicles are driven onto the ship or ferry and then driven off at the other end of the journey.

- **Cruise ships** have become more important and much larger, as demand has increased. They carry millions of passengers per year in many parts of the world.

B Types of ocean vessel

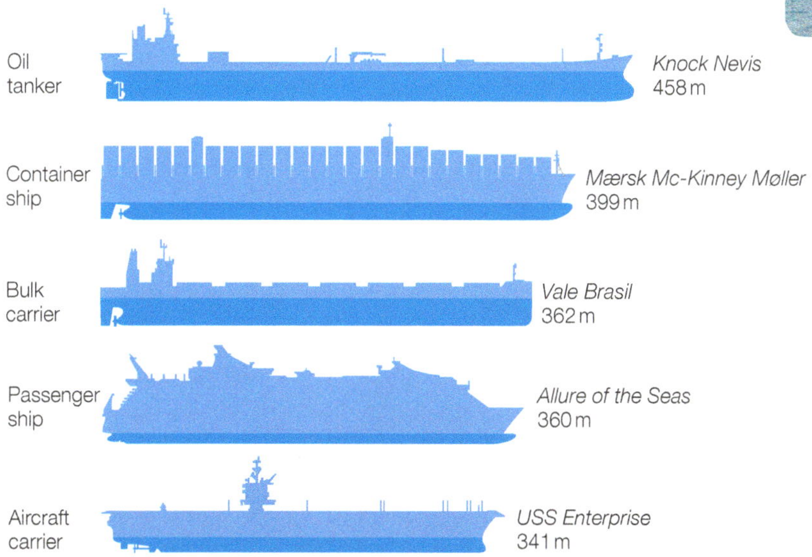

Ship	Name	Length
Oil tanker	Knock Nevis	458 m
Container ship	Mærsk Mc-Kinney Møller	399 m
Bulk carrier	Vale Brasil	362 m
Passenger ship	Allure of the Seas	360 m
Aircraft carrier	USS Enterprise	341 m

C Sizes of different types of ship

Did you know?
A single container ship travels up to 240 000 km per year during its movements across the oceans.

277

Development of ocean shipping and ports

Developments in ocean shipping

Size: Recently built ships are much larger than in the past. This helps to make them more efficient in terms of cost per unit of fuel and staff, as well as saving money on transporting goods. As a result, the major ports have adapted by providing deepwater facilities and large-scale, high-tech equipment. Dockside installations have been upgraded and strengthened to cope with the increased size of vessel.

Automation: Modern shipping depends on automation. This includes the use of computers to aid navigation, global positioning systems (GPS), mechanised loading and unloading. This has improved safety but reduced the number of crew required.

Design: Ship design has changed considerably. Older ships were made from steel and timber. Nowadays, they are made of aluminium and composite materials, which are much lighter and more durable. Latest designs are safer and enable ships to use less fuel and travel more quickly.

Containerisation: A high proportion of dry cargo is carried in containers (photo **D**). They have to be of internationally agreed standard sizes, measured in twenty-foot equivalent units (TEUs). Some of the larger ships can hold over 18 000 TEUs (diagram **E**). Advantages of containerisation include:

- reduced costs as loading and unloading are much quicker
- all processes are mechanised, using cranes, forklift trucks and other equipment
- easy transfer between different types of transport, including railway trucks and lorries
- reduced chance of theft or damage to goods, as items are in secure containers
- less traffic congestion around the port.

Container shipping now accounts for 1.5 billion tonnes of cargo per year.

Specialisation: Ships are now built for a specialised purpose, designed to handle different types of cargoes. This has resulted in greater speed and cost efficiency.

Speed: The mean speed of ocean transport has increased in recent years. Modern ships can travel at approximately 30 knots (50 km/h) or 1200 km/day. Older vessels had a maximum speed of 14–16 knots (30 km/h) or 720 km/day.

Did you know? A single container ship can hold 760 million bananas in 16 000 containers. That is enough for one banana for 10 per cent of the world's population.

278

Communication

D Container storage and loading on to ships

E How container ships have changed over time

length × width × depth below water in metres

Early container ship (1956): 500–800 TEU, 137 × 17 × 9 m

Fully Cellular (1970): 1000–2500 TEU, 215 × 20 × 10 m

Panamax (1980): 3000–3400 TEU, 250 × 32 × 12.5 m

Panamax Max (1985): 3400–4500 TEU, 290 × 32 × 12.5 m

Post Panamax (1988): 4000–5000 TEU, 285 × 40 × 13 m

Post Panamax Plus (2000): 6000–8000 TEU, 300 × 43 × 14.5 m

New Panamax (2014): 12 500 TEU, 366 × 49 × 15.2 m

Triple E (2013): 18 000 TEU, 400 × 59 × 15.5 m

Developments of ports

As the size of shipping and volume of traffic have increased, port facilities have changed. Many small ports have decreased in importance and traffic is concentrated in a smaller number of specialised deepwater ports, often serving particular industries.

In older ports on large estuaries there has been a gradual extension of dock facilities downstream, as specialised handling, more dock space and deep anchorages are required. In the UK, for example, the Port of London has seen its older outdated docks close down and newer facilities, including a container port, located downstream at Tilbury. Some trade has also been lost to the expanded port of Felixstowe on the east coast.

ACTIVITIES

1. Why have some types of ocean shipping decreased in importance?
2. Explain why ocean transport is used to carry up to 90 per cent of the total weight of world cargoes.
3. Using map **A**, describe the distribution of the world's major seaports.
4. Study photo compilation **B**.
   a Identify the types of ocean vessel shown.
   b Describe the purpose of each vessel.
5. Using diagram **C**, compare the maximum size of each type of ocean vessel.
6. Describe changes in the size of ocean ships over time. What are the implications of this changing size of shipping for ports?
7. List the main advantages of containerisation for ocean transport? Are there any disadvantages?
8. Explain the benefits of automation for ocean transport.

Maths skills

1. Study diagram **E**. Draw a line graph to show the changing size of container ships over time.
2. How much larger are the most recent container ships than those built in 1956?

Stretch yourself

Prepare a short presentation on containerisation. When did it start? Why did it revolutionise the transport of goods? What types of cargoes are carried? Why were some people opposed to it? What contribution does it make to ocean transport today? How large are some of the newest container ships?

Practice question

Explain how developments in ocean shipping have caused changes in port location and facilities. *(4 marks)*

20.2 Global patterns of movement by sea

On this spread you find out about global patterns of movement by sea

The busiest shipping routes reflect the patterns of trade between different parts of the world. The most crowded single route is between China and the USA, although exports from China are four times greater than exports from the USA. The China–Europe route is also very important. China exports more containerised cargo than any other country. One reason for this is the decline of manufacturing in the west and the growth of industry in newly emerging economies (NEEs), which have the advantage of cheap labour and modern industrial installations.

Map **A** shows that the main concentrations of ocean traffic are around the ports of western Europe, the eastern seaboard of the USA, the western side of the USA and southern Canada, eastern Australia and eastern Asia (Japan, Singapore, China ports). Congestion points on world shipping routes include narrow straits, such as the straits of Gibraltar, Malacca and Hormuz. These sometimes result in lengthy delays when ships can be susceptible to piracy. Some recently opened routes are helping to speed up transport of goods – these include Russia's north-east passage (for boats travelling from China to Europe) and the northern route across the Arctic north of Canada and Alaska.

Piracy is a threat on some routes, sometimes leading to crews being taken hostage and demands for ransom money. The most vulnerable areas are off the eastern coast of Somalia and the entrance to the Red Sea. Most boats have weaponry and additional security to deter pirates.

Crude oil

Oil represents over 25 per cent of all cargoes transported by sea. The principal suppliers are in the Middle East, including Saudi Arabia, UAE, Iran and Kuwait, accounting for 30 per cent of total world production. The main consumers are located in western Europe, North America and south-east Asia. The USA also obtains oil from west Africa and South America (Venezuela), and western Europe is also supplied by countries in north Africa.

Principal shipping routes from areas of oil surplus are from the Middle East (Arabian Gulf), extending westwards towards Europe through the Suez Canal (photo **B**) or via the southern tip of Africa (Cape of Good Hope). The eastern route, connecting the Arabian Gulf to east Asia and the USA, is also very busy. Other major routes are from north Africa northwards and westwards to western Europe and North America (map **A**).

> **Did you know?**
> Shipping is a male-dominated industry – 98 per cent of sea-going crews are men.

A World shipping routes

Source: Kaluza, P. et al. The complex network of global cargo ship movements, *J R Soc Interface* (2010) 7, 1093–1103.

Communication

B Oil tanker passing through the Suez Canal, Egypt

Did you know?
There are an estimated 18 million shipping containers, one third of which are being transported at any one time.

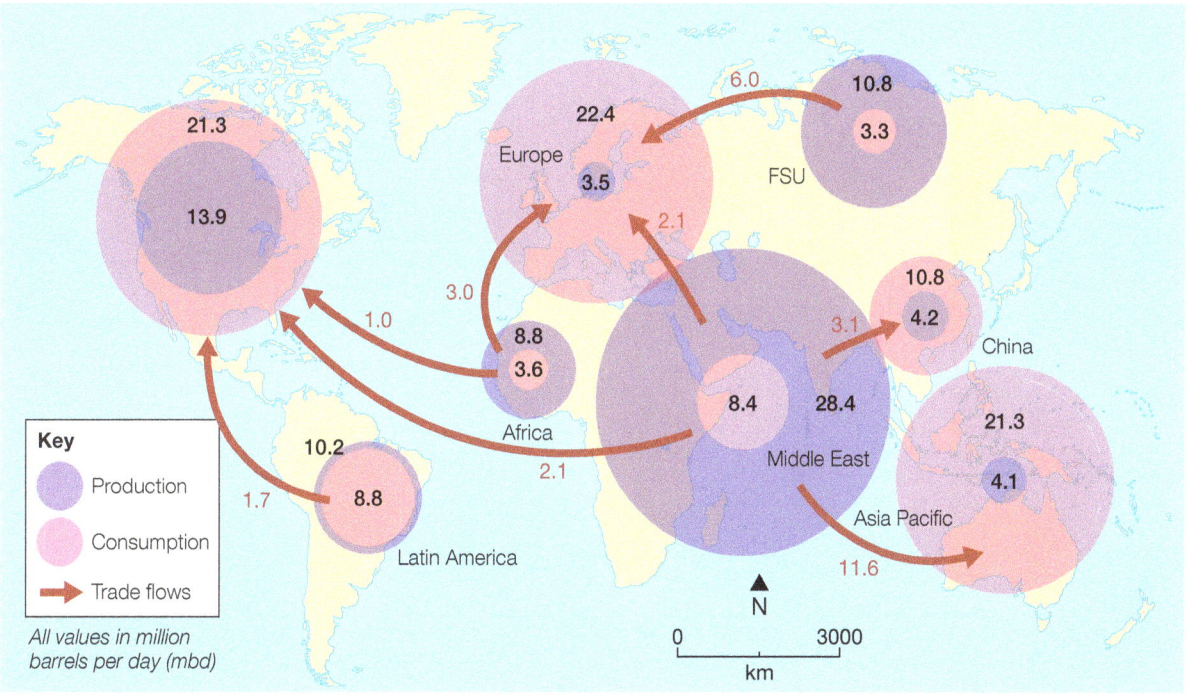

C World trade in oil

Source: Based on data from BP Statistical Review.

Key:
- Production
- Consumption
- Trade flows

All values in million barrels per day (mbd)

ACTIVITIES

1. Using map **A**, describe the busiest routes for ocean shipping. Which parts of the world have relatively few ocean transport routes? Explain the pattern shown.

2. Using map **C**, which regions are the biggest producers and which are the biggest consumers of oil? Describe the pattern of oil transport globally. Explain why some areas have very high oil consumption figures.

3. Suggest why piracy has become a problem for certain shipping routes? What measures are being taken by shipping companies to deter piracy?

4. Explain why some new routes have recently opened up for world shipping, particularly to the north of North America and Asia.

Maths skills

Using map **C**, calculate the total production and consumption of oil (in million barrels per day). Do the figures match up?

Stretch yourself

Using the internet, research the pattern of trade for one other commodity, e.g. wheat or coal. Find out the main exporters and importers and describe the main routes for ocean transport.

Practice question

Assess the factors that affect the number of shipping movements in different parts of the world. *(6 marks)*

281

20.3 The world's leading ports

On this spread you will find out about some of the world's leading ports

The world's leading ports, as measured by their handling capacity in million TEUs, are located in places where global trade connections are strongest (map **A**). These are focused in south-east Asia, where 10 of the top 15 are based, particularly in China. Some way behind are ports in Europe and the east and west coasts of the USA – although only two ports (Los Angeles and Rotterdam) appear in the top 15 listing.

A Location of the world's 30 largest shipping ports, 2014

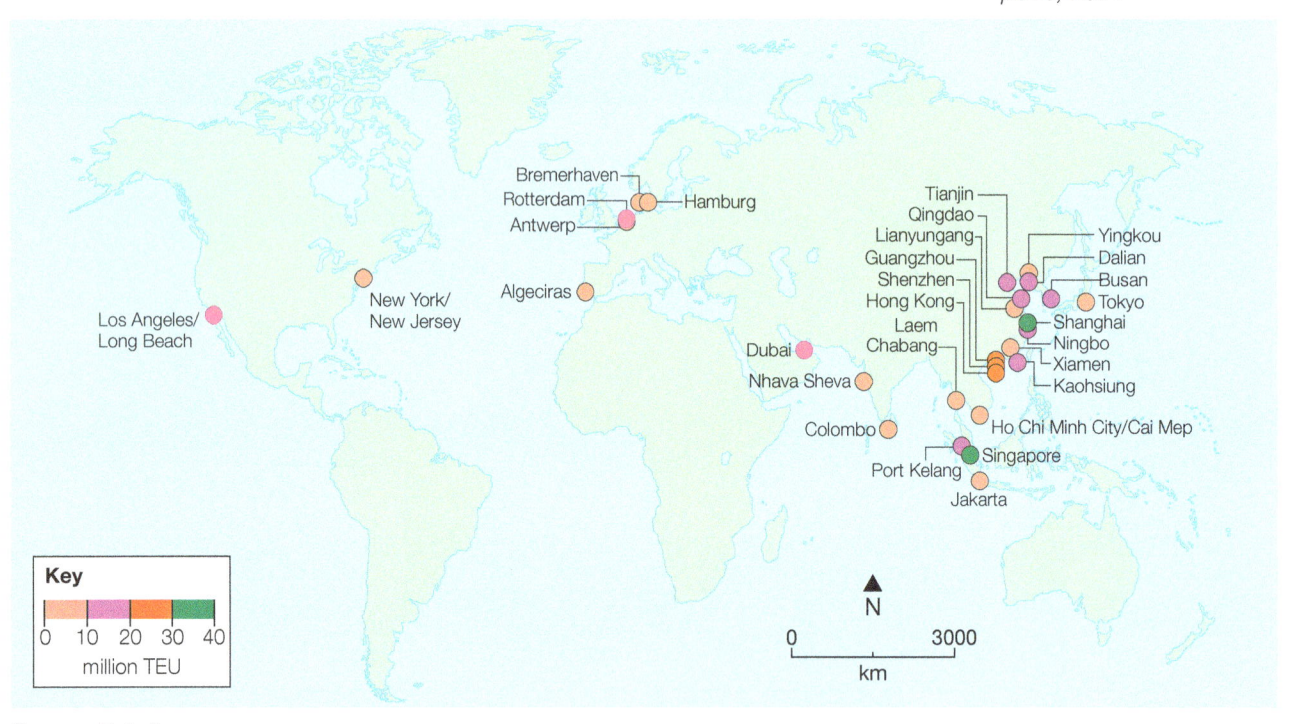

Key: 0 10 20 30 40 million TEU

Source: Alphaliner.

Shanghai (China) – ranked first in the world

The Port of Shanghai has expanded operations enormously in the past few years. A brand new container terminal was opened in December 2017 (photo **B**) – on its own, it is eventually expected to handle a massive 6.3 million TEUs. There is no doubt that Shanghai is the 'gateway' for trade with China, as over a quarter of cargo shipments entering and leaving China pass through the port. This equates to roughly 2000 container ships per month. The port also has large-scale facilities for bulk cargo vessels, roll-on/roll-off ferries and cruise liners. Much of China's trade is focused on Shanghai because of its enormous hinterland, its high population density, rapid economic growth and industrial activity.

B Shanghai's new container terminal

Singapore – ranked second in the world

Singapore was the world's leading port until overtaken by Shanghai in the early 2000s. Singapore is a free port, open to all countries, with seven free trade zones. In these zones, goods can be made or assembled without paying import or export duties, and profits can be sent back to the parent company without paying tax. Many high-tech companies assemble their products here and sell them at very competitive prices.

It is also an important transhipment port, which means that containers are transferred between different vessels. Lots of small feeder boats bring containers into Singapore prior to transhipment onto larger vessels, which will take the shipments to their final destination. Singapore's location at the meeting point of global shipping routes makes this practical and cost-efficient. The port also takes raw materials, such as oil, processes and refines them, then re-exports them to further destinations.

Over 200 shipping lines make use of Singapore as a port, and there are links with upwards of 650 ports in approximately 125 countries. The port now handles over 30 million TEUs per annum.

Rotterdam (Netherlands) – ranked 12th in the world

As the leading port in Europe, Rotterdam handles 11 million TEUs per year. Trading was boosted by the establishment of the EU and the increased bulk and container trade that has since taken place. It has a complex network of waterways as well as fast road and rail links inland. It also has an important transhipment trade (redistribution to other ports) and acts as a transfer point for commodities that are being transported between Europe and the rest of the world.

Rotterdam is one of the world's leading industrial complexes, with heavy industrial petrochemical works, oil refineries and food processing in particular. As vessels have become larger and channels deeper, the port has extended westwards into the sea, where much reclamation has been necessary (map **C**). The port employs over 75 000 people and, not surprisingly, suffers from considerable congestion and some air and water pollution.

ACTIVITIES

1. Using map **A**, describe the distribution of the largest container ports in the world. Explain why some areas have a high concentration of container ports whereas other areas have very few.
2. Explain the need for a new container terminal in the port of Shanghai.
3. Explain how Singapore has been able to expand its port activities so rapidly.
4. Using map **C**, describe the growth of Rotterdam as a port and explain the pattern of development.

Stretch yourself

Plot the following global shipping routes on a world map and explain the pattern shown.

Route	Cargo (million TEUs)
Asia–North America	24.0
Asia–northern Europe	14.0
Asia–Mediterranean	7.0
Asia–Middle East	5.0
Northern Europe–North America	5.0
Australia–Far East	3.0
Asia–east coast South America	2.0
Northern Europe/Mediterranean–east coast South America	2.0
North America–east coast South America	1.5

Practice question

Suggest why many of the world's leading seaports are located in south-east Asia. *(4 marks)*

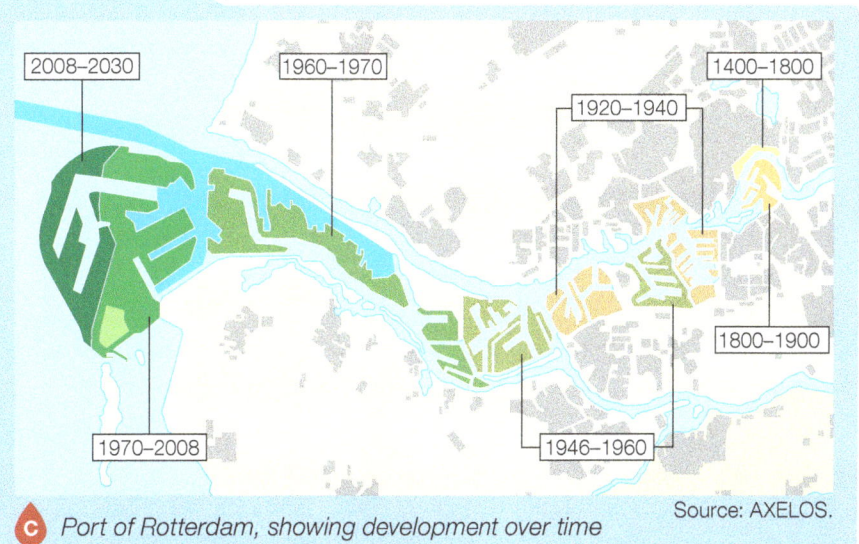

C Port of Rotterdam, showing development over time

Source: AXELOS.

20.4 Comparing ocean transport with air transport

On this spread you will find out about the differences between air transport and ocean transport

	Ocean transport	**Air transport**
Speed–time	Slow	Fastest over longest distances
Distance–cost	Relatively cheap	Generally expensive, but ideal for light goods
Terminal costs	High cost of port duties, port infrastructure and large specialised ships	Very expensive to build and maintain airports High airport fees Much land needed Huge investment in purchasing aeroplanes Requires special preparations, e.g. meteorological stations, flood lights, searchlights
Running costs	Quite economical – costs spread over a large cargo	Speed makes it competitive over very long distances
Number of routes	Relatively few ports Inflexible due to increased specialisation of ships Limited routes to deepwater ports	Often only a few routes, linked to specific airports However, does provide unbroken journey over land and sea
Goods and passengers carried	Heavy, bulky goods, e.g. coal, ores, grains, oil, consumer products Cruise passengers	Mainly passengers Freight is mainly light, perishable (e.g. flowers, fruit) or high value (e.g. watches, diamonds, bullion)
Passenger convenience and comfort	Cruise liners are very comfortable Not very convenient as limited ports	Jet lag if more than three time zones crossed Cramped, tiring and dehydrating over long journeys
Weather	Storms, fog Icebergs in North Atlantic	Fog, icing, snow Airports better if sheltered from wind and away from areas of hills and areas of low cloud
Relief	Harbours need to be deep, wide and sheltered Tidal problems	Large areas of flat land for runways, terminal buildings, hangars, warehousing Firm foundations needed
Environmental problems	Tankers discharging oil Accidental spills at sea (potentially hazardous substances) (photo **A**) Water pollution Noise pollution (e.g. interference with marine mammals' echolocation) Sewage and waste from ships Landscape and ecosystem impacts of port developments	Emissions of NO_2 and CO_2 – high emissions during take-off (chart **B**) Ground-level smog Contribution to ozone depletion Road traffic at airports Runoff from airports containing oil and antifreeze Airport construction putting pressure on land resources and causing landscape degradation

Think about it

*Shipping is the most affordable way to transport cargo. It is cheaper for Scottish cod to be shipped to China 14 000 km and filleted and returned to Scotland, than it is to pay Scottish workers to do the same job (photo **C**).*

Communication

A Worker trying to remove oil that has leaked onto the beaches in the Saronic Gulf near Athens, Greece, from the wreck of the tanker Agia Zoni II in 2017

Did you know?
Plane exhaust fumes kill more people than plane crashes. Approximately 10 000 people are killed annually from toxic pollutants from airplanes.

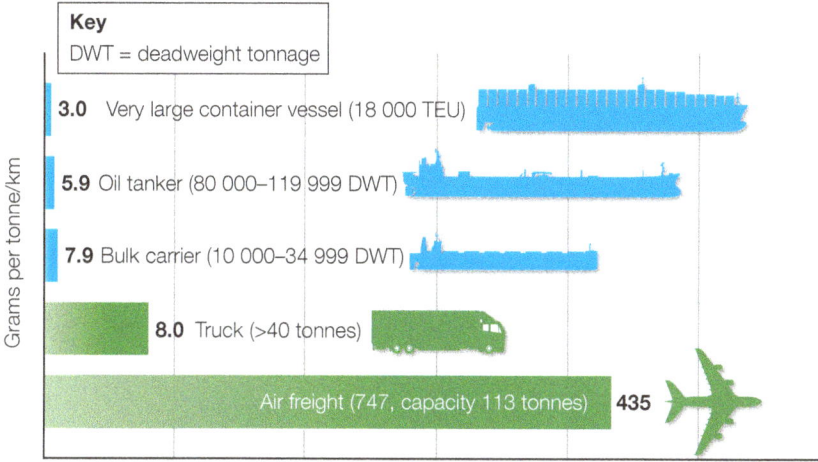

Key
DWT = deadweight tonnage

Grams per tonne/km:
- 3.0 Very large container vessel (18 000 TEU)
- 5.9 Oil tanker (80 000–119 999 DWT)
- 7.9 Bulk carrier (10 000–34 999 DWT)
- 8.0 Truck (>40 tonnes)
- 435 Air freight (747, capacity 113 tonnes)

Source: Second IMO GHG Study, 2014.

B Comparing CO_2 emissions between different types of transport

C Imported fish are descaled, deboned, packaged and refrozen for export in Qingdao, China

ACTIVITIES

1. Why is a huge investment of money required when developing ports and airports?
2. Compare the physical requirements of ports and airports.
3. How might weather conditions affect air and ocean transport?
4. To what extent do ocean and air transport affect the natural environment?
5. Assess the importance of ocean shipping in the transport of goods and passengers between different parts of the world.

Stretch yourself

Find out more about China's transport links with the rest of the world. Search online to find maps showing connections by air and sea. Why is China such an important global transport hub in the twenty-first century?

Practice question

'Air transport is now dominant for both the movement of goods and people.' Do you agree? Explain your answer. (6 marks)

20.5 Development of airports and global patterns

On these spreads you will find out about the development of airports and global patterns of movement by air

Advantages of air transport

The outstanding advantages of air transport are its great speed, the vast distances that can be covered, the directness of routes and the improved accessibility it gives to the most remote locations. It can often operate when other types of transport cannot, for example when providing aid and relief following an earthquake or flood that has disrupted roads and railways. Air transport is particularly suitable for the carriage of goods with low bulk and high value. These include postal mail, high-value electrical equipment, jewellery and precious stones, high-value livestock such as racehorses, and high-value, out-of-season fruits and cut flowers.

Restrictions of air transport

There are a number of restrictions to air transport:

- There is not complete freedom of the air, because air movement has to take place along designated air corridors, and countries place political restrictions on flights within their air space.
- Aircraft have a high depreciation cost and a high operating expenditure.
- All aircraft, despite modern radar and other devices are affected by weather conditions around take-off and landing points. Fog remains a major hazard, as does snow and ice, often causing flight delays.
- Air transport is limited in the volume of passenger and freight traffic it can carry because it remains an expensive form of transport.

Did you know?
Only 5 per cent of the world's population has ever travelled by plane.

Growth of air travel

Over the past decade, passenger and freight traffic have been growing at an annual rate, averaging 7 per cent. In 2017, a total or 4 billion passengers were carried on approximately 35 million scheduled flights. Graph **A** shows the increased volume of air passenger traffic since 2007. The growing importance of air transport is demonstrated by the large modernisation and expansion programmes at many of the world's major airports.

Development of airports

As the number of airports and aircraft has increased, so have passenger numbers. In 2017, there were 3.91 billion passengers worldwide. Several newly emerging economies (NEEs) have built impressive, large airports such as those in Shanghai, Hong Kong, Singapore and Dubai. Altogether, the aviation industry supports 58 million jobs and generates US$2.4 trillion of economic activity per year.

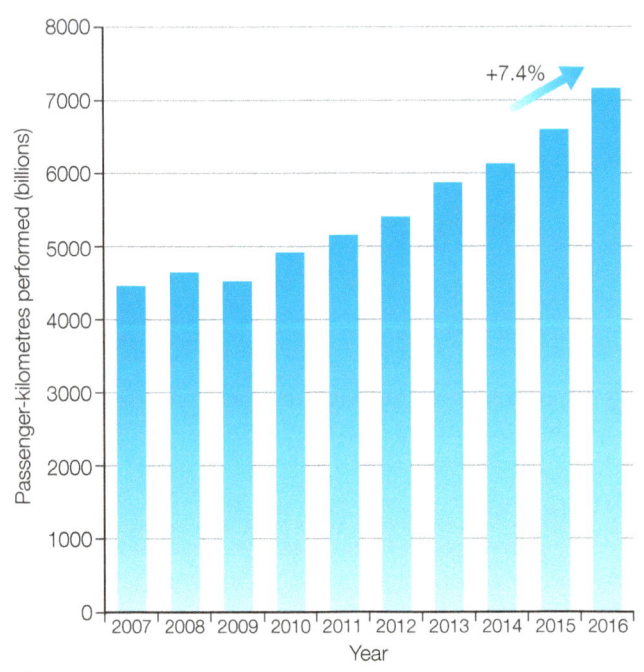

A Growth in air passenger traffic, 2007–16

Airports are facing a number of challenges:

- The latest generation of aircraft are larger and more fuel-efficient, such as the Airbus A380, often requiring longer runways and more infrastructure. This increase in scale affects baggage handling, ticket counters, passenger lounges and queuing areas, parking and terminal design.

- Security has become more stringent as threats from terrorism have grown. To improve safety and increase efficiency numerous digital systems have been introduced, including sophisticated recognition technologies such as biometrics.

- Many airports are already operating at full capacity, such as Düsseldorf, Frankfurt, London Heathrow and Milan. There are often delays to flights caused by problems associated with slow turnaround of aircraft at airports. Road and public transport networks are often stretched to the limit.

- Airports can cause environmental issues, such as noise, air and water pollution, as well as considerable traffic congestion. Many airports in highly populated areas have to make compromises in terms of take-off and landing routes, or by reducing or stopping air traffic at night.

Qatar's brand new Hamad International Airport, built on reclaimed land, replaces the nearby Doha International Airport. The new airport is roughly two-thirds the size of Doha city itself and will soon be able to handle 50 million passengers per year. The airport has installed almost 500 escalators, moving walks, passenger boarding bridges and lifts, all controlled through a central monitoring system. The airport has 29 km^2 of retail space and provides high-quality services such as restaurants, gyms and exclusive hotels.

B *Air traffic control tower of Singapore Changi Airport with construction work for the new development*

Singapore Changi Airport

Singapore Changi Airport is one of the world's leading airports. Over 60 million passengers passed through in 2017, up to 40 per cent of whom were changing to another flight or airline. Changi also handles a huge amount of cargo – approximately 2 million tonnes were transported in 2017.

The airport contributes to Singapore's economy in a number of ways:

- 14 500 people are employed directly as airline workers
- 30 000 are employed in supporting industries and services
- 36 000 work beyond the airport in other sectors, such as hotel accommodation, entertainment, business centres and travel agencies
- the airport is a major hub for local and foreign commercial businesses in the area. They are drawn by access to specialist labour and the lower costs incurred by close proximity to suppliers and customers. Changi has become a major economic centre.

Plans to further development the airport are due to be completed by late 2018. They include a five-storey garden with a 40 m high waterfall, as well as surrounding restaurants, hotels, shops and other facilities leading to the terminal.

Development of airports and global patterns

Global patterns of movement by air

The worldwide growth in air traffic, both for the transport of passengers and carriage of bulk high-value freight, has accelerated in the past few decades – 40 per cent of world trade (by value) is now moved by air.

Region	Percentage of international air traffic in 2016 (%)	Growth rate of international air traffic in 2016 (%)	Annual growth rate in international air freight shipments (%)
Asia Pacific	33	10.2	2.9
Europe	27	6.2	5.7
North America	24	4.3	2.1
Middle East	9	11.2	7.2
Latin America and the Caribbean	5	4.4	−1.9
Africa	2	6.9	2.8

Did you know?
Globally, there are more than 200 000 flights every day. That is almost 73 million every year.

C Global air traffic, 2016

D World airline route map, based on over 50 000 flights

Note that 80 per cent of all international air freight transport takes place along east–west trading routes. These are between Asia and North America, between Asia and Europe, and between Europe and North America.

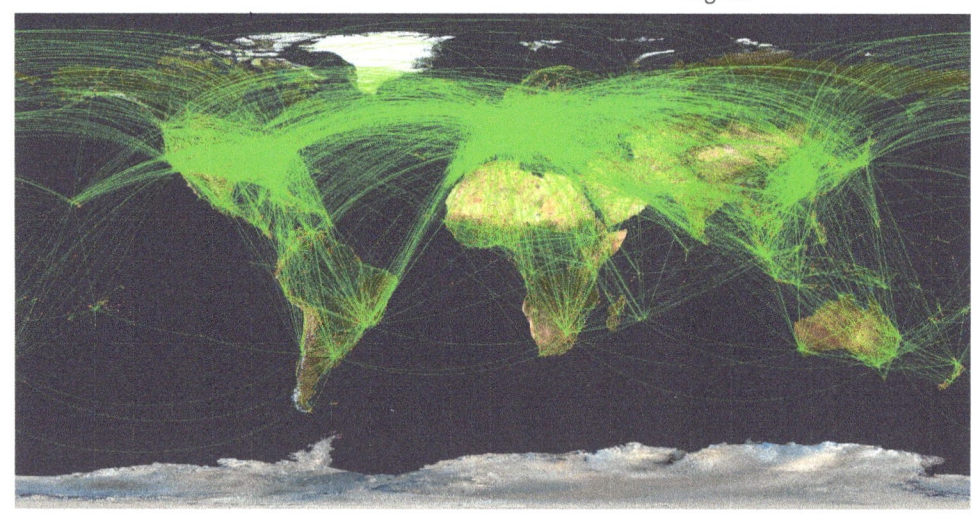

E The link between national wealth and number of flights per head, 2013

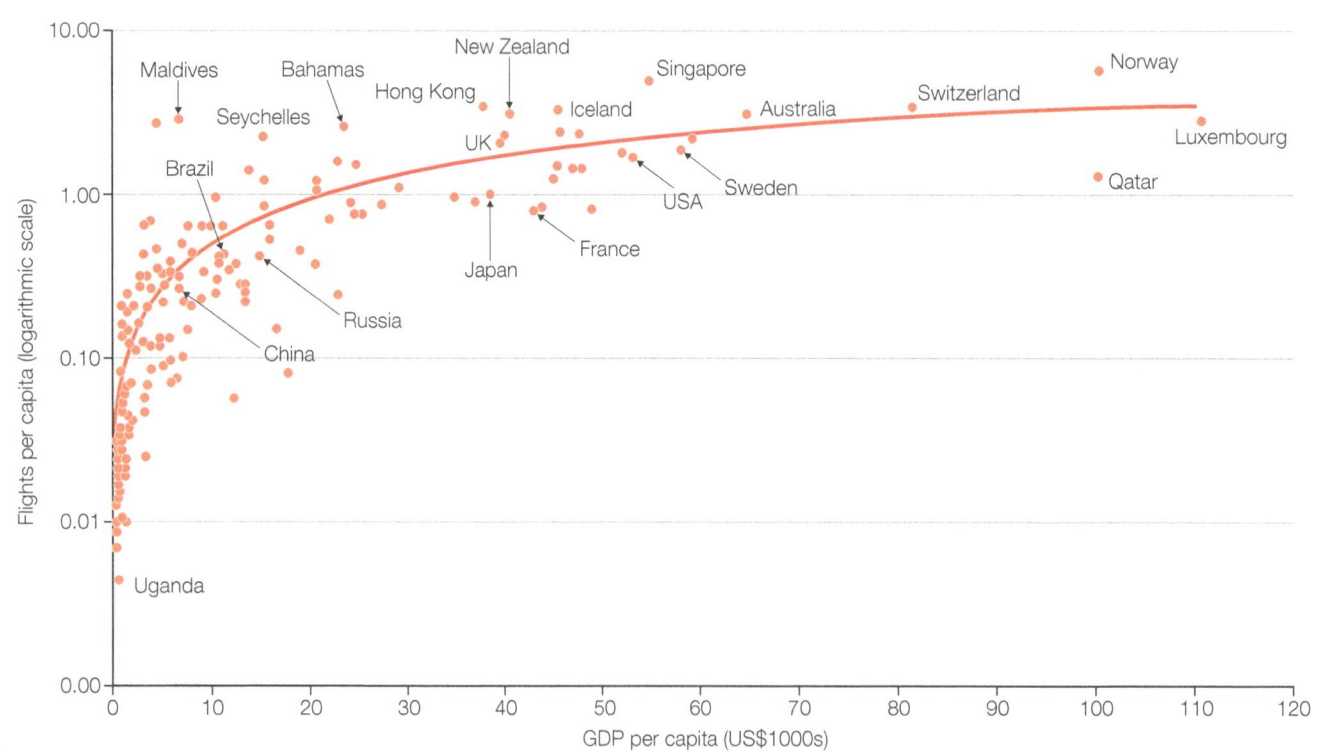

Communication

Factors involved in the expansion of air transport

Increasing levels of disposable income have led to rising demand for air travel, both for tourism and for business travel.

Decreasing costs of air travel. In real terms the price of air travel has decreased by 45 per cent since the mid 1960s (after taking inflation into account). There has been more competition between airlines, which has resulted in lower fares. At the same time, the cost of alternative transport such as road and rail services has increased.

Did you know?
There are almost 42 000 airports in the world, and the USA has 13 500 of them.

Greater number of airports and increased supply of flights. The average distance travelled on flights has doubled from approximately 1000 km in 1980 to 2000 km today. Globalisation has led to greater connectivity between different parts of the world.

Huge investment in business services, freight-handling facilities, larger, quieter and more fuel-efficient aircraft, increased airport capacity and more modern infrastructure.

ACTIVITIES

1. Using graph **A**, describe changes in air passenger traffic since 2007.
2. Explain why some areas have seen rapid rates of growth in air passenger and freight traffic, whereas other areas have grown only very slowly.
3. a Using map **D**, describe the global pattern of air routes. Which areas have the largest number of flights? Why do some parts of the world have very few?
   b Compare this pattern with that of ocean shipping routes (map **A**, 20.2). In what ways is the pattern similar and different?
4. Using graph **E**, state the link between GDP per head (capita) and number of flights taken. Illustrate your answer with examples of different countries.
5. What are the most important factors driving the global growth in air transport?
6. Using an example, explain how an airport can become a major economic centre.
7. Explain why it was considered worthwhile to invest in the new design features at Changi Airport.

Maths skills

Study the statistics shown in table **C**. Draw a divided bar graph to show the percentage of international air traffic as measured by the number of flights in 2016. Describe the pattern of air traffic shown by the graph and the growth rates in 2016.

Stretch yourself

Research the cost of international travel from your home area. What are the costs of passenger travel to different parts of the world on regular scheduled services from your nearest airport? How do the costs change if you travel on different dates? Why do the costs vary so much?

Practice question

Explain the global pattern of major air transport routes. *(4 marks)*

20.6 Advantages of international links for manufacturing, trade and tourism

On this spread you will find out about the advantages of increasing international links for manufacturing, trade and tourism

Did you know?
40 per cent of the value of international manufacturing exports is transported by air.

International links and manufacturing

Air transport is beneficial to manufacturing for several reasons:

- It speeds up delivery times and ensures that goods are delivered reliably and efficiently. These days, industries operate on 'just in time' systems, which means that there is minimal storage and materials and sub-assemblies are delivered just when needed.

- Better transport links extend the market and make industries more competitive, so they may become more efficient as a result.

- As air transport extends to most parts of the world, it becomes feasible to sell goods wherever there is demand. Over one quarter of commercial business sales are linked to air transport worldwide. This has increased markedly since 1990, as markets have expanded and global links increased.

- Air transport has become essential for the delivery of high-value goods such as computer components and pharmaceutical goods.

- Air transport has also helped the development of the express carrier industry, which is able to connect most parts of the world within three days. It is used by almost all transnational companies (TNCs) and uses over 2000 flights per day.

- Air transport provides access to remote areas, opening them up to contact with other communities, providing the means to deliver essential supplies and encouraging economic activity, including manufacturing.

International links and trade

Advances in transport encourage countries to specialise in activities in which they have an advantage, and to trade with countries producing other goods and services. Since 1945, the volume of world trade has increased by about 8 per cent a year on average. The world's trading partners are the USA, Europe and south-east Asia, including Japan and China. Less than 10 per cent of world trade involves low-income countries (LICs). The reduction of tariffs has increased trade, as have improvements in living standards.

Around the world there are trading blocs or groups of countries where there are little or no restrictions between member states on the movement of goods, services, money and, sometimes, labour. Transport between these countries is enhanced because trade barriers are withdrawn and investment can easily take place. Examples include the European Union (EU) and Association of Southeast Asian Nations (ASEAN).

Air transport is vital for trading goods with landlocked and island countries, and for countries that depend on perishable goods and high-value commodities as their main exports.

Passenger air services are instrumental in creating trading opportunities. They ensure that businesses are able to promote their products worldwide and allow companies to meet their customers personally, often at short notice. This helps to forge new sales and improves communication between traders.

Colombia is the biggest supplier of cut flowers to the USA and Canada, with a sizeable percentage carried by air. Clothing and vegetables are also major exports sold to the American market.

Kenya's exports of cut flowers and vegetables are a crucial source of revenue for the Kenyan economy, second only to tourism. It now provides a quarter of the EU's cut flowers and is among the top five exporters in the world. Rapid air transport is essential in getting these perishable commodities to markets in Europe.

A Worker at a rose farm near Nairobi, Kenya, preparing cut flowers for export to Europe

Communication

International links and tourism

Air transport has expanded the range of locations that can be visited – 40 per cent of international tourists now travel by air. A smaller percentage travel by sea, although the international cruise industry is expanding rapidly and there are numerous international ferry crossings.

The air transport industry contributes 8 per cent of global GDP (worth over US$3000 billion). With 30 million jobs linked to the aviation industry, tourism plays an essential role in its success, as well as providing jobs in the destination area, such as those in hotels, transport, farming, retail and other services. Tourism plays a vital part in many economies, including LICs/NEEs, where it may be the largest single source of foreign revenue.

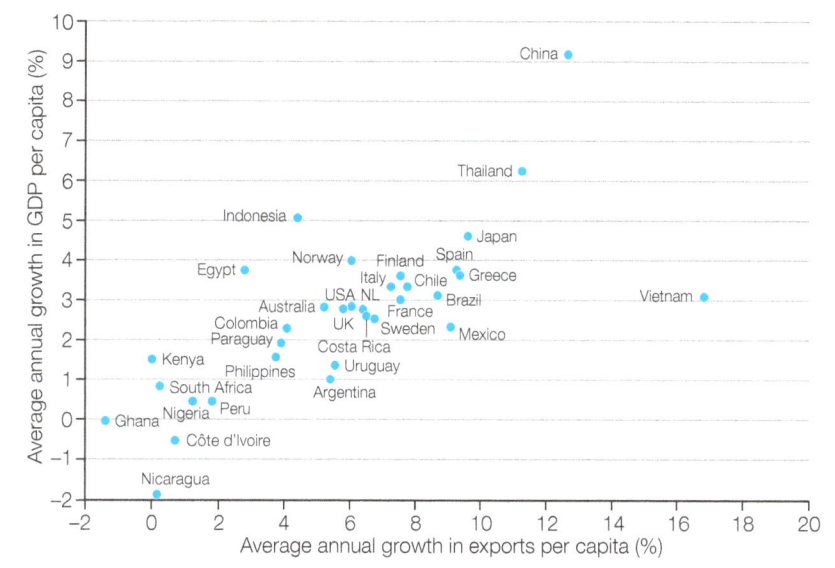

B *Economic growth and trade growth, 1964–2004*

Source: WDI, OEF calculations.

Tourism in Costa Rica

Costa Rica has allowed tourism to develop so that it earns valuable foreign exchange and generates a large number of jobs, but at the same time has insisted on following principles of conservation and environmental protection. Over the past few years, the country has become a major ecotourism destination, which has helped, indirectly, to protect the tropical rainforest environment. Much of the money spent by tourism is reinvested in conservation work and has enabled the country's national parks to be protected. Tourism is now the second largest source of foreign exchange (microchips are the largest).

C *Ecotourist attractions in Costa Rica*

ACTIVITIES

1. Why is air transport becoming increasingly important for manufactured goods?
2. Using graph **B**, explain the link between economic growth and world trade. How does the air transport industry contribute to world trade?
3. Using photo compilation **C**, outline some of the main attractions of Costa Rica for international tourists. Suggest how tourists may contribute to economic growth in Costa Rica.

Stretch yourself

Research an example of an industry that depends on regular air transport for international trade, e.g. flowers or vegetables from Kenya. Find out how quickly the produce is transported from the source to the consumer. What are the costs involved? What proportion is received by the airline? How much goes to the producer? What are the main problems affecting this industry?

Practice question

Assess the importance of air transport to international tourism. *(6 marks)*

291

20.7 Challenges of increasing airport development

On these spreads you will find out about challenges presented by increasing airport development

Challenges presented by increasing airport development

- Air traffic is growing by over 5 per cent per year and may soon approach a total of 4 billion passengers worldwide. This means that airport capacity must continue to expand.
- Aeroplanes are getting bigger. The Airbus A380 and Boeing 747-8 are so large that new terminals are being built to accommodate them.
- Increased legislation is requiring airports to reduce noise levels, construct sustainable buildings and protect the local environment.
- Limiting noise levels may involve reducing the number of night-time hours during which planes can land and take off.
- Transport infrastructure leading to airports may require updating and improvement to cope with rising levels of demand.
- Some airports are considering expansion of airport capacity, including the construction of new runways and terminal buildings (e.g. London Heathrow and Frankfurt).
- Some low-cost airlines have decided to establish routes to new regional airports in areas where on-site costs are lower.
- A few countries have decided to invest in building a new airport close to the site of an existing one. Qatar's recently constructed Hamad International Airport (photo **A**), built on land reclaimed from the Arabian Gulf, replaces Doha International Airport (only 4 km away), and will soon be able to handle 50 million passengers per year.

Airports in the UK

Airports are very important to the economy of the UK, creating vital global links.

- They provide thousands of jobs and boost economic growth, both regionally and nationally.
- The aviation sector accounts for 3.6 per cent of the UK's GDP and employs over 300 000 people.
- Over 2 million tonnes of freight pass through the UK's airports each year.
- More than 750 000 international flights depart from the UK annually, to almost 400 airports in 114 countries.
- Over 420 000 domestic flights provide 35 million seats annually to passengers travelling to over 60 regional airports across the UK.

A *Hamad International Airport, Qatar*

London: a case study of airport expansion

Stretched to capacity

London is one of the world's most visited cities but faces a real challenge in coping with the huge volume of flights needed to bring its visitors. At present, the existing airports cope with 130 million passengers per year, but they are stretched to capacity at times. Heathrow currently operates at 99 per cent capacity – as does Gatwick, the second busiest airport in the UK. In 2014, Heathrow handled over 73 million passengers. More than 76 000 people work at Heathrow and the airport supports many local businesses.

Did you know?
Heathrow handles 76 million passengers a year (2016) – a figure greater than the entire population of the UK. It is the world's second busiest airport in terms of international passenger numbers.

B Airport proposals for south-east England, 1971–2012

Source: UK Department for Transport; Oxera.

Proposed solutions

There has been much controversy about the need to expand London's airport capacity. Over the past 50 years, many options have been proposed to accommodate the growing number of passengers, to compete with European rivals and to stimulate economic growth in the region (map **B**). These include the construction of a new fourth airport in the Thames Estuary and the expansion of either Heathrow or Gatwick. All the options have advantages and disadvantages.

In 2012, a government commission looked into these three options:

- a new runway at Heathrow (costing US$26.1 billion)
- increasing the length of one of the existing runways at Heathrow (costing US$19 billion)
- constructing a new runway at Gatwick (costing US$13.1 billion).

In 2015, the commission published a report recommending a new third runway at Heathrow (map **D**). It was unanimously decided that Heathrow's expansion was the best of the proposals and the north-west runway and terminal plan was approved by government on 25 October 2016. Although approved, work is not likely to start until 2020 or 2021, and it will not be operational until 2025 at the earliest.

The expansion is predicted to create more jobs and make more money for the UK, but the plans are highly controversial, with strong opposition from some interest groups. The report recommends financial support for soundproofing homes and schools, and a ban on night flights. However, many people living nearby are concerned about the noise from planes using the new runway. At peak times aeroplanes land and take off every 30 seconds.

C A housing estate under the flight path of planes approaching Heathrow

293

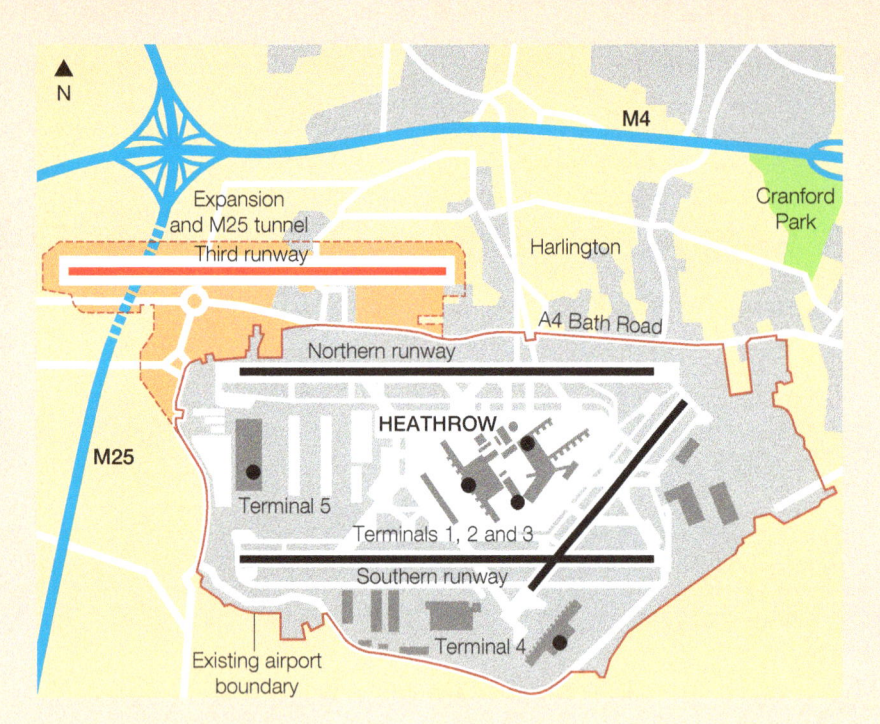

Challenges of increasing airport development

D Proposed expansion of Heathrow Airport

Did you know?
If an aircraft creates too much noise near Heathrow the airline is fined and the money given to local community projects.

Potential benefits

- Up to 180 000 jobs will be created.
- An estimated US$206.7 billion in economic benefit to the UK.
- Improved air connections to many other UK cities.
- Up to 40 new destinations will be possible as the airport increases capacity, e.g. Brazil, Russia, India and China – all important for future trade and economic connections.
- Over 740 000 flights will be possible from Heathrow every year, making it competitive with any other European airport.
- Greater choice of airlines for passengers and lower fares as competition is increased between airlines.
- Heathrow will be able to upgrade and improve its freight facilities, doubling the capacity.
- Rail capacity will increase from 18 to 40 trains (from 5000 to 15 000 seats) an hour.
- Improvements to bus and coach services will mean that 30 million more people will travel to Heathrow by public transport in 2030.
- Improvements to terminal connections connected by an underground passenger transit and baggage system.
- Significant benefits to local shops and businesses, including hotels and conference facilities.
- More flights will also mean London and the UK is more accessible for international tourists.

Arguments against expansion

- Air pollution is likely to increase. It may already account for 9000 premature deaths according to Greenpeace. Expansion of the airport will make Heathrow the biggest source of CO_2 in the country, at 23.6 million tonnes of emissions a year.
- It will cost US$24.7 billion in the short term.
- To construct the third runway, 750 homes will be demolished, mainly in the village of Harmondsworth.
- Altogether, up to 725 000 people will be living directly under the flight paths leading into Heathrow, with all the noise and pollution this brings.
- There will be much disruption to transport links caused by the reconstruction of nearby roads, including the M25 orbital road around London.
- Some believe benefits have been exaggerated, saying only 12 per cent of the travel passing through Heathrow is business-related. The rapid pace of technological development (e.g. teleconferencing) is likely to slow down the need for costly business trips in the future, so the project may not be needed.
- Other alternatives may be preferable, such as an airport in the Thames Estuary or an expansion of Gatwick. These could be less expensive and environmentally less damaging.

Communication

Does this matter to anyone outside of London?

Those in favour of the decision argue that it will benefit the whole of the UK, as any boost to the economy is good for the entire population. Naturally, families and businesses located elsewhere will still be able to make use of the international flights to 40 new destinations.

Why is it taking so long?

The government first proposed a new airport in London in 1968 and many different options have been suggested, accepted and subsequently abandoned since then. Even though the decision has now been made, it will take years to build. Runways are surprisingly complicated constructions, as they need to withstand extremely heavy aeroplanes, landing at high speeds over many years. A poor build will soon need repairs.

Number of passengers	78 million per year 213 668 per day Departures 49% Arrivals 51%
Type of journeys	International 94% Domestic 6% Transfers 30% Leisure 67% Business 33%
Number of flights	474 033 per year 1299 per day
Top destinations	1 New York 2 Dubai 3 Dublin 4 Amsterdam 5 Hong Kong

E Key data about Heathrow Airport in 2017

Did you know?
Every day, 1400 flights take off and land at Heathrow – one every 45 seconds and nearly half a million per year.

F Implications of Heathrow's third runway construction

Opening by	2026
Cost	US$24.8 billion
Road/rail links	US$7 billion
Length	3500 m
Airport total flights (2017)	480 000 per year
Extra flights	260 000 per year
Total with three runways	740 000 per year
Payback to UK economy	US$206.7 billion by 2075
New jobs	70 000

Maths skills

Using table **E**, work out how many passengers per week pass through Heathrow Airport on average. Work out the average number of flights per week.

A third runway would mean Heathrow could provide 740 000 flights a year. How much greater is this number compared with the 2017 total? Convert this figure to a percentage increase.

ACTIVITIES

1. Why has Heathrow been developed more than any other airport in the UK?
2. How is it possible to measure the importance of an airport?
3. With the help of map **A**, suggest why none of the proposed airports were built between 1972 and 2012.
4. Heathrow Terminal 5 was opened in 2008. Why do you think was it needed?
5. Outline the case for the development of the third runway at Heathrow.
6. What are the alternatives if the third runway is not built?
7. Who will lose out if the third runway is built?
8. Who will be the winners if the third runway is completed?
9. Using table **E**, name the most popular destinations of flights from Heathrow.

Stretch yourself

Find out more about the proposed airport development at Heathrow and the other alternatives that have been considered, e.g. increasing the length of one of the existing runways at Heathrow (costing US$19 billion), constructing a new runway at Gatwick (costing US$13.1 billion). Why are the various alternative schemes controversial? Why were the other proposed schemes rejected?

Practice question

Taking into account the arguments for and against development, should the third runway project at Heathrow go ahead? Justify your decision. *(9 marks)*

295

20.8 Developments in ICT

In these spreads you will find out how the development of ICT has led to many worldwide opportunities for development

Have you heard the phrase 'The world is shrinking'? It's often used to describe the way that technology such as satellites, the internet and high-speed travel have reduced the 'distance' between places. Everywhere seems closer together and more interconnected. Consider all the world brands on the high street – many of these can be seen in countries across the world. This increasing connectivity and interdependence in the world is what is meant by **globalisation**. It is partly the result of improvements in global transport, enabling greater interaction between people, and the rapid expansion of information technology, especially digital communication.

Information and communication technology (ICT) refers to ways that technology is used to manage and process information. It generally includes any device that stores, retrieves, transmits or receives information electronically in a digital form, such as personal computers, mobile phones and digital televisions. ICT encompasses all the ways that digital technology can be used to assist people and commercial businesses.

How things have changed

In the early 1990s:

- Online shopping was not available.
- Banking and other services were mainly carried out face to face at the bank in the high street.
- Email communication was in its infancy and very few people used it. Social media websites did not exist.
- Documents were often sent as a fax (or facsimile), where a document is converted into digital format, sent down a phone line and printed at its destination.
- There were very few mobile phones and these tended to be large and bulky (photo **A**). Less than 4 per cent of people in the USA owned a mobile phone. Some people used CB (citizen's band) radio to communicate over short distances.
- Computing was becoming more popular, both for businesses and for personal use (photo **B**). The internet was invented (1990) but it was costly to use – providers often charged by the minute.
- The first webcam was used and the first memory card was produced (1991).
- Most people listened to music on cassette tapes, although CDs became popular during the 1990s.

> **Did you know?**
> The first electronic computer weighed almost 28 tonnes.

A *Motorola released the DynaTAC 8000X in 1983 – the first commercial mobile phone. Costing US$3995, it offered 30 minutes of talk-time, six hours standby and could store 30 phone numbers*

B *The IBM 5160 is a version of the IBM PC with a built-in hard drive. Released on 8 March 1983. The 5100 series are known as one of the first home computers*

296

Communication

ICT has now transformed the ways that people live and work, communicate with each other and are educated:

- Almost all commercial businesses rely on an informative and interactive website to attract customers.
- Teleworking or telecommuting has increased flexibility for business and employees. This involves working remotely from home by using digital technology.
- Most devices now have inbuilt computer chips, ranging from bank and identity cards to mobile phones, thermostats, microwave ovens, supermarket scanners, hospital equipment, TV remote controls and digital cameras. Computer chips are so small they are barely visible.
- Many products have become smaller and lighter or more compact because of microcircuitry. The latest nanotechnology enables items such as smartphones, ultrabooks, smartwatches and smart wristbands to be created.
- Computer-aided design and computer-aided manufacturing programs, often called CAD/CAM, are used by architects and engineers to improve product and building design, especially where plans are very complex, such as large nuclear power plants and space stations.
- Computers have seen a huge increase in processing power. New methods of storage that increase data portability have been invented, such as flash memory.
- Advances in telecommunication allow data to be transferred instantly across the world or locally via wireless technologies.
- Traditionally separate products are being converged into one device, such as a phone, video, camera, address book, music player and internet connection.
- Powerful 'supercomputers' are used, for example, to model and forecast weather, predict climate change and predict the performance of new drugs.
- Computers are now able to manage vital worldwide industries such as food production and transport.
- Computers have become voice-activated and networked together using the internet. They also have digital senses such as speech, which means they can connect with people and other computers.

By 2017, roughly half the world's population (3.6 billion) had access to the internet and an estimated 4.77 billion people owned or had access to a mobile phone. However, vast areas of the world still have very limited access to digital technology, especially in rural parts of LICs.

Development of the internet

The **internet** is a worldwide system of computers connecting with each other anywhere in the world, whereby information such as graphics, voice messages, text, photos and video can be sent and received.

The World Wide Web consists of a collection of websites that can be accessed and searched through the internet. The original World Wide Web (known as Web 1.0) consisted of a number of websites that provided information. There was little opportunity to interact with the websites involved, so it was not possible to comment, leave messages or even log in to the sites.

Web 2.0 refers to the more recent generation of interactive websites. Many of the sites allow the user to upload images and text, make comments and provide feedback, chat and share information (e.g. Facebook), and create new content such as text and videos (e.g. YouTube).

Did you know?
Less than 10 per cent of the world's currency is physical money. The rest only exists on computers.

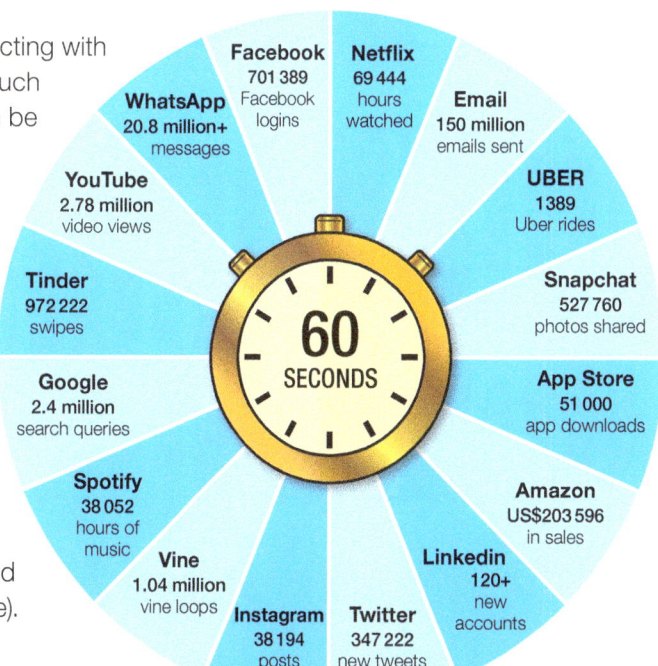

C What happens in an internet minute?

60 SECONDS

- Facebook 701 389 Facebook logins
- Netflix 69 444 hours watched
- Email 150 million emails sent
- UBER 1389 Uber rides
- Snapchat 527 760 photos shared
- App Store 51 000 app downloads
- Amazon US$203 596 in sales
- Linkedin 120+ new accounts
- Twitter 347 222 new tweets
- Instagram 38 194 posts
- Vine 1.04 million vine loops
- Spotify 38 052 hours of music
- Google 2.4 million search queries
- Tinder 972 222 swipes
- YouTube 2.78 million video views
- WhatsApp 20.8 million+ messages

297

Developments in ICT

Increasing access to the internet

World region	Population	Population (% of world)	Internet users (31 Dec 2017)	Penetration rate (% of population)	Growth, 2000–17 (%)
Africa	1 287 914 329	16.9	453 329 534	35.2	9 941
Asia	4 207 588 157	55.1	2 023 630 194	48.1	1 670
Europe	827 650 849	10.8	704 833 752	85.2	570
Latin America/Caribbean	652 047 996	8.5	437 001 277	67.0	2 318
Middle East	254 438 981	3.3	164 037 259	64.5	4 893
North America	363 844 662	4.8	345 660 847	95.0	219
Oceania/Australia	41 273 454	0.6	28 439 277	68.9	273
WORLD TOTAL	7 634 758 428	100.0	4 156 932 140	54.4	1 052

Source: www.internetworldstats.com.

D Internet use in different parts of the world, 2017

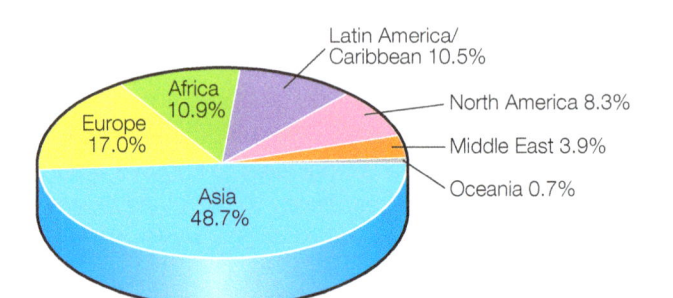

In many advanced economies, access to the internet is available to almost the entire population. It is used in education, business, culture and politics and is also an important means of social contact. However, usage is not the same in all areas of the world (graph **F**). Many poorer countries have limited access to digital technologies. For instance, some of the poorest countries in Africa such as Ethiopia, Sudan, Mali and Uganda all have internet access rates of less than 20 per cent. In general, the lowest access rates are in parts of southern Asia, such as Pakistan, and in Africa south of the Sahara. There is undoubtedly a strong positive link (correlation) between GNI per head and access to the internet (graph **G**).

Pie chart: Asia 48.7%, Europe 17.0%, Africa 10.9%, Latin America/Caribbean 10.5%, North America 8.3%, Middle East 3.9%, Oceania 0.7%

Source: www.internetworldstats.com.

E Internet users in the world by region, 2017

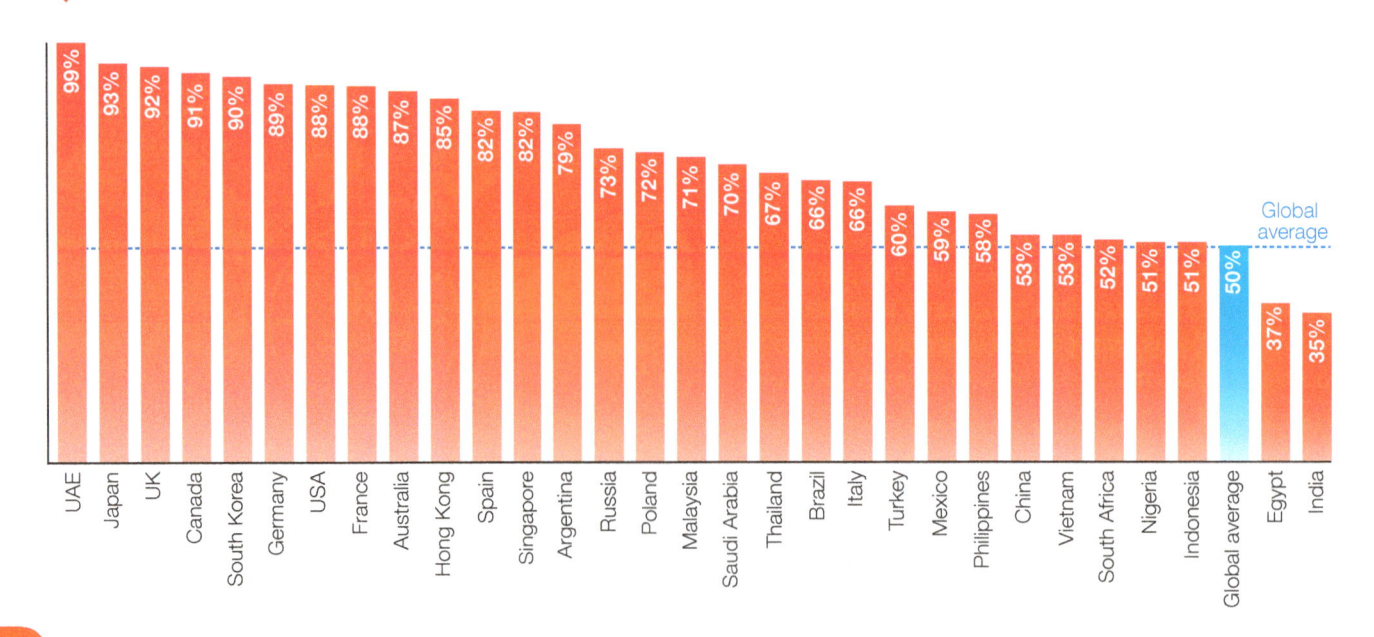

F Internet use by country, 2017

Country	%
UAE	99%
Japan	93%
UK	92%
Canada	91%
South Korea	90%
Germany	89%
USA	88%
France	88%
Australia	87%
Hong Kong	85%
Spain	82%
Singapore	82%
Argentina	79%
Russia	73%
Poland	72%
Malaysia	71%
Saudi Arabia	70%
Thailand	67%
Brazil	66%
Italy	66%
Turkey	60%
Mexico	59%
Philippines	58%
China	53%
Vietnam	53%
South Africa	52%
Nigeria	51%
Indonesia	51%
Global average	50%
Egypt	37%
India	35%

Communication

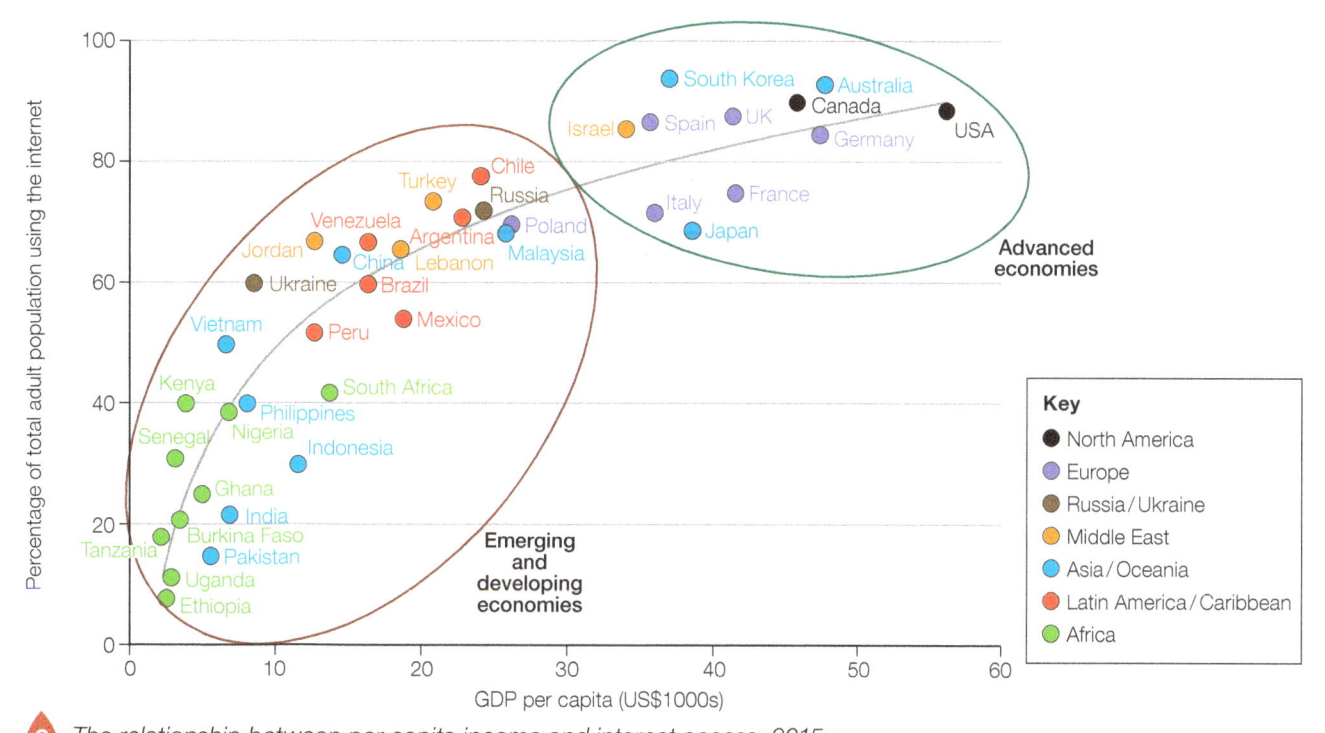

G The relationship between per capita income and internet access, 2015

Factors affecting access to the internet:

- Age: those under 35 are far more likely to use the internet or use a smartphone/tablet.
- Education: the higher the level of education, the greater the use of and access to the internet.
- Income levels: people with higher incomes generally tend to make greater use of the internet. Countries with low levels of wealth tend to have the least access to the internet.

ACTIVITIES

1. Explain the impact of the internet on the ways that organisations do business.
2. What are the reasons a company might prefer to be online instead of on the high street?
3. Explain how the internet has changed over the past 20 years.
4. Using diagram **C**, describe the different ways the internet is used.
5. Study table **D** and chart **E**.
    a   Which regions show the greatest growth in internet use between 2000 and 2017?
    b   Which two regions have the highest proportion of their populations using the internet (internet penetration rate)?
    c   Name the two regions with the lowest rates.
6. Study graph **G**.
    a   Compare internet use between Africa and South America.
    b   Name three countries where internet use is less than 20 per cent of population. What do these countries have in common?
    c   Name three countries where internet use is above 80 per cent and give reasons why the rates are so high in these countries.
7. Study graph **G**. Describe the link between GDP per capita and the percentage of adults using the internet.

Did you know?
The World Wide Web was invented by British computer scientist Sir Tim Berners-Lee in 1989.

Stretch yourself
Research the various ways that the use of ICT is essential to two specific industries.

Practice question
Describe and explain the global pattern of internet use. (6 marks)

299

20.9 Development of international phone links

On this spread you will learn about the development of international phone links

1876	The invention of the telephone by Alexander Graham Bell allowed people to communicate over longer distances.
1927	A telephone service from New York to London was established, transmitted by long wave radio waves. The cost of a telephone call was US$21 for three minutes.
1956	The first transatlantic telephone cable across the Atlantic was set up (TAT1), linking Oban in Scotland with Clarenville in Newfoundland, Canada.
1962	Telstar, the first broadband active communications satellite was sent into orbit on 10 July (photo **B**). Telephone calls could now be 'bounced' off a satellite.
1960s	International direct dialling, eliminating the need for operators, meant that international calls could be made across the world, creating a global network.
1973	Motorola introduced the world's first mobile phone – it weighed over 1.1 kg.
1988	The first transatlantic fibre optic cable (TAT-8) was laid, with 40 000 circuits.
2000	Over 1000 million mobile phones were in operation worldwide. Text and photos could also be exchanged using cellular technology.
2016	Approximately 63 per cent of the world's population had mobile phones. Free or inexpensive calls could now be made worldwide using Wi-Fi rather than a landline phone. Various apps became available across multiple platforms including Apple, Android and Windows phones.
2018	There are over 350 international fibre optic cables (used for linking the global internet and for telephone calls) connecting many parts of the world, covering a distance of over 500 000 km (map **C**).
2019	It is predicted that over 5 billion people will own mobile phones.

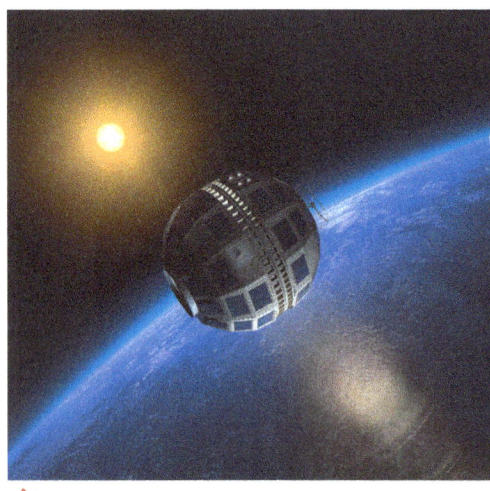

A Timeline of telephone communication

B Telstar 1, the world's first transatlantic broadcast satellite in Earth orbit, 1962

Ownership of smartphones extends to all parts of the globe, but the percentage of people with access to them is much greater in North America, Europe and the Middle East than in other areas such as sub-Saharan Africa, southern Asia and parts of Latin America.

C World undersea cable networks

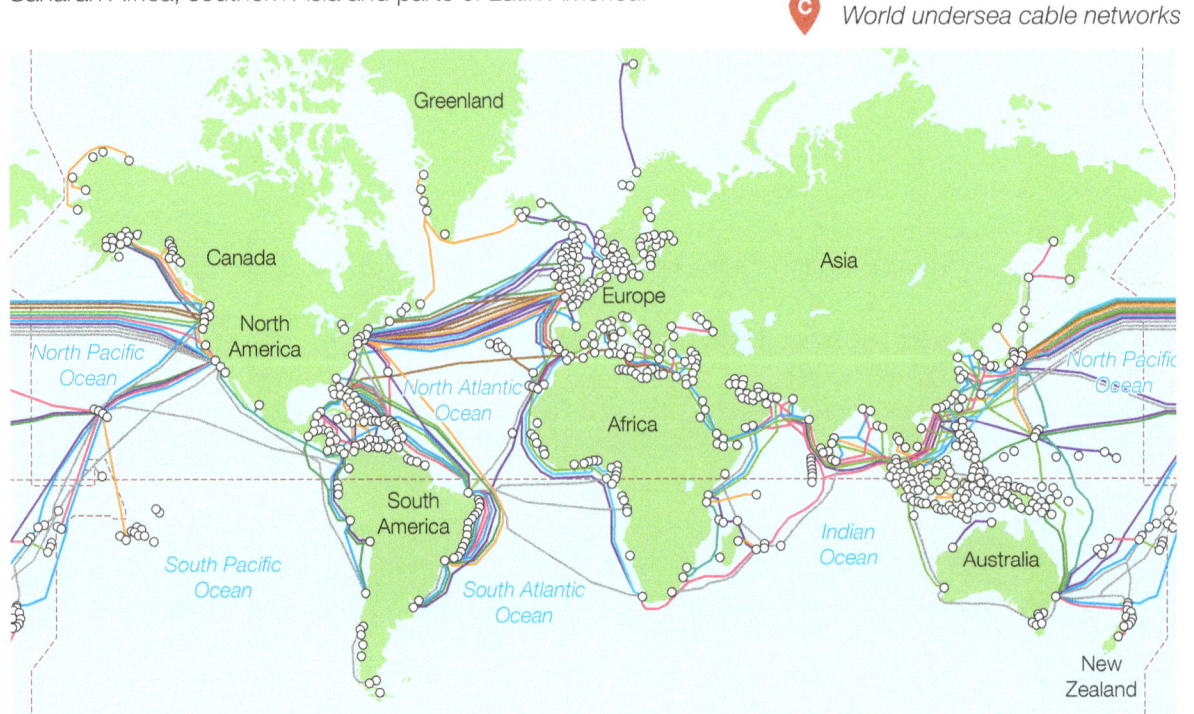

Source: Data from www.submarinecablemap.com.

Communication

Maths skills

Using map **D** calculate the percentage increase in mobile phone use for the various regions of the world. Which regions show the greatest percentage increase between 2013 and 2017?

D *Estimated users of mobile phones worldwide, 2013 and 2017*

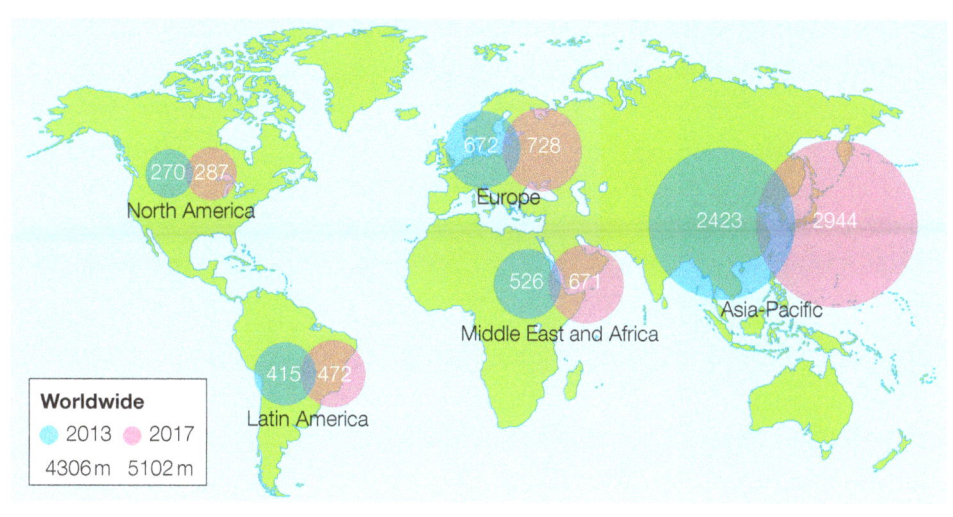

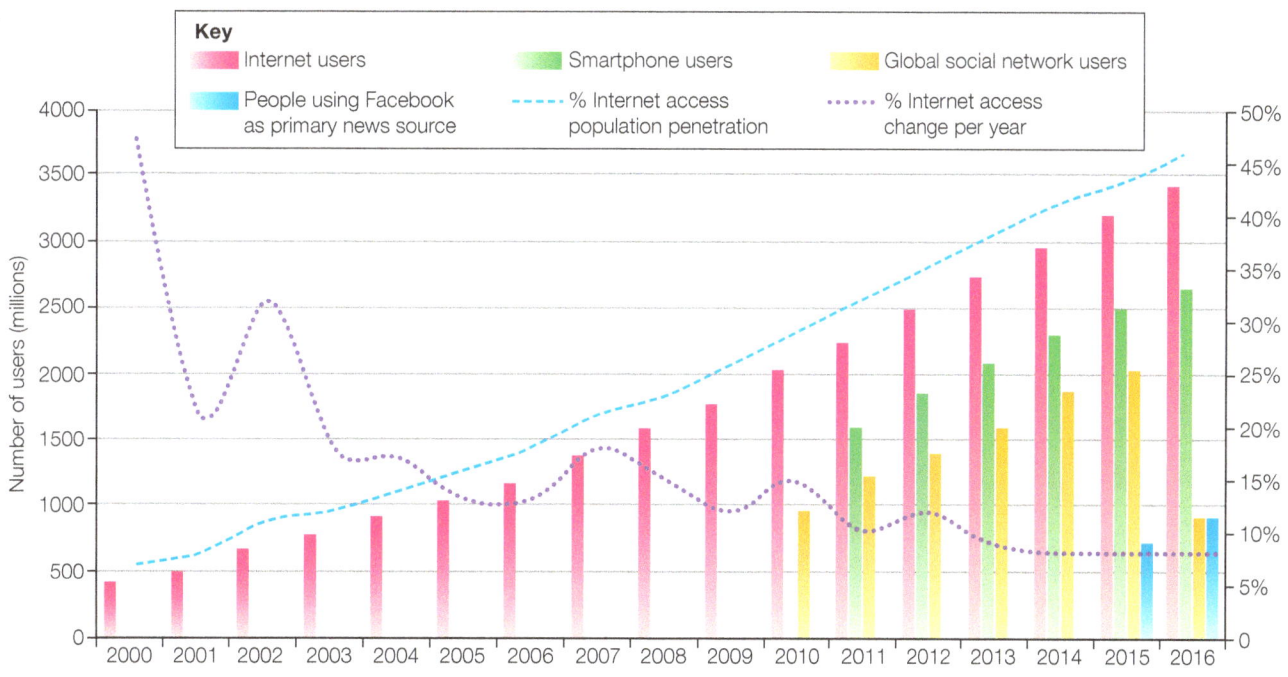

Map data:
- North America: 270 (2013), 287 (2017)
- Europe: 672 (2013), 728 (2017)
- Middle East and Africa: 526 (2013), 671 (2017)
- Asia-Pacific: 2423 (2013), 2944 (2017)
- Latin America: 415 (2013), 472 (2017)
- Worldwide: 4306 m (2013), 5102 m (2017)

E *Worldwide use of social media and smartphones, 2000–16*

Key:
- Internet users
- Smartphone users
- Global social network users
- People using Facebook as primary news source
- % Internet access population penetration
- % Internet access change per year

ACTIVITIES

1. Draw a timeline to show the key events affecting the growth of international phone communications.
2. Explain how making international telephone calls has changed in recent years.
3. Using graph **E**, describe the trends in worldwide use of social media and smartphones since 2010.

Practice question

Explain how access to cheap international phone calls encourages economic development. *(4 marks)*

Did you know?
The number of mobile phones in the world overtook the number of people in 2014.

Stretch yourself

Research the latest data on the use of smartphones in different countries around the world. What is the current rate of growth? Which companies dominate the smartphone industry? Which parts of the world now have the highest rates of increase? What effects does this rapid increase have on economic activity?

301

20.10 ICT and economic growth in NEEs: call centres

On these spreads you will find out about the role of ICT in call centres leading to economic growth in NEEs

Improvements in transport and communications have been largely responsible for the global spread of manufacturing and services. Graph **A** shows how transport and communication costs have fallen in relative terms since 1930. It is now much more economical to transport goods by sea and air and to communicate with places in different parts of the world. Improvements in communication and the growth of satellite technology are partially responsible. There are over 2500 satellites in orbit around the Earth. They are usually built for a specific reason, such as weather or communications satellites (photo **B**, 20.9). Consider how much the media depends on satellites for television (e.g. Sky) and for transmitting sports fixtures 'live' around the world.

A Worldwide transportation and communication costs, 1930–2000

Key
- Transatlantic phone call[1]
- Sea freight[2]
- Air transport[3]
- Satellite charges

1 Cost of three-minute telephone call from New York to London
2 Average ocean feight and port charges per short ton of import and export cargo
3 Average air transport revenue per passenger mile

Source: HM Treasury Transport Study, 2006.

Submarine cables

The development of submarine cables has been important in allowing worldwide communications to take place in the form of high-speed transmission of data and encouraging the development of manufacturing and services. The first transatlantic telegraph cable was completed in 1858. Later, new cables carried telephone communications, then data communications. Modern cables use optical fibre technology to carry digital data, which includes telephone, internet and private data traffic.

Cables can be broken naturally and by human activity, for instance by fishing boats, submarine tremors, sudden mudslides or movements of ocean sediment, and even accidentally by divers or by sharks biting through cables. In some instances they have been sabotaged for political reasons, particularly during the Cold War, or stolen by thieves or pirates to sell as scrap, for instance off the coast of Vietnam in 2007. The Japanese earthquake and tsunami in 2011 broke a series of submarine cables connecting Japan with south-east Asia and the USA. Increasingly, the cables are buried below the seafloor to minimise disturbance.

Distribution of undersea cables

Underwater cables link Europe with North America, south and east Asia, the Middle East and Australasia (map **C**, 20.9). There has been a recent growth in undersea cables across the Pacific, linking North and South America with the emerging economies of south and east Asia. Between 2000 and 2010, over 60 per cent of all undersea cables were across the Pacific Ocean

An increasing proportion of fibre optic undersea cables have been aimed at linking poorer developing economies with the rest of the world. New cables have been constructed to serve southern and east Africa, and the east coast of South America.

Antarctica is the only part of the world that is not served by undersea cables, so all digital communications are transmitted by satellite, which has a restricted capacity.

Communication

The development of call centres in India

A call centre is an office where people respond to telephone enquiries, often relating to banking, insurance, communications (e.g. internet, telephones) and the media. Supermarkets (e.g. ASDA and Tesco), financial institutions (e.g. Barclays, Lloyds TSB, HSBC, American Express, TD Canada Trust), technology (e.g. Microsoft, Cisco Systems, General Electric), motor companies (e.g. Ford), airlines (e.g. British Airways), and telephone companies (e.g. British Telecom) have all set up call centres in India. The larger cities are the main centres for call centre employment, including Bengaluru (formerly Bangalore), Mumbai, Kolkata and Delhi (map **B**). Around 2.8 million people work in call centres in India. However, other countries are competing strongly with India, including South Africa and the Philippines (which now has more call centre workers than India). Manilla, in the Philippines, has huge numbers of call centres dealing largely with customers of American and European companies (chart **C**).

A significant proportion of the population speak English, so are able to communicate effectively with customers in North America, Australia and the UK.

Approximately 80 per cent of people living in urban areas are literate. Almost 20 per cent have a university education.

Overall costs of running a call centre are up to 60 per cent lower in India than in the USA and Europe.

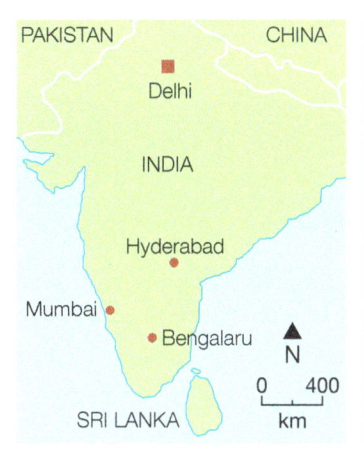

Average wages are up to 90 per cent lower in India than in the UK and USA.

There is little mobility of labour. Most employees remain at the company, working over nine hours per day, at times suited to the host country.

Digital communications including phone calls are fast and clear as a result of improvements in technology.

B *Telephone call centres in India*

Recently, some companies have reversed their decision to outsource work to call centres in India and other countries. Reasons include language, accent and cultural barriers, concerns about poor customer service, call centre employees lacking company knowledge, increasing costs and security issues. Some people argue that the industry does not benefit local people, as many employees are poorly paid, working over 60 hours per week in a highly pressurised environment, with little opportunity for career progression.

The call centre industry brings more investment to India and provides jobs to local people, boosting the country's economic growth by approximately 1 per cent of yearly GDP (US$11 billion). This helps generate more public funds that can be used to establish and create programmes to benefit the local population, including improved infrastructure and spending on transport and services.

| Philippines 26 | India 24 | North America 21 | Western Europe 12 | Latin America 10 | Eastern Europe and Middle East 7 |

Source: Everest Group Research.

C *Locations of call centre employees, 2014 (% of total)*

ICT and economic growth in NEEs: call centres

Case study

Bengaluru: the ICT capital of India

One example of ICT development in an NEE is the city of Bengaluru (formerly Bangalore) in India – a city with 10.8 million inhabitants (2017). The city is nicknamed the 'Silicon Valley of India' because it has become a major hub of communications technology in India.

- Over one third of India's ICT employees are based in Bengaluru. This represents around 900 000 professional jobs.
- The Indian government built a satellite Earth station for high-speed communications, enabling engineers in Bengaluru to communicate instantaneously with companies all over the world and transmit huge computer files within seconds.
- Bengaluru has become the location of 'offshore' head offices – many TNCs that are not Indian-owned have set up major offices there.
- Over 900 ICT companies are located in Bengaluru, concentrating particularly on research and development, software manufacture and many forms of digital communication.
- 'Electronic City', located in the southern part of Bengaluru, is a business park specialising in ICT. Hewlett Packard and Siemens, for example, are located there. There are several other similar business parks scattered across various suburbs of the city.
- Bengaluru is also a major centre for the aerospace industry, with almost two thirds of the country's business concentrated there. Large TNCs such as Boeing and Airbus have companies in Bengaluru, and Hindustan Aeronautics, which makes fighter jets for the Indian Air Force, is based there, employing almost 10 000 people.

D *Bengaluru's location in India*

- Bengaluru has become a centre for car companies, such as Volvo, which has built a car assembly works in the city.
- Apple Incorporated, the largest ICT company in the world, has a manufacturing base in Bengaluru. This is the only plant in Asia apart from China.
- The Indian Space Research Organisation (ISRO) is based in Bengaluru. ISRO has developed satellites and is at the forefront of India's Moon and Mars programme.
- Bengaluru is home to 100 of the 250 biotechnology companies based in India.
- The city is becoming a major financial centre with worldwide connections.
- Call centres in Bengaluru include Avis Cars and the US Government's social security scheme.
- The city boasts 21 engineering colleges.

E *Bagmane Tech Park in Bengaluru – the 'Silicon Valley of India'*

Did you know?
Bengaluru has the highest percentage of engineers in the world, with almost 1 million IT professionals making the city their home.

Communication

Advantages of Bengaluru

- Bengaluru is located almost 1000 m above sea level, which results in a cooler climate, attractive to foreign as well as local workers.
- Businesses that base their operations in Bengaluru can save up to two thirds of their costs compared with their host countries.
- Office space costs are very low compared to equivalent locations in HICs.
- Labour costs for computer programming are much lower than in the USA and Europe.
- Skilled workers in Bengaluru are highly educated and adaptable.
- Due to India's colonial past, most of the graduates can speak English, which suits TNCs in the UK and USA.

Current issues

The dramatic growth of Bengaluru has created a number of environmental problems including severe traffic congestion, with its associated environmental and economic costs. The transport system is stretched to capacity and struggling to cope with the enormous increase in demand. A new integrated transport network is planned, but will take several years to complete. Air pollution is caused by a combination of transport, industrial and domestic sources, and Bengaluru is currently one of India's most polluted cities.

	Population (millions)	Growth rate (%)
Bengaluru district	9.59	46.68
Chennai	4.70	7.65
Mumbai	12.40	4.2
Hyderabad	4.00	4.5
Delhi	16.80	20.96
Kolkata	4.50	−1.74

F Population growth rate in selected Indian cities, 2011

ACTIVITIES

1. Using graph **A**, describe changes in the cost of making a transatlantic phone call since 1930.
2. Explain why transportation and communication costs have fallen worldwide.
3. What are the purposes of:
   a. communications satellites
   b. submarine cables?
4. Using chart **C**, outline the distribution of call centre jobs globally.
5. Explain the recent reduction in call centre jobs in India.
6. Why is Bengaluru nicknamed the Silicon Valley of India?
7. Apart from ICT, which other industries have been established in Bengaluru?
8. Explain the advantages of Bengaluru for the development of ICT-related industries.
9. What problems have occurred as a result of the rapid expansion of Bengaluru as the ICT capital of India?
10. Explain how the development of IT has affected the growth and characteristics of the Bengaluru economy.

Did you know?
Apart from IT, Bengaluru is also the fashion capital of the east. It has as many fashion companies as Paris.

Stretch yourself

Investigate the call centre industry in the Philippines. What factors have been important in encouraging its development? Why has the Philippines overtaken India as the leading country for call centre jobs? What problems have occurred as a result of this development? Why are some TNCs reversing the outsourcing of call centre jobs?

Practice question

Suggest reasons why the call centre industry has become important in one named country you have studied. *(4 marks)*

20.11 ICT and economic growth in NEEs: TNC investment

On this spread you will find out about how investment by TNCs has contributed to economic growth in NEEs

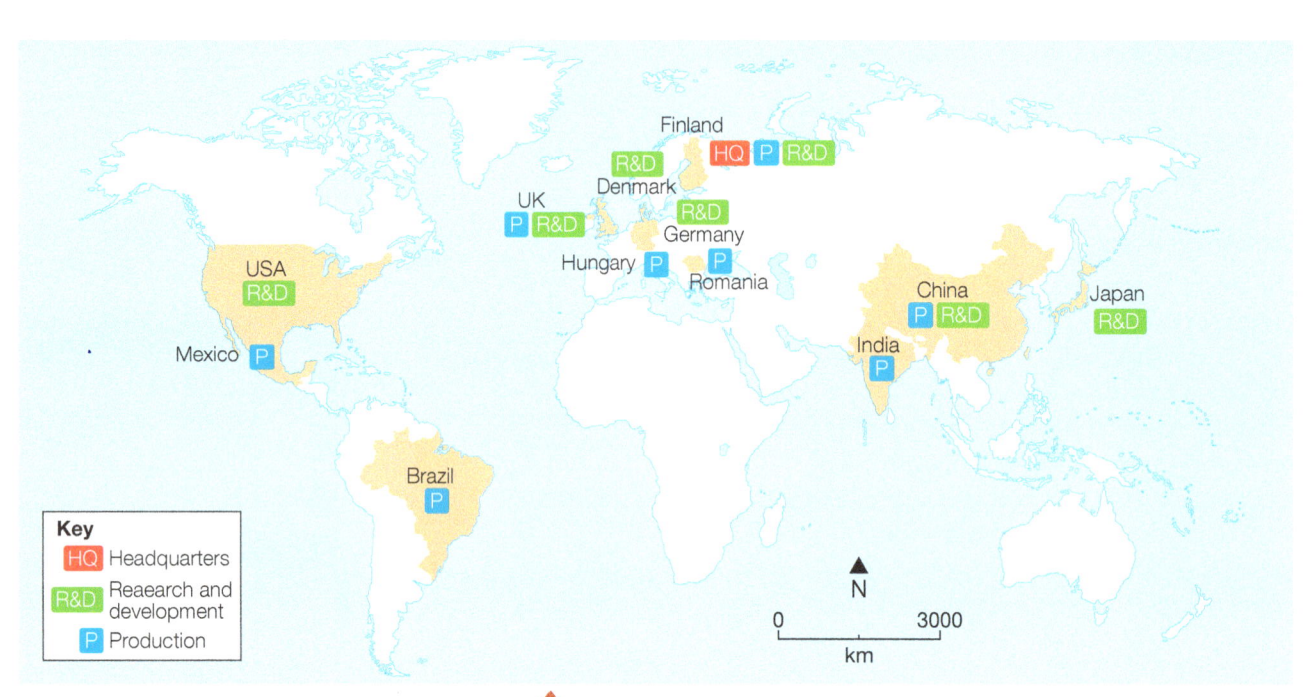

Key
- HQ Headquarters
- R&D Research and development
- P Production

A Worldwide operations of Nokia phone development and production

Investment by TNCs

TNCs are large, generally wealthy international companies. They are businesses that have their headquarters in one country, but often have other branches in several parts of the world. TNCs take many different forms and are based in different economic sectors. As a result of improvements in transport and communications, TNCs have grown steadily over the last 50 years.

Most TNCs have their headquarters in HICs, especially in the USA, UK, France, Germany and Japan, as well as their research and development centres. Production often occurs in poorer areas where labour costs are lower, laws are more lenient, taxes are low or where governments want to seek investment (map **A**). Production may also occur in some richer areas where benefits include a skilled workforce. In almost all cases the use of ICT is essential for the smooth operation of the company, whether it be sales, marketing, worldwide shipments of goods or payment for labour costs and goods sold.

Graphs **B** show that in 2006 the world's largest companies were linked to oil and other types of energy, and the financial sector. By 2016, the principal companies were predominantly concerned with ICT, including Apple, Microsoft and Facebook in the top 10 (photo **D**).

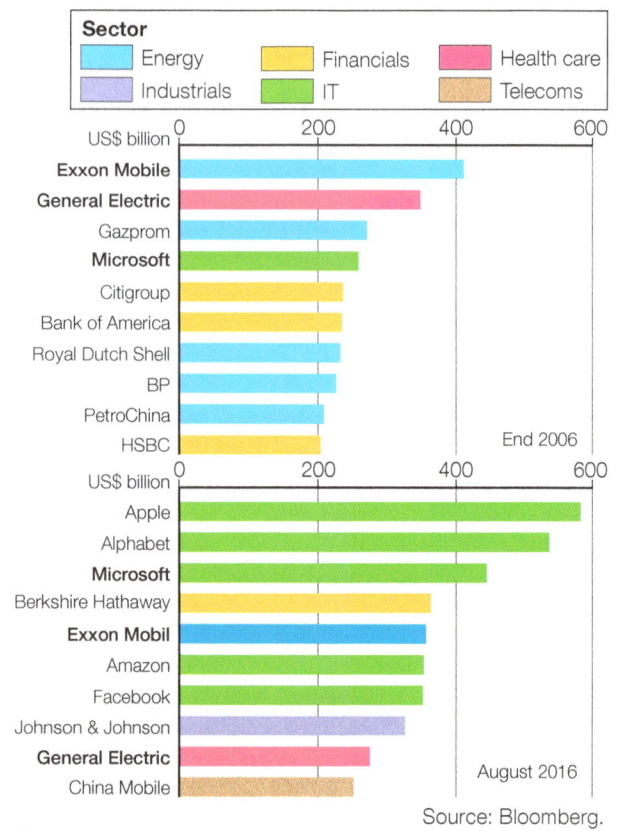

Sector: Energy, Industrials, Financials, IT, Health care, Telecoms

End 2006: Exxon Mobile, General Electric, Gazprom, Microsoft, Citigroup, Bank of America, Royal Dutch Shell, BP, PetroChina, HSBC

August 2016: Apple, Alphabet, Microsoft, Berkshire Hathaway, Exxon Mobil, Amazon, Facebook, Johnson & Johnson, General Electric, China Mobile

Source: Bloomberg.

B World's largest TNCs according to their value, 2006 and 2016

306

Advantages of TNCs

TNCs offer many advantages to the countries where they set up branches. They invest large sums of money in NEEs and LICs, and can help stimulate improvements in the standard of living, generating a multiplier effect and a larger degree of consumer choice. They provide jobs in factories making supplies and in services where products are sold. Training of the workforce leads to the development of skills, including those in ICT. Often, the infrastructure is improved as better access, both within and between countries, and communications are needed. TNC investment may help to diversify the economy, moving away from the reliance on one industry, such as farming or tourism.

They also invest in solutions to problems found in different parts of the world. Facebook has a project called Facebook Aquila, which provides internet access to people living in LICs and NEEs. Johnson & Johnson invested heavily in developing a vaccine for the Ebola disease. It provided training for nurses and other health employees in the control, management and prevention of the disease. This entailed face-to-face messages and extensive online communication.

Disadvantages of TNCs

A significant disadvantage is that of leakage, where the revenue earned by the company is sent back to the country of origin rather than being spent in the host country. In addition, in some locations wages are very low and key jobs go to outsiders. If there are problems worldwide economically or within the company, the branch plants may be closed. In some areas, working conditions can be poor and the labour force is expected to work long hours. Health and safety may be an issue and pollution may be a problem in countries where there are less strict rules and regulations. Large TNCs have been accused of engaging in tax-reduction strategies and have received much negative publicity.

Number of world's largest TNCs	Country
	Key: North America, Central and South America, Africa, Europe, Asia, Oceania
500+	USA
200–300	China, Japan
50–99	Canada
	UK, France, Switzerland
	India, South Korea
20–49	Brazil
	Germany, Ireland, Italy, Netherlands, Spain, Sweden
	Russia
	Australia
10–19	Mexico
	Denmark
	Malaysia, Saudi Arabia, Singapore, Thailand, Turkey, UAE
5–9	Chile, Colombia
	Austria, Belgium, Finland, Greece, Luxembourg, Norway, Poland, Portugal
	Indonesia, Israel
1–4	Argentina, Bolivia, Peru, Venezuela
	Egypt, Morocco, Nigeria, South Africa
	Czech Republic, Slovakia
	Lebanon, Syria, Jordan, Oman, Pakistan, Qatar, Vietnam

C Location of world's largest TNCs, 2017

D Value of technology companies such as Apple overtook other sectors in 2016

ICT and economic growth in NEEs: TNC investment

Nike: a TNC with worldwide operations

Nike is an American TNC that manufactures sports equipment and clothing, especially footwear. The company, started in 1964 and known as Blue Ribbon Sports, was renamed as Nike Inc. in 1971. The main headquarters is in Beaverton, Oregon, but the company employs almost 1 million people in over 740 factories around the world. There are almost 200 factories based in China, 35 in Thailand, and 65 in Vietnam. More than 75 per cent of the workforce work in factories in Asia (map **F**). Many sports stars are paid by Nike to advertise and promote its products, and the company has become highly successful, accounting for almost 40 per cent of the global market in sports shoes. Advances in transport and ICT have enabled the company to expand its worldwide operations.

Use of ICT by Nike

Marketing, sales, design, research and manufacturing all depend on the use of ICT. The company makes extensive use of social media, such as Facebook for each of its major products and Twitter feeds for various sports. Nike+ is a social media platform with 6 million members and the company has an active Instagram platform.

E *Nike key facts*

Value of Nike's sales in 2016	US$32.5 billion
Value of Nike's sales in 2015	US$30.6 billion
Value of Nike's sales in 1996	US$6.4 billion
Percentage share of world sports shoe production	38%
Average number of Nike shoes sold each year	122 million
Number of countries with a Nike office, factory or branch	46

F *Nike's worldwide operations – 1 million workers in 744 factories worldwide, 2014*

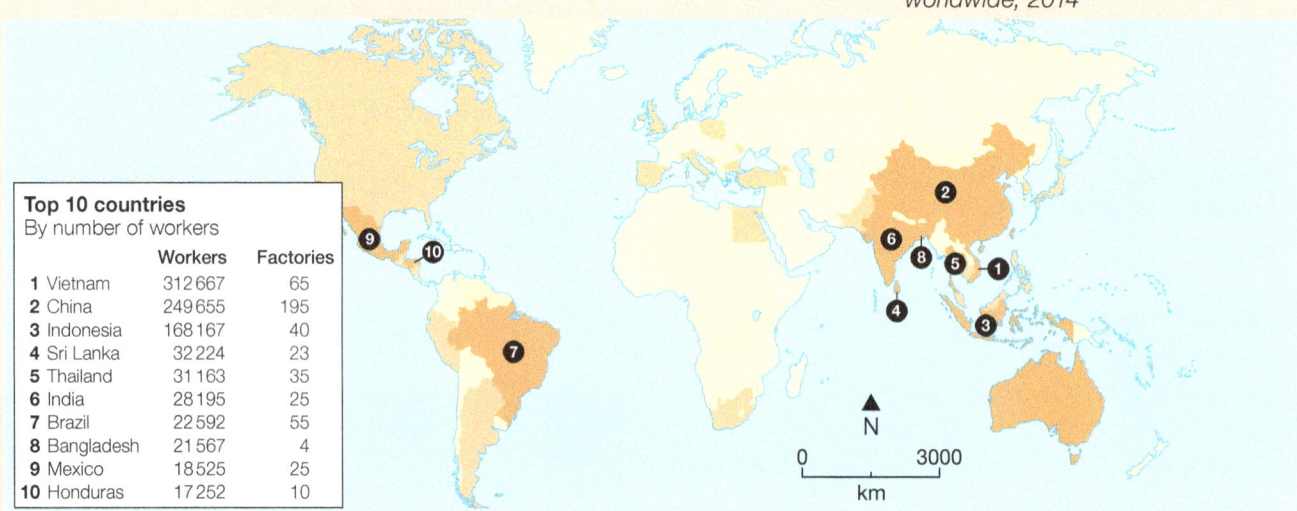

Top 10 countries By number of workers

		Workers	Factories
1	Vietnam	312 667	65
2	China	249 655	195
3	Indonesia	168 167	40
4	Sri Lanka	32 224	23
5	Thailand	31 163	35
6	India	28 195	25
7	Brazil	22 592	55
8	Bangladesh	21 567	4
9	Mexico	18 525	25
10	Honduras	17 252	10

Production

Nike outsources most of its work to independently run factories in order to manufacture its products. Often this takes place in NEEs or LICs, where labour costs are lower than in HICs.

The price paid by customer for a typical pair of sports shoes is US$100. This can be broken down as follows:

- The average price paid to the subcontractor is US$22 per item of footwear. This is subdivided into US$12 for materials used, US$3 for wages, US$4 for additional costs and US$3 for profit.

- Further costs to Nike involve design, research and development, marketing, retailing, advertising, transport, business costs, taxes and profit. This brings the price to US$50.

- Retailers then double the cost to US$100 (on average) to cover wages, insurance, advertising, supplies and services, depreciation, taxes and profit (diagram **G**).

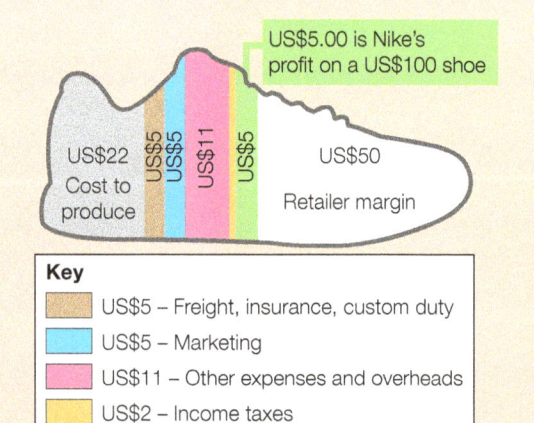

US$5.00 is Nike's profit on a US$100 shoe

US$22 Cost to produce | US$5 | US$5 | US$11 | US$5 | US$50 Retailer margin

Key
- US$5 – Freight, insurance, custom duty
- US$5 – Marketing
- US$11 – Other expenses and overheads
- US$2 – Income taxes
- US$5 – Net profit or income

Source: Solereview.

G *Costs breakdown of a US$100 Nike shoe*

Communication

Impacts of Nike operations on the host country

Advantages – economic benefits resulting from investment by Nike	Disadvantages – criticisms of the way Nike conducts its operations in poorer countries
◆ Substantial employment, especially in south and east Asia, which contains seven of the top 10 countries producing Nike goods (e.g. China, Indonesia and Vietnam) ◆ Outsourcing helps to develop the skills base of the local population. ◆ The slightly higher wages paid by Nike are used to buy consumer goods and contribute to the service sector. ◆ The sale of goods abroad helps the local and national economy and provides valuable foreign exchange. ◆ The company pays taxes, which may be spent by the government on improving services and infrastructure.	◆ Accusations of abuse and exploitation have been made and workers claim that they are forced to work long hours for low pay. It was suggested that some workers were below the legal age of employment in Cambodia and Pakistan. Nike has now signed an international agreement against using child labour and not making people work long hours. ◆ The company has also been accused of moving production at short notice to other countries when costs rise in the host country. For instance, Nike operations were shifted from South Korea to Indonesia as a result of increased labour costs. ◆ Some manufacturing has caused environmental issues, notably air and water pollution and pressures on water supply. Because regulations are lenient in some countries, Nike and other companies have not been prosecuted. The company's CO_2 emissions are over 1.3 million tonnes per year.

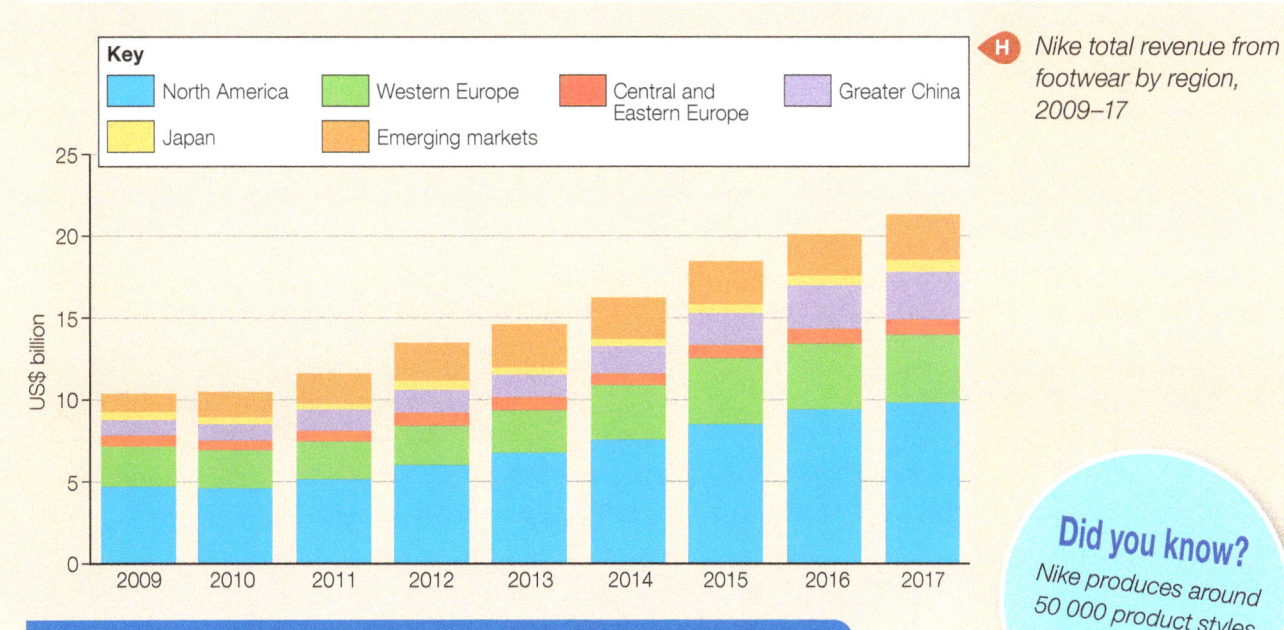

H *Nike total revenue from footwear by region, 2009–17*

Did you know?
Nike produces around 50 000 product styles a year and sells in 160 countries.

ACTIVITIES

1. Suggest why ICT may be important for the smooth operation of TNCs.
2. Explain how investment by TNCs can lead to economic growth in the host country.
3. Using graphs **B**, outline changes in the top 10 TNCs between 2006 and 2016.
4. Outline the main economic advantages and disadvantages of TNCs.
5. When was Nike founded? What does Nike make? Where is Nike HQ? What takes place there?
6. Which countries does Nike operate in? What factories are located in these countries?
7. What are the advantages and disadvantages for Nike of operating in these countries?
8. What are the advantages and disadvantages for the people and government of the host countries?

Stretch yourself

Investigate the global operations of a TNC (other than Nike). What is the role of ICT in the operations of this company?

Practice question

Assess the importance of ICT in the operations of one named TNC.
(6 marks)

20.12 ICT and economic growth in NEEs: trade and tourism

On this spread you will find out how the role of ICT in international trade and tourism contributes to economic growth

Case study

ICT and trade

International trade involves the export and import of goods and services between countries. Its economic importance has increased in recent times, mainly as a result of improvements in the speed and efficiency of transport and communications, greater interdependence between countries in different parts of the world, the growth and influence of TNCs, and the outsourcing of economic activity. Better access to modern ICT with high-speed internet and secured servers, and adoption of e-commerce stimulates trade flows between countries.

For the vast majority of companies, the use of the internet is essential for advertising, sales and marketing. It means that businesses of all sizes can compete effectively for market share. It also means that costs of staffing are reduced, as fewer employees are needed. Selling goods 24 hours a day becomes possible, and selling internationally is financially more secure, using online banking transactions.

NEEs in Asia, Africa and Latin America are now some of the fastest growing economies globally, such as the MINT countries: Mexico (economy growing at 4 per cent annually); Indonesia (5.9 per cent); Nigeria (5.8 per cent); and Turkey (4 per cent). In 2015, the top 10 fastest growing economies were all in Asia or Africa. Much of this growth can be attributed to the expansion of international trade.

Ghana: ICT and trade

Ghana's trade account recorded a surplus of US$646.1 million in 2017, representing 1.4 per cent of GDP, compared to a deficit of US$508 million over the same period in 2016. This surplus was the result of higher export receipts from gold, cocoa and oil along with lower imports (tables **B**).

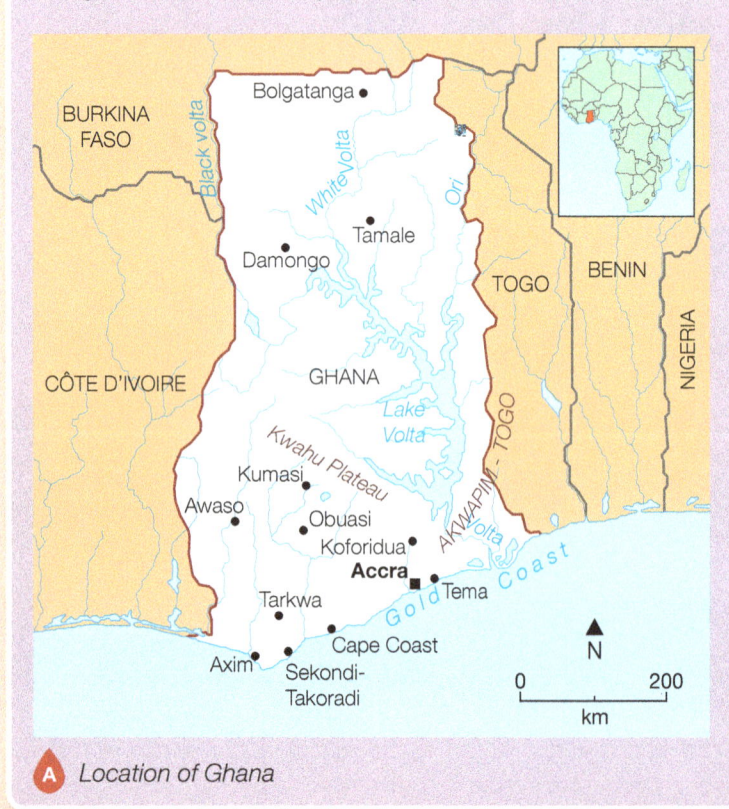

A Location of Ghana

Export	Value (US$ billions)
Gold	4.49
Cocoa beans	1.91
Coconuts, Brazil nuts, cashews	0.99
Crude petroleum	0.96
Sawn wood	0.37
TOTAL EXPORTS	**10.5**

Import	Value (US$ billions)
Cars	0.89
Delivery trucks	0.48
Cement	0.40
Rice	0.29
Frozen fish	0.26
TOTAL IMPORTS	**11.0**

B Some of Ghana's major imports and exports, 2016

The government of Ghana has repeatedly emphasised the need for more trade rather than aid, as the sustainable way to development. The implementation of ICT systems is helping to encourage easy movement of goods and services. ICT applications provide customs automation and supply information through shipping portals and e-business solutions.

Until recently, trading documents were processed manually, which wasted time, was inefficient and required a large number of workers. It involved many face-to-face contacts between business and customs officials, which made the spread of corruption easier.

The introduction of a single-window system, which is an ICT-based concept, provides traders with a one-stop shop for obtaining the necessary clearance and permits for imports and exports. There is also a portal for all trade-related information to aid traders. The implementation of a paperless system took place on 1 September 2017. A paperless environment requires less space, saves costs, aids documents handling and is eco-friendly. E-payment systems also reduce the risk of loss of government revenue.

For an NEE such as Ghana, ICT improves trade in several ways:

- ICT applications ensure that large amounts of information are processed in a quicker and more reliable way.
- Electronic information is available for reuse, eliminating repetitive tasks.
- Procedures are uniform for all traders and the availability of services is not limited to official working hours.
- Customs are able to process higher volumes of cargo efficiently and on time, which has benefits to importers, exporters, customs, government and the wider economy.
- Importers and exporters are served by a transparent and predictable system, avoiding unnecessary rules and formalities.

However, going digital comes with the risks of hacking. There is the need to ensure that the system is robust to prevent it from breaking down often and protect it from cyberattacks. For instance, the 2017 Petya cyberattack caused global outages to the computer systems of Maersk.

In 2017, Ghana's government launched its 'one district, one factory' programme, which focuses on the manufacturing industry rather than dependence on raw materials. In this way the economy should become more balanced. One of the aims of this programme is to improve international trading links by exporting processed goods. This industrial expansion means that efficient management of ports and rapid transfer of imports and exports will be crucial.

C *Export markets of Ghana, 2016*

Egypt 1.5%
France 1.3%
UK 1.5%
Niger 2.3%
Germany 3.8%
Italy 3.8%
USA 6.4%
India 14.1%
China 53.4%
Other 11.9%

D *Farm workers cracking cocoa pods in Ghana*

ICT and economic growth in NEEs: trade and tourism

ICT and the development of tourism

Tourism contributes approximately 10 per cent of global GDP and accounts for up to 9 per cent of employment worldwide.

Malaysia: transforming tourism with ICT

E Location of Malaysia

An example of a country where tourism has expanded rapidly in recent years is Malaysia, with over 27 million international visitors in 2017. The country has a rich diversity of tourist attractions, both physical and human. These are some of the most popular places to visit:

- Langkawi, an archipelago of 99 islands, has extensive beaches, a cable car ride, a tropical forest, an aquarium, coastal resorts and spa centres.
- The Cameron Highlands, provides opportunities for hiking and sightseeing.
- Perhentian Islands, renowned for nightlife and water sports, trekking and wildlife conservation.
- Taman Negara National Park rainforest, which includes animals such as the Malayan tiger and Indian elephant.
- The city of Kuala Lumpur, a mix of Malay, Chinese, India and European influences, has modern skyscrapers, shopping malls and markets. The Petronas Twin Towers building was the tallest in the world until 2004.
- Selangor, including the National Zoo of Malaysia, several large theme parks, an indoor snow park, shopping malls and a Formula One racetrack.
- Penang Island, including many beaches, fishing villages, rice fields and orchards. The city of George Town is a UNESCO world heritage site.
- Malacca Old Town's shops and museums.

F Kek Lok Si Temple on Penang Island, Malaysia

312

Communication

Over the past few years the industry has been transformed by the use of ICT:

- The booking of flights and other forms of travel on the internet, using secured credit and debit card payments. The internet has helped to reduce prices through competition, made information more widely available and allowed travellers to connect with sellers to make financial transactions.

- Booking of hotels and other accommodation through websites. This is often done directly with the hotel but can also be completed via independent websites.

G *Malaysia tourism revenues, 2008–16*

- Use of search engines to compare prices and make reservations for restaurants, trips, car hire, visits and entertainments.

- Information on websites relating to a range of tourist information, including currency, travel insurance, weather forecasts, places of interest, translation services and product advertisements. Some are sponsored by the government, but most are independently run websites.

- Online guides to historical and cultural sites, city tours and similar, which may be in the form of podcasts or audio guides.

- Provision of online videos, maps, photographs about tourist destinations.

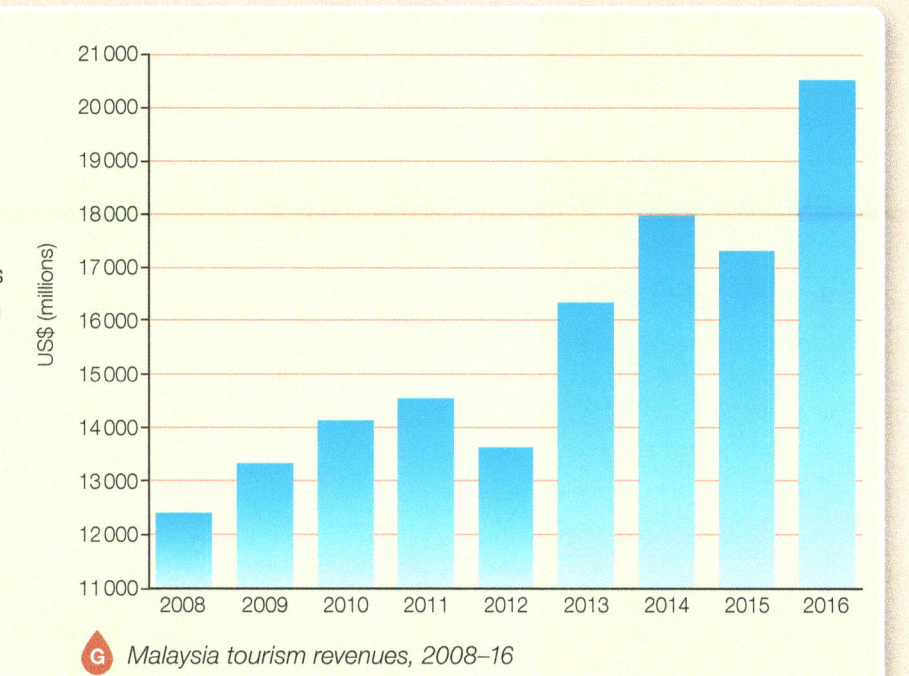

- The development of biometric passports.

- Application for visas and passports completed online.

- Social media reviews on hotels and places of interest, which provide information and up-to-date opinions. Some websites are interactive, allowing comments to be made by both the providers and consumers of tourism services.

- Real-time camera sites showing physical and human attractions, including current weather conditions.

ACTIVITIES

1. Explain how one country has used ICT to improve trade flows. What are the advantages and disadvantages of the new ICT-based system.
2. Draw graphs to show the main imports and exports into and from Ghana. What do you notice about the main types of import and export goods. How might this change in future?
3. Make a list of a ways that modern tourism relies on ICT.
4. Draw a map of Malaysia to show the main tourist attractions.
5. Explain how Malaysia makes use of ICT in its tourism industry. What are the advantages of using the internet to develop tourism?

Stretch yourself

Investigate how increased tourism has a multiplier effect on one named country's development. How do electronic communications affect this development?

Practice question

Using examples of one or more economic activity, evaluate the role of ICT in assisting economic growth. *(9 marks)*

21 Fieldwork

21.1 Investigating river processes and management

On this spread you'll find out how to prepare a fieldwork enquiry to investigate river processes and management

Enquiry questions

Rivers are popular places for people to live near and to enjoy. Photos **A** and **B** shows two contrasting river locations. Think about the kind of questions geographers might ask when they see places like this. For example, they might ask:

- What has happened here?
- How did it happen (short- and longer-term reasons)?
- What might happen to this place in future and why?

Many river (or fluvial) locations are good places for fieldwork since there are lots of questions like these to investigate. This is the starting point for any enquiry. An enquiry is a series of stages that start with a question (diagram **C**, stage 1) and end up with an answer or conclusion (stage 5). You will probably have completed an enquiry in geography (or science) before and have used fieldwork and practical work in the same way.

Each stage is equally important, right from the initial question, to the research and context, through to the overall evaluation. Only at the end can you have an opportunity to reflect on what you have found and what it means.

A *River flowing through rice terraces at Lao Chai village, Sa Pa, Vietnam*

B *Thu Bon river flooding Bach Dang St, Hoi An, Vietnam*

C *The route to enquiry – a planning 'pathway' for your investigation*

(1) Setting up a suitable enquiry question
(2) Selecting, measuring and recording primary and secondary data appropriate to the enquiry
(3) Selecting appropriate methods (e.g. graphs, charts, maps) of processing and presenting fieldwork data
(4) Describing, analysing and explaining fieldwork data
(5) Reaching conclusions and considering their significance
(6) Evaluating and reflecting on the enquiry

Fieldwork

Developing an enquiry question

A good enquiry depends upon having a good question. A good question must be directly linked to the overall theme – in this case, rivers! Consider the following question:

How do different drainage basin and river channel characteristics influence flood risk for people and property along the River Exe?

This question is too broad. It needs to be broken down into sub-questions that are simpler and more workable. For example:

1. What are the main characteristics of the river's channel in its upper course?
2. What places are most at risk from flooding along the River Exe?
3. What impacts does channel shape have on flood risk?
4. What impacts does valley shape and land use have on flood risk?

To complete the enquiry you must use primary data. You can use secondary data if you wish.

Primary data

Fieldwork data which you collect yourself (or as part of a group) are called 'primary' data – first-hand information that comes from you and people you have worked with. There are many different types of primary data and information. You can find out more about these on page 316.

Secondary data

Secondary data are information that another person, group or organisation has collected. Secondary data are very important in providing background information and a context for the enquiry. They help you to understand more about places and the kinds of questions that might be relevant. Past river flow data are one example of secondary data (see graphs **D**).

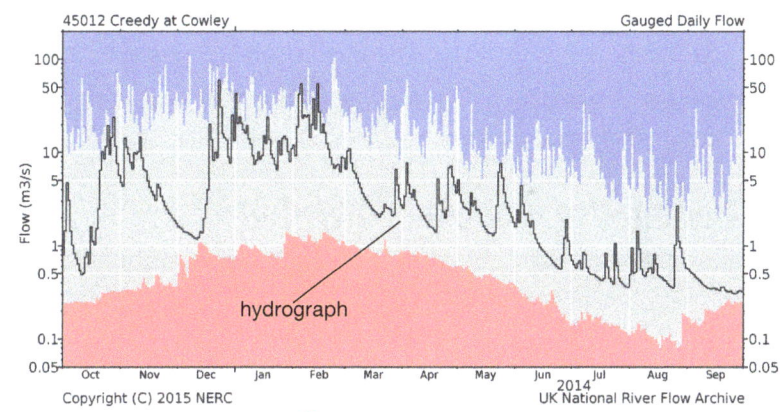

D *An annual hydrograph showing river data for the River Creedy, near Exeter, UK (2013) – this information helps you get a context for the enquiry*

ACTIVITIES

1. Make a copy of this table, which refers to the stages shown in diagram **C**. In pairs, complete the table using each stage.

Stage	Your chosen response
(1) An enquiry question we could investigate for either photo **A** or photo **B**.	
(2) Three methods we could use to collect primary data.	
(3) Two sources of secondary data we could use.	
(4) Three ways in which we could present and process our data.	

2. Explain how the data in graph **D** could help you in your enquiry.

Practice questions

1. Study a river on an OS map. Identify *one* question or aim that could be used to investigate physical processes in this river landscape. *(2 marks)*

2. For your own fieldwork enquiry, explain *two* reasons why particular aims or questions were developed. *(4 marks)*

21.2 Primary data collection in river fieldwork

On this spread, you'll find out about different techniques for collecting primary data in a rivers enquiry

Collecting primary data

The purpose of fieldwork is to collect your own data. The student in photo **A** is using a measuring instrument – a 'pebbleometer' – to find out the size of stones collected in a river. He is investigating river processes and wants to find out about stone size changes along the river.

Data are essential! They help you to understand what is happening in a drainage basin. You can also compare your river fieldwork to what textbooks tell you. It makes good teamwork.

It's very important to consider what data you need when you design your investigation. Any data collected should be as reliable and accurate as possible. In particular, you should think about:

A *Measuring pebble size from a river using a homemade pebbleometer*

- *Sample size* – How many measurements will you be taking, and why? More measurements – for example, measuring more stones – will generally produce more reliable data. But this is time-consuming and group collection of data can save time.
- *Survey locations / sites* – Where will you collect the data and how? Will you collect data along a line (called a *transect*) and how far apart will these locations be?
- *Accuracy* – How can you ensure that your data are accurate? Will you need to measure several samples of stones and calculate an average?

Quantitative and qualitative data

Most data you'll collect on a river investigation involves numbers. There are two types of data – quantitative and qualitative. Whatever data you collect must link directly to the enquiry question that you have set yourself (see page 315).

Quantitative data

River studies include a number of quantitative fieldwork techniques. Table **C** shows data that are commonly collected in river investigations. All quantitative techniques need equipment, like the metre stick shown in photo **B**.

Sample size needs careful consideration. Three types of sampling are used in collecting quantitative data:

- *Random* – where samples are chosen at random, for example every pebble has an equal chance of being selected.
- *Systematic* – means working to a system to collect data, for example every 50 cm across the river.
- *Stratified* – deliberately introducing bias to ensure a sample addresses the question. For example, deliberately selecting samples of different pebble sizes from a point in the river so that the whole range of pebble sizes is included within the sample.

B *Using a metre stick to measure the depth of a stream at intervals across its width*

Fieldwork

Data required	Equipment needed	Brief description and reasons for doing this
River gradient (in degrees)	Clinometer, tapes and ranging poles	The gradient is measured at sites along the river over length of 10 or 20 m. The gradient of a river can, for example, help us to understand more about the processes operating and the influence of geology.
River speed (velocity)	Flow meter or float	Measures how fast the river is flowing. This tells us about the amount of energy in a river and we can investigate whether it conforms to a model.
Pebble size in cm or mm	Ruler or pebbleometer / calliper (photo **A**)	Measures the length of the long axis of a sample of stones. This helps to link processes of river erosion with position within a river catchment.

C Examples of quantitative data used in river investigations

Qualitative data

Qualitative data include a number of techniques that don't involve numbers or counting. They are subjective and involve the judgment of the person collecting the data. Techniques for collecting qualitative data with rivers areas include:

- written site descriptions
- taking photographs
- recording videos
- field sketches (shown in photo **D**).

These techniques can be used to record the use of fieldwork equipment as well as capturing river landscapes and management. When taking a photo, always think carefully about the frame of your picture. Where necessary use an object such as a coin for scale if you are taking close-up pictures of things such as river sediment.

Think about it

What should you consider before taking a photograph to support your fieldwork enquiry?

D A good field sketch. Remember to use annotations to explain the geography of the landscape around you.

Practice questions

1. For your physical geography enquiry, explain two ways that you collected quantitative fieldwork data. *(4 marks)*
2. Explain one way in which you attempted to make your data collection reliable. *(2 marks)*

ACTIVITIES

1. Explain the differences between quantitative and qualitative data.
2. Using the headings in table **C**, complete a table for the four types of qualitative information.
3. In pairs, draw up a table of the advantages and disadvantages of quantitative and qualitative data.
4. Study a river on an OS map.
   a. Choose one location in which you could investigate river processes.
   b. Outline three quantitative techniques that you would use to collect data.
   c. For each technique, decide whether you would use random, stratified or systematic sampling to collect your data. Explain your reasons.

21.3 Processing and presenting river fieldwork

On this spread, you'll find out how to present your data using graphs, photos or maps

Pulling it all together

Managing and organising your data is very important. Make sure that you organise both your own and any group data that you have collected. A spreadsheet which you can complete and share is a good way of doing this.

You might find it helpful to note down how and why you selected your data, and how they link to the enquiry aim or focus.

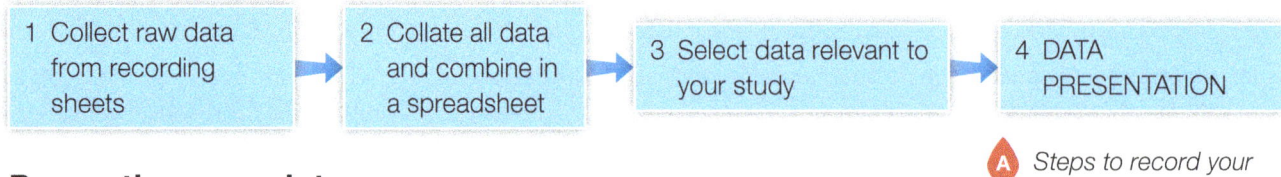

1. Collect raw data from recording sheets → 2. Collate all data and combine in a spreadsheet → 3. Select data relevant to your study → 4. DATA PRESENTATION

A *Steps to record your data*

Presenting your data

When considering how best to present your data, think more widely than just bar charts, histograms and pie charts. Table **B** shows a range of other ways to present your information.

Maps	GIS and photos	Tables	Graphs and charts
• Used to show locations and patterns. • Mini-graphs and charts can be located on maps. • This makes it easier to compare patterns at specific locations. • Consider using isolines or choropleth maps.	• Used to show historic maps or sites which have been lost to erosion. • Useful for aerial shots of rivers to show land use. • Helps to show how places have changed after being affected by storms.	• Can be used to present raw data that you and your group collected. • Useful to highlight patterns and trends. • Can be highlighted and annotated, and can help to identify anomalies (any data which look unusual).	• There is a wide range of graphs and charts available. (Hint: make sure you choose the right chart, e.g. do you know when to use a pie chart or bar chart?) • Can show data and patterns clearly – easier to read than a table of data.

Consider which presentation technique is most appropriate for the data. For example, are you dealing with *continuous data* or *categories*? Are you dealing with numbers or percentages? How can you present your data spatially?

B *A range of data presentation techniques*

◆ *Continuous data* show change along a line of study or over a period of time. River gradients, for example, are continuous, so are best presented using a line graph. An example is shown in graph **C**, which has been created with geographic information systems (GIS) (ArcGIS Online).

◆ *Categories* show classifications – for example, measuring pebble size or long axes and grouping them into sizes. A bar chart would be the best method for presenting this information. An example is shown in graph **D**.

◆ Where your *sample sizes* are different (e.g. 15 pebbles at one location, 17 at another), turn raw numbers into percentages of different sizes. Then you should use a bar chart.

◆ Instead of just presenting graphs, locate them on a map or aerial photo (e.g. using Google Maps or GIS, see map **E**). This makes change easy to spot, and turns simple data into a geographical display.

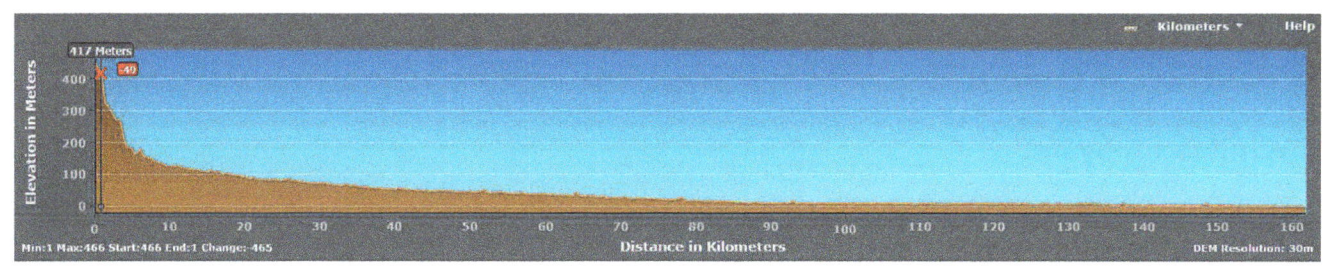

Fieldwork

C *A line graph showing a river valley long profile helps you to understand the drainage basin*

Think about it

What are the most appropriate techniques to present the data that you have collected?

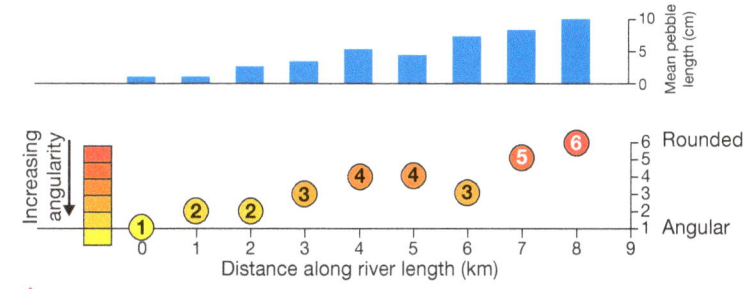

You will find other techniques to use in presenting your fieldwork data. For example:

- **annotated photographs** show evidence of river processes, e.g. erosion on the outer edge of a meander
- **field sketches** highlight the way in which people and property are vulnerable to river flooding.

GIS is another good way of presenting information since it allows you to overlay different types of data (as in map **E**) as well as begin to do some analysis of more complex data. GIS has a number of geo-processing tools that allow you to create specialised maps, as well as look for patterns and relationships.

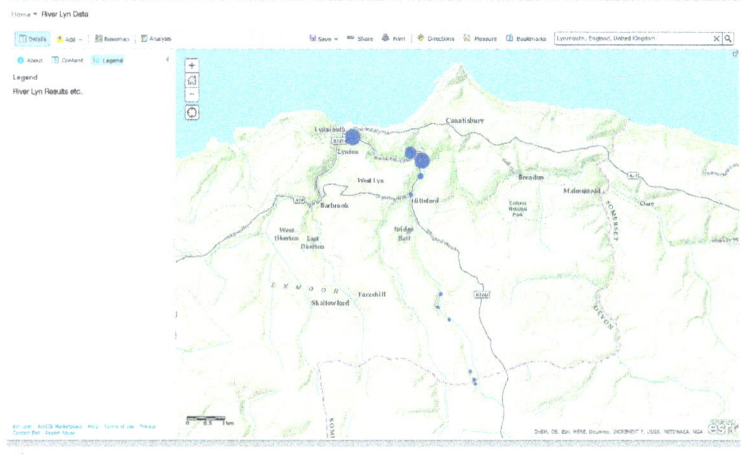

D *These river pebble data show pebble length (top graph) and shape (bottom graph). This is category data (where there are gaps between plot points). The data are plotted on two graphs, one above the other, to aid comparison.*

Practice questions

1. Explain *one* advantage of using a line graph to show the long profile of a river. *(2 marks)*
2. Describe *one* technique that you used to present your river sediment data. *(3 marks)*

E *The data are plotted on a simple base map to aid comparison between the different sites*

ACTIVITIES

1. In pairs, list some examples of when you should use the following: bar charts, pie charts, line graphs and histograms.
2. In pairs, research and identify *two* ways in which you could use GIS to:
   a. research river processes
   b. present fieldwork data collected along a river.
3. Study the data in graphs **C** and **D**. Explain the reasons why the methods used to present the data in each graph are **a** effective, and **b** the most mathematically accurate ways of showing the data.
4. Look at the data in graphs **C** and **D**.
   a. Identify any anomalies which do not seem to fit the general pattern.
   b. Explain possible reasons for these.

21.4 Analysis and conclusions – river enquiry

On this spread you'll find out about how to analyse and draw conclusions

What is analysis?

To analyse your data, you need to:

- identify patterns and trends in your results, and describe them
- make links between different sets of data – for example, how sediment size and roundness seem to change at the same time
- identify *anomalies* – unusual data which do not fit the general pattern of results
- explain reasons for patterns you are sure about – for example, data that might show a process operating along a river, such as deposition
- suggest possible reasons for patterns you are unsure about – for example, why results suddenly change in a way that you can't explain.

Cause and effect	Emphasis	Explaining	Suggesting
as a result of…	above all…	this shows…	could be caused by…
this results in…	mainly…	because…	this looks like…
triggering this…	mostly…	similarly…	points towards…
consequently…	most significantly…	therefore…	tentatively…
the effect of this is…	usually…	as a result of…	the evidence shows…

A *The language of analysis – these words and short phrases are useful to use in analysis*

Writing your analysis

When you write your analysis you should have a clear and logical format. Start with an introductory statement and then write about each point in more detail. Good analysis writing also:

- uses the correct geographical terminology
- uses the past tense
- is written in the third person
- avoids the use of 'I' or 'we'.

Table **A** has some useful phrases you can use, depending on your results.

Analysing data

You need to be able to use both quantitative and qualitative techniques when analysing your data.

Using quantitative techniques

Quantitative techniques are about handling numerical data from different sites, like those shown in table **B**. These can be analysed using statistical techniques – for example, you should be able to calculate the mean (the average of the values in the data).

Site A – upstream section	Site B – middle section	Site C – downstream section
95	24	10
68	19	12
48	16	64
49	15	32
90	29	34
82	18	55
86	6	37
56	10	18
80	19	19
49	20	19
69	13	12
42	9	8
68	15	63
57	18	62
70	19	15
59	21	9

B *River sediment data from three sites A, B and C, measuring the long axis in mm*

Fieldwork

You can also use a dispersion diagram to help you find the following values (see pages 352–3 for more about these values):

- *Median* – to find the median you need to order the data (like the dispersion diagram) and then find the middle value. This divides the data set into two halves.
- *Mode* – the number that appears most frequently in a data set.
- *Range* – the difference between the highest and lowest values.
- *Quartiles* – dividing a list of numbers into four equal groups – two above and two below the median.

Using qualitative techniques

Just like sketches, photos are far more than mere space-fillers. They are examples of qualitative techniques that provide vital clues and evidence about the fieldwork experience, as well as help with the analysis of information. Photo **C** is an example that could be analysed using annotations. Remember – annotations are good for explaining and can also be numbered to show a sequence. Field sketches can also be used to analyse processes as well as change over time.

Writing a good conclusion

A conclusion is almost the end point in your enquiry, with several important features. It is shorter than the analysis, because it is more focused. Remember the following points when writing your conclusion.

- Refer back to the main aim of your investigation (see page 315). What did you find out? Make sure you answer the question!
- State the most important data that support your conclusion – both primary and secondary.
- Is your hypothesis supported / substantiated by the data, or does it need to be modified in the light of your evidence?
- Comment on any anomalies and any unexpected results.
- Comment on the wider geographical significance of your study. Think about why it might be important, whether your results could be useful to others, or whether you think all rivers are like the one you have studied.

C *A section of river with many physical features*

Practice question

Explain *two* ways in which you analysed your physical geography data. *(6 marks)*

ACTIVITIES

1. Using table **B**, calculate the mean sediment size for each of the sites, A, B and C.
2. **a** Draw a dispersion diagram for sites B and C (see pages 352–3).
   b Use your dispersion diagrams for sites B and C to calculate the median, mode and range for each site.
   c Divide each diagram into quartiles. Calculate the mean of the upper quartile and of the lower quartile.
3. Which site has **a** the largest sediment overall, **b** the smallest sediment, and **c** the most variation in size?
4. Using the data in table **B**, explain the overall changes in sediment sizes from upstream to downstream.
5. Are there any anomalies in the river data across the three sites? What possible suggestions could there be for this?
6. Draw an annotated field sketch of photo **C**.

21.5 Evaluating your river enquiry

On this spread you'll find out how to evaluate, reflect and think critically about the different parts of the enquiry process

The importance of the evaluation

The evaluation is the last part of the enquiry process. It is much more than just a list of things that might have gone wrong. It is the part of the enquiry which aims to both evaluate and reflect on:

- the process of collecting data
- the overall quality of the results and conclusion.

Many approaches to fieldwork and research have limitations and errors which can affect the results. It is very important to remember that no study is perfect – even those carried out by university academics and professionals! It is sensible to highlight where you think the shortcomings of your work might be (figure **A**).

What might have affected your results?

Reliability is the extent to which your investigation has produced consistent results. In other words, if you were to repeat the enquiry, would you get the same results? Are your results valid – that is, did your enquiry produce an outcome that you can trust?

Several factors can influence the reliability, validity and therefore the overall quality of your enquiry, as shown in table **B**.

1. What part of my fieldwork design caused errors to be introduced?

2. How might the problems introduced affect the reliability and validity of outcomes?

3. How do my results help me reflect more about geographical knowledge gained?

A Some key questions to ask in an evaluation

Think about it
If I were to repeat my investigation, what would I do to ensure that I obtained more reliable results?

Sources of error	Impacts on quality
Sample size	Smaller sample sizes usually means lower quality data.
Frequency of sample	Fewer sites reduces frequency, which then reduces quality.
Type of sampling	Sampling approaches may create 'gaps' and introduce bias in the results.
Equipment used	The wrong / inaccurate equipment can affect overall quality by producing incorrect results.
Time of survey	Different times of the year will significantly influence the amount of water in the river and may not be representative – may create problems with measurement.
Location of survey	Big variations in river channel depth and width, as well as sediment characteristics, can occur in locations close to each other.
Quality of secondary data	Age and reliability of secondary data affect their overall quality.

B Possible sources of error in a geographical enquiry

Fieldwork

Being critical of your work

Being critical means thinking about any errors that may have affected the results of your enquiry. In a geographical enquiry, researchers generally try to produce the most reliable outcomes possible. They accept the limitations of their study. They may consider the following questions as part of their evaluation:

- How much do I trust the overall patterns and trends in my results?
- What is the chance that these outcomes could have been generated randomly (or by chance)?
- Which of my conclusions are the most reliable compared to other conclusions?
- Which part of my enquiry produced the most unreliable results?

Questions like these, although complex, can be useful when writing an evaluation.

How do your results affect your understanding of river processes?

Another important part of the evaluation process is to link any knowledge you gained from the enquiry back to a theoretical model or idea. It may be helpful to think about the key factors (photo **C**) and then try to develop your own model.

C *Factors that may influence river processes*

- Nature of river course – straight or meandering?
- Length of river course?
- Rock type and rock structure?
- Local settlements and changes of land use?
- Changes in gradient or slope profile?
- Local flood management?

> **Practice questions**
>
> 1 Explain *one* factor about your own primary data which could have affected your results. *(3 marks)*
>
> 2 Evaluate the reliability of your river fieldwork conclusions. *(8 marks)*

ACTIVITIES

1. Explain why an evaluation is the last part of the enquiry process.
2. Explain why an evaluation of one enquiry can be helpful in planning a second enquiry.
3. a In pairs, list the factors in table **B** in order of importance, based on your own fieldwork.
   b Explain your final rank order.
   c Add an extra column to table **B** with the title 'The main sources of error in our enquiry', and add points about your own fieldwork.
4. For your own rivers fieldwork, use photo **C** to add annotations to explain how these factors affect the river.

323

21.6 Investigating variations in urban quality of life

In this section you'll learn how to investigate differences in urban quality of life using fieldwork and research

Enquiry questions

Urban areas are popular for fieldwork as they are familiar and often close to us. Photos **A** and **B** show two very different urban locations. Think about the kind of questions geographers might ask when they see places like this. For example, they might ask:

- Which location offers a higher quality of life?
- Why are they so different?
- What might happen to each place in future, and why?

Many urban locations are good places for fieldwork since there are lots of questions like these to investigate. This is the starting point for any enquiry. An enquiry is a series of stages that start with a question (diagram **C**, stage 1) and end up with an answer or conclusion (stage 5). You will probably have completed an enquiry in geography (or science) before and have used fieldwork and practical work in the same way.

Each stage is equally important, right from the initial question, to the research and context, through to the overall evaluation. Only at the end can you have an opportunity to reflect on what you have found and what it means.

A *The Walk at Jumeirah Beach Residences in Dubai, UAE*

B *Low-income housing in Jakarta, Indonesia*

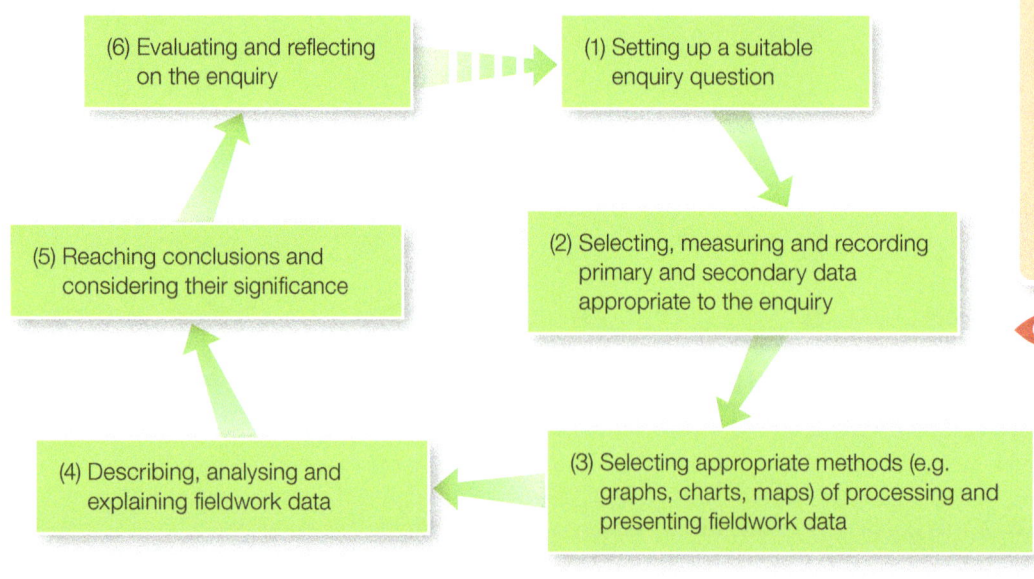

(1) Setting up a suitable enquiry question
(2) Selecting, measuring and recording primary and secondary data appropriate to the enquiry
(3) Selecting appropriate methods (e.g. graphs, charts, maps) of processing and presenting fieldwork data
(4) Describing, analysing and explaining fieldwork data
(5) Reaching conclusions and considering their significance
(6) Evaluating and reflecting on the enquiry

Enquiry means the process of investigation to find an answer to a question.

Fieldwork means work carried out in the outdoors.

C *The route to enquiry – a planning 'pathway' for your investigation*

Fieldwork

Developing an enquiry question

A good enquiry depends upon having a good question. A good question must be directly linked to the overall theme – in this case, urban environments! An example is:

How and why are there variations in quality of life for different census output areas within Leeds in the UK?

This question is too broad. It needs to be broken down into sub-questions that are simpler and more workable. For example:

1. What are the challenges facing some areas of Leeds?
2. What is the primary evidence of differences in quality of life between areas?
3. Does environmental quality affect urban quality of life?
4. What impacts have these differences had on communities?

To complete the enquiry you must use primary data. You can use secondary data if you wish.

Primary data

Fieldwork data which you collect yourself (or as part of a group) are called 'primary' data – first-hand information that comes from you and people you have worked with. There are many different types of primary data and information. You can find out more about these on page 326.

Secondary data

Secondary data are information that another person, group or organisation has collected. Secondary data are very important in providing background information and a context for the enquiry. They help you to understand more about places and the kinds of questions that might be relevant. The UK government's index of multiple deprivation (IMD) is one example of secondary data because it is compiled using census data (chart **D**).

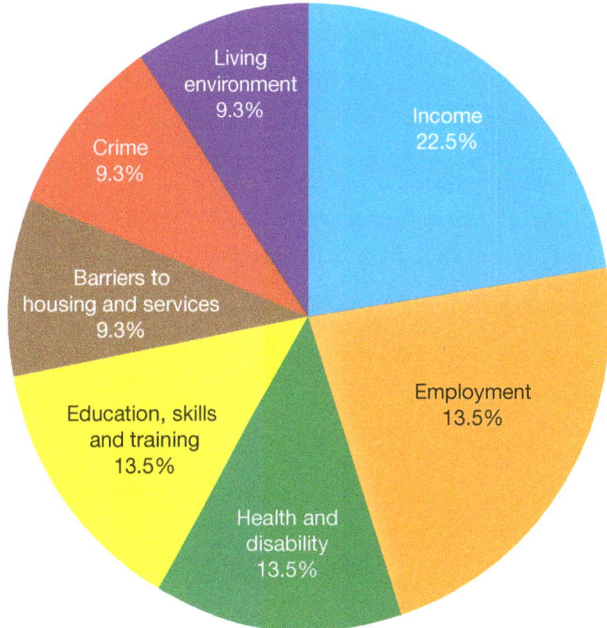

D *Different weightings given to the elements of the IMD. This information helps you get a context for the enquiry.*

- Income 22.5%
- Employment 13.5%
- Health and disability 13.5%
- Education, skills and training 13.5%
- Barriers to housing and services 9.3%
- Crime 9.3%
- Living environment 9.3%

ACTIVITIES

1. Make a copy of this table, which refers to the stages shown in diagram **C**. In pairs, complete the table using each stage.

Stage	Your chosen response
(1) An enquiry question we could investigate for either photo **A** or photo **B**	
(2) Three methods we could use to collect primary data	
(3) Two sources of secondary data we could use	
(4) Three ways in which we could present and process our data	

2. Explain how IMD data (chart **D**) could help you in your enquiry.
3. Design *three* enquiry questions that could be investigated in an urban area such as Bristol or Rio de Janeiro.

Practice questions

1. Identify *one* question or aim that could be used to investigate variations in quality of life. *(2 marks)*
2. For your chosen enquiry, give *two* reasons why particular aims or questions were developed. *(4 marks)*

325

21.7 Primary data collection for urban fieldwork

On this spread you'll find out about different techniques for collecting primary data in an urban enquiry

Enquiry design

The purpose of fieldwork is to collect your own data. The student in photo **A** is using a camera to record the buildings and architecture in a coastal town. She is investigating urban deprivation and wants to use photographic evidence to document the change between different parts of the town.

Data are essential! They help you to understand what is happening in an urban area. You can also compare your fieldwork in a town or city to what textbooks tell you. It makes good teamwork.

It's very important to consider what data you need when you design your investigation, so that any data collected are as reliable and accurate as possible. In particular you should think about:

- *Sample size* – How many measurements will you be taking, and why? More measurements – for example, more questionnaires – will generally get more reliable data. But doing so takes time. This is where group collection of data helps.

- *Survey locations / sites* – Where will you collect the data and how? Will you collect data along a line (called a *transect*) and how far apart will these locations be?

- *Accuracy* – How can you ensure that your data are accurate? Will you need to complete more questionnaires and calculate an average, median or mode?

A Using a camera to record the built environment

Data required	Equipment needed	Brief description and reasons for doing this
Environmental quality survey	Environmental quality survey (**C**)	Measures different characteristics of a place based on personal judgements, with a simple scoring system or using a bi-polar chart
Annotated photos and sketches	Camera or phone and paper for a sketch	Take photos or draw sketches and annotate them to identify features and characteristics that are pertinent to your study

B Examples of quantitative data used in urban investigations

Quantitative and qualitative data

There are two types of primary data – quantitative and qualitative. You could use both types in an urban enquiry. Whatever data you collect must link directly to the enquiry question that you have set yourself (page 325).

Quantitative data

Urban studies include a number of quantitative fieldwork techniques. Table **B** shows data that are commonly collected in urban investigations. Most quantitative techniques need equipment or recording sheets (example **C**).

Sample size needs careful consideration. Three types of sampling are used when collecting quantitative data:

- *Random* – where samples are chosen at random so that every person in a questionnaire survey has an equal chance of being selected.

- *Systematic* – means working to a system to collect data, for example, every 20 m or paces along a road to record land use.

- *Stratified* – deliberately introducing bias to ensure a sample addresses the question. For example, deliberately selecting samples of different people within the town or city so that the whole range of people is included in the sample.

Think about it

What should you consider before taking a photograph to support your fieldwork enquiry?

Fieldwork

Qualities being assessed	High +2	Good +1	Average 0	Fairly poor –1	Very poor –2	
Building design and quality						
1 Well designed / pleasing to the eye						Poorly designed / ugly
2 In good condition – e.g. paintwork, woodwork						In poor condition
3 Houses well maintained or improved						Poorly maintained / no improvement
4 Outside, gardens are kept tidy / in good condition						Outside gardens, or land / open space in poor condition
5 No vandalism, or any graffiti has been cleaned up						Extensive vandalism or graffiti in large amounts
Traffic noise and parking						
6 Roads have no traffic congestion						Streets badly congested with traffic
7 Parking is easy; garages or spaces provided						Parking is difficult; no parking provided / on the street
8 No road traffic, rail or aircraft noise						High noise volume from road, rail, and air traffic
9 No smell from traffic or other pollution						Obvious smell from traffic or other pollution

C *An example of an environmental quality survey that could be used in an urban area*

Qualitative techniques

Qualitative data include a number of techniques that don't involve numbers or counting. They are subjective and involve the judgment of the person collecting the data. Techniques for collecting qualitative data in urban areas include:

- written site descriptions
- taking photographs and videos
- field sketches
- interviews.

These techniques can be used to record use of fieldwork equipment as well as capture different aspects of the urban environment. Always think carefully about the frame of your photo. In urban areas, 360° panoramas work well to illustrate contrasts between areas.

Practice questions

1 For your chosen enquiry, explain *two* ways that you collected quantitative fieldwork data. *(4 marks)*
2 Explain *one* way in which you attempted to make your data collection reliable. *(2 marks)*

ACTIVITIES

1 Explain the differences between quantitative and qualitative data.
2 Using the headings in table **B**, complete a table for the four types of *qualitative* information.
3 In pairs, draw up a table of the advantages and disadvantages of quantitative and qualitative data.
4 Use a detailed map of your local area.
   a Choose one location in which you could investigate issues of urban deprivation.
   b Justify your choice of location.
   c Outline *three* quantitative techniques that you would use to collect data there.
   d For each technique decide whether you would use random, stratified or systematic sampling to collect your data. Explain your reasons.

21.8 Processing and presenting urban fieldwork data

On this spread, you'll find out how to present your data using graphs, photos or maps

Pulling it all together

Managing and organising your data is very important. Make sure that you organise both your own and any group data that you have collected. A spreadsheet which you can complete and share is a good way of doing this.

You might find it helpful to note down how and why you selected your individual and group data, and how they link to the enquiry aim or focus.

1 Collect raw data from recording sheets → 2 Collate all data and combine in a spreadsheet → 3 Select data relevant to your study → 4 DATA PRESENTATION

A *Steps to record your data*

Presenting your data

When considering how best to present your data, think more widely than just bar charts, histograms and pie charts. Table **B** shows a range of other ways to present your information.

Maps	GIS and photos	Tables	Graphs and charts
• Used to show locations and patterns • Mini-graphs and charts can be located on maps • This makes it easier to compare patterns at locations • Consider isolines or choropleth maps	• Used to show historic maps to show change in an urban area • Useful for aerial photos of the town / city to show land use • Helps to show deprivation and / or 'health' of a place	• Can be used to present raw data that you and your group collected • Useful to highlight patterns and trends • Can be highlighted and annotated, and can help to identify anomalies (any data which look unusual)	• There is a wide range of graphs and charts available (hint: make sure you choose the right chart, e.g. do you know when to use a pie chart or bar chart?) • Can show data and patterns clearly – easier to read than a table of data

Consider which presentation technique is most appropriate for the data. For example, are you dealing with *continuous data* or *categories*? Are you dealing with numbers or percentages? How can you present your data spatially?

B *A range of data presentation techniques*

- *Continuous data* show change along a line of study or over a period of time. Pedestrian flows might be continuous, for example, so are best presented using a line graph.

- *Categories* show classifications – for example, putting environmental quality scores into classified groups (shaded circles have been used on map **C**).

C *Locations in Ipswich, UK, on a GIS map where EQA (Environmental Quality Assessment) data have been displayed as circles. Circles are colour coded with a 'colour-ramp' (values are in the centre).*

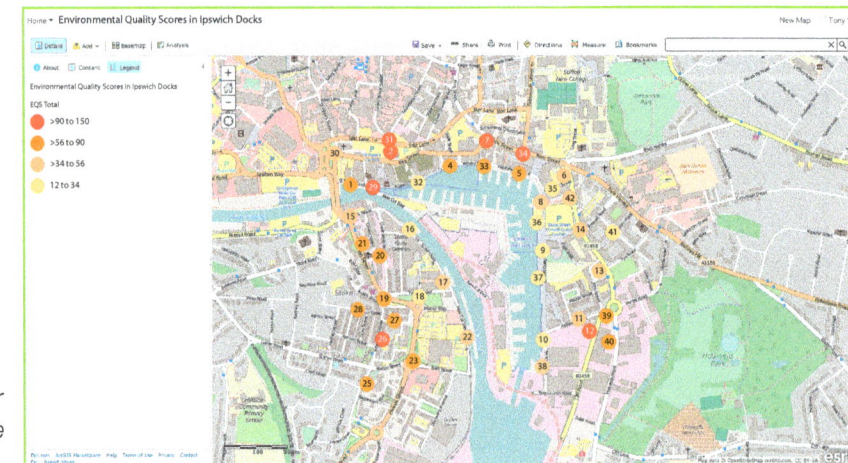

328

Fieldwork

- Where your *sample sizes* are different (e.g. 15 quality scores at one location, 17 at another), turn raw numbers into percentages of different sizes. Then you should use a pie chart.
- Instead of presenting graphs individually, locate them on a map or aerial photo (e.g. using Google Maps or geographical information systems (GIS) (map **C**)). This makes differences easy to spot, and turns simple data into a geographical display.

There are other techniques that you may find helpful in presenting your fieldwork data. For example:

- *annotated photographs* show evidence of dereliction and decay, possibly indicating a lower quality of life
- *field sketches* highlight the way in which people and property are influenced by areas of changing environmental quality.

We have already seen that GIS is another good way of presenting information since it allows comparisons (as on map **C**). It also allows more sophisticated presentation tools to be used, such as digital choropleth maps. GIS also has a number of geo-processing tools that allow you to create specialised maps, as well as look for patterns and relationships.

> **Respondent: 65-year-old retired person, discussing changes in their local town.**
>
> 'I have lived in Tiverton, Devon, all my life and there has been a lot of change. For a start, many of the smaller local shops have gone; the big supermarket near the river was to blame. I'm less mobile than I was and there are also fewer bus services so I need to reply on my car (but parking is free for a short period in the town). The town has been improved I think. It's better for people as they have stopped cars driving through the middle like they used to, plus I like the coffee shops where I can relax and they have outside seating. I don't like the fact that there are fewer banks and book shops but that's probably just an age thing. I don't really do internet shopping!'

D *A coding technique is useful for a variety of text-based data, whether primary or secondary information. Colour highlighting can be used to show positive (yellow) and negative (blue) comments. This example helps to analyse results from a questionnaire about attitudes to quality of life.*

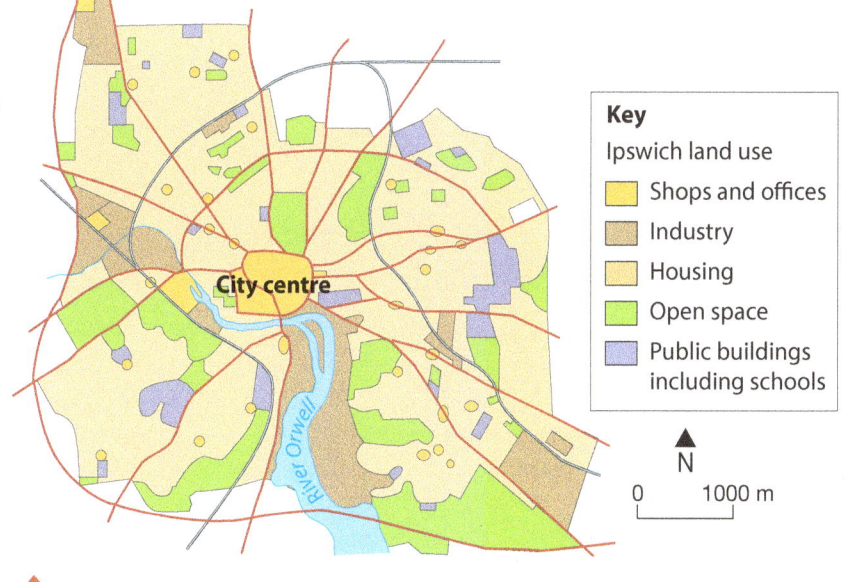

E *Land use maps are common presentation techniques for a variety of urban studies and can be linked to urban quality of life*

Practice question

Give reasons for the choice of data presentation techniques in your enquiry. (2 marks)

ACTIVITIES

1. In pairs, explain the differences between bar charts, pie charts, line graphs and histograms.
2. In pairs, research and identify *two* ways in which you could use GIS to **a** research urban quality of life, **b** present fieldwork data.
3. Choose *two* ways of presenting your urban fieldwork data. In pairs, make a table of the advantages and disadvantages of each of these methods.
4. Study collated data from your class fieldwork. Are there any anomalies or data which do not seem to fit the general pattern?

21.9 Analysis and conclusions – urban enquiry

On this spread you'll find out how to analyse and draw conclusions

What is analysis?

To analyse, you need to:

- identify patterns and trends in your results, and describe them
- make links between different sets of data – for example, how sediment size and roundness seem to change at the same time
- identify *anomalies* – unusual data which do not fit the general pattern of results
- explain reasons for patterns you are sure about – for example, data that might show a process operating in a town or city, such as spatial change in land use
- suggest possible reasons for patterns you are unsure about – for example, why results suddenly change in a way that you can't explain.

Writing your analysis

When you write your analysis you should have a clear and logical format. Start with an introductory statement and then write about each point in more detail. Good analysis writing also:

- uses the correct geographical terminology
- uses the past tense
- is written in the third person
- avoids the use of 'I' or 'we'.

Table **A** has some useful phrases you can use, depending on your results.

Analysing data

You need to be able to use both quantitative and qualitative techniques when analysing your data.

Using quantitative techniques

Quantitative techniques are about handling numerical data from different sites, like that shown in table **B**. These can be analysed using statistical techniques – for example, you should be able to calculate the *mean* (the average of the values in the data).

Cause and effect	Emphasis	Explaining	Suggesting
as a result of…	above all…	this shows…	could be caused by…
this results in…	mainly…	because…	this looks like…
triggering this…	mostly…	similarly…	points towards…
consequently…	most significantly…	therefore…	tentatively…
the effect of this is…	usually…	as a result of…	the evidence shows…

A The language of analysis – these words and shorts phrases are useful to use in analysis

Site A	Site B	Site C
95	24	10
68	19	12
48	16	64
49	15	32
90	29	34
82	18	55
86	6	37
56	10	18
80	19	19
49	20	19
69	13	12
42	9	8
68	15	63
57	18	62
70	19	15
59	21	9

B Totalled environmental quality scores (/100) for three different urban locations: A, B and C. A variety of different indicators have been measured in each location; higher scores indicate a better environmental quality.

Fieldwork

You can also use a dispersion diagram to help you find the following values (see pages 352–3 for more about these values):

- *Median* – to find the median you need to order the data (like the dispersion diagram) and then find the middle value. This divides the data set into two halves.
- *Mode* – the number that appears most frequently in a data set.
- *Range* – the difference between the highest and lowest values.
- *Quartiles* – dividing a list of numbers into four equal groups – two above and two below the median. You could use quintiles (five groups) as well.

Using qualitative techniques

Just like sketches, photos are far more than mere space-fillers. They are examples of qualitative techniques that provide vital clues and evidence about the fieldwork experience, as well as help with the analysis of information. Photo **C** is an example that could be analysed using annotations. Remember – annotations are good for explaining and can also be numbered to show a sequence. Field sketches can also be used to analyse processes as well as change over time.

C *Congestion in Wan Chai District, Hong Kong*

Writing a good conclusion

A conclusion is almost the end point in your enquiry, with several important features. It is shorter than the analysis, because it is more focused. Remember the following points when writing your conclusion.

- Refer back to the main aim of your investigation (see page 325). What did you find out? Make sure you answer the question!
- State the most important data that supports your conclusion – both primary and secondary.
- Comment on any anomalies and any unexpected results.
- Comment on the wider geographical significance of your study. Think about why it might be important, whether your results could be useful to others, or whether you think all urban locations are like the one you have studied.

Practice question

Explain *two* ways in which you analysed your fieldwork data. *(6 marks)*

ACTIVITIES

1. Draw an annotated field sketch of photo **C**.
2. Use table **B** to calculate the mean environmental quality survey (EQS) scores for each of the locations, A, B and C.
3. **a** Draw a dispersion diagram for sites B and C.
   b Use the diagrams to calculate the mean, median, mode and range for each site.
   c Divide each diagram into quartiles. Calculate the mean of the upper quartile and of the lower quartile.
4. Which site has **a** the highest overall EQS score, **b** the smallest EQS score, and **c** the most variation?
5. Using the data in table **B**, suggest possible reasons for the variations in EQS between locations.
6. Are there any anomalies in the EQS data between the three locations? What possible explanations could there be for this?

21.10 Evaluating your urban enquiry

On this spread you'll find out how to evaluate, reflect and think critically about the different parts of the enquiry process

The importance of the evaluation

The evaluation is the last part of the enquiry process. It is much more than just a list of things that might have gone wrong. It is the part of the enquiry which aims to both evaluate and reflect on:

- the process of collecting data
- the overall quality of the results and conclusion.

Many approaches to fieldwork and research have limitations and errors which can affect the results. It is very important to remember that no study is perfect – even those carried out by university academics and professionals! It is sensible to highlight where you think the shortcomings of your work might be (figure **A**).

What might have affected your results?

Reliability is the extent to which your investigation has produced consistent results. In other words, if you were to repeat the enquiry, would you get the same results? Are your results valid – that is, did your enquiry produce an outcome that you can trust?

Several factors can influence the reliability, validity and therefore the overall quality of your enquiry, as shown in table **B**.

1. What part of my fieldwork design caused errors to be introduced?

2. How might the problems introduced affect the reliability and validity of outcomes?

3. How do my results help me reflect more about geographical knowledge gained?

A *Some key questions to ask in an evaluation*

Think about it
If I were to repeat my investigation, what would I do to ensure that I obtained more reliable results?

Sources of error	Impacts on quality
Sample size	Smaller sample sizes usually means lower quality data.
Frequency of sample	Fewer sites reduces frequency, which then reduces quality.
Type of sampling	Sampling approaches may create 'gaps' and introduce bias in the results.
Equipment used	The wrong / inaccurate equipment can affect overall quality by producing incorrect results.
Time of survey	Different days or times of day might influence perceptions and pedestrian flows, for example.
Location of survey	Big variations in environmental quality can occur between places very close to each other.
Quality of secondary data	Age and reliability of secondary data affect their overall quality.

B *Possible sources of error in a geographical enquiry*

Fieldwork

Being critical of your work

Being critical means thinking about any errors that may have affected the results of your enquiry. In a geographical enquiry researchers generally try to produce the most reliable outcomes possible. They accept the limitations of their study. They may consider the following questions as part of their evaluation:

- How much do I trust the overall patterns and trends in my results?
- What is the chance that these outcomes could have been generated randomly (or by chance)?
- Which of my conclusions are the most reliable compared to other conclusions?
- Which part of my enquiry produced the most unreliable results?

Questions like these, although complex, can be useful when writing an evaluation.

How do your results affect your understanding of urban deprivation?

Another important part of the evaluation process is to link any knowledge you gained from the enquiry back to a theoretical model or idea. It may be helpful to think about the key factors (photo **C**) and then try to develop your own model.

C *Factors that may influence urban deprivation and quality of life*

Home ownership?
Overcrowding?
Availability of green spaces?
Access to services (e.g. electricity, water, sanitation)?
Hazards (e.g. fire, trains)?
Social conflict/cohesion?
Availability of employment?

Practice questions

1. Explain *one* factor about your own primary data which could have affected your results. *(3 marks)*
2. Evaluate the reliability of your fieldwork conclusions. *(8 marks)*

ACTIVITIES

1. Explain why an evaluation is the last part of the enquiry process.
2. Explain why an evaluation of one enquiry can be helpful in planning a second enquiry.
3. a In pairs, list in order of importance the factors that may be possible sources of error in your own fieldwork.
   b Explain your final rank order.
   c Create a table similar to table **B** with the title 'The main sources of error in our enquiry', and add points about your own fieldwork.
4. For your own fieldwork, use photo **C** to add annotations to explain how these factors influence quality of life.

333

22 Geographical skills

22.1 Cartographic skills

In this unit you will find out how to use and interpret the information on different kinds of maps and photos

Atlas maps

Latitude and longitude

Any place on the Earth's surface can be located by its latitude and longitude (map **A**).

- *Lines of latitude* run *parallel* to the Equator. This divides the world into the northern and southern hemispheres. Latitude increases north and south of the Equator to reach 90° at the north and south poles.

- *Lines of longitude* run between the north and south poles. The prime meridian, 0° longitude, passes through Greenwich in London. Values are given east and west of this line.

Remember!
Both latitude and longitude are measured in degrees (using the symbol °). Each degree is subdivided into 60 minutes (using the symbol '). So, '30 minutes' (30') equates to half a degree.

The location of a place is expressed as follows:

Manchester: 53° 30' N 2° 15' W

On map **A**, Mumbai is located at 18° 56' N 72° 51' E

Using atlas maps

Atlas maps are useful sources of information for geographers.

- Basic maps of countries and regions of the world show physical relief, settlements and political information.

- Thematic maps show factors such as climate, vegetation, population, tourism and tectonics.

- Maps can show global issues such as pollution, global warming, desertification and poverty.

- Atlases also include tables of statistics and useful data.

Different thematic maps can be used to find links between patterns, such as those between physical and human factors.

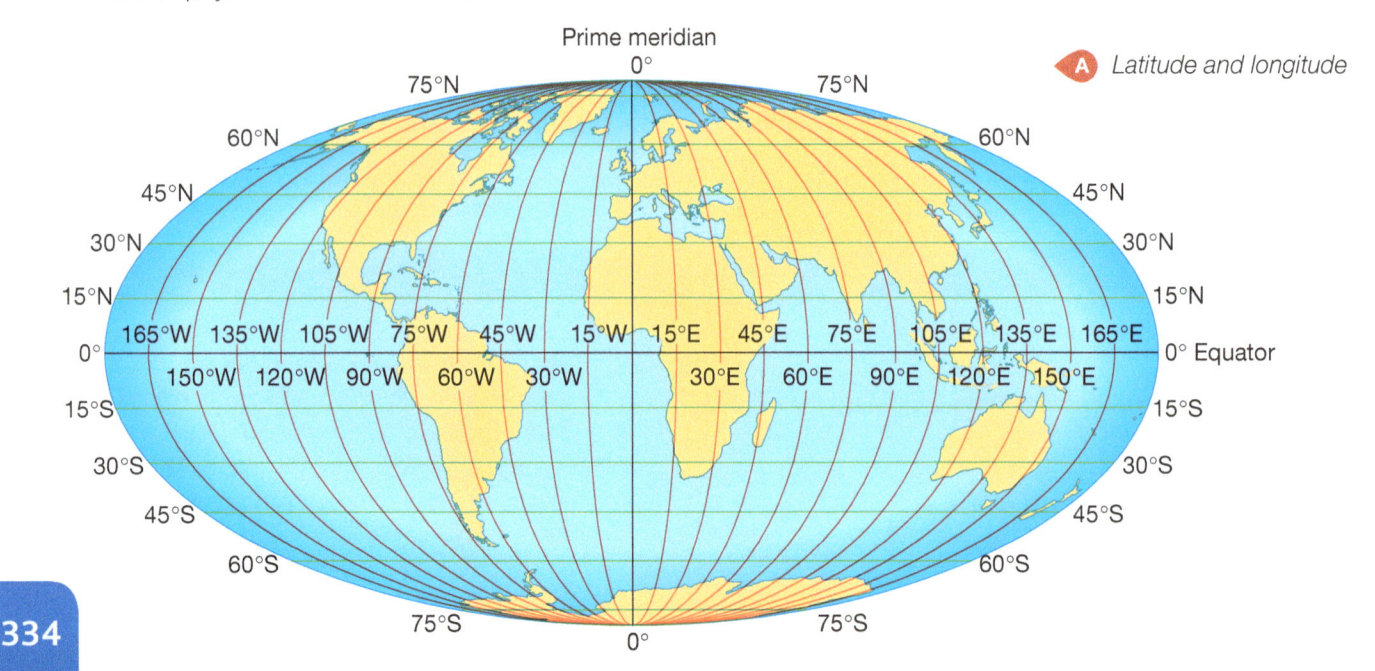

A *Latitude and longitude*

Geographical skills

You will make use of a range of atlas resources while studying Geography and you may be asked about an atlas map in your exam. You may be asked to identify patterns or distribution on maps, so make sure you practise these skills.

- A *pattern* means there is some regularity or connection between things, for example population concentrated along the coast or industry concentrated along a river valley. Terms such as *radial* (spreading outwards from a central point) or *linear* can be used to describe a pattern. For example, earthquakes tend to form a linear pattern in the North Atlantic by following the North American–Eurasian plate margin.

- *Distribution* is a term used more broadly to describe where things are. There may or may not be a regular pattern. For example, the distribution of population in Kenya shows that most people live in the highlands where the climate is less extreme and soils are good for farming. Fewer people live on the lower ground in eastern Kenya because it is very hot and dry.

Atlas maps include a range of physical and human features such as:

- population distribution
- population movements
- transport networks
- settlement layout
- relief
- drainage.

Practise identifying and describing these features on an atlas map. You may be asked to make use of two different maps to consider links and inter-relationships between physical and human factors, for example between population distribution and relief in Kenya.

Ordnance Survey maps

You need to be confident using Ordnance Survey (OS) maps at a range of different scales, including 1:50 000 and 1:25 000. You should be able to identify and describe both physical and human features and to use key mapwork skills.

Four-figure and six-figure grid references

OS maps have numbered gridlines drawn on them. The lines that run up and down and increase in value from left to right (west to east) are called *eastings*. Those that run across the map, and increase in value from bottom to top (south to north), are called *northings* (diagram **B**).

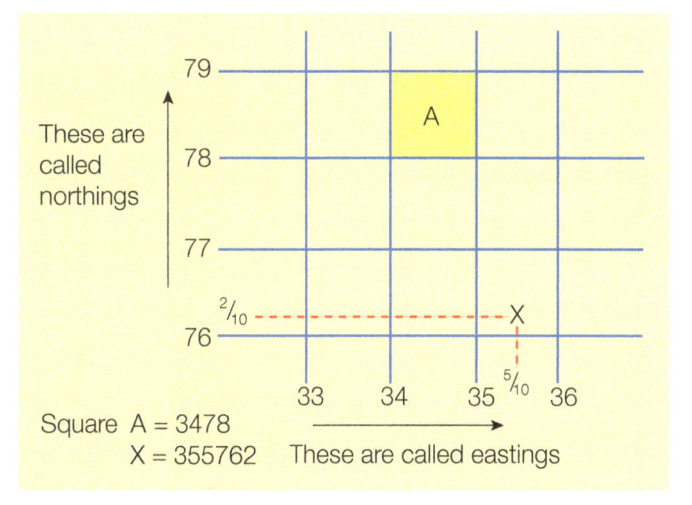

Square A = 3478
X = 355762

B *How to use grid references*

To locate a point rather than a square, each square is split into tenths to give a six-figure reference. Look at diagram **B** and notice that point X is at grid reference 355762. Notice how the eastings value is represented by the three digits 355 and the northings value is represented by the digits 762. It is the third digit of each set that gives the 'tenths' value. Thus the eastings value is 35 and 5/10ths and the northings value is 76 and 2/10ths.

To locate a grid square on a map, we use a four-figure reference:

- the first two digits refer to the *easting* value
- the second two digits give the *northing* value.

Remember to give the *eastings* value *first* and then the northings. Think of the phrase '*along* the corridor and *up* the stairs'!

For example: The four-figure reference for grid square A on diagram **B** is 3478; grid square A is the square after the values 34 and 78.

335

Geographical skills

Scale

OS maps are drawn to scale. This means they are an accurate representation of the real world, but reduced to fit onto a sheet of paper. Scale can be shown using a *ratio* or a *linear scale*.

- A scale of 1:25 000 means that 1 unit on the map equals 25 000 units on the ground.
- 1:50 000 means that 1 unit on the map equals 50 000 units on the ground.

Distance

Distance can be measured as a 'straight-line' or 'curved' distance (for example, along a road or a river). You need to be able to measure both straight and curved distances.

Straight-line distance

Every map has a scale, usually in the form of a linear scale – a straight line with distances written alongside. To calculate a straight-line distance, simply measure the distance on the map between any two points, using a ruler or the straight edge of a piece of paper. Then line up your ruler or paper alongside the linear scale to find out the actual distance on the ground in kilometres (diagram **C**).

Curved distance

A curved distance takes longer to work out. Use the straight edge of a piece of paper to mark off sections of the curved line, converting the curved distance into a straight-line distance (diagram **C**).

> **Remember!**
> On a 1:25 000 map, 1 cm equals 25 000 cm on the ground, or 250 m. 1 km on the ground equals 4 cm on the map.
>
> On a 1:50 000 map, 1 cm on the map represents 0.5 km and 2 cm equals 1 km.
>
> The distance between gridlines on any OS map is 1 km. On a 1:25 000 map the gridlines are 4 cm apart. On a 1:50 000 map they are just 2 cm apart.

C Measuring distance

Straight-line distance

1 Use a ruler to measure the distance between two places on the map, in centimetres.

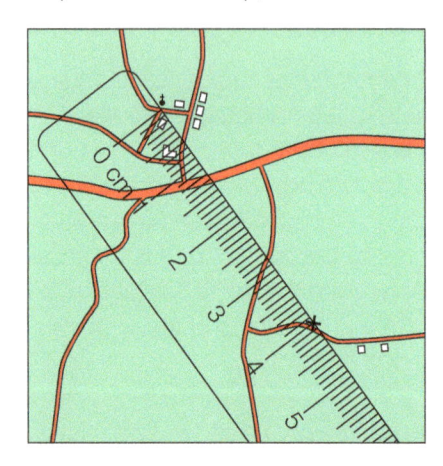

2 Measure out the distance on the map's linear scale to discover the distance on the ground in kilometres.

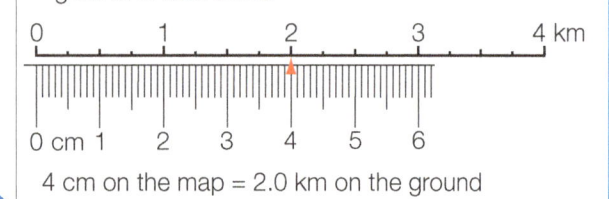

4 cm on the map = 2.0 km on the ground

Curved-line distance

1 Place the straight edge of a piece of paper along the route to be measured. Mark the start with the letter S. Look along the paper and mark off the point where the route moves away from the straight edge.

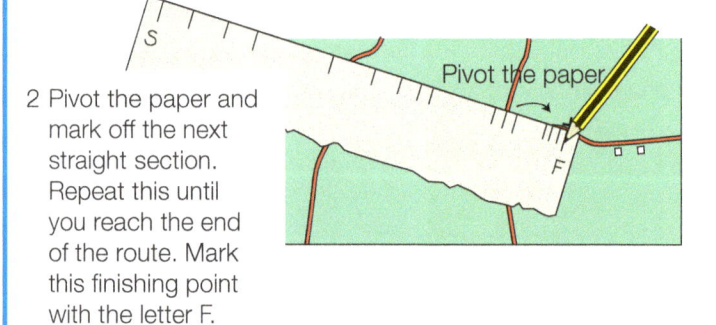

2 Pivot the paper and mark off the next straight section. Repeat this until you reach the end of the route. Mark this finishing point with the letter F.

3 Place the edge of the marked paper alongside the linear scale on the map and convert the total length to kilometres. Remember to always give the units when writing your answer!

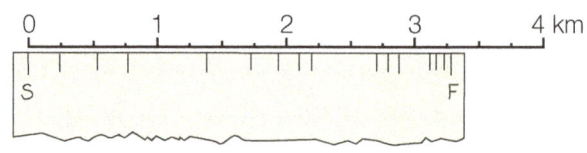

Compass directions

On most maps the direction 'north' is straight up – but not always! You should always check this in the key when using maps and diagrams, and make sure you understand the eight points of the compass (diagram **D**). Always use compass directions carefully and precisely, for example, 'Settlement X is to the north-west of Settlement Y'.

Identifying and describing landscape and relief features

Contour patterns on maps can be used to identify basic physical features, such as river valleys, ridges and plateaus (diagram **E**). Having identified these features, you need to be able to describe them by referring to size, shape, height and orientation (direction).

Example

'The ridge is about 2 km wide, is orientated roughly north–south and rises to a maximum height of 232 m at GR 376490. It has a steep eastern side and gentle western side.'

D *The eight points of the compass*

Skills in context

You can find out more about identifying and describing relief features in Chapters 9–11. Turn to page 338 to see how cross-sections can be used to identify physical features.

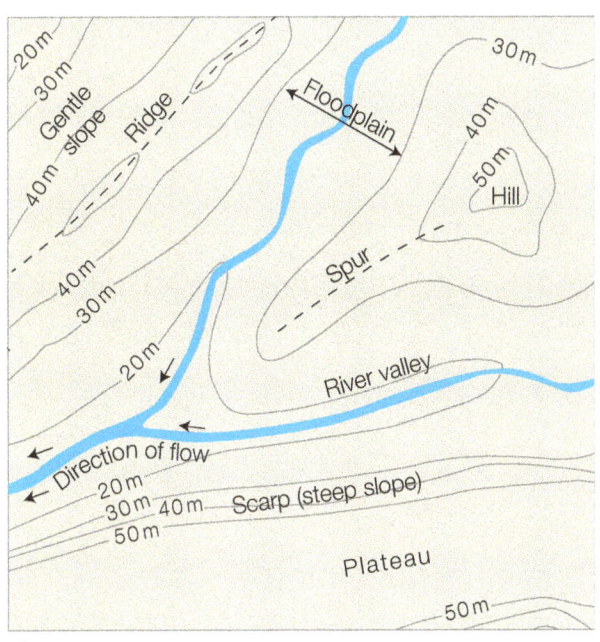

E *Using contours to identify basic landscape features*

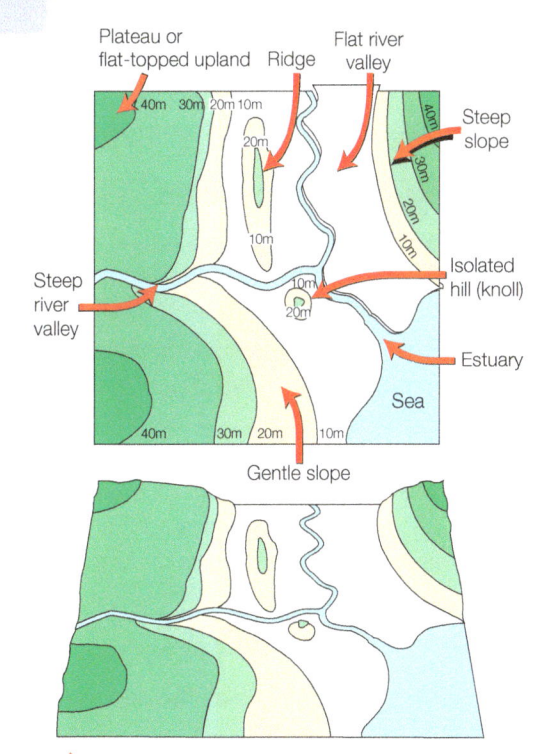

F *Interpreting cross-sections and transects of physical and human landscapes*

Contours, spot heights and gradient

The height of the land is indicated by:

◆ *contours* – lines on the map (usually brown) joining points of equal height above sea level

◆ *spot heights* – usually indicated by black dots with a height above sea level written alongside.

Skills in context

You can find out about how to interpret cross-sections and transects in Chapters 9–11.

337

Geographical skills

The closer the contours, the steeper the gradient of the slope. Gradient can be calculated by measuring the change in height over a known distance:

1 Measure distance and height change using the same units (e.g. metres).
2 Divide the height change by the distance.
3 Express gradient as a percentage or ratio.

Example

Height change (H) of 20 m over a distance (D) of 100 m:

H/D = 20 m/100 m = 0.2

Ratio is 20% (or 1:5).

Numerical and statistical information

OS maps contain numerical and statistical information ranging from road numbers to values of height on contours and alongside spot heights. Grid references also provide numerical detail when locating a place. Be sure to use this information to add extra depth and detail to your map interpretation.

Drawing cross-sections

A cross-section is an imaginary 'slice' through a landscape. It helps to visualise what a landscape actually looks like. Make sure you can identify and label the main physical features of a landscape, for example, steep and gentle slopes, ridge, escarpment and valley. Drawing a cross-section is an important skill for a geographer. You need a piece of paper, a sharp pencil, a ruler and an eraser (diagram **F**). When you complete your section, check that you have:

- copied height values accurately
- made your vertical scale as realistic as possible (don't exaggerate it so much that you create a totally unreal landscape!)
- completed the section to both vertical axes by carrying on the trend of the landscape
- labelled any features
- labelled axes and given grid references for each end of your section
- given your section a title.

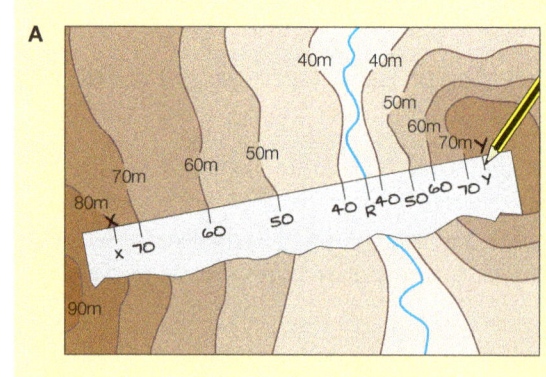

A

1 Place the straight edge of a piece of paper along the chosen line of section.
2 Mark the start and finish of your section.
3 Mark contours and features, e.g. rivers.

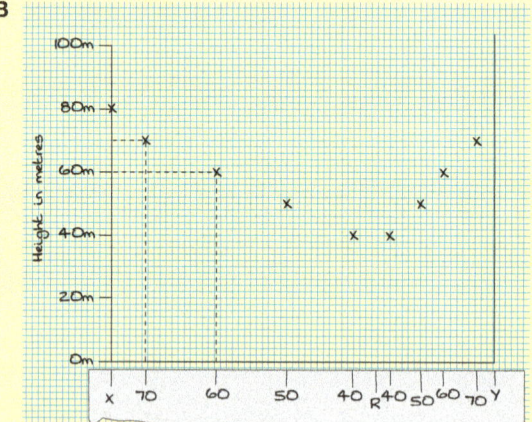

B

1 Draw the axes of a graph, and choose an appropriate vertical scale.
2 Lay your paper along the horizontal axis.
3 Mark each contour value on the graph paper with a cross.

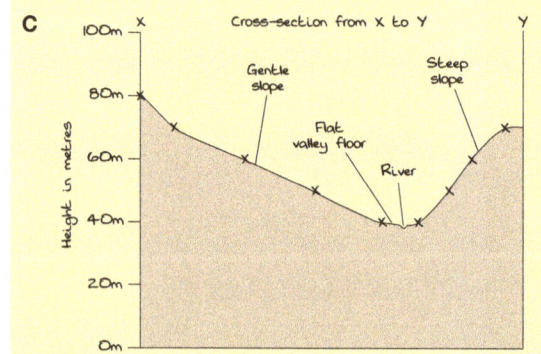

C

1 Join the crosses with a freehand curve.
2 Label any features.
3 Give your cross-section a title.

F How to draw a cross-section

Geographical skills

Interpreting physical and human features

Relief

Relief is the geographical term used to describe the height of the land and the different landscape features created by changes in height. When describing relief it is important to refer to simple landforms such as river valleys, hills and ridges. You should use adjectives to develop your description, for example: 'There is a *steep* river valley with *asymmetrical* (not the same on each side) valley sides'. To give a good answer you should comment on certain features:

- The height of the land, using actual figures taken from contours or spot heights to support your points. *Using words such as 'high' and 'low' is meaningless without using actual figures.*

- The slope of the land. Is the land flat, or sloping? Which way do the slopes face? Are the slopes gentle or steep? Are there exposed, bare cliffs? *Remember to give precise information such as grid references and compass directions.*

- Features such as valleys or ridges. *Refer to names and grid references.*

Drainage

Drainage is the presence (or absence) and flow of water. When describing the drainage of an area, you should comment on:

- The presence or absence of rivers. Which way are they flowing? (Hint: look at the contours.) Are the rivers single or multi-channelled? *Give names of the rivers, and use distances, heights and directions to add depth to your description.*

- Drainage density – the total length of rivers in an area, usually expressed as 'km per km^2'. High drainage densities are typically found on impermeable rocks, whereas low densities suggest permeable rocks.

- The pattern of rivers (diagram **G**).

- The influence of people on drainage channels, for example straightening channels or building embankments. Straight channels are rare in nature and usually indicate human intervention.

- Evidence of underground drainage, in the form of springs or wells.

- The presence of lakes, either natural or artificial.

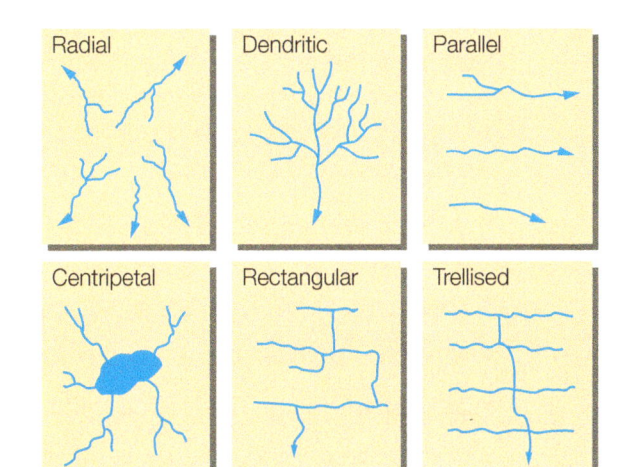

G *Drainage patterns*

Settlement

When describing patterns and types of settlement (diagram **H**) you should understand the following geographical terms:

- *Dispersed settlements* – low-density settlements spread out over a large area and typical of rural agricultural regions.

- *Nucleated settlements* – high-density settlements, tightly packed and often focused on a central point such as a major road intersection. The settlement typically spreads out in all directions.

- *Linear settlements* – these typically extend alongside a road, railway or canal. 'Linear' means 'line', so a linear settlement tends to be long and narrow.

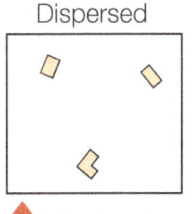

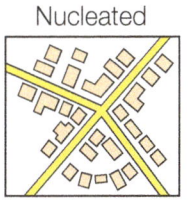

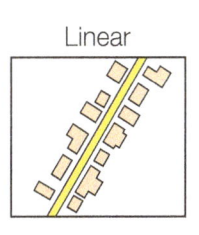

H *Settlement types*

339

Geographical skills

Communication

Communication networks include many kinds of transport, such as:

- roads (of various types)
- railways and footpaths
- ferries (river and cross-channel)
- airports
- cycleways.

You should be able to describe these networks, giving locational details such as length and orientation or compass direction and referring to patterns and density. For example, roads may radiate out from a settlement or form a series of concentric ring roads and by-passes around it.

Communication networks frequently reflect the relief of an area.

- Major transport arteries such as roads, canals and railways tend to follow flat, low ground, which explains why they are often located in river valleys.
- Footpaths often follow river valleys, as well as linking settlements and following ridge-lines or escarpments. Look out for named footpaths, such as the Pennine Way, and remember to refer to them by name when answering a question.

Land use

Land use refers to the way in which land is used or has been modified or managed by people. In writing a good answer about land use you should always refer to the map key and try to give specific examples from the map to support your statements. A typical land use map may contain information about the following land uses:

- different types of woodland (for example, coniferous or non-coniferous)
- coastal deposits (mud, sand or shingle)
- vegetation (for example, scrub, bracken or marsh)
- urban areas (be prepared to describe settlement patterns)
- fields (often just shown white on maps)
- quarries
- industrial areas
- tourist sites
- recreation areas.

Indeed, land use includes all aspects of the Earth's surface! When describing land use you should refer to:

- the specific location (don't forget to use grid references)
- the size and shape of the area.

Inferring human activity from map evidence

As a geographer, you will be expected to describe and interpret features on a map extract. You can use map evidence to infer human activity as well as simply identifying it. For example, you might use map evidence to infer what type of settlement or what type of urban zone you are looking at.

> **Remember!**
> You may be asked to explain why land at a specific location is used in a particular way, for example why an area or slope has been planted with coniferous trees. Remember to use the word 'because' when you are asked to explain a land use.

> **Skills in context**
> *Describing physical features of coastlines, fluvial and glacial landscapes*
> You need to be able to identify and describe two of these three landscape types with reference to OS maps. You can find out more about how to do this in Chapters 10–12.

Inference is all about reaching informed conclusions using the evidence available to you. For example:

◆ If you are asked to identify the 'inner city', look for the appropriate evidence on the map and then use it to support your suggestion (map **I**).

◆ At the coast, the presence of a sandy beach, sand dunes and clifftop footpaths infer that tourism may well be important in the area. Look for the symbols that indicate tourist facilities.

◆ In a glacial landscape, the presence of a lake could be used to infer that people might take part in water sports, fishing or bird watching. The same applies to woodlands or mountains.

Skills in context

Comparing maps

Two or more maps can be compared to see how things have changed over a period of time, for example, the growth of a settlement. The similarities and differences between two maps can also be considered where there may be an association, for example earthquake epicentres and plate boundaries.

Remember!

- The term 'compare' means similarities and differences.
- 'Contrast' means differences only!

Drawing sketch maps

A sketch map is drawn to produce a simplified version of a map. It should focus on just a few key elements, such as patterns of roads or rivers, without lots of other information.

To draw a sketch map, follow these steps:

1 Start by drawing a frame, either to the same scale as the map or enlarging/reducing it as required.

2 Divide the frame into grid squares as they appear on the map and write the grid reference numbers around the edges of your frame. These will act as your guidelines when you draw your sketch.

3 Using a pencil, carefully draw just the features that you need onto your sketch.

4 When your sketch is complete, use colour and shading if you wish, although black and white sketches are often the most successful.

5 Label and annotate your sketch as necessary.

6 Don't forget to include a scale (which can be approximate), a north point and a title.

You will gain the most credit for your labels and annotations (detailed labels with some explanation), which show your ability to interpret the map.

I Characteristics of a small UK market town – Alnwick (a nucleated settlement)

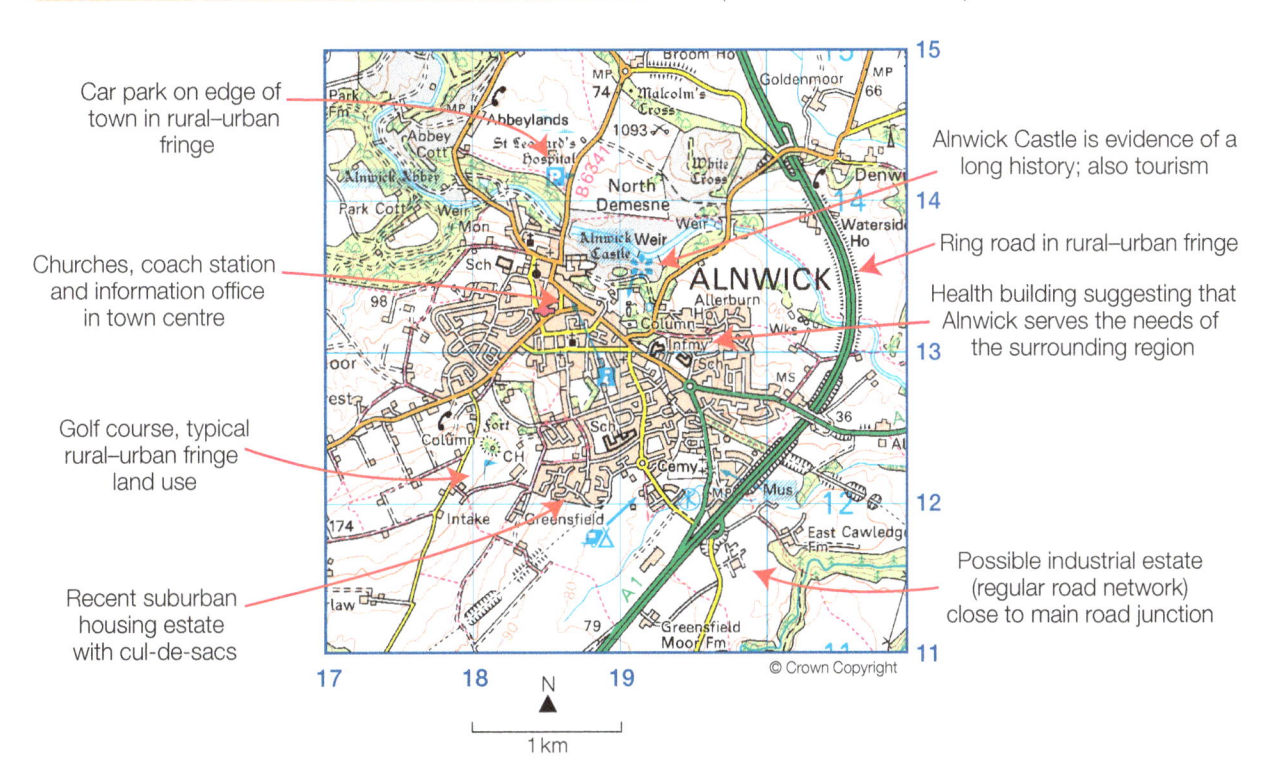

Car park on edge of town in rural–urban fringe

Churches, coach station and information office in town centre

Golf course, typical rural–urban fringe land use

Recent suburban housing estate with cul-de-sacs

Alnwick Castle is evidence of a long history; also tourism

Ring road in rural–urban fringe

Health building suggesting that Alnwick serves the needs of the surrounding region

Possible industrial estate (regular road network) close to main road junction

© Crown Copyright

Geographical skills

341

Geographical skills

Using photos

Photos are widely used in the study of geography. They can be used on their own or in association with maps.

Geographers make use of three different types of photo.

Ground photos

Photos taken on the ground (**J**) are the most common types of photo and are usually used to focus on a particular physical feature or characteristic, such as a building or a waterfall.

Aerial photos

These are usually taken from aeroplanes, helicopters or drones, looking down on a landscape. They often show large areas that can be related directly to maps – for example showing settlements or stretches of coastline. There are two kinds of aerial photos:

◆ *Vertical* aerial photos (**K a**) look directly down onto the ground and therefore give no indication of relative height – so everything looks flat!

◆ *Oblique* aerial photos (**K b**) give a sideways view of the landscape. They are used more often than vertical aerial photos. They can distort size, with objects in the foreground appearing larger than those in the distant background.

Satellite photos

Like vertical aerial photos, these look directly down onto the Earth (**L**). Satellite photos may be digitally processed with enhanced colours to make certain land uses and features show up more clearly. These 'false-colour' images can be used to show environmental factors such as pollution and deforestation. They are also widely used to show weather features, such as hurricanes.

J *A ground photo*

a *A vertical aerial photo*

K b *An oblique aerial photo*

L *Satellite photo*

Geographical skills

Describing human and physical landscapes

Photos are widely used by geographers to record, investigate and understand physical and human landscapes such as landforms, natural vegetation, land use and settlement.

When describing what a photo shows, you should:

- use directional language – for example 'in the foreground' and 'in the background', as well as 'right' and 'left'
- use juxtaposition – for example 'just behind and to the right of the stack' – to enable you to identify and describe features accurately.

You may be asked to use photos and maps alongside each other. You could, for example, be asked to identify the direction that a photo is looking. Take your time to orientate the photo on the map, possibly by turning it to line it up correctly – look for evidence in the foreground and the background on the photo to help you do this. Once you have orientated the photo, it should be quite easy to work with both resources.

Drawing sketches from photos

The purpose of a sketch is to identify the main geographical characteristics of the landscape (figure **M**). It is not necessary to produce a brilliant artistic drawing – clarity and accuracy are all that are needed so that labels and annotations can be added.

To draw a sketch, follow these steps:

1. Draw a frame that is the same shape as the photograph.
2. Draw one or two major lines that will subsequently act as guidelines for the rest of your sketch. For example, you could draw the profile of a slope, a hilltop, a road or river.
3. Consider what it is that you are trying to show and concentrate on that feature or aspect – it may be river features or the pattern of settlements.

Labels and annotations

You should always add labels or annotations to diagrams, maps, graphs, sketches and photos, where appropriate.

- Labels – these are usually single words or phrases that identify features, for example the peak on a hydrograph, a river cliff on a meander or a roundabout in a town.
- Annotations – these give more detail and may include some detailed description and explanation, for example 'The cliff is vertical and high, probably because it is made of hard rock and is being actively eroded and undercut at its base by the sea.'

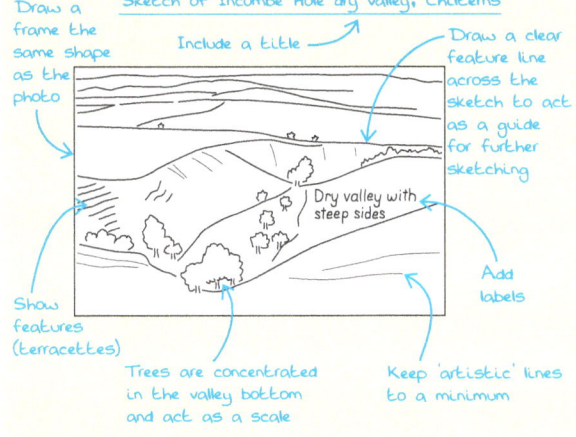

M Sketching from a photo

Remember!

- Don't waste time drawing a lot of unnecessary detail.
- Always use a good sharp pencil and don't be afraid to rub things out as you go along.
- Always use labels or annotations (detailed labels) on your sketch, to identify the features.
- Give your sketch a title.

343

22.2 Graphical skills

In this unit you will find out how to interpret and construct graphs and diagrams

As a geographer, you need to be able to read and interpret information that is presented in a variety of ways. This includes written text, photos and maps of different types and scale. You should also be able to interpret and construct a variety of basic graphs and diagrams.

How to interpret a graph or diagram

Graph **A** is a line graph showing world population growth. Notice the following points:

- The scales have equal intervals between each line (2 billion people on the *y* axis and every 50 years on the *x* axis). If different intervals were used, the graph would be distorted.

- The top line of the graph shows total world population. It increases slowly from about 1 billion in 1800 to about 3 billion in 1950. From 1950 it increases very rapidly before levelling off at about 10 billion by 2050.

- The graph has been subdivided into *developing* regions and *developed* regions. It can be called a 'divided' or 'compound' graph. Take care to read values from the correct section of the graph. So, population for developing regions in 1950 is about 2 billion.

Remember!
It can be easy to miss these practical activities in an exam because there are no lines for writing an answer!

Remember!
The *three* stages of a description:
1. Describe the overall trends and patterns – the 'big picture'.
2. Provide some evidence to support your description (quote a few facts and figures).
3. Consider any anomalies (exceptions) to the overall trends and patterns.

When explaining:
- give reasons for trends, patterns and anomalies (use the word 'because')
- consider links and connections between different variables that might help your explanation (for example, a war might affect the shape of a population pyramid).

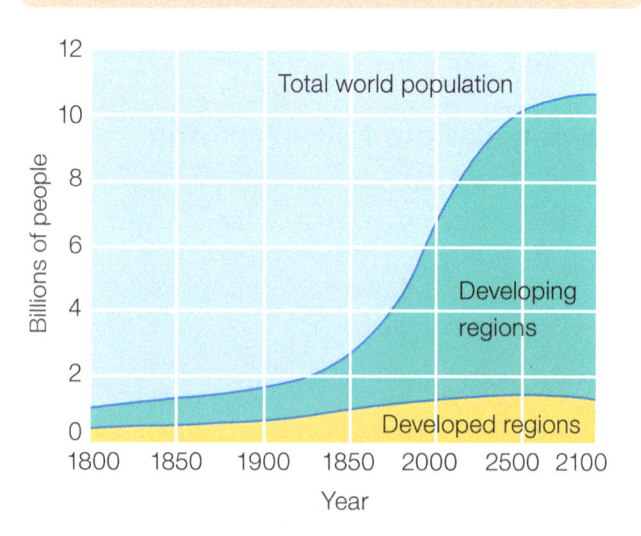

A World population growth line graph

How to construct graphs and diagrams

You may be asked to construct or complete a partly drawn graph, diagram or map. When doing this, make sure you look closely at the scales and plot the data accurately and precisely. Use a sharp pencil and double check that you have plotted the information correctly.

Line graphs

A line graph shows *continuous* changes over a period of time – for example, stream flow (hydrograph), traffic flow or population change. Remember that time, shown on the horizontal axis, must have an equal spacing – for example for periods of time (graph **A**).

Bar graphs and histograms

Bar graphs and histograms are one of the most common methods of displaying statistical information. You should use the one best suited to your data.

Geographical skills

Bar graphs

A bar graph is a way of comparing quantities or frequencies in different categories, such as types of vegetation, or places. The bars are drawn in different colours with gaps between them, because they are unconnected (graph **B**).

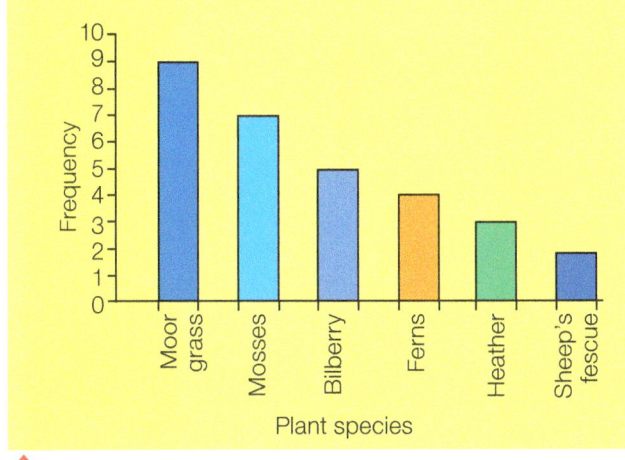

B A bar graph

It is possible to subdivide individual bars in order to show multiple data. In graph **C** the bars are sub-divided to show different species. This type of graph is called a *divided* bar graph.

C A divided bar graph

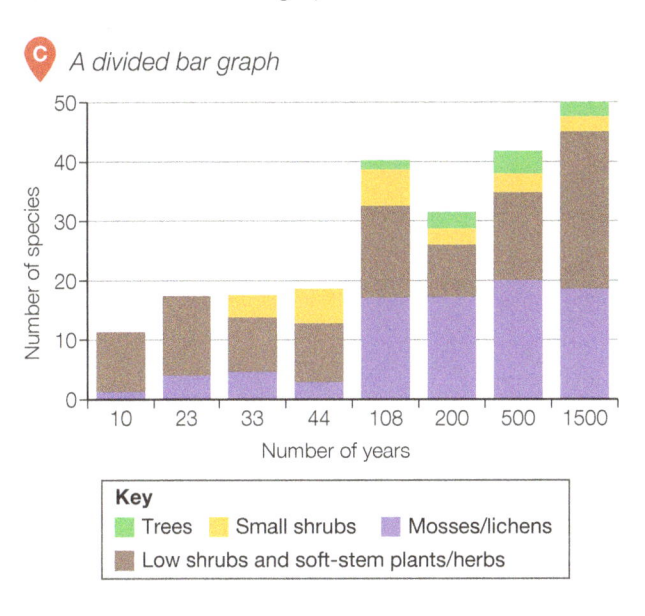

Key
- Trees
- Small shrubs
- Mosses/lichens
- Low shrubs and soft-stem plants/herbs

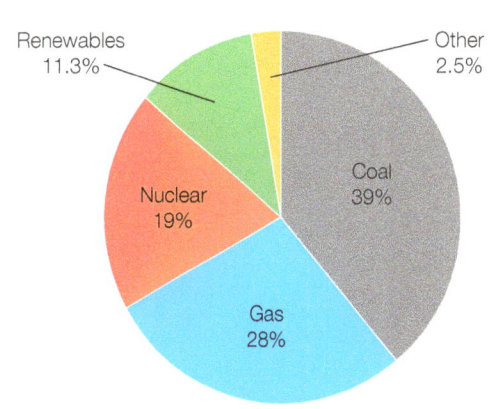

E Pie chart showing fuel used for UK energy generation

Remember!
To convert percentages into degrees for pie charts, multiply the value by 3.6.

Histograms

A histogram also uses bars but with no gaps between them. This is because:

- a histogram represents *continuous* data (such as daily rainfall values over a period of a month)
- the values may be all part of a single sample, for example, the sizes of particles in a sediment sample (graph **D**). As the bars are effectively connected, a single colour or type of shading is used. Notice that there are equal class intervals between the bars.

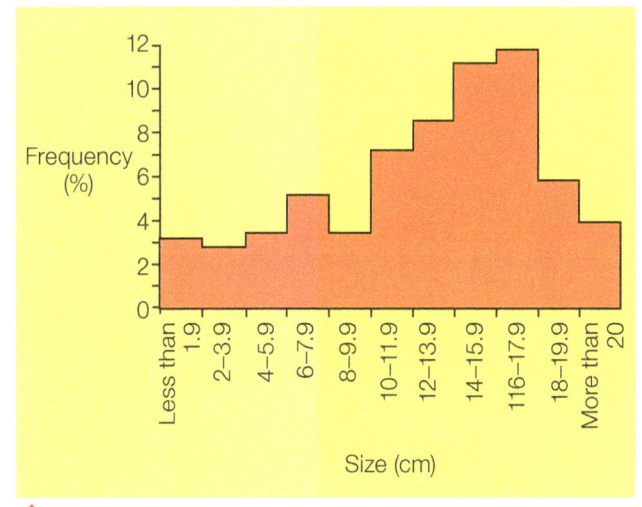

D A histogram

Pie charts

A pie chart is a simple circle divided into segments, rather like the slices of a pie. It shows the proportions of a total. Percentage figures are written alongside the segments to help interpret the diagram. For example, chart **E** shows that in 2012, 39 per cent of UK electricity was generated by burning coal, and 11.9 per cent from renewable sources.

Pie charts work best when there are between four and six 'segments'. Don't draw a pie chart as just one segment!

Geographical skills

Pictograms

A pictogram uses a pictorial symbol or icon instead of a bar (graph **F**). It is an effective visual technique although it may be difficult to extract precise data from the diagram. All icons must be the same size. Fractions of icons can be used to represent values in between those represented by a full icon. For example, if an icon of one person represents 100 tourists, then 50 tourists would be represented by half a person!

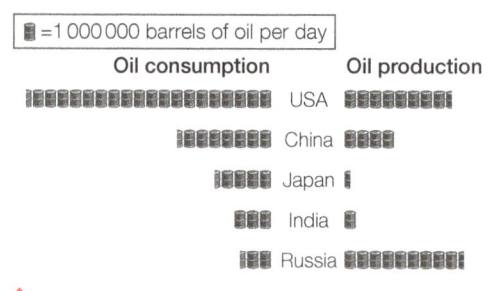

Scattergraphs

If two sets of data are thought to be related, they can be plotted on a graph called a scattergraph. To complete a scattergraph follow these steps:

1 Draw two axes in the normal way, with the variable thought to be causing the change (called the independent variable) on the horizontal (*x*) axis. On graph **G**, GNP (gross national product, the wealth of a country) is thought to be responsible for average car ownership.

2 Use each pair of values to plot a single point on the graph using a cross.

3 Draw a best-fit line to show the trend of the points if there is one. Your best-fit line should pass approximately through the middle of the points, with roughly the same number of points on either side of the line. Use a ruler to draw a straight line through the points. Best-fit lines may also be curved, and for these you need to draw a line by hand. Remember: the best-fit line does not need to pass through the origin.

4 Describe the resulting pattern (diagram **H**).

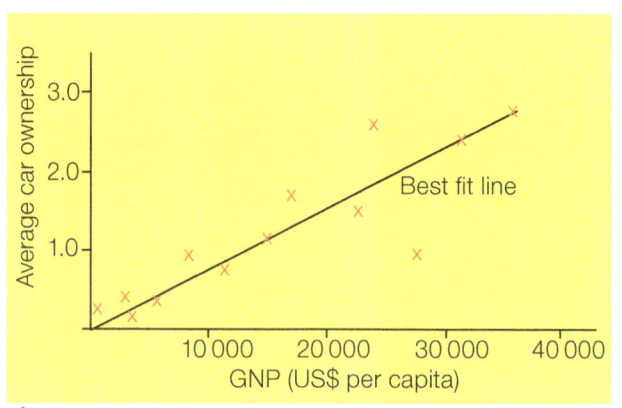

F *Pictogram showing oil consumption and production in the top five oil-consuming countries*

G *Scattergraph and best-fit line*

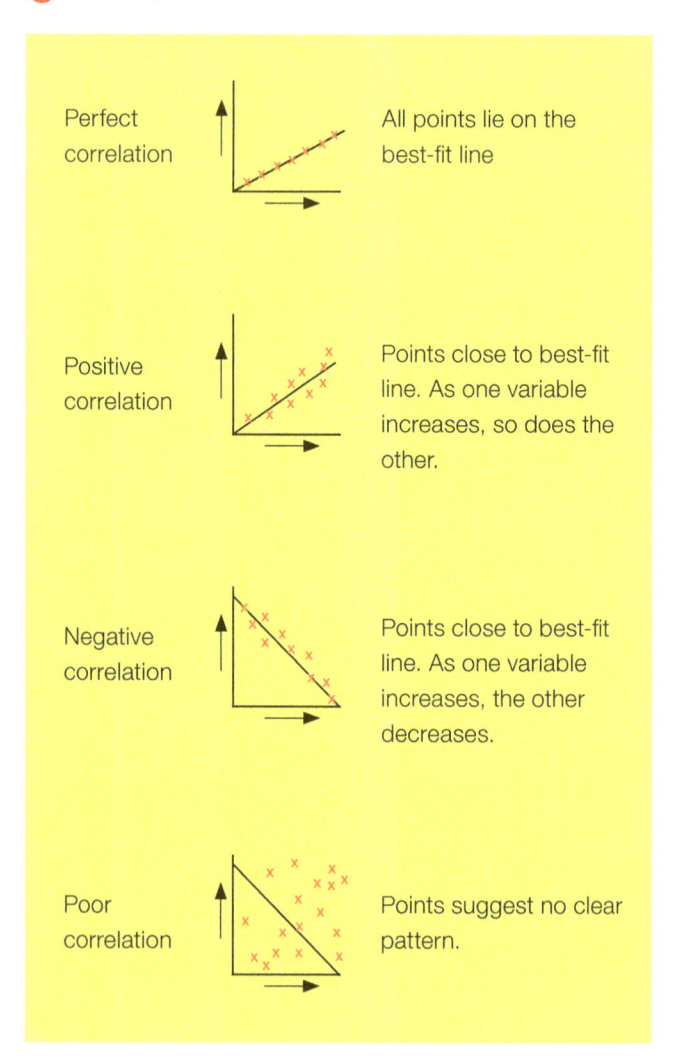

H *Interpreting scattergraph patterns*

Perfect correlation — All points lie on the best-fit line

Positive correlation — Points close to best-fit line. As one variable increases, so does the other.

Negative correlation — Points close to best-fit line. As one variable increases, the other decreases.

Poor correlation — Points suggest no clear pattern.

Geographical skills

Population pyramids

A population pyramid is a type of histogram showing the proportions of a population in different age and gender categories. Graph **I** shows males on the left and females on the right. Each age group – with equal intervals – is represented by a bar.

A population pyramid represents the structure of a population and its shape provides valuable information for a government planning for the future provision of health care, schooling and housing. The labels on graph **I** show how to interpret a population pyramid. (For more about population pyramids see pages 184–5.)

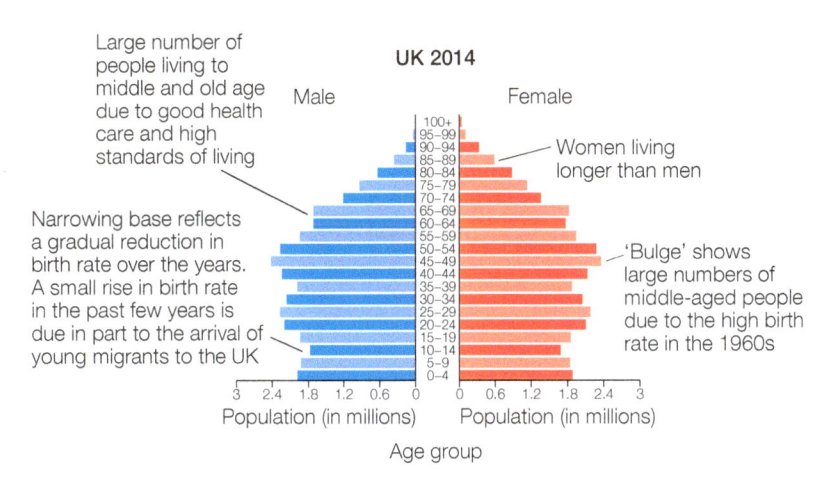

UK 2014

Large number of people living to middle and old age due to good health care and high standards of living

Narrowing base reflects a gradual reduction in birth rate over the years. A small rise in birth rate in the past few years is due in part to the arrival of young migrants to the UK

Women living longer than men

'Bulge' shows large numbers of middle-aged people due to the high birth rate in the 1960s

I Population pyramid for the UK, 2014

Choropleth maps

A choropleth map uses different colours or different densities of the same colour to show the distribution of data categories (map **J**). A choropleth map has the following features:

- The base map shows regions or areas – in map **J** it is countries of the world.

- Data are divided into groups or categories. Ideally there should be 4–6 categories. Notice that the category values do not overlap and that the intervals are equal (for example, 2–2.9, 3–3.9, etc.).

- The darker (or denser) the shading, the higher the values. This is a key characteristic of a choropleth map and makes it easy to interpret. White (blank) or grey can be used for the lowest category or to show areas on the map for which no data are available.

Choropleth maps are a good way of showing variations between areas. However, they can be misleading, as there will often be significant variations at a local scale within each area. They also imply sudden changes at area boundaries, which is often not the case in reality.

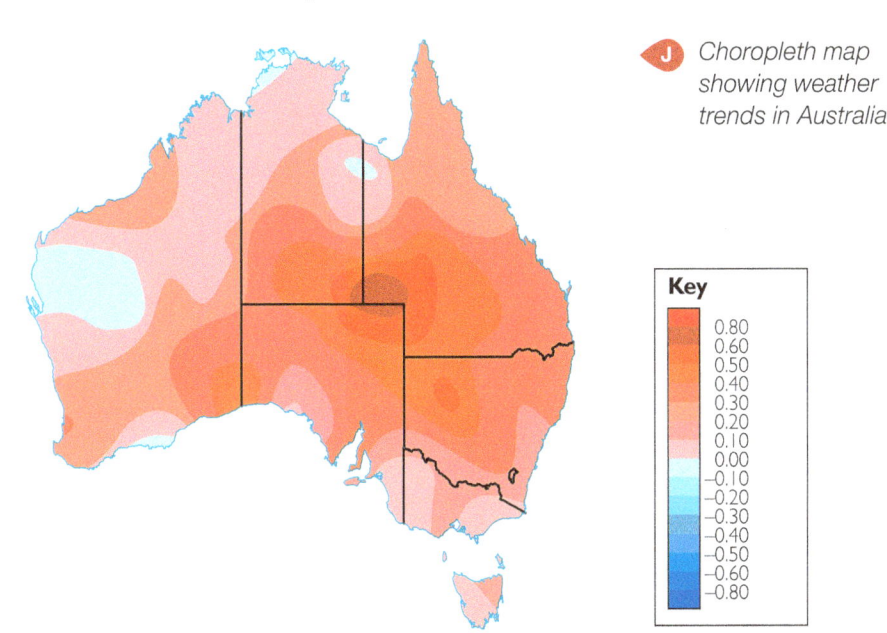

J Choropleth map showing weather trends in Australia

Remember!
Note the spelling of choropleth – don't make the common mistake of spelling it 'chloropleth'!

347

Geographical skills

Isoline maps

An isoline map uses lines of equal value to show patterns ('iso' means 'equal'). Some of the most common types of isoline map show aspects of weather and climate. For example, isobars show pressure and isotherms show temperature.

Isoline maps can be tricky to draw but they are a good way of showing patterns when superimposed on a base map, for example, pedestrian counts at different places in a town (map **K**).

K Isoline map showing pedestrian counts in Blackburn's CBD

To draw an isoline map, mark your observed data onto a base map or sheet of tracing paper. Then consider how many lines to draw and at what intervals you will draw them, for example every 10 units. This decision is largely 'trial and error' and you might like to draw the lines in rough first.

Map **L** shows how isolines are drawn. They pass between values that are higher and lower than the value of the line. All values to one side of a line will be higher and all those to the other side will be lower.

Each map will be individual – don't worry if yours looks different to other people's.

L Drawing isolines

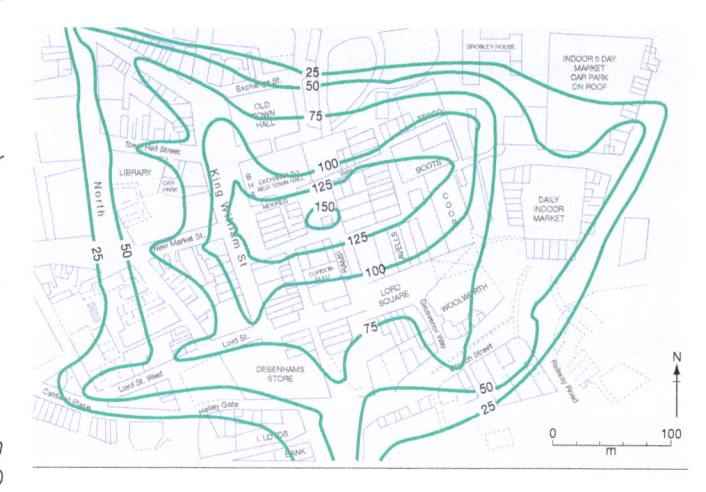

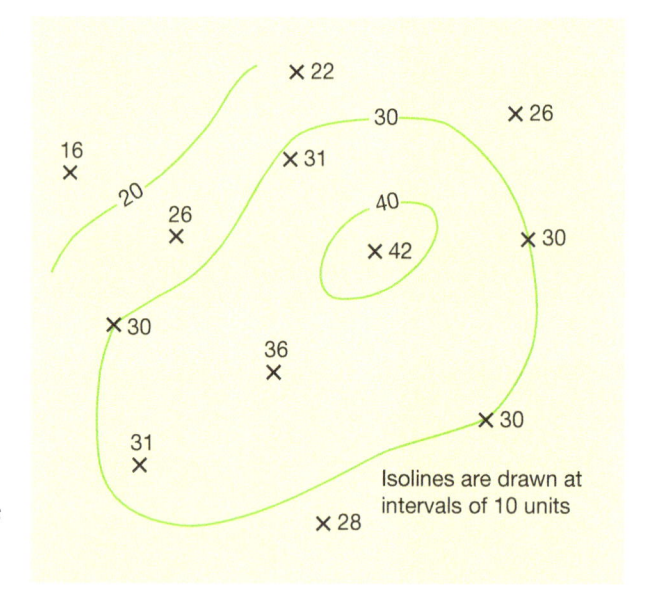

Dot maps

Dots are used to represent a particular value or number (for example, a population of 1 million) and are located accurately on a map. The number and density of the dots conveys the information on the map (map **M**), but it can be difficult to extract accurate information from them.

M Dot map showing global population distribution

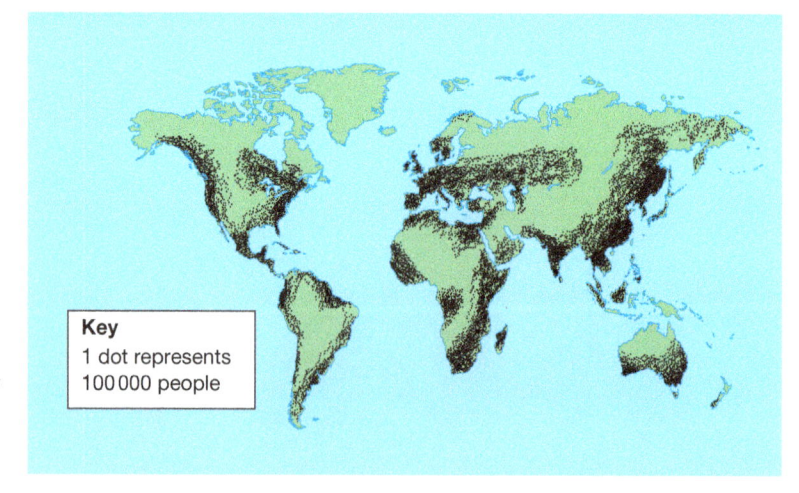

Geographical skills

Desire line maps

Desire lines show movement of people or goods between places (map **N**), for example commuters travelling to a nearby town or city from the surrounding area. They may also be proportional, and show trends in the distance travelled between places (for example, most people might commute short distances) and the spatial density of the travellers (for example, where people commute from). They are similar to flow lines, but show only direct movement from A to B, while flow lines show the exact path of movement.

N *Desire line map of international flights from Heathrow*

When drawing a desire line map, each line should be positioned accurately to show its source and its destination.

Flow line maps

Flow lines indicate direction and volume of movement, with thickness representing volume. They show movement between places by connecting the source with the destination. Desire lines show lots of individual movements, while flow lines are drawn proportionately to show grouped data. For example, 10 separate desire lines might be drawn to show the movement of commuters from Village A to Town B; or a single flow line with the width drawn proportionately to show 10 commuters.

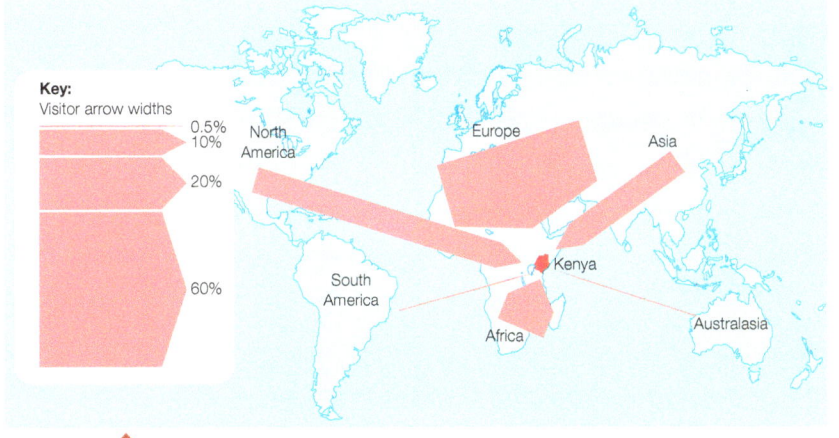

Map **O** shows the origin of tourists visiting Kenya. Each flow line connects the continent of origin and the destination (Kenya). The width of each line is in proportion to the percentage of tourists.

O *Flow line map showing the origin of tourists to Kenya*

P *Map with proportional circles*

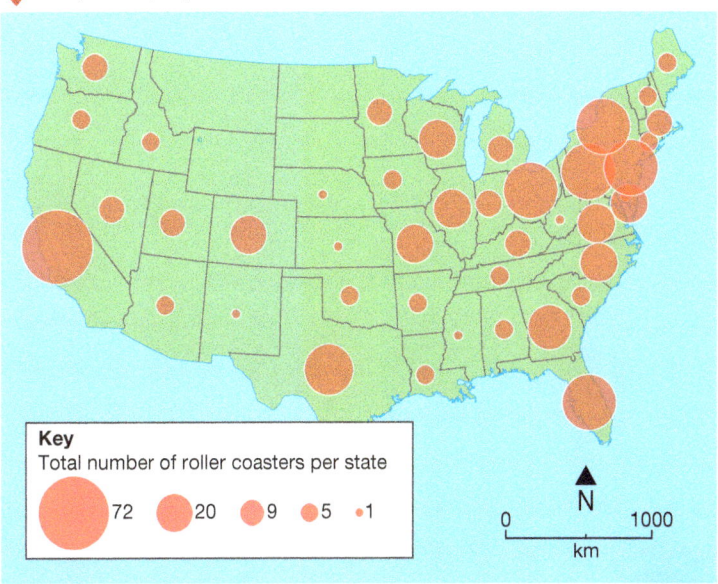

Flow lines can be drawn on a base map, but an appropriate scale is needed to avoid flow lines crossing over each other. Don't forget to write the scale on your map.

Proportional symbols

Proportional symbols (for example, circles) are a useful way to show data on a base map where spatial variations can be seen (map **P**). They can be difficult to draw and you will need to choose your scale carefully.

When using proportional circles, select a scale for the radius of your circle. The area of the circle should be proportional, so use the square root value as your radius distance.

349

22.3 Statistical skills

> In this unit you will find out how to use a range of statistical methods to measure the average and spread of a data set, calculate percentage change over time and describe relationships between variables

Using statistics in geography

Geographers frequently use numbers and data sets. The use of statistics is an important part of any geographical investigation. They can help you to interpret patterns and trends.

In an exam you should be prepared to spot weaknesses in the presentation of selected data. This might involve spotting incorrect labelling of axes or inaccurate interpretation of trends.

Measures of central tendency

Central tendency is a description of the 'average' within a data set. There are three ways of measuring central tendency: mean, median and mode.

Mean

Mean is calculated very simply, by summing (adding up) all the values in a data set and then dividing by the number of values. This is the most commonly used measure of central tendency and the one that is normally associated with the term 'average'. However, it can be skewed by one very high or one very low value and doesn't always fairly represent the majority of the values.

Example
10, 14, 8, 16, 14, 9, 12, 18, 10, 9
Mean is 120 divided by 10 = 12

Median

This is the central (middle) value in a ranked data set. If there is an odd number of values, identifying the middle value is easy. If there is an even number of values, the median lies midway between the two central values.

Example
Odd number of values:
13, 13, 13, 13, **14**, 14, 16, 18, 21
The median is the 5th value = 14

Even number of values:
8, 9, 11, 13, **14, 16**, 16, 18, 21, 24
The median lies midway between the 5th value (14) and 6th value (16). This can be calculated by adding the two values together and dividing by two.
14 + 16 = 30 / 2 = **15**

Mode

This is the most common value in a data set. If there are no repeated values then there is no mode in the data set.

Example
13, 13, 13, 13, 14, 14, 16, 18, 21
Here the value 13 is stated four times whereas the value 14 is only stated twice. The mode value is **13**.

Modal class

If data are grouped into categories, the category with the highest frequency is called the modal class. Look back to the histogram on page 345 (**D**). The modal class is 16–17.9 cm, with the highest bar representing the greatest frequency.

Measures of spread

The measures of central tendency are useful in identifying 'average' values. However, they give no indication of how the values in a data set are spread around the average. Look at the data sets in the example. They both have the same mean but very different values!

Example

Data set A: 11, 15, 17, 22, 24, 26, 34, 35

Mean = 184 / 8 = **23**

Data set B: 2, 3, 4, 6, 6, 7, 56, 100

Mean = 184 / 8 = **23**

Range

The *range* is the difference between the highest and lowest values. It gives us a good measure of the spread of the values in a data set and provides another means of description to use alongside the 'average'.

Example

Data set A: 35 − 11 = **24**

Data set B: 100 − 2 = **98**

Quartiles and inter-quartile range

The median is the middle value in a ranked data set. It splits the data set into two halves – an upper half and a lower half. These two halves can be split again into quarters at a value called the quartile.

There is an upper quartile value (that splits the upper half of the values) and a lower quartile (that splits the lower half). So, if there are 20 values, the median would lie midway between the 10th and 11th values. The upper quartile value lies between the 15th and 16th values. The lower quartile value lies between the 5th and 6th values. With the median, this divides the data set (20) into four groups of five.

The *inter-quartile range* (IQR) is the difference between the upper quartile and the lower quartile. It is useful for showing degree of clustering or dispersal of values around the median.

Turn to page 352 (figure **A**) to see how the range can be applied to values displayed on a dispersion graph.

Example

3, 3, 3, 4, 6, 7, 7, 8, 8, 10, **14**, **14**, 16, 20, 21, 21, 22, 24, 25, 30

Median = 10 + 14 = 24 / 2 = **12**

Lower quartile = 6 + 7 = 13 / 2 = **6.5**

Upper quartile = 21 + 21 = 42 / 2 = **21**

Inter-quartile range = 21 − 6.5 = **14.5**

Using a formula:

Assuming the highest value is ranked as 1, the upper quartile (UQ) is calculated using the formula:

UQ = n+1 / 4 th position in the rank order.

The lower quartile (LQ) is calculated using the formula:

LQ = 3(n+1) / 4 th position in the rank order.

LQ is then subtracted from UQ to give the IQR.

Geographical skills

Dispersion graphs

Dispersion graphs shows the *spread* of data. They are a useful way to make comparisons between different sites, for example locations along a river or across a beach. They can be used to identify a number of statistical measures including the range, median, quartiles and inter-quartile range.

Graph **A** shows comparisons between pebble sizes across a beach. The degree of overlap of the graphs can be used to assess difference between data sets.

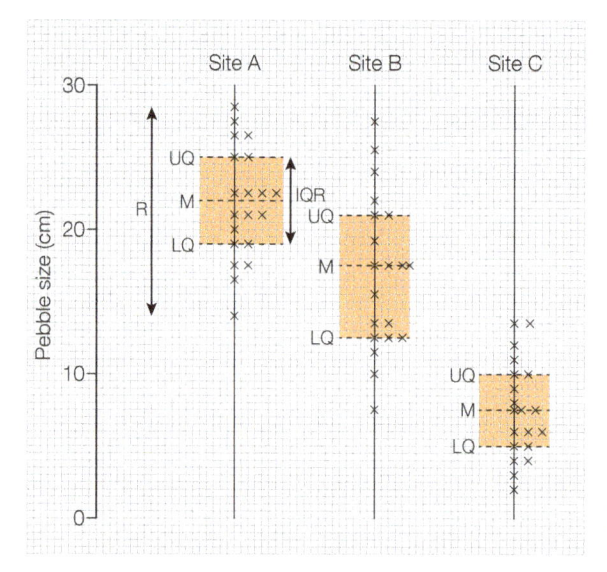

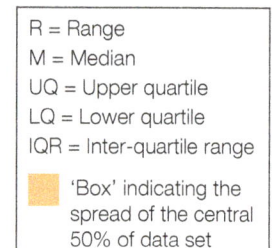

R = Range
M = Median
UQ = Upper quartile
LQ = Lower quartile
IQR = Inter-quartile range

'Box' indicating the spread of the central 50% of data set

(Notice that there is *no* overlap of the box for site C with sites A and B. This means there is a significant *difference* between the data for site C and data for sites A and B.)

A Dispersion graphs showing pebble sizes across a beach

Calculating percentage change and using percentiles

Percentage change

You have probably heard comments like 'the cost of a ticket has increased by 20 per cent' or 'there has been a 50 per cent fall in attendance'. Geographers often want to make comparisons between things or describe how something has changed over a period of time. Percentage change is a good way to do this.

To calculate the percentage increase between two numbers:

1. Work out the difference (increase) between the two numbers you are comparing.
2. Divide the increase by the *original* number.
3. Multiply the answer by 100 to give you a percentage.

If your answer is a negative number then this is a *percentage decrease*.

Example

The number of bus routes in a town increased from 24 in 2010 to 31 in 2016.

31 − 24 = 7

7 / 24 = 0.29

0.29 × 100 = 29%

There has been a 29% increase (just less than one third) in the number of bus routes between 2010 and 2016.

Percentiles

A *percentile* is used to indicate the value below which a given percentage of observations fall. So, for example, the 80th percentile is the value in a data set below which 80 per cent of the observations occur and above which 20 per cent of the observations occur.

You have already come across the term *median*. This is a point half way along a ranked data set, so is in effect the 50th percentile (50 per cent). The upper quartile is the 75th percentile and the lower quartile the 25th percentile.

Geographical skills

Describing relationships in bivariate data

The term *bivariate data* means data for two variables that may be considered to be related, for example GDP and energy consumption. (*Univariate* data involve a single set of data and might be displayed in a dispersion graph.) In the case of GDP and energy consumption, the amount of energy consumed might be expected to increase as the wealth of a country (GNP) increases. Energy consumption is dependent on GNP. Therefore, GNP can be said to be the dependent variable and GNP the *independent* variable.

Bivariate data are usually plotted as a scattergraph (see graph **G** on page 348). The dependent variable is plotted along the side (*y* axis) and the independent variable along the bottom (*x* axis).

A *best-fit* line can be drawn to indicate a relationship (if one exists) and the relationship can be described. In most cases best-fit lines are drawn with a ruler to show a linear relationship. However, a curved line may be used to show an *exponential* relationship.

Remember!
Using a small data set may be unreliable. For example, if a scattergraph only has four or five points, the trend or relationship shown by a best-fit line could be misleading. You should try to plot at least ten points on your graph if possible.

Trend lines

A sketch trend line can also be used to suggest a trend in bivariate data. This line is drawn through the scatter plots to suggest the overall trend, such as an increase or a decrease. It is commonly used on a graph where changes take place over time (graphs **A** and **B**). A stretch trend line may be a curved line.

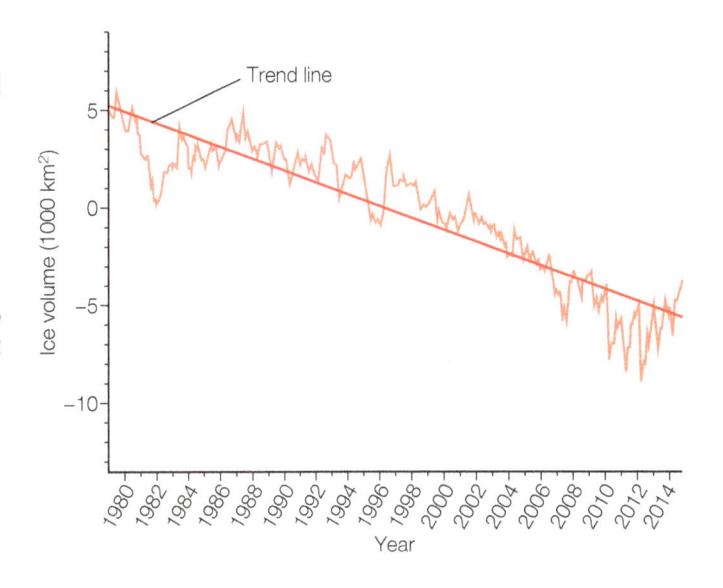

B *Trend line showing a decrease in Arctic sea ice 1980–2014*

How to interpolate and extrapolate

To estimate an unknown value you first need to *interpolate* or *extrapolate* a trend. Then you can use the trend line or best-fit line to estimate the unknown value (graph **C**).

- Interpolation involves estimating an unknown value from *within* the data set.
- Extrapolation involves estimating an unknown value that is *outside* the data set.

Graph **C** shows how the use of a best-fit line enables interpolation and extrapolation to take place.

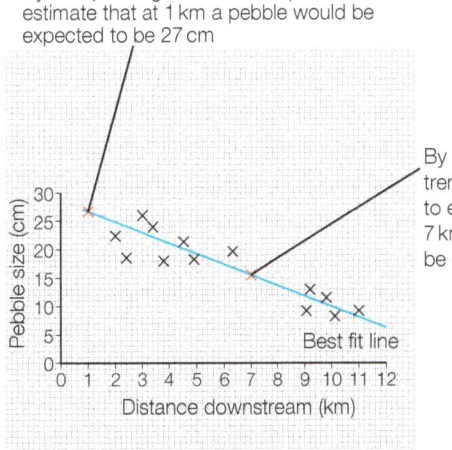

By *extrapolating* the trend it is possible to estimate that at 1 km a pebble would be expected to be 27 cm

By *interpolating* the trend it is possible to estimate that at 7 km a pebble would be expected to be 16 cm

C *Using a best-fit line to interpolate and extrapolate*

Glossary

Abrasion (1) Rocks carried along a river wear down the riverbed and banks; (2) the effect of wind sand-blasting rock surfaces in a desert

Adaptation Actions taken to adjust to natural events such as climate change, to reduce damage, limit the impacts, take advantage of opportunities, or cope with the consequences

Age structure The proportion of each age group in a population

Allotment A shared open space where people grow their own food

Alluvial fan Triangular fan-shaped alluvial deposit formed at the edge of a mountain front at the outlet of wadis and canyons

Anti-natalist policy A government initiative designed to reduce birth rates, usually because the country is overpopulated or the population is growing too rapidly, with a high percentage of young people

Appropriate (or intermediate) technology Technology suited to the needs, skills, knowledge and wealth of local people and their environment

Arch A wave-eroded passage through a small headland. This begins as a cave which is gradually widened and deepened until it cuts through

Asylum seeker Person who believes that their life is at risk if they remain in their home country and who seeks to settle in another (safe) country

Badlands Desert landscape typically formed in horizontally bedded rocks

Bar Where a spit grows across a bay, a bay bar can eventually enclose the bay to create a lagoon

Barchans Crescent-shaped sand dunes formed when there is a strongly dominant wind direction

Beach A zone of deposited material that extends from the low water line to the limit of storm waves

Beach nourishment Adding new material to a beach artificially, through the dumping of large amounts of sand or shingle

Biodiversity The variety of life in the world or a particular ecosystem

Biomass Renewable organic materials, such as wood, agricultural crops or wastes, especially when used as a source of fuel or energy

Birth rate The number of births a year per 1000 of the total population

Brownfield site Land that has been used, abandoned and now awaits reuse; often found in urban areas

Carbon footprint Measurement of the greenhouse gases individuals produce, through burning fossil fuels

Cave A large hole in a cliff caused by waves forcing their way into cracks in the cliff face

Chemical weathering The decomposition (or rotting) of rock caused by a chemical change within that rock

Child mortality The number of children that die under five years of age, per 1000 live births

Cliff A steep, high rock face formed by weathering and erosion

Climate change A long-term change in the Earth's climate, especially a change due to an increase in the average atmospheric temperature

Commonwealth The Commonwealth is a voluntary association of 53 independent and equal sovereign states, most being former British colonies

Conservation Managing the environment in order to preserve, protect or restore it

Conservative plate margin Two plates sliding alongside each other, in the same or different directions – sometimes known as a transform plate margin

Constructive plate margin Tectonic plate margin where rising magma adds new material to plates that are diverging or moving apart

Consumer Organism that eats herbivores and/or plant matter

Country of origin The country from which a migration starts

Cross profile The side-by-side cross-section of a river channel and/or valley

Dam and reservoir A barrier built across a valley to interrupt river flow and create an artificial lake to store water and control river discharge

Death rate The number of deaths in a year per 1000 of the total population

Debt crisis When a country cannot pay its debts, often leading to calls to other countries for assistance

Debt relief Cancellation of debts to a country by a global organisation such as the World Bank

Decomposer Organisms such as bacteria or fungi that break down plant and animal material

Deflation The effect of wind action removing loose sediment on the desert floor to form a hollow

Deforestation The cutting down and removal of forest

De-industrialisation The decline of a country's traditional manufacturing industry due to exhaustion of raw materials, loss of markets and overseas competition

Deposition Occurs when material being transported by the sea is dropped due to the sea losing energy

Dereliction Abandoned buildings and wasteland

Desertification The process by which land becomes drier and degraded, as a result of climate change or human activities, or both

Glossary

Destructive plate margin Tectonic plate margin where two plates are converging and the oceanic plate is subducted – there could be violent earthquakes and explosive volcanoes

Development The progress of a country in terms of economic growth, the use of technology and human welfare

Development gap Difference in standards of living and well-being between the world's richest and poorest countries

Discharge Quantity of water that passes a given point on a stream or riverbank within a given period of time

Displaced person A person forced to move from their home but who stays in their country of origin

Dune regeneration Building up dunes and increasing vegetation to prevent excessive coastal retreat

Earthquake A sudden or violent movement within the Earth's crust followed by a series of shocks

Economic impact Effect of an event on the wealth of an area or community

Economic migrant Person who moves voluntarily to improve their standard of living

Economic opportunities Chances for people to improve their standard of living through employment

Ecosystem A community of plants and animals that interact with each other and their physical environment

Ecotourism Nature tourism, usually involving small groups, with a minimal impact on the environment

Embankments Artificially raised river banks often using concrete walls

Emigrant Someone leaving their country of residence to move to another country

Energy conservation Reducing energy consumption by using less energy and existing sources more efficiently

Energy exploitation Developing and using energy resources to the greatest possible advantage, usually for profit

Energy mix Range of energy sources of a region or country, both renewable and non-renewable

Energy security Uninterrupted availability of energy sources at an affordable price

Environmental degradation The deterioration of the environment through depletion of resources, such as air, water and soil. It includes the destruction of ecosystems, habitat destruction, the extinction of wildlife and pollution

Environmental impact Effect of an event on the landscape and ecology of the surrounding area

Erosion Wearing away and removal of material by a moving force, such as a breaking wave

Estuary Tidal mouth of a river where it meets the sea – wide banks of deposited mud are exposed at low tide

European Union A politico-economic union of 28 European countries – the UK is a member state

Exponential growth A pattern where the growth rate constantly increases – often shown as a J-curve graph

Extreme weather When a weather event is significantly different from the average or usual weather pattern, and is especially severe or unseasonal

Fairtrade Producers in LICs given a better price for their goods such as cocoa, coffee and cotton

Famine Widespread, serious, often fatal shortage of food

Fertility rate The average number of children each woman in a population will bear. (If this number is 2.1 or more the population will replace itself.)

Flood Where river discharge exceeds river channel capacity and water spills onto the floodplain

Floodplain Relatively flat area forming the valley floor either side of a river channel that is sometimes flooded

Floodplain zoning Identifying how a floodplain can be developed for human uses

Flood relief channels Artificial channels that are used when a river is close to maximum discharge; they take the pressure off the main channels when floods are likely

Flood warning Providing reliable advance information about possible flooding

Fluvial processes Processes relating to deposition, erosion, and transport by a river

Food chain Connections between different organisms (plants and animals) that rely upon one another as their source of food

Food insecurity Being without reliable access to enough affordable, nutritious food

Food miles The distance covered supplying food to consumers

Food security Access to sufficient, safe, nutritious food to maintain a healthy and active life

Food web A complex hierarchy of plants and animals relying on each other for food

Formal economy/sector The type of employment where people work to receive a regular wage, pay tax, and have certain rights, i.e. paid holidays, sickness leave

Fossil fuel A natural fuel such as coal or gas, formed in the geological past from the remains of living organisms

Fragile environment An environment that is both easily disturbed and difficult to restore

Freeze-thaw weathering (or frost shattering) A common process of weathering in a glacial environment involving repeated cycles of freezing and thawing that can make cracks in rock bigger

Glossary

Gabion Steel wire mesh filled with boulders used in coastal defences

Gender structure The balance between males and females in a population

Geothermal energy Energy generated by heat stored deep in the Earth

Global ecosystem (biome) A community of plants and animals that have common characteristics for the environment they exist in. They can be found over a range of continents

Globalisation Process creating a more connected world, with increases in the global movements of goods (trade) and people (migration and tourism)

Green belt The area around a city where development is restricted so that towns and cities do not merge

Greenfield site A plot of land, often in a rural area or on the edge of an urban area that has not been built on before

Green revolution An increase in crop production, especially in poorer countries, using high-yielding varieties, artificial fertilisers and pesticides

Grey water Recycled domestic waste water

Gross national income (GNI) Measurement of economic activity calculated by dividing the gross (total) national income by the size of the population

Groundwater management Regulation and control of water levels, pollution, ownership and use of groundwater

Groyne A wooden barrier built out into the sea to stop the longshore drift of sand and shingle, and allow the beach to grow

Hard engineering Using concrete or large artificial structures to defend against natural processes, either coastal, fluvial or glacial

Hazard risk Probability or chance that a natural hazard may take place

Headlands and bays A rocky coastal promontory (highpoint of land) made of rock that is resistant to erosion: headlands lie between bays of less-resistant rock where the land has been eroded by the sea

High-income country (HIC) A country with GNI per capita higher than US$12 746 (World Bank, 2013)

Host country The country where a migrant settles

Hot desert Parts of the world that have high average temperatures and very low precipitation

Human development index (HDI) A method of measuring development where GDP per capita, life expectancy and adult literacy are combined to give an overview

Hydraulic power Process where breaking waves compress pockets of air in cracks in a cliff; the pressure may cause the crack to widen, breaking off rock

Hydroelectric power (HEP) Electricity generated by turbines that are driven by moving water

Hydrograph A graph which shows the discharge of a river, related to rainfall, over a period of time

Immediate responses Reactions of people as the disaster happens and in the immediate aftermath

Immigrant Someone entering a new country with the intention of living there

Industrial structure Relative proportion of the workforce employed in different sectors of the economy

Inequalities Differences between poverty and wealth, as well as wellbeing and access to jobs, housing, education, etc.

Infant mortality Number of babies that die under one year of age, per 1000 live births

Informal economy/sector Employment outside the official knowledge of the government

Information and communication technology (ICT) Computer, internet, mobile phone and satellite technologies

Infrastructure The basic equipment and structures (such as roads, utilities, water supply and sewage) that are needed for a country or region to function properly

Integrated transport system Different forms of transport are linked together to make it easy to transfer from one to another

Interlocking spurs Outcrops of land along the river course in a valley

Intermediate (or appropriate) technology Simple, easily learned and maintained technology used in LICs for a range of economic activities

International aid Money, goods and services given by single governments or an organisation like the World Bank or IMF to help the quality of life and economy of another country

Internet A worldwide system of computers connecting with each other anywhere in the world whereby information such as graphics, voice messages, text, photos and video can be sent and received

Irrigation Artificial application of water to the land or soil

Landscape An extensive area of land regarded as being visually and physically distinct

Land use conflicts Disagreements between interest groups who do not agree on how land should be used

Lateral erosion Erosion of river banks rather than the bed – helps to form the floodplain

Levee Raised bank found on either side of a river, formed naturally by regular flooding or built up by people to protect the area against flooding

Glossary

Life expectancy The average number of years a person is expected to live

Literacy rate Percentage of people in a country who have basic reading and writing skills

Local food sourcing Food production and distribution that is local, rather than national and/or international

Logging The business of cutting down trees and transporting the logs to sawmills

Long profile The gradient of a river, from its source to its mouth

Longshore drift Transport of sediment along a stretch of coastline caused by waves approaching the beach at an angle

Long-term responses Later reactions that occur in the weeks, months and years after the event

Low-income country (LIC) A country with GNI per capita lower than US$1045 (World Bank, 2013)

Managed retreat Controlled retreat of the coastline, often allowing flooding to occur over low-lying land

Management strategies Techniques of controlling, responding to, or dealing with an event

Mass movement Downhill movement of weathered material under the force of gravity

Meander A wide bend in a river

Mechanical weathering Physical disintegration or break up of exposed rock without any change in its chemical composition, i.e. freeze–thaw

Megacity An urban area with a total population of more than 10 million people

Mesa A table-like relic landform formed in horizontal rocks

Microfinance loans Very small loans which are given to people in the LICs to help them start a small business

Migration The movement of people from one permanent home to another, with the intention of staying at least a year. This move may be within a country (national migration) or between countries (international migration). In many LICs people move from rural to urban areas (rural–urban migration)

Mineral extraction Removal of solid mineral resources from the earth

Mitigation Action taken to reduce the long-term risk from natural hazards, such as earthquake-proof buildings or international agreements to reduce greenhouse gas emissions.

Monitoring (1) Recording physical changes, i.e. tracking a tropical storm by satellite, to help forecast when and where a natural hazard might strike; (2) using scientific methods to study coastal processes to help inform management options

Natural change/decrease/increase The difference between birth and death rates per 1000 people per year

Newly emerging economies Countries that have begun to experience high rates of economic development, usually along with rapid industrialisation

Nuclear power Energy released by a nuclear reaction, especially by fission or fusion

Nutrient cycling Ongoing recycling of nutrients between living organisms and their environment

Over abstraction When water is used more quickly than it is being replaced

Over-cultivation Where the intensive growing of crops exhausts the soil, leaving it barren

Overgrazing Feeding too many livestock for too long on the land, so it is unable to recover its vegetation

Oxbow lake An arc-shaped lake on a floodplain formed by a cut-off meander

Pediment Gently sloping, usually concave rock surface at the foot of a mountain front

Planning Actions taken to enable communities to respond to, and recover from, natural disasters

Plate margin The border between two tectonic plates

Playa Salt lake formed on flat clay deposits on a desert plain characterised by high levels of salinity

Pollution Chemicals, noise, dirt or other substances which have harmful or poisonous effects on an environment

Population structure The proportion of males and females in a country, usually in the form of age distributions

Post-industrial economy The shift of some HIC economies from producing goods to providing services

Precipitation Moisture falling from the atmosphere – rain, sleet or snow

Prediction Using historical evidence and monitoring, scientists can make predictions about when and where a tectonic hazard may happen

Primary effects Initial impact of a natural event on people and property, caused directly by it, i.e. the buildings collapsing following an earthquake

Producer An organism or plant that is able to absorb energy from the Sun through photosynthesis

Pro-natalist policy A government initiative designed to increase the birth rate, usually because the country has an ageing population and total numbers of people are falling.

Protection Actions taken before a hazard strikes to reduce its impact, such as educating people or improving building design

Pull factors The attractions and opportunities of a place that encourage people to move there

Glossary

Push factors The negative aspects of a place that encourage people to move away

Redevelopment The improvement of an area that is in poor condition, especially an area of old buildings in a city

Refugee Person who has proven to the authorities that they would be at risk if returned to their home country, have had their claim for asylum accepted by the government and can now stay in the receiving country

Renewable energy sources A resource that cannot be exhausted, i.e. wind, solar and tidal energy

Resource management Control and monitoring of resources so that they do not become exhausted

Rock armour Large boulders deliberately dumped on a beach as part of coastal defences

Rural–urban fringe A zone of transition between a built-up area and the countryside, where there is often competition for land use

Saltation Hopping movement of pebbles along a riverbed, seabed or desert floor

Salt lake See 'playa'

Sand dune (1) Coastal sand hill above the high tide mark, shaped by wind action; (2) Sand deposits formed by wind in deserts

Sanitation Measures designed to protect public health, such as providing clean water and disposing of sewage and waste

Science park A collection of scientific and technical knowledge-based businesses located on a single site

Sea wall Concrete wall aiming to prevent erosion of the coast by reflecting wave energy

Secondary effects After-effects that occur as indirect impacts of a natural event, sometimes on a longer timescale, i.e. fires due to ruptured gas mains, resulting from the ground shaking

Seif dunes Elongated sand dunes formed parallel to the prevailing wind direction

Selective logging sustainable forestry management where only carefully selected trees are cut down

Service (tertiary) industries The economic activities that provide various services – commercial, professional, social, entertainment and personal

Shale gas Natural gas that is found trapped within shale formations of fine-grained sedimentary rock

Sliding Loose surface material becomes saturated and the extra weight causes the material to become unstable and move rapidly downhill

Slum A squalid section of a city, with inferior living conditions, poverty and overcrowding

Social deprivation The extent an individual or an area lacks services, decent housing, adequate income and employment

Social impact The effect of an event on the lives of people or communities

Social opportunities The chances available to improve quality of life, i.e. access to education, health care, etc.

Soft engineering Managing erosion by working with natural processes to help restore beaches and coastal ecosystems or to reduce the risk of river flooding

Soil erosion Removal of topsoil faster than it can be replaced, due to natural (water and wind), animal and human activity

Solar energy Sun's energy exploited by solar panels, collectors or cells to heat water or air or to generate electricity

Solution (or corrosion) Chemical erosion caused by the dissolving of rocks and minerals by river or seawater

Spit Depositional landform formed when a finger of sediment extends from the shore out to sea, often at a river mouth

Squatter settlement An area of (often illegal) poor-quality housing, lacking in services such as water supply, sewerage and electricity

Stack Isolated pillar of rock left when the top of an arch has collapsed

Subsistence farming A type of agriculture producing only enough food and materials for the benefit of a farmer and their family

Surface creep Wind transport involving large particles being rolled along the desert floor

Suspension Small particles carried in river flow or seawater (i.e. sands, silts and clays) or by the wind across a desert

Sustainability Actions that meet the needs of the present without reducing the ability of future generations to meet their needs

Sustainable energy supply Energy that can potentially be used well into the future without harming future generations

Sustainable food supply Food production that avoids damaging natural resources, providing good quality produce and social and economic benefits to local communities

Sustainable water supply Meeting the present-day need for safe, reliable and affordable water without reducing supply for future generations

Tectonic hazard Natural hazard caused by the movement of tectonic plates (i.e. volcanoes and earthquakes)

Traction Where material is rolled along a riverbed or by waves

Trade Buying and selling of goods and services between countries

Traffic congestion When there is too great a volume of traffic for roads to cope with, and traffic slows to a crawl

Glossary

Transnational corporation (TNC) A company that has operations (factories, offices, research and development, shops) in more than one country

Transportation The movement of eroded material

Tropical storm (hurricane, cyclone, typhoon) An area of low pressure with winds moving in a spiral around a calm central point called the eye of the storm – winds are powerful and rainfall is heavy

Tundra A vast, flat, treeless Arctic region of Europe, Asia, and North America where the subsoil is permanently frozen

Undernutrition When people do not eat enough nutrients to cover their needs for energy and growth, or to maintain a healthy immune system

Urban farming Growing food and raising animals in towns and cities; processing and distributing food; collecting and re-using food waste

Urban greening Process of increasing and preserving open space in urban areas, i.e. public parks and gardens

Urbanisation When an increasing percentage of a country's population comes to live in towns and cities

Urban regeneration Reversing the urban decline by modernising or redeveloping, aiming to improve the local economy

Urban sprawl Unplanned growth of urban areas into the surrounding rural areas

Urban sustainability A city organised without over reliance on the surrounding rural areas and using renewable energy

Vertical erosion Downward erosion of the riverbed

Volcano An opening in the Earth's crust from which lava, ash and gases erupt

Wadi A dry river channel, gully or valley formed by periodic water erosion, commonly cut into a desert plateau

Waste recycling Process of extracting and reusing useful substances found in waste

Waterfall A step in the long profile of a river usually formed when a river crosses over a hard (resistant) band of rock

Waterborne diseases Diseases such as cholera and typhoid caused by micro-organisms in contaminated water

Water conflict Disputes between different regions or countries about the distribution and use of freshwater

Water deficit When demand for water is greater than supply

Water insecurity When water availability is insufficient to ensure the good health and livelihood of a population, due to short supply or poor quality

Water security Availability of a reliable source of acceptable quantity and quality of water

Water quality Measured in terms of the chemical, physical and biological content of the water

Water stress When the demand for water exceeds supply in a certain period or when poor quality restricts its use

Water surplus When water supply is greater than demand

Water transfer Matching supply with demand by moving water from an area with water surplus to another with water deficit

Wave cut platform Rocky, level shelf at or around sea level representing the base of old, retreated cliffs

Waves Ripples in the sea caused by the transfer of energy from the wind blowing over the surface of the sea

Wilderness area A natural environment that has not been significantly modified by human activity

Wind energy Electrical energy produced from the power of the wind, using windmills or wind turbines

World city A city that has influence over the world; they are ranked by importance of global trade, politics, culture, science and the extent to which they are integrated with the global economy

Yardang Elongated ridge separated by deep grooves cut into the desert surface

Zeugen Pedestal-shaped flat-topped rock formations formed in horizontally bedded rocks

Symbols on Ordnance Survey maps (1:50 000 and 1:25 000)

ROADS AND PATHS

M1 or A6(M)	Motorway
A35	Dual carriageway
A31(T) or A35	Trunk or main road
B 3074	Secondary road
	Narrow road with passing places
	Road under construction
	Road generally more than 4 m wide
	Road generally less than 4 m wide
	Other road, drive or track, fenced and unfenced
	Gradient: steeper than 1 in 5; 1 in 7 to 1 in 5
Ferry	Ferry; Ferry P – passenger only
	Path

PUBLIC RIGHTS OF WAY

(Not applicable to Scotland)

1:25 000	1:50 000	
		Footpath
		Road used as a public footpath
+++++++	--------	Bridleway
		Byway open to all traffic

RAILWAYS

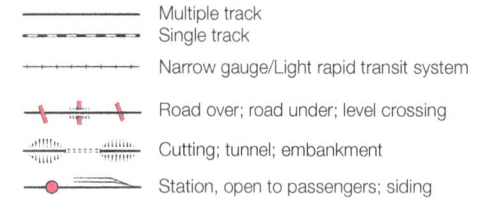

- Multiple track
- Single track
- Narrow gauge/Light rapid transit system
- Road over; road under; level crossing
- Cutting; tunnel; embankment
- Station, open to passengers; siding

BOUNDARIES

- National
- District
- County, Unitary Authority, Metropolitan District or London Borough
- National Park

HEIGHTS/ROCK FEATURES

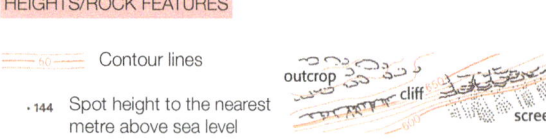

- Contour lines
- ·144 Spot height to the nearest metre above sea level

outcrop, cliff, scree

ABBREVIATIONS

P	Post office	PC	Public convenience (rural areas)
PH	Public house	TH	Town Hall, Guildhall or equivalent
MS	Milestone	Sch	School
MP	Milepost	Coll	College
CH	Clubhouse	Mus	Museum
CG	Coastguard	Cemy	Cemetery
Fm	Farm		

ANTIQUITIES

- VILLA Roman
- Castle Non-Roman
- Battlefield (with date)
- Tumulus/Tumuli (mound over burial place)

© Crown copyright.

LAND FEATURES

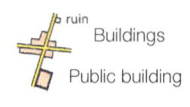

- Buildings (ruin)
- Public building
- Bus or coach station
- Place of Worship { with tower / with spire, minaret or dome / without such additions }
- Chimney or tower
- Glass structure
- Heliport
- Triangulation pillar
- Mast
- Wind pump / wind generator
- Windmill
- Graticule intersection
- Cutting, embankment
- Quarry
- Spoil heap, refuse tip or dump
- Coniferous wood
- Non-coniferous wood
- Mixed wood
- Orchard
- Park or ornamental ground
- Forestry Commission access land
- National Trust – always open
- National Trust, limited access, observe local signs
- National Trust for Scotland

WATER FEATURES

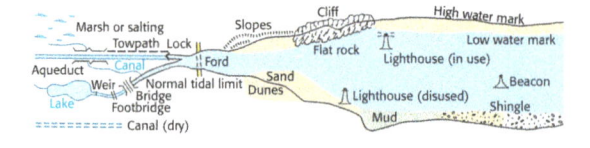

Marsh or salting, Towpath, Aqueduct, Canal, Weir, Bridge, Footbridge, Lake, Canal (dry), Lock, Ford, Normal tidal limit, Slopes, Cliff, Flat rock, Sand, Dunes, Mud, High water mark, Low water mark, Lighthouse (in use), Lighthouse (disused), Beacon, Shingle

TOURIST INFORMATION

- P Parking
- P&R Park & Ride
- V Visitor centre
- i Information centre
- Telephone
- Camp site/Caravan site
- Golf course or links
- Viewpoint
- PC Public convenience
- Picnic site
- Pub/s
- Museum
- Castle/fort
- Building of historic interest
- Steam railway
- English Heritage
- Garden
- Nature reserve
- Water activities
- Fishing
- Other tourist feature
- Moorings (free)
- Electric boat charging point
- Recreation/leisure/sports centre

Index

A
abrasion 70, 84, 87, 100
accessibility 97
Achuar people, Peru 53
aeolian processes 84–5
agriculture *see* farming
aid 194, 251
  different types of aid 194
  Nigeria 212–13
  reducing the development gap 194
air pollution 135, 173, 285
air transport 286
  development of airports 286–7, 292–5
  factors involved in the expansion of air transport 289
  global patterns of movement by air 288
  growth of air travel 286
  international links and manufacturing 290
  international links and tourism 291
  international links and trade 290
  ocean transport and air transport 284–5
airports 286–7, 289
  airports in the UK 292–5
  challenges of increasing development 292
alluvial fans 86, 93
Amazon 53, 99, 239
arches 73
Arctic 234
asylum seekers 266
  migration into Europe 269–71
atlas maps 334–5
atmosphere 18, 32
attrition 70, 100

B
backwash 71
Badia, Jordan 59, 60
badlands 92
Bakun Dam, Sarawak, Malaysia 49
Bangladesh 27
bar graphs 344–5
barchans 90, 91
bars 75
bays 72
beaches 74, 76
  beach nourishment and re-profiling 81, 82
Bengaluru, India 304–5
Berners-Lee, Sir Tim 299
bicycle hire 155
biodiversity 47, 53
  loss of biodiversity 50
biomes 44
birth rate 180, 248
bivariate data 353
Bodo oil spills (2008/09), Nigeria 215
Bollywood 124
Brazil 52, 257
brownfield sites 152–3
Buddhism 262
bulk carriers 277
Burma 267
business 146, 166

C
call centres 302
  development of call centres in India 303–5
  submarine cables 302
carbon dioxide 33
  carbon capture 34
  carbon sinks 55
  planting trees 35
carbon footprint 32

cartographic skills 334–43
caves 73
Chambamontera micro-hydro scheme, Peru 242
  benefits to the local community 243
changing economic world 176–7
  development gap 178–201
  Nigeria: a newly emerging economy 202–17
channel straightening 109
children 252, 254
Chile earthquake (2010) 10
  immediate and long-term responses 12
  primary and secondary effects 11
China 223, 246
  Huai River Basin 112–13
  Shanghai 282
  south–north water transfer scheme 225
choropleth maps 347
cliffs 72, 77
  what causes cliffs to collapse? 68–9
climate 46, 53, 56
climate change 5, 28, 53, 257
  adaptations 36
  deforestation 50
  desertification 59
  economic impacts 35
  evidence for 29
  global effects 28
  global impacts 35
  human causes 32–3
  international agreements 35
  management 34–5
  managing water supply 36–7
  natural causes 30–1
  reducing risk from rising sea levels 37
  tropical storms 22–3
  warming trends 29
Clywedog reservoir, Llanidloes, Wales 108
coastal deposition 71
  landforms 74–5
coastal erosion 70
  landforms 72–3
coastal landscapes
  erosion and deposition 70–5
  Indonesia 76–9
  management strategies 80–3
  wave types and their characteristics 66–7
  weathering and mass movement 68–9
coastal management 80
  hard engineering strategies 80
  Mactan Island, Philippines 82–3
  managed retreat 80, 81
  soft engineering strategies 80, 81
coastal realignment 81
coastal transportation 70
  longshore drift 71
cocoa 196
coffee 197
Colombia 290
colonialism 187
commercial farming 49, 95, 97, 214
Commonwealth 206
compass directions 337
conflict 233, 235
conservation 52, 54
container ships 277, 278, 279
contours 337–8
copper 187

coral reefs 77
corrasion 70
Costa Rica 291
costs 233, 289
crime 133
cross profile of rivers 99
cruise ships 277
culture 141, 147, 167, 205, 251

D
dams 108, 113, 223, 224
data
  data analysis 320–1, 330–1
  data presentation 318–19, 328–9
  describing relationships in bivariate data 353
  primary data 315, 316, 325
  qualitative data 317, 321, 326, 327, 331
  quantitative data 316–17, 320–1, 326, 330–1
  secondary data 315, 325
death rate 180, 248
debt reduction 55, 198
  debt relief 198–9
  how have poor countries built up debt? 198
  microfinance 199
deflation 84
deforestation 48–9, 106
  Brazil 52, 257
  impacts 50–1
  Nigeria 214
  rates of deforestation 52
demographic transition model (DTM) 182
  countries at different stages of development 183
  economic development 182
  population pyramids and the DTM 185
dependency ratio 184
dereliction 152
desalination 225
desert landscapes 84
  water deposition 87
  water erosion 87
  water landforms 92–3
  water processes 86
  water transportation 87
  wind deposition 85
  wind erosion 84
  wind landforms 88–91
  wind transportation 85
desertification 58
  appropriate technology 61
  Badia, Jordan 59, 60
  causes 58–9
  national parks 60
  water and soil management 60–1
  where is desertification a problem? 58
deserts, hot 19, 56
  adaptations to living in the desert 57
  climate 56
  development challenges 96–7
  development opportunities 94–5
  people 56
  plants and animals 57
  soils 56, 94
  where are hot deserts found? 56
desire line maps 349
development gap 178–9
  aid 194–5
  debt relief 198–9
  disparities in health 189
  economic causes 186–7

historical causes 186–7
how does uneven development lead to disparities in wealth? 188
imbalance between rich and poor 188
limitations of economic and social measures 181
measures of development 180
migration 190–1
physical causes 186
reducing the development gap 192–201
tourism 200–1
trade 196–7
dispersion graphs 352
displaced persons 190
distance 336
  curved-line distance 336
  straight-line distance 336
dot maps 348
drainage 339
drainage basins 98, 113

E
Earth's orbit 30
  axial tilt 30
  eccentricity 30
  precession 30
earthquakes 6
  immediate responses 12–13
  living with risk 14–15
  long-term responses 12–13
  monitoring 16
  planning 17
  predicting 16
  primary effects 10–11
  protection 17
  secondary effects 10–11
economic development 51, 141
  aid 194–5
  debt relief 198–9
  demographic transition model 182–3
  energy consumption 233
  formal economy 127
  gains and losses 51
  industrial development 192–3
  informal sector 127, 129
  intermediate technology 195
  investment 192
  measures of development 180–1
  measuring development 178–9
  measuring quality of life 179, 181
  Mumbai, India 126–7, 129
  Nigeria: a newly emerging economy 202–17
  population 254
  population pyramids 184–5
  tourism 193, 200–1
  trade 196–7
  uneven development 188–91
  what is development? 178
economic migrants 190, 191, 264, 266
  freedom of movement within the EU 271
  migration into Europe 269–71
ecosystems 40
  Avington Park lake, Winchester, Hampshire 43
  changes due to human activities 42
  freshwater ponds 40–1, 43
  global ecosystems 44–5
  impacts of change 42–3
  natural changes 42
ecotourism 55, 201
education 54, 125, 132, 151, 252

361

Index

embankments 109
emigrants 190, 272
employment 148, 168, 201
energy 95
　alternative energy sources 34, 236
　energy conservation 157, 174
energy exploitation 234
　costs of exploitation and production 233
　exploiting energy resources in the Arctic 234
energy insecurity 234
　exploiting resources in difficult and sensitive areas 234
　food production 235
　industry 235
　potential for conflict 235
energy mix 236
energy security 232
energy supply 125, 131
　Chambamontera micro-hydro scheme, Peru 242–3
　factors affecting energy supply 233
　global energy consumption and supply 232
　increasing efficiency of fossil fuels 241
　increasing energy consumption 233
　natural gas 238–9
　non-renewable energy sources 237
　reducing energy demand 241
　renewable energy sources 236
　sustainable energy 240
　sustainable energy developments in Malmo, Sweden 240
enquiry design 326
　quantitative and qualitative data 326–7
enquiry questions 314, 324
　developing an enquiry question 315, 325
entertainment 149, 169
environment 201
　climate change 35
　environmental degradation 257
　impact of economic growth in Nigeria 214–15
Equator 19
estuaries 105
European Union 271
extrapolation 353

F Fairtrade 197
Far East 64–5
farming 5, 106, 207, 222
　agricultural adaptations to climate change 36
　commercial farming 49, 95, 97, 214
　hot deserts 95, 97
　Nigeria 214
　subsistence farming 49, 95
Federal Reserve Bank, New York, USA 166
fertility rates 251
fieldwork
　evaluation of results 322–3, 332–3
　investigating river processes and management 314–23
　investigating variations in urban quality of life 324–33
　writing conclusions 321, 331
finance 126, 146, 166
flood relief channels 109
flood storage areas 110
flood warnings 111
flooding 24, 106
　hard engineering 108–9

hydrographs 107
　physical and human factors 106
　soft engineering 110–11
　what causes flooding? 106
floodplains 105
　floodplain zoning 110
flow line maps 349
fluvial processes 100–1
food supply 154, 174, 222, 235, 256
Forest Stewardship Council (FSC) 55
forests see tropical rainforests
fossil fuels 34, 233, 237, 241
freeze-thaw weathering 68, 69
fuelwood 59

G gabions 80
gas 238
　extracting natural gas 239
　extracting natural gas in the Amazon 239
　reserves of natural gas 238
geothermal energy 233
Ghana 196
　ICT (information and communication technology) and trade 310–11
Givaudan 54
glaciers 29
　artificial glaciers 37
global atmospheric circulation 18
　effect on the world's weather 18–19
　how does global atmospheric circulation work? 18
global ecosystems 44
　characteristics 45
global issues 218–19
　communication 276–313
　energy supply 232–43
　population 244–75
　water supply 220–31
globalisation 148, 296
Goat Aid Oxfam 195
gorges 103
gradients 337–8
Grameen Bank, Bangladesh 199
graphical skills 344–9
graphs 344, 352
　describing relationships in bivariate data 353
　how to construct graphs or diagrams 344–5
　how to interpret graphs or diagrams 344
　interpreting population growth graphs 245–6
green belts 152
greenfield sites 152–3
greenhouse effect 32–3
greenhouse gases 32
　impact of human activity 33
grey water 229
gross national income (GNI) 178, 188
groundwater management 228, 229
groynes 80

H hardwood forestry 55
hazard risk 5
　living with tectonic hazards 14–15
　reducing risk from tectonic hazards 16–17
headlands 72
health care 125, 128, 132, 151
　Aduwan Health Centre, Nigeria 213
　disparities in health 189
　improved medical care 249
　improved sanitation 250
Heathrow Airport, UK 293

benefits and drawbacks of third runway construction 294–5
high-income countries (HICs) 178
histograms 344–5
housing 150, 171
Huai River Basin, China 112–13
　Huai River Basin Flood Management and Drainage Improvement Project (2010) 113
human development index (HDI) 179
hurricanes 22
　Hurricane Catarina (2004) 23
　Hurricane Patricia (2015) 4
hydraulic power 70, 87, 100
hydroelectric power (HEP) 236
　Chambamontera micro-hydro scheme, Peru 242–3
hydrographs 107

I ice, melting 29
Iceland 8
　life on a plate margin 15
ICT (information and communication technology) 296
　development of call centres 302–5
　development of the international phone links 300–1
　development of the internet 297–9
　how things have changed 296–7
　submarine cables 302
　trade and tourism 310–13
　transnational corporations (TNCs) 306–9
immigrants 190, 271
income 178, 208, 289
India 222, 229, 246, 258
　development of call centres in India 303–5
　Mumbai 118, 120–39
　population policies 258–9
　population policies in Kerala 260–1
　Thar Desert 94–7
　Wakel River Basin Project, Rajasthan 230–1
Indira Gandhi Canal, Rajasthan, India 95, 97
Indonesian coast 76
　beaches 76
　cliffs 77
　coral reefs 77
　Krakatoa Islands 78
　Mahakam Delta, Kalimantan 79
　mangroves 76
industrial development 192, 223, 235
　China 223
　Malaysia 192
　Nigeria 208, 214
infant mortality 180, 249, 254
infrastructure 51, 192, 201
inter-quartile range 351
interlocking spurs 102
intermediate technology 195
　reducing the development gap 195
international migration 144–5, 164–5
　impacts on country of origin 265, 274
　impacts on host country 265, 274
　major international migrations in the twenty-first century 266–75
　Mexican migration to the USA 272–5
　migration into Europe 269–71
　push and pull factors 264
　reasons for international migration 264–5
international phone links 300–1
internet 297
　increasing access to the internet 298–9

interpolation 353
investment 192
　foreign investment in Africa 192
　investment in air transport 289
　transnational corporations (TNCs) 306
irrigation 60, 95, 97
　Adis Nifas, Ethiopia 195
isoline maps 348

J Jamaica 200
　tourism and economic development 200–1
Japan 142, 185
Jordan 59, 60
Jubilee River, Maidenhead, Berkshire, UK 109

K Kathmandu earthquake (1934) 12
Kenya 290
Kielder Water, Northumberland, UK 224
Ko Tapu, Thailand 73
Krakatoa Islands, Indonesia 78

L land use 106
landslides 68, 69
lateral erosion 100, 104
latitude and longitude 334
leisure 124
Lesotho Highland Water Project 226–7
levees 105
life expectancy 179, 246, 248
line graphs 344
literacy rate 180
living world 38–9
　ecosystems 40–5
　hot deserts 56–61
　tropical rainforests 46–55
logging 49
　replanting 54
　selective logging 49, 54
London, UK 142
　airport expansion 293–5
　brownfield and greenfield sites 152–3
　business 146
　culture 147
　education 151
　employment 148
　energy and water conservation 157
　finance 146
　food supply 154
　green belt 152
　health 151
　housing 150
　impacts of international migration to London 145
　location and development 142–3
　M25 155
　national and international migration 144–5
　Olympic Park urban regeneration project 158–61
　politics 147
　population timeline 144
　recreation and entertainment 149
　trade 147
　traffic congestion 154–5
　urban deprivation 150
　urban greening 148–9
　waste disposal, reducing and recycling 156
long profile of rivers 98–9
longshore drift 71
low-income countries (LICs) 178

M Mactan Island, Philippines 82
　coastline management 82
　effects of coastline management 83
Mahakam Delta, Kalimantan, Indonesia 79

362

Index

malaria 189
Malaysia 48
  impacts of deforestation 50–1
  industrial development in Malaysia 192
  Main Range, Peninsular Malaysia 50
  threats to Malaysia's rainforests 49
  transforming tourism with ICT (information and communication technology) 312–13
Maldives 37
management strategies
  climate change 34–7
  coastal management strategies 80–3
  energy supply 236–43
  population growth 258–63
  reducing desertification 60–1
  reducing flooding 108–13
  tectonic hazards 16–17
  traffic congestion 137, 155
  tropical rainforests 54–5
  water supply 224–31
mangroves 76, 81
manufacturing 126, 209, 290
maps 334–41, 347–9
  communication networks 340
  compass directions 337
  distance 336
  drawing cross-sections 338
  drawing sketch maps 341
  identifying and describing landscape and relief features 337–8
  inferring human activity from map evidence 340–1
  interpreting physical and human features 339
  land use 340
  numerical and statistical information 338
  scale 336
Marriott hotels 241
mass movement 69
mean 350
meanders 104
measures of central tendency 350–1
measures of spread 351–2
median 350
medicine 53
megacities 119, 140
  why do cities grow? 118
methane 33
Mexico 184
  Mexican migration to the USA 272–5
microfinance 199
Middle East 64–5
  refugee crisis (2015) 190–1
migration 116, 190
  international migration 144–5, 164–5, 264–75
  national migration 144–5, 164–5
  rural–urban migration 118, 122
Milankovitch cycles 30
mineral extraction 49, 94
  Nigeria 215
mobile phones 300–1
mode 350
  modal class 351
monitoring 16
  tropical storms 26
  volcanoes and earthquakes 16
Mount Tambora eruption (1815) 7, 31
mudflows 69
Mumbai, India 118
  air and water pollution 135

causes of growth 122
communal land trust 139
Dharavi 118, 128–9, 138–9
economic opportunities 126
education 125, 132
energy supply 125, 131
financial sector 126
health 125, 128, 132
improving quality of life for the urban poor 138–9
leisure 124
location and geographical features 120
manufacturing and services 126
Mumbai Electrification Project 139
population distribution and diversity 123
reasons for importance 121
reducing unemployment and crime 133
shops 124
Slum Sanitation Project 139
slums and squatter settlements 128, 138–9
social opportunities 124
traffic congestion 136–7
waste disposal and recycling 134
water supply 125, 130

N national migration 144–5, 164–5
national parks 60
natural hazards 2–3
  different types of natural hazard 4
  factors affecting risk 5
  hazard risk 5
  tectonic hazards 6–17
  weather hazards 18–27
  what is a natural hazard? 4
Nepal earthquake (2015) 10
  immediate and long-term responses 13
  primary and secondary effects 11
Netherlands 283
New York, US 162
  business and finance 166
  culture 167
  dealing with waste 175
  deprivation in Morrisania and Crotona, the Bronx 170
  employment 168
  energy conservation 174
  food supply 174
  housing inequality 171
  impacts of national and international migration 164–5
  location and growth of the city 162–3
  politics 167
  recreation and entertainment 169
  strategies to reduce congestion and air pollution 173
  trade 166–7
  transport 172
  urban deprivation and inequality 170–1
  urban greening 169
  urban sprawl 173
  water conservation 174–5
  wealth and low social deprivation in Brooklyn Heights, Brooklyn 171
newly emerging economies (NEEs) 178
  call centres 302–5
  trade and tourism 310–13
  transnational corporations (TNCs) 306–9
Nigeria 202
  Aduwan Health Centre 213
  cultural context 205
  economy 208

environmental context 205
global importance 202–3
global trading relationships 206–7
impact of economic growth on the environment 214–15
importance in Africa 203
international aid 212–13
manufacturing 209
political context 204
political links 206
quality of life 216–17
regional variations 205
social context 204
sources of income 208
transnational corporations (TNCs) 210–11
Nike 308
  impacts on the host country 309
  production 308
  use of ICT (information and communication technology) 308
Nile 99
nitrous oxides 33
nomads 57
nuclear power 237

O ocean shipping 275
  developments in ocean shipping 278
  developments of ports 279
  global patterns of movement by sea 280
  ocean transport and air transport 284–5
  types of vessel 277
  world's leading ports 282–3
oil 207, 211, 215
  shipping crude oil 280
Olympic Park urban regeneration project, London, UK 158–61
orang-utans 48
Ordnance Survey maps 335
  four-figure and six-figure grid references 335
  numerical and statistical information 338
over-abstraction 221
over-cultivation 59
overgrazing 58
ox-bow lakes 104
Oxfam 195

P Pakistan 194
  Thar Desert 94–7
Participatory Groundwater Management (PGM), India 229
percentage change 352
percentiles 352
Peru 53, 242–3
Phillippines 82–3
photos 342
  aerial photos 342
  describing human and physical landscapes 343
  drawing sketches from photos 343
  ground photos 342
  labels and annotations 343
  satellite photos 342
physical landscapes 62–3
  coastal landscapes 66–83
  hot desert landscapes 84–97
  Middle and Far East 64–5
  river landscapes 98–113
pictograms 346
pie charts 345
planning 16
  tropical storms 27

volcanoes and earthquakes 17
plastic waste 254
plate margins 6
  conservative (transform) margins 8, 9
  constructive margins 8, 15
  destructive margins 8, 9
  living with risk 15
playas 93
politics 141, 147, 167
  energy supply 233
  Nigeria 204, 206
pools 104
population 244
  ageing population 255
  demographic transition model (DTM) 182–3, 185
  dependency ratio 184
  economic development 254
  energy consumption 233
  environmental degradation 257
  exponential growth 244
  factors explaining population change 249–53
  food supply 256
  future trends 244–5
  how population growth varies in different parts of the world 246–7
  international migration 264–75
  interpreting population growth graphs 245–6
  managing population growth 258–63
  natural change 248
  natural decrease 248
  natural increase 118, 122, 248
  population and resource balance 254
  population pressure 49, 59
  youthful population 255
population pyramids 184–5, 347
  age structure 253, 255
  gender structure 253
population structure 253
  population structure in Japan 185
  population structure in Mexico 184
ports 279
  world's leading ports 282–3
Portugal 68
poverty 5, 128–9, 150
  improving quality of life for the urban poor 138–9
  urban deprivation 150, 170–1
Praia de Luz, Algarve, Portugal 68
precipitation 106
prediction 16
  tropical storms 26
  volcanoes and earthquakes 16
proportional symbols 349
protection 16
  volcanoes and earthquakes 17

Q quality of life 179, 181, 201
  Nigeria 216–17
quartiles 351

R rainforests *see* tropical rainforests
range 351
recreation 149, 169
recycling 134, 156
  water 229
refrigerated ships 277
refugees 264, 266
  migration into Europe 269–71
  Myanmar 267
  sub-Saharan Africa 266
  Syria 190–1, 268–9

363

Index

relief 64, 339
   landscapes of the Middle and Far East 64, 65
religion 251
reservoirs 108, 224
resources 53
   energy exploitation 234
   overpopulation 254
riffles 104
river courses 100
river deposition 101
   landforms 105
river discharge 107
river erosion 100
   landforms 102–4
river flooding 106–7
   hard engineering strategies 108–9
   Huai River Basin, China 112–13
   preparing for floods 111
   soft engineering strategies 110–11
river landscapes 98
   cross profile of a river and its valley 99
   drainage basins 98, 113
   fluvial processes 100–1
   long profile of a river 98–9
river restoration 110
river transportation 101
road building 49
rock armour 80
rockfalls 68, 69
Rogun Dam, Tajikistan 223
Rohingya 267
roll-on/roll-off (Ro-Ro) ships 277
rotational slip 69
Rotterdam, Netherlands 283
rural–urban migration 118, 122
   push and pull factors 118

S Saffir–Simpson scale 22
salinisation 60
salt lakes 93
saltation 70, 85, 87, 101
sand dunes 74, 90–1
   dune regeneration 81
sanitation 139, 250
scale 336
scattergraphs 346
sea levels, rising 29
   Maldives 37
   reducing risk from rising sea levels 37
sea walls 80
seasonal changes 29
seif dunes 90, 91
settlement 339
shale gas 238
Shanghai, China 282
Shell Oil 211, 215
ships 276, 177
   automation 278
   containerisation 278
   design 278
   size 278
   specialisation 278
   speed 278
sideways erosion 100, 104
Singapore 283
   Singapore Changi Airport 287
sliding 69
slums 128–9, 138–9
smartphones 300–1
social impact 4
soil erosion 50, 58, 59
solar activity 30–1

solar energy 233, 236
solution 70, 87, 100, 101
spits 75
spot heights 337–8
squatter settlements 128–9, 138, 269
stacks 73
statistics 350–3
   describing relationships in bivariate data 353
   measures of central tendency 350–1
   measures of spread 351–2
   percentage change and percentiles 352
storms *see* tropical storms
submarine cables 302
subsistence farming 49, 95
surface creep 85
suspension 70, 85, 87, 101
swash 71

T tankers 277
technology 233, 241
   appropriate technology 61
   information and communication technology (ICT) 296–313
tectonic hazards 6–15
   management strategies 16–17
tectonic plates 6
telephone links 300–1
temperature extremes 96
Thailand 73
   population policies 262–3
Thar Desert, India and Pakistan 94–5
   development challenges 96–7
   tree planting 61
Tokyo, Japan 142
tourism 94, 193, 291
   Costa Rica 291
   ICT (information and communication technology) 312–13
   Jamaica 200–1
traction 70, 87, 101
trade 147, 166–7, 178, 196, 290
   cocoa from Ghana 196
   copper in Zambia 187
   development gap 186–7
   free trade 196–7
   ICT (information and communication technology) 310–11
   Ugandan coffee farmers 197
trade winds 18
traffic congestion 136–7, 154–5, 172–3
   congestion charging 155
   strategies to reduce traffic congestion 155
transnational corporations (TNCs) 210–11
   advantages and disadvantages 307
   investment in ICT (information and communication technology) 306
   Nike 308–9
transport 141, 155, 172
   see air transport; ocean shipping
tree planting 35, 61
trend lines 353
tropical rainforests 46
   adaptations to life in the rainforest 47
   climate 46
   deforestation 48–53
   international agreements 55
   plants and animals 47
   soils 47
   sustainable management 54
   where are tropical rainforests found? 46

   why should tropical rainforests be protected? 53
tropical storms 20
   climate change 22–3
   distribution 23
   frequency 23
   how do tropical storms form? 21
   intensity 23
   monitoring and prediction 26
   planning 27
   protection 26
   structure of a tropical storm 22
   Typhoon Haiyan 24–5
   where do tropical storms form? 20
tundra 44
Typhoon Haiyan (2013) 24
   immediate and long-term responses 25
   primary and secondary effects 24

U Uganda 197
UK 19, 109, 224
   aid 194
   aid to Pakistan 194
   airports in the UK 292–5
   economic migration to the UK 191
   London 142–61
underseas cables 302
unemployment 133
Unilever 210
urban deprivation 150, 170–1
urban greening 148–9, 169
urban issues and challenges 114–15
   urban growth 120–39
   urban world 116–18
   world cities 140–75
urban regeneration 158–61
urban sprawl 123, 152, 153, 173
urbanisation 5, 106
   distribution of the world's urban population 117
   how does urbanisation vary around the world? 117
   Nigeria 214
   what is urbanisation? 116
USA 289
   Mexican migration to the USA 272–5
   New York 162–75

V valleys 99
vertical erosion 100
volcanoes 7
   distribution of volcanoes 7
   living with risk 14
   monitoring 16
   pattern of volcanoes 7
   planning 17
   predicting eruptions 16
   protection 17
   volcanic activity 31

W wadis 92
Wakel River Basin Project, Rajasthan, India 230–1
waste disposal 134, 156, 175
waste reduction 156
water 53
water conservation 157, 174–5, 228
   grey water 229
   groundwater management 228
   recycling 229
   saving water at home 228
water deposition 87
water erosion 87
water insecurity 220
   food production 222

   impacts 222–3
   industrial output 223
   water conflict 223
   water shortages in Europe 222
water landforms 92–3
water pollution 135, 222, 228
   River Ganges, India 222
water quality 228
water supply 36, 125, 250
   dams and reservoirs 224
   desalination 225
   diverting supplies and increasing storage 224
   increasing consumption 221
   Lesotho Highland Water Project 226–7
   managing water supply in the Himalayas 37
   sustainable water supplies 228–9
   Thar Desert, India and Pakistan 96–7
   Wakel River Basin Project, Rajasthan, India 230–1
water availability 221
water security 220
water stress 220–1
water surplus and deficit 220
water transfers 225–7
water transportation 87
waterborne diseases 221, 222
waterfalls 103
waves 66
   constructive waves 67
   destructive waves 67
   wave-cut platforms 72
   what happens when waves reach the coast? 66, 71
weather 18
   cloudy and wet in the UK 19
   hot and dry in the desert 19
   hot and sweaty at the Equator 19
   tropical storms 20–7
weathering 68–9
   biological weathering 68, 69
   chemical weathering 68, 69
   mechanical (physical) weathering 68, 69
wetlands 110
wind 18
   wind deposition 85
   wind energy, 236 233
   wind erosion 84
   wind landforms 88–91
   wind transportation 85
women 252
world cities 140
   cultural features 141
   distribution of world cities 140
   economic features 141
   political features 141
   transport features 141
World Wide Web 297–9

Y Yangtze 99
yardangs 88

Z Zambia 187
zeugen 89